MW01620546

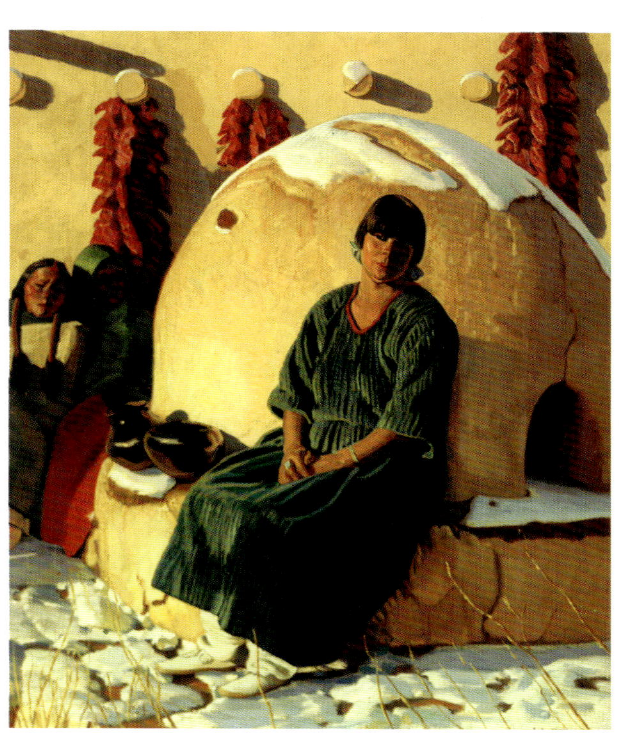

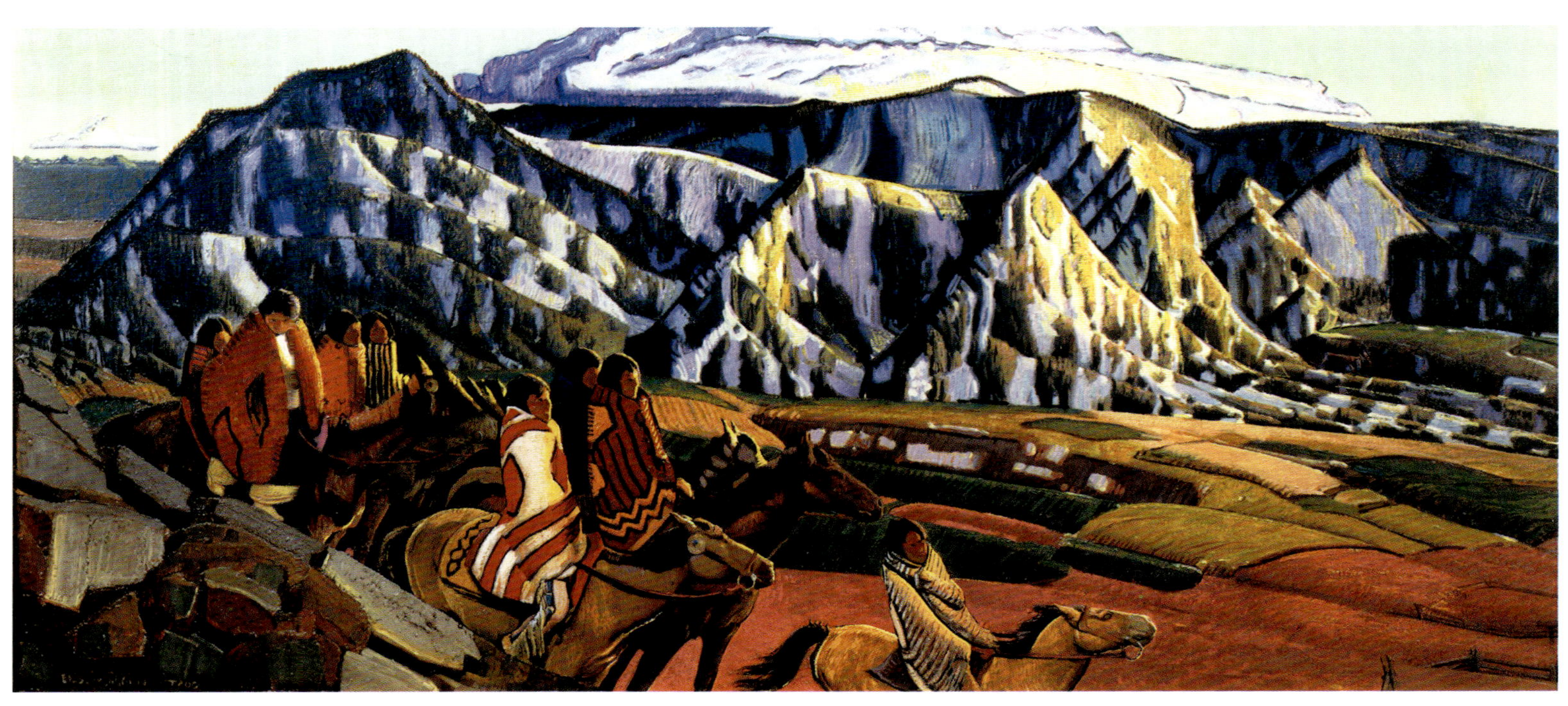

In Contemporary Rhythm

The Charles M. Russell Center Series
on Art and Photography of the American West
B. Byron Price, General Editor

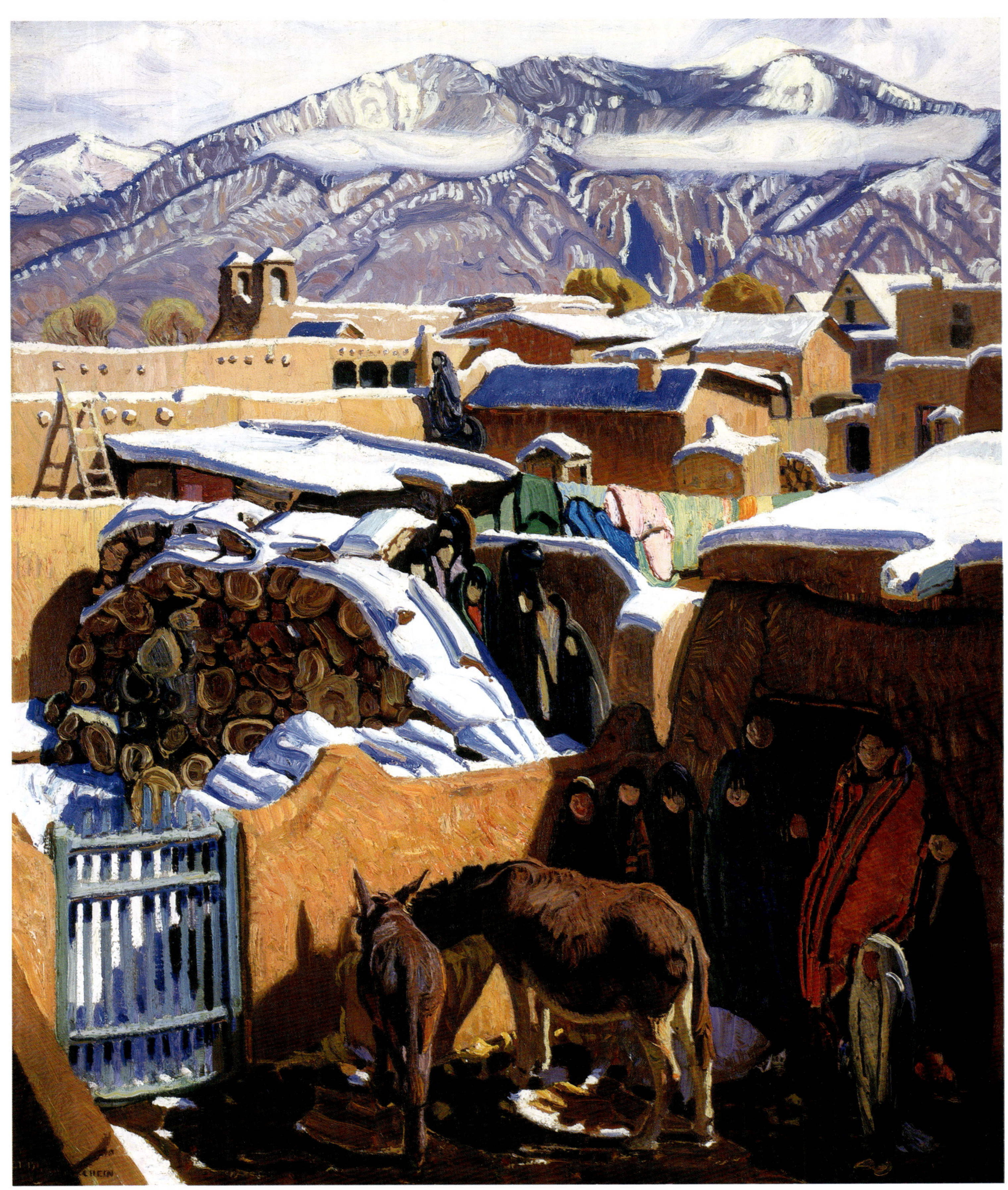

In Contemporary Rhythm
The Art of Ernest L. Blumenschein

By Peter H. Hassrick and Elizabeth J. Cunningham

With contributions by Sarah E. Boehme, Skip Keith Miller,
James Moore, and Jerry N. Smith

Foreword by James K. Ballinger,
Lewis I. Sharp, and Cathy L. Wright

University of Oklahoma Press : Norman
In cooperation with The Albuquerque Museum of Art and History,
Denver Art Museum, and Phoenix Art Museum

In Contemporary Rhythm: The Art of Ernest L. Blumenschein is organized by The Albuquerque Museum of Art and History, Denver Art Museum, and Phoenix Art Museum. Funding for this exhibition is provided by the National Endowment for the Arts, the Albuquerque Museum Foundation, the Henry Luce Foundation, and the Western Art Associates of the Phoenix Art Museum.

Dates of the exhibition

The Albuquerque Museum, June 8–September 7, 2008
Denver Art Museum, November 15, 2008–February 15, 2009
Phoenix Art Museum, March 15–June 14, 2009

Library of Congress Cataloging-in-Publication Data

Hassrick, Peter H.
In contemporary rhythm : the art of Ernest L. Blumenschein / by Peter H. Hassrick and Elizabeth J. Cunningham ; foreword by James Ballinger, Lewis I. Sharp, and Cathy L. Wright.
p. cm. — (The Charles M. Russell Center series on art and photography of the American West ; 2)
Catalog of an exhibition at The Albuquerque Museum, June 8–Sept. 7, 2008; the Denver Art Museum, Nov. 7, 2008–Feb. 8, 2009; and the Phoenix Art Museum, Mar. 15–June 4, 2009.
Includes bibliographical references and index.
ISBN 978-0-8061-3937-1 (hardcover : alk. paper)
1. Blumenschein, Ernest Leonard, 1874–1960—Exhibitions. 2. Blumenschein, Ernest Leonard, 1874–1960—Criticism and interpretation. I. Cunningham, Elizabeth J., 1951– II. Blumenschein, Ernest Leonard, 1874–1960. III. Albuquerque Museum. IV. Denver Art Museum. V. Phoenix Art Museum. VI. Charles M. Russell Center for the Study of Art of the American West. VII. Title.
ND237.B717A4 2008
759.13—dc22
2007049310

In Contemporary Rhythm: The Art of Ernest L. Blumenschein is Volume 2 in the Charles M. Russell Center Series on Art and Photography of the American West.

The paper in this book meets the guidelines for permanence and durability of the Committee on Production Guidelines for Book Longevity of the Council on Library Resources, Inc. ∞

2 3 4 5 6 7 8 9 10

Contents

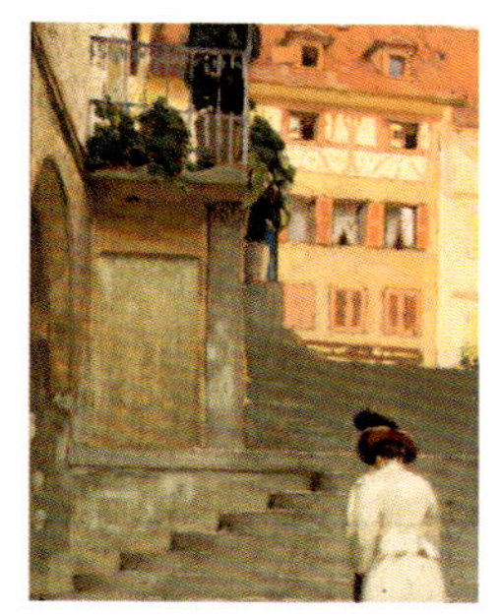

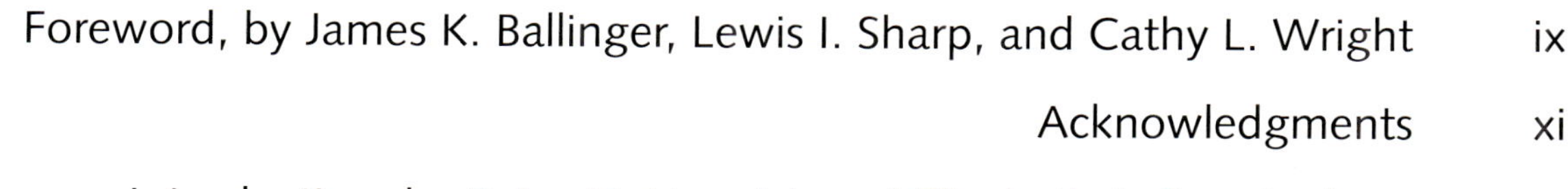

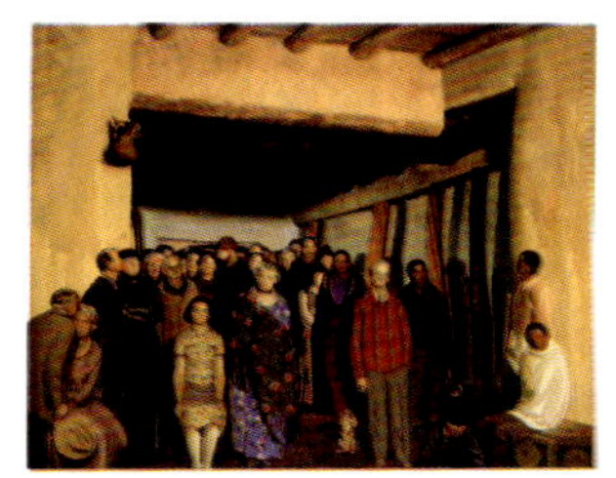

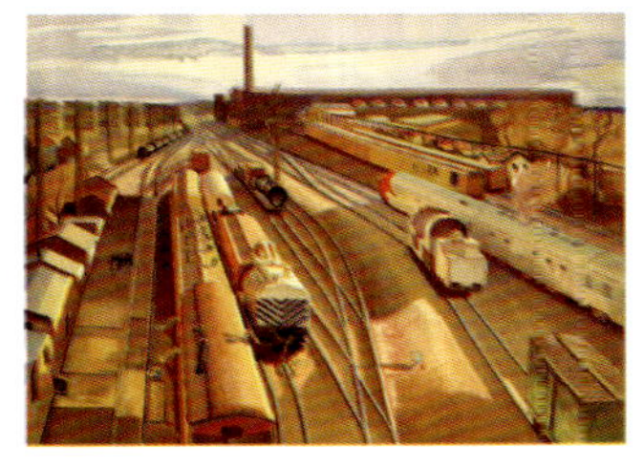

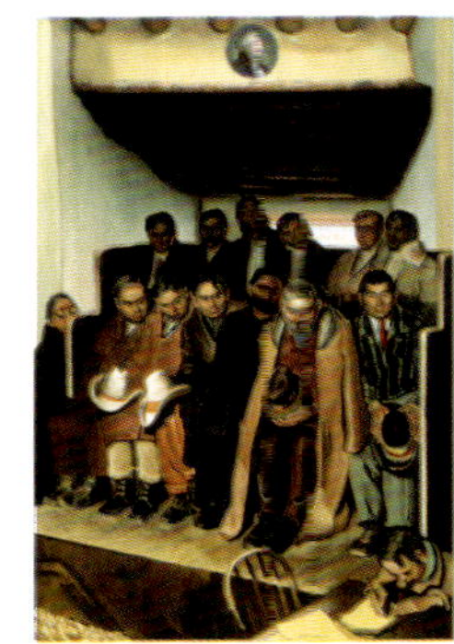

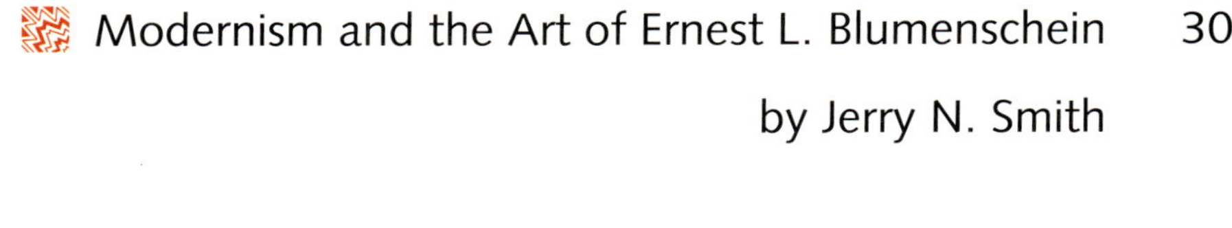

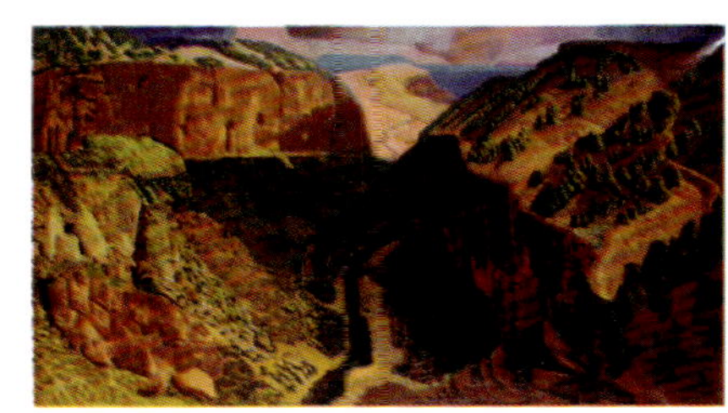

Foreword

The paintings of Ernest L. Blumenschein have been treasured by collectors and museums for much of the past hundred years. With Bert Phillips, Blumenschein is credited with founding the famed Taos art colony at the turn of the twentieth century. Why have curators and critics since then considered him the most distinctive of the scores of Taos artists in his own time and afterward? The exhibition In Contemporary Rhythm: The Art of Ernest L. Blumenschein was organized with the goal of answering that question.

Blumenschein was not a prolific painter during his long career, choosing instead to create significant works for the major national competitive exhibitions of his time, and thus establishing a solid national reputation. He was a complex, talented, thoughtful artist whose work was infused with modern tendencies. He embraced Post-Impressionist color and texture, abstract organic pattern, and structural design to build the foundations for his work depicting the people and geography of the Southwest. The popularity of western American art in recent years has unfairly categorized this sophisticated painter. During his lifetime, museums as diverse as the Dayton Art Institute, the Metropolitan Museum of Art, and the Museum of Modern Art acquired major paintings. This exhibition is intended to celebrate Blumenschein's achievements and reestablish his career in the broader context of American art.

An undertaking such as this exhibition and book takes a great deal of time, effort, dedication, and resources. Our three institutions—The Albuquerque Museum of Art and History, Denver Art Museum, and Phoenix Art Museum—have joined together to better ensure this project's success. Peter H. Hassrick, director of the Petrie Institute of Western American Art, and independent scholar Elizabeth J. Cunningham first envisioned this retrospective exhibition in 2004 in concert with James Moore, then director of The Albuquerque Museum of Art and History. They were later joined by Douglas Fairfield, curator at The Albuquerque Museum, and Jerry N. Smith, associate curator of American art at Phoenix Art Museum, these five forming the core team for the project. These talented scholars have been joined by two other contributors, Sarah Boehme, director of the Stark Museum of Art in Orange, Texas, and Skip Keith Miller, former curator and codirector of the Blumenschein Home, Taos Historic Museums, to create a handsome volume documenting Blumenschein's life and art.

The importance of this project has been recognized by significant funding from the National Endowment for the Arts American Masterpiece initiative, the Henry Luce Foundation, and The Albuquerque Museum Foundation. Western Art Associates of Phoenix Art Museum also made an organization grant. Our thanks go to them all for their assistance.

Likewise, we thank the many lenders who answered our call to bring together Blumenschein's greatest works for this timely investigation. Without their shared vision, there would be no exhibition.

It has been gratifying for the staffs of our three institutions to collaborate on such a worthy endeavor. We, in turn, wish the visitors to our respective museums who see the exhibition and the readers of this book to be equally rewarded and invigorated.

James K. Ballinger
Lewis I. Sharp
Cathy L. Wright

Acknowledgments

This exhibition and publication have spanned many years and taken many forms before reaching this final state. In the 1980s The Albuquerque Museum and the Phoenix Art Museum opened discussions with the Dayton Art Institute to organize a retrospective exhibition of Ernest L. Blumenschein's work. While those efforts never came to fruition, a seed was planted that would ultimately blossom into its present form here.

In the course of developing ideas and pursuing the attendant research for this project, several previous (and sometimes ongoing) efforts have played significant roles. Several artists and writers commented on Blumenschein's work before 1960, documenting it during his lifetime. After her father's death, Helen Blumenschein created the first public resource by allowing the Archives of American Art to select correspondence and commentary on his life and work from the family files. Acquisition of the remaining Blumenschein family material at the New Mexico History Museum/Palace of the Governors, Santa Fe, and groundbreaking research by Forrest Fenn and Sherry Clayton Taggett, along with the Blumenschein files at the Archives of American Art and the Arizona State University Library, have provided another key informational component on which the scholarship of this project has been built. Of most recent significance has been the Blumenschein catalogue raisonné initiated by Jerry Peters at the Gerald Peters Gallery in Santa Fe. Peters has most generously shared his research files with the museums and their guest curators so that the catalogue for the exhibition and the selection of works might represent the best-informed product possible. These assembled Blumenschein records provided the core scholarly resources for this book.

Fellow museum curators and American art scholars have also contributed much to our understanding of Blumenschein, his art, and his times. Of special note are William T. Henning, Jr., and his ambitious Ernest L. Blumenschein Retrospective exhibition at the Colorado Springs Fine Arts Center in 1978, James C. Moore's and Charles C. Eldredge's seminal writings on individual Blumenschein paintings, and Laura M. Bickerstaff's recognition of Blumenschein's critical stature as a New Mexico artist as revealed in her landmark 1955 book, *Pioneer Artists of Taos*. Blumenschein has garnered many enthusiasts among art aficionados today, and a group of them have been especially supportive of this project. These include Virginia Couse Leavitt of Taos and Tucson, Dean A. Porter of Granger, Indiana, and Robert R. White of Albuquerque, each of whom deserves our profound thanks.

The three museums hosting this exhibition are particularly grateful to the Henry Luce Foundation, its board and executive director, Ellen Holtzman, The Albuquerque Museum Foundation, and the National Endowment for the Arts for their munificence that has made this catalogue and exhibition possible. We would also like to single out the Western Art Associates of the Phoenix Art Museum for their gracious support. Thanks also go to the Charles M. Russell Center for the Study of Art of the American West, B. Byron Price, Director, for its support of this catalogue.

Along the way, many individuals and institutions have contributed to the scholarship that underpins the conclusions we make here about Blumenschein and his world. We would like to extend thanks to The Albuquerque Museum, James C. Moore, Douglas Fairfield, Connor O'Laughlin, and Patricia Gonzales; Arizona State University Art Museum, Heather Lineberry and Tiffany Fairall; Arizona State University Library Special Collections, Marilyn Wurzberger and Carole Moore; Arizona West Galleries, Scottsdale, A. P. Hays; Arrowsmith Galleries, Rex Arrowsmith; Art Students League of New York, Stephanie Cassidy; Museum of the American West, Autry National Center, Los Angeles, Amy Scott; Alisa Branham, Lawrence, Kansas; The Bancroft Library, University of California, Berkeley, Emily Balmages; J. N. Bartfield Galleries, New York, Michael Frost; Cincinnati Art Museum Library, Mona L. Chapin and William K. Clark; The Corcoran Gallery of Art, Washington, D.C., Marisa Bourgoin; Dallas Art Museum Library, Mary Leonard; Dayton Metro Library, Dayton, Ohio, Nancy Horlacher; Denver Art

Museum, Mindy Besaw, Holly Clymore, Megan Cooke, Nicole Parks, Lisa Steffen, and Nancy Simon; Denver Museum of Nature & Science, Joyce Herrold and Ryntha Johnson; Denver Public Library, Western History Department, Kay Wisnia, Phil Panum, and Josie Teodosijev; The Detroit Institute of Arts Archives, Deborah Rice; Eiteljorg Museum of American Indians and Western Art, Sara Summers, Robert Tucker, and Betsy Hutchins; Charles C. Eldredge, University of Kansas; The Fred Jones, Jr., Museum of Art, Eric M. Lee, Susan S. Squires, and Gail K. Anderson; Free Library of Philadelphia, Karen Lightner and Janine Pollock; Gerald Peters Gallery, Santa Fe, Nicole Crawford, Julie Schimmel, Ashley Waechter, and Debbie White; Gilcrease Museum, Tulsa, Oklahoma, Anne Morand, Tobie Cunningham, and April Miller; The Nita Stewart Haley Memorial Library, Midland, Texas, James Bradshaw; Margaret S. Hart, Chicago, Illinois; The Harwood Museum of Art, University of New Mexico, Taos, Charles Lovell; Indiana Historical Society, Indianapolis, Suzanne Crowe; Indianapolis Museum of Art, Maureen Tucker and Harriet Warkel; Andrew Jewell, Lincoln, Nebraska; David A. Kiehn, Collierville, Tennessee; Los Angeles County Museum of Art, Ted Greenberg, Deborah Smedstad, and Anne Smith; McFarlin Library, University of Tulsa, Katie Lee; Memorial Art Gallery of the University of Rochester, New York, Lu Harper; Metropolitan Museum of Art, New York, Lisa Messinger; The Museum of Modern Art, New York, Laura Rosenstock and Allyson Wolfe; National Academy Museum, New York, David Dearinger, Kathy Fieramosca, Wendy Rogers, and Mark D. Mitchell; National Archives and Records Administration, Civil Branch, Washington, D.C., Eugene Morris; National Arts Club, New York, Carol Lowrey; National Museum of American History, Washington, D.C., Nancy L. Card; Barbara Neary, Raton, New Mexico; Nedra Matteucci Galleries, Santa Fe, Nedra Matteuci, John Schild, and Harry McKee; New Mexico Museum of Art, Santa Fe, Michelle Roberts and Joan Tafoya; New Mexico Museum of Art Library, Santa Fe, Susan Poorbaugh and Mary Jebsen; New Mexico History Museum/Palace of the Governors, Museum of New Mexico, Santa Fe, Daniel Kosharek; Palace of the Governors, Fray Angélico Chávez History Library, Santa Fe, Tomas Jaehn; Oklahoma City Museum of Art, Hardy George and Jim Meeks; Panhandle-Plains Museum of Art, Canyon, Texas, Michael Grauer; Ruth Pasquine, Little Rock, Arkansas; Margot Peters, Lake Mills,

Wisconsin; Phoenix Art Museum, Leesha Alston and Jerry N. Smith; Robert L. Parsons Fine Art, Taos, New Mexico, Robert Parsons; Rosenstock Fine Arts, Denver, Steve Good; St. Louis Art Museum, Clare M. Vasquez; Sangre de Cristo Arts and Conference Center, Pueblo, Colorado, Natasia Brandstatten and Holly Paulman; Smithsonian American Art Museum, Washington, D.C., William Truettner, Sandra Levinson, James Souza, Pat Lynagh, Cecilia Chin, and Kelly Johannes; Smithsonian Institution, Archives of American Art, Washington, D.C., Wendy Hurlock-Baker and Judy Throm; Smithsonian Institution, Research and Scholars Center, Washington, D.C., Andrew L. Thomas, Juley Photographic Collection, and Joan Stahl; Southwest Research Center of Northern New Mexico, Taos, Nita Murphy; Stark Museum of Art, Orange, Texas, Sarah Boehme, David Hunt, Jennifer Hudson Connors, Janis Becker, and Tom Eckert; Taos Historic Museums, New Mexico, David Cunningham, Cheri Vitez, Seth Dalby, Annie McDaniel, Karen Young, and Joan Phillips; Taos Public Library, Judith Bronner; University of New Mexico, Center for Southwest Research, Albuquerque, Ann Massman; University of New Mexico, Fine Arts/Zimmerman Library, Albuquerque, David Herzel and Dena Kinney; University of New Mexico, University Art Museum, Albuquerque, Tyler Anderson, Bonnie Verardo, and Kathleen Howe; University of Oklahoma, Charles M. Russell Center for the Study of Art of the American West, B. Byron Price; Whitman College Archives, Walla Walla, Washington, Michael Paulus; David L. Witt, Taos, New Mexico; Wright State University Libraries, Dayton, Ohio, Lynda Kachurek; Zaplin-Lampert Gallery, Santa Fe, Mark Zaplin, Richard Lampert, and David Clemmer. Special thanks to the following individuals for personal recollections and interpretations regarding Blumenschein's life career: Shirley G. Davis, Nancy Butler Waller Nadler, Grace Rowe, Gail Curry Fish, Nick Kilmer, Miriam Kilmer, Annie Cohen-Solal, Jennifer Donnelly, George Carlson, Sally (and John) Schrup, Ellen Waterston, Gib Curry, Melissa Rowe, and those persons who wished to remain anonymous or whose names and kind assistance we may have overlooked.

We would also like to acknowledge our fellow authors for the essays they contributed about singular Blumenschein works. They were assisted in their research by Noel Anderson, Humanities Librarian, and Gary Spurr, Labor and Political Collections Archivist, University of Texas at Arlington Library; Peggy Ann Brown,

Alexandria, Virginia; Charles C. Eldredge, Hall Distinguished Professor of American Art and Culture, University of Kansas, Lawrence; Betsy Fahlman; Sarena Fletcher, Head Librarian, Delaware Art Museum, Wilmington; Tomas Jaehn, Curator, Fray Angélico Chávez History Library, Palace of the Governors, Museum of New Mexico, Santa Fe; Helen Lucero, Director Emeritus, Visual Arts, National Hispanic Cultural Center, Albuquerque; Enrique Lamadrid, Director, Chicano/Hispano/Mexicano Studies, University of New Mexico, Albuquerque; Eugene Morris, Archivist, Civil Records, National Archives and Records Administration, Washington, D.C.; Marilee Nason; Sascha Scott, Pre-doctoral Fellow, Smithsonian Institution American Art Museum, Washington, D.C.; Samuel Sisneros, Senior Archivist, New Mexico State Records Center and Archives, Albuquerque; Gray Sweeney, Professor of Art History, Arizona State University, Tempe; Tessa Veazey, Archives of American Art, Smithsonian Institution, Washington, D.C.; Allyson Wolfe, Collection Management and Exhibition Registration, The Museum of Modern Art, New York.

We cannot thank enough the many institutional and private lenders to the exhibition: The Albuquerque Museum of Art and History; The Anschutz Collection; Arizona State University Art Museum; BNSF (Burlington Northern/Santa Fe) Railway; Carlsbad Museum and Art Center, New Mexico; Cheekwood Museum of Art, Nashville; Dallas Museum of Art; The Dayton Art Institute, Dayton, Ohio; Denver Art Museum; Denver Museum of Nature & Science; Eiteljorg Museum of American Indians and Western Art, Indianapolis; The Fred Jones, Jr., Museum of Art, including the Eugene Brady Adkins Collection, University of Oklahoma, Norman; Free Library of Philadelphia; Michael and Andrea Frost; Gerald Peters Gallery, Santa Fe; Gilcrease Museum, Tulsa, Oklahoma; Indianapolis Museum of Art; J. N. Bartfield Galleries, New York; The Kelly Collection of American Illustration, Great Falls, Virginia; The Lunder Collection, Colby College Museum of Art, Waterville, Maine; The Metropolitan Museum of Art, New York; Museum of the American West, Autry National Center, Los Angeles; National Academy Museum, New York; National Cowboy & Western Heritage Museum, Oklahoma City; New Mexico Museum of Art, Santa Fe; North Carolina Museum of Art, Raleigh; Phoenix Art Museum; a Private Collection; Private Collection, Washington, D.C.; Rockwell Museum of Western Art, Corning, New York; Smithsonian American Art Museum, Washington, D.C.;

Robert Stamm; Stark Museum of Art, Orange, Texas; The Steinway Collection; University of New Mexico Art Museum, Albuquerque; The Wichita Center for the Arts.

And, finally, our sincere thanks to the staff at the University of Oklahoma Press, including Charles Rankin, Bobbie Canfield, Steven Baker, and Emmy Ezzell, and to copyeditor Renae Morehead, Lincoln, Nebraska, and indexer Debbie Lindblom, Apple Valley, California.

James K. Ballinger, Sybil Harrington Director, Phoenix Art Museum
Elizabeth J. Cunningham, Blumenschein Scholar
Peter H. Hassrick, Director, Petrie Institute for Western American Art, Denver Art Museum
Cathy L. Wright, Director, The Albuquerque Museum of Art and History

November 9, 2007

In Contemporary Rhythm

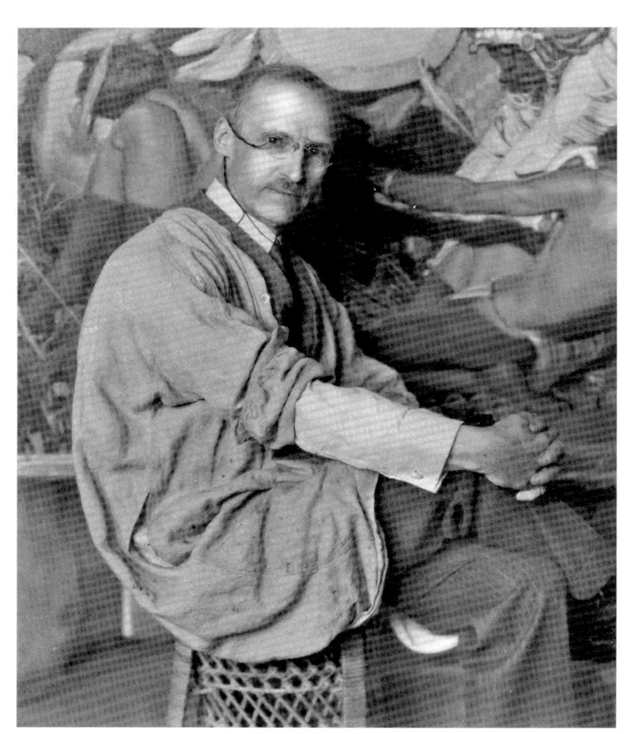

Introduction

Peter H. Hassrick and Elizabeth J. Cunningham

The world of art has long recognized American painter Ernest L. Blumenschein (1874–1960) as one of the founders of the Taos, New Mexico, art colony and the Taos Society of Artists. Many consider his work the most artistically complex, innovative, and accomplished within the beaux arts painting tradition. Less widely recognized are the modernism of his mature work, his early, influential perspectives on modern art, and his deep and lasting association with the leading artists, writers, and intellectuals of the first half of the twentieth century.

Like his fellow Taos artists, he cherished a legendary affection for the brilliance and physicality of the light and the extraordinary diversity of landforms and cultures in New Mexico. The Southwest certainly informed and expanded his art and spirit. However, his record of major prizes and commissions, coupled with the critical acclaim he received nationally and internationally, transcends those regional parameters and confirms his stature as a significant American artist.

Students of his art are also familiar with his dual early career as a master illustrator and art teacher, and they occasionally celebrate him as a champion and practitioner of nascent twentieth-century modernist trends. Those who have examined his life more thoroughly believe that his creative ambitions and extraordinary quest for excellence went beyond painting to include virtuoso skills as a violinist and a competitive obsession with physical and mental acuity. These pushed him to champion status as an angler and as a tennis, baseball, and bridge player.

Driven by perfectionism, Blumenschein was not especially prolific. His entire output, had it survived, would have numbered just over four hundred works—

including sketches, drawings, illustrations, studies, and small works painted for pleasure, as sketches for unrealized larger works, or as gifts for friends or potboilers that tourists could afford. Today only a few signature paintings remain. Blumenschein disposed of those canvases with which he was less than fully satisfied. A small note written by Blumenschein states, "150 paintings destroyed" before the family moved to Taos, New Mexico, in 1919, and an anecdotal account from one of his housekeepers relates receiving his cast-off canvases to help keep the dirt from dropping through the ceiling boards of an adobe home. His ledger books attest to others that he destroyed, cut down, or repainted. Blumenschein considered only about fifty paintings, many of which are reproduced in this book, to be truly worthy of representing him to posterity. Some of these won national awards and landed in major museum collections during his lifetime.

Due to the relative paucity of his pictures, not many museums or private collectors own examples of Blumenschein's art. To view his work takes an effort: paintings are scattered throughout the country, mainly in the West, in museum, corporate, and private collections. The largest number of museum-quality paintings created specifically for competition, about 20 percent, is in the Stark Museum of Art in Orange, Texas, and the Gilcrease Museum in Tulsa, Oklahoma. In the eastern United States, the Smithsonian American Art Museum owns two, as does the National Academy of Design in New York. The Metropolitan Museum of Art, the National Arts Club, the Rockwell Museum in Corning, New York, and the Dayton Art Museum in Ohio each possess one major painting. Farsighted collectors recognized the value of Blumenschein's paintings beginning in the 1970s, a time when museums and corporate collections were de-accessioning works that did not fit their constantly evolving missions. Thus, such major paintings as *Jury for the Trial of a Sheepherder for Murder* from the Museum of Modern Art, *The Chief Speaks* from the Cincinnati Art Museum, *Sangre de Cristo Mountains* from the Toronto Art Museum, and *Taos Indian Holding Water Jug* and *The Peacemaker* from the Santa Fe Railway's corporate collection ended up in private hands. In Denver, Philip Anschutz and William Foxley acquired several remarkable such paintings from these sources at the time.

The purpose of this book and the accompanying retrospective exhibition is to explore in depth the dimensions of Blumenschein's multifaceted life and to build upon the broad public and academic enthusiasm that has followed the artist for many years. In particular, a debt is owed to the early recognition of Blumenschein's talents by Denver Art Museum and the Museum of New Mexico, the latter of which hosted not one but two retrospective exhibitions of his work during the artist's lifetime. Also, much credit must be extended to the considerable insight and observations of William T. Henning, Jr., then curator at the Colorado Springs Fine Arts Center, who initiated and organized the Ernest L. Blumenschein Retrospective exhibition, held at the center in 1978. Henning and others before him understood what a formative artist Blumenschein was and how forcefully he served as a spokesman and catalyst for multiple voices in art in his time.

When, in 1955, Laura Bickerstaff set out to write *Pioneer Artists of Taos*, she asked Blumenschein, one of the few surviving members of the Taos Society of Artists, to write the introduction, offering his thoughts on several of the colony's leading painters. His observations and recollections heavily influenced Bickerstaff's writings and have continued to have a significant effect on current understanding of the Taos artists. When *Century* magazine searched for someone to offer a balanced view of the contentious Armory Show in 1913, the editor turned to Blumenschein for a critique. And when the members of the Taos Society of Artists sought to promote their collaborative efforts beyond the borders of New Mexico, Blumenschein not only published one of the first articles on the group from within its ranks but also procured permission from the State Land Office for use of a 1917 film on New Mexico that included engaging, efficacious promotional footage on the society. This helped earn the society its place in the American art scene nearly twenty years before critics and art historians coined the term "regionalism" to describe works by such artists as Grant Wood and Thomas Hart Benton.

Blumenschein bridged divergent worlds. The geographies he enjoyed were spread widely from the Rocky Mountain West to New York City and Paris, France. He intentionally elected to live and find inspiration among various groups of people. Taos, with its mix of Anglo, Hispanic, and Indian lifeways, was as complex socially and culturally as New York or Paris. Additionally, he embraced a diverse range of aesthetic constructs, espousing general understanding of and appreciation for a variety of traditions and movements. His own paintings were at once based on academic figuration and realism but were so strongly crafted on principles of formalist rigor, abstract design, and color as a fundamental determinant of form that his peers and many of the nation's leading critics considered him a "modern."

Like John Sloan, Maynard Dixon, William Glackens, Frederic Remington, and other American artists active in the 1890s and 1900s, Blumenschein first made his living as an illustrator. The magazines sought works that complemented the stories they illustrated with a pictorial narrative. This experience later influenced the artist's painting, which had a story or internal narrative that often only the artist understood. Several of his great works, however, record the history and culture of northern New Mexico. Although viewers in his day (and today as well) may not have comprehended all the hidden meanings, the emotional essence and regional narratives are compelling. Critics, museum staff, artists, and audiences recognized their power and aesthetic—the work of a consummate master.

Musical training, discipline, and passion from his early years infused Blumenschein's mature paintings from the 1910s through the 1950s. Movement, composition, rhythm, pattern, harmony, and color appear in nearly every mature signature painting. All of these combined to create accomplished finished works deserving of the term "decorative"—then an expression of high praise for an artist in total control of his craft and aesthetics.

With such distinctive paintings, Blumenschein won numerous awards at the Panama Pacific International Exposition, the Art Institute of Chicago, the Philadelphia Sesquicentennial Exhibition, the National Academy of Design, the Carnegie International, the National Arts Club, and the Salmagundi Club. Blumenschein is known to have participated between 1896 and 1959 in over five hundred local, regional, national, and international exhibitions, including two solo shows at New York's Grand Central Art Galleries in 1927 and 1934 and, in 1948, the Museum of New Mexico's first solo retrospective exhibition honoring the state's outstanding artists.

Blumenschein was, throughout his career, more enlightened in his treatment of American Indians than most of his contemporaries. Even so, his work shows evolution in his interpretation of Indians. During his years as an illustrator, Blumenschein had numerous opportunities to portray the Indian people of the West and Southwest. Assignments to illustrate the writings of Hamlin Garland, Dr. Charles Eastman, and other Indian advocates acquainted the artist with the plight of Native peoples in the 1890s and early 1900s. Invariably, he chose to depict Indians as defenders of their way of life and, unlike most illustrators of the previous generation, to present them from their own perspective. By the 1910s Blumenschein was concentrating on large easel paintings with Taos Indians as central subjects. In these works he painted Taos Pueblo people in ceremonial dress and posed them in classical stances, investing them with symbolic grandeur that evoked stirring metaphorical implications.

During the 1920s Blumenschein witnessed Indian cultures in transition, their traditions endangered by the Anglo-Christian dominant culture. The artist took explicit steps through his paintings and writings at this time to counter destructive trends in cultural dominance. *Dance at Taos* (ca. 1923), for example, was both an exercise in aesthetic experimentation and a political statement. It put him in direct opposition to the Bureau of Indian Affairs' efforts at acculturation. More precisely, through his art he strove to thwart legislative attempts to expropriate Pueblo lands and restrict Indian dances and religious ceremonies. At a time when many government officials, religious conservatives, and segments of the general public believed that Indian ceremonies were backward if not lewd and fundamentally injurious, Blumenschein joined liberal thinkers from New Mexico and beyond to fight for Indian rights.

True to his aesthetic aspirations, in the 1920s Blumenschein also began to experiment with Native pictorial forms and musical patterns to find design structures that honored Indian art. His reverence for Native art led him to incorporate Indian design into his vision of Native peoples as inseparable parts of the larger scheme of nature. When the artist turned to landscape painting in the 1930s, he often integrated Indian subjects and designs into those canvases.

In the 1930s, however, leading historians of American art such as Virgil Barker (*A Critical Introduction to American Painting*) and Eugene Neuhaus (*The History and Ideals of American Art*) pigeonholed Blumenschein as an illustrator or a painter of Indians. Some have recognized him strictly as a portraitist. Yet from the mid-1920s through the 1940s his paintng broadened to include monumental landscapes as well as two signature figure paintings. He received lofty recognition for his achievement when, during his lifetime, the Metropolitan Museum of Art purchased *Taos Valley* and the Museum of Modern Art acquired *Jury for the Trial of a Sheepherder for Murder*. In the 1940s and 1950s, the cold winters and altitude of Taos forced him to the milder climate of Albuquerque. There he found a fresh landscape to paint in the surrounding Sandia Mountains, as well as a built environment that inspired his last series—urban landscapes of the downtown area and the railroad yards.

Blumenschein is often thought of strictly as a western artist, yet he influenced a broad spectrum of American cultural life. As an illustrator, he fashioned a graceful, art nouveau image of national life that elevated the standard of pictorial interpretation in popular magazines and books. His later reflections on the Armory Show helped many to reconcile their traditional view of art with the more avant-garde trends of Post-Impressionism, Fauvism, and Cubism. In the 1920s, for example, he persuaded his colleagues at the conservative National Academy of Design in New York to admit "moderns" into their ranks and their exhibition programs. And through his art, with its western subject matter and experimental design-oriented style, he promoted a modern way of viewing themes that had traditionally been presented in strictly academic terms.

One of the difficulties in analyzing Blumenschein's oeuvre is how to categorize it. Critics, fellow artists, and museum people have noted both conservative and modernistic elements in his paintings. While his work was considered "radical" among National Academy conservatives, the modernist ranks, including Alfred Barr, director of the Museum of Modern Art, viewed Blumenschein's paintings as examples of "objective description" (in the realistic narrative or realistic storytelling tradition, a sidebar within the modernist painting tradition). Yet in the 1950s, when modern art began focusing on expression rather than craft, even Barr realized what Blumenschein had accomplished in his work—a blend of aesthetic discipline and exquisite craftsmanship governed by academic tradition but with distinctly modernist tendencies. In the end, Blumenschein was an original, true to his own art and vision.

This book and exhibition provide an unprecedented opportunity to reevaluate, through the work of one of the region's most commanding artistic figures, the traditionally academic realm of western American art. To consider that realm as a harbor that accommodates progressive, Post-Impressionist experimentation and production is to move beyond the former limiting categorization of not only Blumenschein's work but, in a broader sweep, art of the American West.

At mid-century, Blumenschein predicted that abstract painting would overshadow and nearly obliterate representational painting for at least the next fifty years. History validated his assessment. In 1958, the year of Blumenschein's last retrospective during his lifetime, Erwin Barrie made another prediction. Noting the originality and individuality of Blumenschein's paintings, Barrie, director of New York's Grand Central Art Galleries, declared his work deserving of "a place in American art for all time." This book intends to do just that: to give Blumenschein his deserved place in American art.

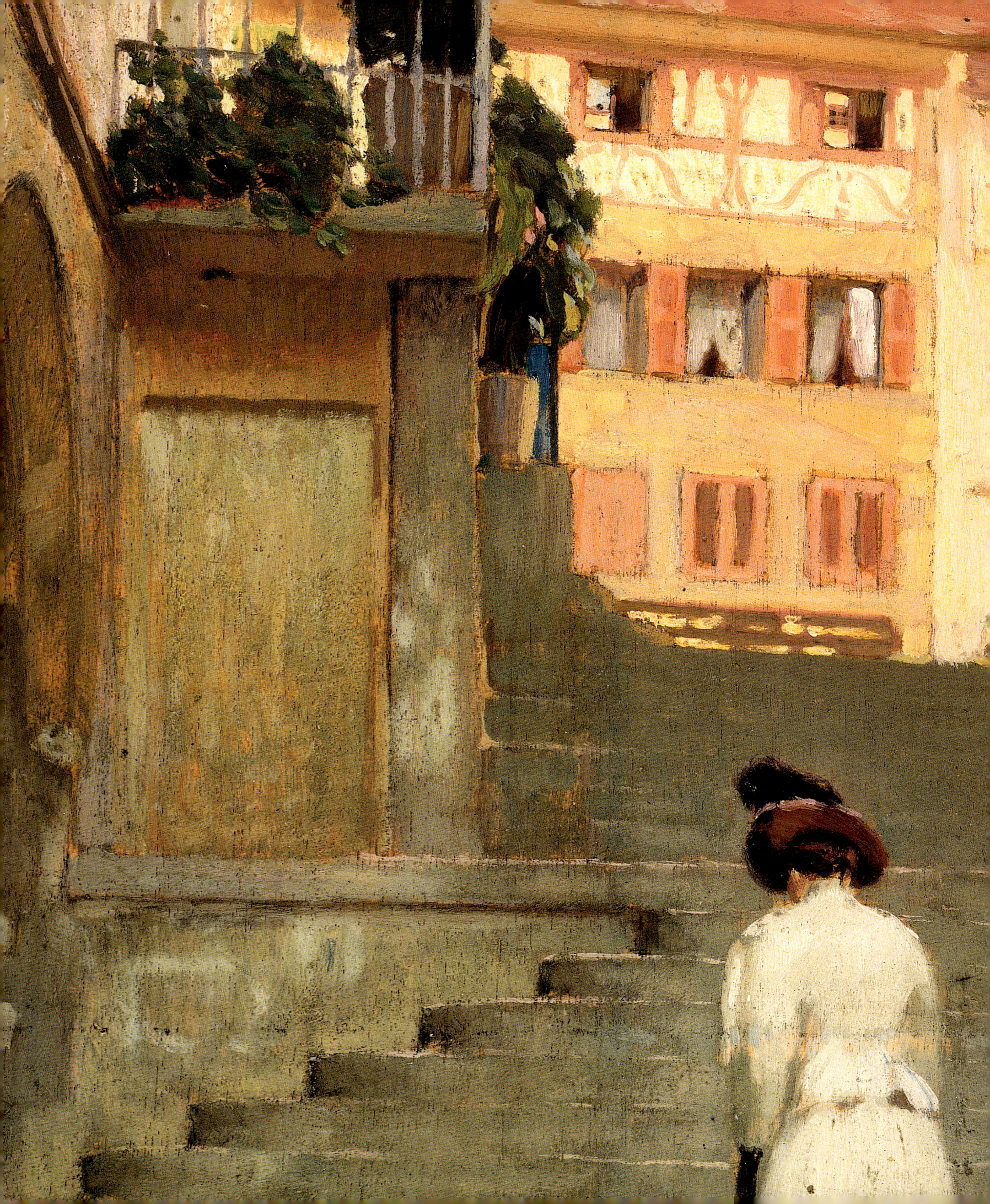

Chapter 1

Building Color Muscle

The Path to Painting, 1874–1909

Elizabeth J. Cunningham

The artist is artist to the death," wrote Ernest L. Blumenschein in January 1904. At age thirty, while pursuing advanced studies in Paris, he stood at a personal crossroads. With his intent to become a painter firmly in mind, he had to decide between his chosen profession and the love of a woman, a fellow art student. In a poignant letter to her, he voiced his doubts and insecurities. How could he support them financially when he did not yet know his trade? What if he could not make a living once he had learned it? If he directed his energies along a more practical path, would he awake one day full of regret, revulsed by his choice? In the calm air of the night, away from her, he came face to face with the truth. Art was more necessary to him than the love of a woman. Art would always have the prior claim. Art had his soul. For art, his old mistress, he would endure "all the struggles, the disappointments and discouragements" of work that would "demand and compel a life of servitude, a life of excruciating pleasure and pain."[1]

Thus was Blumenschein's very being defined, both as a person and as a painter. At times humanistic, compassionate, and conciliatory, he could also be insecure, uneasy, and downright contentious. His self-imposed demands established a perfectionist standard by which he judged himself and others equally. When driven by his muse, these high ideals—and Blumenschein's unequivocal candor—often created conflict with others, including his family. Art came first: his passion for painting commanded his consummate effort always.

Ernest Leonard Blumenschein, born May 25, 1874, in Pittsburgh, Pennsylvania, descended from a long line of European-trained musicians. The family legacy and discipline of music would influence his early years and resonate profoundly throughout his career. His grandfather and great-uncle formed their own band, known as Jung's Orchestra, and played in and around Darmstadt, Germany, before immigrating to the United States in 1850. His father, William Leonard Blumenschein, left gainful employment in Pittsburgh to study composition and theory in Leipzig, Germany, in the early 1870s. At the time, Leipzig enjoyed a reputation as the finest musical training center in Europe. While studying there, William Leonard met and fell in love with fellow student Leonore Chapin from Springfield, Massachusetts.

Music and love bound the two young musicians' hearts, and following their betrothal, they returned to Springfield to be married in the bride's family home on August 5, 1873. The Blumenscheins moved to Pittsburgh, where William Leonard taught piano and gave voice lessons. Following the births of their two sons, Ernest and George, and their only daughter, Florence, born in 1874, 1876, and 1878, respectively, William Leonard sought more lucrative employment to support his growing family. The year that Florence was born, he accepted the Dayton Philharmonic Society's offer to conduct their orchestra, so they again sought a new home. During his tenure with the Philharmonic Society from 1878 to 1909, William Leonard also wrote and composed over 150 works for choir, voice, and piano. Many of his scores were published by such firms as Schirmer, one of the leading musical publishers of the day, and he often performed them in Dayton and in Cincinnati, where he appeared as guest conductor from time to time. Between 1882 and 1896 William Leonard taught piano and voice at the Dayton Conservatory of Music, where he was principal, and played the organ and directed the choir at a Presbyterian church to supplement the family's income.

In 1881, three years after their move to Dayton, Leonore Blumenschein died of puerperal fever. Young Ernest had little more to hold onto than her photo and his memories of her enchanting songs and of bedtime readings from books like *The Swiss Family Robinson*. Her death fundamentally altered the family's home life even though William Leonard did his best to care for and nurture his young children. He hired a housekeeper to look after them while he was working and took them to services at the Presbyterian church where he was the organist. From him they learned the value of money and the importance of family. He stayed in touch with Leonore's family, and when Ernest was eleven, they traveled to Grandmother Chapin's home in Springfield. Ernest never forgot that visit—he went fishing for the first time and got his first dose of poison ivy.[2]

The family's grief may have been the reason that William Leonard started Ernest on the violin at age seven, and Ernest later remembered that violin practice and school kept him busy. William Leonard set musical standards for his son similar to those he established for the symphonies and choirs he conducted. Becoming a successful musician required unwavering discipline, faultless technical proficiency, and a deep love of music in general. Years after his father's death, Ernest wrote, "His life was preaching the beauty and nobility of the great composers, for which his children and many others will be very thankful. . . . He was much loved and respected by the people of Dayton where his quest for better music made a deep impression upon the entire surrounding country."[3] Through his father, Ernest learned about the lives and music of great composers—including Mozart, Bach, Handel, Beethoven, and Haydn—and developed a profound and enduring appreciation for and understanding of music. The legacy of excellence and dedication that his father left with him helped instill in young Ernest a sense of discipline and an enlightened cultural passion.

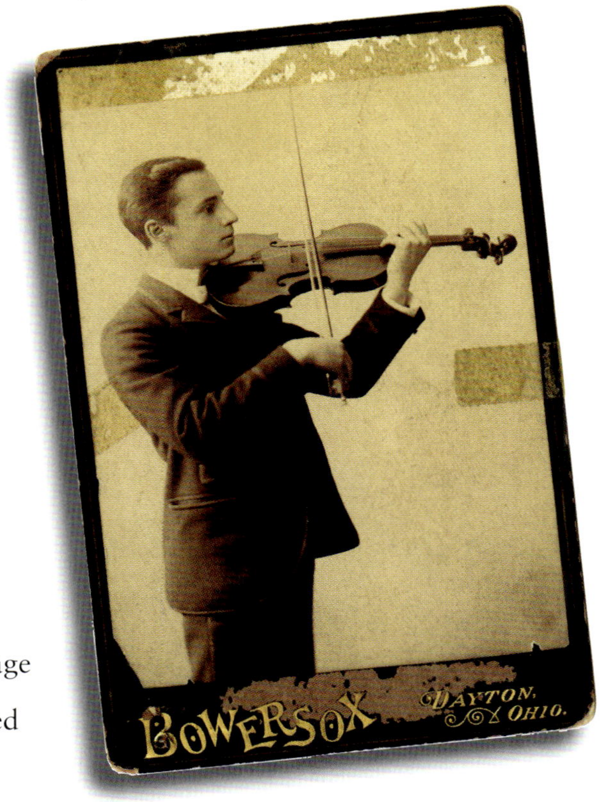

A precocious child, Ernest had been enrolled in public school at age five. Several years later, when the boy got in trouble in class, he received a whipping from the school principal, Marie Jacque.[4] This unpleasant happenstance took an abrupt and unexpected turn. Jacque, it happens, soon married a Dayton attorney, Charles Kumler. About the same time, Ernest's father met Kumler's sister, Jennie. She became Ernest's stepmother, and Marie Jacque Kumler became his aunt.[5]

Blumenschein at the violin, ca. age 17. Courtesy of the Palace of the Governors, Museum of New Mexico, New Mexico Department of Cultural Affairs, Santa Fe (neg. HP05.25-K).

Athletics and music occupied most of Ernest's teenage years. He recalled exposure to an "ordinary common school education" at Dayton's Central High School. Hours spent practicing music were balanced with playing baseball, football, and tennis. He brought the same determination and discipline to sports as he did to playing the violin. In early boyhood he learned to play tennis and later won medals at YMCA meets in Ohio and Indiana. For a year or two he was captain of the high school football team—an honor conferred upon him for his skill at the game. Baseball, tennis, and fishing would become lifelong passions, as would another pastime, chess. At age seventeen his ability and ambition took him to the state chess championship in Cleveland; he later boasted that he "came close to winning."[6]

In later years, Blumenschein would mention fellow students who became well-known Daytonians. When Blumenschein was a high school freshman, Orville Wright was a senior. He remembered that the Wright brothers ran the bicycle repair shop where the two gifted mechanics later constructed their aircraft. Another companion, Jacob Ritter, invented and developed the National Cash Register machine and tried on several occasions to entice Ernest into joining the business. Paul Laurence Dunbar, the first nationally acclaimed African American poet, was in Blumenschein's graduating class and shared his artistic aspirations.[7]

The *Dayton Herald* published one of Dunbar's first poems in June 1888.[8] Dunbar was the editor of Central High School's monthly paper, the *High School Times*, and also the president of the Philomathean Society, the literary organization responsible for publishing it.[9] Perhaps his fellow student's publication success inspired Blumenschein to produce, edit, and illustrate his own magazine called *Tomfoolery*. He modeled this weekly broadside on *Puck* and *Judge*, two popular magazines of the time. It consisted of one copy on four sheets of manila paper. Subscriptions cost fifteen cents, and subscribers were expected to pass each issue from hand to hand. Listed as editor, Blumenschein created the first issue in September 1888 and the last in April 1891. One of his drawings was of Dunbar and his fellow Philomatheans at one of the society's meetings.[10]

Pictures by Gustave Dore, found in his father's volumes of Dante, first captured Blumenschein's youthful imagination. Later, the works of Zim (caricaturist Eugene Zimmerman) claimed his "first great admiration in art."[11] By his senior year, Blumenschein's artistic tastes had advanced so that he could appreciate the fine drawings of two of America's premier illustrators, Charles Reinhart and Edwin Austin Abbey, then the budding artist's most inspiring influences.

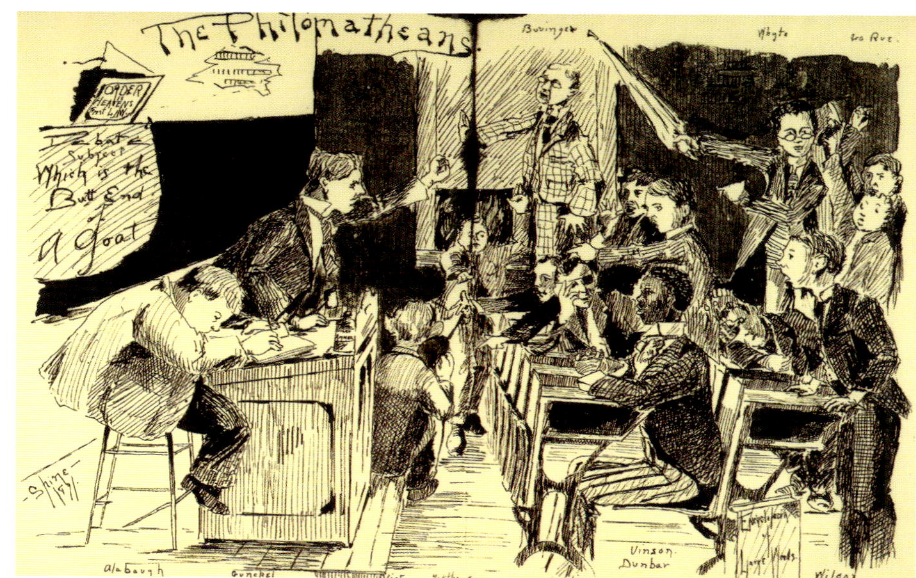

The Philomatheans, drawing, 1891. Courtesy of the Paul Laurence Dunbar Collection, Dayton Metro Library, Dayton, Ohio.

William Leonard's greatest wish for his son was that he might become a professional musician. By the time Ernest graduated from high school in 1891 (at age seventeen), he had played many concerts in Dayton and in the surrounding small towns, often performing with the Ayght Concert Company. His father discussed Ernest's musical future with the principal of Central High School. They weighed the merits of traditional college versus musical school, then settled on a compromise, concurring that a musical college would be best. Ernest's proficiency on the violin easily earned him admittance to Ohio's best, the Cincinnati College of Music. After producing his editions of *Tomfoolery*, however, Ernest wished to become an illustrator. Hoping to dissuade his son from such a course, William Leonard decided to consult someone in the field to test the viability of Ernest's chances. He wrote the editors of *Harper's Young People* for an opinion of his son's work. Just two weeks before his graduation from high school, Ernest received the editor's response:

> Dear Master Blumenschein:—Your father wished to know our opinion of your effort at drawing. In reply, the art editor of *Harper's Young People* directs me to say that the specimens which you submit show enough talent to warrant, in his opinion, further study. You need careful

> instruction in practical work. When the experiment is carried out for, say, a year, you can then decide whether there is enough promise to continue. The ranks of illustrators are very full—overcrowded in fact, but talent always commands success. You show talent which is promising.[12]

Since the Blumenschein clan had flourished as musicians for two generations, the prospects of a visual artist in the family appeared uncertain. The cautionary note about the overcrowded ranks of illustrators further strengthened the elder Blumenschein's resolve for his son to stay with music. However, during the 1891–92 academic year, while pursuing music at the Cincinnati College of Music, where he had won a violin scholarship, Ernest continued to sketch. The following year he persuaded his father to let him enroll simultaneously in drawing classes at the Art Academy of Cincinnati.

At the time that Blumenschein began his art studies, Cincinnati was an emerging national center for the visual arts. The Art Academy of Cincinnati, founded in 1887, had named Thomas Nobel its director. A painter trained in the European academic tradition, Nobel believed in providing students with a solid grounding in rudimentary skills. Beginning students started out by drawing elementary forms, first recording simple outlines, then working on the effects of light and shadow. Next they focused on the still life, adding the study of texture. From there they advanced to drawing heads, then antique casts of statuary, ending with portraiture and the human figure. Nobel discussed his teaching philosophy with a Cincinnati paper: "Occasionally I have a pupil who wants to soar, but after I have held him back for a while he will thank me for teaching him thoroughness. That is what gives strength. Insufficient rudimentary training leaves the artist weak, and when he begins to compose and sketch, his compositions and sketches are weak. Hence we do not let our students go faster than they are prepared to go."[13]

The academy's 1892–93 enrollment roster shows Blumenschein in four classes: two elemental drawing and two pen-drawing classes. As ambitious as that sounds, the curriculum apparently did not meet his expectations: "I was put to drawing and shading cubical and cylindrical boxes painted white. It was a frightful task and nearly extinguished my desire to become an illustrator."[14] When Blumenschein complained to Nobel, the director sent him back to the elementary class, with its white boxes and messy charcoal, with the encouraging words that "God's light is just as beautiful on an ash can as on the human form divine."[15] Blumenschein never forgot this counsel and later advocated a similar academic approach in his own teaching.

Fortuitously, study at the school included visits to the Cincinnati Art Museum. Founded in 1880, the museum had opened its doors to the public in 1886. Since Blumenschein had limited prior exposure to the visual arts, the museum provided an introduction to the first sophisticated oil paintings and sculptures he had ever seen. The works of several prominent Cincinnati painters—Henry Farny, Edward Potthast, Joseph Henry Sharp, J. H. Gest, Frank Duveneck, and Fernand Lungren—graced the walls. Members of the Cincinnati Art Club, many of these local worthies taught at Cincinnati's art schools, including the academy. Several would have direct influence on Blumenschein's student life and his later career.

These works by European and American artists not only came as a revelation to Blumenschein but they also provided the impetus for him to continue with his drawing classes. He had a particular fondness for rendering statuary he saw in the galleries. His pursuit of art was further sustained when the academy offered a special trial class in late 1892. "I was about ready to give up the disgusting study of art," he later admitted, "when a class in illustration was opened under Fernand Lungren. It was at last a chance to exercise my imagination." The course description spelled out a potential future for Blumenschein: "This class is designed for the practical instruction in all branches of illustration—to prepare the student to compete with those already engaged in the occupation. The best examples of illustration furnished in our newspapers, magazines, and books will be considered and instruction given in the use of all methods employed in making drawings for reproduction in black and white."[16]

Lungren, an established illustrator, had published work in most of the major New York magazines by the 1890s. He had also visited the West a couple of times and found particular success with illustrations that featured western scenes. Lungren's class opened at an opportune time for Blumenschein. His enthusiasm shone, and so did his talent when he won the class competition for best illustration.

A Cincinnati paper chose one of Blumenschein's works to illustrate a story, an achievement that finally proved Ernest's mettle to his father.[17] Although it may have been painful to witness his son's diversion from a career in music, William Leonard now recognized where Ernest's passions lay and realized that his son just might have a chance at success. To further Ernest's artistic aspirations, he agreed to pay for a year's study at the Art Students League of New York, provided Ernest continue his music study at the National Conservatory of Music, where philanthropist Jeannette Thurber, its founder, offered worthy young musicians professional training to further their public careers. In this venue his talents evidently earned him the privilege of playing first violin under the celebrated Anton Dvořák, the conservatory's second director.[18]

In the fall of 1893 Ernest set out for his new adventure in New York with Charles Ebert, a classmate from the Art Academy of Cincinnati. The two found a room with meals for seven dollars a week in the vicinity of the Art Students League, which offered a program that seemed perfectly suited to him.

Considered the nation's leading art school, the Art Students League was founded in 1875 when young artists rebelled against the conservatism and favoritism at the National Academy of Design. The country's only independent art school at the time, the Art Students League offered a fresh alternative to the strictly ordered curriculum at the academy. Its objective as stated in foundation documents was the "encouragement of a spirit of unselfishness among its members" that would allow the "free exchange of information and ideas."[19] Students could choose their own classes and enter any class so long as the instructor consented. Students also had a say in critiquing teacher performance, lending a sense of democratic structure to the institution. The regimen was rigorous but generally rewarding to individual students, who came from all over the country. By 1893, when Blumenschein enrolled, an estimated five hundred students were in attendance, many of whom were women.[20]

Blumenschein arrived at the Art Students League at an exciting time. The school had moved into its new, permanent home at 215 West Fifty-seventh Avenue in 1892. The modern, well-lit, and well-ventilated classrooms and studios were considered the best in the world.[21] The instructors, trained in Europe, dedicated themselves to teaching the newest foreign methods to the next generation. William Merritt Chase, Kenyon Cox, and J. Carroll Beckwith, who had represented their country at the Paris Salon of 1889, determined that they would adapt the lessons they had learned abroad to the depiction of the landscape and people of the United States, thus creating a manner of painting that was cosmopolitan, rather than insular, and recognizably American. They and other league instructors were early members of the Society of American Artists, formed in 1877 in reaction to the National Academy of Design's rejection of some younger progressive members from that year's exhibition. When comparing exhibitions between the two groups in 1893, a *New York Times* review found that the cosmopolitan society's "beauty of workmanship and vigorous personality" vied with current painting at the new Salon of Paris. The insular academy showed many interesting works, but, the critic predicted, it was liable to lose more of its membership due to the "narrow spirit shown by the older men toward the painters of sunlight and the impressionists."[22]

League instructors and their students exhibited at the 1893 Columbian Exposition in Chicago. There a reporter compared the students' work with that of the students at the Pennsylvania Academy of Fine Arts. In contrast with their Philadelphia brethren, the "pictures made by the life classes of the New York League [were] taken from living things."[23] In those days, most beginning classes drew from plaster casts. At the Art Students League, both men and women could draw from the nude figure as soon as they graduated from the antique classes. That was considered progressive.

Blumenschein began his study in John Twachtman's preparatory antique drawing class.[24] He later recounted that his distinguished mentor, a founding member in 1897 of the Ten American Painters (a group that espoused an American style of impressionism), failed to inspire him as a teacher. This was not true for other students. Allen Tucker, for example, felt fortunate to begin under Twachtman.

In Tucker's opinion, "not only was he one of the great men of his time, but one of the best teachers that ever was, somehow instilling into people the idea of the greatness and nobility of the thing called art."[25] For Blumenschein, Twachtman proved to be generally unsympathetic, ill-tempered, and brutal with his charges. His irate temperament, Blumenschein surmised, stemmed from Twachtman's lack of critical recognition and a problem with drinking.[26] One of Blumenschein's fellow students, however, may have created the atmosphere for Blumenschein's bad experience with Twachtman. Lionel Barrymore got into a fight in class with another student. They crashed into easels, "scattering color like an explosion in a paint factory." The fight ended with the classroom in shambles and an uncertainty as to when it could be restored to its former condition.[27] No doubt after the two miscreants were expelled from Twachtman's class, the damage they had done left him cranky.

In any event, the young student from Ohio bore Twachtman's instruction for only two months, then switched to a similar class offered by J. Carroll Beckwith. There Blumenschein found the inspiration and understanding he needed. With another league instructor, William Merritt Chase, Beckwith had exposed American audiences to major trends in French art when they organized an exhibition of the Barbizon school and Impressionists at the National Academy of Design in 1883. Teaching was another of Beckwith's missions: at the Art Students League he could pass on the pleasure in craftsmanship and dedication to producing works of the highest quality to his students.[28] Blumenschein did not mention Beckwith's skill as a teacher, but sculptor Alexander Phimister Proctor transferred from the National Academy of Design to the Art Students League just to take his antique class. Under Beckwith, Proctor "really began to learn how to draw."[29]

Blumenschein also took life classes with Kenyon Cox, who was known for "his rigid and exacting system of instruction."[30] Some students found Cox too demanding, but for Blumenschein, accustomed to the discipline music had instilled, this was not a problem. He evidently learned a technique from Cox that became an enduring practice. The instructor would pose the model in a studio separate from the classroom, which forced students to leave their easels, go up one floor, look at the model, and return to the easel and draw their impressions, repeating the process until they could reproduce the figure from memory. This exercise helped students become analytical, so that their compositions conveyed the function and structure of the figure as well as the feeling it evoked.[31] Blumenschein would utilize memory sketches in his work throughout his career.

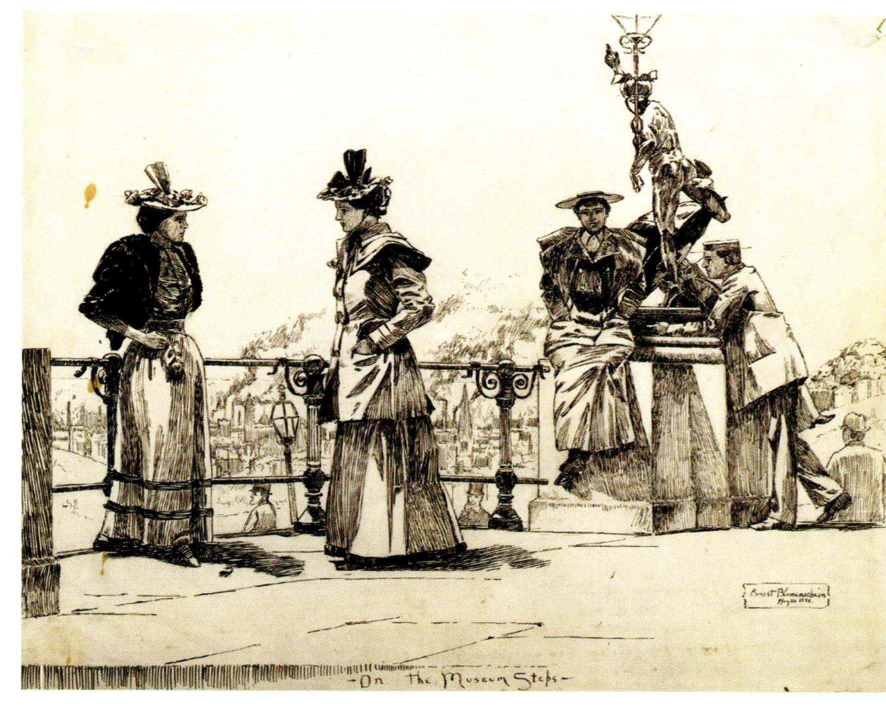

On the Museum Steps, 1893, ink on paper, 13½ × 16¾ inches. Collection of the New Mexico Museum of Art, Santa Fe. Gift of Helen Greene Blumenschein.

Kenyon Cox and William Merritt Chase may have shared prestige as two of the league's outstanding personalities in the 1890s; however, their philosophies stood in direct opposition. Cox, who adhered to strict academic traditions, was conservative, while Chase, who was open to experimentation and continued growth, was progressive. In another setting this may have forced students into one camp or the other, but at the Art Students League, which stressed cooperation and fostered a free exchange of new ideas as well as the maintenance of the old standards, they learned to embrace all styles of art.[32]

Although Blumenschein later claimed that he found little of interest in his year's study at the Art Students League, his experience there left a deep impression—it centered him in his craft. Certainly one remarkable opportunity grew out of his training. At the close of classes in 1894, Blumenschein landed his first illustration job. He took his portfolio to the offices of *McClure's* magazine in Lafayette Place. After perusing the young artist's portfolio, A. F. Jaccaci, the art editor, commissioned him to execute four pages: two for Gilbert Parker's article "The Finding of Fingall," featured in the September 1894 issue, and two more to enhance "The Romance of Dulltown," by James W. Temple, which appeared in February 1895. For a young artist with only two years' training, it was a portentous assignment. Blumenschein earned ten dollars per page for these illustrations, a modest stipend compared to an established illustrator like Frederic Remington, who earned at least ten times as much in those years. It was enough, though, to impress Ernest's father, who finally, once and for all, relinquished his dream of a musical career for Ernest and decided that his son should now receive the finest available schooling, the kind that had launched his own career. That meant European training. He would send Ernest to Paris.

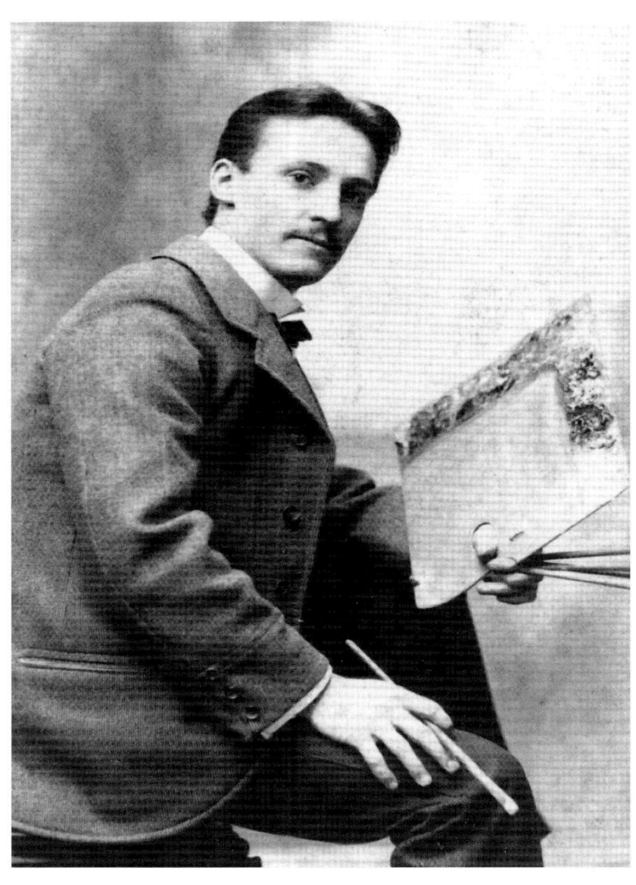

Blumenschein as an art student, ate 1890s. Courtesy of the Palace of the Governors, Museum of New Mexico, New Mexico Department of Cultural Affairs, Santa Fe (neg. HP05.25-M).

Just as Leipzig had attracted young Americans as a musical center in 1850, Paris had become the mecca for young American painters and sculptors by the end of the century. Blumenschein joined their ranks, sailing for France in September 1894 with fellow art students Charles Allan Gilbert, Ernest Kaiser, Oscar Lentz, and his former roommate Charles Ebert. The five found lodgings at 9 rue Falguierre. Despite his father's monthly stipend of fifty-nine dollars (about three hundred francs), a sum that made him the "richest member in the Latin Quarter," Blumenschein initially had to share a studio and an apartment with his four friends; and with them he also frequented "a certain cheap restaurant."[33]

Blumenschein's training at the Art Students League prepared him for the rigors of his art studies in Paris. He enrolled at the Académie Julian under Jean-Joseph Benjamin-Constant, known for his portraits and orientalist paintings, and Jean-Paul Laurens, largely a history painter. Esteemed for his easel work and large state commissions, Laurens was also an accomplished illustrator. He favored tightly drawn, richly colored grand genre scenes inspired by French and Spanish history. His teaching focused on the careful study of anatomy, which, according to Alphaeus Cole, one of Blumenschein's fellow students, Laurens considered "a most important asset to an artist's knowledge, especially when drawing figures in action from imagination."[34] Blumenschein, recognizing their importance to his art, quickly absorbed these lessons.

Benjamin-Constant, Blumenschein's other teacher, was known more as a colorist whose chosen subject—Arabic themes—connected him with exotic cultures of North Africa. It was Benjamin-Constant who, according to Blumenschein, encouraged him to paint American Indians. Blumenschein had become enamored with James Fenimore Cooper's *Last of the Mohicans*, and Benjamin-Constant's urgings fell on receptive ears.[35] The American naturalist Ernest Thompson Seton, a former student at the Art Students League and at the Académie Julian, had a studio in Paris at the time. Like Blumenschein, he had a lifelong interest in American Indians, and he purportedly held mock Indian dances in his studio, which he invited Blumenschein and his compatriots to watch.

Of the two instructors, Laurens was considered the more affable and was regarded by his many American pupils as "among the most famous of modern French masters."[36] Lionel Barrymore, who also took classes with Laurens, perhaps best expressed the *cher maître*'s repute among students: "I looked at Jean-Paul Laurens' works with admiration and awe and upon him with awe and terror."[37] The two instructors as a teaching team, however, did not present a particularly harmonious presence. Their methods differed to such a degree that students often felt perplexed. On the simple matter of how to prime one's canvas before starting to work, for example, there was fundamental disagreement. As Cole recollected, "One, Jean-Paul Laurens, gets angry if we tone our canvases: the other, Benjamin-Constant, if we do not. We try to please them both. It happened one month to be Benjamin-Constant's, he was sick and Jean-Paul turned up in his place and he had the shock of his life and said he would only criticize the drawings that month as the painters preferred the old way of working."[38] The two professors shared one basic philosophy, however: they were both firm traditionalists. Laurens taught drawing in the spirit of Jean-Auguste Dominique Ingres, precise and unfaltering. Benjamin-Constant exploded with expletives when any of his pupils wavered toward the influence of artists who practiced outside the beaux arts tradition, such as the Impressionists, whom he referred to as "those 'sal con' [sons of bitches]" who "only exist to destroy the young."[39]

Over the next ten months, Blumenschein worked long hours on his drawing, attending classes by day and sketching around Paris in his free time. Blumenschein remembered it as "a very happy life." The classroom, a "high-ceilinged, crowded, smoky, ill-smelling painty art studio," was crowded "with male students from all over the world—most of them wearing heavy beards and large flowing black neckties. They were a jolly lot: insolent, disrespectful, proud to defy most of society's conventions. Some, extremely gifted with the brush; others could sing well or act well. Many were descendants of the great men of Europe. A son of Alphonse Daudet was in this class." On cold days and throughout the winter, a big coal stove heated the room. There was no ventilation because cold air discomforted the models. "The French," Blumenschein remarked, "in those days before the war, were not strong on fresh air and hygiene." Windows topped the classroom's high walls, providing light, and palette scrapings plastered the walls as high as the hand could reach. Paintings and drawings of the nudes completely covered one wall.[40]

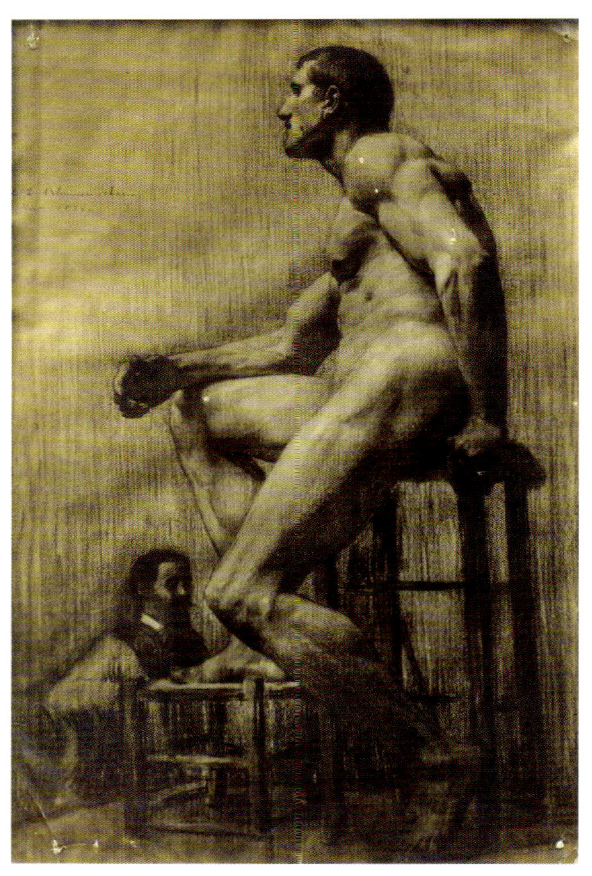

Prize-winning drawing by Blumenschein at the Académie Julian in Paris, ca. 1893. Photograph by Em. Crevaux, 16 × 11 centimeters. Courtesy of the Ernest L. Blumenschein Papers, 1889–1960, Archives of American Art, Smithsonian Institution, Washington, D.C.

Laurens and Benjamin-Constant awarded Blumenschein three prizes—one for composition and two for drawings of the nude. One of the two prize-winning drawings showed a male model posed on a stool with a footstool at his feet; the other presented a frontal pose of a bearded old man sitting on a stool. Such powerful drawings, with their forceful linear definition, supported Laurens's contention that through faithful anatomical rendition an artist might capture the true spirit of art. On a practical scale, such lessons were, in the master's mind, also fundamental for the illustrator who would have to work often without the benefit of a model.

After the *concours*, or competition exams, at the end of the term, art students followed the lead of French painters and departed Paris for the summer. Blumenschein joined the flow in the summer of 1895 and escaped the city heat in the nearby country town of Crecy-en-Brie (known as the birthplace of French writer Charles Etienne Louis Camus). There he relaxed and painted the picturesque rural scene. In the fall he returned to Paris for another year's study with Laurens and Benjamin-Constant.

Although he took his studies seriously, Blumenschein found time for pleasure and to make friends through his music. While he had by now abandoned the academic pursuit of music, he still played the violin well enough to garner an invitation to perform at the American Mission in Paris. On a more mundane level, he produced and acted in a minstrel show at the American Art Club, serving also on the Committee of Arrangements with three other students. The playbill, dated April 10, 1896, reveals the breadth of his thespian skills. He played the part of Bro' Michael for the first act and appeared again in the second as "Mlle. Lilly Blossom-Shine, The Première Danseuse."[41] He participated in Parisian cultural life, attending artists' balls such as the Quatres Arts Bal and Bal Julian.

The two seasons Blumenschein spent studying at the Académie Julian and copying paintings in the Louvre bore results when two of his works, a painting titled *Le Flutiste* (*The Flute Player*) and *Le Lac* (*The Lake*), a watercolor, were accepted in the Paris Salon of 1896. News of his accomplishment reached newspapers in Dayton and Cincinnati. In Dayton a Blumenschein admirer, L. B. Gunkel, wrote a letter to the editor in May 1896. He had recently visited Paris and seen the salon. There he discovered, to his surprise and delight, two of Blumenschein's works. *Le Flutiste*, he was proud to report, hung in a conspicuous position in one of the salon's largest rooms. Since French juries were perceived to be prejudiced against foreigners, Gunkel felt Blumenschein had received a great honor. Nonetheless, he ended his letter with a caveat: "Mr. Blumenschein has undoubted talent, and if he will keep himself free from the temptations that surround an artist's life in Paris, and add to his gift continued perseverance and industry (for talent without application is worse than nothing) he will do honor to himself and his native city. Let us hope that he will be equal to the occasion."[42]

Already a hometown hero in Dayton, now Cincinnati also claimed him as one of their own: "Mr. Blumenschein, another of the Cincinnati colony, and one of the strongest American students in Paris, has two pictures in the Old Salon," boasted a Cincinnati paper. The paper also reported on the city's other prominent artists, Joseph Henry Sharp, Elizabeth Nourse, Frank Duveneck, and Henry Farny, who also had paintings in the salon. To illustrate the article, the paper chose one of Sharp's Paris paintings, *Devaut St. Antoine*.[43] Alongside it and printed larger—taking up nearly a fourth of the article's space—was Blumenschein's *The Flute Player*.[44]

In September 1896 Blumenschein returned to New York. Attired in his French corduroy suit and flowing tie, he again sought out A. F. Jaccaci, now art editor with *Scribner's Monthly*. He received a commission to illustrate an article on the New England cotton mills and traveled to Lawrence, Massachusetts, and stayed two months to do the drawings on site. His next assignment took him to the Southwest. By way of the Santa Fe Railway, he arrived at Ft. Wingate, New Mexico, on January 2, 1897. Even blizzard conditions and a gruff army officer could not dispel the magic he felt at glimpsing his first American Indians—the Navajos—and the life and landscape of the West. He attended his first Indian dance and observed a Navajo medicine ceremony. The great spaces, snow-covered mountains, and dusty deserts peopled by Indians, Mexicans, and cowboys made such a strong impression on Blumenschein that he completely forgot to record local color for the story. His first pictures were a failure; he had to rework the whole job. The trip stood in stark contrast to student and studio life in Paris: it gave him a taste of outdoor life and imbued him with the desire to paint impressions of his own. Without a doubt, this experience laid the foundation for his future work.[45]

McClure's magazine kept Blumenschein busy for the rest of the year. Of his numerous assignments, three focused on the West: "Behind the Scenes at the 'Wild West' Show"; "The Bride Comes to Yellow Sky," by Stephen Crane; and "General Custer's Last Fight as Seen by Two Moon," by Hamlin Garland. The latter commission had far-reaching significance for Blumenschein. It was Blumenschein's initial contact with Garland (who made the "most systematic study of the red man" in American literature between 1895 and 1905), who would begin to shape his view of American Indian people within the context of social critique.[46]

Following a research trip to gather information on the Ute Indians in southern Colorado and the Pueblo people of New Mexico and Arizona in 1895,

Garland wrote about the injustices Indians suffered due to the federal government's allotment and assimilation policies and began to champion Indian rights. In 1897 the writer traveled to the Standing Rock Reservation in the Dakotas to learn more about the Sioux leader Sitting Bull. From there he traveled to the Lame Deer Reservation in Montana, where he met and interviewed the Northern Cheyenne leader Two Moon, witness to General George Armstrong Custer's defeat in 1876. Garland's narrative, based on this interview, compelled the American people to view the momentous battle at the Little Big Horn not as a story about the disaster that befell General Custer and his men but rather as an account from the perspective of the Cheyenne chief. Garland began and ended his article with a description of Two Moon, a tall, old man of regal bearing who personified the Cheyenne character in all its strength and distinction. The author also used the story to indicate the poverty that had been forced on reservation Indians, who, like Two Moon, were "patient under injustice, courteous even to [their] enemies."[47] Garland's writings allowed the American public to see Indian peoples as strong, dignified individuals with a culture of their own and provided an important contrast to the negative, often lurid, portrayals of Indians as savages and heathens produced by assimilationists and religious leaders bent on destroying their customs.

In this and other Indian stories, Garland continued his reformist writing, advocating for the downtrodden on government reservations. The writer, like any good interviewer, let the subject tell the story directly and served as the conduit between Two Moon, in this instance, and the American public. Blumenschein would take Garland's point of view to heart, not only in future works produced for other Garland stories, but in his whole view of Indians' place in the larger scheme of things.[48] He would adapt this technique to his own social commentary paintings in later years.

Blumenschein would illustrate two more of Garland's Indian stories for *McClure's*. Evidently his depictions impressed the author, who probably saw Blumenschein's illustration *Wards of the Nation*, published a few months later in *Harper's Weekly*.[49] Garland, who would later express disapproval of Frederic Remington's illustrations, could not help but admire Blumenschein's honest and sympathetic visual portrayal of the dilemma caused by the federal assimilation policy that took young Indian children away from their parents and culture to attend government boarding schools.[50] Blumenschein's work with Garland probably earned him future commissions for works by other Indian sympathizers. Blumenschein would later illustrate an article by American anthropologist James Mooney, whose support of Native people caused assimilationists to label him "a reactionary Indian-lover," and a book by Dr. Charles A. Eastman, an early advocate of Native rights.[51]

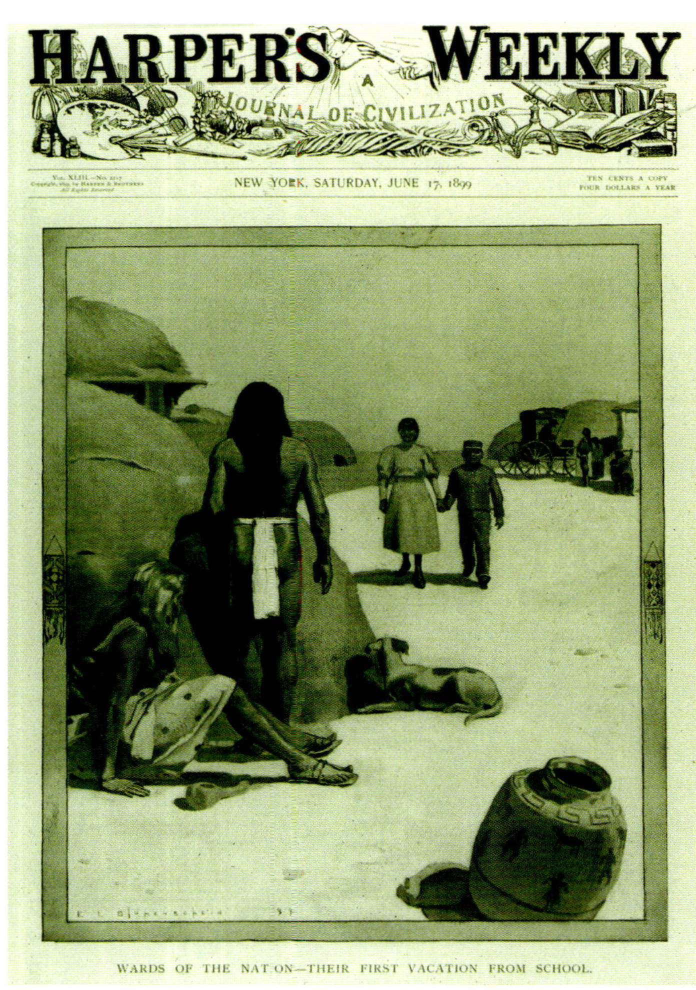

Wards of the Nation — Their First Vacation from School, *Harper's Weekly,* June 17, 1899. Courtesy of the Taos Historic Museums, Taos, New Mexico.

In April 1898 *McClure's* commissioned Blumenschein to interview the renowned journalist William Allen White in Kansas. In May he went to Emporia to discuss the story—"a county-seat war and theft of a courthouse"—with White; rode sixty miles by buckboard to the county seat; made a detour to Dodge City, Kansas, where he made sketches; then returned to New York. As it happened, neither the story nor the illustrations were ever published. What endured, however, was Blumenschein's lifelong friendship with White.[52]

Blumenschein entered the field of illustration during its golden age. New technology had created high-speed printing presses, and the invention of the halftone printing plate for photoengraving replaced the old, cumbersome wood engraving process. These advances made reproducing artwork fast, accurate, and inexpensive. Magazines could increasingly use pictures to enhance circulation. The economic boom following the Civil War accommodated the publishing surge. When Blumenschein began illustrating, magazines, books, and newspapers were the major sources of information and entertainment, while the technological advances and the rise of the middle class created conditions that supported the publishing industry. As the industry grew, publishers, editors, writers, and artists became the "celebrities of the day."[53]

By spring 1898, with $250 in his pocket and another Southwest assignment, Blumenschein decided to return to the Rockies to sketch for several months. His enthusiasm for the West convinced his New York studio mate, Bert Geer Phillips, to accompany him.[54] In June 1898 two of the "greenest *gringos* that ever struck the Southwest," as Phillips referred to the two tenderfeet, arrived in Denver.[55] They knew nothing of camp life or horses, so they sought advice regarding purchase of provisions for their western journey. They ended up with three horses, a shotgun and a pistol (which they never used), camping gear, and a dog to keep them warm. Their inexperience driving horses came to light when they hitched up their team for the first time, having observed the liveryman's job only once. An irate farmer stopped and cursed their ineptitude, shouting that they would have a runaway the way they had fastened the harness. He helped them with the necessary adjustments. Blumenschein later reminisced: "We painted and camped in Colorado for three months, had our first experiences with horses, cloudbursts, cooking, sleeping in the open, and the many delights of outdoor life."[56] The two artists thrived in the "glorious" mountain air, while "learning to love the great nature of the West."[57] Theirs combined a youthful exuberance and physical quest for the vigorous life with a philosophical, spiritual union with nature. Blumenschein carried a copy of Emerson's *Essays* in his bags.

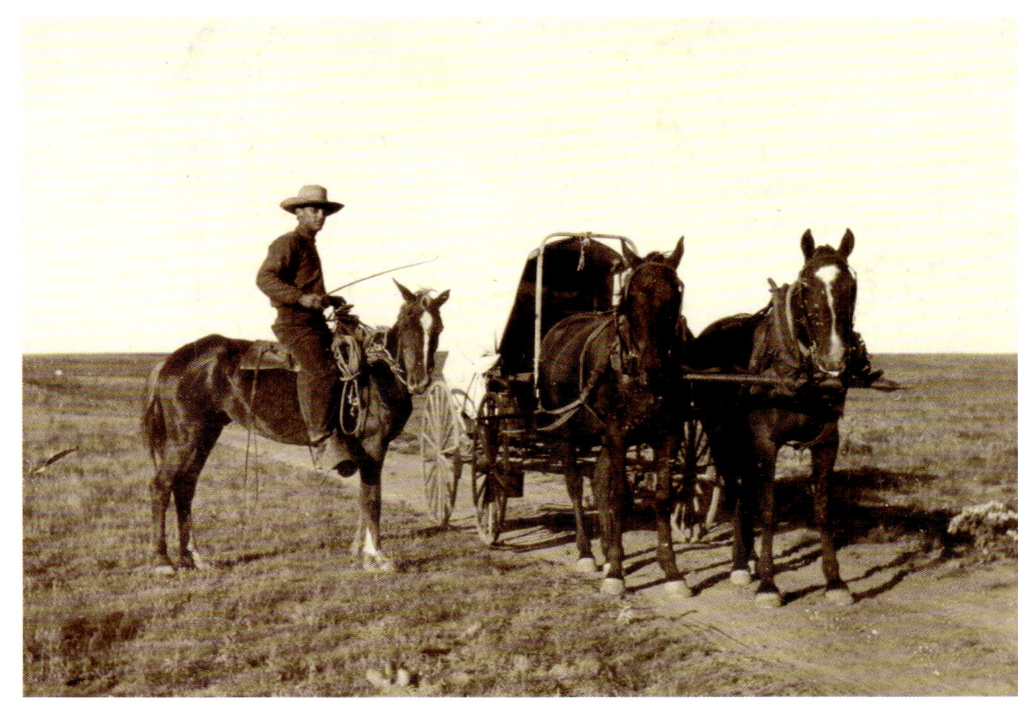

Blumenschein and Bert Phillips with horses and wagon, August 1898. Courtesy of the Palace of the Governors, Museum of New Mexico, New Mexico Department of Cultural Affairs, Santa Fe (neg. HP05.25-I).

By late August the two artists felt they had exhausted the painting possibilities of Colorado. They decided to head south toward Mexico, "just [to] sketch and paint and drift" until they found "something that might hold" them. When they crossed the high mountain pass from Colorado into New Mexico, the roads steadily worsened and eventually caused their John Deere Light wagon, heavily loaded with camping and painting gear, to break down. At first the two artists managed to make repairs. They learned to "substitute a spruce limb for a double tree and many other little tricks." But after crossing a second mountain pass in early September, their luck and ingenuity ran out.[58] The rear wheel broke. "We 'tossed up' to see who would carry the wheel to the nearest blacksmith." Blumenschein won the toss.[59]

It took Blumenschein two days to cover what turned out to be twenty-two miles to the nearest blacksmith. After spending the night with a hospitable Spanish-speaking family, he arrived in Taos. The magnificent Taos Valley spread out before him, bounded on three sides by mountains and yielding to high desert plateau and the Rio Grande gorge on the fourth. Among these "superb mountains" and the "moving grandeur of great plains," Blumenschein discovered singular pictorial appeal. He later recalled, "This, I knew at once, was what I wanted to paint and where I wanted to live. But on return to camp with the mended wheel I concealed my impressions from my partner, for I wanted to see if he would react as I did."[60] Together with Phillips, the two men retraced the route to Taos. They agreed that here was an extraordinary scene, forever spellbinding, something to hold them for all time.

Captivated by the architecture of Taos Pueblo and excited by the proximity of Indian subjects to paint, they camped, unknowingly, on Indian land. Tribal officials asked them to break camp and go somewhere else. The two soon rented a house, sold the horses and wagon, and settled in the town of Taos, where they painted the Indians and ceremonials at the pueblo, the adobe buildings, and the volcanic-torn landscape bathed in its "continuous sunshine."[61] Phillips never left Taos. The region literally possessed him. Blumenschein, who had commissions to fulfill, stayed only three months. In November he moved on to the Mojave Desert to gather subject matter for an article for *Harper's* and then returned to New York.[62] The material he gathered from this trip appeared over the next two years in *McClure's* and *Harper's*.

Blumenschein's fresh impressions of Taos appeared in the December 10, 1898, issue of *Harper's Weekly*. The magazine dedicated a two-page spread to his illustration titled *A Strange Mixture of Barbarism and Christianity—The Celebration of San Geronimo's Day among the Pueblo Indians*. This was not the first visual depiction of Taos Pueblo—Henry Rankin Poore, for example, used an etching by Peter Moran of the North House for an article in 1883—but Blumenschein ostensibly produced the first images of the feast day of San Geronimo seen by the American public. *Harper's* also published his description of the festivities, the first written record of this event by an artist. Blumenschein described the footraces between the South and North houses, the drumming and singing that "stirs you like the great movement in a Beethoven symphony," the trade fair and barter between the Pueblos, their Spanish-speaking neighbors and American tourists, and the *chiffonetes*, or sacred clowns, whose antics he likened to a comic opera. This was Blumenschein's first direct exposure to the history of Taos Pueblo. Before the races, he spoke to a Taos Pueblo man, Swift Arrow, who related the people's early history.[63]

The following year, 1899, marked what Blumenschein called "a very busy and successful year in illustrating work."[64] In May the fruits of his labors appeared in a weeklong exhibition at the Dayton Club. The show featured thirty-six paintings and sixty drawings created over the past three years for *Scribner's*, *Harper's Weekly*, and *McClure's*, revealing a developing penchant for western themes. It featured illustrations for two stories by Garland, "The Trail of the Golden North" and "Rising Wolf—Ghost Dancer."[65] A Dayton reviewer concluded that "in the variety of subject and the strong power of execution there is the evidence of his talent which has won for him such laudable recognition.

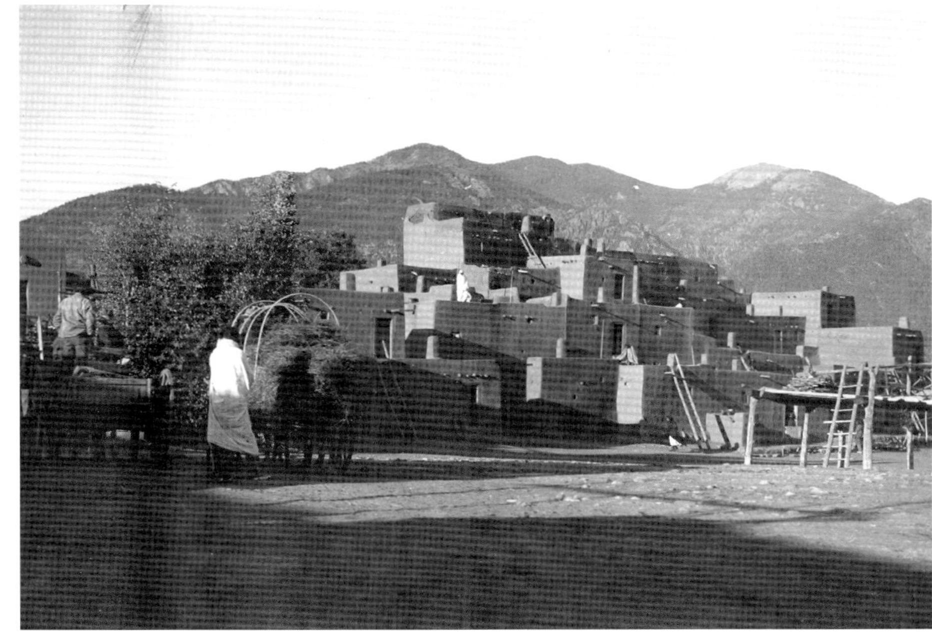

Taos Pueblo, North House, with hay wagon. Courtesy of the Palace of the Governors, Museum of New Mexico, New Mexico Department of Cultural Affairs, Santa Fe (neg. HP05.25-J).

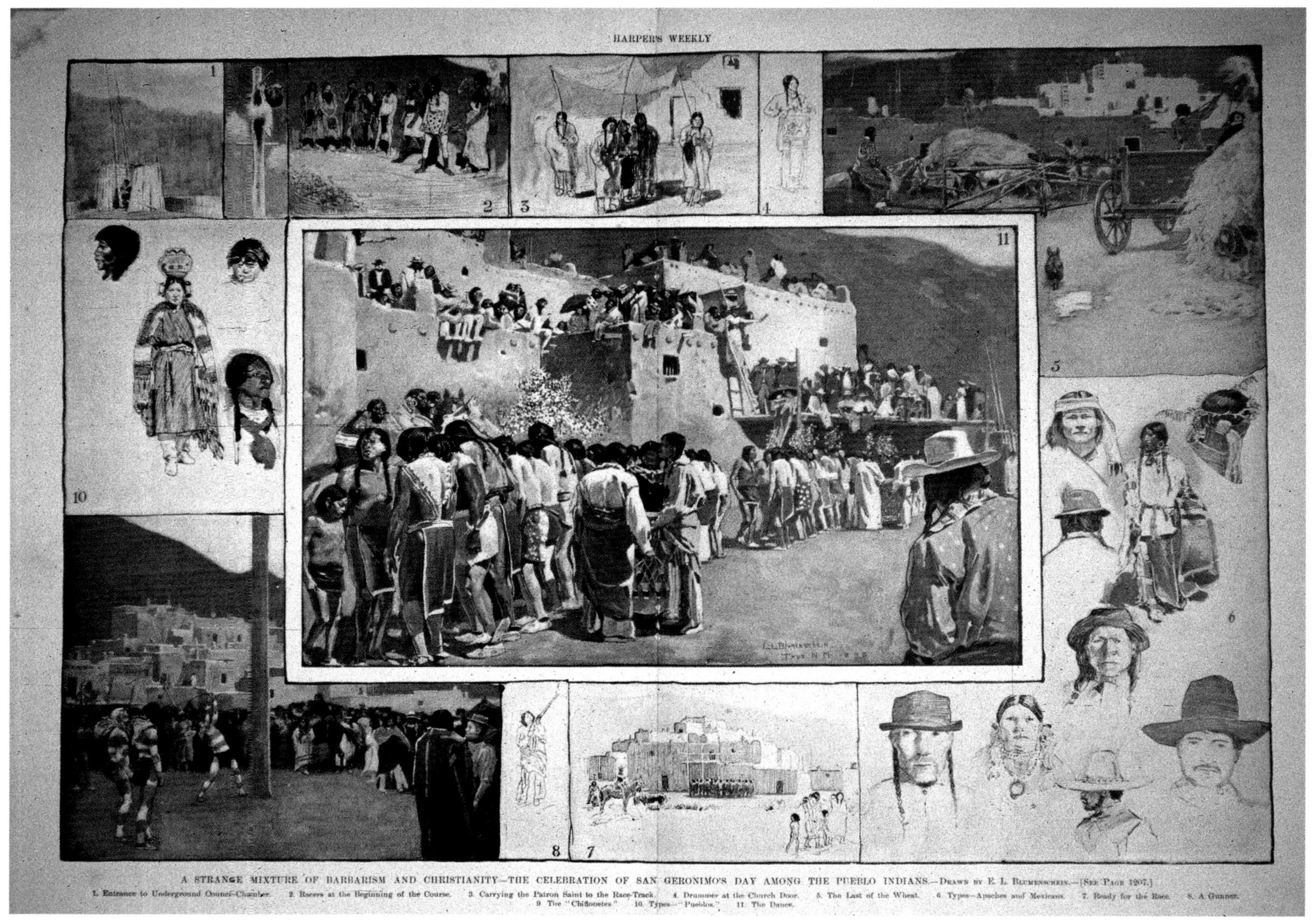

A Strange Mixture of Barbarism and Christianity—The Celebration of San Geronimo's Day among the Pueblo Indians, Harper's Weekly, December 10, 1898. Courtesy of the Taos Historic Museums, Taos, New Mexico.

There is indication that his work has been done along the lines of personal thought, and especially is this fact noticeable in his pictures of Western life." Blumenschein's work, one paper reported, was "owned by connoisseurs." The names included art editor A. F. Jaccaci, a Mr. Bigelow of Boston, and Aime Dupont of New York.[66]

In New York artists also recognized Blumenschein's talent: in 1899 he was elected a member of the Salmagundi Club. Begun as the New York Sketch Club in 1871, the Salmagundi Club served as a gathering place for artists in Blumenschein's day. It was there that painters and sculptors rendezvoused to converse about art issues, to be among peers, and to test aesthetic ideas. Although Blumenschein disliked its attendant artistic politics, the club remained a social and professional vortex for him for many years.

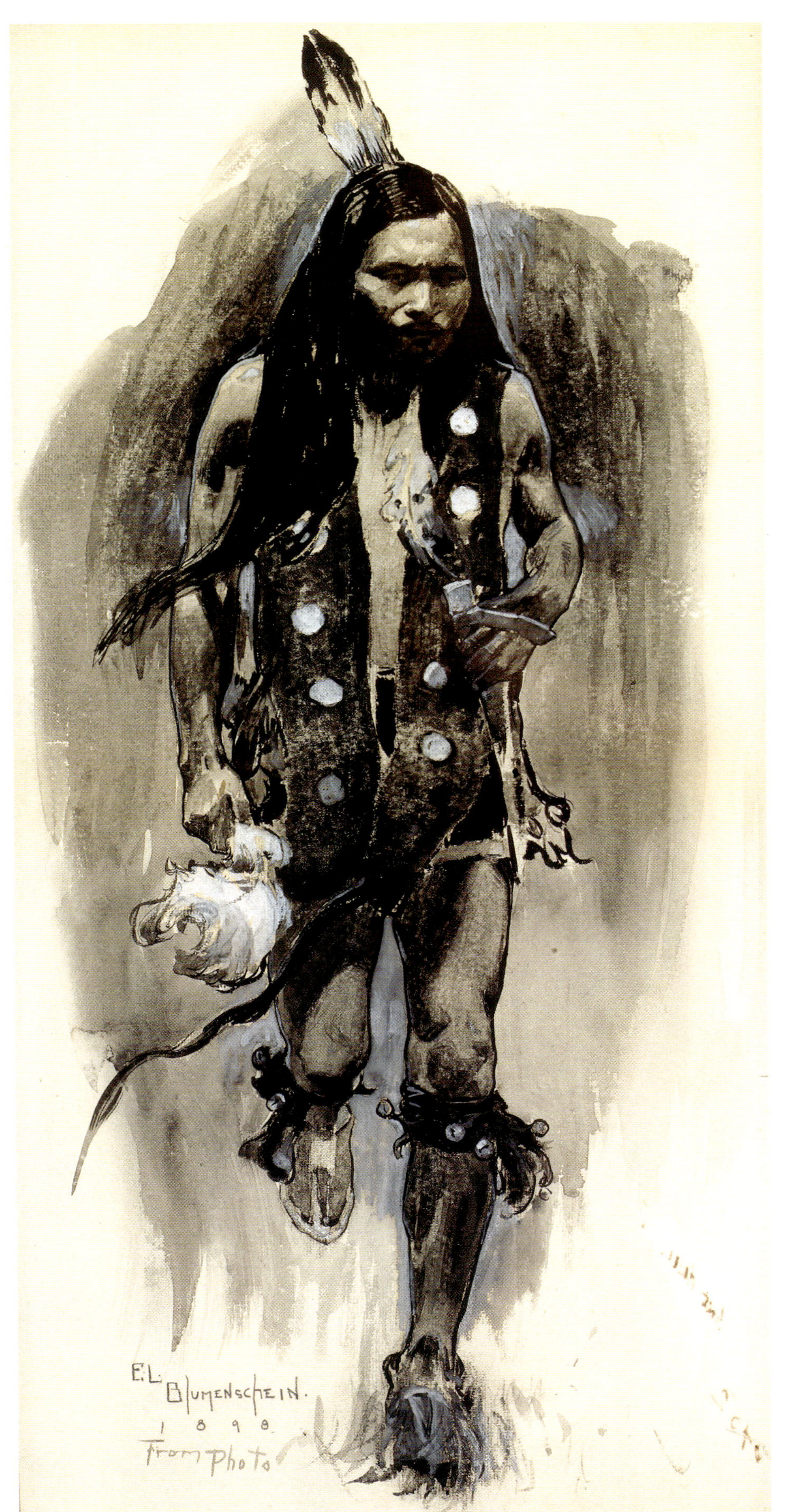

Ghost Dancer, 1898.
Illustration for "Rising Wolf, Ghost Dancer," by Hamlin Garland, *McClure's Magazine*, 1899, gouache and ink on paper, 32 × 20 inches. Collection of Cheekwood Museum of Art, Nashville, Tennessee.

That year Blumenschein also met the writer Booth Tarkington, when *McClure's* hired him to illustrate the serial edition of Tarkington's first novel, *The Gentleman from Indiana*. Tarkington was, like Blumenschein, a midwesterner. Trained in literature at Princeton, Tarkington rose to become one of America's most popular novelists and dramatists. According to Blumenschein, the two met when Tarkington came to his studio to read him the first installment of the novel because Blumenschein was too rushed to do so himself.[67] In their haste to get the serial to press, however, *McClure's* decided to forego visual supplementation, and Blumenschein's illustrations were never published. He did glean a reward from his efforts, however, a friendship that lasted until Tarkington's death in 1946.

Around the time he met Tarkington, Blumenschein had become friends with another midwestern author, the "Foremost Humorist in America," Ellis Parker Butler.[68] *Puck* and *Judge*, two of the humor magazines that inspired Blumenschein's earliest work, had purchased Butler's early work and had given him his start. The writer had just sold his first piece to *Century* magazine and decided to relocate to be closer to the great publishing houses that also drew Blumenschein to New York. They met in 1897 when Butler rented a room in the same boarding house where Blumenschein resided. Among other commonalities, both were struggling to establish themselves in their respective fields. Just as Blumenschein would later gain recognition as a painter, Butler became one of the most popular comic writers of his day. Over his forty-year career, he would produce over two thousand books and articles—many written while he managed a bank in Flushing, New York—and cofound a trade magazine, *The Decorative Furnisher.*[69]

These early struggles and their shared love of literature, humor, and New York's cultural life created a close friendship that endured until Butler's death in 1936. The two corresponded in the early 1900s while Blumenschein was on assignment in the United States and studying and living in Paris. The artist entrusted his friend with his finances and the packing and shipping of illustrations and paintings while he was away. Butler, in turn, sought out Blumenschein in Paris after both had married and both lost a child. Their wives, and later their families, enhanced their friendship.

The *Dayton Daily Journal* observed Blumenschein's intent to return to Paris for further painting studies in January 1899. His future career hopes lay "not in making pictures for books [but] with the palette and brushes."[70] By September 1899 Blumenschein had saved enough money to return to Paris for a year. Lodged at 9 rue des Fourneaux, he enrolled for a second time in the atelier of Laurens and Benjamin-Constant at the Académie Julian. He intended to work on the "color muscle" in his painting, to lay down "some good solid stones and mortar." He also wanted to do "something in the picture line," painting more for the sheer joy of it. He wrote Butler of his plans to revisit Taos and perhaps stay for good the following September, also that he had heard from Phillips, who was enthusiastic about their "scheme to form a Barbizon school of painters and writers."[71] That fall, though, for the first time in his life, he felt unsettled and unhappy. The gray skies of winter and the people and customs of Paris oppressed him. He longed for the sunsets of Taos. He wanted to go home.[72]

As the months progressed, Blumenschein's state of mind improved. He was working "well and seriously" in school and independently, and, like most art students of the day, in his spare time he studied the grand pictures in the Louvre. Blumenschein's schedule was probably similar to his classmate Alphaeus Cole's, who reminisced years later that he spent mornings at Julian's and afternoons in the Louvre, where he made "small studies from the great paintings" with the promise that this "would strengthen [his] sense of color and design."[73]

When at the Louvre, Blumenschein copied some paintings and made notes on others. Velasquez, according to his notes, represented "the flesh" most realistically, while Carolus-Duran approached "near to it." Sir Thomas Lawrence's color paralleled that of Velasquez. Botticelli achieved "a flat effect produced by tones; often with lines around them" and used a "delicate color scheme, harmonious with surroundings, often repeating." In Titian, Blumenschein observed strong drawing, beautiful color, and strength of composition, a strength that would be lost "without the simplicity and contrast in the lights and darks." The arrangement of light and dark masses made for a fine composition. Rembrandt modeled his light tone "so solidly because he has a big range for his half-tones . . . resulting from the darkness (contrast) of his shadows." In his *Mona Lisa*, Leonardo da Vinci had forced blacks to extremes to allow the light tones to be "highly modeled."[74]

As fall came on, the exterior Paris, "brilliant as ever," inspired him. Further, the Exposition Universelle was taking shape, and in September 1899 the Seine near the Eiffel tower was, according to Blumenschein, "remarkably picturesque with the multitude of exposition buildings hidden behind networks of European scaffolding." It would "surely be great," he thought, and by November he decided to remain in Paris to experience the extravaganza. Exposure to exhibits from all over the world, especially in art, would provide an invaluable education, but one obstacle remained: he lacked work assignments. Unless a "good angel" came along, he wrote Butler, he would be "dead broke" by June. In hopes of getting a commission, Blumenschein had sent some illustrations to New York by way of Butler. The good angel arrived in March when *Harper's Weekly* assigned him, along with a cadre of illustrators like E. C. Peixotto, Thur de Thulstrup, and Charles Curran, as an artist-correspondent to the Paris Exposition. He lightheartedly reported the good news to Butler: "I have plenty jobs now make a de picht, maybe make a da mon."[75] He produced half a dozen impressive views of life in and around the fair, typical among them his spirited drawing for a centerfold, *The Sunday Crowd at the Paris Exposition,* for the May issue.[76]

The Paris Exposition also attracted American dancer Isadora Duncan to the City of Light in 1900. After observing the dance styles of American-born Loie Fuller and the Japanese company of Kawakami Otojiro and Sadko Yacco, Fuller's protégées, Duncan adapted what she had learned into her own style of dancing. She was soon introduced into Parisian society and took Paris by storm. Blumenschein had the opportunity to observe her and practice his "color muscle." His oil sketches capture in a few brush strokes Duncan's essence and the movement of the dance.

Once finished with his Paris assignments, Blumenschein decided to go home. Immediately after his return to New York, *Century* commissioned Blumenschein to illustrate a series on the iron industry. He traveled to Minnesota's Mesabi Range to see the mines and observe the extraction of iron ore for the first article.

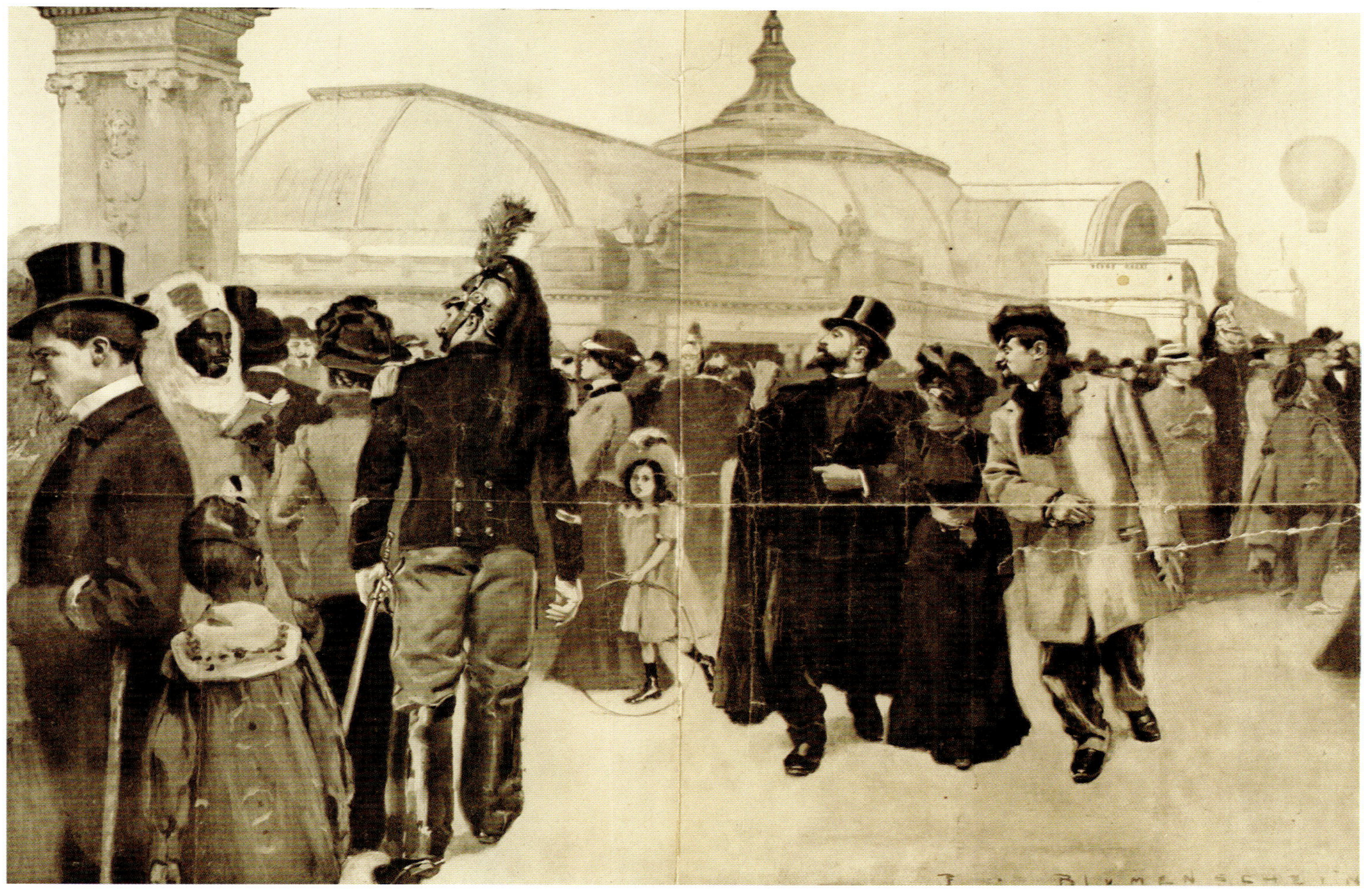

The Sunday Crowd at the Paris Exposition, *Harper's Weekly*, May 5, 1900, 41 × 58 centimeters. Courtesy of the Ernest L. Blumenschein Papers, 1889–1960, Archives of American Art, Smithsonian Institution, Washington, D.C.

He then turned south to visit the Homestead Steel Smelter near Pittsburgh, where he gathered material for the next two articles. He completed the assignment in Duluth.[77] During this trip, Butler served as his corresponding secretary to *Harper's*, *Scribner's*, and other publishers in his absence and forwarded his mail. Blumenschein wrote him from the "rough and crude" mining town of Eveleth, enthused by the region's "grand material for stories and pictures." Though feeling dwarfed at times by his experiences, he nonetheless embraced his adventures: witnessing a devastating explosion, watching a miner cough himself to death, and suffering his own embarrassment of getting "neatly skinned" in a poker game. It was all part of a "valuable experience" that brought life and excitement to the profession of illustrating.[78]

Blumenschein commented that these "highly successful" illustrations led to his meeting Richard Watson Gilder, editor of *Century*. Gilder had been responsible

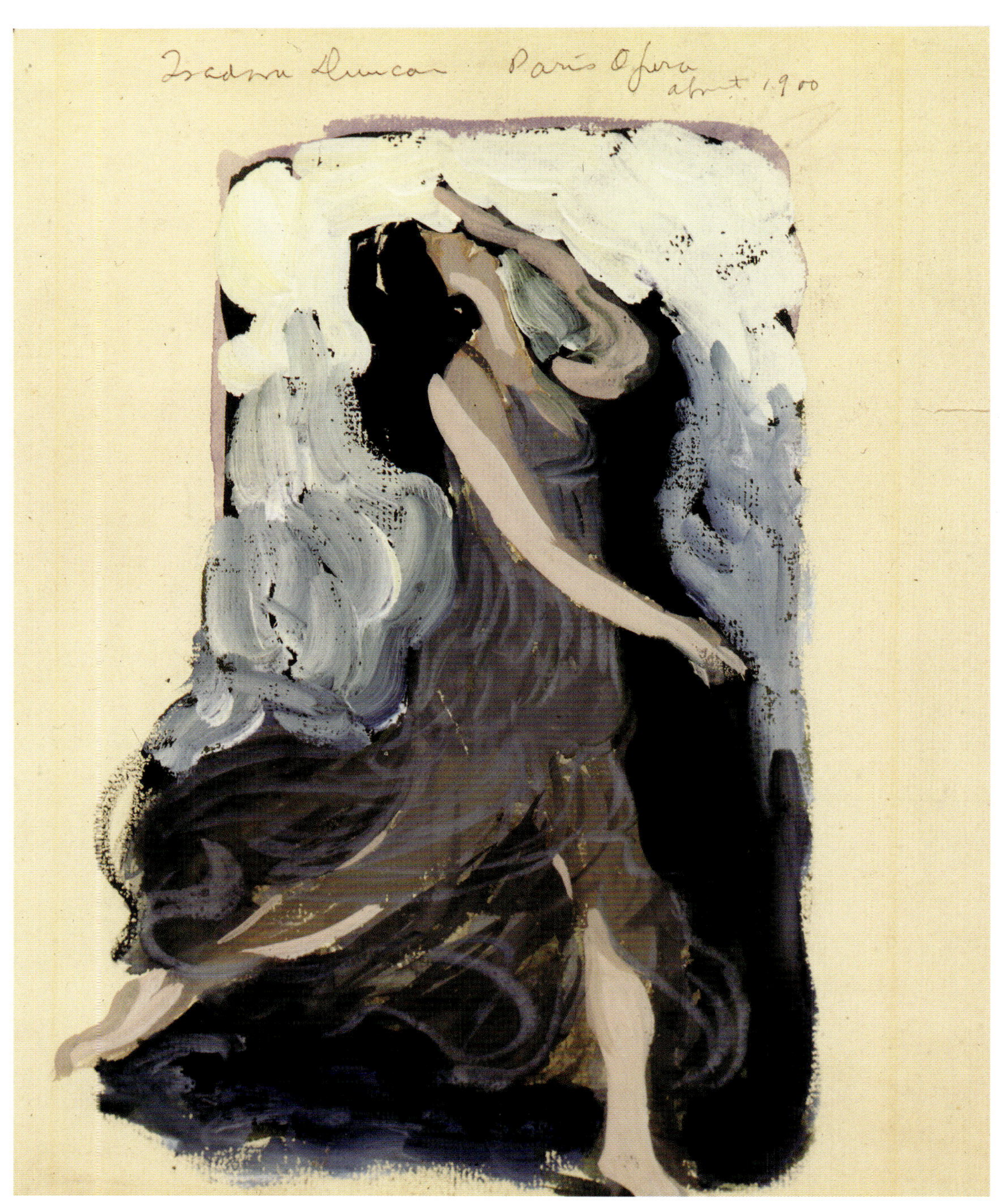

Isadora Duncan — Paris Opera, 1900
Gouache on paper, 9 × 5 inches
Collection of the New Mexico Museum of Art, Santa Fe
Gift of Helen Greene Blumenschein, 1964

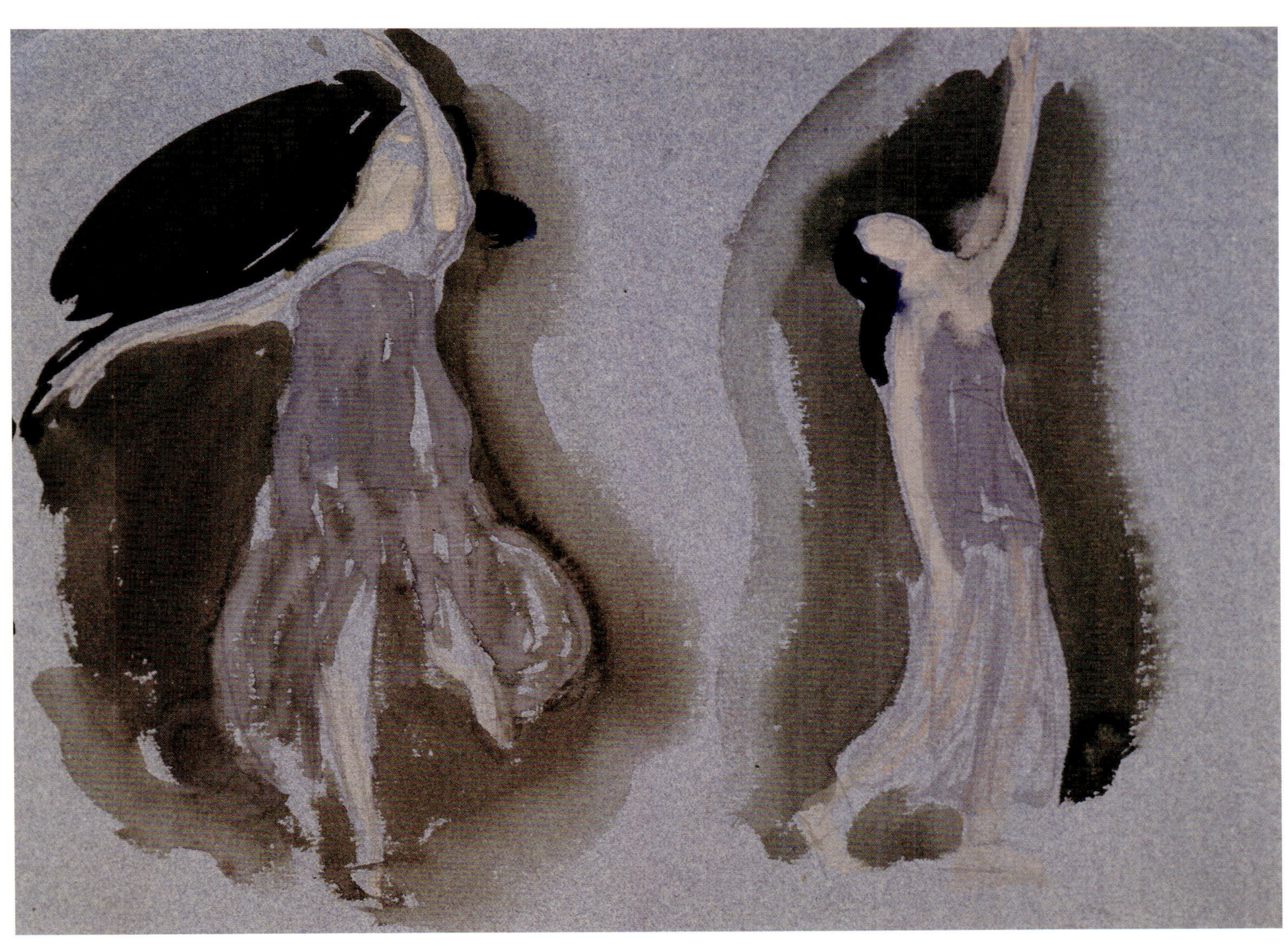

Untitled (Isadora Duncan), 1900
Gouache on paper, 9 × 11½ inches
Collection of the New Mexico Museum of Art, Santa Fe
Gift of Helen Greene Blumenschein, 1964

for creating *Century* two decades earlier. In it, he sought a magazine that would address "living, practical questions" of American life and popular history.[79] Such an ambitious, novel program required the best possible pictorial augmentation. Gilder retained Alexander Wilson Drake, founding art editor of *Scribner's*, to oversee the new art department. They proved to be a formidable pair in the publishing world, and together they developed a warm professional friendship with Blumenschein. They particularly admired him because, in their minds, Blumenschein took illustration so seriously, "never drawing to make money." Blumenschein would go to "great trouble and expense" in gathering material for his illustration and work always toward advancing his art. In Gilder especially, he found a devoted champion. The editor was interested in helping to mature his talent, not in exploiting him as a financial asset to the magazine, and encouraged him to "get as much painting quality into the illustrations" as possible; he "wanted a man to give the art that was in him."[80] Most editors demanded that artists stick to strict commercial requirements. The danger in that, Blumenschein felt, was that there was no opportunity for growth. That Gilder allowed him artistic freedom became vital to his continued advancement.

Gilder and Drake recognized Blumenschein's talent in another way. They felt he had been underpaid in the past. They raised his salary from $75 a page to $100 a page. Within six months, they were paying him $150 a page. Blumenschein said they had given him raises voluntarily. He was touched by their actions, and now, he knew, he was professionally competitive. While at *Century,* Blumenschein felt that the editors believed thoroughly in his work, and in his judgment they gave him a free hand. That offered him—a young, ambitious artist—the greatest encouragement of all.[81]

Century sent Blumenschein to Sioux country in the Dakotas in the summer of 1901. He was assigned to illustrate Dr. Charles Eastman's book *Indian Boyhood.* Eastman, a Wahpeton Sioux and grandson of frontier artist Seth Eastman, attended to the tribe's medical needs. He had graduated from Dartmouth before attaining his medical degree at Boston University in June 1890. The Bureau of Indian Affairs (BIA) hired him in October as physician to the Sioux at the Pine Ridge agency.

In December he had the grisly task of caring for the forty-four survivors of the Wounded Knee massacre. Eastman's discovery of financial remuneration abuses that the Sioux survivors suffered at the hands of Indian agents, and the resulting dispute, led to his departure some months later. He spent the next years working on the text for what became *Indian Boyhood* and on Indian reform, until the BIA persuaded him to return to the Dakotas in 1900, this time as physician to the Sioux at the Crow Creek Reservation.

Eastman often took Blumenschein with him as he called on the sick throughout the large reservation. They carried shotguns with them to shoot any prairie chickens they flushed along the way. Wild game was always welcome at Indian tables. While they rode, Eastman would tell him stories, "legends of wild creatures, and sometimes of man."[82] Through Eastman, Blumenschein became acquainted with the "Sioux Nine."[83] Throughout that August these young baseball players took him with them to play against "clubs of the neighboring cities and towns." As they drove over the prairies, the young men sang "almost incessantly."[84] As Blumenschein made friends among the Sioux, he got insights into their lives. These experiences and his time with Eastman, who had been raised traditionally, then was sent to Indian boarding school before studying medicine and who had experienced the atrocities inflicted on Indian people at Wounded Knee and the abuses that followed, would later fuel Blumenschein's defense of Native rights in New Mexico.

Everywhere Blumenschein went on the reservation he carried his sketchbook. He stayed for two months, then left for Taos, where he began work on his illustrations. The work took four months to complete. Forty years later, the artist remarked that the book had been in print since 1902. He believed it "would live longer, because of its sincere quality and the charming simplicity of its style."[85]

The *New York Times* reviewed *Indian Boyhood* in September 1902. Eastman's first book told of "work and play, education, the superstitions, the traits, and training of the Indian boy such as he himself was, and includes much lore and legend of the Sioux."[86] The review also cited Blumenschein's illustrations. One of them, *Ohiyesa and Chatanna,* depicts Eastman and his brother as boys. This was the first of several books that Blumenschein illustrated.

While Blumenschein labored in Taos, he had a letter from Drake offering him his next assignment, to work side by side with the popular travel writer Ray Stannard Baker. Blumenschein was a fan of Baker's, especially relishing the author's descriptions of the Southwest. In a letter to Drake, Blumenschein lauded the "splendid articles" that Baker had written and said the author had expressed what Blumenschein himself had "long wanted to write." This would, as he wrote Drake, leave him "free of the responsibility of saying more than pictures would say."[87]

Yet if pictures rather than words were his selected method of communication, when it came to describing his beloved Taos, Blumenschein was downright eloquent. In near-poetic terms, he described the people and the countryside—Indians who still practiced the old customs that made them "real and themselves," the landscape with its deserts and vast sky, the "colored cañons with happy vigorous streams," and the great mountain ranges, "as dear to him as a friend"—the source of inspiration for his work.[88] In Taos, Blumenschein never felt alone but rather a part of all he described. He did miss music, but he even found that "in the storms that tune all the instruments of nature to noble harmonies and in the quiet nights that fill a man's soul with a calm rhythm in accord with all that is serene and beautiful."[89] He saw his beloved music manifested visually in all aspects of nature. Blumenschein remained in Taos until November and then returned to New York.

By now Blumenschein's professional struggles were over, and he considered himself a "prosperous illustrator."[90] He had commissions from the nation's three major publishers—*Harper's*, *Century*, and *McClure's*—and, indeed, had more than he could handle. In fact, when *Century* offered him a commission to illustrate articles on the Southwest by Ray Stannard Baker, Blumenschein had to decline because he had to finish a set of illustrations for *McClure's* that included another story by Garland, "Sitting Bull's Defiance," relating western history from the Indian perspective. When a popular illustrator had too much work, that circumstance allowed new artists to enter the ranks. Since Blumenschein could not take on this

Century commission, it went to a then-unknown artist, Maxfield Parrish, who, according to Blumenschein, "made his reputation on these pictures."[91]

At Christmastime, Gilder engaged Blumenschein to travel with Baker for a series of articles on the Northwest. This time his schedule permitted him to accept the commission. The only instruction that Baker and he received from *Century* was to send for funds as they needed them. Otherwise, the author set the itinerary that guided them. In June they covered "the many mines on the barren hill" in Butte, Montana. From there the duo embarked on a wide-ranging adventure that included forest fires in Washington State, a Wyoming land rush, and tourists in Yellowstone. They were gone for nearly a year.

One of Blumenschein's last illustrations for the six articles Baker wrote is titled *Sitting for a Photograph on Pulpit Terrace*. It reveals the artist's sense of humor blended with his energetic, stylized manner of drawing. As an effective illustrator, he established a tension between the human figures and their setting, one of Yellowstone's most famous thermal features.

By the end of summer 1903, Blumenschein realized that, despite his successes, his painting had suffered at the expense of "the limitations of illustration as a satisfying creative art."[92] With three thousand dollars in his pocket from the *Century* commission, he turned his back on the American scene and sailed once more for Europe. Before resuming study in Paris, Blumenschein spent two months in Italy. He later wrote of this trip as his "greatest experience in art" and of Italy in particular, with its "great beauty of the past" and its engaging paintings of the Italian primitives, as having profound influence on his subsequent work.[93]

Once settled in Paris at 18 rue Boissonade in October 1903, Blumenschein wrote Butler that he had done the "very best thing in getting down to hard study in this atmosphere of real art, not clever illustration."[94] Even so, he relied on illustration commissions to support him while studying in France. Because American magazines had increasingly focused on illustrating their pages with color at the turn of the century, Blumenschein benefited. He had determined to improve his "color muscle," and the magazines' new direction provided him with renewed impetus to learn afresh how to paint in color. He took "twelve or more"

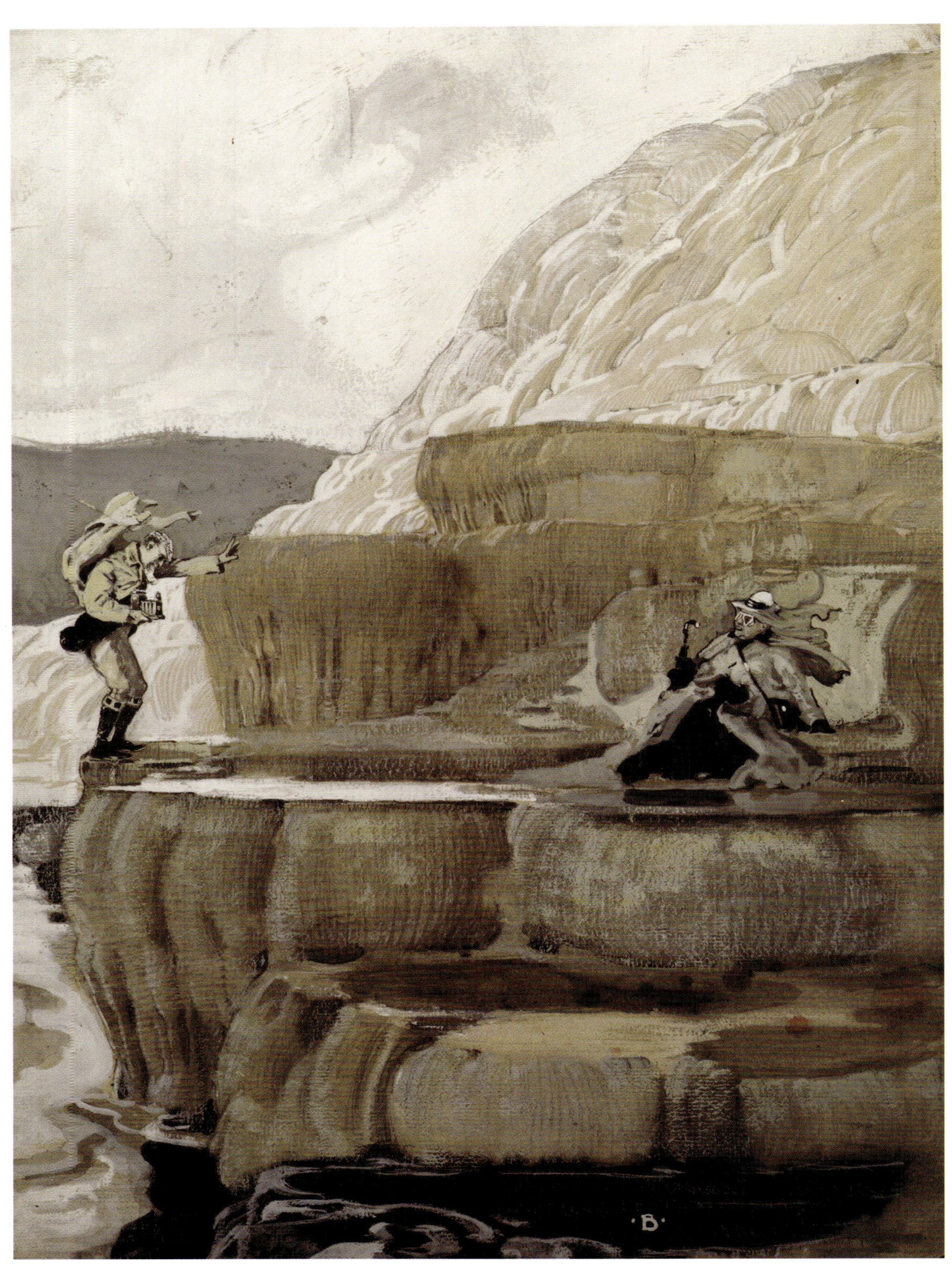

Sitting for a Photograph on Pulpit Terrace, 1903
Gouache on paper, 17½ × 12⅞ inches
Courtesy of the Print and Picture Collection
Free Library of Philadelphia, Philadelphia, Pennsylvania

criticisms at the Académie de la Grande Chaumière from Lucien Simon and Rene Menard. Blumenschein referred to Menard's work, with its rich and harmonious palette, as a nearly religious "rapport with color."[95] Simon also had a reputation for the warm, colorful palette that imbued his views of French country life. The Impressionists referred to Menard and Simon as the Nubians, whose poetic, tonally balanced works allied them with the Symbolists. Blumenschein, who particularly appreciated the mood their works evoked, applied himself to discover the secrets of color handling. Through observation and experimentation he began to master the mixing of oil paint. He discovered how many color shifts he could obtain by mixing two complementary colors—like cadmium red and viridian green—together and how, by adding white, he could create a range of shades, from light to dark.[96]

Blumenschein's focus on color found him back at the "glorious" Louvre to study its great masters. He was "happily painting—not pictures—but studies." By December he suffered again from the "miserable climate" of Paris. Homesick for the camaraderie of intelligent friends and the Salmagundi Club, he hired people to read Dante and philosophy aloud to him at night. In February he began planning a painting trip that he hoped might end his winter slump. He would travel from Spain up the Mediterranean to Naples and again through Italy on what would be a second grand tour. Two months later, however, something happened that changed his plans, something that made him decide to stick it out in Paris until summer.[97]

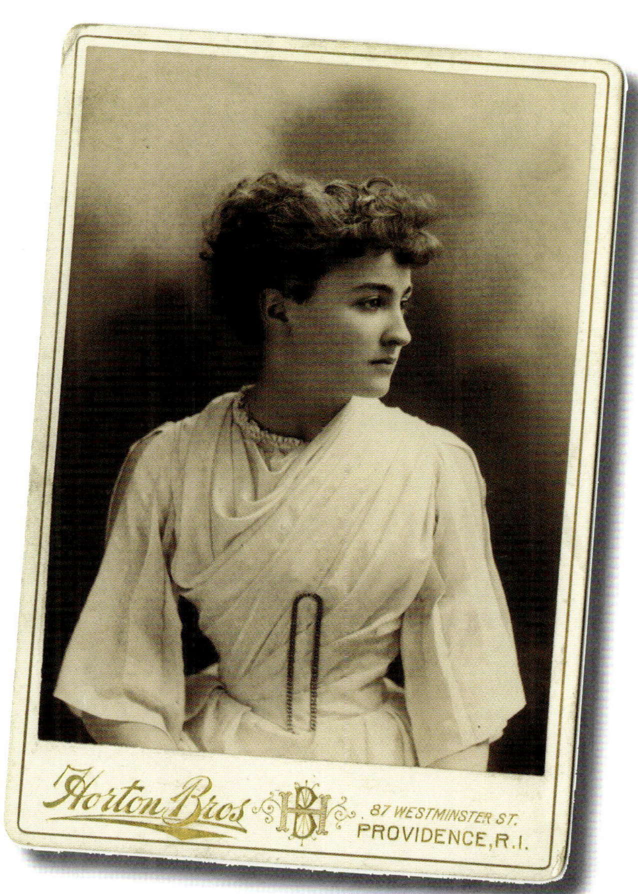

Mary Shepard Greene, ca. age 17.
Courtesy of the Palace of the Governors, Museum of New Mexico, New Mexico Department of Cultural Affairs, Santa Fe (neg. HP05.25-N).

For years the extroverted Blumenschein had participated in the Associated American Artist's minstrel shows in Paris. The April 1904 show proved momentous. In attendance was the American painter Mary Shepard Greene, who took notice of the "cute little guy in black face, the song and dance man in the role of 'Bro' Michael'" and asked to be introduced.[98] Within weeks, the two had fallen in love. Blumenschein could not yet know that a strong adversary would test his limits. Just a month later, in a letter to Butler, he revealed having endured "the depths of hell" after getting "twisted up with an ambitious mother with an only daughter." Only one obstacle stood in the way of Blumenschein's love for Mary—her mother, the formidable Mrs. Greene.[99]

When Greene and Blumenschein first met, she had already won medals at the Paris Salon in 1900 and 1902 and was about to receive her first medal in an international art exhibition at the 1904 St. Louis World's Fair. With her rudimentary studies completed at Brooklyn's Pratt Institute a decade earlier, she had evinced sufficient artistic ability to persuade her mother to take her to Paris for further art training. She began classes with French academic painter Raphael Collin sometime in the mid-1890s. By 1896 her talent and Collin's sponsorship won her a spot in the Paris Salon. Following her 1900 salon medal, for *Une Regard Fugitive* (*A Fugitive Glance*), she was invited to exhibit the work in the Pennsylvania Academy of Fine Arts' Seventieth Annual Exhibition in 1901. A Philadelphia paper published the painting in a two-page spread alongside works by John Singer Sargent, Cecilia Beaux, and Winslow Homer. Greene's second medal in 1902 brought even more notice, both in New York and in Paris. The prestigious journal *Revue Bleu* deemed her "une exquise artiste." In an article critiquing her winning painting, *Une Petit Histoire* (*A Little Story*), which showed a young woman lying prone and reading, a reviewer praised her skill in handling the interior space and mood. It was a "modest subject," a *petit genre* painting, with its "subtle harmony of creamy whites and pale greens."[100]

From another quarter, Elizabeth Nourse, a seasoned American painter championed by Puvis de Chavannes and recognized by the French for "painting like a man," sent her congratulations: "Hurrah! . . . I knew you would get a medal for your lovely picture."[101] Nourse knew what this medal meant to the younger painter: it made her *hors concours*, meaning future salon submissions would bypass the jury. The acclaim brought Greene to the attention of potential patrons.[102]

Greene's success meant even more to her mother. Her daughter's artistic talent, hard work, and resounding successes had placed her in good company. Her salon awards elevated her to a level with leading American artists in Paris like

Frederick Frieseke, Alfred Maurer, Elizabeth Nourse, Henry O. Tanner, and Mary's friend and former classmate Susan Watkins.[103] The medal from the World's Fair in St. Louis earned her wider recognition among artists at home. She commanded exhibition space next to such giants as John Singer Sargent and John LaFarge.[104] No wonder Mrs. Greene balked at the possibility of her daughter marrying a mere illustrator.

Blumenschein's position with Mrs. Greene improved little over the summer of 1904, even after he received a letter from *McClure's* applauding some of his recent submissions as truly "stunning pictures" and the substantial check that followed. These accolades and the resulting gain in financial status evidently made him impatient, for through the fall, Greene entreated him to show restraint and understanding for her mother. Blumenschein lasted until December. He worked hard to be "virtuous . . . clean under the arm-pits, careful of [his] fingernails, and considerate of old ladies' feelings," but to no avail. The situation remained like a game where only Mrs. Greene knew the rules. At month's end a desperate Blumenschein wrote his father, asking for his help with the necessary

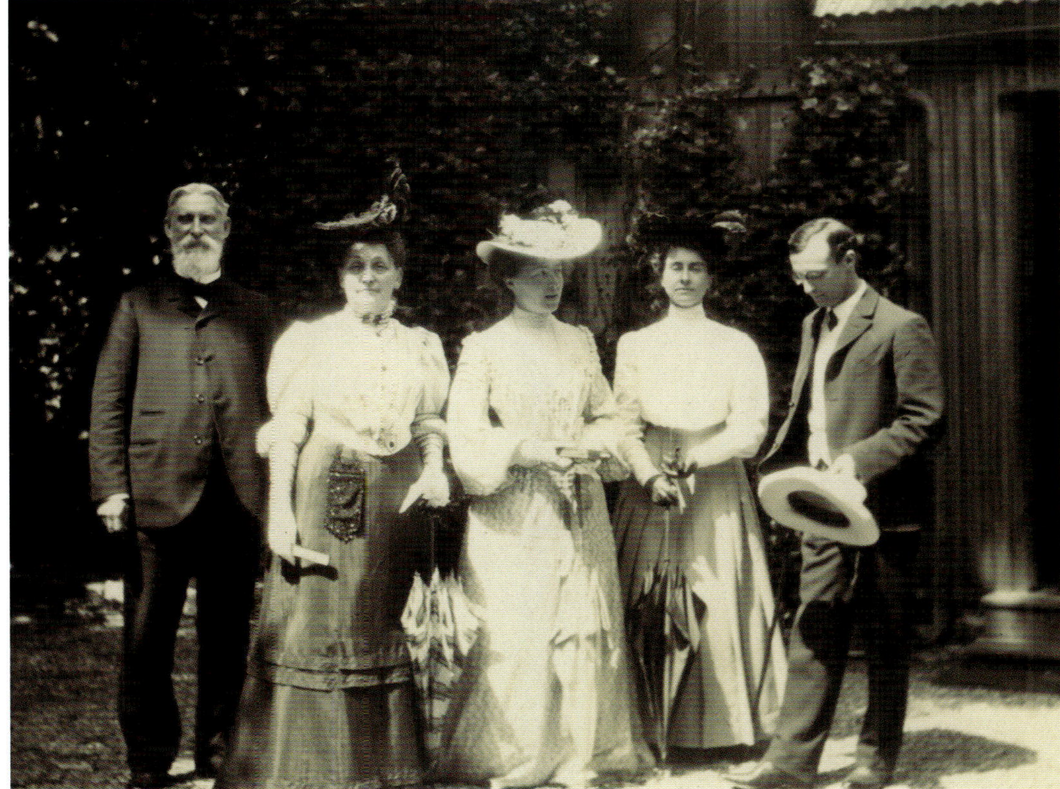

Blumenschein-Greene nuptials, June 29, 1905 (Mrs. Greene to left of Mary, at center, Blumenschein far right). Courtesy of the Palace of the Governors, Museum of New Mexico, New Mexico Department of Cultural Affairs, Santa Fe (neg. HP05.25-0).

marriage papers. The reply from Dayton arrived in January 1905 and provided no help. After reading his son's "Vesuvius eruption script," the elder Blumenschein vented on the "infernal nuisance" of mothers-in-law yet refused to take any action until Ernest completed his intended studies. He advised his son to see Greene less often, put his love to the test, and take care of himself.[105] Mrs. Greene gave her daughter the same advice.

At the end of April, when Mary and Ernest announced their intention to marry, Mrs. Greene had "a grand blow off," then "let her engines cool off," and eventually had wedding invitations printed.[106] The ceremony on June 29, 1905, was reported as one of the prettiest in the recent history of the American colony in Paris. Susan Watkins was maid of honor, with Raphael Collin, Elizabeth Nourse, Frederick Frieseke, and several other artists and close friends of the family attending the nuptials at St. Luke's Church in the Latin Quarter. The *Brooklyn Daily Eagle* reported that Mrs. Greene would travel to the United States during her daughter's honeymoon.[107]

By September the newlyweds had settled in to an apartment at 19 rue le Verrier. In response to a congratulatory note from Butler, Blumenschein pronounced himself a "lucky dog," having drawn "the first prize in the lottery." He described his wife as splendid, modest, sweet—"a little lady with a good level head, and much ability."[108] She would improve his art and his manners. Blumenschein had worked hard at painting over the last year, and Mary's canvases, such as *Une Petit Histoire,* probably benefited his work as much as his classes with Simon and Menard. She soon took over the duties that her husband had formerly relegated to Butler. In subsequent decades she often handled matters around crating and shipping and even helped with painting sales. She would support him as wife, artist, model, and critic. He trusted her judgment and often invited her opinion of his work. Her devotion would sustain him throughout his career. As with many women of her time, Mary sublimated her artistic life to help further her husband's. She did this with the same grace with which she lived her life, and somehow managed to keep her own creative ability, albeit diminished by the demands of family life, intact.

Days after they settled into their new place that September, the couple hosted Albert A. Boyden, managing editor of *McClure's,* at dinner and learned that the magazine would publish Blumenschein's "big story" in the Christmas 1905 issue.[109] Boyden wrote an exuberant letter two months later. Blumenschein's illustrations for Jack London's compelling story "Love of Life," a tale of a man set against nature and his battle to survive in the wilderness, appeared in the December issue. They were "the hit of the month." Many artists had come forward to praise the "wonderful drawings" as well as the magazine's superb printing job. London too was ecstatic over the illustrations: "They are magnificent! He has imagination! Vision!"[110] To Blumenschein he penned, "They are of that rare sort that *help* the text," and added a final compliment by buying one of the paintings.[111]

The Dayton press agreed with London. The illustrations were "noteworthy for strength, virility, and artistic expression," wrote one hometown reporter. Another championed them as "great works of art [even] without their connection with Jack London's pen pictures. . . . When one of the adventurers finally found the bones of his lost companion, the words of even Jack London make no such impression on the reader as the illustration of Blumenschein." The commentary ended by stating that the artist showed remarkable talent in both the execution and conception.[112] A fan, Annis Pound, conveyed the effect of illustrations like *Yet the Life That Was within Him* might have on the average reader. She wrote, "For days now, ever since the December *McClure's* came, your illustrations of London's 'Love of Life' have haunted me. You have made many other pictures, but in these you have succeeded in laying bare a soul . . . a human soul in the hour of its nakedness."[113]

April 1906 found the Blumenscheins relocated to 246 boulevard Raspail, in a "civilized apartment with bath and elevator."[114] At the turn of the century, new roads and residences were under construction. The section of Boulevard Raspail between Boulevard Montparnasse and Boulevard Saint-Jacque had recently been completed by the time the couple settled there. The new buildings provided a fresh canvas for Blumenschein to work from, and the play of light on architectural surfaces must have reminded him of the sunlight on adobe walls in Taos. During

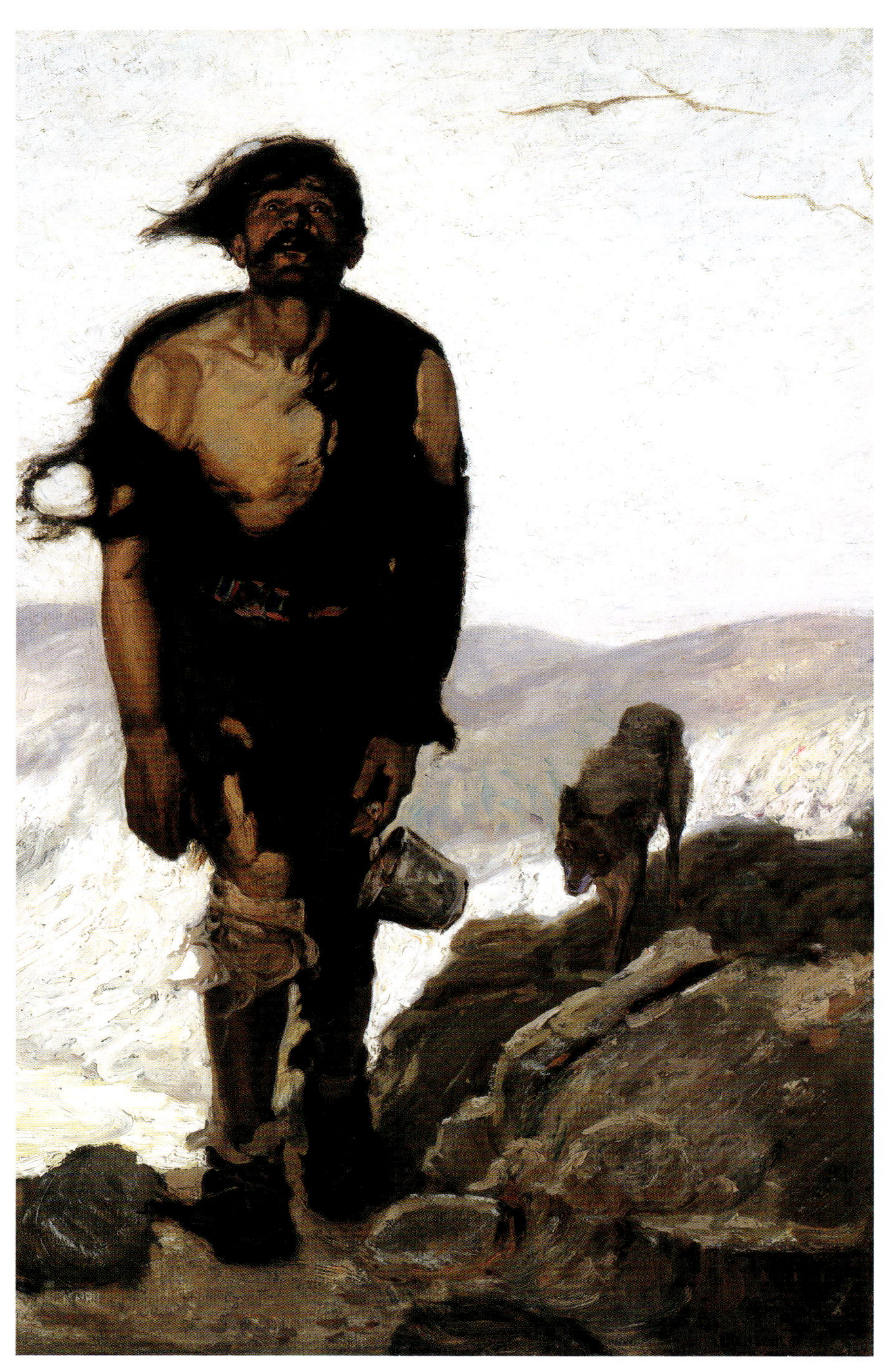

Yet the Life That Was within Him, 1904
Oil on canvas, 30 × 19 inches
Used with permission of the Kelly Collection of American Illustration

this time Blumenschein worked on small oils and revealed a renewed interest in Parisian streets and architecture, as shown by his rosy, glowing views of the couple's apartment and Notre Dame.

These oil studies show the artist's keen sense of composition as he transforms complex subjects, especially a building with a line of windows, into their bare essentials and distills them into basic elements and shapes. Through use of a long horizontal line, and set off by shadows, the mountain of the Notre Dame cathedral emerges, the space broken up by the vertical mass of the trees. The way Blumenschein designs and builds the foreground, middle ground, and background in this study foreshadows what would become a signature characteristic of his later work.

The paintings of the apartment reflect the domestic turn in Blumenschein's work. He and Mary usually painted during the day. Mrs. Greene, who lived nearby at Rue Boissonade, joined them regularly evenings for dinner. Afterward they would often read aloud, frequently the humorous stories of Ellis Parker Butler. Butler's book *Pigs Is Pigs*, about one family's acquisition of guinea pigs and their rapid proliferation, kept them laughing for days. In much the same tone, Blumenschein congratulated and thanked his friend, who had sent them each a copy. The King of Sweden had awarded his copy, he joshed, "with the Nobel Prize for being peaceful." He ended the letter: "I hope to bring my own wife (and family? we'll know about Xmas) . . . we'll have a good time making friends of the ladies and children."[115]

Weeks later, on December 26, Mary gave birth to a son. The parents and Mrs. Greene's joy was short-lived. Two days later, baby Ethan Allen died. Blumenschein shared the news with Butler in February 1907. The Butlers' infant son had died the previous year. Blumenschein's expression of condolence at his friend's tragic loss—"It must be a fierce experience to have a child just long enough to become attached to it"—now applied to his own family.[116] The grief was shared but not mitigated. Blumenschein was especially concerned for Mary at their loss. Keeping busy with their art was their only relief.

From the time he returned to Paris in 1903, and throughout his courtship and marriage years there, the mail continued to bring Blumenschein numerous

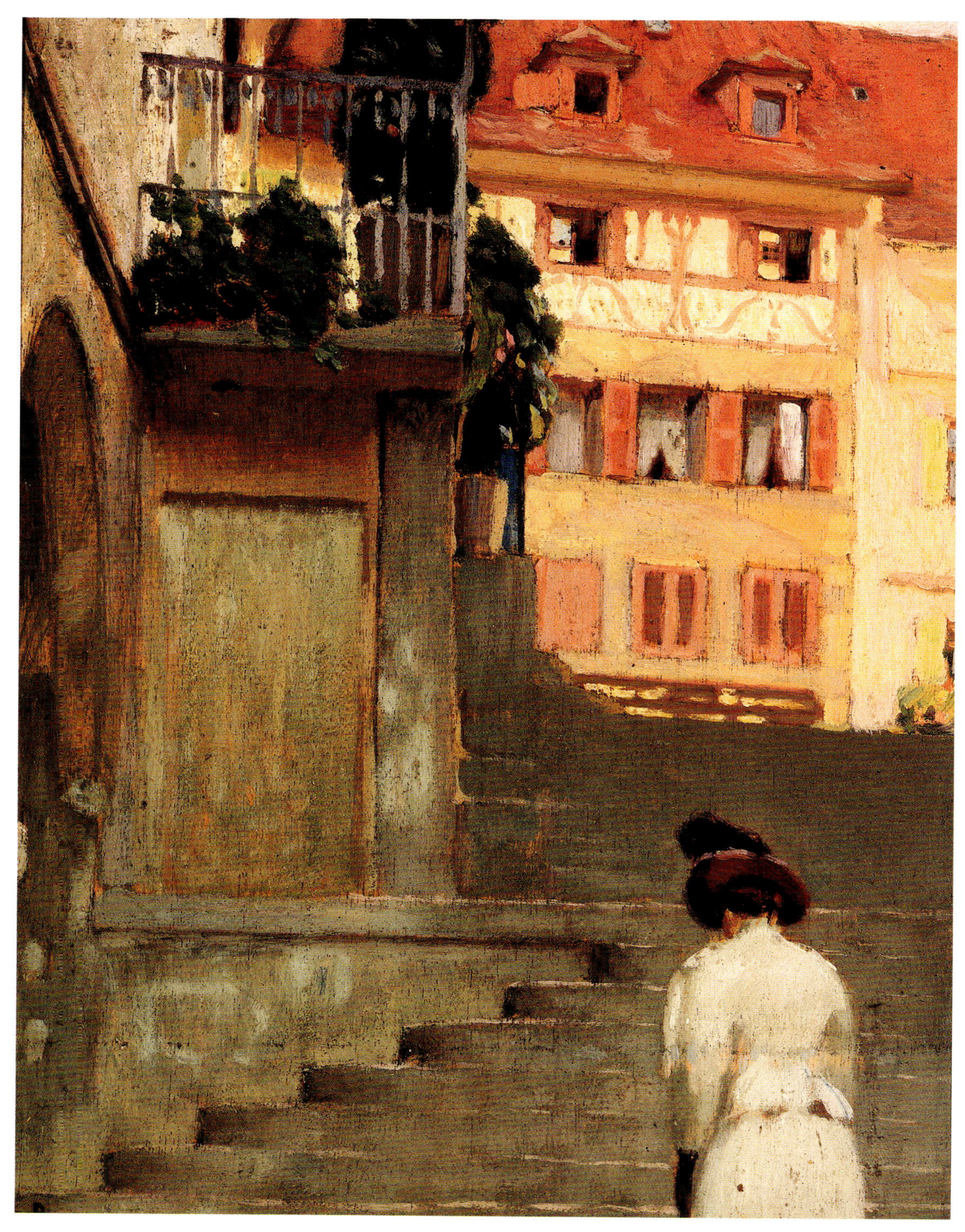

Paris Apartment, ca. 1906
Oil on panel, 10 × 8 inches
Courtesy of the Fred Jones Jr. Museum of Art, the University of Oklahoma, Norman
Purchase, Richard H. and Adeline J. Fleischaker Collection, 1996

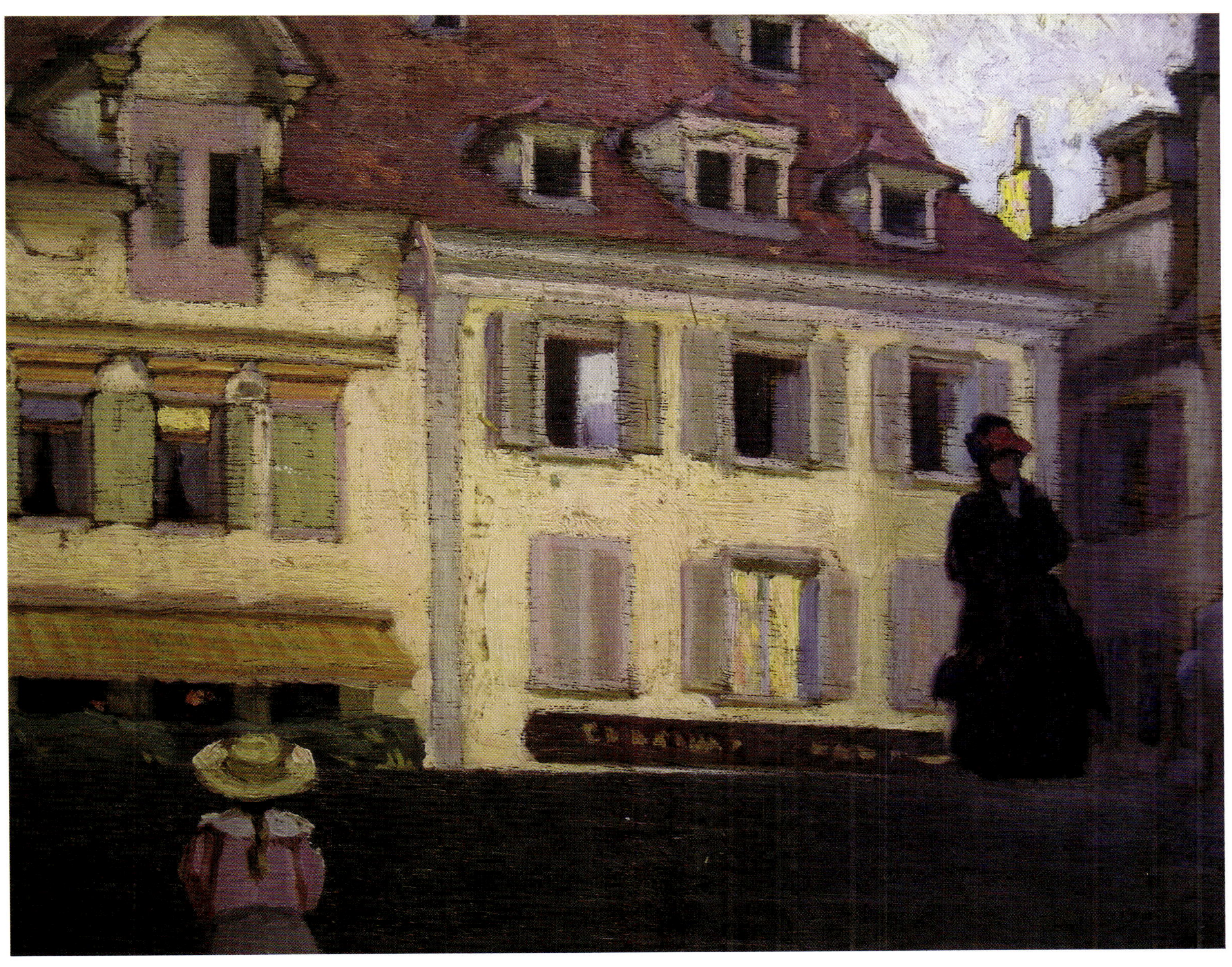

Our Paris Apartment, ca. 1906
Oil on board, 13 × 9¼ inches
Courtesy of the Carlsbad Museum and Art Center, Carlsbad, New Mexico (CMAC 1047)
Gift of William and Christine McAdoo

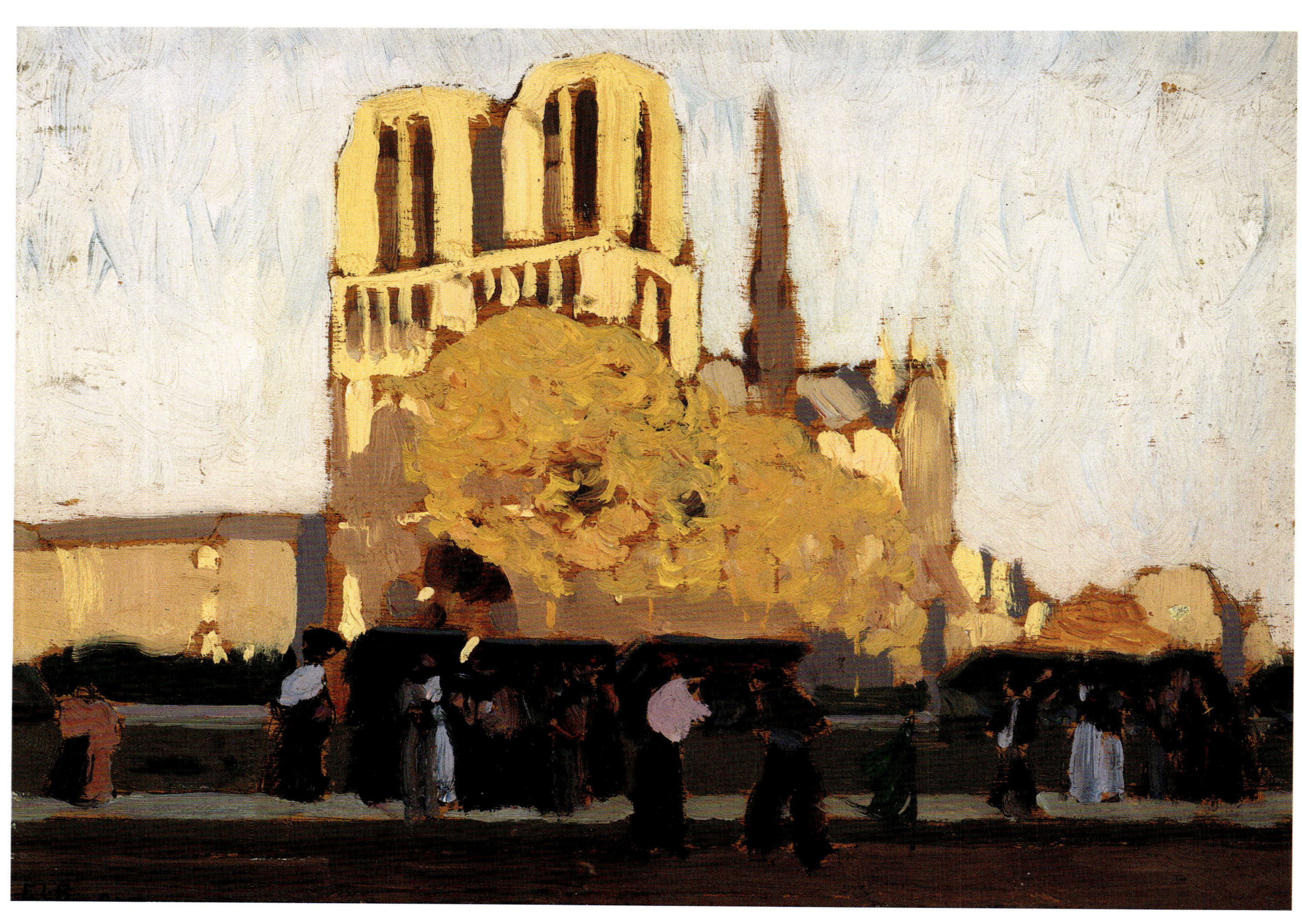

Notre Dame, Paris, 1906
Oil on canvas, 10½ × 14¼ inches
Courtesy of the University of New Mexico Art Museum, Albuquerque (74.204)
Gift of Mrs. Julius L. Rolshoven

illustration commissions, including another one for Jack London in 1906. Many of the writers' names from that period are no longer familiar, but some became part of the American literary canon. In 1907 Blumenschein illustrated stories for O. Henry, Joseph Conrad, and Willa Cather.[117] He also received commissions for several book illustrations. Of the known volumes, the most notable from that period was *Tales* (1909), Edgar Allen Poe's centenary book of stories.[118] Mary reported that Blumenschein worked on "Red Deaths, Folies Ushers, Rue Morgans" while she did "pink roses, pink ribbons, pink nightcaps and small mirrors."[119]

The income from Blumenschein's illustrations helped finance his goal of becoming a painter. He continued to work on color and concentrated on painting portraits. He completed a three-quarter-length likeness of his friend Booth Tarkington in 1904. The following year *Bookman* magazine used the painting to illustrate an article on the author in its March issue. Mary stood model for her husband for several illustrations, including a Jack London story titled "The Unexpected," which appeared in *McClure's* in 1906.[120] A year later Mary apparently was the model for one of his smaller works, *Nude with Drapery*. Ever conscious of design and composition, Blumenschein frames her torso, slightly offset from center, against the long, patterned curtain in their apartment. The deep, darker tones in the curtain and background wall contrast with the rosy, alabaster tones of her skin.

This small portrait helped prepare him for a more ambitious endeavor, a portrait of Tarkington's wife, Louisa.[121] The painting, *Portrait de Mme Tarkington*, was accepted for the 1907 Paris Salon. Modeling for her husband, however, did not interfere with Mary's own painting. She had two pieces in the same salon, one of which, *The Blouse*, was subsequently invited to the Art Institute of Chicago's 1907 annual. The Carnegie Institute showed Ernest's *Portrait of a Man* and Mary's *A Little Story* that same year.

Weeks after the Paris Salon, the season ended, and artists sought out quieter environs away from the bustle, heat, and noise of the city. That summer the Blumenscheins accompanied their friends Frederick and Sadie Frieseke to Giverny. Their friendship with the Friesekes had begun before 1905, when each of the

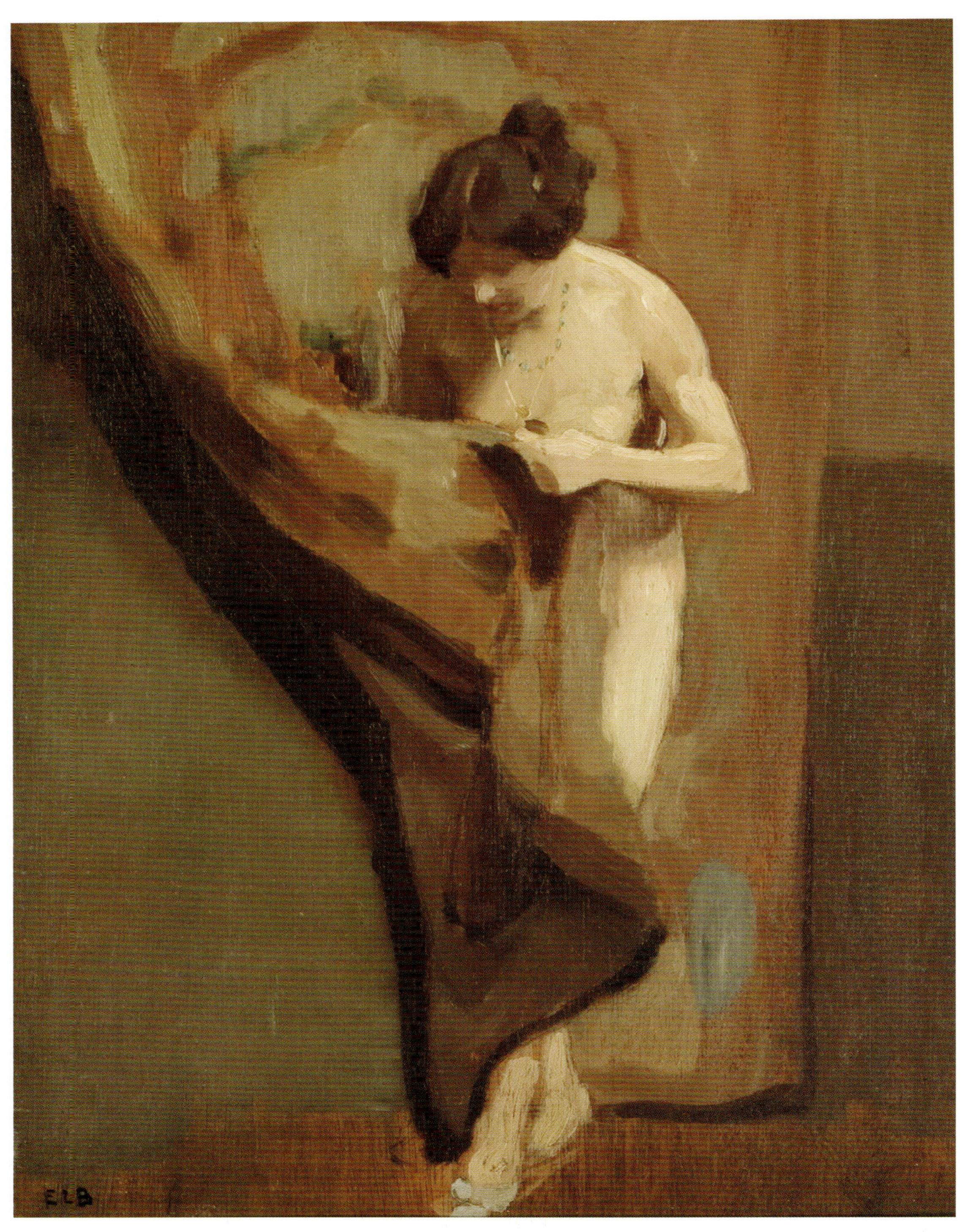

***Untitled (Nude with Drapery)*, 1907**
Oil on canvas, 15 × 12 inches
Courtesy of The Albuquerque Museum, Albuquerque, New Mexico (1994.15.1)
Museum purchase, 1993 General Obligation Bonds

couples married. Ernest played violin at a dinner that Sadie's family hosted in 1904 and lent assistance when her father died unexpectedly in March 1905.[122] Frederick had spent a month in Giverny in 1905 and found a place to rent for the next summer. Beginning in 1906, the Friesekes began spending the months of April through October in Giverny and invited friends to join them. Artists among the "American regulars" included the Blumenscheins; the sculptor Frederick MacMonnies; painters Edmund Graecen, Guy Rose, and Rose's wife, Ethel; and the illustrator A. B. Frost and his family. They would gather for tennis, fishing, afternoon teas, musical evenings, and other recreational activities. They also did some work. The artists hired Parisian models to pose nude for them in protected gardens.[123] This was a much sunnier, more open environment than afforded by Blumenschein's previous summer haunts around Crecy-en-Brie.

In July 1906 Blumenschein sailed to New York for a month. He apparently renewed personal contacts with magazine editors and acquaintanceship with his fellow artists at a Society of Illustrators smoker at Carnegie Hall.[124] He sailed back to France with new assignments. Mary and he spent time in Giverny that summer. There, in MacMonnies's studio, Blumenschein worked on illustrations for "The Namesake," a story by Willa Cather. The most accomplished painting of the series carried the lengthy title *Despite the Dullness of the Light, We Instantly Recognized the Boy of Hartwell's "Color Sergeant."*[125] In palette the painting reflects the Nubian sway of lyrical, soft tones. Perhaps Mary's work also influenced his delicate harmonies. The composition and intellectual tension of the picture, however, suggest the famous Henri Fantin-Latour painting *A Study in the Batignelles Quarter,* which hung in the Louvre. Fantin-Latour, an academic painter acceptable to the Paris Salon, was trying to reveal himself as sympathetic with the rebels of his day, the 1870s. Manet was Cather's favorite painter, and Blumenschein, while at work in MacMonnies's studio, was trying to make similar connections to modern innovations and trends of his own time.[126]

When they returned from their second Giverny visit in the summer of 1907, the Blumenscheins welcomed Ellis, Ida, and little Elsie Butler, who arrived that October. The Butlers had found lodging at 23 rue Boissonade, the same building

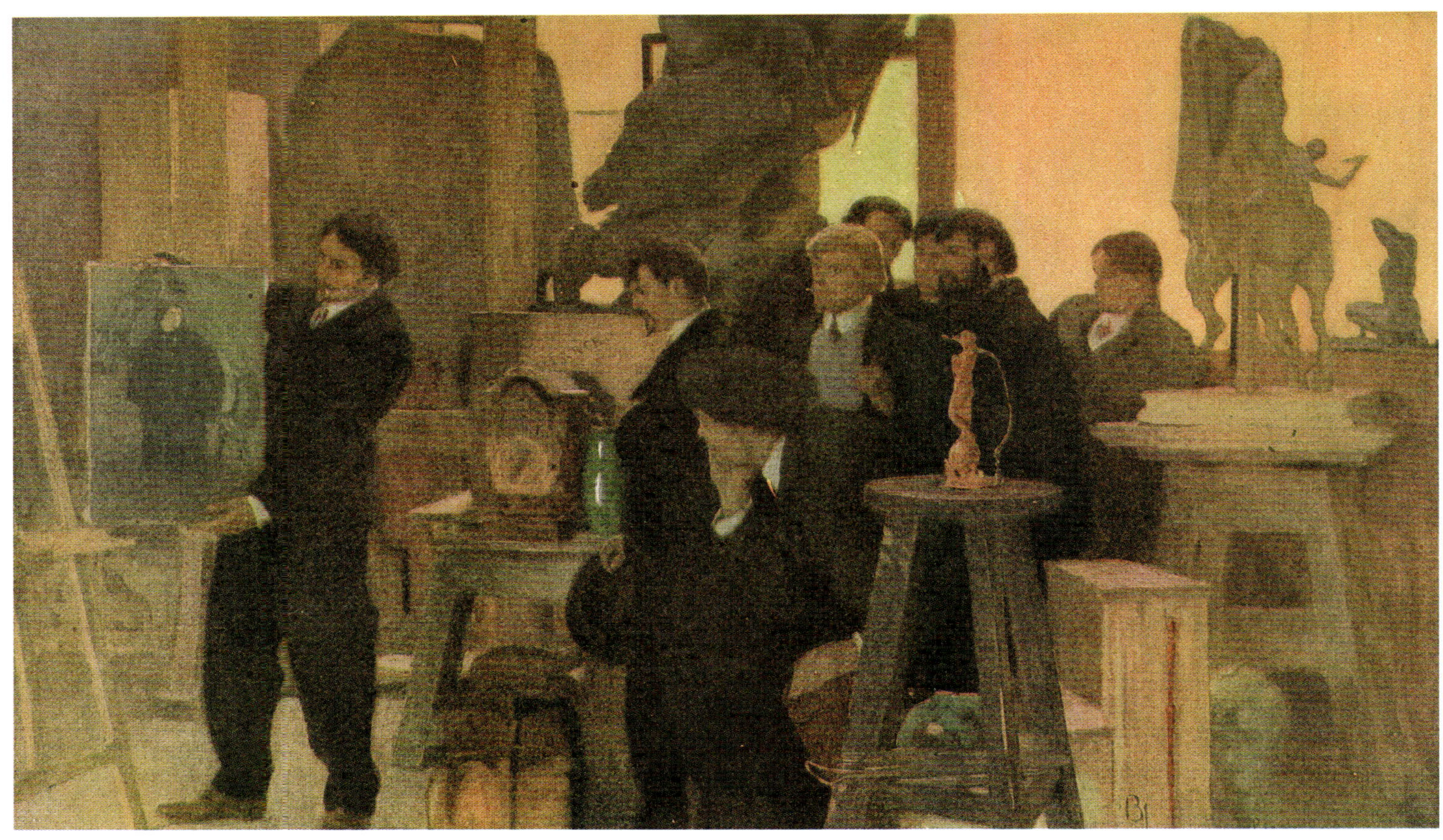

Despite the Dullness of the Light, We Instantly Recognized the Boy of Hartwell's "Color Sergeant," *McClure's*, March 1907, illustration for "The Namesake," by Willa Sibert Cather. Courtesy of Whitman College and Northwest Archives, Penrose Library, Whitman College, Walla Walla, Washington.

where Mrs. Greene kept an apartment, and enrolled Elsie in French kindergarten. Between working on paintings and writing, the two couples found time for taking in the atmosphere of Paris. It must have been a joy to introduce the Butlers to their museums, galleries, restaurants, and cafes. They would have gone on outings and picnics in the surrounding environs, maybe played tennis and bridge. Blumenschein told Butler that it would take Ida "about a month to know 2500 Americans, more or less" at the various afternoon teas the women would attend together.[127] Butler already knew Booth Tarkington and had possibly met Louisa. The Butlers probably also met the Friesekes, who lived in the same building as the Blumenscheins. When the two families parted in May 1908, they had "the pleasantest of memories" of their time together.[128]

The Butlers may have seen Blumenschein's next salon entry before returning to New York. In 1907 a stranded Austrian actor was working for a few painters while he was between jobs in Paris. Blumenschein hired him to pose for a full-length portrait. The French jury chose the resulting painting, *Portrait d'un artiste dramatique*, later retitled *The German Tragedian*, for the 1908 salon. It was later invited to show at the Carnegie Institute's annual in 1909.

With *The German Tragedian*, Blumenschein took another step toward presenting the unconventional. Instead of posing the actor in his studio, he chose instead to lend levity to the scene by situating his subject in his family's dainty reception room. The sitter's comedic expression and pose enlivened the portrait's effect, making it both popularly pleasing and substantively provocative. As a *New York Times* reviewer claimed, "Altogether, it is a work of living art which hardly can fail to capture the most rebellious fancy by its originality and force."[129]

Around this time Blumenschein encountered other unconventional artwork. One day while out walking, he crossed paths with a man whose long black cloak, profusion of red whiskers, and bare feet in sandals marked him as one who had "the courage to be himself." The man, Leo Stein, issued an invitation to his apartment nearby at 27 rue de Fleures, where a dozen people stood around the room enthusiastically discussing paintings and sculpture by Matisse and a painting by Picasso.[130] The works startled Blumenschein—he considered them "freakish and disordered." After the visit, he reflected on what he had seen and concluded that "these men were going far back in order to go forward." He tucked this experience away for future reference.[131]

In December 1908 Blumenschein reflected on a "happy" year of painting and study. He had made good, rapid progress. He had started a new painting commission, a family portrait of the Butlers, by far the most ambitious and complex portrait he had ever attempted. Fellow artists thought his portrayal of Elsie was "way ahead of anything" he had previously painted. Blumenschein had placed the little girl in the foreground at the center. Hers was, according to the artist, the "best head" he had ever painted.[132] Blumenschein had placed the little girl in the foreground just off center; her light hair and complexion and her white dress in light tones make her nearly step out of the canvas. Blumenschein uses the same pinks as in the rosy color of Elsie's cheeks in her hair ribbon and hat as well as the tone of the blue ribbon around her teddy bear's neck to create a harmony of lights in her figure and uses darker lavender to unify the portrait of her mother.

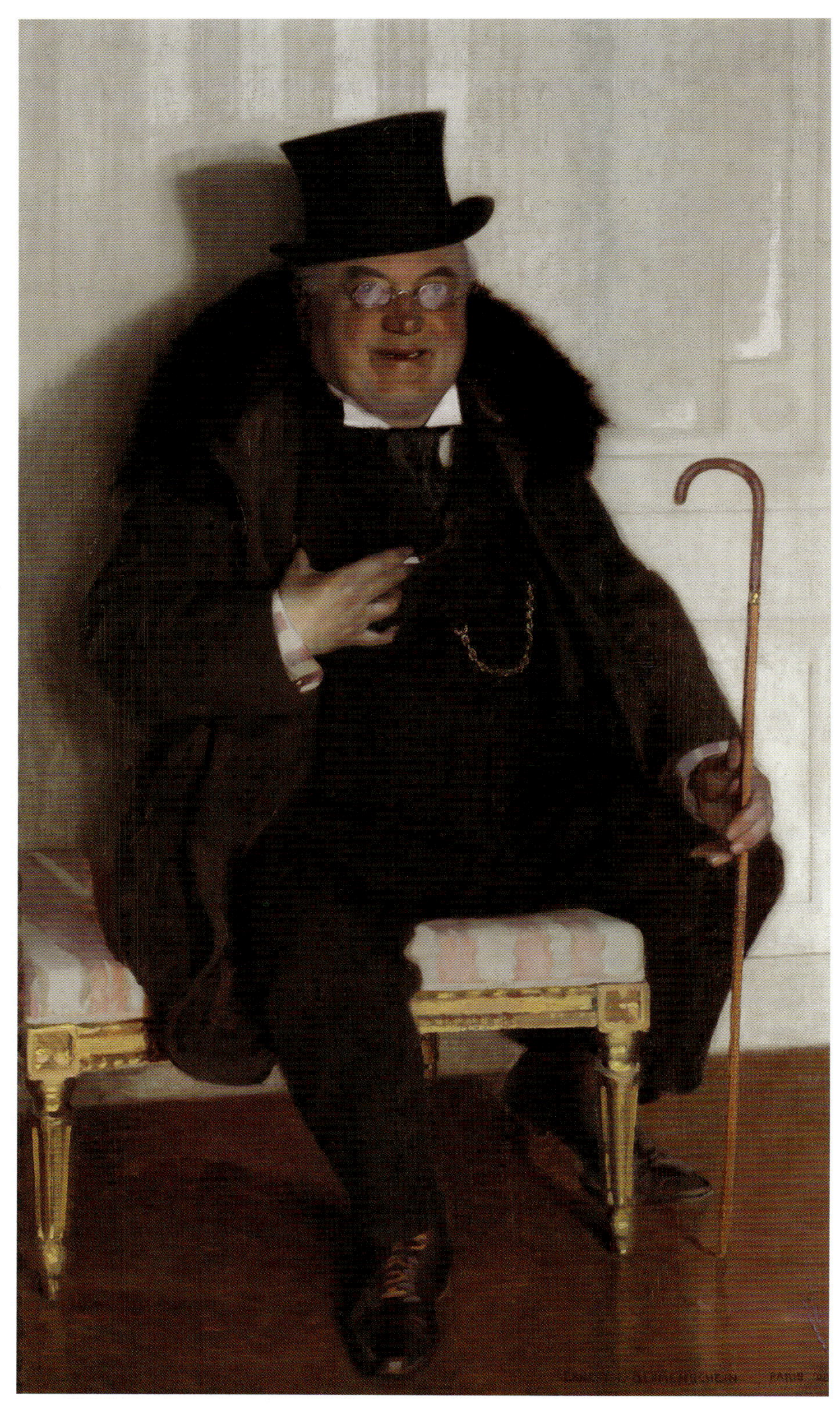

Portrait of a German Tragedian, 1907
Oil on canvas, 57½ × 33 inches
Courtesy of the Indianapolis Museum of Art, Indianapolis, Indiana (41.32)
Gift of Booth Tarkington

Off to the left side, Ida recedes slightly to middle ground through the purposeful use of midtones, beginning with her darker hair, to help place her there, while the dark blond of Ellis's hair helps frame his face, the dark tones of his suit jacket fading into the near-black background. This masterful use of tones and few colors creates a three-dimensional effect. The painting shows Blumenschein's skill in academic portraiture, using a limited palette of just a few colors to maximum effect. This portrait exudes the quality Blumenschein referred to as depth, where he used "vigorous, full" design to create balance and full, rich color, comparable to a full rich tone in music, to establish his planes in his paintings.[133]

Over the course of its creation, he and Mary had grown fond of the painting, and Blumenschein asked Butler for permission to borrow it for exhibition purposes. The portrait made its debut in January 1909 at the Pennsylvania Academy of the Fine Arts' annual. Blumenschein sent the Butlers tickets to the opening, and he gave them another surprise as well. *Century* magazine had decided to feature their portrait in its December 1909 issue as part of their American Artist series.[134]

Encouraged by his success with the Butlers, Blumenschein began a family portrait of the Lionel Barrymores in March 1909. By that time he had also completed a "good" portrait of Mark Luther, a portrait of Mrs. Greene "in glad rags," and "a nude lady in scarlet gauze playing sadly upon a well-painted harp." Mary, in the meantime, had painted what she regarded as her "chef d'oeuvre," *The Princess and the Frog*, drawn from Grimm's Fairy Tales.[135] As other artists prepared for the next Paris Salon, however, the Blumenscheins made other plans. With the advent of Mary's second pregnancy in April, thoughts of returning to New York solidified. They spent the next weeks putting finishing touches on paintings, selling furniture, settling bills, and visiting the Louvre, which made Ernest feel he was "about to lose a dear friend." On May 29 they sailed from Europe aboard the SS *St. Paul*.[136]

Once in New York, the Blumenscheins accepted the Butlers' offer to stop a while in Flushing. Mary could settle in and visit with Ida while Ernest found lodgings. By mid-June he had rented an apartment at 22 West Ninth and a double studio in New York that fit their needs.[137] To escape the city's summer heat, they

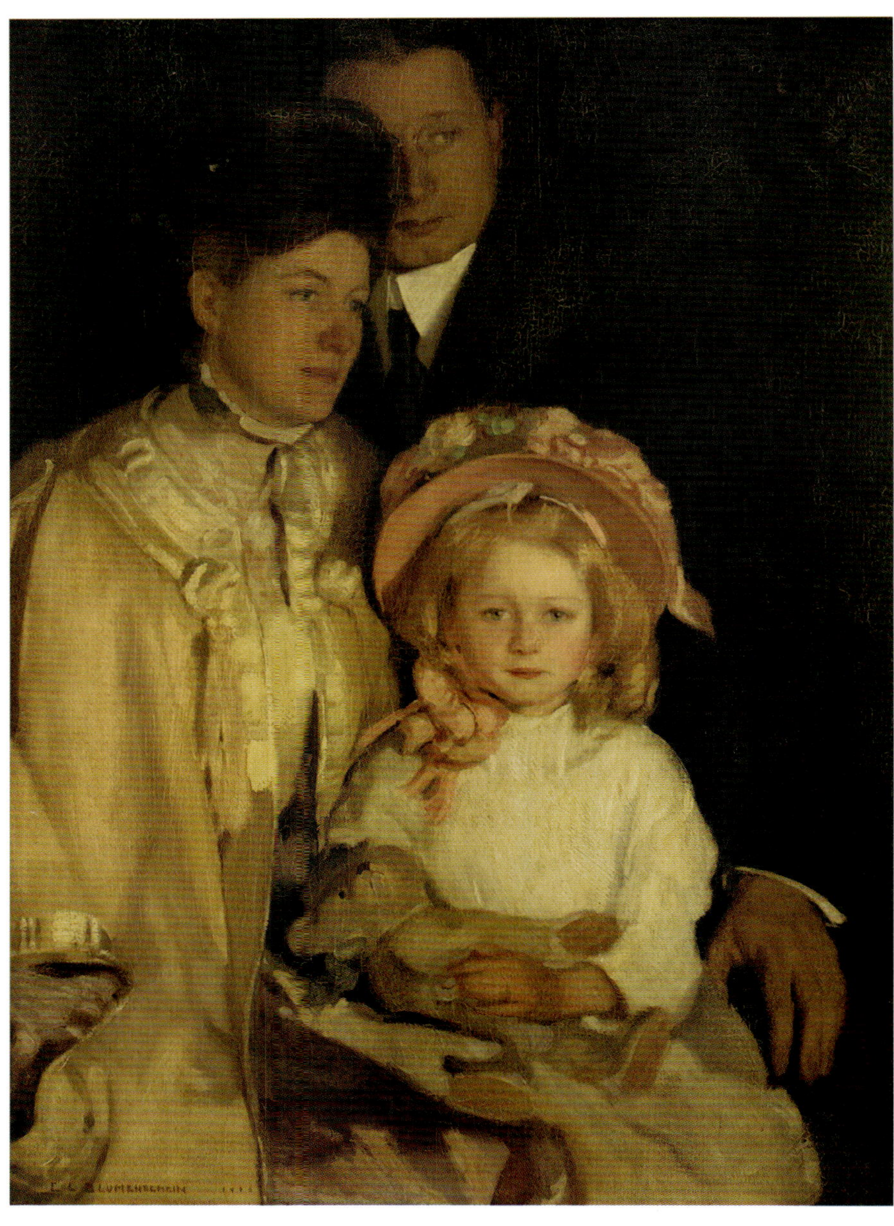

Portrait of Ellis Parker Butler and Family
1908, oil on canvas, 37½ × 28 inches.
Private collection.

took in the sea air at Brighton, until "blind luck" took them to Ogunquit, Maine. On the cool and beautiful New England coast, they painted, clambered over rocks to the beach, swam, and rested. Just as Ogunquit's artist receptions were about to commence, Blumenschein added a musical note: he played a violin solo at the annual Methodist church concert held on August 9, 1909.[138]

Commissions from *American Magazine*, *Scribner's*, and *Century* called Blumenschein back to the New York studio at the end of August. He announced another creation in November. On the twenty-first, "an infant appeared. A short investigation showed that it had to be named Helen." The family was thankful for the baby's safe arrival, and Blumenschein was equally grateful for "the good health of the mother" (age forty). He had reason to be "much pleased."[139]

Two other propitious events followed Helen's birth. The Butler portrait was reproduced in full color on its own page in the December issue of *Century*, and days later the *New York Times* singled out the painting at the National Academy of Design's winter exhibition:

> It is not often that an exhibition strong on the side of portraiture contains many figure subjects that are not portraits. . . . Mr. Blumenschein's "Portrait of Ellis Parker Butler and Family," . . . has many beauties that promise permanence of appeal. It is arranged in three planes, the man

> in the background, the woman in the middle distance, and the child in the foreground, making the child's head the most vivid object in the composition, a quaint little head, seen quite simply and painted with delightful freshness of color and brushwork. The whole picture is a thoroughly competent performance, the paint is skillfully handled, and the surface is neither worried nor dull, but delicately expressive of the character of the pigment as well as of the sitters.[140]

This review informed the New York art world for the first time of Blumenschein's change of direction. The critic understood how the artist had mastered his craft and that from an art historical perspective, this painting would withstand the test of time. However, a Dayton reporter, untrained in art criticism, comprehended something more. He wrote about the quality of Blumenschein's work from a layman's perspective: "His pictures strike you right between the eyes because they are life: large, vivid, palpitating." Each painting contained not one but two messages—"one on the surface that you see first; the next 'between the lines,' as we say of a piece of writing. There is a subjective and objective side to everything he paints."[141] This insight on Blumenschein's work proved prophetic as he embarked on his new career as a painter.

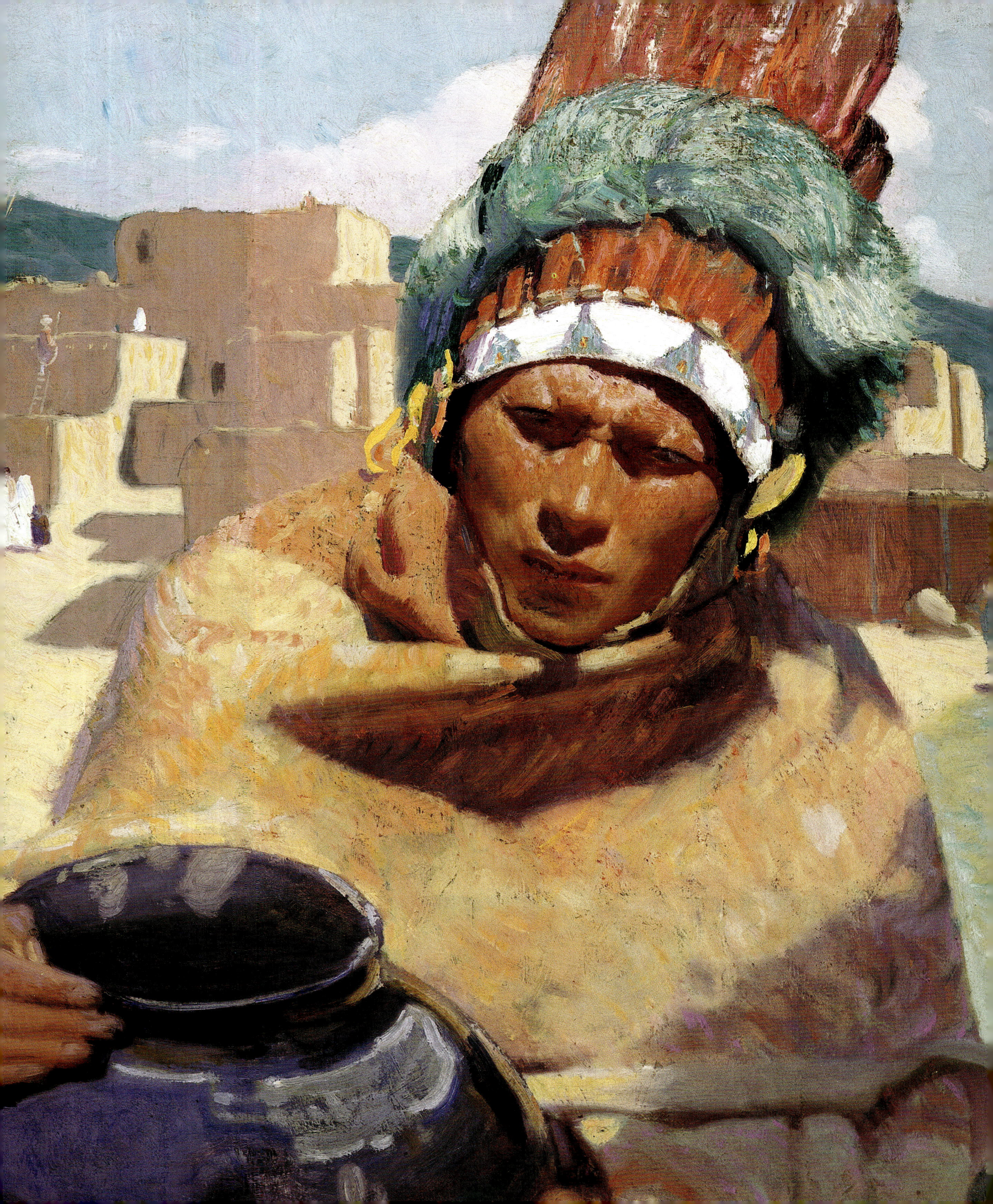

Chapter 2

In Search of the Real Thing

Blumenschein in the 1910s

Peter H. Hassrick

The Blumenscheins' return to New York in 1909 would represent what Ernest called a "totally different place" in their lives.[1] The biggest change, of course, involved switching their intellectual roots from Paris to New York. This they accomplished by actively embracing New York's art scene, despite Mary's need to share with her mother the nurturing of their newborn infant daughter, Helen. In that year's winter exhibition of the National Academy of Design, Ernest presented his 1908 *Portrait of Ellis Parker Butler and His Family*, and the following spring, they each showed paintings at the academy's annual exhibition.[2] Of the two painters, Ernest received the more laudatory recognition from the critical press, thus garnering international acclaim for his French work.

Competing with such purveyors of charmed elegance as John Singer Sargent and the academy's president, John White Alexander, Blumenschein earned special praise for his Butler portrait as "one of the best shown." Its appeal, wrote one New York newspaper, held the promise of permanence. "Quite simply," the portrait exuded "delightful freshness," "the paint was skillfully handled," and the surface was "delicately expressive of the character of the pigment as well as of the sitters."[3] But what impressed most observers was the sophisticated method of presenting his group portrait in a series of planes, with the child, in the foreground, assuming prominence. This was a technical tour de force and deserved praise. It was also a confirmation of how the artist felt about family and how important children, in particular, were to his vision of what constituted familial accord.

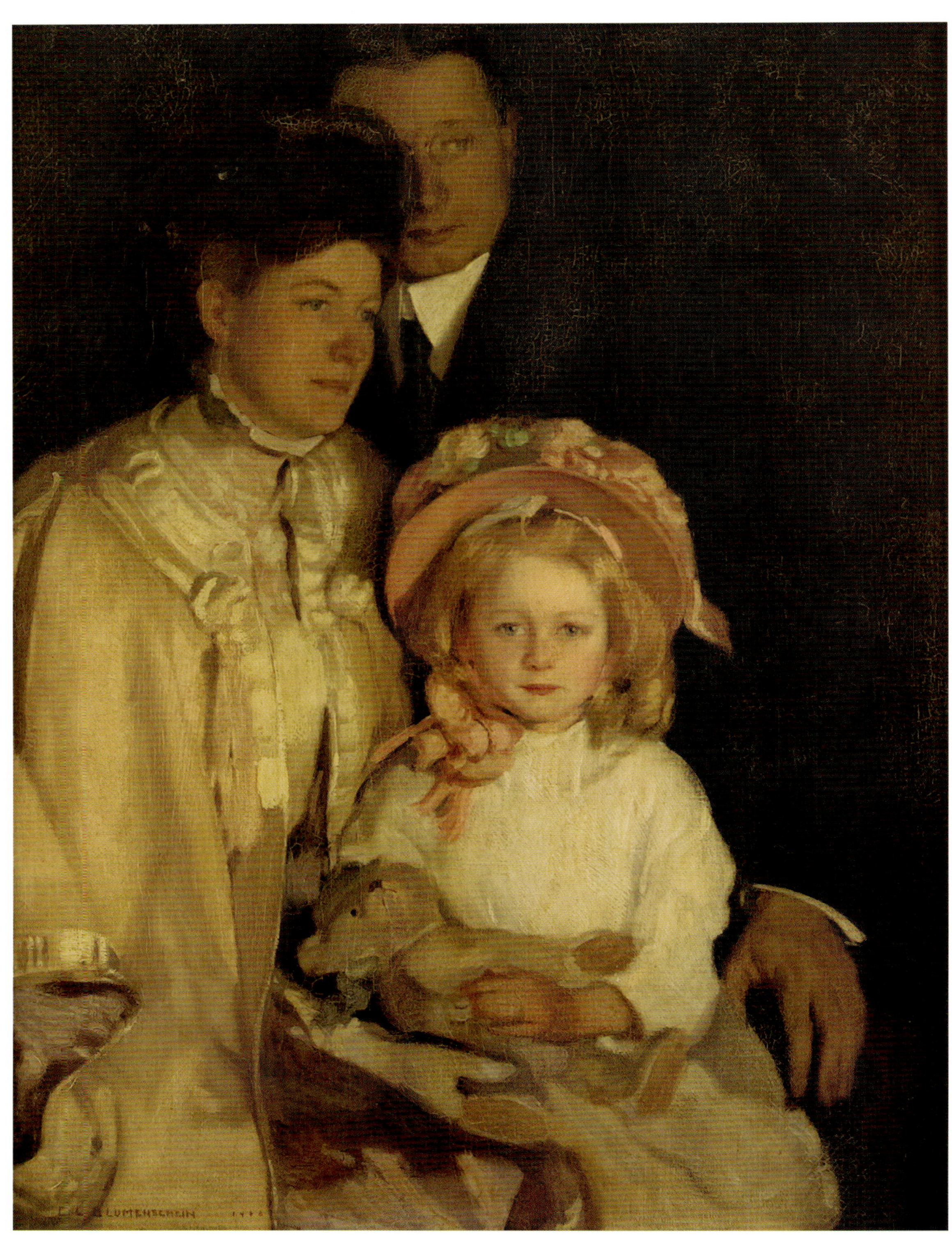

Portrait of Ellis Parker Butler and His Family, 1908
Oil on canvas, 37½ × 28 inches
Private collection

Blumenschein, although he had exhibited at the academy as early as 1903, was considered a newcomer. Perhaps to mitigate that image and to win formal approval as a painter (or maybe simply out of wishful thinking), Blumenschein gave the impression to some that he was prepared to forsake illustration now that he had come back to the United States.[4] The critic Arthur Hoeber wrote that Blumenschein, "who has returned after some years in Paris," was bent on "quitting illustrative work."[5] At the Salmagundi Club, where he exhibited his Butler family painting in 1910 and won a one-hundred-dollar prize for best portrait, Blumenschein also reputedly counseled other artists, such as young William Herbert Dunton, to abandon illustration.[6]

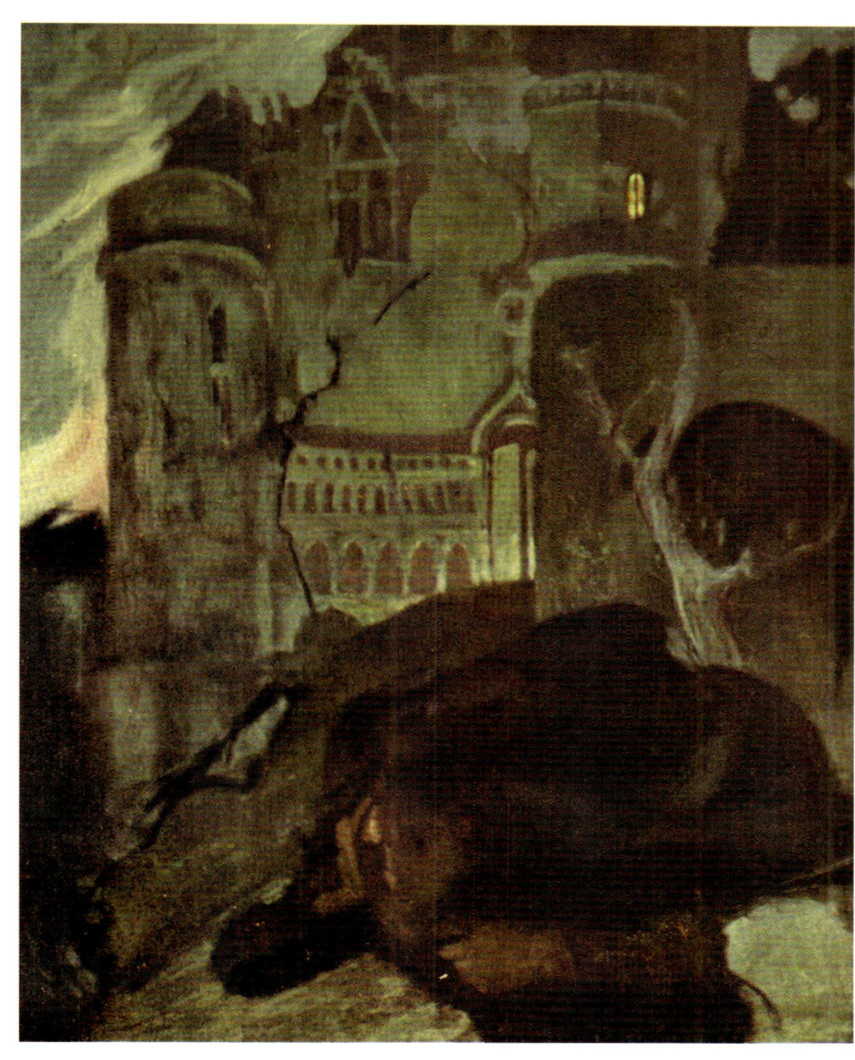

The Fall of the House of Usher, 1909, illustration from Edgar Allan Poe, *Tales* (New York: Duffield, 1909). Courtesy of the Rare Book Collection, Dayton Metro Library, Dayton, Ohio.

In fact, although Blumenschein contended that he "was anxious to devote all my time to painting," financial realities precluded such a course. Especially with a new daughter to support, he actually found less and less time to paint.[7] Fortunately for him, given his recent years of study in color, his pictures could be reproduced in color, as with his 1909 illustrations for the centenary edition of Edgar Allan Poe's *Tales*.[8] Illustrations like *The Fall of the House of Usher* proved what Blumenschein's friend and *Century* editor Richard Gilder said that year, namely, that an "extraordinary change" had just taken place in terms of commercial illustration. Much to the pleasure of artists and the reading public, "color [had] come in with a subtlety" that seemed all but impossible only a few years earlier. Even "so delicate a painter as Mr. Robert Reid," the American Impressionist, was "delighted with the reproduction of a painting by him" that appeared as a frontispiece in the March 1909 issue of *Century*.[9]

Beyond the audience of appreciative readers who enjoyed Blumenschein's illustrations through the ensuing years of the 1910s, there was also some occasional academic acknowledgement of his efforts in the commercial world. When in 1910 he exhibited his series of gouaches from Jack London's "Love of Life" story at the Pennsylvania Academy of the Fine Arts, he came away with the Beck Prize for best watercolor. The prize carried with it a cash award of one hundred dollars, equal to that presented by the Salmagundi Club.

As part of Blumenschein's effort to become enmeshed in the New York scene, he reengaged his association with the Salmagundi Club. He had been a member there since 1900 but now could become more deeply involved. Blumenschein later said that the club had played an important part in his education, but not in an expected way. It had nothing to do with enhancing his artistic education, he reported, but the club was influential in "touching my knowledge of the ways of men—and here I made many of my New York friends." What art talk there was at the club focused either on the commercial side of things, which "distressed" him with its purely mercenary inclination, or the Tonalist landscapes of J. Francis Murphy, which annoyed him even more as he felt them to be so stylistically contrary to his own. But the "social side" of the club and "the good camaraderie of . . . artist friends" made up for the deficiencies.[10]

Within a few months of his successful showing of the Butler family painting at the National Academy of Design, Blumenschein exhibited two more portraits in the academy's annual spring show. One of them was his increasingly famous and well-received *Portrait of a German Tragedian* of 1907 (see p. 000). As earlier, the Blumenschein canvas was paired with one by John White Alexander but in this case was more highly lauded for its "clever analysis of character as well as for draughtsmanship and brushwork" that went, as the *New York Times* judged, "way beyond the ordinary."[11] Even so, in its very devotion to characterization and draftsmanship, the work showed a continued reliance on Blumenschein's skills as an illustrator. "It is one of the best things, if not the best thing, he has accomplished thus far," observed another critic: "Essentially an illustrator, Mr. Blumenschein has a lively sense of character, and has caught with unerring precision the soul and body of the smiling, self-satisfied old chap, who has dumped his fat little body on a stool, hat cocked on the side of his big head, a cigarette between his fingers, a cane in his hand. . . . The quality of the paint is better than we have learned to expect from Mr. Blumenschein."[12] The painting was purchased in 1910 by the Pulitzer Prize–winning author Booth Tarkington for one thousand dollars.[13]

Building his image as an artist with close connection to writers and actors, Blumenschein's second painting to be shown at the academy in 1910 was one listed simply as *Portrait Group*. It was probably a family portrait later retitled *Allegory in Honor of a Barrymore Child* and subsequently exhibited at the Pennsylvania Academy and the Art Institute of Chicago. The portrait featured the actor Lionel Barrymore with his wife, Doris, one of their children, and a nursemaid. Unlike the Blumenscheins, the Barrymores had lost not one but two children in their early marriage. Their first daughter, Mary, is thought to have died in Paris, where Barrymore and Blumenschein were both art students. This painting is probably a celebration of Mary's short life. In March 1910, however, when the painting was on display at the National Academy of Design, the Barrymores' second daughter, eighteen-month-old Ethel, also died, so the painting could have expanded meaning as a tribute to both children. In any event, Doris may be pictured here symbolically handing over her child to heavenly care with a bouquet of memorial flowers in the foreground.[14]

In the same way that Blumenschein related to writers and actors of his generation, he also established genuine bonds with his fellow pictorial artists. He worked hard to earn and sustain their personal friendships and their professional approbation. His peers formally recognized him in the spring of 1910 when they elected him an associate member of the National Academy of Design.

In early April Blumenschein received a letter from his old friend and mentor Joseph Henry Gest, director of the Cincinnati Art Museum, inviting him to submit a couple of canvases to their annual group show of American artists.[15] Blumenschein had to decline. All his paintings were tied up elsewhere, and he had nothing to share with his Ohio admirers. His artistic larder had run low, and the only creatively rewarding way to remedy the problem was to return to Taos.

Bert Phillips had been imploring him to return for years, hoping that, as they had dreamed a dozen years earlier, they might be able to establish a viable art colony there. Blumenschein's heart had always been overwhelmingly drawn to New Mexico, even in his years away in France. He told the writer Blanche Grant in later years that during the early 1900s "there seemed to be but two places in the world for me, Paris and Taos."[16] Now that had changed. Now they were New York and Taos. And now it was time to find his way back to the truest of his muses, that little adobe town at the foot of the Sangre de Cristo Mountains.

By August 1910 Blumenschein was ready to travel west again, and with this sojourn he established a pattern that he would follow over the next nine years. As described some years later, the routine went like this: "I religiously visited New Mexico every summer. During each vacation, I would do no illustration. Some years I had three months—sometimes less—one year I recall having only six weeks, but these short stretches were devoted entirely to painting. The Santa Fe Railroad gave me passes and later purchased pictures in order to help pay the expenses of those trips."[17] During the 1910s, he said, "conditions did not change," so for the remainder of the year he had to rely on illustration to pay the bills. Over this period the family never suffered, he said; they "had none of the struggles of terrible strain which some artists have to undergo." Yet he also confessed that "we never got ahead financially" over that whole decade.[18] Thus, although his Taos reprieves were brief and had become intensely focused on his larger ambition to achieve success as a painter, they were hardly, as he called them, "vacations." He was there to "work feverishly on serious painting," to challenge himself on a higher plane than illustration afforded, and to escape into his dream of the West as his most potent and enduring inspiration.[19]

The local newspaper suggests that Blumenschein arrived in Taos in mid-August 1910. He was a welcome sight, adding to the "interesting and charming group of summer workers, who are doing so much to keep Taos country consistently on the map."[20] The dream of a New Mexico art colony, one that he and Phillips had defined as "a Barbizon school of painters and writers," took a measured step forward with Blumenschein's presence that summer.[21]

Blumenschein settled into a house and studio on Pueblo Road that for several years had been owned and used by E. Irving Couse. The current owners now rented it to itinerant artists, including Oscar Berninghaus, who had been coming out from St. Louis for the summers since 1899. The writer and indefatigable champion of the Southwest Charles Lummis had two years earlier called upon artists to explore the region as a fertile artistic inspiration. Whole trainloads of them had responded, including a half dozen painters under the aegis of the Toledo Museum of Art who saw their journey to the Grand Canyon in 1910 as a nationalistic pilgrimage. "The pastoral painter, the painter of picturesque genre, the imaginative and dramatic landscapist," wrote the trip's organizer, Nina Spalding Stevens, "are here offered all that can delight the eye or stir the imagination and emotions." Lummis had cherished the hope of someday seeing the Southwest, Arizona and New Mexico, discovered by "artists big enough to try it—at least big enough to dare to Try to try." And when they do, he concluded, they will not simply find a wonderland, "they will begin to discover themselves."[22] Blumenschein had come to Taos specifically on those orders, to rediscover himself.

It worked. Comments he made after 1903 about that first summer back in Taos suggest that he had truly found himself. "A wonderful Indian summer is on here with gorgeous color in the mountains and plains," he wrote to William Simpson, the Santa Fe Railroad's advertising agent who had helped his cause by providing free passage. "I'm having a very happy time working out of doors with my Indian model on horse-back standing in the sage brush. I'm after the real thing, Indian in his own landscape, painted on the spot."[23] A few weeks later, the *Taos Valley News* affirmed the success of his efforts. His landscape studies, the editors opined, were "especially winning" and the rendition of atmosphere was "well nigh perfect." The paintings that Blumenschein had described to Simpson drew special attention: "Two pictures covering the sage brush landscape with an Indian figure on a pinto were very strong. They were the same subjects, but depicting different hours of the day and the artist brought this out with remarkable fidelity, the shadows and atmosphere telling their own story."[24]

Blumenschein had dared to try. There was no serendipity here; the results were hard earned, profoundly gratifying, and immediate.

One of the paintings that Blumenschein must have returned to New York with in November 1910 was an oil painting that he submitted to the National Academy of Design's winter exhibition. Titled *Indian Boy with Jar,* it may have been a prototype for or an early rendition of a painting known as *Taos Indian Holding a Water Jar,* which was purchased a year later by the Santa Fe Railroad and later cut down by the artist. The railroad paid him four hundred dollars, the first such patronage that Blumenschein received. Railroad customers over the next several years would enjoy this image on pamphlets, posters, and postcards featuring the company's logo in the upper left-hand corner and as part of a portfolio of reproductions, *Indian Album,* published by the Detroit Publishing Company for the Fred Harvey Company of Kansas City.[25] What made this such a popular and versatile image was its powerful composition with the figure so boldly presented, the fresh, light palette that was employed, and the breathless clarity of the atmosphere that envelops the scene. The railroad had been purchasing paintings from western artists since 1903 and publishing images in ad promotions, such as calendars, since 1907. But never had Simpson or his staff seen such brilliance of expression, such cheeky artistic self-confidence.[26]

By comparison, works that the railroad had purchased to date from Couse and Phillips were rather somber treatments of Indian life. Some might explore exotic peril as seen in Couse's graphic treatment of the *Moki Snake Dance—A Prayer for Rain* (1903), while another, by contrast, might weigh in on the shadowy side of things, as with Phillips's *Taos Indian* (ca. 1907). Blumenschein's *Taos Indian Holding a Water Jar* provides a sunny, largely decorative respite from the relatively gloomy presentations of his colleagues. He had come west to study and paint the New Mexico light, and he had the facility to accurately respond to it. The light and color shown in his resulting paintings would serve to attract other painters to the area.

The theme Blumenschein chose to portray, an Indian contemplating a Tewa pot, however, was nothing new among the Taos ranks. Couse had used the motif in

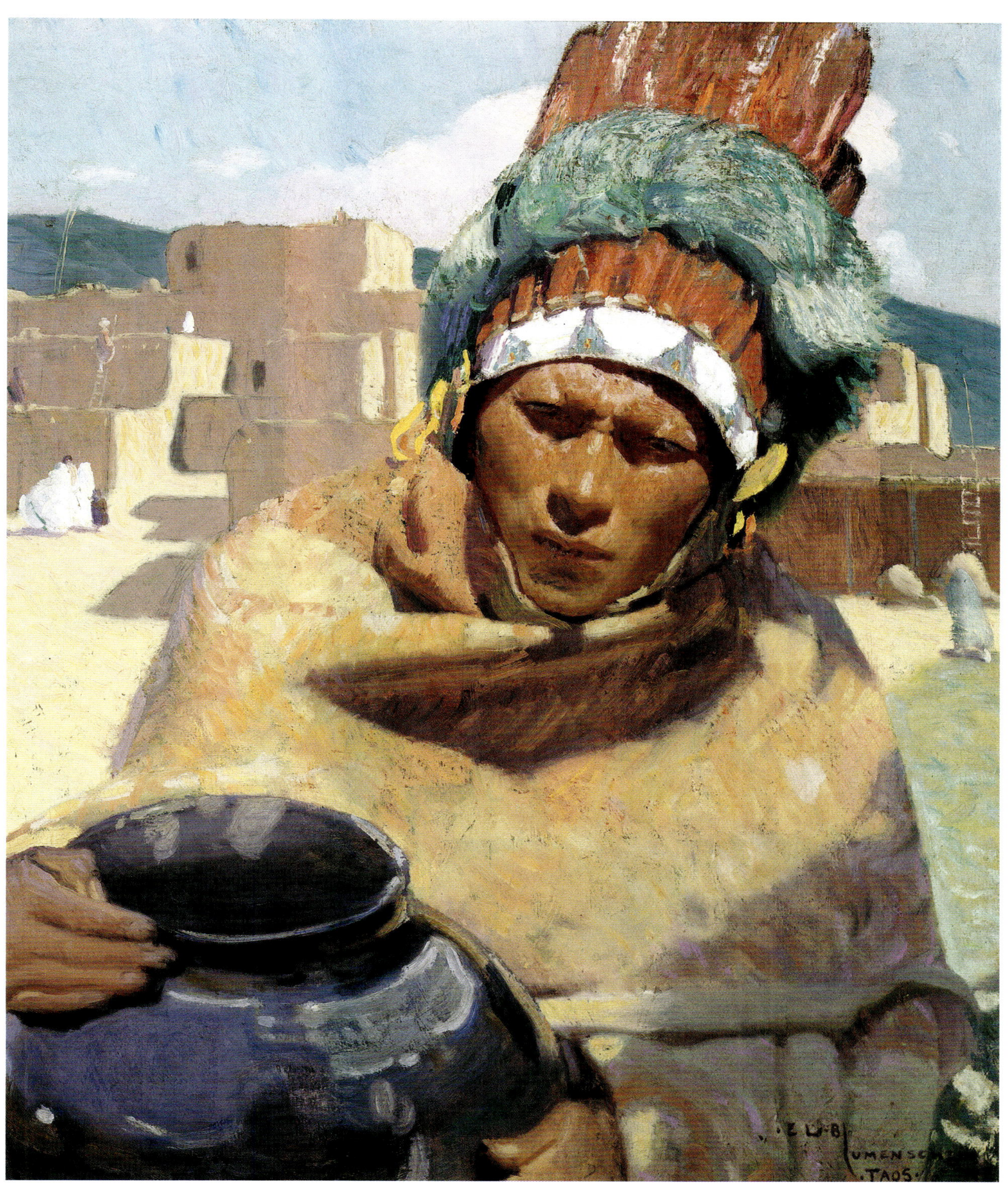

Taos Indian Holding a Water Jar, 1911
Oil on canvas, 30 × 25¼ inches
Courtesy of the Gerald Peters Gallery, Santa Fe, New Mexico.

one of his masterpieces, *San Juan Pottery* in 1911, and Phillips had repeated the idea likewise in 1913 with his oil *Relics of His Ancestors*. Thematically and metaphorically, all three works are idealized, contemplative exercises in which a young Indian male reflects on the beauty of traditional Pueblo crafts. Couse's rendition appears to privilege this sentiment more than those of his fellow painters. In later years, he was recognized more than any of his Taos associates for picturing Native people in the creative process.[27] Phillips's painting is more of a memorial of sorts, a melancholic view to the past that poses a Pueblo youth in the role of an archaeologist.[28] In Blumenschein's version, the boy regards the shiny olla with sincerity and anticipation. He extends it toward the viewer as if offering it for another's delectation—perhaps he is trying to sell it? If so, in comparison with the other two paintings, this work exudes immediacy and modernity. It carries an extra quotient of vivacity and relevance. It is also, on a more apparent level than the others, an undisguised commodification of Native people and their art.

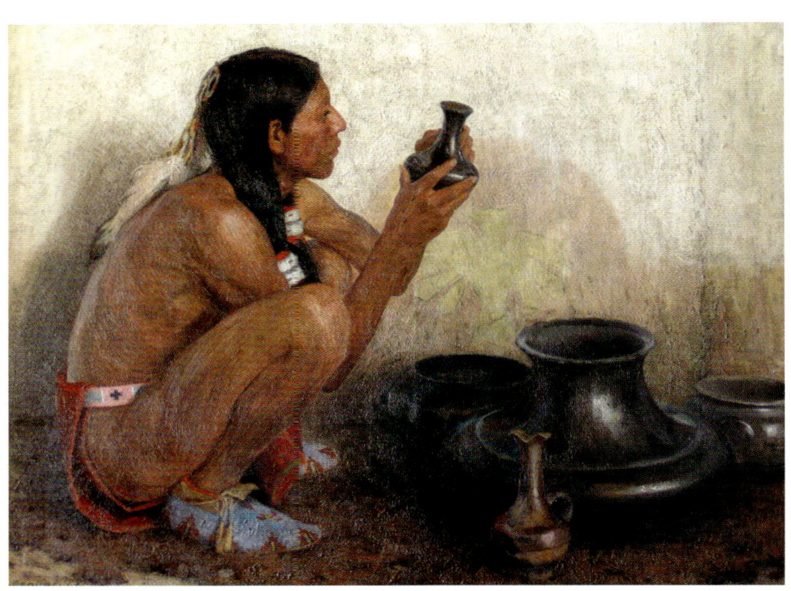

E. Irving Couse, ***San Juan Pottery***, 1911, oil on canvas, 35¼ × 46¼ inches. Private collection. Used with permission of Couse Family Archives.

Blumenschein did not limit his aspirations to sales to the railroad. He had larger dreams, including the hope that Simpson might cotton to the notion of a traveling exhibition made up of works by his compatriot artists in Taos. "I've thought several times in the last year," he wrote his patron, "that the thing to do was to form an organization of the painters who would find their subjects in that region" and organize "unusual exhibitions that could tour the country to the advantage of both the artists and the Santa Fe R. R."[29] Such innovative thinking, although it apparently did not strike a receptive chord with Simpson, provided a seed of inspiration for the circuit shows organized later by the Taos Society of Artists.

Blumenschein spent the summer and fall of 1911 in Taos, this time taking up residence in the Teresina Scheurich residence on present-day Bent Street, one block north of Taos Plaza. In and of itself, the house with its courtyard, which became the subject of one of Blumenschein's paintings that summer, provided an "unrivaled" natural beauty and romantic interest that national authors were beginning to write about by then.[30] Like the home the Blumenscheins later owned, it dated to the late 1700s and was one of the oldest houses in town, a residence once belonging to Charles Bent, New Mexico's first territorial governor, and his family.[31]

Phillips was thrilled when Blumenschein showed up in August for a second successive stint in New Mexico. By this date Joseph Henry Sharp had settled into a studio next door to Couse. Phillips, "the Pioneer" of the group as he called himself, lived on North Pueblo Road across the street from Dr. T. P. Martin. Frank Sauerwein (1871–1910) lived across the street from Phillips, and Berninghaus's studio and home were nearby. To this roster, Phillips added Blumenschein who, lamentably, had "no permanent studio here as yet" but was unquestionably "one of the foremost, in points of talent . . . one of the most enthusiastic and one of the best trained artists of the group." In the thirteen years since he and Blumenschein had first "discovered" Taos, Phillips's consuming dream had been for a sympathetic association of artists "who by their various talents and genius could make complete the record of beauty." Aided by Blumenschein, who from New York worked to recruit artists like Couse and Dunton to New Mexico, Phillips was now in a position to claim satisfaction for the duo that the "splendid results of the united efforts, of the 'Taos Colony' for the past few years, predict the ultimate success of his highest ideals."[32] Although frustrated that he could not join the colony full time, Blumenschein must have been gratified that he served as the first as well as the last part of the equation that equaled a full-blown artist colony in their beloved Taos.

In the spring of 1911, before leaving for New Mexico, Blumenschein received formal notice of his acceptance as an associate national academician. He later recalled that this accolade had come his way as a result of critical favor lavished on his jovial portrait of the German tragedian.[33] The requisite self-portrait he submitted to become a formal member of the academy was far from the charmed conviviality shown by his German thespian. Here Blumenschein presents himself as skeptical and aloof, his pince-nez spectacles bridging a scowling brow as if questioning his professional recognition or the academy itself. His demeanor, so cantankerous and austere, seems in direct opposition to his persona as viewed by many in Taos at the time. In later years, for example, Jacopo Bernal, a Spanish teacher and Taos County superintendent of schools, recounted his impressions of Blumenschein. One of the first things the artist did after he settled permanently in Taos, according to Bernal, was to join the Grays, one of the two local baseball teams. They played every Sunday afternoon, and Blumenschein served as shortstop and coach. In these roles he earned considerable favor among local townsfolk. To fellow players like Bernal, his was an endearing style. The artist became for "each one of us on the team . . . our hero and friend." Blumenschein appeared sufficiently at ease with himself to embrace comradeship with fellows from all walks of life.[34] And beyond his cordiality, he also showed himself to be a dedicated and energetic sportsman and athlete. Like Frederic Remington and others of his generation, Blumenschein took heart with Theodore Roosevelt and his call for American participation in the "strenuous life."

In order to keep abreast of his financial obligations, Blumenschein assumed a teaching post at the Art Students League of New York that fall. He joined an eclectic and passionate faculty that sought to provide a wide-ranging art curriculum privileging innovation over tradition and recognizing illustration and fine painting as equally lofty pursuits. One of his students, for whom he became a close friend and mentor, was Herbert Dunton. Dunton was drawn to Blumenschein, over other teachers at the league like Frank Vincent DuMond and Frederick Yohn, because of Blumenschein's dedication to innovative thinking. As a result of Blumenschein's exuberant accounts of Taos and its burgeoning art colony, Dunton would visit New Mexico the next summer and become a full-time resident there two years later.[35]

As an illustrator, Blumenschein continued to thrive, fulfilling half a dozen book and magazine commissions in 1911. The critic Royal Cortissoz wrote an introduction to the *Annual Society of Illustrators* that year. Although he noted that the halcyon days of American illustration had passed with men like Edwin Abbey and Frederic Remington, he reasserted Richard Gilder's contention that with

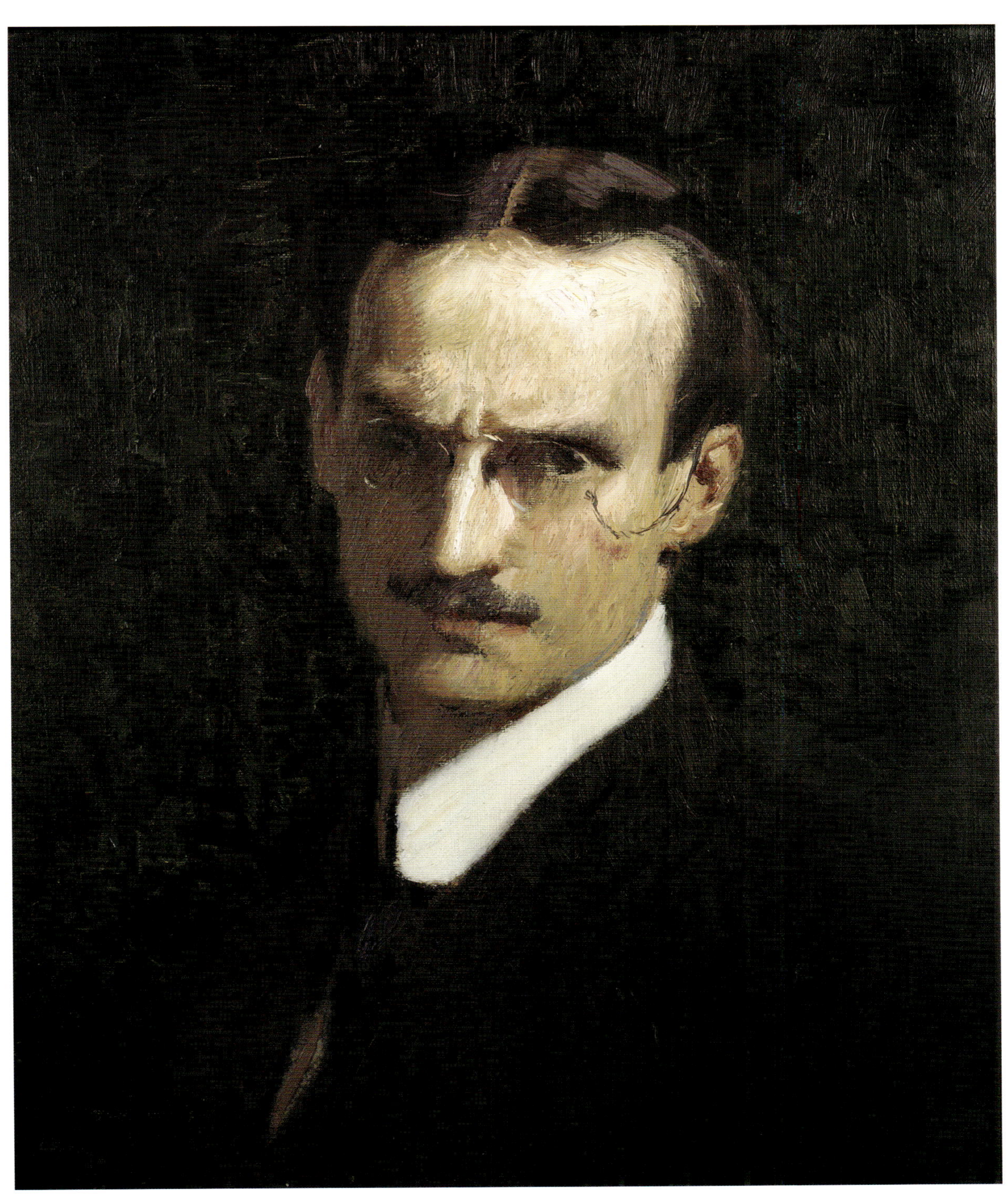

Self-Portrait, 1911 (detail)
Oil on canvas, 30 × 20 inches
Courtesy of National Academy Museum, New York (111-P)

the quality of color reproduction available, illustrators could now "do practically anything they like." Even so, he cautioned, "it takes a rare man of genius to break through the prosaic crust of things and embody in his work something like inspiration."[36] Illustrations by Blumenschein, such as his frontispiece for Randall Parrish's *Molly McDonald: A Tale of the Old Frontier,* which appeared in 1912, resonated with Cortissoz's remarks. They effectively engaged the reader, not with the matter-of-fact cheeriness of Abbey's work or the raw candor of Remington's, but with a design vigor and compositional ingenuity that at times would enchant and at others truly stimulate those who turned the pages to his color plates. In composition, brushwork, palette, and vitality, his illustrations fit the critic's conclusion that "we reap our reward in an abundance of character, of human interest, and of movement. Our illustrators have plenty of 'go.'"[37]

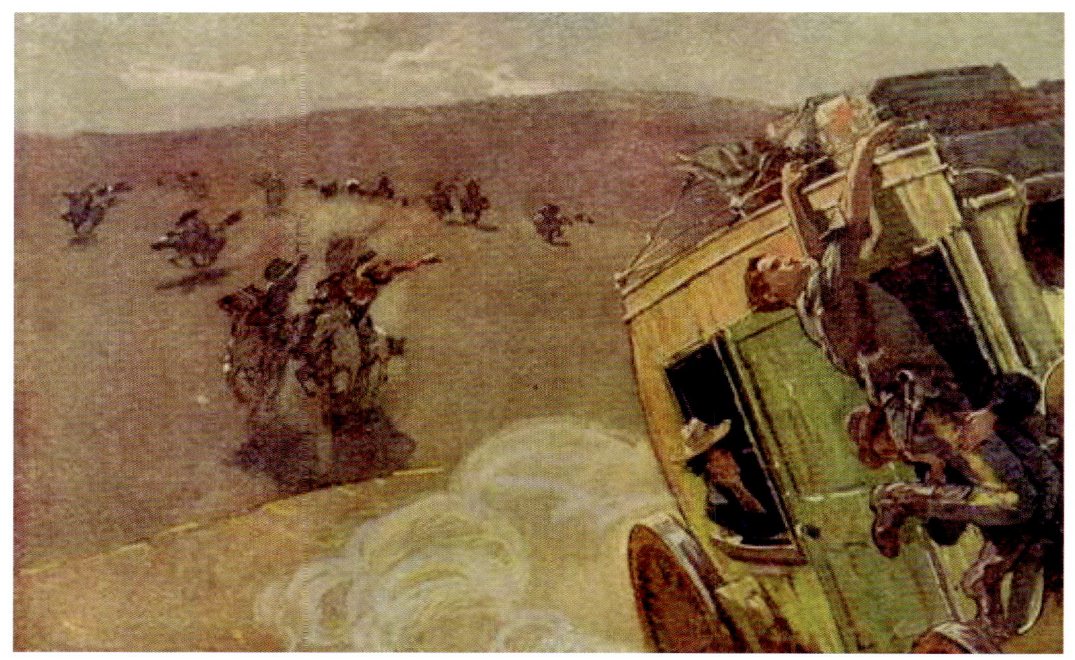

Frontispiece for Randall Parrish, ***Molly McDonald: A Tale of the Old Frontier*** (Chicago: A. C. McClurg, 1912). Courtesy of Denver Public Library, Western History Collection, Denver, Colorado.

Blumenschein's prime submission to the National Academy of Design's winter 1911–12 exhibition was the antithesis of his western illustrations. It had little or no "go" to it but rather a sense of pervasive quiet and cherished affection in which unspoken familial bonds weave together in an elegant interplay of the artist and his family—Mary, Ernest, Helen, and the artist's mother-in-law, Mrs. Rufus Greene. He titled it *A Family Portrait*. Helen, who was featured prominently, later described the group as being executed "about 1912 . . . with his mother-in-law and baby daughter in her lap. Blumy [a nickname for Blumenschein that had come into popular use by this time] with his violin and Mary, his wife, with a palette in her hand were painted in a subdued manner behind Mrs. Greene, while at the top of the painting in muted colors soared the winged figure of Victory!"[38]

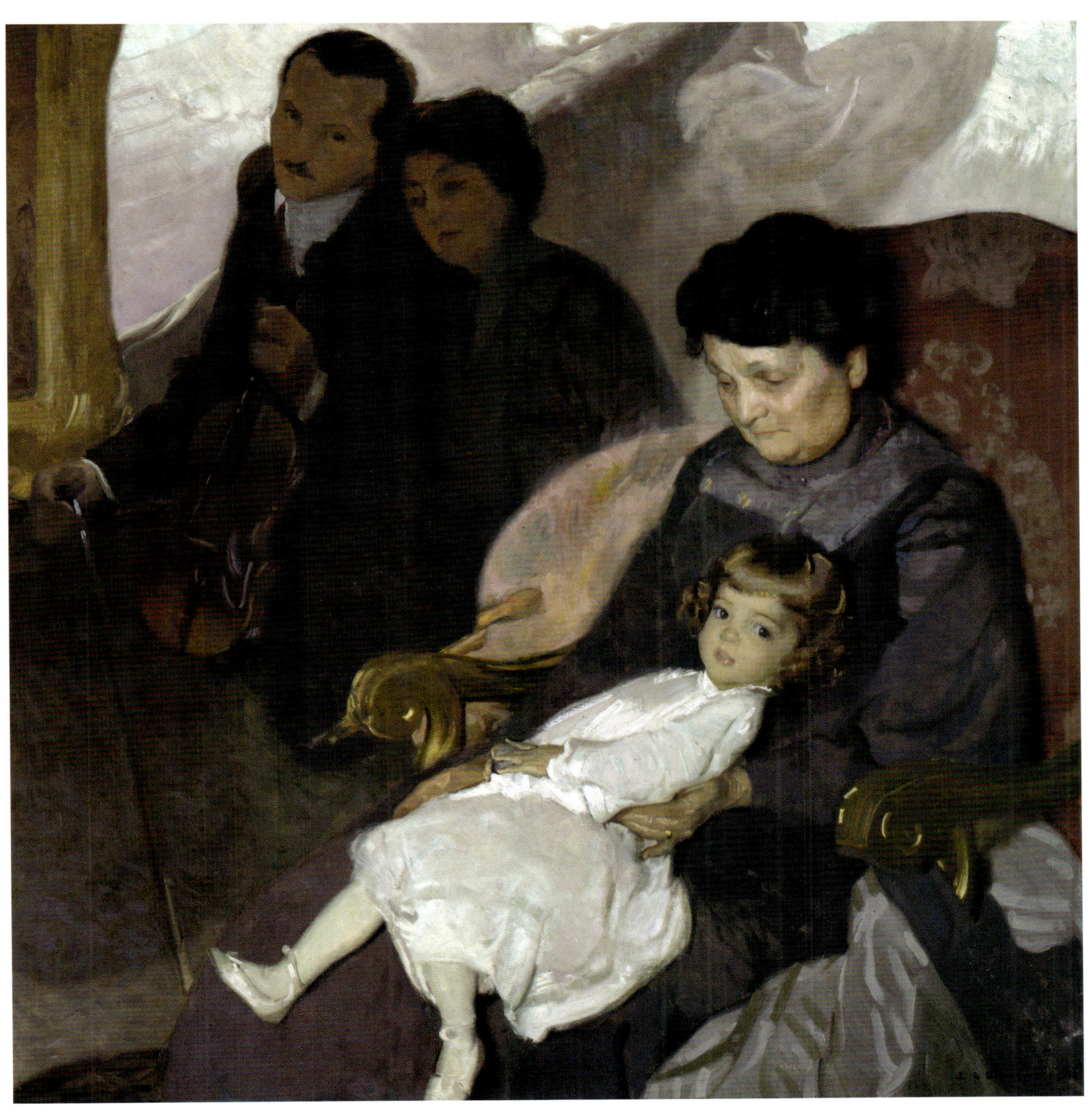

Portrait of the Artist and Family, 1913
Oil on canvas, 46 × 45 inches
Collection of the New Mexico Museum of Art, Santa Fe
Gift of Helen Greene Blumenschein, 1982

Blumenschein said on a number of occasions that his prime influences as an artist were his visits to the Louvre and later his exposure to the Impressionists in Paris.[39] And while he disdained the analytical pursuit of truth in color espoused by the Impressionists, he did seem to sympathize with the honest presentation of sentiment achieved by painters like Mary Cassatt. In Cassatt's depictions of mothers and children in the late 1890s, increasingly complex compositional devices such as diagonal axes are brought into play to accentuate the primacy of the portrayed child. This is apparent in her pastel *Nurse and Child* of 1896 in which the child, with her gesture, glance, and expression, establishes the emotional tone of the picture.[40]

How well, if at all, the Blumenscheins knew Cassatt is not known. Mary Blumenschein shared an important accolade with her in that she was the only other American woman of her time to have received a medal at the Paris Salon. Nonetheless, the ascendant presence of the child in Blumenschein's family portrait and the compositional complexity of the work suggest a more than casual familiarity with Cassatt's pictures.

What informed Blumenschein's portrait stylistically, however, was what he would refer to as the prime tenets of Post-Impressionism: "large masses of harmonious color" brought to bear in the service of "the decorative picture."[41] Sinuous lines weave the composition together with an art nouveau elegance that is balanced by a soft, atmospheric cushion. The painting also demonstrates, as one art historian has noted, the artist's "architectonic sense of pictorial design," a structural discipline that requires sophisticated axial constructs to support the interplay of figures and emotions.[42] These highly ordered geometric foundations became the structural support for many of Blumenschein's most ambitious oils produced over the next decade and beyond.

Although three-year-old Helen is the central focus of the painting, with her dark almond eyes peering evocatively out at the viewer and her right foot tipped up to accent her father's violin bow, a complex orchestration of emotions resolves the highly successful, unified ensemble. Each figure has its place—the nurturing grandmother, the affectionate artist-wife, the artist himself who may be deferring to his wife by holding a violin rather than a palette or certifying music as the primary art when it comes to formal, decorative, abstract (nonillustrative) aesthetics, and the flirtatious child whose white-clad innocence infers that the ideal qualities of the adults may someday be invested in her character.[43]

The larger mystery of the painting involves the diaphanous figure of Victory. No clear explanation of the victory figure has been forthcoming, leading one scholar to suggest, rather plausibly, that it involves the winning of familial accord. Mrs. Greene had not originally approved of Mary's marrying Ernest. The child resolved that tension, and the artist, in subordinating himself in the composition, won favor with the mother-in-law.[44] Blumenschein had earlier flattered Mrs. Greene by painting her portrait, variously known as *Portrait of Madame G* or *Lady in Black*, for the National Academy of Design winter exhibition in 1910. It would subsequently earn him the Isidor Prize and one hundred dollars for best portrait at the Salmagundi Club in 1911.

The other side of Blumenschein's life in these years consisted of his months as a bachelor in Taos. He arrived early in June 1912 and spent a most productive two and a half months generating what the doting Taos newspaper referred to as "art treasures that will live for centuries."[45] Late in his stay the members of the art colony received an invitation, probably through Phillips, to exhibit a group of paintings at the Artists' Club of Denver in the fall. That Colorado organization, precursor to the Denver Art Museum, would thus serve as one of several facilitators for the artists of Taos to begin thinking beyond the notion of an art colony to the idea of a collaborative group that might work together in a concerted effort at mutual promotion and collaborative unity.[46] It would be another three years before they allied as the Taos Society of Artists, but the Denver opportunity caused them to consider early on the advantages of group efforts. Blumenschein, who like Phillips would have encouraged such an effort, saved back two of his summer's paintings for the Denver show. But for unknown reasons, the show never took place.

Blumenschein had promised Taos friends that he would bring his wife and daughter to New Mexico for the summer of 1912. That did not happen either.

Mary and Helen instead went to Maine, where Mary painted scenery along the coast. Blumenschein joined his family there in August when he left Taos. Then he returned to New York and spent much of the fall working on an ambitious figure study, *Wise Man, Warrior, and Youth*, to be sent in December to the National Academy of Design's winter exhibition. As an early Christmas present, he learned that he had won the Isidor Medal for best figure composition, the same prize Couse had won a year earlier with his *San Juan Pottery*. Their creative talents and energies, as neighbors in Taos during the summers and at the Sherwood Building in New York over the winter, must have been mutually synergistic.[47] Blumenschein owed much to Couse, who over the years opened many doors for him, in the East and in the West. The two had met in 1903. Blumenschein had suggested to Couse, because he was having a difficult time finding good Indian models in the Northwest where he spent summers, that he might consider Taos as a field for study. It proved a felicitous recommendation, and Couse soon was spending summers in New Mexico.

As with his family portrait, Blumenschein's *Wise Man, Warrior, and Youth* is a statement of generational bonding and emotional support. Three idealized, heroically proportioned men sit facing the viewer in three-quarter view. Their faces, as with Mary and Ernest in the family portrait, are in shadow. The sun still strikes them from the back and seems to lift them above a distant, distinctly low horizon line. The young man holds the warrior's bow as if preparing to accept the latter's life mission. The wise man, like Mrs. Greene, stares forward with a sense of interiority that projects wisdom. He wears a *manta,* or white cotton blanket, which was common attire for mature, kiva-indoctrinated men from Taos Pueblo.

Wise Man, Warrior, and Youth went on tour following its celebrated debut in New York. It would subsequently be seen in 1913 at the Pennsylvania Academy of the Fine Arts in Philadelphia and at the Art Institute of Chicago. In the meantime, the Santa Fe Railroad was again looking for a painting from Blumenschein. Among the sketches that the artist had come home with the past summer was an ethereal study of men and animals in front of Taos Pueblo and the Sangre de Cristo Mountains. This he worked up into a large and melodic genre scene with Indian horsemen gathered on one side and an ox-drawn hay wagon being unloaded on the other, titled *Evening at Taos Pueblo*. In a letter to Simpson dated March 26, 1913, Blumenschein said he could provide a 25-by-30-inch version of the scene for six hundred dollars or a 34-by-40-inch version for eight hundred dollars.[48] Simpson chose the larger dimension; yet after much dickering back and forth, he paid the artist only seven hundred dollars.[49] By the time he received his check, Blumenschein had been to Taos and back again.

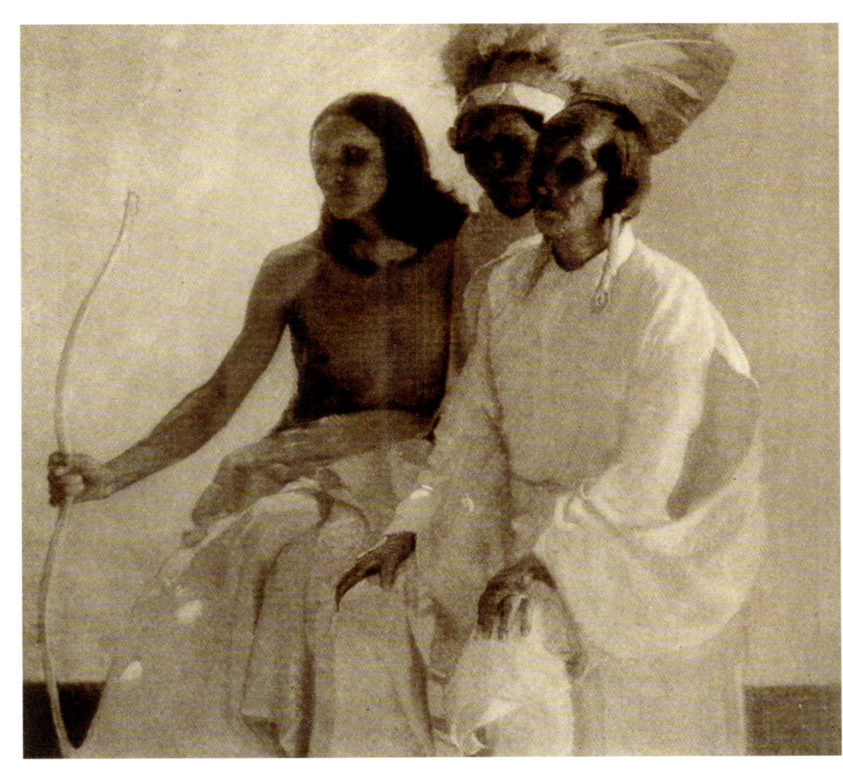

Wise Man, Warrior and Youth, 1912, from the *American Art Annual*, volume 11, copyright 1914 by the American Federation of Arts. Courtesy of McCracken Research Library, Buffalo Bill Historical Center, Cody, Wyoming.

When Blumenschein arrived in Taos for the summer of 1913, he proudly had Mary and Helen in tow. The art colony members were happy to add a second Blumenschein artist to their ranks. Mary was touted as "one of the most popular magazine illustrators" of her day, "her cover pages in colors being amongst the finest and most artistic that appear in any of our monthly magazines."[50] But while the newspaper said that the Blumenscheins planned to stay well into September, that sadly did not transpire. From the time the family left Paris, Ernest had made every effort to persuade Mary to go west. As Helen told it:

> He painted glowing pictures of the fine American group of artists in Taos, just two miles from a pueblo of some 500 Indians! He did not mention that after you left the railroad station at Barranca, you would descend a sudden and precipitous gorge 1,000 feet deep, while riding in a surrey with a fringed top, drawn by four horses over twenty-five miles of rough dirt and rocky road!! This was after a four-day and night train ride from New York City to Chicago, to Lamy, New Mexico, and then on the Chili Line to Barranca Station!
>
> A photo taken in 1913 behind the Ranchos Church shows a most disconsolate me weeping, and a most happy mother, game for

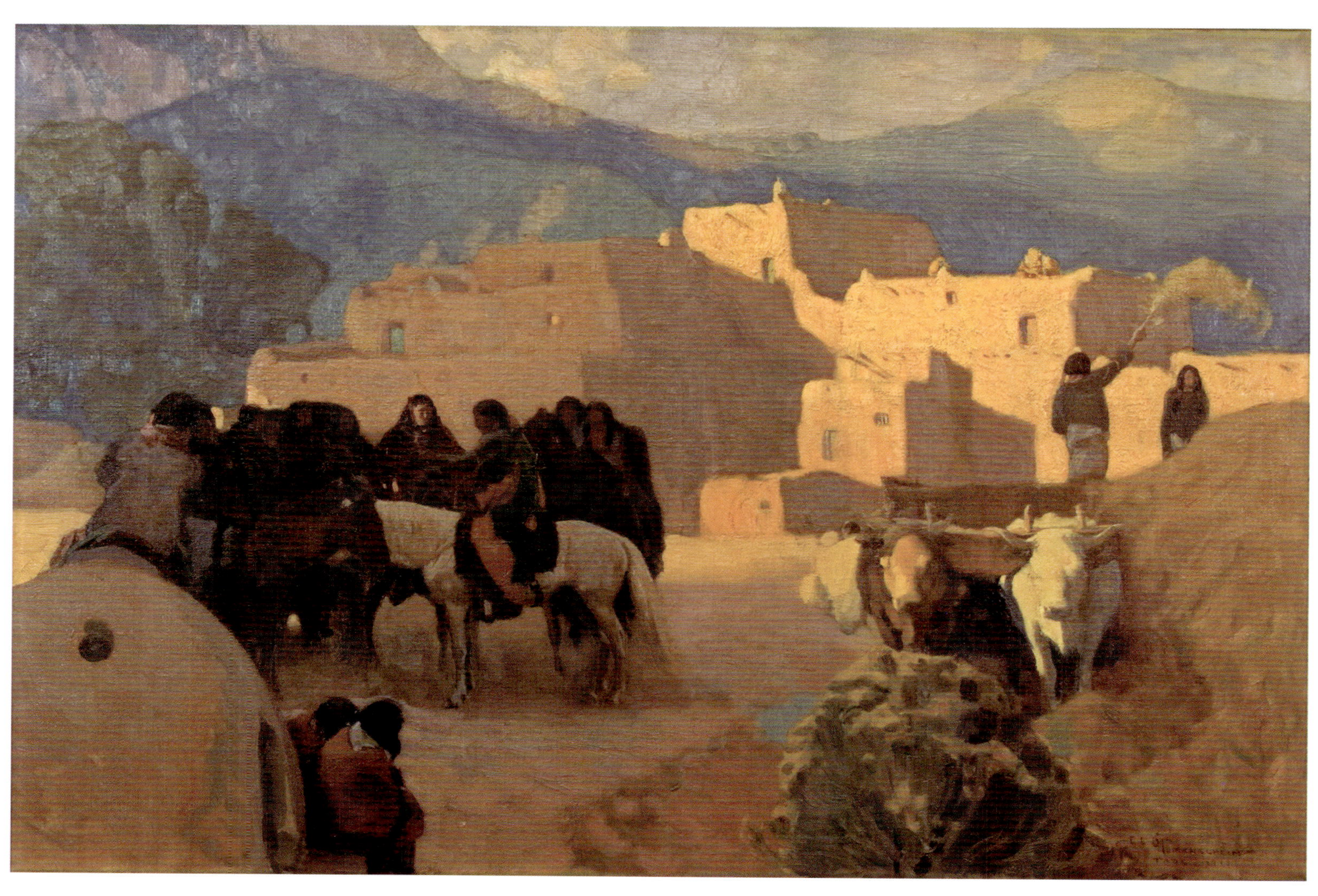

Evening at Pueblo of Taos, 1913
Oil on canvas, 30 × 40 inches
Courtesy of the BNSF Railway

> anything—except there was no milk nor fresh food for daughter Helen. A diphtheria epidemic reared its ugly head while we were all staying at the Wengert boarding house. . . .
>
> Mother flung down the gauntlet—a house and dairy milk or no Taos for the two of us. A week later, back to New York we went.[51]

"It was a regular frontier experience," wrote one art critic several years later, "and the artists proved to be good frontiersmen."[52] Their spouses, at least at first blush, were not always so accommodating or adventuresome.

Despite this setback, Blumenschein stayed in Taos until late October. Just before leaving for New York he opened his studio to friends and associates to view the Indian paintings he had completed over the summer. It was such a significant group of works that the Palace of the Governors in Santa Fe persuaded him to present a one-man exhibition of his summer's work in its reception room. The recent ex-mayor of Santa Fe, Arthur Seligman, acquired two of these paintings, thus lightening the load of Blumenschein's shipment home. Local "connoisseurs," according to the *Santa Fe New Mexican*, pronounced the display "superb," especially appreciated for the "color, arrangement, form, execution, and character" of the canvases.[53] In the West, as on the East Coast, Blumenschein was now being recognized for the aesthetic, stylistic, and technical elements that defined his protean vision as a painter. New Mexico audiences were no less astute or observant than those in New York.

One painting in the show that visitors described as "a dream" was, according to the *Santa Fe New Mexican*, a "semi-decorative picture which stamps the artist as an idealist."[54] It was titled *The Peacemaker* and was one of the largest and most striking of Blumenschein's pieces. When displayed subsequently at the National Academy of Design's winter exhibition (1913–14) and at the Pennsylvania Academy of the Fine Arts (1914) it carried a full title of *Semi-Decorative Composition: The Peacemaker,* suggesting that Blumenschein wished viewers to respond first to its formal aesthetic elements and then to its narrative component.

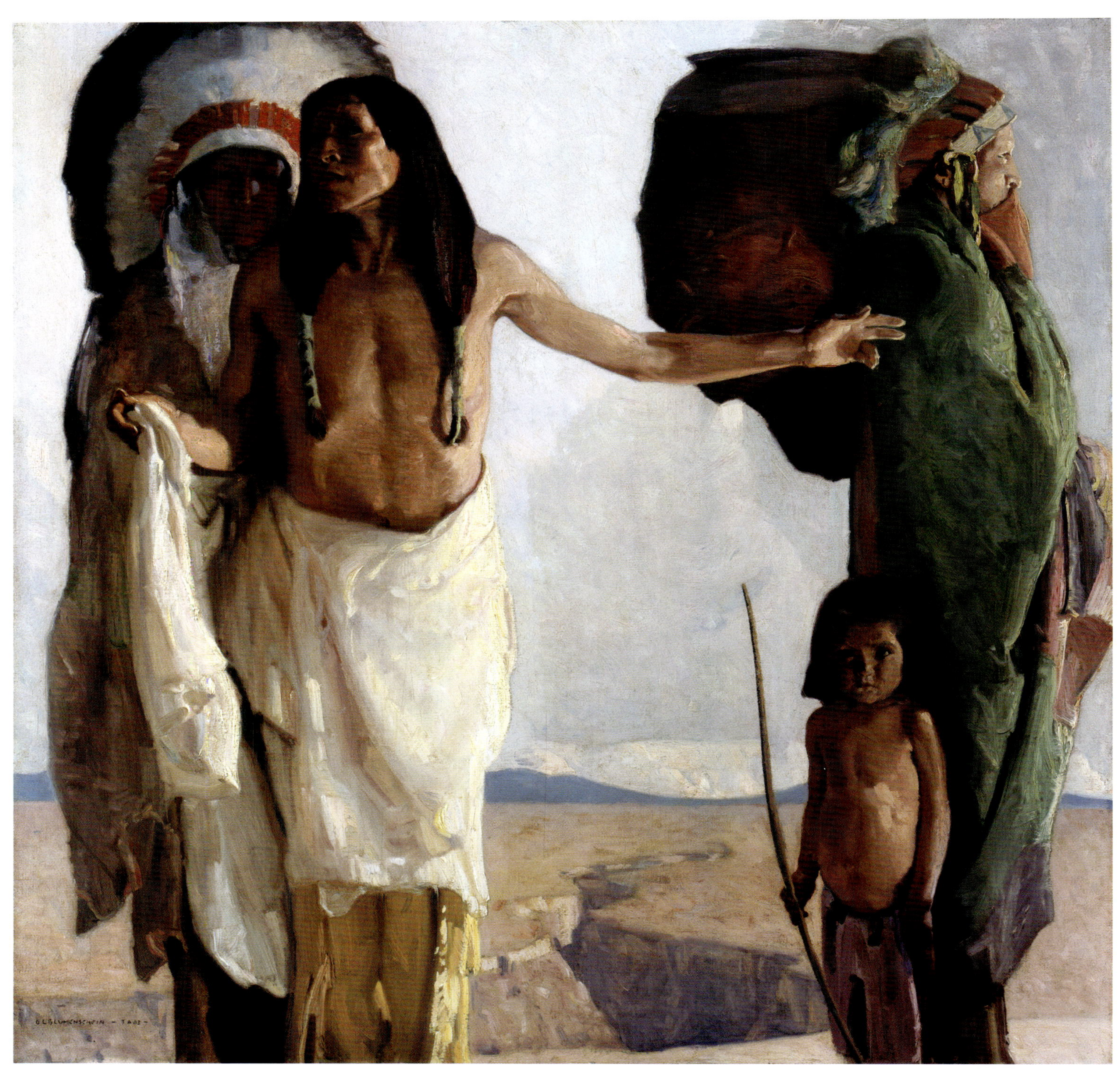

The Peacemaker (The Orator), 1913
Oil on canvas, 44¼ × 45 inches
Courtesy of The Anschutz Collection

The painter and critic Ernest Peixotto recognized that primary dimension of the canvas when he commented on it in 1913. Blumenschein "does not content himself merely with the picturesque side of Indian life," he wrote, "but is preoccupied with harmony of line, mass, and color, building compositions that 'carry' and please the eye with fine decorative effect." Peixotto observed that Blumenschein's approach, the search for "truly decorative value" to be discovered in Native subjects, was essentially unprecedented in American art. It was a "field rich in possibilities."[55] With this, as with *Wise Man, Warrior, and Youth*, Blumenschein was setting ambitious new standards.

Blumenschein composed the painting with two large masses, essentially inanimate, bonneted chiefs connected by the extended arm of a young warrior who reaches across to link the two shadowy, peripheral figures. Raking morning sunlight accents the warrior's hands, one of which holds a white drape denoting peace. A violet blue sky separates the figures, as does a tawny distant landscape, itself divided by a vast cleft in the earth, the Rio Grande Gorge west of Taos. The scene is unified by a harmonized, soft palette and invigorated by the artist's lively brushwork. These were all stylistic components of what he referred to as "primitive art," or one of "the side streets of Impressionism," that he attributed to Cézanne, Gauguin, and Van Gogh, whose works he saw and wrote about later that year at the Armory Show in New York. In primitive art, or Post-Impressionism, the figures assume an "unobtrusive place in the scheme of decoration"; in other words, they are subservient to the design function of the work. The Post-Impressionist, Blumenschein observed, deals in "large, flat masses," simple, harmonized colors, "decorative composition," and "imaginative" expressions that reflect "personal feelings."[56]

The Peacemaker has also been broadly interpreted over the years for its message. Sadly, Blumenschein, who considered this one of his best paintings and kept it proudly in his studio for a dozen years as a prop and an alter ego, left no explanation of its meaning. It may simply be, as art historian Patricia Trenton has suggested, emblematic of a schism, symbolized by the Rio Grande canyon, a geological rift, between two chiefs at the Taos Pueblo.[57] Or, on a larger scale, it

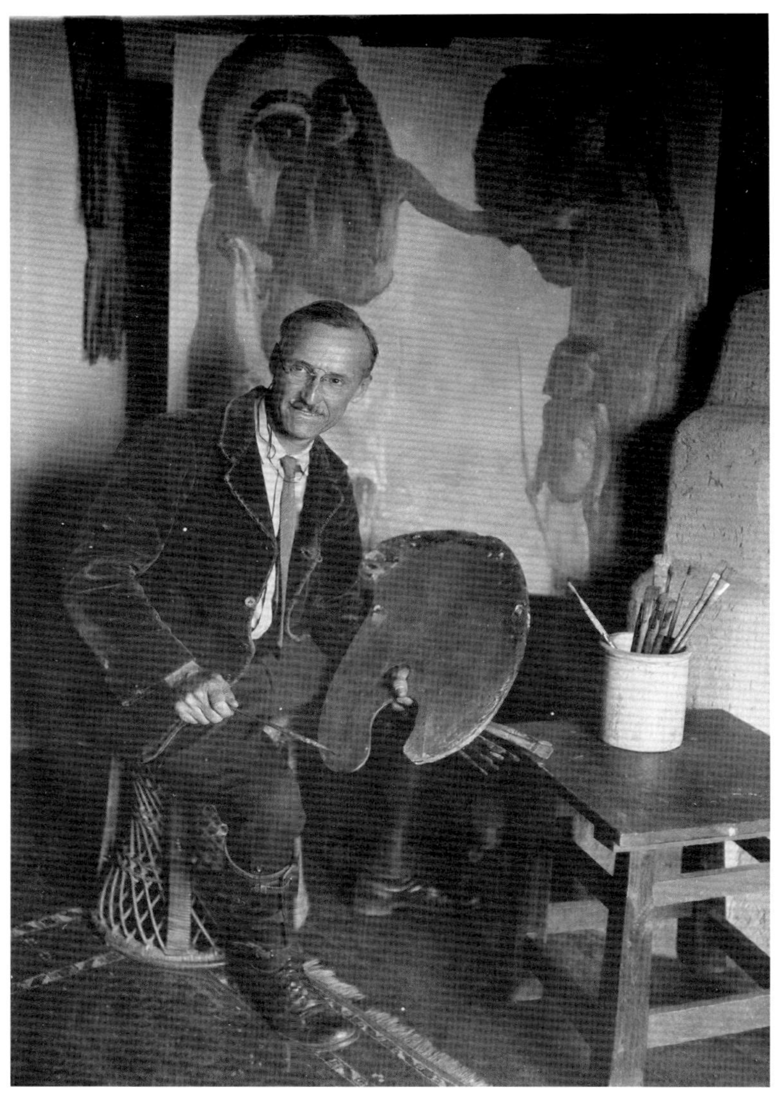

Blumenschein in his studio, ca. 1923. Photograph courtesy of the Taos Historic Museums, Taos, New Mexico.

may relate to the political battle lines then being drawn in Europe. In all these scenarios, the child, who represents future generations that will learn from the outcome, is positioned to interphase with the viewer and call upon the viewer to share responsibility and accountability with the participants.

American art scholar Charles Eldredge has made elaborate arguments for the painting being a statement of "hope for a renascent native culture, for survival of traditions without Anglo interference," that found promise in alterations to the Dawes Act (which had threatened tribal land rights) that had occurred in 1912.[58] Perhaps even the pervasive color, violet, is symbolic. Blumenschein identified violet as the color of shadows at dawn; thus the dominant hue in this work may imply fresh beginnings for himself and his art, for the Taos art colony, or for Native people of New Mexico.[59] At a time when the federal government was trying to make Native people wards of the nation, Blumenschein strove to prove that the Pueblos at least, through their cultural longevity, deserved to be recognized as full-fledged American citizens. Whatever its metaphorical core, its idealized classical beauty (the arbitrating warrior has often been likened to the Greek god Apollo and the white blanket associated with Roman citizenry) and its boldly decorative aesthetic proclivities, *The Peacemaker* remained one of the artist's most highly acclaimed early Taos paintings. When in 1914–15 it was displayed in San Francisco at the Panama-Pacific Exposition, it, along with *Wise Man, Warrior, and Youth*, won a coveted silver medal.

Blumenschein resumed teaching classes at the Art Students League that fall. Perhaps he used lessons learned in painting this canvas when he counseled his pupils. He once summarized his philosophy of painting, and one of the many points he made may well have served as his instruction for others: "Ask yourself when contemplating your work: are your masses large? Is your design vigorous? Are your proportions or spaces beautiful in the relations? Is the brush craftsmanship able? . . . Is your picture like many, many others—or have you said something that is your own? Is it decorative as well as realistic?"[60] At this point in his career, these precepts certainly defined at least his own vision as a painter. He had brought himself to a middle ground in terms of modernism and had found a comfortable and worthy niche.

Blumenschein had attended the Armory Show in New York prior to his summer's stay in Taos. He had come away, as with his earlier visits to Leo and Gertrude Stein's Paris apartment, amused and inspired. His friend Richard Gilder, editor of *Century* magazine, invited Blumenschein to join five other American artists in writing articles about the exhibition. The expatriate painter and critic Walter Pach, who had helped organize the show's European component, wrote the essay "The Point of View of the 'Moderns,'" which essentially mirrored Walt Kuhn's dream that the show would mark "the starting point of the new spirit in art, at least as far as America is concerned."[61] The president of the National Academy of Design, John White Alexander, weighed in with an essay titled "Is Our Art Distinctively American?" in which he defended the academy and bemoaned a perceived arrogance of the moderns saying they had a tendency to "cry down the achievement of the great men of the past."[62] Others, like the traditionalist Kenyon Cox, later demurred that modernism was nothing more than artistic abandonment of social obligation, a whim practiced by artists whose primary pursuit was historically rootless "novelty" and egocentric "self-advertisement."[63]

Gilder, who wrote an introduction to the series of essays, was more balanced in his assessment yet observed a set of particularly "radical" or "revolutionary extremes" among the Post-Impressionist and Cubist work. Blumenschein did not share Gilder's view any more than he did the perspectives of Cox and Alexander.[64] When he sat down to author his own piece, Blumenschein embraced most of what he had seen, especially the Post-Impressionists, reading into their work much of what he considered the fundamental premise behind his own. "There's a big truth in their point of view," he contended. He hesitated when it came to Impressionism because he felt art should step beyond mere analysis of light and color, and he faulted Cubism and Futurism on the premise that they too were overly analytical and suggested more about the artist than the object or idea portrayed.[65] For Blumenschein, concepts like Max Weber's cubist "fourth dimension" were simply too abstract, too introverted as intellectual constructs to have meaning beyond the artists themselves.[66] By dismissing such ideas, Blumenschein, though a declared modernist, abandoned his chances at joining the ranks of the avant-garde. Many savants of the newest trends believed that the fourth dimension equated with a "harmonic use of what may arbitrarily be called volume."[67] But Blumenschein was convinced that volume and harmonic resolution in painting should still be defined more naturalistically through color and contour delineation.

His article on the Armory Show, with its openly gracious accommodation for modern trends, earned for Blumenschein a reputation over the ensuing few decades as an authority on modern art and postmodernism.[68] Certainly the article itself, in its emphatically didactic tone, would suggest that he was genuinely trying to persuade the public, and perhaps his students, to expand their view of art to include new means of expression.

In 1915, during his annual summer stay in Taos, Blumenschein tried a new approach to the theme of Indians. He painted an ambitious oil, 34-by-70 inches in size, depicting two bonneted young men standing side by side. In contrast to *The Peacemaker*, or perhaps as a sequel to it, this work, *The Chief's Two Sons*, featured the next generation. Instead of old men being separated by political rifts, the youths have come together. They enjoy shared stature, each wearing a feather headdress and each carrying an eagle wing fan, symbols of power. They look at each other as if communicating, something the Taos Pueblo elders in *The Peacemaker* were loath to do. In the background are adobe dwellings and cottonwood trees, connoting shady settlements and prosperity. Although it never received the critical acclaim of *The Peacemaker*, this painting was exhibited by Blumenschein at the Pennsylvania Academy of the Fine Arts, the National Academy of Design, and the Art Institute

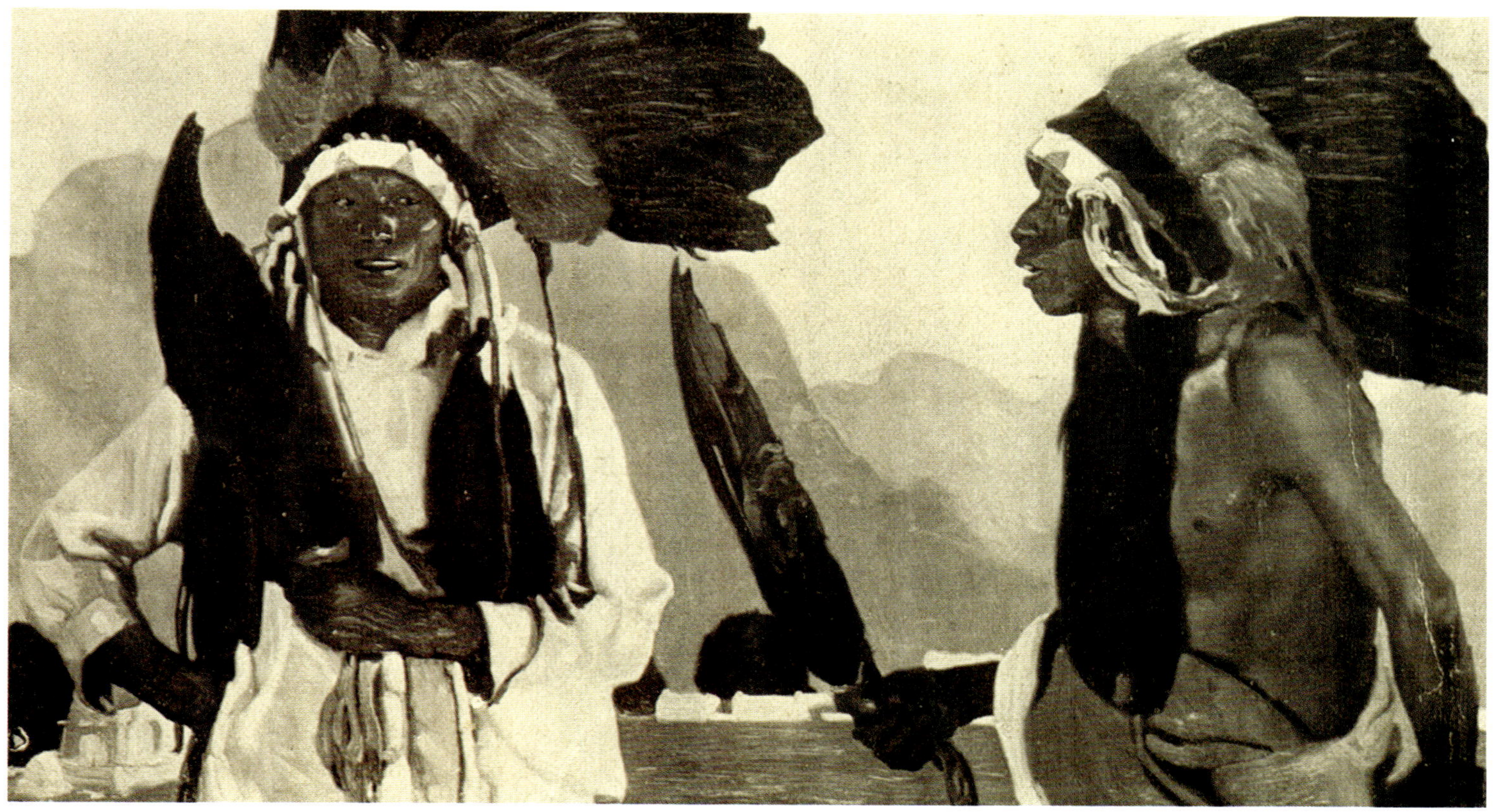

The Chief's Two Sons, 1915, from a newspaper clipping. Courtesy of Mary R. Schiff Library and Archives, Cincinnati Art Museum, Cincinnati, Ohio.

of Chicago over the next three years. When offered for sale at those venues it commanded the same price as *The Peacemaker*, two thousand dollars.

Sometime after 1920 *The Chief's Two Sons* was cut in half by the artist and the scenic background painted out. The two resulting paintings are now known as *Eagle Fan* and *Eagle Feather Prayer Chant*. The artist elected to paint the backgrounds of each a different neutral color, thus making it difficult to fathom that they were once a unified, single composition.

The Blumenscheins had, back in 1914, moved into the Sherwood Studio Building at 58 West Fifty-seventh Street. Built in the late 1870s as the first apartment house in the city designed specifically for artists, it was seven stories high and contained forty-four apartments, each with a fifteen-foot-high studio as well as living accommodations. It was known to be comfortable, some said even luxurious. The Blumenschein family lived there for three years, carrying on their busy schedules and ambitious workloads.

Blumenschein spent the months of July and August 1915 in Taos. He had made arrangements to stay at the home of Dr. T. P. Martin, Taos's medical and

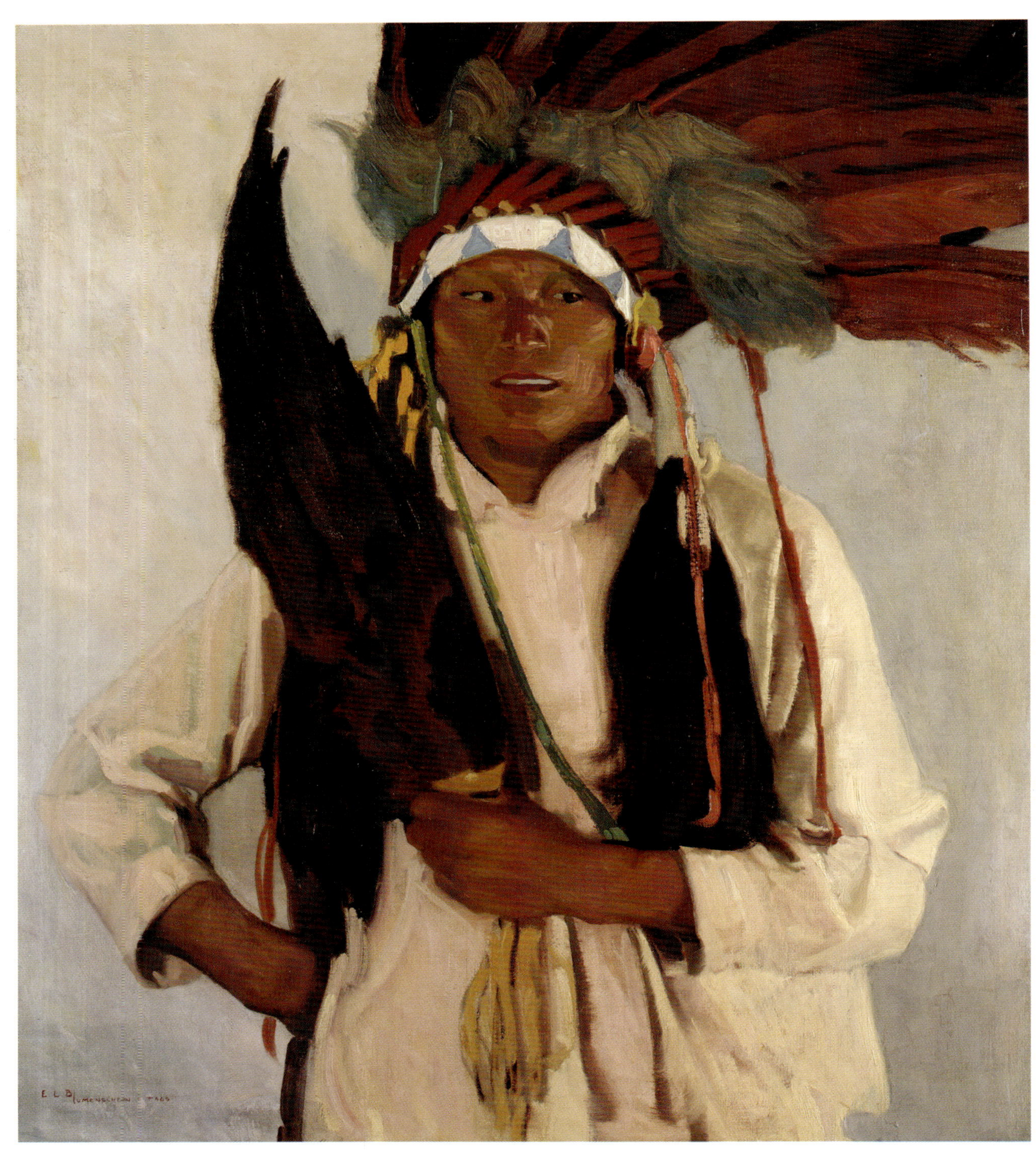

Eagle Fan (originally the left half of *The Chief's Two Sons,* 1915), reworked 1920s
Oil on canvas, 34 × 40 inches
Courtesy of the William Sr. and Dorothy Harmsen Collection,
Denver Art Museum, Denver, Colorado (2001.446)

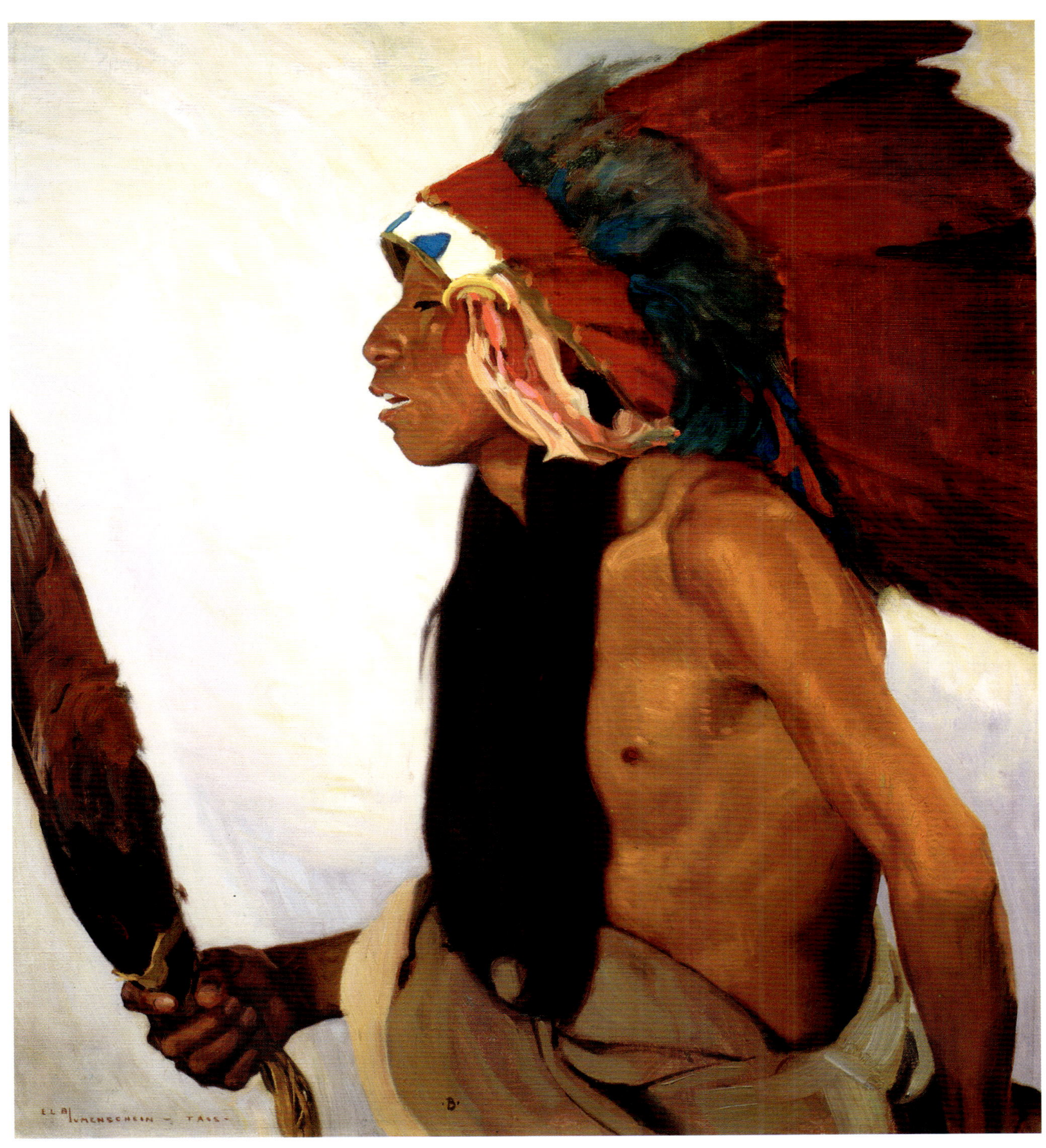

Eagle Feather, Prayer Chant (originally the right half of *The Chief's Two Sons,* 1915), reworked 1920s
Oil on canvas, 34 × 30 inches
Courtesy of The Lunder Collection,
Colby College Museum of Art, Waterville, Maine

cultural mainstay.[69] "I'm here again in Taos and find the colony augmented and enthusiastic," he wrote to Simpson shortly after his arrival.[70] There were many other artists in town that summer—by some accounts as many as one hundred showed up to share the scene. So popular had the town and pueblo become, in fact, that the small cadre of painters who had followed Phillips's and Blumenschein's lead in establishing a colony in Taos decided to band together, in part, no doubt, to distinguish themselves from the creative masses that had begun to assemble.[71] There were six members who originally banded together under the name of the Taos Society of Artists. They met at Dr. Martin's house in July and drafted something of a charter for a formal collegial association. Although Blumenschein was not in attendance, he was elected a member along with Phillips, Couse, Dunton, Berninghaus, and Sharp. A formal constitution was not adopted until 1918, but the essential guideposts were in place from the start: to promote the highest possible standards in painting, to educate the public about the western scene through their art, to circulate joint exhibitions for the purpose of sales and mutual promotion, and to encourage excellence in allied forms of art such as sculpture, architecture, music, and literature.[72] "The fame of the Society, was not a slow and painful growth," wrote Kenneth Adams, a member in the organization's later years. "Recognition and favorable publicity came to the Taos group immediately after its organization."[73] Blumenschein reported that the society contemplated an exhibition in New York at the end of the season, "to which all of us will contribute."[74] In reality, their initial group effort was considerably more modest, a collection of works by the six painters was presented at the end of the season in Albuquerque at the New Mexico State Fair.[75]

On his way home at the end of the summer in 1915, Blumenschein stopped in Dayton to visit his father. In an interview he granted to the *Dayton Journal*, he spoke at great length about Mary and the considerable success she was making of herself as a painter and illustrator. As for himself, he mentioned that most of his time during the winter, when he was forced to be away from his beloved "scenery of the Rockies" and the "many sides of the character of the American Indian" that appealed so strongly to his imagination, was spent primarily in the pursuit of portrait painting.[76] The previous winter and spring he had won acclaim at the National Academy with a portrait of Mary and another of an unknown sitter, *The Violinist*. The Dayton article mentioned another from 1915, a portrait of Mr. Andrew Cooper from Bridgeport, Connecticut.

The Dayton interviewer asked Blumenschein what advice he might have for young, aspiring artists. In one breath, the artist replied that they essentially needed to follow his lead in pursuing formal academic training in America or France in order to obtain "a solid foundation under the guidance of a first class artist, in the study of form, anatomy, color, and composition." In the next breath, Blumenschein let it be known that he would not be one who could provide such instruction, as he was leaving his position at the Art Students League. The job was too time consuming and sapped his energy, he said. The reporter considered this to be "a serious, almost . . . damaging loss to the art school, for it was because of Blumenschein's affiliation with the institution that many of the students chose to go there."[77] Blumenschein had taught at the league for only three years.

Nowhere in the article does Blumenschein remark about his own illustration work. Perhaps he considered illustration such rudimentary bread and butter production that it did not merit mention. Nonetheless, he was an active member of the National Arts Club and the Society of Illustrators, participating regularly in their exhibitions.[78] In the next year, 1916, between *Scribner's Monthly* and *American Magazine*, the artist illustrated at least a half dozen different stories. Yet recognition for the interpretive skill he showed in illustration and painting would come with a prestigious commission from Steinway and Sons. Sometime in the mid-1910s, Steinway and Sons decided for promotional purposes to commission works from leading American painters that would provide visual interpretations of music by the great composers. Blumenschein's 1918 painting interpreted Edward Alexander MacDowell's orchestral work *Indian Suite*. Like the Santa Fe Railway, Steinway and Sons used the painting in its advertisement. The painting would go on to win the first medal ever awarded for best figure painting at the New York Art Directors Show in 1922. Such acclaim came to Blumenschein in the 1920s just as the art world began to recognize him as a painter.[79] Illustration, not just Taos

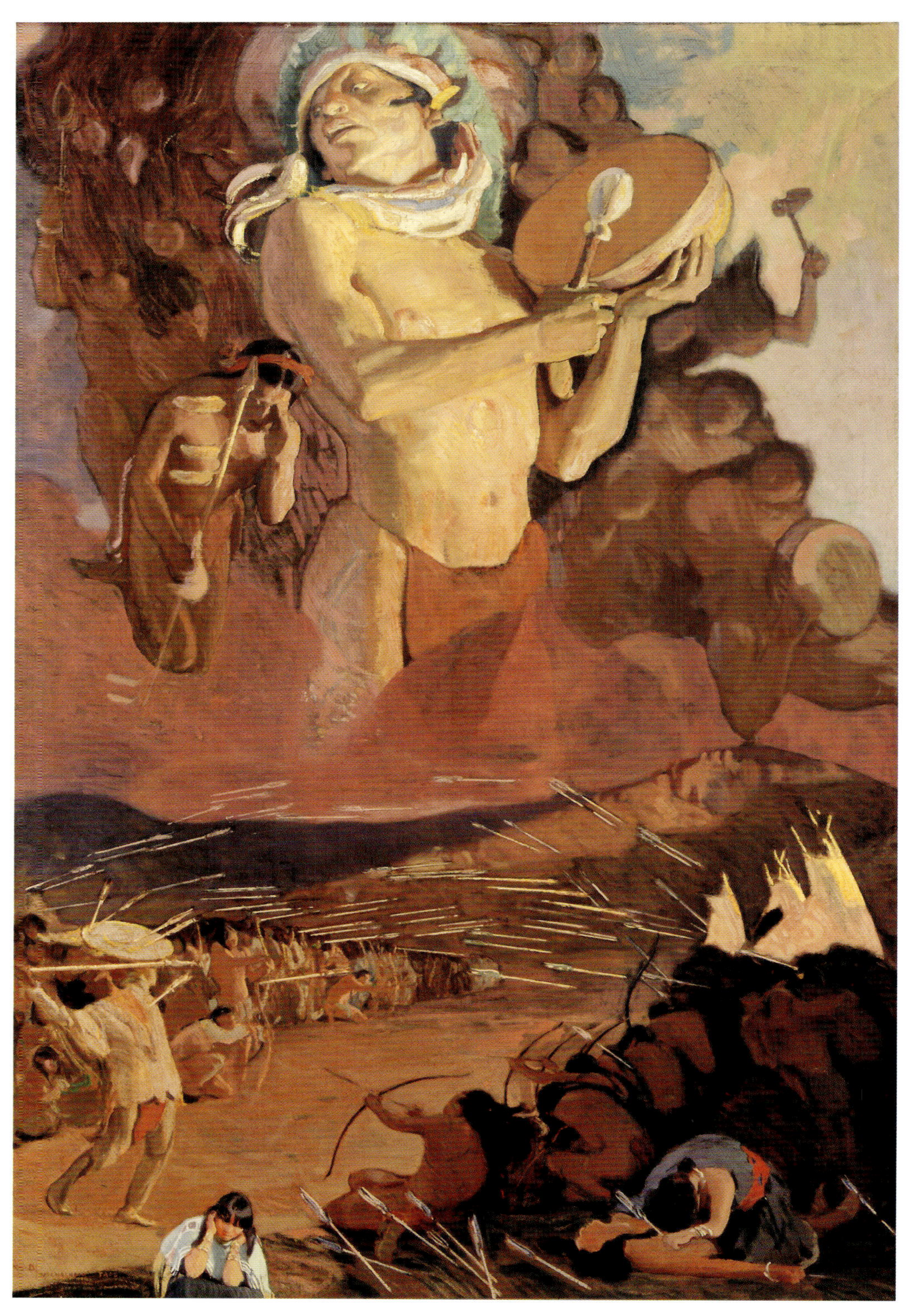

Indian Suite, 1918
Oil on canvas, 55½ × 37½ inches
Courtesy of the Steinway Collection, New York

subjects and portraits, remained a vital part of Blumenschein's creative output in the twentieth century. Even so, his heart was in Taos and his pride in his portraits. The illustrations could speak for themselves.

In late 1916 Santa Fe's sometime art museum curator Paul A. F. Walter offered a testament to the Taos artists. Quoting the Arizona Grand Canyon landscape painter Louis Aiken, who had visited there in 1903, Walter concluded: "It is simply too good to leave. It's the best stuff in America and has scarcely been touched."[80] So compelling were the ambiance and the material that, in Walter's mind, the southwestern art movement proclaimed a novel trend in the national art scene. "Virile and prophetic is the new note in American art," Walter opined. The participants were to be regarded as nothing short of "prophets of an American renaissance."[81]

Such hyperbole made good reading and might have puffed up the egos of Blumenschein and his cohorts. It also confirmed what the Taos Society of Artists had hoped to achieve as a group. They had dreamed of making their art colony the foundation of a uniquely American art statement and movement. Many other art colonies across the country, from Cos Cob in Connecticut to Laguna in California, aspired to accomplish the same goal, but New Mexico as a muse held something special.[82] An associate member of the Taos Society of Artists, the Post-Impressionist painter Birger Sandzen from Kansas had written in 1915 that, although "everybody loves and admires . . . the Barbizon-Woodstock theme, . . . and the East and West [coasts] have many charming subjects in common, . . . the atmospheric effects peculiar to the high plateau of the Southwest give them a somewhat new setting."[83] Phillips had referred to it as the development of "a distinctive American art idea."[84] Walter Ufer, who became a member of the society in 1917, later proclaimed it a truly unparalleled school of American art, one that was so unique that it certified the supremacy of American culture over Europe's.[85]

Over the summer of 1916 Blumenschein endeavored to take that challenge to heart. In a boldly idealized portrayal of a Taos chief enveloped by what Sandzen referred to as the region's "scintillating light and mystic color,"

Blumenschein presented what he conceived of as the quintessential American painting.[86] Titled *The Chief Speaks*, the painting was the perfect pictorial reification of the artist's underlying sense of Native grandeur and pristine natural environment.

Formally, the painting presents the central figure arrayed in a dazzling morning light, his face and darkened war bonnet set off against a brilliantly highlighted, billowing cloud. The Taos elder, possibly the war chief, is buttressed on one side by two fellow Indians—similar to the composition with the warrior and youth in another painting, *Wise Man, Warrior, and Youth*—and on the other side by a distant, sun-raked adobe church. The Sangre de Cristo Mountain backdrop adds majesty to an already regal scene. Muted colors are applied with vigorous brushstrokes, establishing the broad planes and masses that Blumenschein considered decorative and modern. Thirty some years later, in a major 1948 retrospective exhibition hosted by the Museum of New Mexico, *The Chief Speaks* served as a centerpiece. Blumenschein's friend and fellow artist Howard Cook, who viewed it in the galleries at that time, regarded the colors as somewhat "hesitant" and the masses "still limited to the flatter decorative aspects of the [painter's] early period." Cook felt, however, that it presaged Blumenschein's most accomplished, mature work, especially in the deft treatment of the chief's head.[87]

Blumenschein proudly presented the painting in what was becoming for him a standard exhibition tour for major works—the winter exhibition of the National Academy of Design in New York, beginning in mid-December 1916, the Pennsylvania Academy of the Fine Arts in the spring of 1917, and finally the Art Institute of Chicago in the fall of 1917. The variety of critical response to the painting suggests that Blumenschein's was perhaps, even in this early phase, pushing some bounds within the standard beaux arts vernacular. Edward Watts-Russell in the *American Art News* magazine proclaimed *The Chief Speaks* a "rather labored composition, with bad perspective and even worse texture quality in the painting."[88] Yet Lena McCauley of the *Chicago Evening Post* saw it in the opposite light, referring to it as "a fine monumental composition," inspiring as an

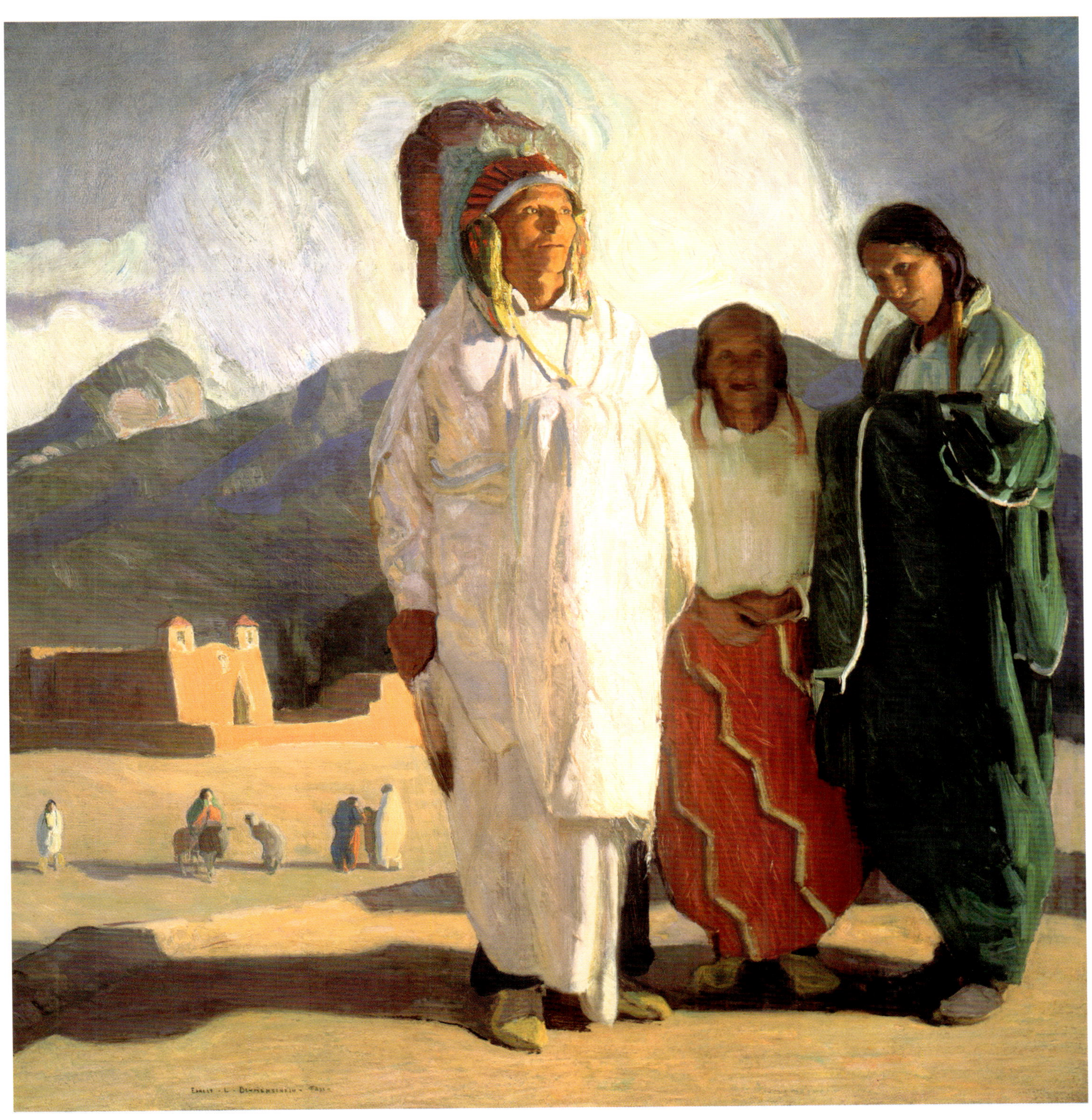

The Chief Speaks, 1917
Oil on canvas, 47 × 44½ inches
Private collection

"honest effort in picture making" and absolutely without rival in the Art Institute's annual show: "It easily ranks first in the exhibition."[89] The staff of the Art Institute concurred, awarding it the coveted Potter Palmer Gold Medal and a cash prize of one thousand dollars. Blumenschein would later remember it as his first major award.[90] The painting was purchased a year later, in 1918, by the Cincinnati Art Museum for its permanent collection. On that occasion, the Cincinnati newspapers praised the painting for its innovative composition, which they regarded as "big in feeling" and pleasing in its "decorative completeness." And "though at times the artist has a tendency to lay on his paint too thickly, thus somewhat deadening texture, the new canvas is entirely free from that quality."[91] Blumenschein was thinking at the time along the lines of John Sloan, who sought to have his students recognize the difference between what he called "the texture of realization," that is, the essence of the subject portrayed, and "realism" per se.[92]

As Blumenschein's magnum opus for 1916, *The Chief Speaks,* was more than a technical and stylistic tour de force. It embodied a strong metaphorical message as well, one that spoke eloquently to the high esteem in which the artist held the Taos Indians and their traditions. In 1917 he wrote about Taos and its artists for the *American Magazine of Art.* Much of the article, and by far its most passionate message, dealt with his Indian neighbors:

> The Indians of Taos, pocketed in the north west corner of New Mexico, have resisted all enemies for these many centuries during which they gradually developed the grand little democracy of the Pueblos, self-governing, self-supporting and self-respecting. They have been influenced by the northern plains Indians and by the Spaniards, but have always maintained their customs and their religion even until now, when they are struggling against the mighty white race that threatens to swallow them up and spit them out again, servants with short hair and clad in overalls! In their executive underground councils the officers elected by the people make rules to counteract all outside influences that might destroy their traditions, change their native costume, bring a mixture of

white blood into the race, upset the beautiful nature worship. And so far, the old wise men have done well.[93]

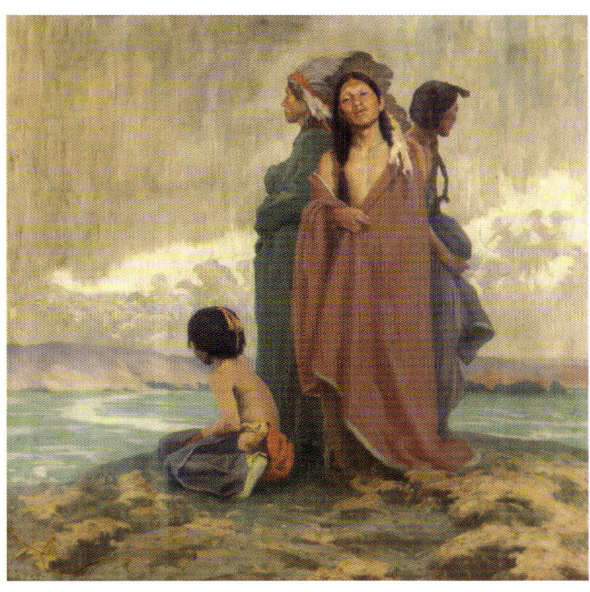

E. Irving Couse, ***A Vision of the Past,*** 1916, oil on canvas, 59 × 59 inches. Collection of the Butler Institute of American Art, Youngstown, Ohio. Used with permission of Couse Family Archives.

As a celebration and defense of Pueblo democracy and cultural independence, *The Chief Speaks* pays homage to the Taos elders who spoke for their people and, in Blumenschein's words, helped to "counter-act the impression so common in our country that our Indians are not quite respectable."[94]

This gesture was not unique to Blumenschein among the Taos artist group. Couse, for example, painted a similar, slightly larger, survival allegory, *Vision of the Past*, in 1916. Created in conjunction with a movie being produced by J. Stuart Blackton of Hamlin Garland's novel *The Captain of Gray Horse Troop,* Couse's oil shared the author's mission of addressing issues of modern reservation life. The three central figures in the painting, compositionally bound together as if captives of bygone days, were, in the emotive force of their reticence, intended to change public attitudes about Indians. As Couse phrased it, he hoped "to remove the misconception in which the Indian has been held, and to show that they are human beings worthy of consideration and a place in the sun."[95]

Some critics of the period held that more matter-of-fact interpretations, as found in the works of Walter Ufer, for example, came closer to a "sympathetic understanding of the Indian as he is now" and were thus more effective purveyors of the position.[96] Yet allegories such as *The Chief Speaks* and *Vision of the Past* had broad public appeal and garnered highly publicized critical notice. Blumenschein's work, as mentioned, won the Potter Palmer prize in 1917, and Couse's oil brought him the revered Altman Prize at the National Academy of Design. Blumenschein continued throughout most of his career to write, paint, and speak in support of Pueblo cultural independence and political hegemony. *The Chief Speaks* was a large, famous, and important early expression of the artist's admiration for Native people. For him they were far more than props and artistic commodities. They had provided the primary impulse for him to be in Taos, and they would be a fundamental reason for him to stay.[97]

When Blumenschein returned to New York in the fall of 1916, he sent a sketch of one of his summer's most successful works to Simpson with hopes of interesting his patron in another purchase. Simpson was impressed with what he saw and encouraged the artist to work up a finished oil. It turned out that the painting Blumenschein had in mind, a 45-by-47-inch canvas, was already completed. It had, in fact, according to Blumenschein, been done "on the spot at Ranchos de Taos," a church several miles south of town.[98] Featuring a group of mounted Pueblo Indians, perhaps in celebration of the annual Saint Francis Day, the painting was titled *Church at Ranchos de Taos*. By virtue of that title, it served as a pictorial recognition of an architectural gem that ultimately came to be recognized not only as a symbol of Hispanic Catholicism but of all New Mexico.[99]

The Hispanic community had built the San Francisco de Asis church about a century before Blumenschein came along to paint its portrait. Considered the "Notre Dame" of mission churches in New Mexico and perhaps the finest example of American Indian building techniques and early-nineteenth-century American-Franciscan ecclesiastical architecture, the building has inspired myriad painters and photographers to record its sensuous, organically flowing contours. Blumenschein was one of the first serious artists, if not the first, to put this intriguing shape on canvas and to explore the way light and shadow played across its adobe surfaces to produce an engaging and dramatic abstract form.

Blumenschein had always felt a special draw to New Mexico's architecture. When in 1917 he recalled his first visit to Taos and the realization that "here was work for a lifetime," he remembered too that the remarkable architecture of the Pueblo and Hispanic people had impressed him deeply.[100] As early as 1913, he began to be recognized as a keen observer and defender of New Mexico vernacular architecture. Like many inhabitants and visitors, he believed that these singular adobe structures were the nation's only purely indigenous form of architecture.[101] A movement was already afoot in Santa Fe, under the guidance of the chamber of commerce and Museum of New Mexico director Edgar L. Hewett, to protect the city's adobe buildings and to perpetuate the look of the community, the architectural style that would become known as Pueblo Revival. Blumenschein

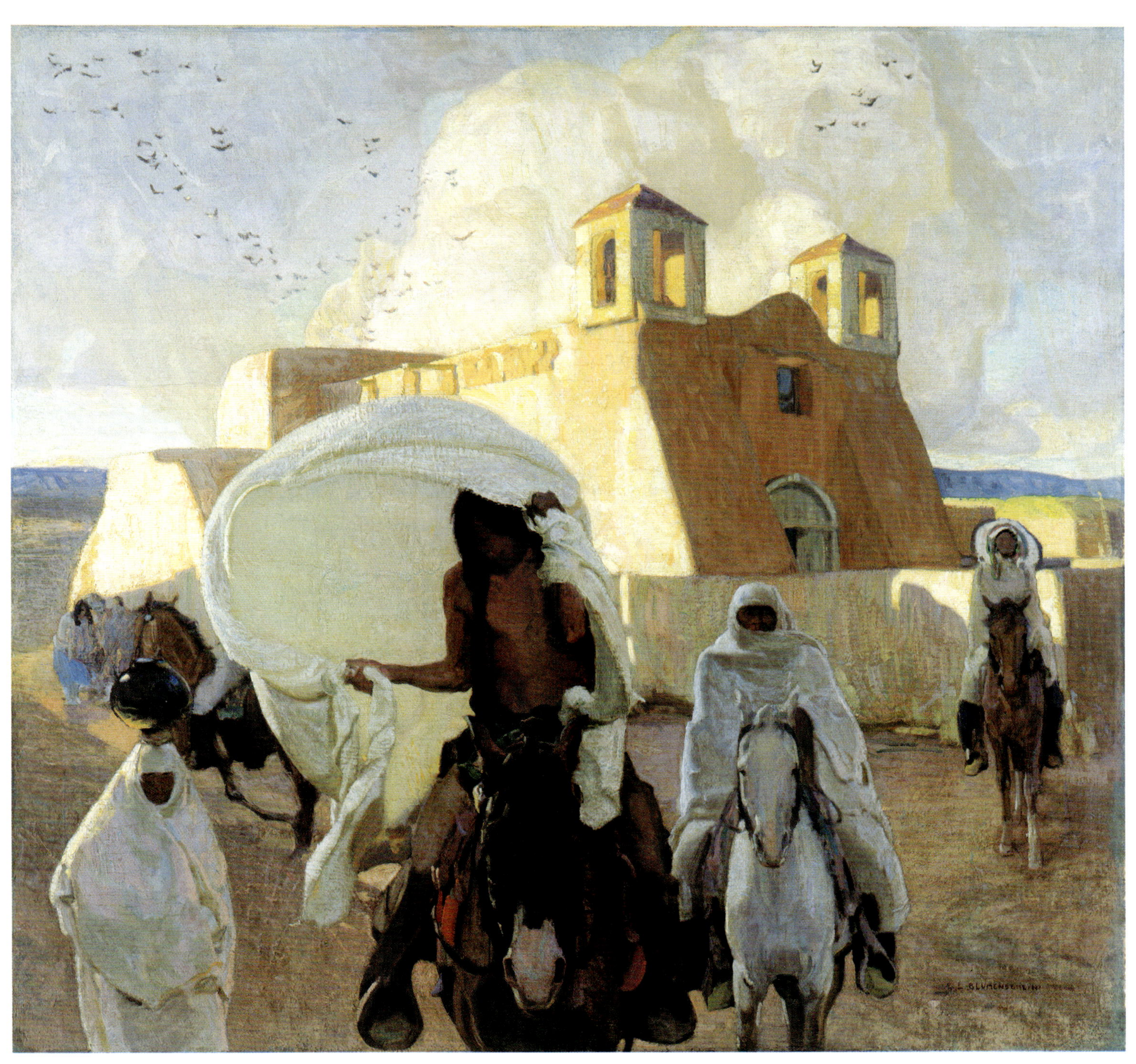

Church at Ranchos de Taos, 1916
Oil on canvas, 45½ × 47½ inches
Courtesy of the Anschutz Collection
Photograph by William J. O'Connor

warned the people of Taos that "if the commerce club of Taos doesn't soon take some action like the Santa Fe chamber of commerce with its New-Old Santa Fe committee, Taos will soon lose its charm."[102] Around the time Blumenschein first selected the church at Ranchos de Taos as a subject, Hewett also had a new museum building under construction in Santa Fe. It would reflect, in its massive adobe features and undulating, graceful lineation, the best of both Pueblo and Hispanic traditions. In Hewett's "Spanish Pueblo Revival," mission churches, specifically the church at Acoma Pueblo, had served as the principal models. Most would recognize, as Victor Higgins did in 1917, that Pueblo architecture was "the only naturally American architecture in the nation today. All other styles were borrowed from Europe."[103] The artist Carlos Vierra described the mission church style in 1918 as a "free-hand architecture with the living quality of a sculptor's work, and that pliant, unaffected and unconfined beauty characteristic of natural growth . . . bearing the closest relations to the surrounding landscape."[104] Blumenschein relished the opportunity to go back to such a distinguished source and to explore the connections between the synthetic forms of the church and its natural propinquity with earth and sky.

In his painting, Blumenschein places the church prominently but harmoniously between the earth, with its corporeal figures, and the sky, with its ethereal, spiritual essence. Sunlit, in a late-afternoon display of brilliant grandeur, the church connotes strength, solidity, and, with its open door, accessibility. The implied synergy between these two realms, however, is broken by the directional flow of the Indians, who have all turned away from the church rather than toward it. Their faces are cast in shadow as they uniformly turn their backs to the structure and set out for Taos Pueblo. The billowing white cotton sheet enveloping the most prominent rider suggests a closer affinity with the spiritual province of the bulging cumulus cloud than with the physicality of the structural intermediary, the church. Perhaps this painting provided, as had *The Chief Speaks,* a forum for Blumenschein's sincere wish to see the Pueblos be able to preserve and affirm their own sacred and cultural traditions outside of Catholicism.

In style and metaphor, Blumenschein's rendition of Ranchos church contrasts in mood and possibly also in intention with that of his fellow Taos painter Berninghaus, who depicted a similar scene a few years later. Although Berninghaus preserves the structure's majesty, the people in his painting have a more comfortable relationship with the church. As the predominately Hispanic congregation emerges from the open door, instead of turning their backs on the church, they mingle contently in the sunlit courtyard.

To distance the Indians from the church in Blumenschein's rendition even further, many art historians have associated this painting with the influence of the French Orientalists—among them Blumenschein's teacher Benjamin-Constant—who depicted the Arab people and culture of North Africa.[105] This subject inspired canvases by Julius Rolshoven, an associate member of the Taos Society of Artists, during his years spent in Paris. Blumenschein himself remarked about the exotic appeal of the white cotton blankets. Following an accepted perception that the Southwest was the American Near East, he told an interviewer in the 1920s that the Taos Indians were "the only Indians who wear a white sheet in the summer, and to these costumes I attribute a great deal of the attraction of Taos—to their white Arab-like sheet."[106]

Another, less exotic population and architecture with which Blumenschein was intimately familiar by 1917 was his hometown, New York. He and his family had been living in the Sherwood Studio Building for three years, and his little view up his snowy block, *Fifty-seventh Street, New York,* offered a somber contrast to his past summer's New Mexico scene. Even so, it was affectionately and sympathetically rendered, giving the feeling that Blumenschein connected not only with the architectonic shapes of metropolitan spaces that would fascinate him for the next three decades but with what he called "the comforts and attractions of great cities" as well.[107] There was also a directness in his pictorial response to the city, absent in some of his allegorical western work. The skyscrapers that rose beyond the picture plane were regarded by many as examples of a true American architecture just as unique as what he had found in Santa Fe and Taos.

Two of Blumenschein's favorite American painters, John Sloan and George Bellows, were also energetically painting the Manhattan scene in those years, but they enjoyed exploring less refined neighborhoods than Blumenschein's in their

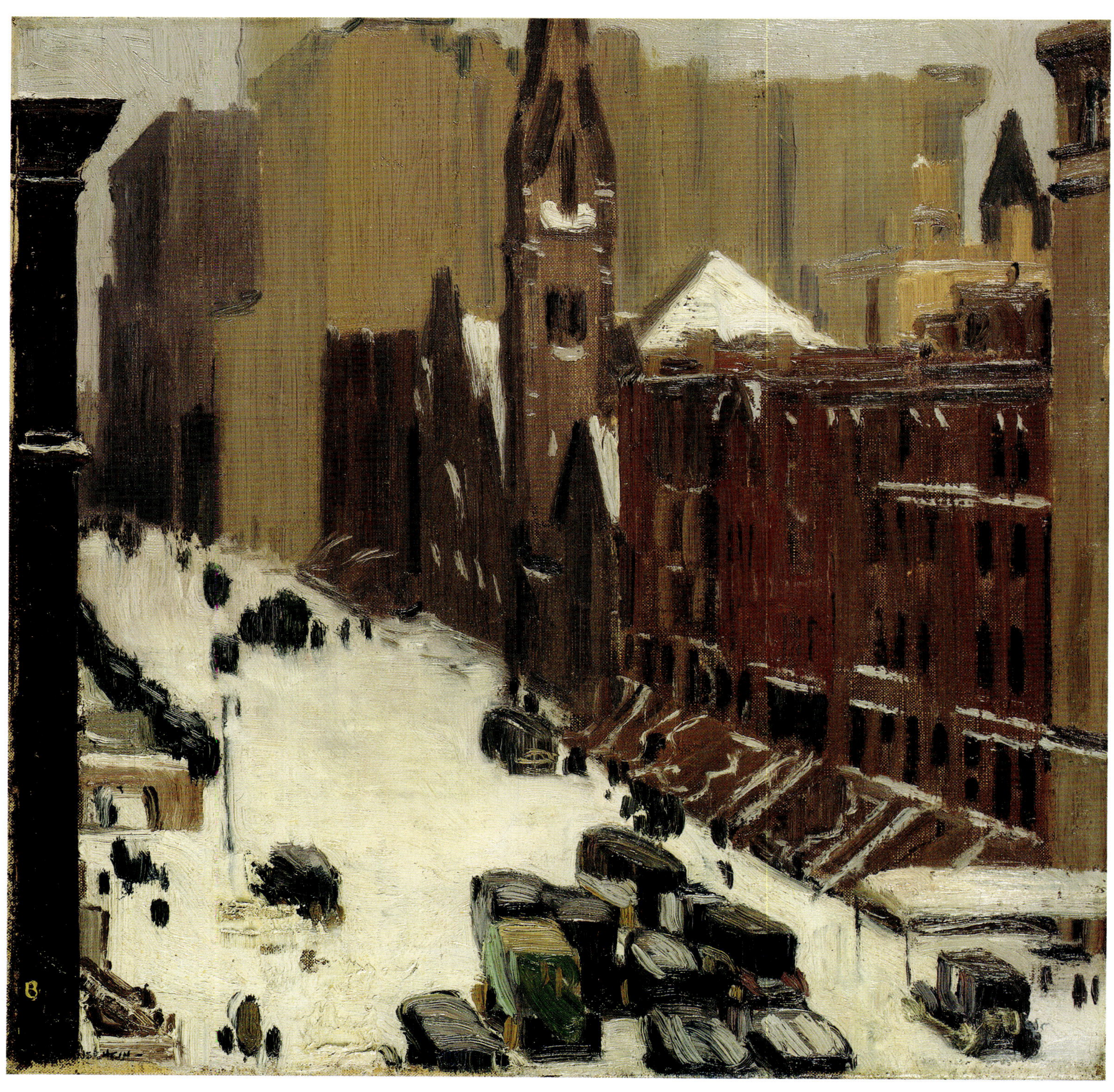

Fifty-seventh Street, New York, 1917
Oil on canvas, 14 × 14 inches
Courtesy of the North Carolina Museum of Art, Raleigh
Gift of the North Carolina Art Society (Robert F. Phifer Bequest)

art, searching for potent evocations of mass culture and the urban experience. When Blumenschein sought what Bellows called "big ideas" in art, he retreated to the West. As critic Royal Cortissoz said of Blumenschein and his New Mexican cronies, they "cultivated an Americanism having a more primitive picturesqueness than that of the great cities."[108] Yet there is at least a qualified picturesqueness to Blumenschein's city views just as there is a certain primitive quality to Bellows's cliff dwellers.[109]

In 1917 Mary Blumenschein's mother, Mrs. Rufus Greene, passed away, leaving Mary with a considerable inheritance and her Brooklyn house at 273 Ryerson Street. The Blumenscheins promptly abandoned their Sherwood apartment and studio and moved to the Brooklyn home. Mary's new income was, according to Ernest, "sufficient to make her and the daughter independent of me, and at this time I gave up illustrating entirely and devoted all my time to painting." He was about forty years old. It was now his turn to focus exclusively on his dream and what he called "my love . . . [of] the material in the Southwest."[110] But sadly, his dream of a future of painting in New Mexico full-time was a fleeting one. The United States entered into World War I in April 1917. Because of exigencies at home and the uncertainties brought on by the war, Blumenschein may have spent less than six weeks in Taos that year.

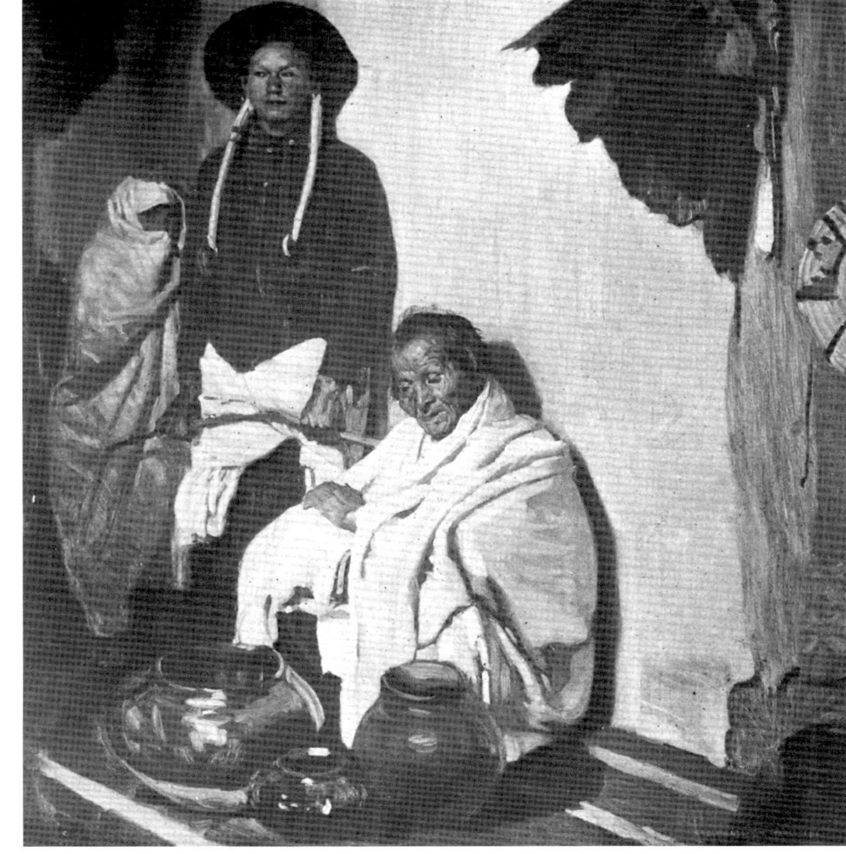

The Medicine Man, 1917, oil on canvas, from the *American Magazine of Art,* September 1917. Courtesy of Denver Public Library, Magazine and Newspaper Collection, Denver, Colorado.

At the spring annual exhibition of the National Academy of Design in 1917, Blumenschein had submitted a complex interior scene called *The Medicine Man*. He used this painting to illustrate his essay "The Taos Society of Artists" and to illuminate his point that someday soon Taos would be, like New York, "the great American school" of art.[111] His model for the painting had been a Taos Indian

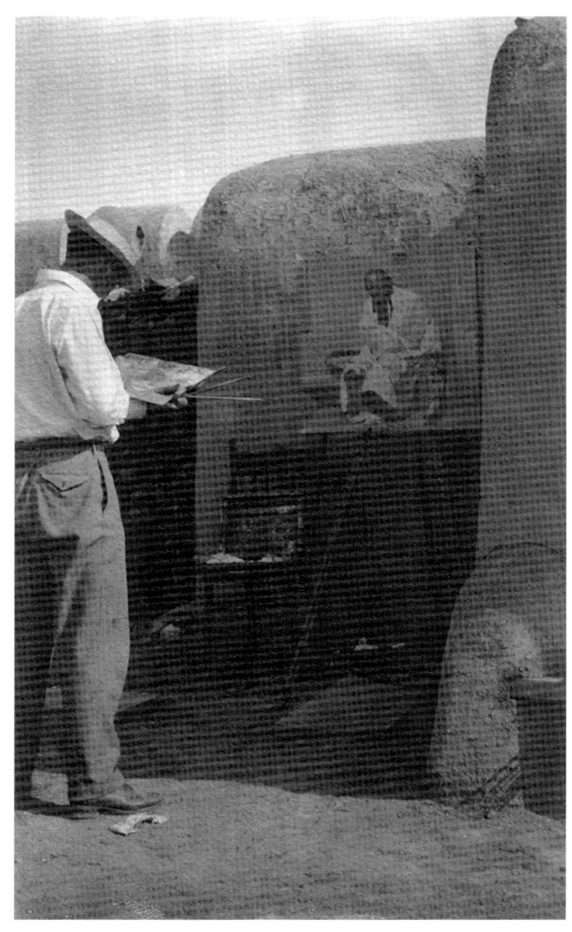

Blumenschein study for *Old Man in White*. Collection of Chesta Wrenn. Used with permission of Couse Family Archives.

named Marcio Martínez, also known among locals as the "medicine man," no doubt the same older gentleman who appeared in *Wise Man, Warrior, and Youth*.[112]

One of his principle works of summer 1917 was a single portrait of Martínez, *Old Man in White*. Blumenschein first painted a small sketch in oil picturing Martínez leaning against an adobe wall with no trappings or props. Working from that compositional study, he reposed his model, added a black Tewa pot and an eagle wing fan, and doubled the size of his canvas. Martínez, who was reputedly over one hundred years old at the time of this portrait and at least partly blind, slumps forward as if asleep or in deep contemplation. He neither reflects on the pot nor suggests any purpose for the fan. The neutral backdrop serves little in terms of contextualizing the scene aside from being a sunlit, tawny adobe wall. On his blanket appear a few drawings, perhaps showing some of Martínez's exploits as a younger man. Beyond that, this is a study in harmonized color, bold massing of shapes and contours, and a general statement about the dignity of age. One art historian has viewed this painting as a transitional work, bridging Blumenschein's style that wed muted palette with large, decorative compositions in the 1910s and the more hearty color schemes and rhythmic design patterns of the 1920s.[113] In addition to celebrating Martínez's life and searching for new methodologies of portraiture, this painting explores the fragility of humankind and their cultural traditions. In earlier works like *The Chief Speaks* and *The Medicine Man* Blumenschein buttressed the old man with someone from a younger generation. Here, Martínez sits alone, drooped and holding on to the last vestige of his power, the eagle fan that hangs passively at his side, thus accentuating his vulnerability.

By the end of the 1917 season, the members of the Taos Society of Artists were—rather miraculously, considering the war—beginning to find genuine success. Bert Phillips served as secretary and treasurer for the society and had helped plan an ambitious national traveling tour of their art. They had received numerous

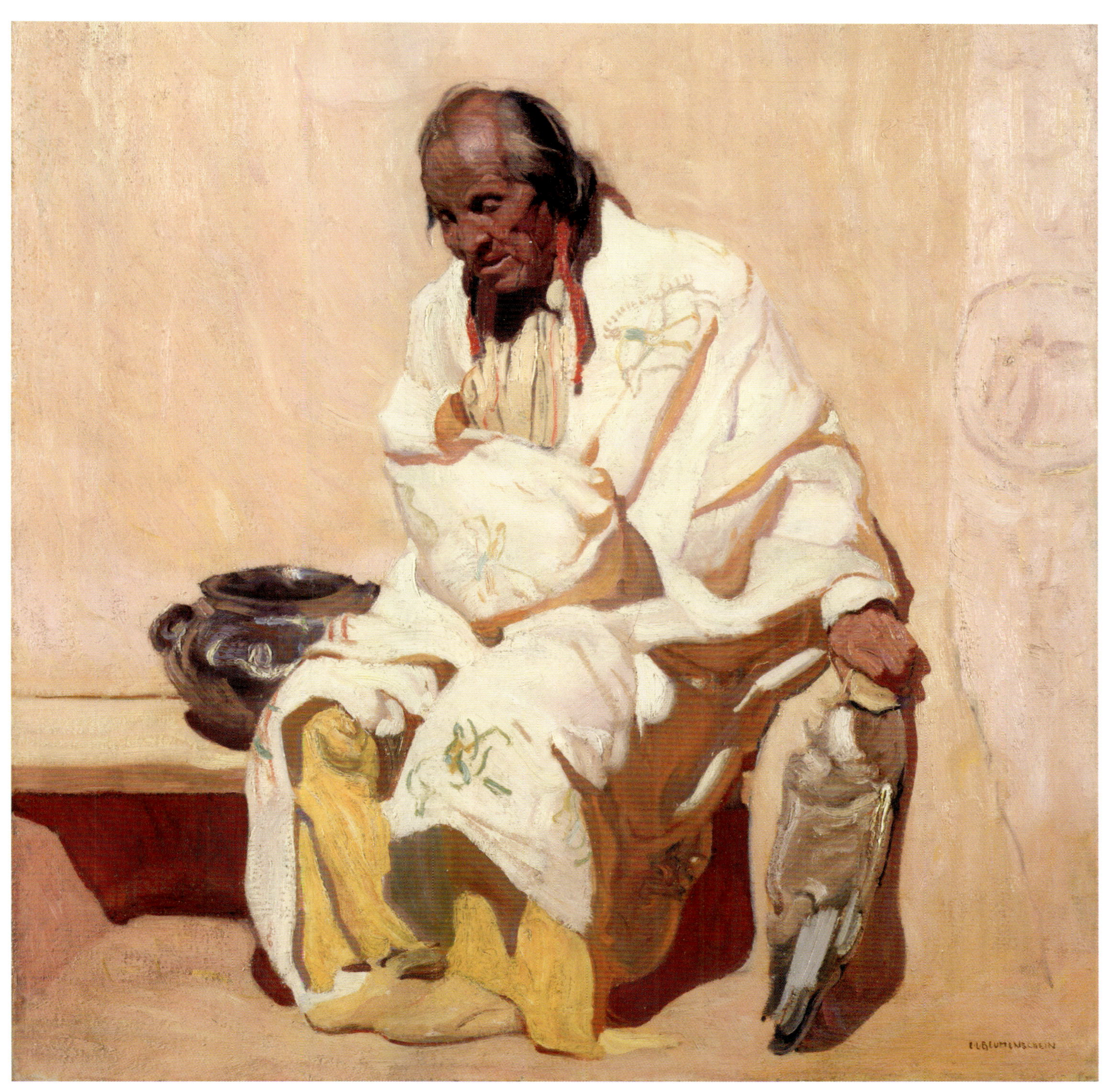

Old Man in White, 1917
Oil on canvas, 25½ × 25½ inches
Courtesy of the Museum of the American West and the
Institute for the Study of the American West, Autry National Center,
Los Angeles, California (98.108.1)

notices in the national press, including Blumenschein's article "The Taos Society of Artists" in the *American Magazine of Art*, and were flooded with letters of inquiry from museums and galleries to show their work and explain their mission. Phillips wrote in his 1917 report, hoping to persuade the group to work together, that "the growing reputation of the Society and the increasing demands for its usefulness at home and abroad should encourage us to realize that no effort is wasted which we can employ for its advancement."[114] Great success was imminent, thanks in large measure to Phillips's hard work.

Thus, when it was announced in the fall of 1917 that Blumenschein had won a prize of one thousand dollars with the Potter Palmer Gold Medal at the Art Institute of Chicago for his painting *The Chief Speaks*, he took immediate steps to mitigate any negative reactions that might stir among fellow artists and the Taos townsfolk. "Mr. Blumenschein wants the people of Taos to understand," wrote the *Taos Valley News*,

> that such a prize only comes once or twice in a life time and that of course many years pass in which no prizes or as far as that goes no good sales of pictures occur. He does not want it thought that the artists of Taos are in the habit of receiving so much money for their pictures. He has been here for 12 summers and most of those summers he has spent every cent of his money to pay the expenses of the long trip from N.Y. to Taos and return. So you see to receive one prize of a thousand dollars after 12 years of work is not very good pay. Of course, the money part of the prize is very little compared to being awarded the honor in competition with the best painters in the U.S.[115]

The broader critical acclaim that Blumenschein sought started to clear the path collectively as the society exhibitions traveled. They began with a special show for the dedication of the new Museum of New Mexico in Santa Fe, an institution that would provide the catalyst over the coming years for a vastly expanded artistic scene in New Mexico. Over the following months the society saw its group exhibitions displayed and acclaimed in New York, Boston, Chicago, St. Louis, Kansas City, Des Moines, Denver, Los Angeles, and Salt Lake City. The artists enjoyed such welcome exposure that Phillips, at the 1918 meeting of the society the next summer, could hardly restrain himself: "Our pictures have met with no little appreciation from thousands of people and a great deal of advertising matter has been printed and circulated until it would be difficult to find a person in the whole country making any pretension to being posted in art matters who has not heard of Taos and the 'Taos Artists.'"[116] As Paul Walter had conjectured the year before, "who can say that the . . . Taos school . . . may not in the near future mean to American art what the Barbizon school has meant to France?"[117] The group had by now claimed that status, and nearly all observers concurred in full. "Perhaps a new school of American art has come to the fore," proposed the *Kansas City Times,* while the *Denver Times* suggested that the prophesy of "a great American school of artists" from Taos had evidenced itself in "one of the most colorful exhibits that has been sponsored by the Denver Art Association."[118]

Yet for Blumenschein, as enthusiastic as he probably was about the flourishing state of the society, the war effort superceded any advances taken or accolades received by the group. "The great fight," he wrote, "is a much, very much, bigger cause than the production of beautiful art works."[119] And so he would begin to curtail his normal production in favor of expending energy for the cause. He initially participated in what was called the Liberty Loan program, which used art to generate support for the war. Patriotically symbolic paintings such as his portrait of Charles H. Lembke, a first lieutenant, Purple Heart veteran, and *Long Range Gun, Paris* (alternatively titled *Good Friday in a Paris Church* to express the poignancy of the French people's war situation) proved useful in this way.

In the fall of 1918 Blumenschein wrote to Walter at the Museum of New Mexico: "It has been one H—— of a summer for production, of course, but now our loss is mighty, mighty slight compared to the sacrifice of many others. It's fine to think that the artists have been of use to the war, just doing the last liberty loan, we lined 5th Ave. windows with war paintings, and some of them were striking."[120] Perhaps the Lembke portrait and *Long Range Gun, Paris* were

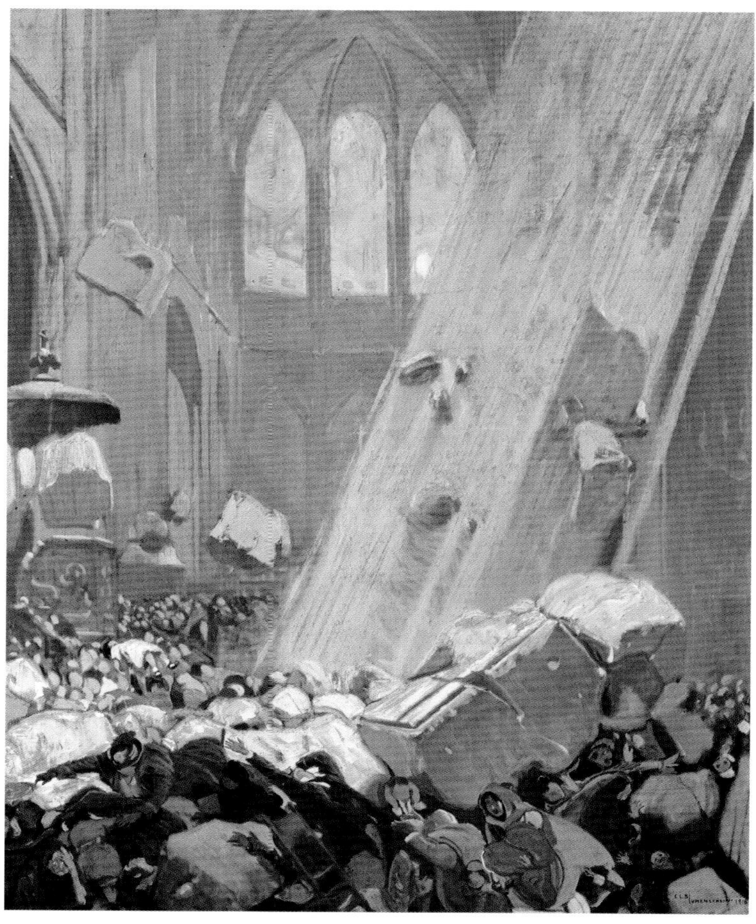

Long Range Gun, Paris, 1918, oil on canvas, 52¼ × 34 inches. Courtesy of the National Museum of American History, Smithsonian Institution, Washington, D.C.

included in that display. The latter was exhibited at the Salmagundi Club as part of a war display and was subsequently acquired by the publicity department of the Liberty Loan Committee to be used as a poster.

Couse mentioned during the winter of 1918 that "the war . . . seems to have knocked the bottom out of art here [in New York]."[121] It was especially tough on artists with German heritage like Blumenschein and Ufer. Couse and Blumenschein had hoped, for example, to bring Ufer's name forward as a candidate for an associate membership of the National Academy of Design. After testing the water, however, they concluded that the times were not propitious for such a move. "Couse and I talked it over," Blumenschein wrote Ufer, "and decided it would be a very risky thing for you to be proposed by me, with my German name."[122] It would have proven to be a double liability.

On the premise that exposure for one's art held promise for potential sales, Blumenschein joined with Ufer, Higgins, and the American animalier sculptor Alexander Phimister Proctor to circulate a small, select exhibition to major eastern and midwestern institutions at the behest of the Association of Museum Directors. In addition, the Cincinnati Art Museum's director, Joseph Henry Gest, invited Blumenschein to send two paintings, *The Chief Speaks* and a new work, *Taos Entertains the Cheyennes,* to a special summer show at the Cincinnati Art Museum. Gest ended up buying *The Chief Speaks* for $750, to Blumenschein's profound pleasure. It represented Blumenschein's first major museum purchase and encouraged his nurturing of similar relationships over the coming years. But Cincinnati was also special because of his sentimental ties to that museum. "I highly appreciate the honor of having a canvas in the museum," he wrote. "I feel my child has a good home forever. I am particularly delighted, because my art study began [there] at the museum."[123]

Much of Blumenschein's time was spent, especially during the summer of 1918, in organizing a program for producing range finder paintings for the military. These were large, 50-by-70-inch landscape paintings picturing European scenes that were used as targets for sighting and determining distance for machine gunners. The effort began at the Salmagundi Club in February 1918, and Blumenschein was involved from the beginning. When he went to New Mexico that spring, he carried the program west, promoting it in Santa Fe as well as in other western states and in Chicago and organizing artists to participate with him in Taos.[124] A fellow painter, Burt Harwood, allowed the use of his commodious studio for the artist to work in, and Blumenschein made a valiant effort to coordinate the production. It was said that "no other group of artists threw itself so enthusiastically and generously into the task as the men and women of the Taos–Santa Fe Circle."[125] It was not easy, though, and not everyone could afford to abandon their normal work or agreed about the level of dedication. Couse, for example, had contributed a range finder to the Salmagundi Club endeavor and thus felt his contribution had been already been made. Others were frustratingly difficult, either not as keen on the project as Blumenschein or, in their own minds, just too busy to cooperate. His level of chagrin was such that by fall Blumenschein voiced his displeasure publicly with the *American Art News*:

> I make this statement, which a month ago I would not have thought necessary, because of my experience with painters in the last few weeks. Out here in the war work was hardly thought of a month ago. The men were wrapped up in their paintings, in the usual course of a summer's labor, some, in their supreme egotism, feeling that their genius should be unhampered; others in plain selfishness, simply painting because they loved to paint; others producing "pot-boilers" for the winter's market. So when we sent out a call, a private letter to each painter asking him to pledge himself to so many days for one month, and in those days to produce range finders for the Western camps, we began to see that the painter, with a few exceptions was not so anxious to help with this

métier, and really sacrifice some of his precious summer days for the benefit of the men who were willing to sacrifice their precious lives. The responses were very slow in coming. One artist said (and it is actually the most outrageous example of egotism I ever encountered) that "he considered his work more important than the war!" Another said he had given this and that and had painted a range finder back East, owned Liberty Bonds and had given generously to the Red Cross, all of which I knew to be true, and now he was going to work for himself until next winter, when he would again help in war work.

But the war isn't waiting until next winter and the soldiers must be developed. And so I hope that other artists who have reasoned the same way may see this letter, be moved to contribute a range finder, and realize, as Gen. Johnston has said, that it will be of "inestimable value to us in our musketry and machine gun instruction," and realize also that with their hands and brains and talents they are actually of great service in winning the war.

The Taos painters came around beautifully in the end, and inside of two weeks we had 15 completed canvasses, 50 x 70, landscapes and village scenes of France, which are now on their way to help lick the Kaiser.[126]

Although Blumenschein genuinely felt that his uncensored thoughts reflected the truth and were a reflection of the high standard of perfection and patriotism that he expected of himself and of others—an outlook that plagued him throughout his life—his fellow artists probably considered it self-righteous vitriol. And although he may have been motivated by a desire to distance himself from his German ancestry, that did not matter either. The fallout was swift and bitter. At a special meeting of the Taos Society of Artists, Blumenschein was summarily chastised for painting his fellow members with such a caustic, patriotically embarrassing brush. Blumenschein was forced to publish a retraction or be run out of town.[127] Blumenschein, instead of the range-finder paintings, had become the target.

Blumenschein had also been integrally involved in Red Cross work, especially through his assistance with organizing and presiding over a local benefit art raffle in the fall of 1918. Most of the society's painters contributed one or two of the twenty-two works auctioned, so they all seemed in concert with this subsequent enterprise.[128]

At the end of the summer, the Museum of New Mexico hosted its Fourth Annual Exhibit of the Taos Society of Artists in Santa Fe. Except for Blumenschein, the members each were able to present half a dozen or more new works. He had but one painting (plus two range finders) to offer, no doubt due to the attention he had given the war effort, as well as the general distraction of the times. "We cannot get down to real creative work," complained one of the society members. "This War pervades everything, makes us restless, causes everything we do to seem futile."[129] But what Blumenschein did exhibit was truly masterful.

Titled *Albedia of Taos*, the small oil was a portrait of Albedia Marcus, one of Taos's most striking and enchanting models.[130] It is not simply an arresting study of character, with the sitter's tightly fixed lips and her determined, enigmatic gaze focused out beyond the viewer, but an exquisite interplay of line and mass with a richer-than-usual, more saturated palette. A critic in Santa Fe noticed in it a change worth mentioning. "Mr. Blumenschein is represented by only one portrait, 'Albedia of Taos,' differing in style from what one expects from this brilliant artist, especially effective in color and arrangement."[131] According to museum staff, some visitors mistook Blumenschein's portrait for a Robert Henri. In fact it was said that there were "strong resemblances between the superb portraits that Henri produced at Santa Fe the past two years and this painting by an academician to whom Henri is supposed to be anathema."[132]

It was thought that Blumenschein might resent the comparison, but nothing could have been further from the truth. Henri had been elected as an associate member of the society that summer and might well have been invited to full membership had he put in enough time in Taos to be considered. It was probably Blumenschein who proposed his name, since of all the society members (all academically trained and all allied with fundamental beaux arts traditions) he, along

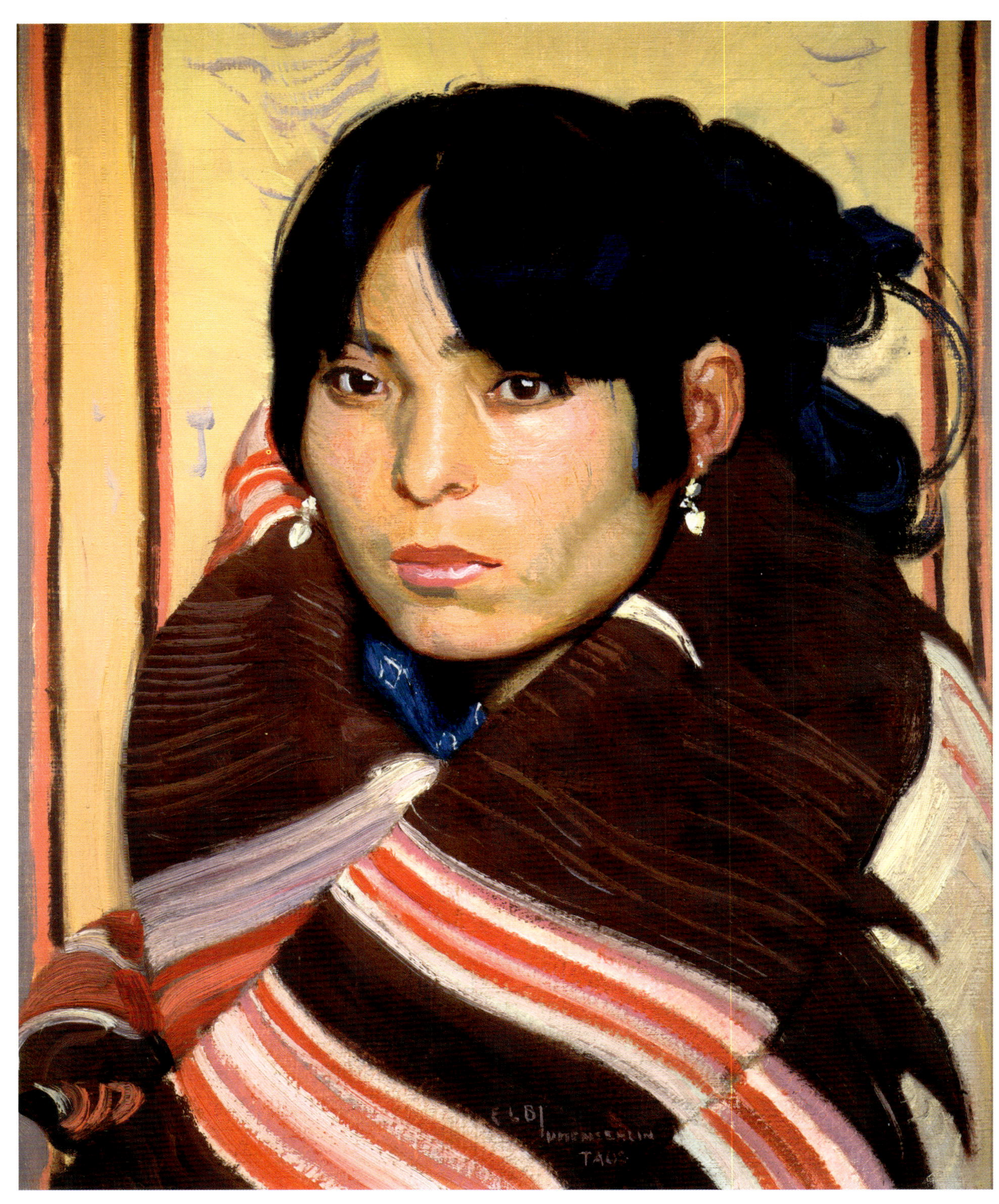

Portrait of Albedia, ca. 1918
Oil on canvas, 20 × 16 inches
Courtesy of the Gerald Peters Gallery, Santa Fe, New Mexico

with Higgins and Ufer, was the most receptive to new ideas. While Henri had openly rebelled against the academy and Blumenschein by this date had not, Blumenschein had publicly professed sympathy for fresh thinking and nonconventional modes of aesthetic expression ever since his visit to the Armory Show.

Blumenschein surely would have noticed and appreciated changes occurring in Henri's painting after 1913 as Henri's progressive methods, based on lessons from Edouard Manet and Franz Hals, began to shed historical antecedents in favor of a more intense, almost Fauvist, palette and complex, geometrical compositional arrangements.[133] These changes assumed special prominence after Henri's exposure to western subjects, California in 1914 and New Mexico in 1916 and 1917. It was Henri's paintings such as *Indian Girl (Julianita)* of 1917 that would have attracted Blumenschein's attention and alerted him to Henri's potentially innovative contribution as a member of the society. Both painters were in transition at the time, each seeking to enrich their color, to integrate Native decorative elements into their compositions, and to explore in greater depth the character of their sitters. And while *Indian Girl* would provide a coda for Henri's Indian themes, *Albedia of Taos* offered Blumenschein a next step forward.

Blumenschein painted a second, profile version of *Woman of Taos (Albedia)* that summer. More organic, with its art nouveau swirls in the background and flamelike decorations on the blanket, it was as if Blumenschein were composing an abbreviated musical sonnet in counterpoint—the first movement with staccato formality and the second with flowing, melodic beauty. He would exhibit the two as an ensemble the next year in Santa Fe's fifth annual exhibit of the society.[134]

Sometime during the summer of 1918 Blumenschein had a visit from an old Cincinnati friend, the sculptor Clement Barnhorn. Barnhorn had been connected with the art school when Blumenschein was a student there in the 1890s. Now he was in Taos to experience the art colony and to see one of the artists who had made Cincinnati famous. There may even have been some discussions about the art museum's impending acquisition of Blumenschein's *The Chief Speaks*. Barnhorn had dropped in on most of the other artists who resided in Taos, but Blumenschein's studio (he was renting Frank Sauerwein's old studio on Pueblo

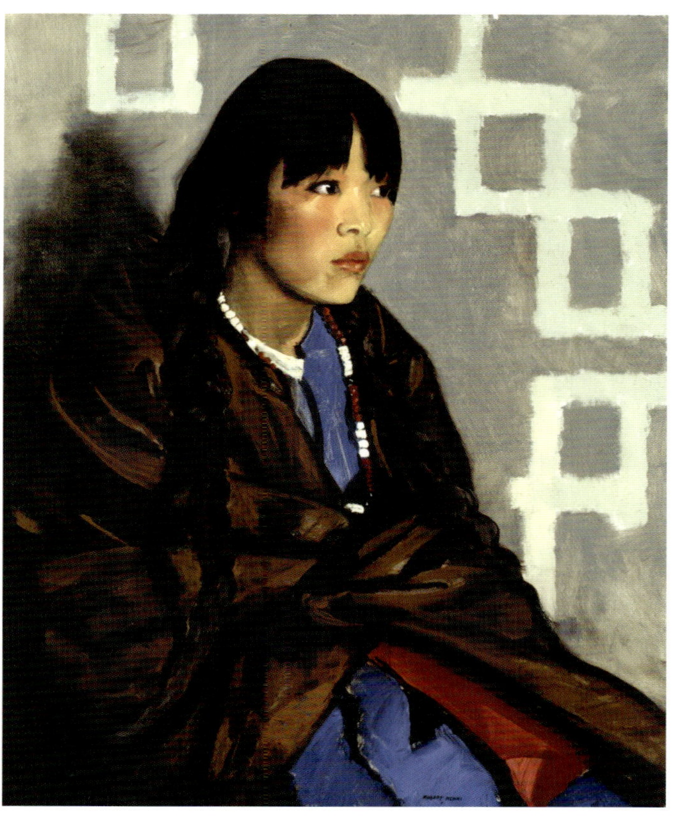

Robert Henri, ***Indian Girl (Julianita)***, ca. 1917, oil on canvas, 32 × 26 inches. Courtesy of the Indianapolis Museum of Art, Indianapolis, Indiana. Gift of Mrs. John N. Carey.

Avenue that summer) drew him back again and again. At the conclusion of his New Mexico stay, Barnhorn would reckon that Blumenschein was probably *the* leading figure among the Taos art colony.[135]

Blumenschein would leave for Brooklyn in late October, after spending about seven months in the land of his inspiration. He had been there since April, having arrived in time to play fielder in the opening game of the baseball season. He had won local celebrity for such community activities along with his extraordinary patriotic service to the range finder and Red Cross efforts. Somehow, by October he seemed to have salved over the rough feelings among his artistic cohorts caused by his inopportune letter to the *American Art News* magazine. And, regarded as "one of America's foremost painters," he had produced what the *Taos Valley News* referred to as "many beautiful canvases . . . [as] the result of his stay in the picturesque and historical village." Blumenschein, according to the newspaper, had "many friends [who] regret his going" and who were gratified by his assurances that he would return another season.[136]

Phillips's dream of an art colony in the shadow of the Sangre de Cristo Mountains had by this time come to pass. Its evolution into a formal society had suffered its share of vicissitudes, good and bad squabbles, offset by its good times and downright fun, but with Blumenschein's help, vision, dedication, and aesthetic flexibility it had engaged an ever-widening cadre of creative personalities. Blumenschein and Phillips had been the exemplars. Theirs was the model to follow—to come to Taos to stay or, if not that, to come to Taos for as long and often as possible. As Blumenschein would reminisce years later: "We all drifted into Taos like skilled hands looking for a good steady job. We found it, as it grew into an urge that pushed us to our limits, a joyous inspiration to produce and give to the deepest extent of each man's own caliber. We lived only to paint. And that is what happens to every painter who passes this way."[137]

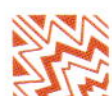

Superstition and the Artist's Defense of Native Rights

Skip Keith Miller

The year 1921 proved a landmark year in productivity and creativity for Ernest L. Blumenschein. In this year he defied the convention of both his fellow Taos artists and the more widely accepted depictions of Native American subject matter when he painted *Portrait of Jim Romero, Star Road and White Sun,* and *Superstition.*[1] Instead of creating unthreatening scenes of Indian life—people working the fields, making pottery, riding in the woods—like those of Eanger I. Couse, Oscar Berninghaus, Joseph H. Sharp, or the general works of Bert G. Phillips, which were often nostalgic and romanticized, Blumenschein chose to place his subjects in distinctly confrontational postures. He skillfully created canvases in which the Indians speak for themselves and confront the viewer directly. In the three paintings noted, the Taos Pueblo people are articulating unequivocally in their own voice to the American public that something is very wrong.

Blumenschein, unlike many of his fellow artists, was familiar with the plight of Native Americans, having spent time in his twenties traveling in the West and illustrating Indian people for *Harper's* and *McClure's* magazines.[2] As an illustrator he created images for the early advocate for Native rights Hamlin Garland as well as for Great Plains anthropologist James Mooney. However, the time Blumenschein spent with and the friendship he developed with Dr. Charles Eastman (grandson of western artist and soldier Seth Eastman) in 1901 had to have been central in the development of his sensitivity to the predicament

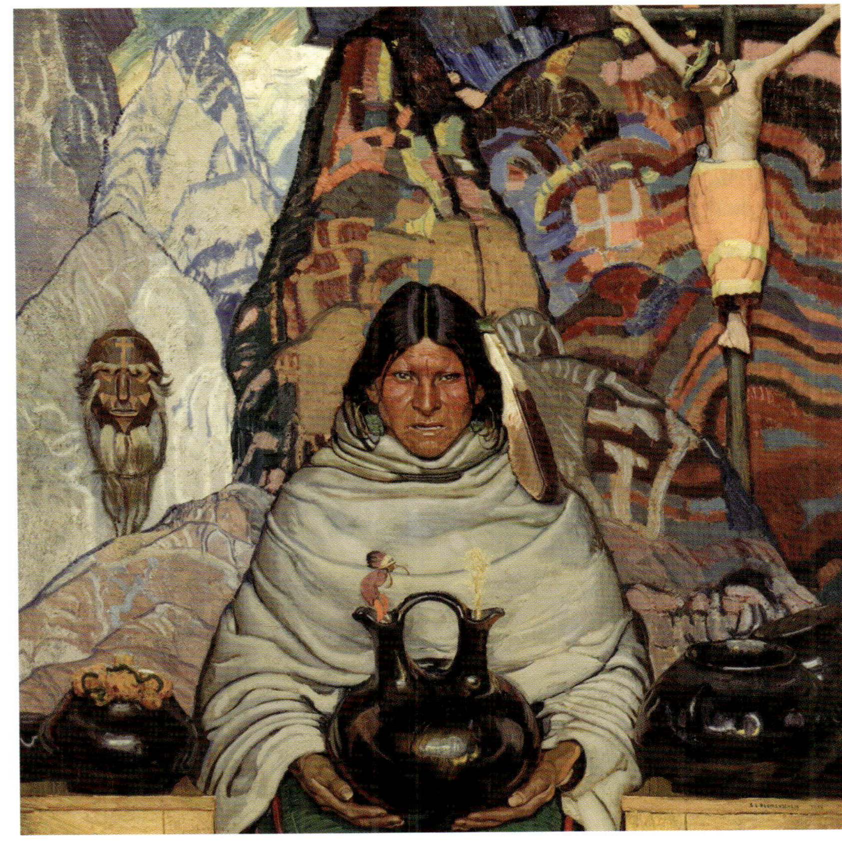

Superstition, 1921, oil on canvas, 41¼ × 45 inches. Courtesy of the Gilcrease Museum, Tulsa, Oklahoma.

of Indian people. He spent two months living and playing baseball among the Sioux while gathering ideas and preparing sketches to illustrate Eastman's book *Indian Boyhood*.

Working for the Bureau of Indian Affairs (BIA), Eastman was the only doctor available to treat the victims of the Ghost Dance massacre of Wounded Knee, December 29, 1890. This and the appalling conditions on the reservations at the time forced Eastman to oppose the often inhumane and corrupt policies and practices of his employer.[3] Blumenschein absorbed much from his relationships with these capable defenders of Native rights and continued to develop his appreciation for the issues facing Indian people with his sustained association and friendship with the people of Taos Pueblo.

With the creation of *Superstition*, Blumenschein took his stand against the ignorance and prejudices of the latest in a series of BIA edicts perpetrated against the Pueblo people of New Mexico and Arizona. *Superstition* is an incomparable work of art in which the subject veritably glares, challenges, and threatens the viewer from the painting's surface. Blumenschein places his model, Jim Romero (a camping and fishing companion and friend), at eye level with the viewer, and Romero's demeanor is anything but mild. Staring out of the canvas, Romero conveys, according to Pueblo social customs, that he does not believe or trust the viewer. To Pueblo and other southwestern tribal people, staring is considered extremely ill-mannered, so when staring is intentionally used, it is to defy or to convey an affront or direct challenge. Romero's emotionally laden countenance is the focal point of the painting and literally bursts from dead center of the pictorial plane to confront the viewer straight on. The viewer, in this case the American nation, is at the root of his problem. Here Pueblo people defy and challenge dominant society. The confrontation revolves around the 1921 release of BIA Circular 1665, a prejudiced bureaucratic insult and outrage to all Native people. In a country that guarantees certain inalienable rights, American citizens are being challenged to explain how and by what right the Pueblo people can be denied the right to practice their millennia-old religion.

An additional justification for Romero's angry confrontation is yet another consequence of federal assimilation policies. Boarding schools took children away from the Pueblos at a time when the young boys should all have been participating in kiva. This instruction transmitted time-honored sacred knowledge and provided the religious training they required in order to become men and leaders within their Pueblo society. Often, upon returning to their people, the young men and women who had been systematically indoctrinated in the whites' religions (predominately Protestant) and social concepts at boarding schools were no longer comfortable with the traditional lifeways of their culture. This alienation frequently resulted in a schism between generations and the formation of conservative and progressive factions within the Pueblo communities.[4]

The figure of Romero is positioned in a deliberately flattened and compressed space between two small end tables containing Tewa blackware pottery, while the backdrop is composed of a richly painted and textured surface that gives rise to a brilliantly colored complex of shifting Navajo and Hispanic Rio Grande blanket designs.[5] These designs then transform into an equally patterned display, albeit more subdued in color, of the repetitive mountainlike forms, and reminiscent of the blankets, they are rendered without any illusion of perspective or depth.[6] Furthermore, the overall patterning of the background replicates the powerful outline and form of the central figure. In this elaborately composed and colorful setting a Seri-style mask with a crosslike symbol carved into the forehead signifies the ancient belief system of yet another indigenous people. Its juxtaposition with a Penitente crucifix reiterates the question posed by the painting's title.[7]

The crucifix represents the belief system of the Catholic Church; in New Mexico the "skirt" on the Cristo carries additional meaning. It represents the tradition of the Penitentes, a Catholic lay brotherhood that has roots in the early Franciscan influences and the *genízaro* and *mestízo* heritage of northern New Mexico.[8] The Penitentes attach more significance to the passions and sufferings of the living, breathing Christ and therefore to the reenactment of his human agony than to the celebration of his resurrection. In the same manner that the Pueblo dances were being outlawed by the American government, the American Catholic Church attempted repeatedly from the mid-1800s under the influence of French-born Archbishop Lamy and those non-Hispanic clerics who followed him to abolish the Penitentes and their rituals as barbaric practices.[9] Of the images Blumenschein situated before the viewer, which would be considered "superstitious" and by whom and by what right could such a judgment be made?

Blumenschein has deliberately placed a Tewa "wedding vase" in Romero's hands. The wedding vase is a pottery form with little precontact precedence and is thought to have developed out of the Pueblo pottery revival associated with the coming of the railroad and the burgeoning southwestern tourist market after 1880. The vessel form had come to represent the union of two within one body. Here Blumenschein portrays the very issues at the heart of the governmental desire for assimilation, not as divisive, but as a solution, the union of lifeways. In one spout of the vase he has depicted a Native American in full ceremonial regalia dancing—anathema to the government—while in the other spout is a beautiful and robust sheaf of grain, representing the desire of the BIA for the Indians to become assimilated as self-sufficient farmers on their own lands. The great irony of the attitude expressed by the BIA at this time is that Taos Pueblo was from the early Spanish colonial period forward one of the great wheat-producing communities in all of New Mexico.[10] Romero holds the resolution to the government-imposed dilemma in his hands.

When *Superstition* won the Altman Prize at the National Academy of Design in November 1921, a perceptive reviewer for the *New York Times* commented:

> Most of the prizes of the National Academy of Design are taken by works that meet you half way. The first Altman prize of $1000, which rambled about with false starts until

> it reached Ernest Blumenschein, is given to a richly patterned Indian subject from the now famous region of Taos. The colors are not high in key, but the color scheme carries far, and the detached objects that give the composition its title, "Superstition," are like bits of raised embroidery on a patchwork. The Indian figure in the centre of the composition is strongly characterized without emerging from the flat plain of the background. It is a good painting and not the worst for suggesting adaptability to a fabric design.[11]

Another reviewer, this one from the *New York Herald,* stated, "Mr. Blumenschein's 'Superstition' [is a] cheap and tawdry Indian picture. The Indians have suffered a great deal from the white man in times past, but it begins to seem as though we were destined to hound them to the very end."[12]

Superstition received wide public notice almost everywhere it was shown. Most critics, but certainly not all, recognized the inherent power and superb quality of the painting, but few understood the latent meaning behind this extraordinary image. For example, in a review of Blumenschein's 1927 exhibit in Dayton, Ohio, one critic noted, "Superstition, one learns from press comments elsewhere, shows an interesting arrangement of pagan and Christian symbols grouped about the figure of an Indian, in whose expression of half fear and half mystery, lies the keynote of the composition."[13]

However, the painting had a far deeper meaning, one of great significance to the Taos Pueblo Indians, the figures portrayed in both *Superstition* and *Star Road and White Sun.* These works were Blumenschein's personal manifestations of his need to make important social statements regarding the horrendous treatment by the American government of his Pueblo friends and neighbors.

Blumenschein's paintings were the first volley of protest that erupted as artists and writers of New Mexico launched a rigorous, systematic attack on the devastating federal assimilation policies of the 1920s that so demoralized Native peoples. His protest of Circular 1665, published by the BIA in April 1921, motivated his creation of *Superstition.* The document was the proverbial final straw in a long line of governmental policies that forced assimilation on Indian people. The process dated back forty years to when Captain Richard Henry Pratt convinced the secretaries of war and the interior to support the creation of the off-reservation boarding schools in 1879. The concept of total immersion based on military subjugation called for the removal of Native American children from their homes to attend schools where they were dressed in uniforms, had their hair cut off, and were not allowed to speak their Native languages. Instead they were taught menial domestic and craft skills by which they might eventually find employment in the dominant society. Thus began a new and disturbing experiment in what would amount to cultural genocide—for all intents and purposes a war on the minds and souls of the children of Native America. Another tactic of acculturation followed in 1883, when Secretary of the Interior Henry M. Teller attempted to repress religious practices and eliminate forever the immoral "heathenish rites" of Native people through the creation of the Courts of Indian Offenses. The "offenses" directly related to dances, especially those involving ceremonial clowns, would be commonly referred to as the Religious Crimes Code.[14]

From the 1880s through the 1930s the BIA, in concert with a variety of Protestant missionaries and moral reform groups, created a scandalous document of approximately two hundred pages. It contained often-lurid "testimony" by religious and moral reformers describing what they perceived to be the immoral and anti-Christian dances of several of the Pueblo tribes. This testament was never printed or circulated through the mail. They considered it too indecent and disgusting. It became known as the Secret Dance File. John Collier would later call the file "subterranean propaganda," because word spread through intimation, gossip, and hearsay rather than in print.[15]

In April 1921 Commissioner of Indian Affairs Charles Burke, encouraged by the various reform groups, used the Secret Dance File to support the creation and issuance of Circular 1665. This BIA policy statement denounced Indian dances and required that all BIA reservation superintendents ban dances that involved "immoral relations between the sexes and any disorderly or plainly excessive performances that promotes superstitious cruelty, licentiousness, idleness, danger to health and shiftless indifference to family welfare." Circular 1665 fundamentally denied Native Americans First Amendment rights by attempting to make the practice of Indian religion and participation in traditional ceremonies and dances against the law.

Superstition then becomes one of several social commentary paintings by a scant few New Mexican painters creating art in the 1910s and early 1920s—Walter Ufer, Gerald Cassidy, Bert G. Phillips (especially in *Relics of His Ancestors*)—who addressed these cruel and culturally repressive federal mandates. Later, Texas and California painters would comment on the devastating effects of the Depression and the Dust Bowl in the 1930s. Unlike works by the Ashcan school in the early 1900s, which were more familiar and easily read by an East Coast or urban population, Blumenschein's and Ufer's paintings were more difficult to read without the context in which they were created. Therefore, these artists intentionally scripted exacting titles, essentially narratives, to help establish the cultural perspective by which the works might be made comprehensible to viewers often unfamiliar with the seemingly exotic settings and characters portrayed.

The level of ambiguity in the social commentary aspects of *Superstition* was also a predicament in two contemporaneous paintings by Blumenschein's friend and colleague Walter Ufer. *Hunger* depicts a Penitente Cristo and Indian subjects, and *Strange Things,* also features a Penitente Cristo as the central element to the composition, but here the model is probably a *genízaro* Penitente. Both are considered exceptional paintings, but their full meaning has yet to be fully revealed.[16] Ufer completed *Hunger* in 1919, and it is thought to be his interpretation on the physical, emotional, and spiritual devastation wrought by the First World War.[17] Although Ufer depicts a northern

New Mexican style crucifix, his strong anti-Catholic or anti-Christian sentiment was persuasively demonstrated in a letter in which he discussed the Cristo as a "dead carved thing [that] really can not give to anything living."[18] Ufer goes on to say that the painting is not really about Indian life but rather "means the world at large."[19] Art historian and Ufer scholar Dr. Dean Porter notes that "Ufer's dealer and 'general agent,' John E. D. Trask, understood *Hunger* as well as anyone when he wrote that it 'was too tragic for public approval.'"[20]

Strange Things was painted in 1921, the same year as *Superstition,* and there is every reason to presume that Ufer and Blumenschein were aware of what the other had going in the studio and even that they discussed their compositions and ideas. In *Strange Things,* Ufer depicted a fine example of a Penitente altar from a morada (a Penitente meeting house) with an assortment of classic New Mexican and Mexican *santos,* or saints, and a Hispanic, or genízaro, Penitente in the immediate foreground. Unlike the confrontational aspect of Romero in *Superstition,* the solitary figure in Ufer's work is depicted in prayer or contemplation, perhaps seeking guidance from the social and political threats to his faith and very cultural identity. Ufer would have understood and appreciated the significant role the Penitente Brotherhood played in maintaining the social, economic, and spiritual fabric of the remote mixed-blood communities of northern New Mexico and southern Colorado. Similarly, the coyote skull on the wall to the right of the Cristo may be a visual play on the word "coyote," which from Spanish colonial times up through the early twentieth century frequently referred pejoratively to a "half-breed" or a *genízaro.*

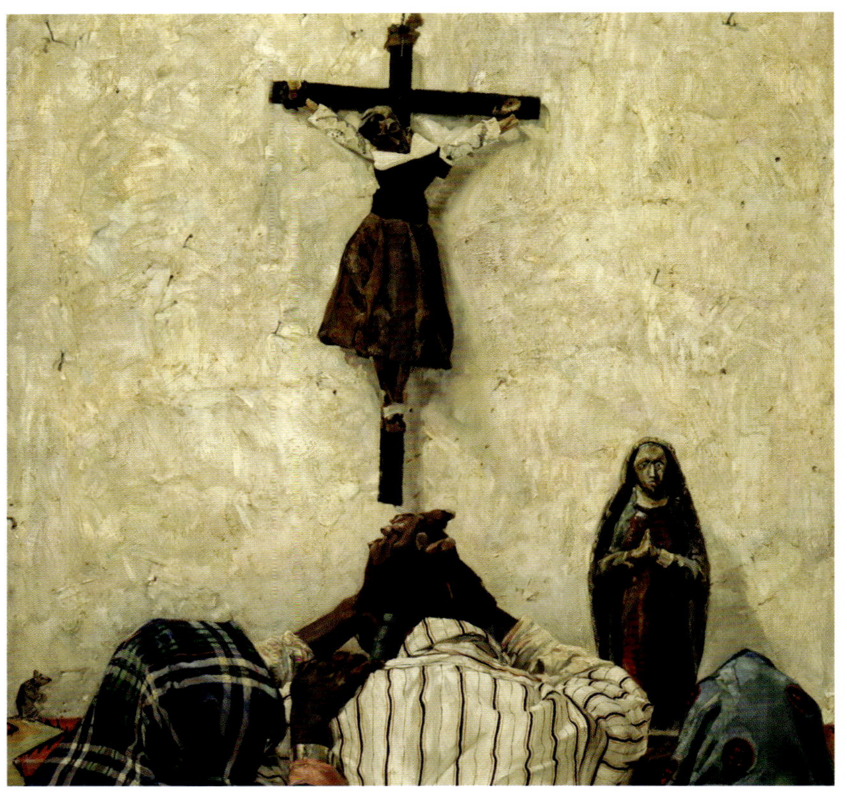

Walter Ufer, ***Hunger,*** 1919, oil on canvas, 50½ × 50¼ inches. Courtesy of the Gilcrease Museum, Tulsa, Oklahoma.

During the latter part of the 1910s, when the federal government was attempting to eradicate the Native belief system and force assimilation on Native Americans, there were similar, albeit regional, efforts underway in New Mexico to eradicate the Penitente Brotherhood, which was also equated with "'superstition . . . irresponsibility' in the form of the Catholic Church, family ties and every-day culture if they get in the way of making money."[21] The period was made doubly difficult for the rural Hispanic communities of the region as the prejudices were directed toward the Penitente Brotherhood from within by the American Catholic Church and from without by the national predominantly Protestant political and economic base and in the new state's administration, which espoused staunchly anti-Catholic sentiments. In *Strange Things,* Ufer may be defending the rights of the general Hispanic population, and the Penitentes specifically, to maintain their cultural identity, traditions, values, and belief system in the face of these external cultural and racial biases. That Ufer was a staunch socialist is readily evident in the large number of his fine works that epitomize his unique form of hard-core social realism (see, e.g., *In Taos, The Land of Mañana,* and *Manuel La Jeunesse*); by and large, he did not reach for symbolic meaning, with the rare exceptions of *Hunger, Strange Things,* and a number of his brilliant self-portraits.[22] Like Blumenschein, Ufer was defending the rights of another of New Mexico's traditional cultures from the threat of assimilation from the dominant society in the early twentieth century.

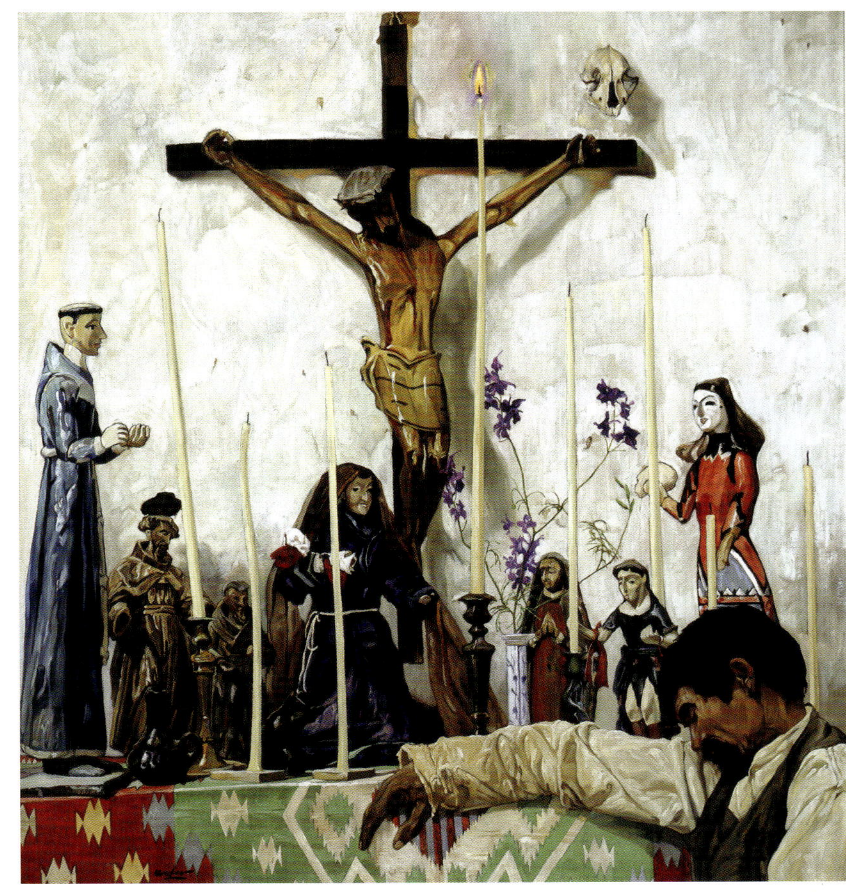

Walter Ufer, ***Strange Things***, 1921, oil on canvas, 40 × 36½ inches. Courtesy of the Nedra Matteucci Galleries, Santa Fe, New Mexico.

Knowledge of Circular 1665 had to have been widespread, as all of the Pueblos and Jim Romero certainly knew about it, and Romero must have conveyed his feelings to Blumenschein. This is suggested in the artist's attempt to explain *Superstition* over thirty years after its creation: "I can't say anymore with words than I have with paint. In fact I have tried—and all I do is confuse more than ever. I just wrote a description of why this, why that, and—tore it up." He then attempts a second explanation, noting, "Add to that his own Indian religion in which the beautiful Indian dances are so important, and the result is even more confusing than I can depict in my picture with its vivid colors and shapes." He then relates Jim Romero's disappointing experiences with a medicine man from outside of the Pueblo and his own dissatisfaction with a Catholic priest. But he brings the discussion back to the primary concerns disturbing his model and friend: the latest federal push for cultural assimilation, Circular 1665. "So I tried to paint the Indian friend's feelings—and maybe my own. . . . It grew into this picture, which will be interpreted according to the intelligence of the onlooker."[23]

Blumenschein's paintings *Superstition* and *Star Road and White Sun* were the first onslaught in a battle to sway both public opinion and federal policy regarding Native rights through the visual arts. These two powerfully confrontational paintings were exhibited extensively in national and international venues almost continuously from 1921 well into the late 1930s, when intellectual forces were gathering to support American Indians and oppose the increasing attacks on Native America from both the federal government and Christian reform groups. It is not surprising that Commissioner of Indian Affairs Charles Burke was feeling threatened by the pressure that the arts were bringing to bear against his campaign of assimilation. A year after the publication of the supplement to Circular 1665, Burke made a surprise appearance at Taos Pueblo, as noted by a young linguistic anthropologist visiting Mabel and Tony Luhan at the time.[24] Jaime de Angulo, who worked and corresponded with Carl Jung among others of the intelligentsia of the time, captured the undisguised animosity and consequences of Burke's visit in his journal.[25]

> Taos. Easter Sunday [1924].
>
> The pueblo is very sad and all upset. Yesterday, the Commissioner of Indian Affairs, Burke, came thru here on a tour of inspection and told the Indians that they must put a stop to their ceremonies. What a stupidly cruel thing to do.
>
> It is hard to keep calm and not to believe as all the hot heads in the Indian Defense Association do that the Government is willfully trying to kill off the Indian and thus put an end to the too onerous and too bothersome trust.
>
> For my part I do not believe it. I think it is just another case of American bullying, of the hundred percent variety, that combined with the traditional ignorance of the Bureau of Indian Affairs in all that is Indian. I will not do them the honor of believing them capable of understanding that to take away his religious ceremonies from the Indian is to take away his heart, and leave him a corpse, ready for quick disintegration.
>
> It is just plain stupid, brutal, arrogant, Nordic superiority.
>
> But there is some meanness, too, in this case. For here is what Burke did . . . he came here in a machine, assembled the old men in the school house and delivered his ukase and then sped on to another pueblo. . . . He told them that they must stop their ceremonies and all that nonsense and give their energy to ploughing. And the boys who are in retreat preparatory to initiation must be sent to school immediately. And they must discourage all those artists and fellows with long hair . . . discourage all those people from coming to the pueblo and don't listen to them. It is their interest to keep the Indian ignorant and unprogressive. They make their money out of him.[26]

Thus, it was in response to the oppressive demands and intentions of Circular 1665 in 1921, the Bursum Bill in 1921–22, and the supplement to

Circular 1665 in 1923 that many of the writers and other artist activists joined Blumenschein and took up pen or paint to bring national exposure to and recognition of the plight of the Pueblo and other Native people and to advocate for the protection of their religious freedoms, human rights, and even traditionally held and occupied lands and water rights.[27] Blumenschein and his fellow artists and writers well understood and utilized the awesome power of art to effect positive change in their world.

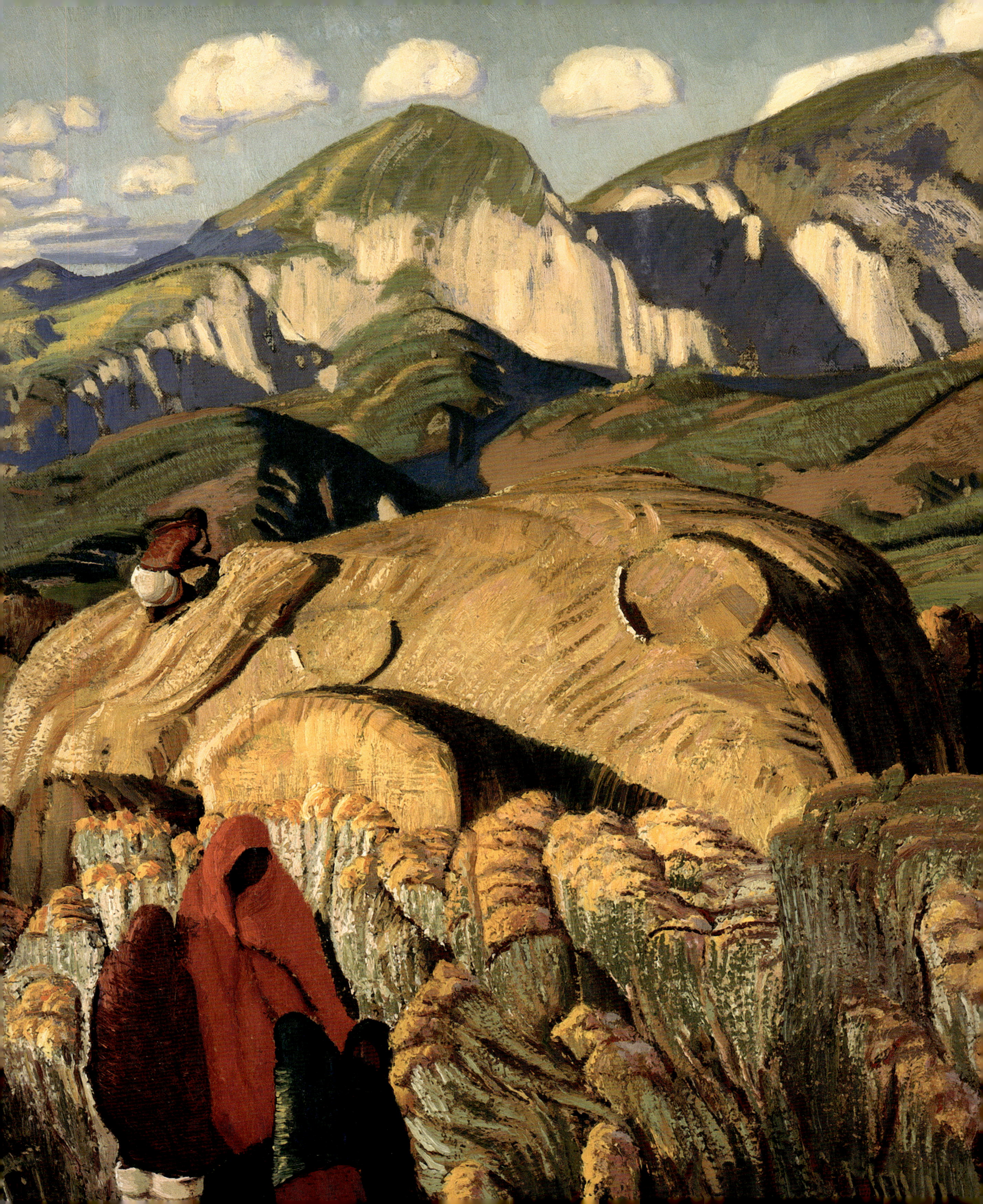

Chapter 3
Chasing Rainbows
Taos in the 1920s

Peter H. Hassrick

The Blumenscheins ushered in the year 1919 with newfound joy and resolve. The Great War had come to an end in late 1918, and a new epoch was about to unfold. While some, like the British journalist and pundit William Bolitho, would see 1920 and the coming age it spawned as infected with a Zeitgeist of the "endlessly sorrowful yet endlessly unsentimental" narratives of people "with no past, no memory, no future, no hope," Blumenschein was considerably more sanguine.[1] If he were at all attracted to popular music (it is known that he disliked jazz) and if he ever sang in the shower, Blumenschein would more likely have crooned the current Harry Carroll hit "I'm Always Chasing Rainbows," especially appropriate for the classical maestro, given its derivation from Chopin's "Fantasie Impromptu."

The arch of Blumenschein's rainbow stretched, of course, from New York to Taos, that enchanting little adobe town in northern New Mexico that was at last about to become his permanent home. As he told an interviewer almost fifty years later, 1919 was a major turning point for him and the family. "The great decision of our lives," he commented, was "to locate in Taos." He said he was "inspired by the primitive and picturesque surroundings," but he also reveled in the liberating notion that, thanks to Mary's inheritance, he might go west now with assurance that he could "devote [his] entire time to painting."[2] It was the end of a twenty-five-year period of illustrating, and for Blumenschein it had come none too soon.

The war caused Americans to seek utopian visions and accommodate Spartan idealism. It rallied public opinion against all things German, including people with

German names, no matter how patriotic they were. And the war made the nation, according to one historian of the times, "impatient for immediate results."[3] All these caused Blumenschein to share the dream with the boy-heroes in Douglas Fairbanks's movies of the mid-1910s, *Wild and Wooly* and *The Knickerbocker Buckaroo*, of going west for good.

Blumenschein's impatience manifested itself in the speed with which he decided to make the move west after the war. Facilitated by Mary's windfall, his diminished need of proximity to the New York publishing houses, and his financial successes just before the war (the Potter Palmer Award from the Art Institute of Chicago and the sale of his painting *The Chief Speaks* to the Cincinnati Art Museum, which had cumulatively netted him $1,750), he was prepared to act impulsively. The immediate results that Blumenschein envisioned included the utopian life in an artist colony with Spartan primitivism at its core (and Taos was plenty ascetic with neither electricity nor plumbing available for another decade). Perhaps too he felt that his Germanness would be a bit less visible in the West.

By late January 1919, Blumenschein had already arrived in New Mexico. He took a studio in Albuquerque and began working among the Southern Pueblos. As spring approached, his optimism and wanderlust occasioned the purchase of a new Ford automobile. As Mary and Helen could not join him until June, the end of the New York school semester, he summoned his old friend Bert Phillips, along with rations and camping gear, and embarked on a six-week tour of New Mexico going as far west as Zuni.[4] He wrote to Mary just before starting on his trip: "I really can't understand why people want to live so many months a year in houses and cities. This great western country is so inspiring, makes your thoughts [move] along large lines, and your life full of joy. You are living, sharing a thankful existence with all of nature, while out of doors in the desert sand and mountains under a great sky. There is no gloom."[5]

Blumenschein's New Mexico rendezvous with Mary and Helen ultimately took place in June, and as a family they extended the trip into Colorado. When the threesome eventually rolled into Taos on July 8, the local newspaper reported that "they are looking fine and prosperous and their many friends in Taos rejoiced to see them."[6]

A few years later, Blumenschein related the story of his family's move a bit differently. He told the artist DeWitt Lockman in an interview:

> In 1919 we sold the Brooklyn house and I induced Mrs. Blumenschein to make her first trip to the west. She had always had a prejudice against life on a frontier. She also had been told she had a weak heart and she feared Taos which has an altitude of 7000 feet. We went to Albuquerque, bought a Flivver [a generic term for an inexpensive car, usually a Model T Ford] and started a camping trip through New Mexico and Colorado with the principal object of getting the wife acclimated and interested in the Rocky Mountains. At the end of a month we reached Taos. At Taos she found the artistic atmosphere that she so much enjoyed and she was soon planning with me to purchase a house and move our valued Paris furniture to New Mexico. All this was accomplished within six months.[7]

In many ways Blumenschein's spring tour of New Mexico with Phillips had been a spiritual reunion. Twenty-one years had passed since those two pioneers had first found themselves in Taos. They could take pride in having established the "Taos School of painting," as the *Albuquerque Evening Herald* called it in a published interview with Blumenschein in March. That school had, by 1919, "probably done as much as any other publicity agent in the booming of New Mexico."[8] As he so often did publicly, Blumenschein relived their "discovery" of Taos, but he was also unreserved in his claim that Albuquerque would someday be an art hub. "A few years more," he speculated, and the tourists will "be coming to Albuquerque to visit the artists' studios and the scenery and people they make famous."[9]

On the heels of their travels, the *Albuquerque Evening Herald* requested an interview with the two artists. As reprinted in May in *El Palacio* and titled "Appreciation of Indian Art," it provided opportunity for the two artists to vent about troublesome trends in the management of Indian affairs. Of particular urgency for Phillips and Blumenschein were policies being fostered by the Bureau of Indian Affairs that would compromise the integrity of Pueblo culture, and especially their art. The threat had been apparent for several years, and the artists' time together afforded them a chance to formulate a unified response. They felt the government's acculturation program then being touted would result "in a discouragement of racial customs which will eventually destroy their [the Indians'] wonderful art," a particularly loathsome development since "their contribution to art has been invaluable." Phillips compared Indian art to the great creative traditions of the world. "Their conceptions are as individual and full of racial character as those of the Japanese," for example, "and should be cultivated as such." Phillips, who for a time ran an Indian curio business to generate income and so understood such matters, contended that their art was additionally important from an economic standpoint. "There is a great future in Indian art; of this we artists are confident," he contended. "It will be recognized and appreciated and will prove of definite commercial value."[10]

Blumenschein was less material and more eloquent: "If in the adoption of a 'higher' civilization the Indian gives up his own remarkable gifts to the world, the loss will be irreparable. . . . The art of the Indians is not only beautiful, but it is unique. Originality is a priceless donation to all human endeavor and the aboriginal American has actually contributed more to that than two hundred years of 'civilized' occupation of North America has produced."[11]

This was one of numerous salvoes against the BIA that echoed across New Mexico during these years. Other artists, like Victor Higgins, had asserted two years earlier that the state's Anglo artists would be helpless without the creative genius of Native people to inspire them. The Pueblo Indians in their lifestyle and in their art presented the Anglo artist with "a host of fresh and original ideas."[12] Writers including Mary Austin, D. H. Lawrence, Mabel Dodge Luhan, and Alice Corbin Henderson also took up the cause of cultural preservation.

The campaign had two sides, though. Zealots for change, such as Indian Commissioner George Vaux, saw Blumenschein, Phillips, and the Taos art colony in general as having a "deleterious and undesirable effect upon the Pueblo Indian in that [they encourage] him to retain his immemorial manner of dress and spoils him by offering him easy money to pose for paintings when he might be better employed at the handles of a plow. . . . Painters are merely clogging the wheels of progress by making the Indian lazy and shiftless."[13] The battle would rage well into the next decade.

As the summer of 1919 came to a close, the Blumenscheins hosted a party for their fellow Taos artists. The painter no doubt showed off his summer's work, including a handsome portrait of Adam Trujillo titled *Red War Bonnet*. Its red, white, and blue color scheme, if nothing else, was a metaphor for patriotism. The Indian represented not only valiant cultural self-determination and, through its geometric patterns, a natural union with the landscape but was also a symbol of America itself and a token of victory in a larger, foreign world conflict.

In October the *Taos Valley News* ran an article on the popularity of Taos as an artist colony, listing different painters who had enjoyed the town's ambiance over the summer.[14] As mentioned, Blumenschein had told the Albuquerque paper earlier that spring that the Taos colony was both nationally important as a school of painting and regionally valuable as an economic stimulant.[15] Certainly, over the year of 1919, the Taos Society of Artists had made every effort to expand its own and the town's visibility. They had induced Robert Henri, a powerful force within the national art community, to join their ranks as an associate member. Their exhibition had toured in New York, Detroit, Chicago, Saint Louis, Kansas City, and Colorado Springs and was soon to be featured in Santa Fe's new museum. "The exhibitions of the Society have become an event of the year in many cities," Oscar Berninghaus, the society's secretary proudly reported, and twelve canvases would sell by the end of the tour.[16] Blumenschein had headed a committee in charge of promoting the society by showing film footage produced and provided by the New Mexico State Land Office in conjunction with the exhibitions. He would work at this with varying success over the next several years.[17] It presented a picture of open minded, collegial fellowship, not unlike the impression offered up in the *Christian Science Monitor* earlier that year: "The men at Taos are a congenial group, all marked by strong individuality and each working independently in the direction of his own ideals. There has been no attempt to make the society stand for any set creed, any particular cult or theory of art methods. The association is stimulating but in no way restricting."[18] It was a rosy view, and these were sunny times.

But all was not entirely harmonious in what Blumenschein called his "little mud town in New Mexico."[19] The three most modern-leaning of the society, Higgins, Ufer, and Blumenschein, joined forces in 1919 with the American animalier sculptor Alexander Phimister Proctor to circulate a major collaborative exhibition to the Art Institute of Chicago and the Cincinnati Art Museum. Titled Paintings and Sculptures by Four Artists of Taos, it included many of Blumenschein's most significant works. Organized by the Museum Directors' Association, it was, according to the artist, "my first big chance to show what I can do, and I think it will mean a great deal in building my reputation."[20] The Taos Society of Artists exhibition that ran concurrently with this show went mostly to commercial galleries, with the exception of the second venue at the Detroit Institute of Arts. It is interesting that in spite of Blumenschein's desire for financial validation through sales, it was the museum exhibition with his modernist cohorts that inspired his most ambitious self-expectation. This amounted to the first serious breakaway exhibition from the society.

As the year came to a close, Blumenschein's rainbow-length separation from New York became more permanent. The family purchased a house for themselves on Ledoux Street that November, with anticipation of moving in the following spring. The low-lying adobe structure had been owned by Blumenschein's friend and former student Herbert Dunton. Over time, it would grow to accommodate additional studio space for both Mary and Helen as well as guest quarters.[21] No sooner was the sale consummated than Dunton departed for New Jersey for the winter and Blumenschein returned to Brooklyn to join his wife and daughter, where the family began preparations for their move to New Mexico.

Blumenschein made a busy life for himself over the winter in New York. He exhibited an exclusive selection of his works from the Paintings and Sculpture by Four Artists of Taos show at the Fakir Club. A *New York Times* writer applauding the decorative quality of his new work suggested that here was a "brilliant encouraging note."[22] Henry McBride of the *New York Sun*, a critic who generally found little favorable to say about Blumenschein's work, which he considered old-fashioned, recanted by praising Blumenschein's treatment of Indian subjects, especially in his restraint and his painstaking and careful execution.[23] So pleased was the artist with his showing at the Art Students League's Fakir Club that he placed his dual portrait *The Chief's Two Sons* on loan there.[24]

At the same time, the Taos Society of Artists exhibition was featured at Milch Galleries in Manhattan, and Blumenschein sent a recent work, *Indian Battle*, to the Pennsylvania Academy of the Fine Arts in Philadelphia. Later that spring, Ufer, Higgins, and Blumenschein (this time without Proctor) would repeat their performance at the Milch Galleries in a three-man exhibition of fresh material.[25] That the triumvirate of Taos's most modern painters would break out of the fold for a second time and present their paintings at the same gallery within months of the larger organization's New York show may well have been viewed as a divisive move, especially given the disparity in styles between this trio and the others of the society. Blumenschein, Ufer, and Higgins were elected as the governing board of the society in July 1920, with Blumenschein as president and Ufer as secretary and treasurer.[26]

The Blumenscheins were back in Taos by mid-April, having departed New York six weeks earlier to motor across the country to California and then back to New Mexico.[27] They enjoyed their new car. And, no doubt, once they got furniture arranged and walls painted, they also enjoyed their new home. In late July they entertained seventy-five of their neighbors for a house warming, a lecture on Southwestern Indians by Bureau of Ethnology anthropologist J. A. Jeançon, and an evening of dancing.[28]

Mary had found a welcome niche for herself in Taos. As Helen recalled,

> [She] put her mind and body to making this adobe a home for all of us, keeping its simplicity, its Indian fireplaces and Spanish vigas and latias [*sic*], increasing the light by putting in windows that were horizontal rather than the few vertical ones. She added shelves, Japanese prints

in the library room and the Southwest Indian watercolors in the cool, white-washed dining rooms.

Mother had our fine Indian carpenter, Geronimo Gomez, Taos War Chief, who was also a model for father, paint the walls of the library with a Muresco hand-mixed Venetian red color. She placed a chaise lounge in front of the fireplace, a tapestry over a New Mexican bed on the east wall and an oval mahogany table opposite.[29]

The Blumenscheins' guest must have been impressed with Mary's accomplishments. Her taste and savoir faire continually grew in the community's esteem.

Visitors to the Blumenschein home probably saw the artist's most serious new painting in progress, a dual portrait like *The Chief's Two Sons* but much more edgy. He called it *Star Road and White Sun*. So significant was this canvas in the artist's mind that over the next year, carrying a price of between $2,000 and $2,500, it toured on its own to the National Academy of Design in New York and to the Detroit Institute of Arts.[30]

Unlike Higgins, Blumenschein established close bonds with his Indian models. This portrait of his handyman and carpenter Geronimo Gomez (Star Road) and an older man known as Juan de Jesus Martinez or by his Pueblo name, White Sun, suggests an abiding personal relationship.[31] The painting is really about Star Road, with White Sun serving primarily as a generational foil, but it is also about changing times as well as friendship. Star Road, a self-declared user of peyote, was a proud resister of multiple social and cultural forces at play in 1920. He wanted to be recognized as a modern Indian, on his own terms. Thus, in his peyote practices he countered three authorities: the BIA, which viewed peyote as anathema to its dream of acculturating the Pueblos; the Catholic Church, which sought control of his spiritual self; and even his tribal elders, who opposed peyote use on religious grounds.[32] The Peyote Cult introduced a tradition that was not consonant with the traditional ways at Taos Pueblo. The "peyote boys," as Star Road and his fellow practitioners were called, were just that within the pueblo—boys. They had spent years away at Indian boarding schools, keeping them from

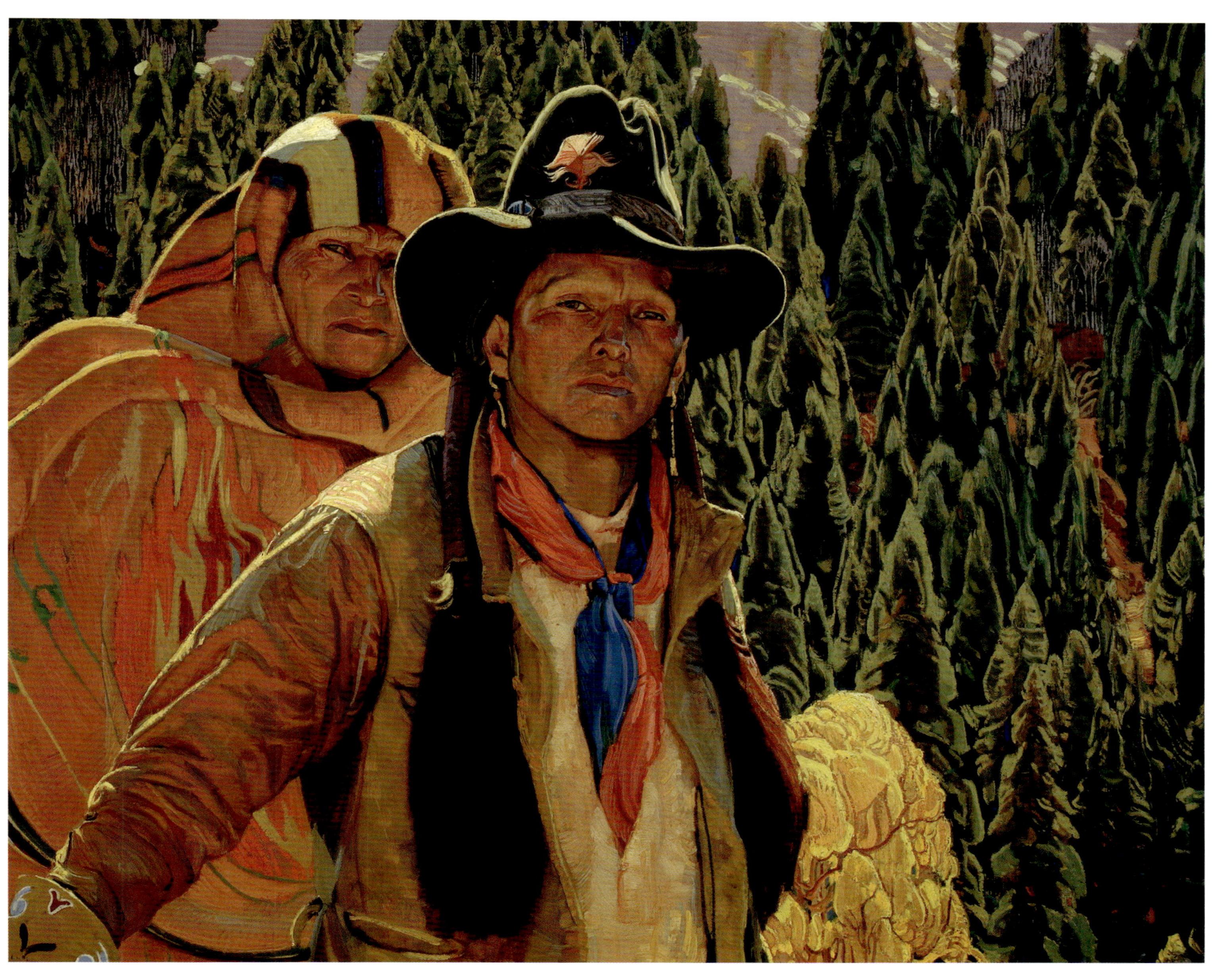

Star Road and White Sun, 1920
Oil on canvas, 42 × 51 inches
Courtesy of The Albuquerque Museum, Albuquerque, New Mexico
Museum purchase, 1985 General Obligation Bonds, Albuquerque High School Collection (1986.50.3)
Gift of the classes of 1943, 1944, and 1945

participating in the kiva, which would have taught them the traditional ways of the tribe, including manhood rites. The Peyote Cult became the only way these boys could find transcendence into manhood. This split the pueblo, a division cause by the government's acculturation program. Star Road and White Sun, representing the elders who opposed the introduction of nontraditional religious practices, glare out at the viewer with unmistakably accusative expressions.

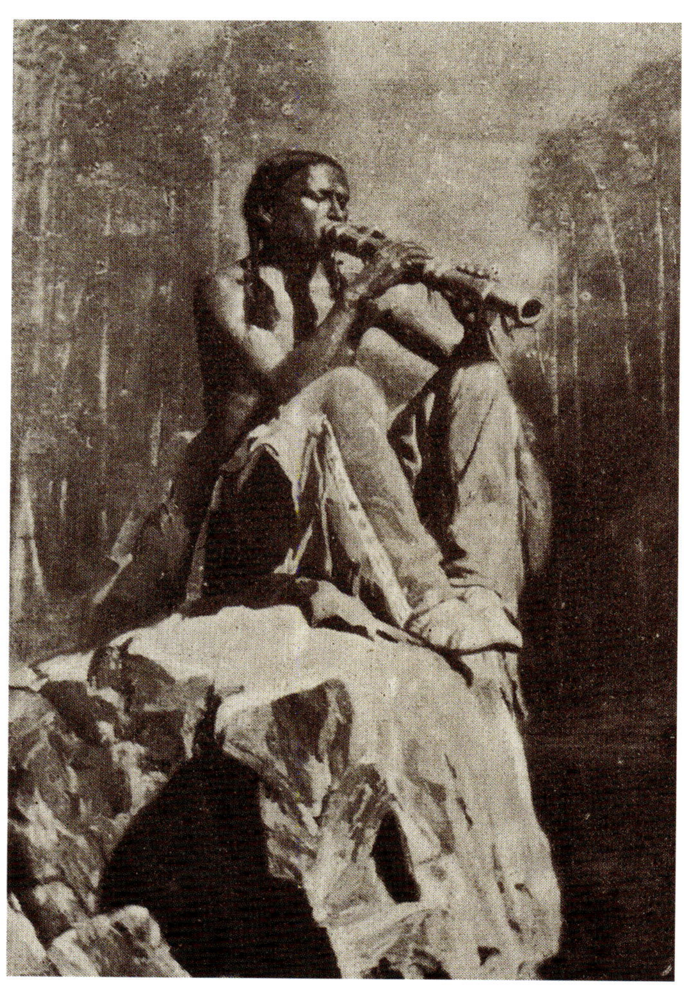

Bert Phillips, ***Moonlight Lake Song***, 1924, oil on canvas, from an illustration in *Art and Archaeology*, December 18, 1924. Courtesy of University Libraries, University of Colorado at Boulder.

Note: Present location unknown; painting's orientation unverifiable.

This was a change in the way Blumenschein pictured Indian people. He was directly taking sides. Blumenschein, who had so wanted to herald traditional Native culture and art, was equally driven to champion modern Indian life. In this he was joined by his cohort in modernism Walter Ufer. Rather than focusing on idealized, historicized images of Indians, as did most of the Taos Society painters, the three modernists preferred instead to concentrate on contemporary life. Comparing Phillips's 1924 painting *Moonlight Lake Song* with Blumenschein's *Star Road and White Sun* and a similar composition by Higgins, *Apaches* (1918), suggests the latter two painters' affinity for living Indians as opposed to the rather stereotypical images of Native people in harmony with nature.

Star Road and White Sun also demonstrates the transformations that became evident in Blumenschein's painting after his move full time to Taos. The whole approach to his art changed, according to art historian Mary Carroll Nelson: "He adopted a brighter palette and he gave rein to an intuitive, mystical understanding of his Indian subjects, portraying not just their appearance but also their emotions."[33] Helen would write of her father's early years as a Taos resident that, now "completely happy," he finally realized his "real potential" by beginning to produce "large oil paintings, all of them now more and more symbolic. Suddenly they were intense in color, three dimensional in their rendition. They included the faces of his Indian models

[and] workers."[34] The painting's brilliant, saturated colors are what attracted a reviewer in Cincinnati a few years later when it was shown at the art museum. "The artist has made of it a wonderful harmony of rich orange-brown color, and the conventionalized background gives it the quality of imagination and spirit that it has. It is one of the finest things Blumenschein has ever sent."[35]

Beyond matters of scale and color, this painting was also an experiment in orchestrated design. Gomez holds the center third of the canvas. His right arm extends at an angle in front of Martinez, and the brim of his hat obscures part of Martinez's face. And Gomez, with his self-assured expression and confident stance, stands in the forefront.

Despite the fact that *Star Road and White Sun* ultimately enjoyed one of the most ambitious traveling histories of any of Blumenschein's works, and even though the price was gradually reduced over the years, it never sold. Late in his life, the artist sacrificed the painting to the Albuquerque High School, charging them $250, or what he considered his costs in materials.[36] The market for such works in 1920 and beyond was weak. As Joseph Henry Sharp wrote to the Los Angeles dealer J. F. Kanst that year, Blumenschein "is about the strongest from our point of view but his stuff is not of the gallery *salable* sort as some of the others."[37] Blumenschein asserted the same thing late in life when he remembered, "those whose pictures were principally picturesque subject matter had a good income. The rest of us, with high ideals of art, had to fight it out, and we never could have won but for prizes at shows and purchases by museums."[38]

Two paintings that traveled with the Higgins, Ufer, and Blumenschein exhibition in 1920, *War Captains in Time of Peace* (later repainted and titled *The Gift*) and *White Blanket and Blue Spruce*, soon found homes in American museums. Both canvases feature a single, standing, face-forward, draped figure who takes up approximately one-third of the composition. *White Blanket and Blue Spruce* is particularly compelling with its contrast of tinted cobalt blue bows that flow forward in Art Nouveau elegance and the stark white blanket that wraps the subject. *The Gift*, though more complex as a picture, shares a static, classical quality with its companion work. A couple of years after its creation, Blumenschein described *The Gift* to a colleague at the National Academy of Design. "The story is nothing," he wrote; "perhaps there is a fiesta and the principle figure is about to present to a visiting guest the deerskin beaded bag as a token of friendship between tribes." What was important to Blumenschein was the conceptual organization of the picture: "the composition of masses and colors and the rhythm of line give the sentiment I wish to express."[39]

By the fall of 1920, the "Three Artists of the Taos Group," as they called themselves, were feeling a bit overwhelmed. In addition to their three-man show, each was circulating solo exhibitions and participating in the traveling shows of the Taos Society of Artists. When, in October, Blumenschein wrote to the Albright Art Gallery in Buffalo, the final venue for the three-man exhibition, he advised that "the group disbands now—for the present at least—as there are too many requests for paintings—more than we can supply—but we shall continue to exhibit with the Taos Society of Artists of which Mr. Ufer has been elected secretary and myself President."[40]

The society's traveling show closed out the year in New York at the Kingore Galleries. The members expressed overwhelming pleasure at its reception, reporting a "very great success among the people there" and a media reaction that "did it great justice."[41] Yet the modernist art critic Henry McBride reacted mockingly. With the exception of Ufer, McBride contended, these artists had given considerable attention "to the most showy outward events of the Western Indian's existence, such as the religious and other dances that the tribes still keep up, but there is no recorded expression of deep feeling upon the part of the artists at these manifestations."[42]

Such criticism perhaps induced Blumenschein to embark in 1921 on a profoundly emotional and aesthetically and spiritually complex work titled *Superstition*. It was a work of social commentary in which he expressed the cultural plight of Native people that resulted from acculturation. Thirty years after creating this picture, Blumenschein endeavored to explain its rather irreverent essence to his patron Thomas Gilcrease. "I tried to paint the Indian friend's feelings—and maybe my own," he wrote, and then continued sympathetically: "The Indian's mind is partly made up by Medicine Men who are often fakers who play off on all superstitions that come into his life—and in addition he

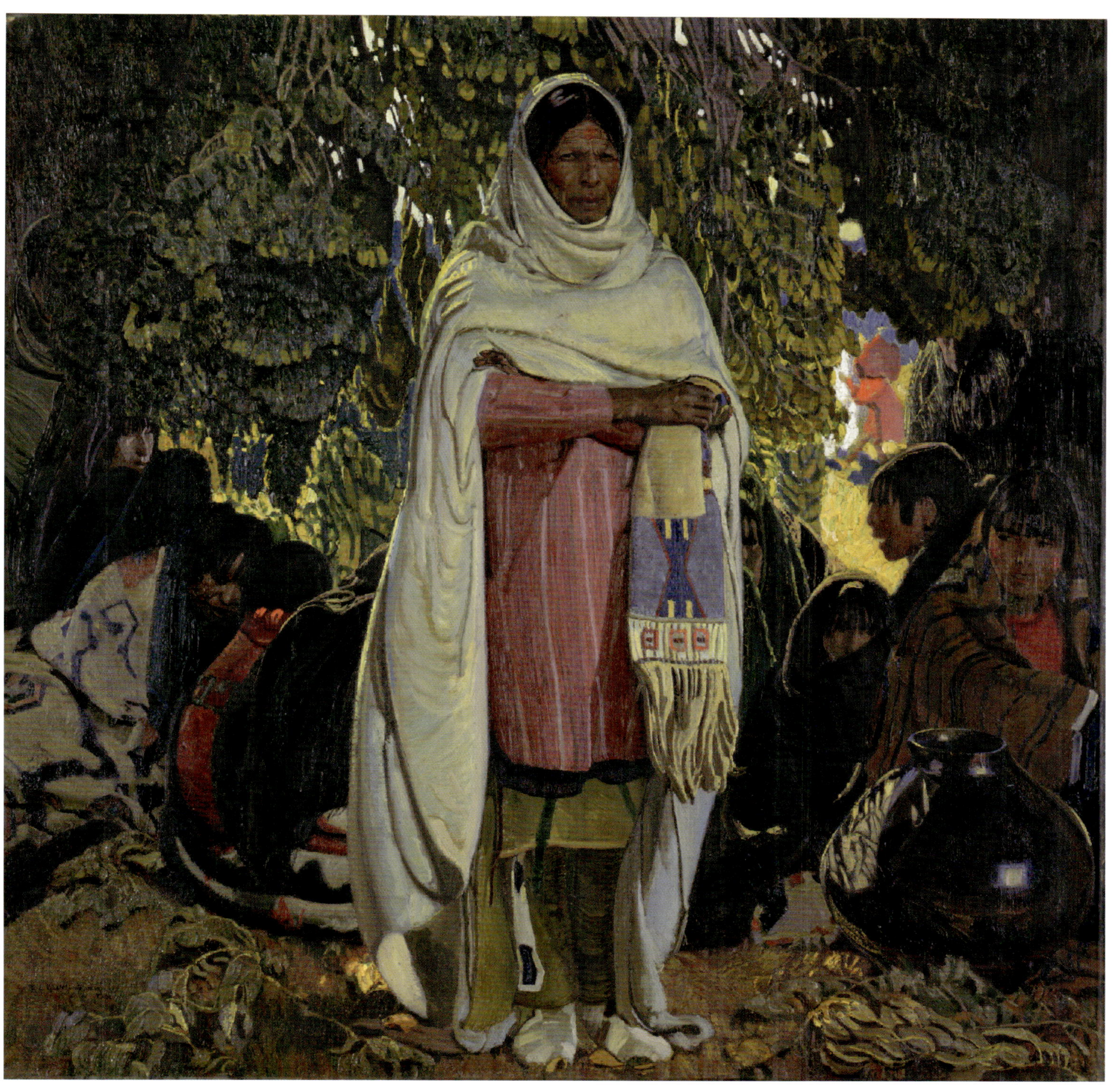

The Gift (originally ***The War Captain in Times of Peace,*** 1919), reworked 1922
Oil on canvas, 40½ × 40¼ inches
Courtesy of the Smithsonian American Art Museum, Washington, D.C. (1975.86)
Bequest of Henry Ward Ranger through the National Academy of Design

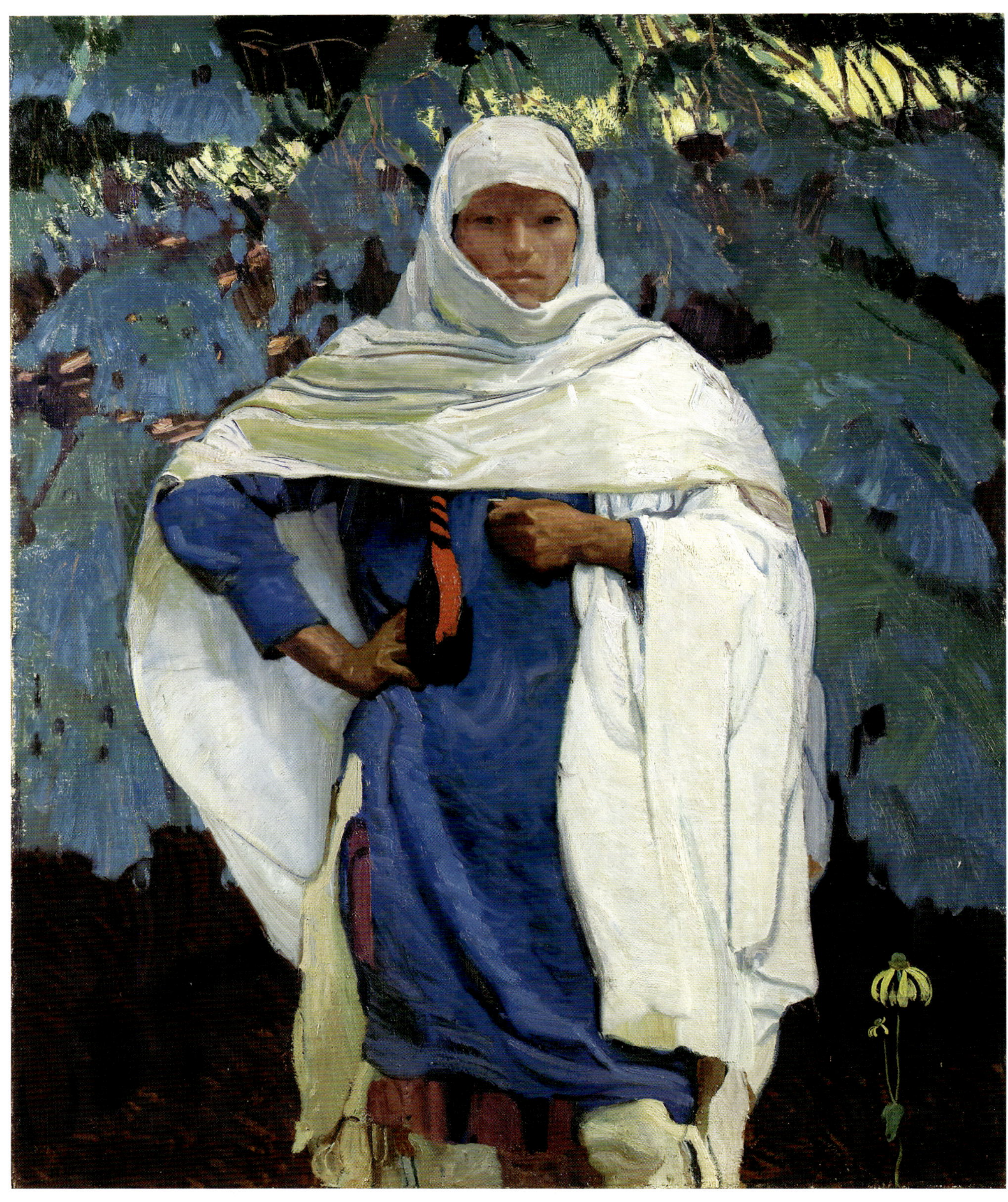

White Robe and Blue Spruce, 1922
Oil on linen mounted on paperboard, 34 1/8 × 28 1/8 inches
The Wichita Center for the Arts Collection, Wichita, Kansas (1928.1)
Purchased with funds provided by the Wichita Art Association Patron Group Subscription

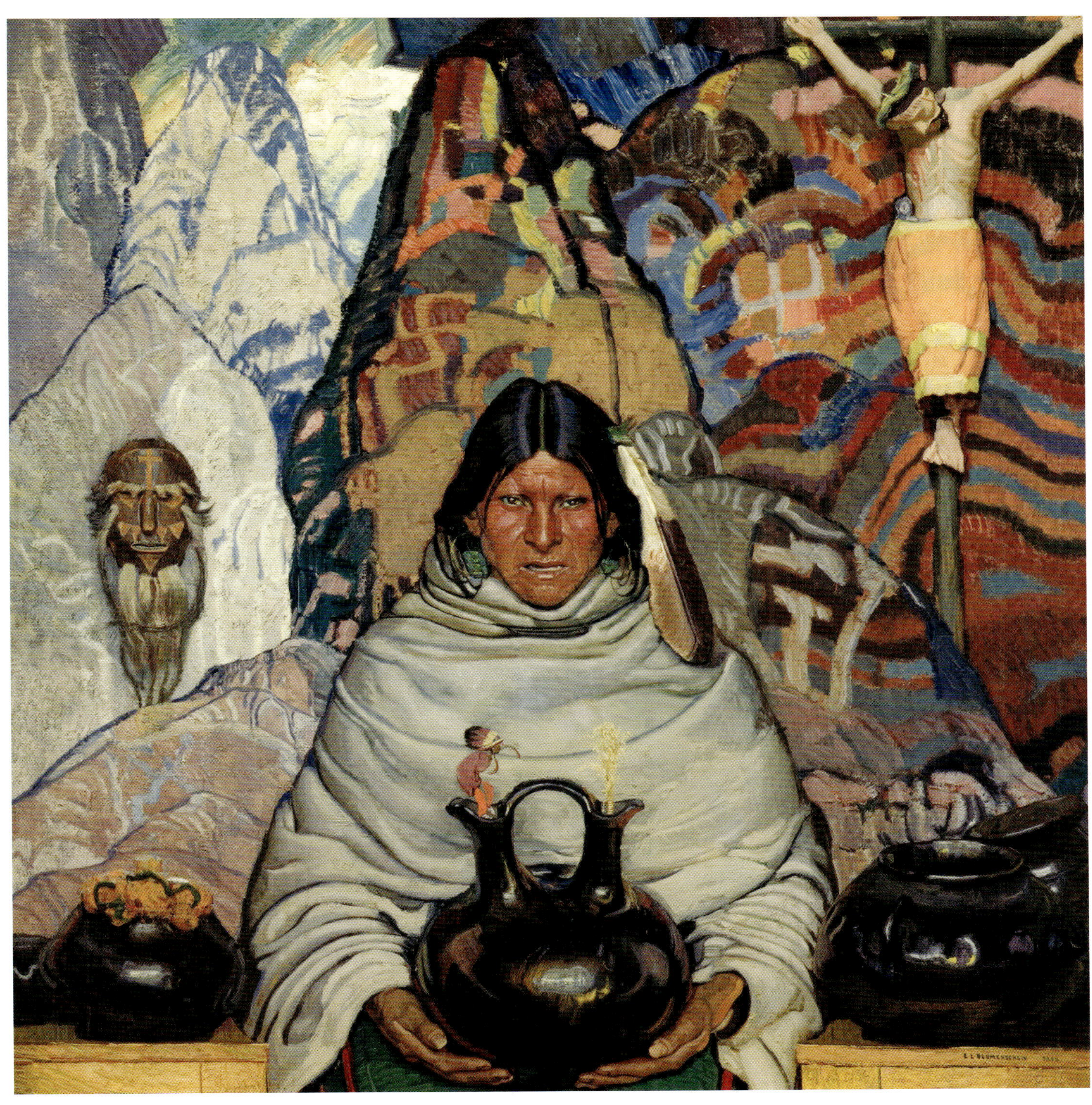

Superstition, 1921
Oil on canvas, 41¼ × 45 inches
Courtesy of the Gilcrease Museum, Tulsa, Oklahoma

has the religion of the white man which he gets from a priest that is not always conscientious. Add to that his own Indian religion in which the beautiful Indian dances are so important, and the result is even more confusing than I can depict in my picture with its vivid colors and shapes."[43] For Blumenschein, the conflicting spiritual ideologies were the Indians' bane. Using visual irony, he makes the point that one person's religion may be viewed by another as superstition, while at the same time calling for attention to basic human rights such as those addressed in the First Amendment—including freedom of religion. The omnipresence of the crucifix in the upper third of the painting suggests the fundamental political underpinning for this painting. It was in 1921 that the commissioner of Indian affairs stormed the tribal council at Taos Pueblo, denouncing the Taos Indians as being "half animals" and "pagan worshippers" and forbidding any dances or ceremonials, except for those approved by the BIA.[44] Obviously Blumenschein was saying that the Pueblo religion was no more rife with paganism than the Christian faith.

Blumenschein placed his subject, Jim Romero (his model, handyman, and frequent fishing and camping companion), in the center lower half of the composition. Romero looks squarely at the viewer with a hostile glare. He cradles a black wedding vase in his hands, out of which rises an Indian dancer from one spout and a sheaf of wheat from the other. Behind the central figure are two recognizable icons, a Seri mask and a *bulto*, or three-dimensional carved and painted Penitente-style crucifix, that silhouette themselves before a highly abstracted series of precipitous architectonic mountains. The Cézannesque brushwork in the peaks is reminiscent of elements from Marsden Hartley's New Mexico still lifes such as his oil *El Santo* (Museum of Fine Arts, Museum of New Mexico), done in Santa Fe in 1919. The message, related to the conflated negative effect of religion on the human spirit, was cross-culturally iconoclastic. The cacophony of brilliant colors and sensate textures that define two-thirds of the nearly vertical hills add visual confusion to Romero's turbulent emotional state.

But if the painting was confounded with emotional tension and pathos, the critical assessment of it was not. When exhibited in New York at the winter exhibition of the National Academy of Design, it won the Altman Prize and a one-thousand-dollar purse. One reviewer reacted to the painting rather frivolously, claiming that Blumenschein, though lacking a certain "sense of beauty," had the redeeming qualities of "wit and humor."[45] But it was a serious painting with a profound message of gravitas and pathos. It was also for Blumenschein his second major cash award in five years. Its combination of academic portraiture, emotive power, political polemic, and abstract painting caused his fellow New Mexico artist Theodore Van Soelen to refer to this piece as a turning point in Blumenschein's artistic career.[46] In this way it may be viewed as a pendant to *Star Road and White Sun*.

Blumenschein gave his favorite model of the time a more secular countenance in *Portrait of Jim Romero*, thought to have been painted in 1921. Here Romero, with no less an inscrutable gaze, is pictured beneath a soft-brimmed felt hat with his braids falling over a rich red blanket that clothes his stooped shoulders. He is positioned before an adobe fireplace in the artist's studio. A window on Romero's left casts a glow on one side of the sitter's face, effectively dividing the man and the composition into light and dark. The dichotomy may, as in *Superstition*, suggest a conflicted man.

Because Blumenschein, like Ufer, was intrigued with contemporary life in Taos, he selected his neighbor to the east, Epimenio Tenorio, as the subject for his painting of *The Plasterer*.[47] Long regarded by the artist as "one of my best," the painting juxtaposed the weary laborer with Pueblo pottery, thus honoring both Indian as well as Hispanic traditions.[48] Here he celebrates the values of hard work and the dignity of labor with an image that transcends time and place. He proves with this work that he could create significant art with humble, quotidian subjects. Tenorio carries the burden of his life task on his sloped shoulders and also bears the legacy of a craft tradition that went back to the first Spanish settlers, who adopted the adobe architecture as their own—again an expression of cultural union. As such, Blumenschein paid homage to the uniqueness of the past, much as artists like Grant Wood were doing contemporaneously in other parts of America.[49]

Less adventurous in brushwork than *Superstition*, yet more harmonious with its muted cerulean blue and yellow ochre, this approach represents an aesthetic retreat to a more academic mode. Yet his friend and fellow artist Howard Cook

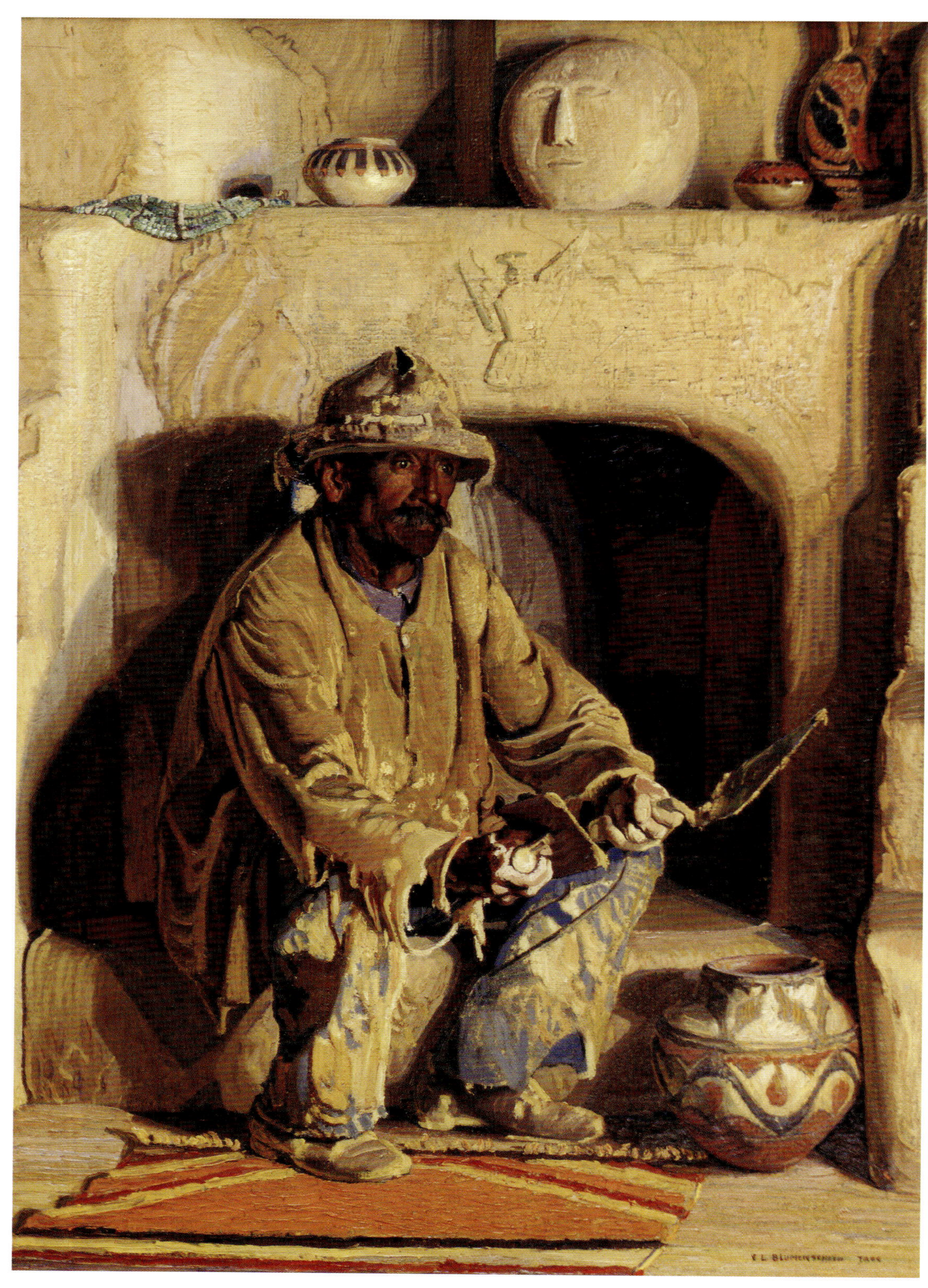

The Plasterer, 1921
Oil on canvas, 48⅛ × 30⅛ inches
Courtesy of the Eiteljorg Museum of American Indians and Western Art,
Indianapolis, Indiana

regarded this mellow tribute as not only his "high mark in the treatment of genre" but also "surprisingly modern," with its "feeling of basic design" and its "rhythm of movement through the objects."[50] Blumenschein's propensity for the primacy of orchestrated design was beginning to show itself in a most powerful way.

In the late 1940s, during an interview with Reginald Fisher, director of the Museum of New Mexico's art museum, Blumenschein summarized the 1920s as "a period of high production, considerable success in prizes and one-man shows and sales."[51] It was a decade in which some paintings, like *Superstition*, were conceived, painted, and exhibited and received critical acclaim within months. Other paintings, though, might take almost the whole decade to mature. Such was the case with the stunning portrait of the area's most revered and frequently depicted architectural icon, *Church at Ranchos*, which was begun in 1921 but worked and reworked until it was finally finished in 1929.

Blumenschein operated under the premise that "a picture must work: it should be well composed and slowly constructed until it has grown to completion."[52] *Church at Ranchos* was one of many that came to life over an extended period. In this work Blumenschein adopted a motif that also changed, the Ranchos church, which may explain why the final version took so long to produce. The church had appeared as a distant sunlit element in his 1917 masterwork, *The Chief Speaks*. It served there as an intermediary between a group of Indians in the middle distance and the verdant mountains beyond, suggesting that the chief was not the only voice to be heard in the land.

One small but highly finished oil on panel, *Ranchos Church with Indians,* may have been the first study for this work. It, like *The Chief Speaks*, situates the church between a mass of people in the foreground and a billowing cloud over the horizon—the sacred structure interposing the humble corporeal beings with the ethereal forces of heaven. The stark white steeples, though, seem oddly antithetical to the harmonious mood that characterizes the rest of the scene. In a larger study for *Church at Ranchos,* titled *Feast Day, Ranchos Church, Taos,* the steeples are more in accord with the overall tone of the painting. A larger crowd has gathered in front of the church walls, but the sky is lackluster and the symbolism is lost.

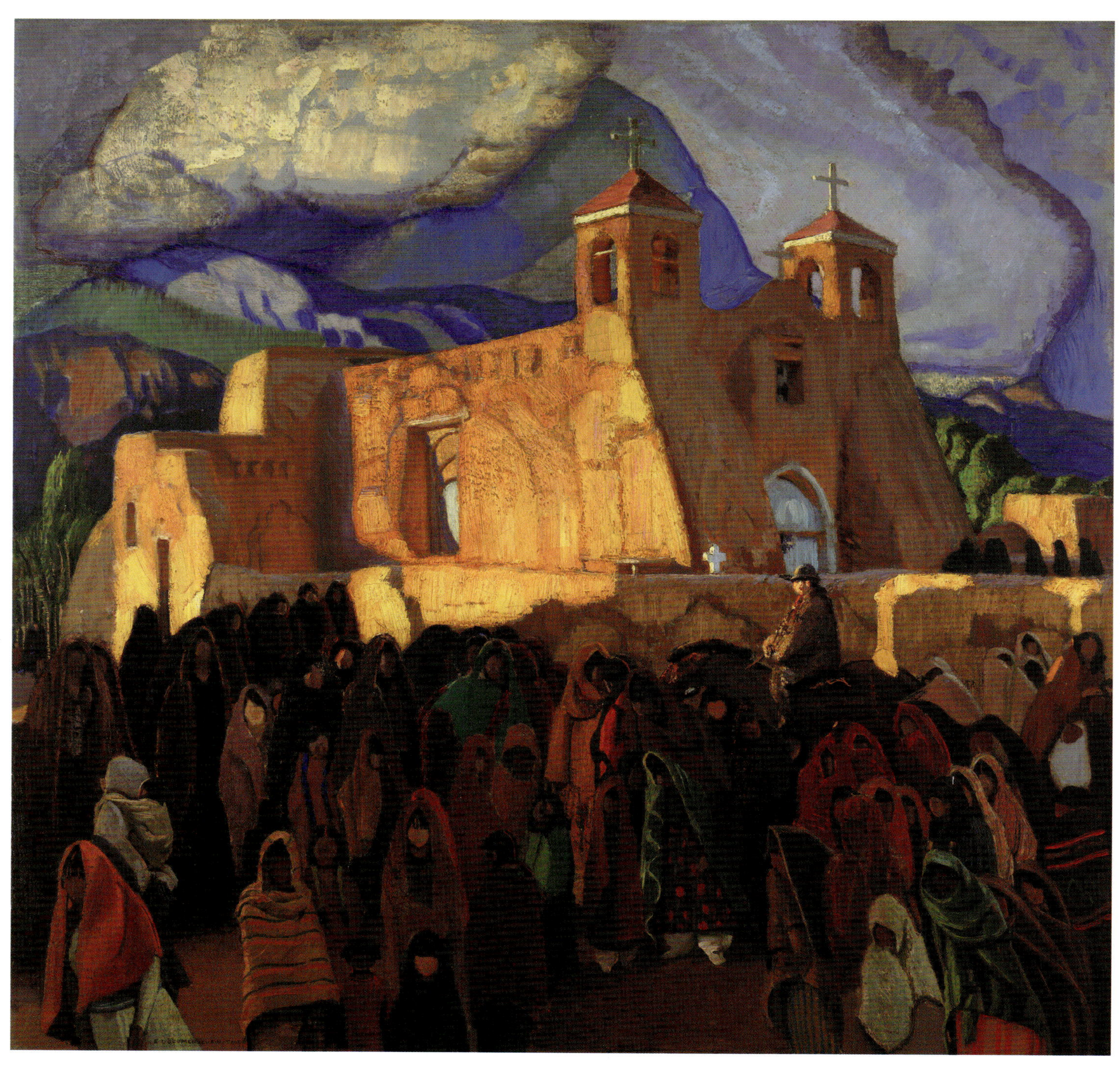

Church at Ranchos, ca. 1921, repainted 1929
Oil on panel, 30 × 31 inches
Courtesy of Taos Historic Museums

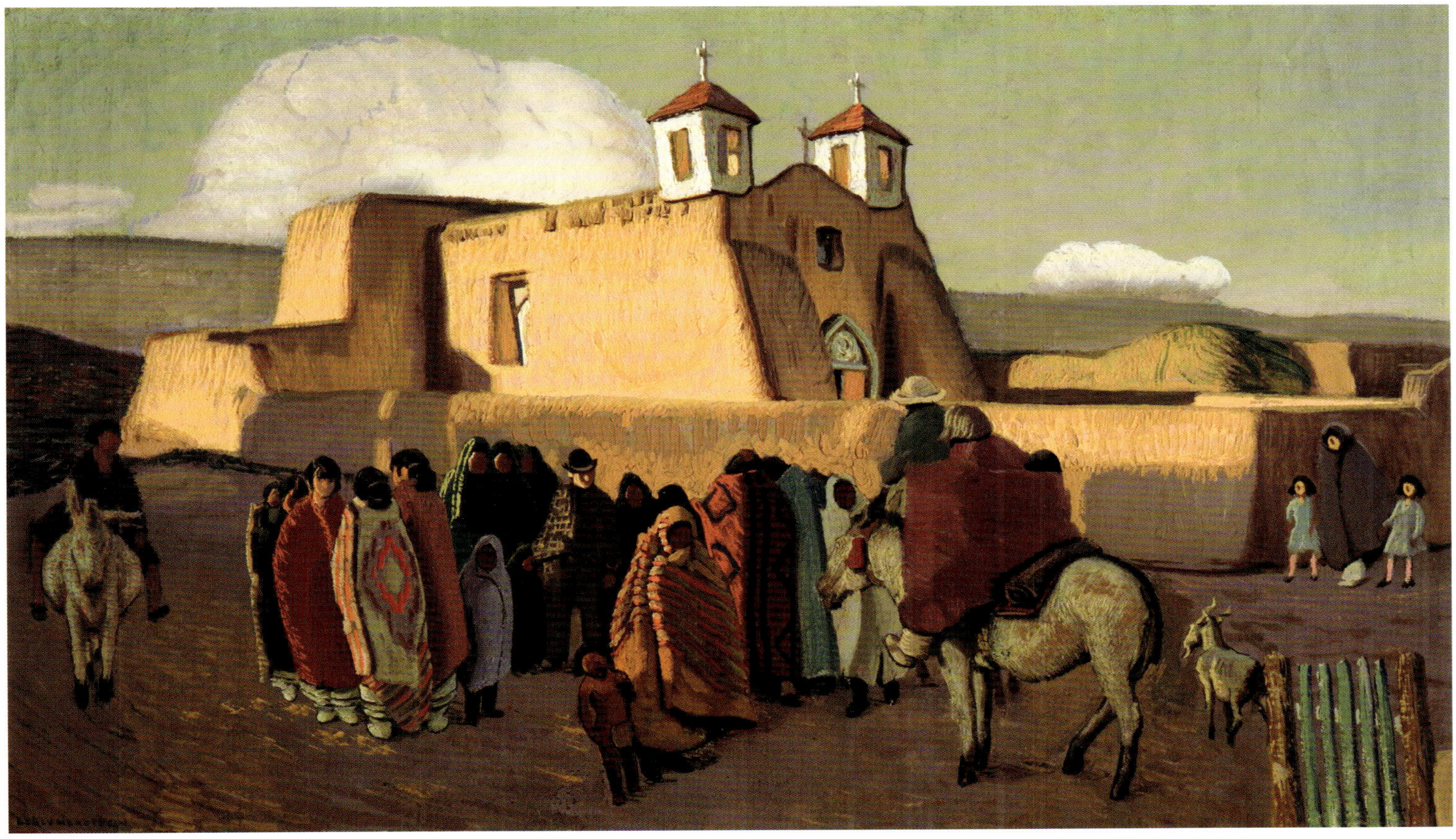

Ranchos Church with Indians, ca. 1925; oil on panel, 14⅜ × 23¾ inches. Courtesy of the Gilcrease Museum, Tulsa, Oklahoma

The final painting resolved all the shortcomings of the studies and proclaims the symbolic message with eloquence. A substantial throng of supplicants is assembled before the adobe churchyard wall. A horseman overlooks the faceless crowd. His head, significantly, is spotlighted and placed directly in the doorway at the front of the church. Blumenschein has cast the church in a brilliant evening glow. Its steeples, now, by 1929, have been plastered and conform to the rest of the structure. Each thrusts its cross into the sky—one silhouetted against the clouds and the other against a lofty peak. Blumenschein used considerable artistic license here, as with many of his works, having moved the Sangre de Cristo Mountains into a position not seen from that vantage point. The clouds, enshrouding the lush blue and green peaks, resolve the composition. Emblematic of much the same theme as expressed in *Superstition*, this painting, with its Indians organized chaotically in the dark and the church oppressively, though splendidly brilliant, overwhelming all but the heavenly realm above, speaks to the separate worlds of the Pueblo Indians and the Catholic Church.

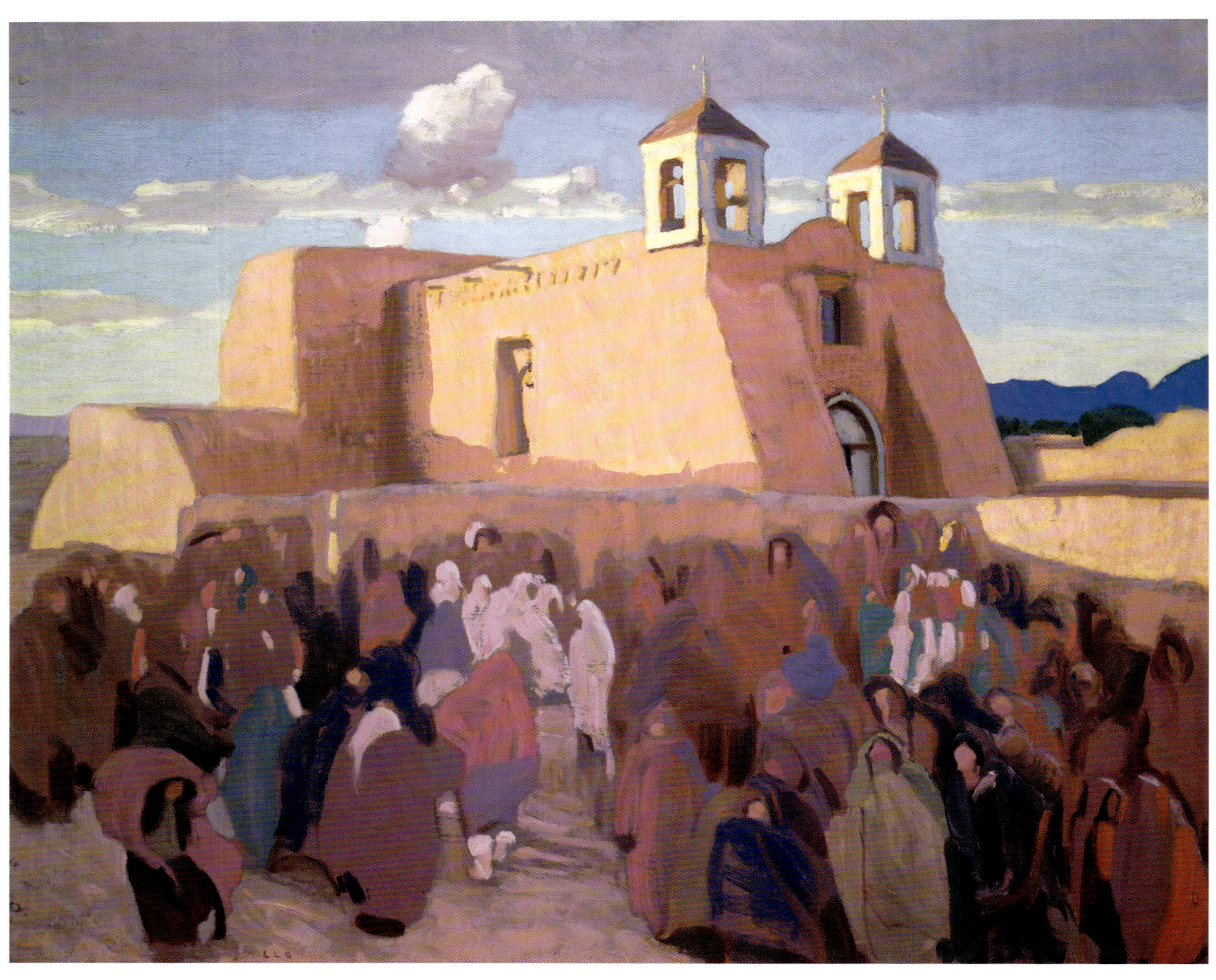

Feast Day, Ranchos Church, Taos, ca. 1925
Oil on canvas, 25 × 30 inches
Courtesy of the Gerald Peters Gallery, Santa Fe, New Mexico

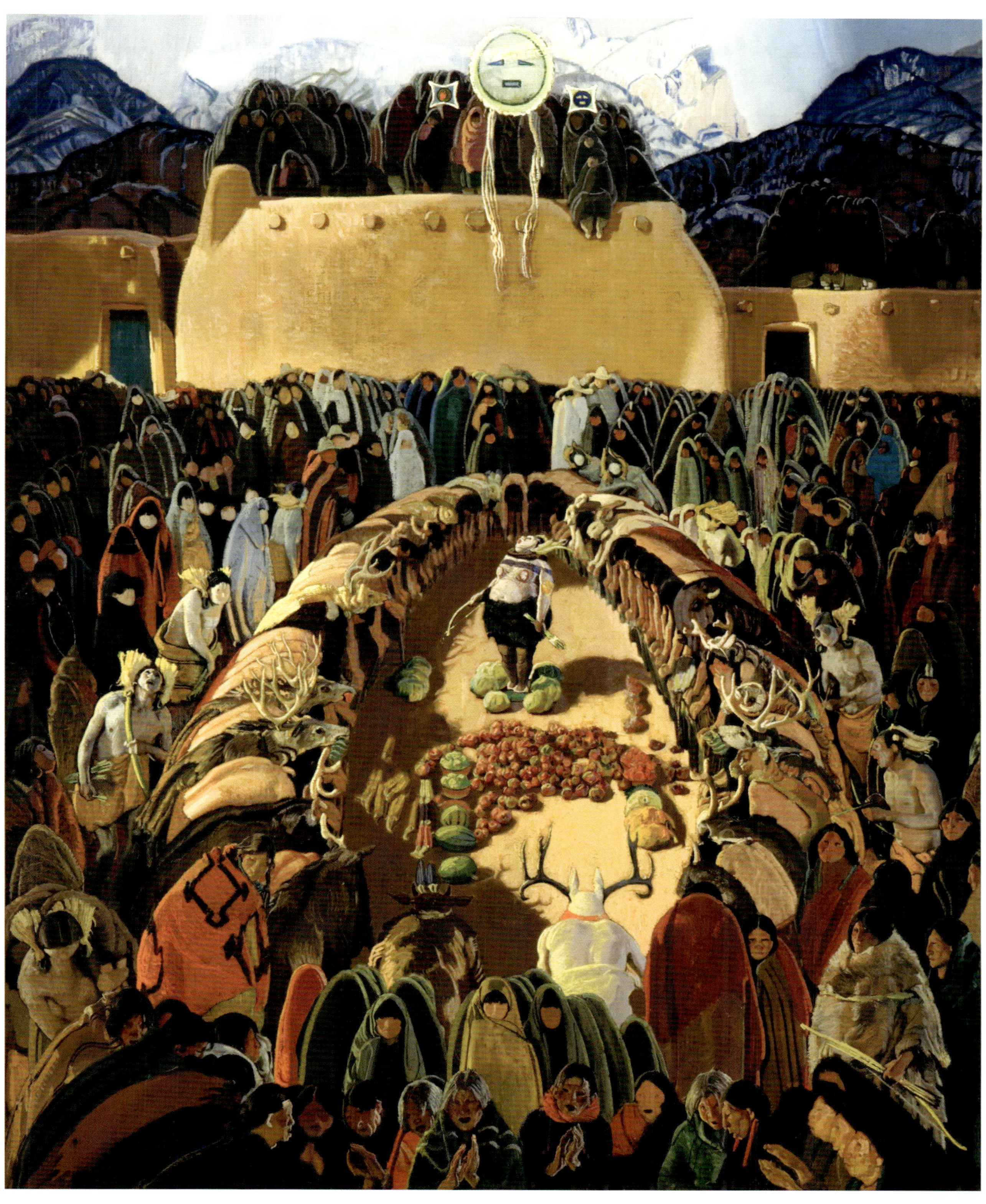

Moon, Morning Star, and Evening Star (originally ***Legend,*** 1923), reworked 1931
Oil on canvas, 50 × 40 inches
Courtesy of the Gilcrease Museum, Tulsa, Oklahoma

When the Indians were allowed to practice their own religious ceremonies, however, Blumenschein was prepared to lavish upon them the richest of colors and to reveal their world as purposeful and highly ordered, pulsing with rhythm and life and essentially joyful. Such is the case with the painting *Moon, Morning Star, and Evening Star* (originally known as *Legend*), which, according to the *Taos Valley News* was completed in March 1922. The local reviewer thought it to be a "very unique painting." Original and daring in composition and modern treatment, it shows the artist to be a close student of Indian life and thought.[53] He proved to be a profoundly empathetic student as well.

Blumenschein has produced a truly generative work. The Deer Dance celebrants, forming an oval around representative elements of the harvest, bow to the earth from which the harvest has come. A *chifonete* or sacred clown, looks skyward at three celestial symbols that hover above the pueblo. The oval might represent birth, fecundity, and renewal, while the moon and stars, replacing the three crosses on Ranchos Church, suggest the wonder of the seasonal cycles.

The artist regarded the painting as possessing a special "virility."[54] Blumenschein described the scene and his depiction of it to Thomas Gilcrease, the painting's eventual owner: "As a dance it is very beautiful; as a story or legend, it will always live: as a work of art, it is the American Indian at his top. The complicated weaving of these fifty or sixty figures, the intricate counter play of the 'Chifonetes' (or clowns), the mobility of slow dance movement and the accompaniment of the singers and drummers produce a whole that, in my mind, equals any folk lore dance in the world."[55] The *Christian Science Monitor*, certainly much to the artist's pleasure, claimed that these Indians were "painted from within . . . not as interesting studio models, but as an inherent part of their surroundings."[56]

Blumenschein's student and fellow painter Alexandre Hogue once wrote that while Blumenschein's portraits were faithful renditions, "when he is interested in the great gatherings at Indian ceremonials he turns to the abstract."[57] This probably occurred with *Moon, Morning Star, and Evening Star* as a reaction to a growing critical ennui with figurative Indian subjects that began to appear in the press. (A *New York Times* review of the 1921 winter exhibition at the National Academy of Design complained that "nowadays there is no Academy without its Indians.")[58] This may have been Blumenschein's way of retaining the association with some of his fellow Taos painters, such as Couse, who that year exhibited *The Corn Ceremony*, a distinctly academic work, next to Blumenschein's *Superstition*.

The Taos Society of Artists, in operation since 1915, made allowance for both approaches to art, modern and academic. To promote the philosophical unity of its members, Blumenschein as president had asked Dunton to write an article on the society, its vision, and its accomplishments.[59] Dunton's essay appeared in the August 1922 issue of the *American Magazine of Art* and sought to answer the question "What does the artist see in Taos?":

> Between Montana and Mexico unquestionably there are spots as beautiful as Taos, where the painter can *think* and stumble upon or dream out his motifs uninterrupted. But to each one of the little group who, a few years ago, organized the Taos Society of Artists there was no other place which lent to them so enduring an appeal—remote from commercialism and the sordid, restful in its peaceful isolation, quiet along its crooked alleys, in the soft shadows of the adobe walls. The mountain rivers sung of happiness. The pines of the peaks breathed a lullaby of sleep.

Beyond that, the Indian and Hispanic people, the "nooks and crannies of the town," the spectacular Rio Grande Canyon, and the dramatic Sangre de Cristo Mountains all appealed to the painter. And, "everywhere the sage, the adobes and the cottonwoods melt together in one harmonious symphony . . . [under] that marvelous, unchanging blue canopy of the sky."[60] When Blumenschein had written on the same theme for the same magazine back in 1917, he had stressed the creation of a "great American School" in Taos, but Dunton's focus was more on unity of mission and harmony of spirit.[61] Yet, in reality, nothing could have been further from the truth. Dunton had resigned from the society before his own article appeared, because of acrimonious interaction between members (Ufer had, in Blumenschein's absence, called him a "bald headed S.O.B." during a meeting), and Blumenschein threatened to quit at the same time, using the excuse that he and Mary had not been properly thanked by the members for his service as president.[62] Blumenschein remained a member, unlike Dunton, but then was forced out for refusing to accept the secretary's post in 1923.

One of the underlying reasons for Blumenschein's departure from the society had to do with the discord between the academic and modernism. The efforts could be seen in a review of the society's 1922 traveling exhibition when it reached St. Louis. There, a critic named Mary Powell put her finger on the problem. "Couse and Sharp show their usual quota of illustrative paintings which have strong popular appeal," she wrote, "[but] B. J. Nordfeldt [a Post-Impressionist painter from Santa Fe and a newly appointed associate member of the society] has burst into Modernism and many . . . turn hurriedly away from the three paintings [he has] shown here."[63] Blumenschein did not care to be a painter of cliché and increasingly found kindred spirits among more radical modernists like Nordfeldt. At the summer meeting of the society that year Blumenschein, Ufer, and Higgins nominated William P. Henderson and Jozef Bakos, two more modernist painters from Santa Fe, to become associate members. They were voted down, however, causing the widening of a rift that had been evident for several years. Blumenschein, Ufer, and Higgins subsequently met with some Santa Fe modernist painters, of which Nordfeldt was a prominent player, and formed the New Mexico Painters. Blumenschein, the organization's founder, became their secretary and used this as an excuse for not being able to take the secretary post of the society, which, by alphabetical rotation, should have been his appointment. He was thus summarily bounced from their ranks.[64]

Blumenschein often took the initiative in his career—he made things happen. This was a prime example of his undaunted ambition. In his role as secretary of the New Mexico Painters, Blumenschein worked hard. He has not only been regarded as the catalyst behind the organization but as its driving force.[65] He presented himself as an enthusiastic and resolute advocate of the group's mission and its members. As an example, he wrote to the Albright Gallery in Buffalo, New York, where he had arranged for their touring exhibition to go in early 1924. His letter included a gracious introduction to the relatively unheralded painter Jozef Bakos whose merits he wanted to bring to the museum's attention. "Personally, I believe he is a great artist," he proffered, "a man of high ideals and willing to 'die for them,' as he says in a recent letter to me."[66]

The New Mexico Painters was described as a "group of men [that] represents the Progressive or Radical Conservative element," according to the *Taos Valley News* in 1923.[67] Blumenschein was proud of the affiliation. "I am not a hard boiled academic," he wrote emphatically to the New York critic Royal Cortissoz that year, and "I have been working for the past year along lines that fellow artists think indicate a big step ahead toward sound art. . . . I was searching to create works of art, not for commerce, but because I had it in me to express."[68] His striving for recognition as a modernist manifested itself in word as well as deed. He was invigorated by his new association, and, over the next few years, the critics began to miss him at the Taos Society of Artists shows, claiming that the exhibitions were substantially weakened by his absence. One reviewer lamented, "now the Society can hardly claim to have the greatest of the Taos artists on its roster."[69]

When people visited Blumenschein's studio during the summer of 1923, they were surprised by the novel direction his paintings had begun to take. A writer from the *Taos Valley News* observed, "The work that this artist is doing now is of a different nature. We do not know for sure but it seems of the cubist character."[70] If not exactly cubist in the formal sense, his paintings like *Dance at Taos* were sufficiently bold in abstract design and reductive in figural treatment to be considered expressionistic. Here four lines of child dancers weave toward the viewer, who looks down on the ceremony as if perched like the women onlookers on an adjacent rooftop. The tilted plane of the picture flattens the perspective, and the deep rich colors of the sinuous processions evoke a sense of rhythms provided by the unseen drums propelling the dance. This personalized treatment of richly saturated color and undulating forms was used by Blumenschein to express the sense of rhythm the dance movements conveyed. To explore this expressionist evocation of rhythmic dance patterns, he painted a companion piece, *Indian Dance,* at the same time.

Dance at Taos was also something more than aesthetic experimentation. It showed, as had *Moon, Morning Star, and Evening Star*, that he, in support of cultural relativism, was firmly against the BIA's efforts at acculturation and, more precisely, eschewed their attempts through legislation to expropriate Pueblo lands (the Bursum Bill of 1921) and restrict Native dancing and religious ceremony (Circular 1665 of 1921 and Supplement to Circular 1665 of 1923), under the mandate of Charles Burke, then commissioner of Indian affairs.[71] Burke and his Christian missionary followers felt that Indian ceremonies were lewd and injurious. Children, he felt, would be negatively influenced by what he called "Indian offenses." Blumenschein joined a large group of liberal thinkers from Taos and beyond to fight Burke's program. Writers, artists, and activists like Mabel Dodge Luhan, Mary Austin, Charles Lummis, John Collier, and D. H. Lawrence spearheaded the campaign to preserve Indian land and ceremonial rights. Blumenschein's paintings of such rituals as the Taos Children's Dance and the Deer Dance seen in *Moon, Morning Star, and Evening Star* were part of his contribution to the cause.

The Blumenscheins hosted a big dinner dance in September, then departed for Brooklyn later that fall to see that Helen settled into the rhythm of school with her eastern peers. Mary attended classes in jewelry design and silversmithing at the Pratt Institute over the winter, and Blumenschein worked on sketches for a set of three murals being commissioned for the Missouri State Capitol in Jefferson City.

The mural project was the brainchild of Oscar Berninghaus. He had completed two murals for the building in 1921, and the Capitol Decoration Commission was searching for other artists to participate. In 1923 the president of the commission, Dr. John Pickard asked Berninghaus where he might find additional qualified painters to help complete the job. Berninghaus replied, "Come to Taos next summer and I'll show you a whole colony of them."[72] Following an August visit to Taos, the committee selected Berninghaus and six other painters, including Couse, Phillips, Ufer, Higgins, Dunton, and Blumenschein (the latter two who were no longer members of the society), each to submit three sketches for large lunette murals for interior arches. By February 1924 the *Taos Valley News* proudly announced:

> The members of the Taos Society of Artists have been recognized with an honor never before extended to a single association. . . . The Capitol Decoration Committee, after scouring the whole country, has decided to give the honor of this artistic work to the artists of Taos. . . . More and more the talented artists of Taos are being recognized all through the country and those who know them best will recognize the fact that nowhere in this country of any other are there more gifted canvas decorators than in our own unique town. . . . They are the front ranks of today's artists, and . . . this honor extended is a well deserved recognition of exceptional ability of the Taos Art Colony.[73]

Completing those commissions would keep all the artists busy for months and would provide a common cause for a group of men who were often rather rancorous by dint of divergent personality and competitive impulse.

Blumenschein's three murals were illustrated together in the final report of the commission in 1928. They bore the cumbersome titles of *Meeting of Washington Irving and Kit Carson at Arrow Rock Tavern*, *The Indian Trader at Fort Carondelet*, and *Return of the French Officer and His Indian Bride to Fort Orleans*. Of these, *The Indian Trader at Fort Carondelet*, although perhaps the least compelling of the narratives, was considered the "masterpiece."[74] According to the Pickard Commission's report, "The rich deep color, the dramatic movement, the well balanced composition, make this one of the most notable of this entire series of historical paintings."[75] Everything that Blumenschein wished to have recognized in his paintings—color, design, rhythm, and balance—was here applauded. As a later extension on the commission, Blumenschein was asked to produce two full-length portraits of two of the state's most distinguished historical figures: the pioneer master painter George Caleb Bingham, from his imagination, and General John J. Pershing, who posed for the artist twice.

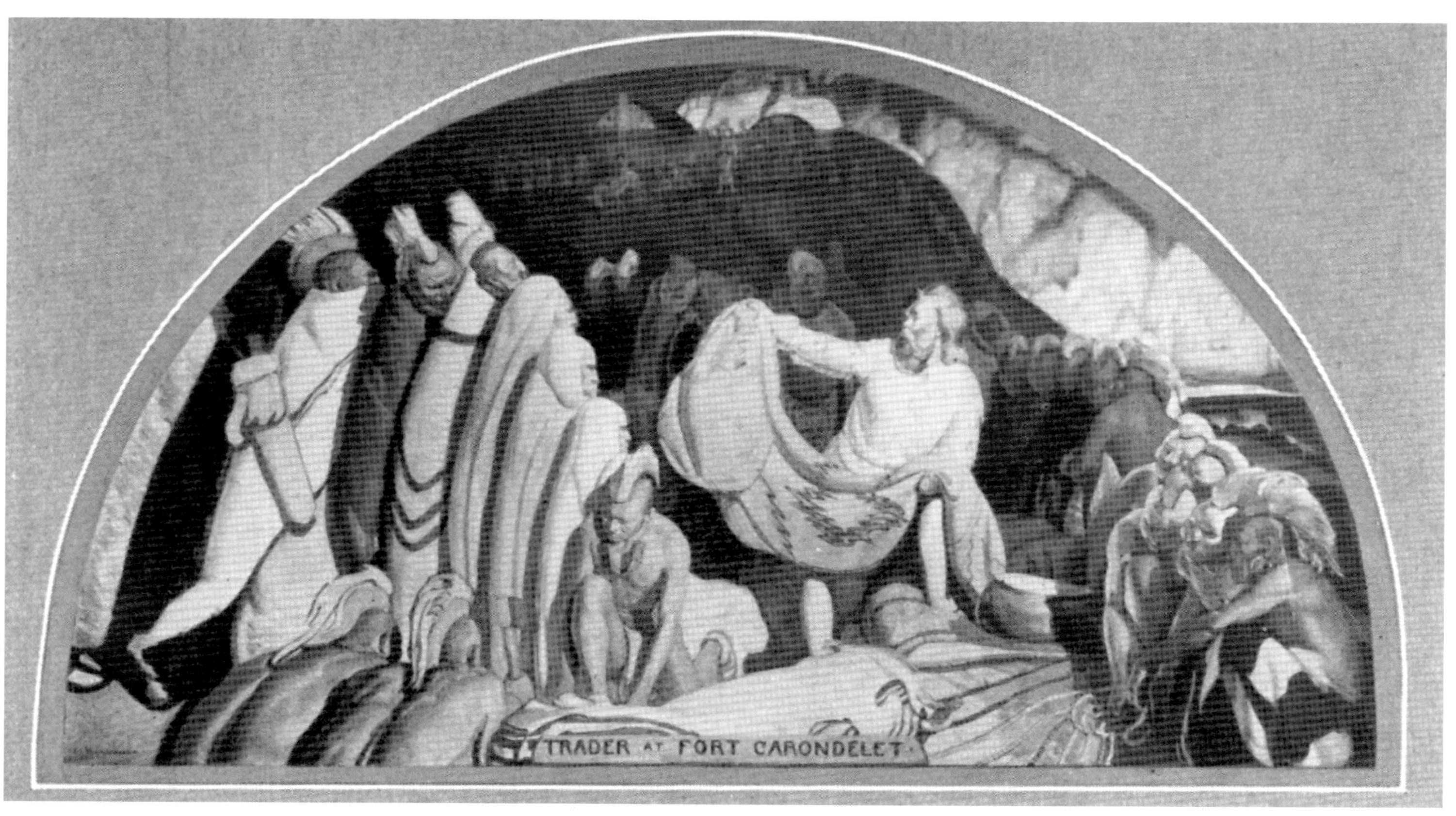

Trader at Fort Carondelet, mural at Missouri State Capitol, from John Pickard *Report of the Capitol Decoration Commission, 1917–1918* (1928). Courtesy of the Missouri State Archives, Jefferson City.

The summer of 1924 must have been a golden time for Blumenschein. "Crazy," he wrote, "to get [to] the snow on the mountains"—a landscape feature with the kind of patterning and light that would later inspire two prize-winning paintings. Driving west in a new Cadillac, he arrived in Taos in early May.[76] Helen and Mary arrived a month later. They declared their intention to do something novel—spend the coming winter in Taos, allowing Helen to try the local schools. Blumenschein brought with him three new baseball bats, looking forward to an exciting season.[77]

Taos increasingly attracted art advocate writers other than the painters themselves. One such author, J. Pennington wrote for *The Mentor* that Taos was "the painter's paradise of the South-West." The artists, beginning with Blumenschein and Phillips, "found in Taos not only the primitive ways of life and art, the dream of every artist the world over; they found not only color so dazzling and so pure that it defies and eludes the brush; not only native models crowding about their very thresholds; but above all they found a simple, unrestrained, inexpensive, and unpretentious way of living."[78] The artists,

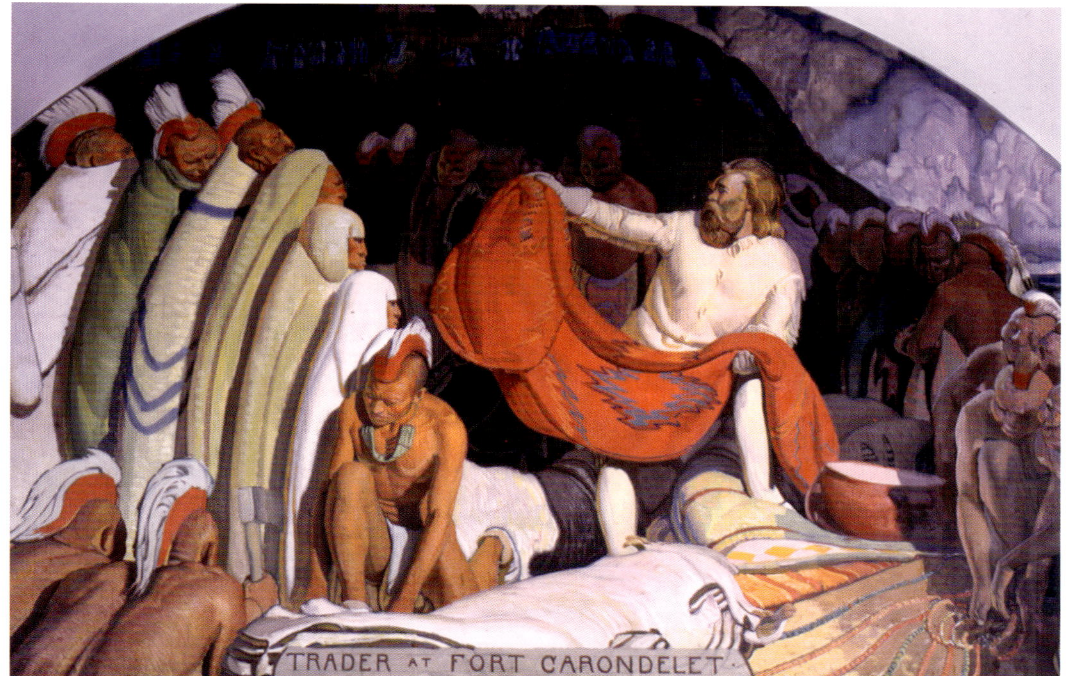

Trader at Fort Carondelet, 1924, oil on canvas. Missouri State Capitol Art Collection. Courtesy of the Missouri State Archives, Jefferson City.

Pennington observed, lived in harmony with their surroundings. They all resided in adobe structures—Sharp in an abandoned church and Dunton with a Pueblo-style studio "having a ladder by which one entered the upper story." He noted that "Ernest L. Blumenschein has transformed one of these native mud houses into a low, flower wreathed villa."[79] Helen, in later years, described their house and its evolving presence:

> Our house, built of adobe, was one that was strung out in a straight line forming part of the south wall of town. Father bought four rooms of this old place from [Herbert] 'Buck' Dunton, who had settled there several years before. As time went on and the old occupants of the rooms on either side of us died, we would purchase those rooms, until finally we had 11 rooms, enough to supply a studio room for each of us and have bedrooms for our summer guests. Of course, in those days you had plenty of hired help, and in that way we became acquainted with our Spanish and Indian neighbors.
>
> Many New Mexicans seemed to be accomplished carpenters in those days. So it was no problem re-roofing our 3,000 sq. feet and adding,

after 1931, a kitchen, two baths, plus a workshop for my mother, who had switched her profession from oil painting to jewelry making in 1922. We furnished the house with a combination of European furniture and simple New Mexico couches, chairs, and a cedar dining room that Mr. Sharp had ordered made, and did not like! We planted hollyhocks on the south side of the house from which we had an unbroken view of the Taos Valley, all the way to the Picuris Peaks. To the southwest we could see the cut-off top of the Pedernal Mountain, some 50 miles away as the crow flies.[80]

Epimenio Tenorio died at about this time, allowing Blumenschein to add a twelve-foot addition to his studio, with a new large north window to accommodate the mural work for the Missouri State Capitol.[81]

Not all of Blumenschein's time was taken up with murals, though. In the National Academy of Design exhibition of winter 1924, Blumenschein exhibited a large landscape titled *Trail through the Canyon* (it was repainted in 1929 and retitled *Landscape with Indian Camp,* and no record exists of how it originally looked). This was an exhilarating swirl of light and form, where the figures, though engaging in their movement and prominent in their foreground positioning, are rather subservient to the billowing trees and the landscape. The year before, his academy submission had been a pure landscape picture, *The Lake*, and this trend in Blumenschein's work may have been a response to the fact that Indian themes in art continued to be disparaged. An *Art News* review of the Taos Society of Artists exhibit in Detroit in March 1924 had claimed, "The Indian, as a painter's subject, has gone a bit stale, and it is too bad to let the ubiquitous Couse red skin dominate in the Taos exhibition. Most of the other men are doing more interesting work."[82] A visitor to Phillips's studio in March indicated that he, like Couse, had either not gotten the message or did not care. On Phillips's easel and walls were six new paintings, all of them strong Indian subjects.[83] Though Blumenschein was no longer a member of the society, and therefore was not represented in their shows, he definitely fit with the other men

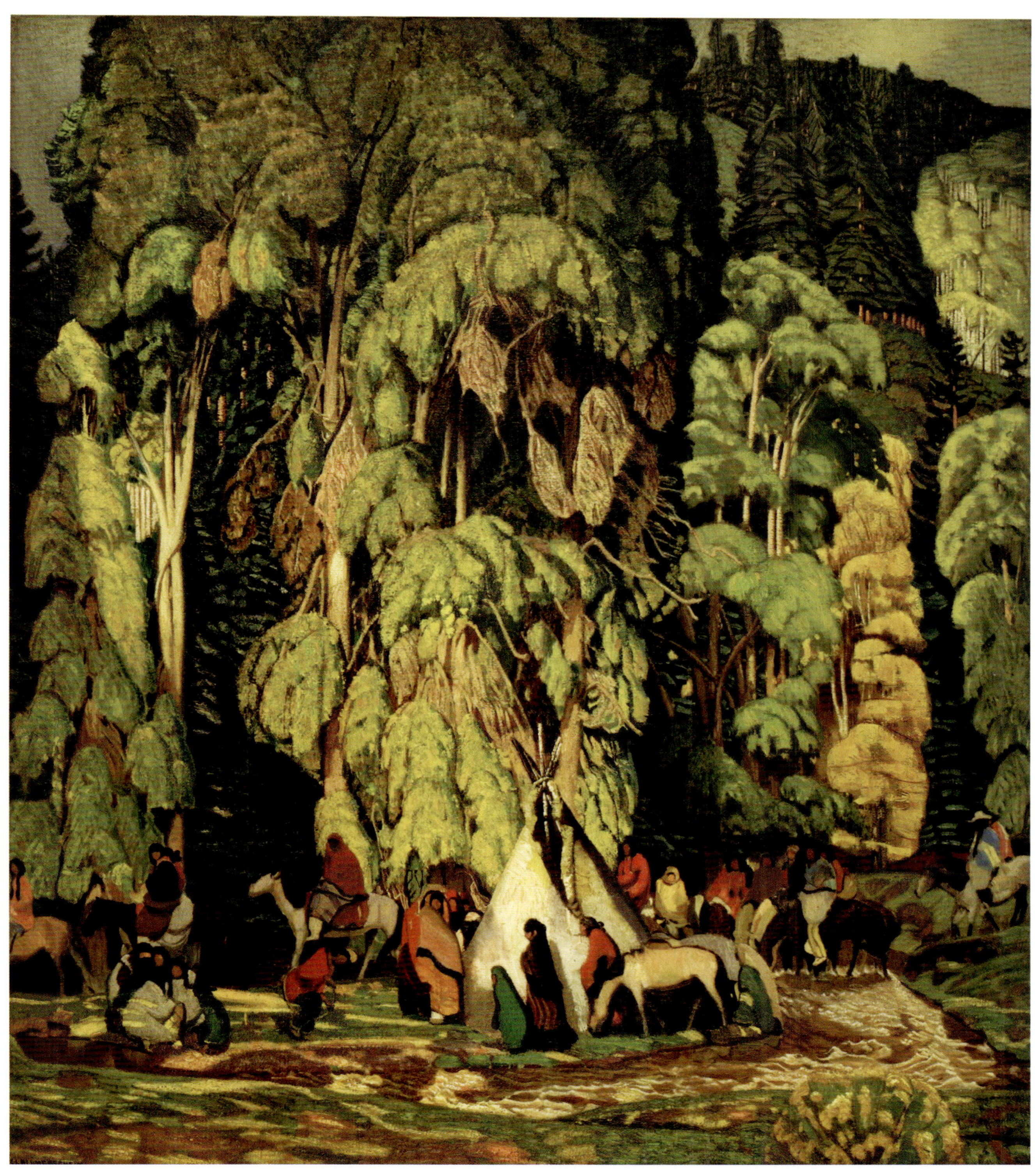

Landscape with Indian Camp (originally *Trail through the Canyon,* 1920), reworked 1929
Oil on canvas, 50 × 43 inches
Courtesy of the Denver Museum of Nature & Science,
Denver, Colorado (A1822.1)

and, arguably, was doing more interesting work. He had begun to concentrate attention on landscapes.

The Lake, though half the size of *Trail through the Canyon* and nearly three times less expensive ($900 as opposed to $2,500), was also a remarkable tour de force. Heavy thunderclouds with crisp, silvery linings and deeply shadowed lower contours dominate a rocky, high mountain ridge. In the foreground sage-dappled hills roll toward a placid lake, providing an impressive contrast in nature's moods. The painting pulsates—its air is as electric as it is fresh. The academy must have cherished it, for after it traveled to Worchester, Salem, and back to New York in the mid-1920s, Blumenschein offered it as his diploma presentation in 1927 when the academy made him a full member.

Helen's pet burros and the windmill next door at the Harwood home inspired Blumenschein to paint a large, exhibition-size painting, *Three Burros—Extravaganza*, in the mid-1920s. According to the artist's ledgers, after the painting was exhibited at the National Academy in 1926 and at the Art Institute of Chicago in 1927, the Metropolitan Museum of New York requested it for purchase consideration. The trustees rejected the painting, and its later destiny remains unknown. However, one smaller work, *Two Burros*, conveys a feeling of color and mood the artist set forth in the larger painting.

Snow-blanketed land had aroused Blumenschein's interest months earlier and resulted in two paintings, both initially titled *First Snow.* In one of these small works, an unseasonal autumn snowfall covers golden cottonwood and still-green willow and fruit tree leaves on the neighboring Randall property. The encroaching low light of winter accentuates the masses created by the house and outbuildings. The rounded shapes of the snow-covered trees set against the square forms of the buildings create fresh patterns and forms, and the mountains rise up in the picture frame to become monumental in scale. This familiar landscape is renewed in the artist's eyes by the advent of winter, yielding a transitional work in which Blumenschein worked out several formal problems.

As he had promised when he arrived in New Mexico in spring 1924, Blumenschein planned to spend the following winter in Taos. Helen and

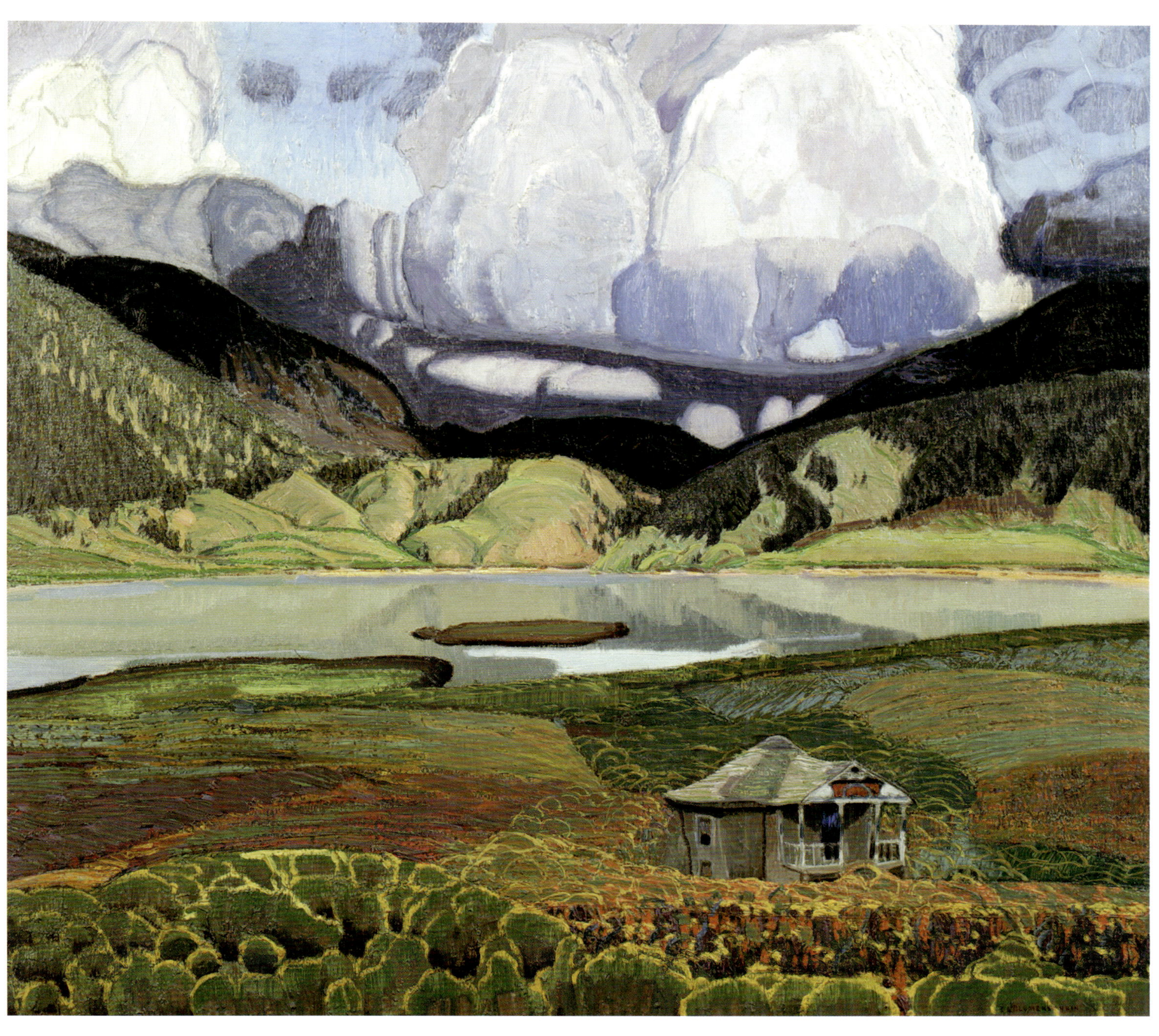

The Lake, ca. 1927
Oil on canvas, 24 1/8 × 27 inches
Courtesy of the National Academy Museum, New York (112-P)

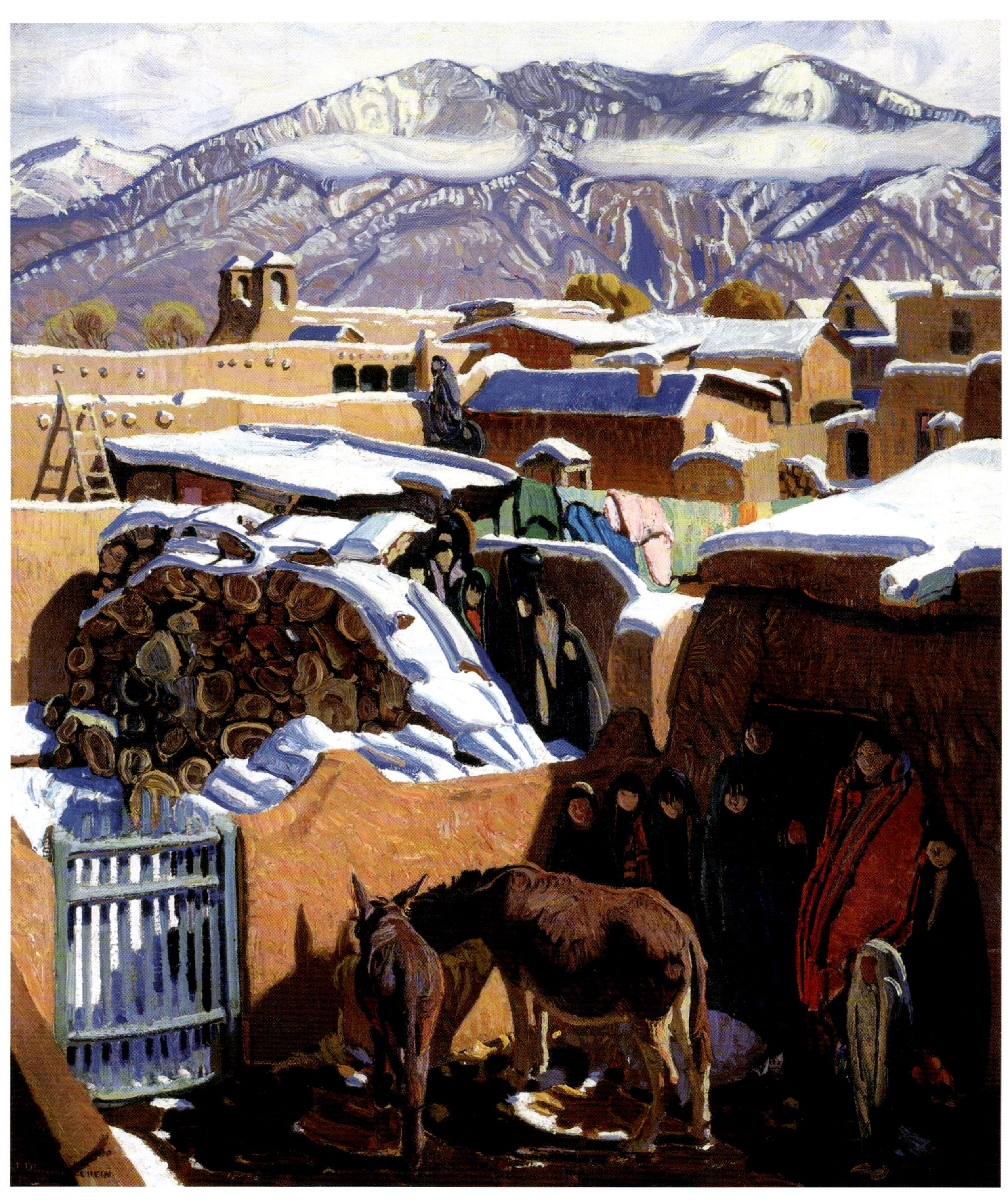

Two Burros, ca. 1925
Oil on canvas, 30 × 25 inches
Private collection

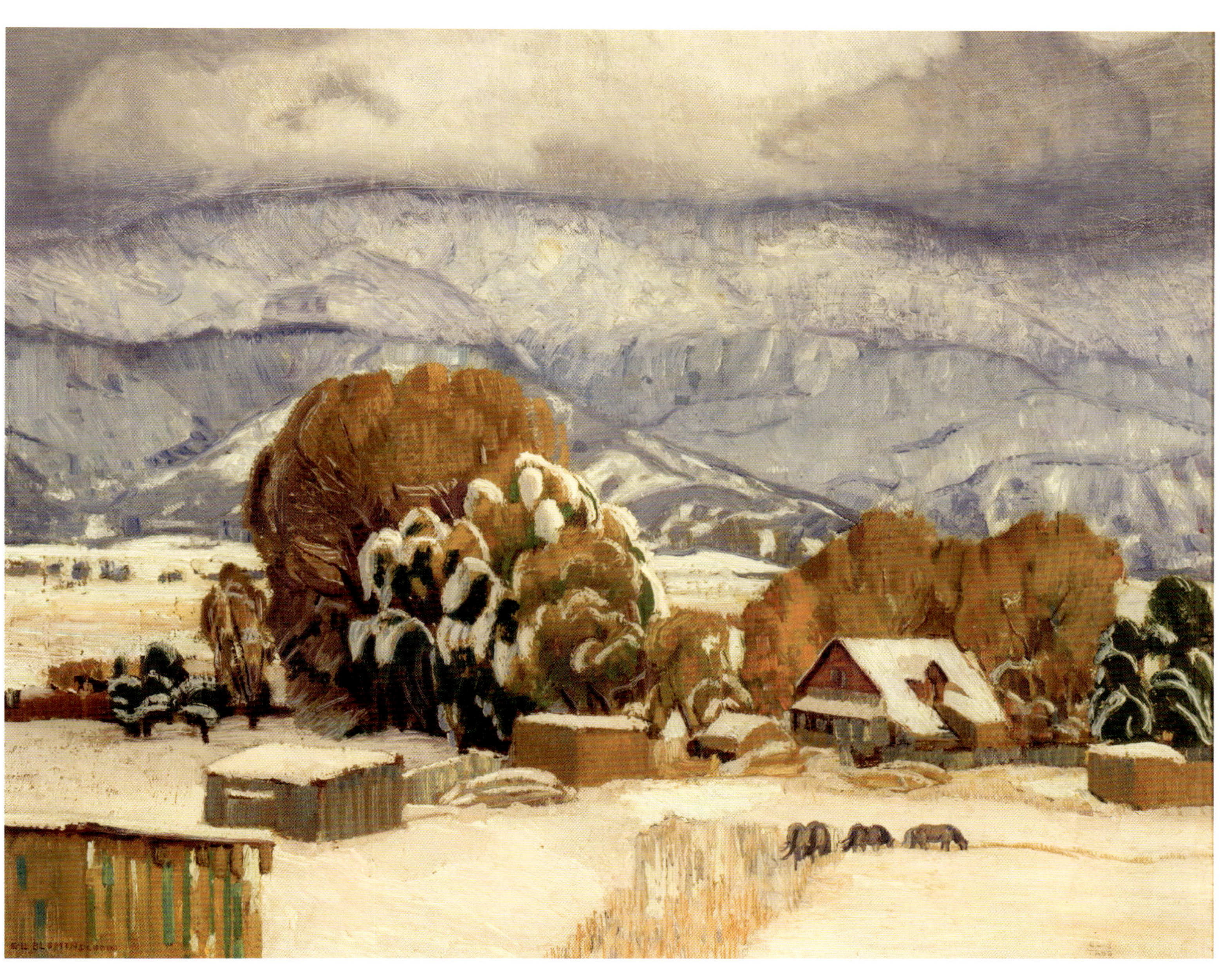

First Snow, ca. 1924
Oil on canvas, 17⅛ × 21 inches
Courtesy of Robert Stamm

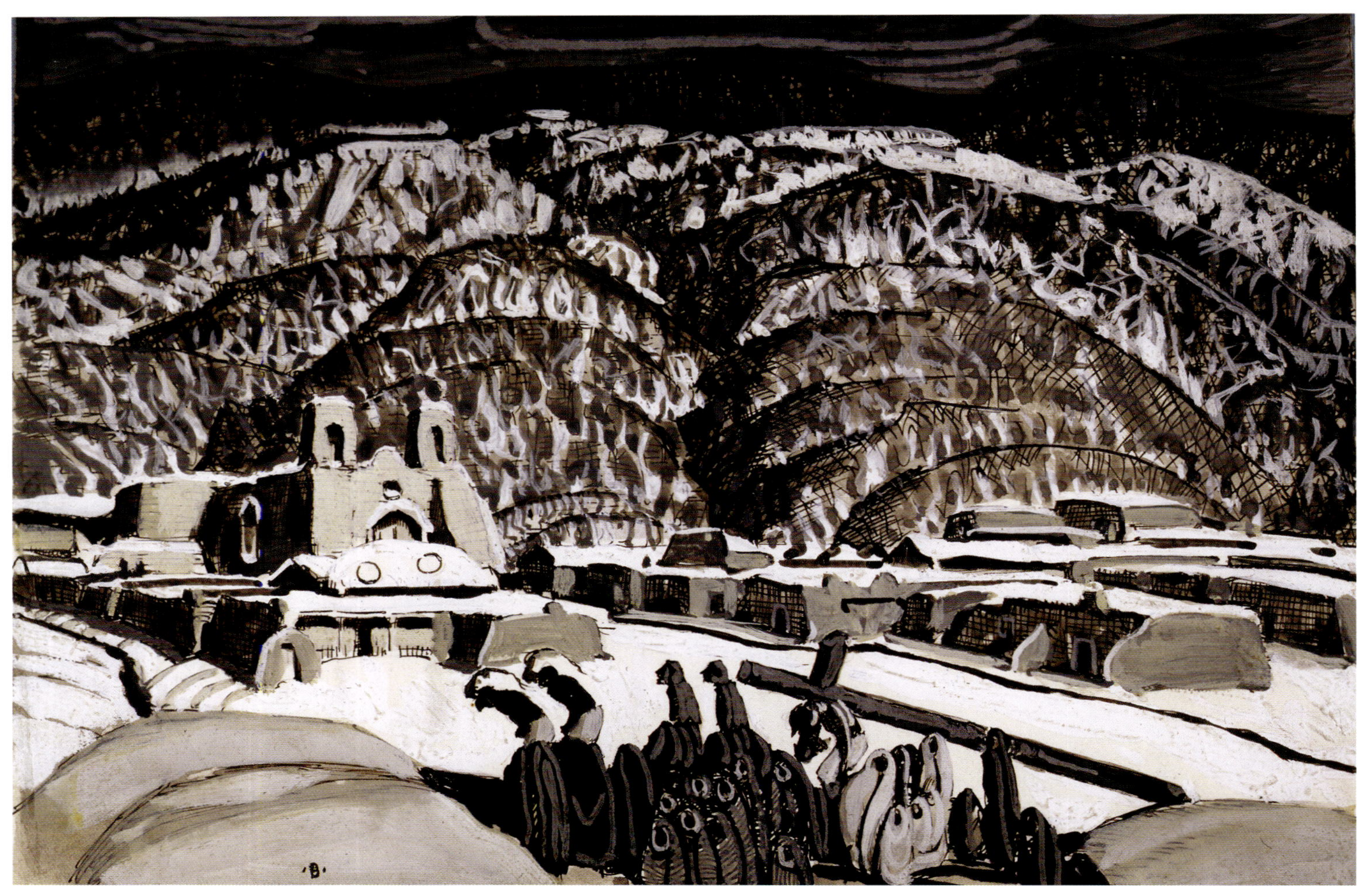

Penitente Procession (study for *Sangre de Cristo Mountains*), ca. 1925; ink, watercolor, Chinese white on paper mounted on paper; 12 × 8⅞ inches. Collection of the New Mexico Museum of Art, Santa Fe. Gift of Helen Greene Blumenschein, 1985.

Mary remained until late January, but the artist persevered well into March. It was during those winter months that he produced one of his true landscape masterpieces, *Sangre de Cristo Mountains*.

Actually, the painting was probably started in 1924. Blumenschein once described the process behind the production of this large oil to an enthusiastic, hometown Dayton audience. As reported in the *Dayton Journal*:

> The inspiration for this rendering came one late afternoon following a day of snowfall. A peculiar light fell over the little Mexican village leaving the mountainous background in shadow. The next day Mr. Blumenschein made a small [color] sketch of his impression. This appears in the present exhibition near the large painting. With the sketch in hand, the large 50x60 canvas was begun. The village was arranged to

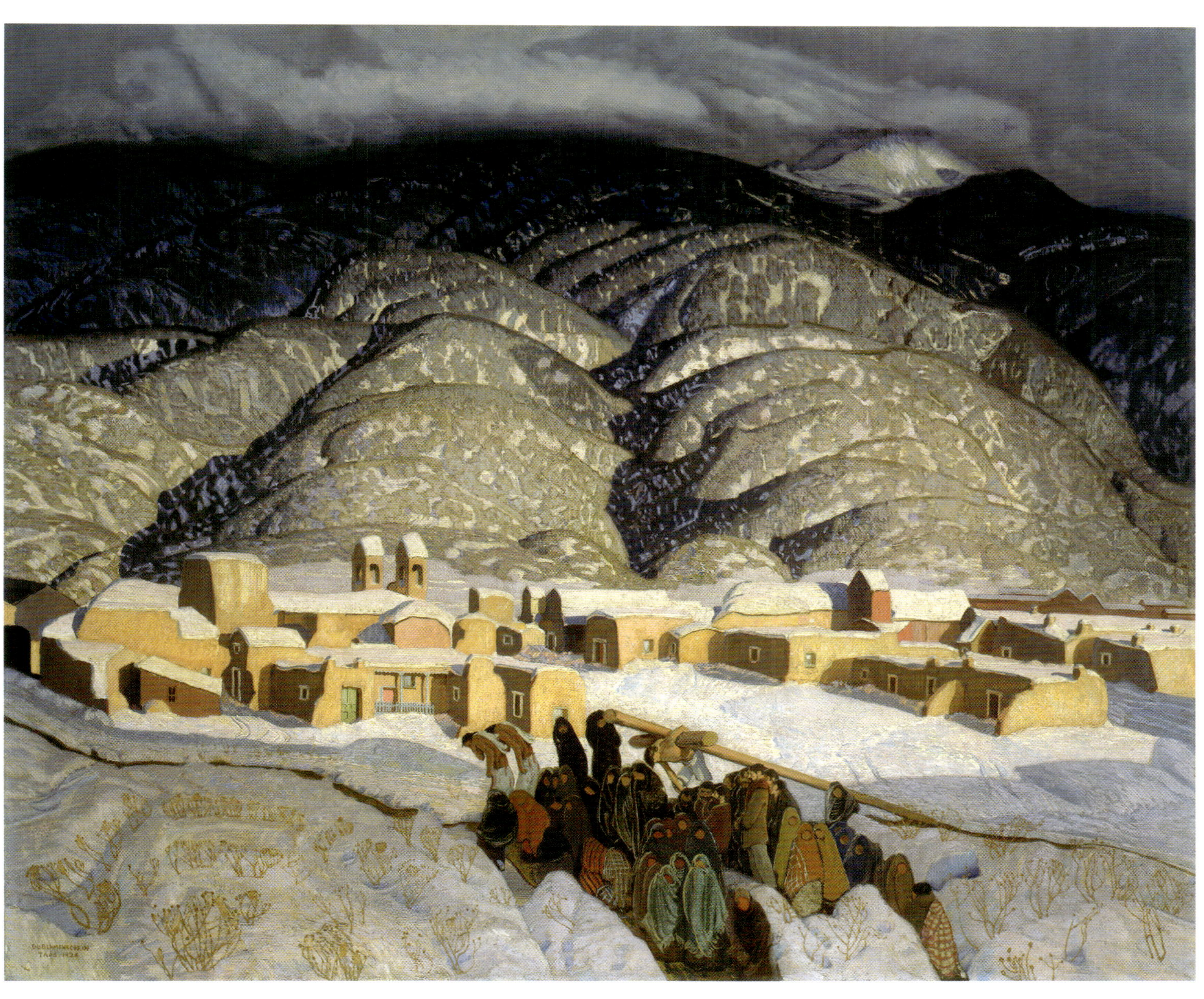

Sangre de Cristo Mountains, 1925
Oil on canvas, 50⅛ × 60 inches
Courtesy of The Anschutz Collection
Photograph by William J. O'Connor

> suit the composition and the color spotting developed through feeling. In the midst of the work Mr. Blumenschein realized he could go no further until he might again study a similar occasion of snow and light. For this he had to wait a year. When the same phenomenon of light appeared the artist was ready to study it. The picture was finished after four months of actual work upon it.[84]

So it would seem that at least part of the reason for his extended winter stay was to finish this painting. According to Blumenschein's records, the work was completed in early March 1925. He put a tag of three thousand dollars on it, a price that was soon raised to five thousand (the highest value of any painting in this period) after it won a second Altman Prize for him at the spring National Academy of Design exhibition in 1925.

Sangre de Cristo Mountains is historic in narrative and modern in treatment. According to Hogue, the canvas portrays the old Hispanic village of Taos as it was long before Phillips and Blumenschein ever saw it.[85] Called Don Fernando de Taos, the old town appealed to the artist historically as part of his efforts to preserve adobe architecture in northern New Mexico. As such, it was a tribute to the area's past and a plea for continuance of its architectural integrity into the future. The Penitentes and their onlookers, who somberly process across the foreground of the painting, speak also to historic traditions. By 1925 the religious practices of this sect had been outlawed by the Catholic Church. In the painting, the celebrants are depicted in shadow, their bowed figures mirrored in the contours of the distant hills and darkly shrouded mountains.

Hogue felt that Blumenschein had employed a "highly sophisticated technique" adapted to "a superb composition."[86] One art critic of the day, Jean Mowat of the *Chicago Evening Post*, emphasized that scenes like this of New Mexico's winter season grasped something different. "It may be the newer trend of modernism," she concluded.[87] Since by definition, Blumenschein equated the ascendancy of design over narrative with the notion of modernism, Taos's winter color and light along with the mountains' bold reliefs and the architectectonic

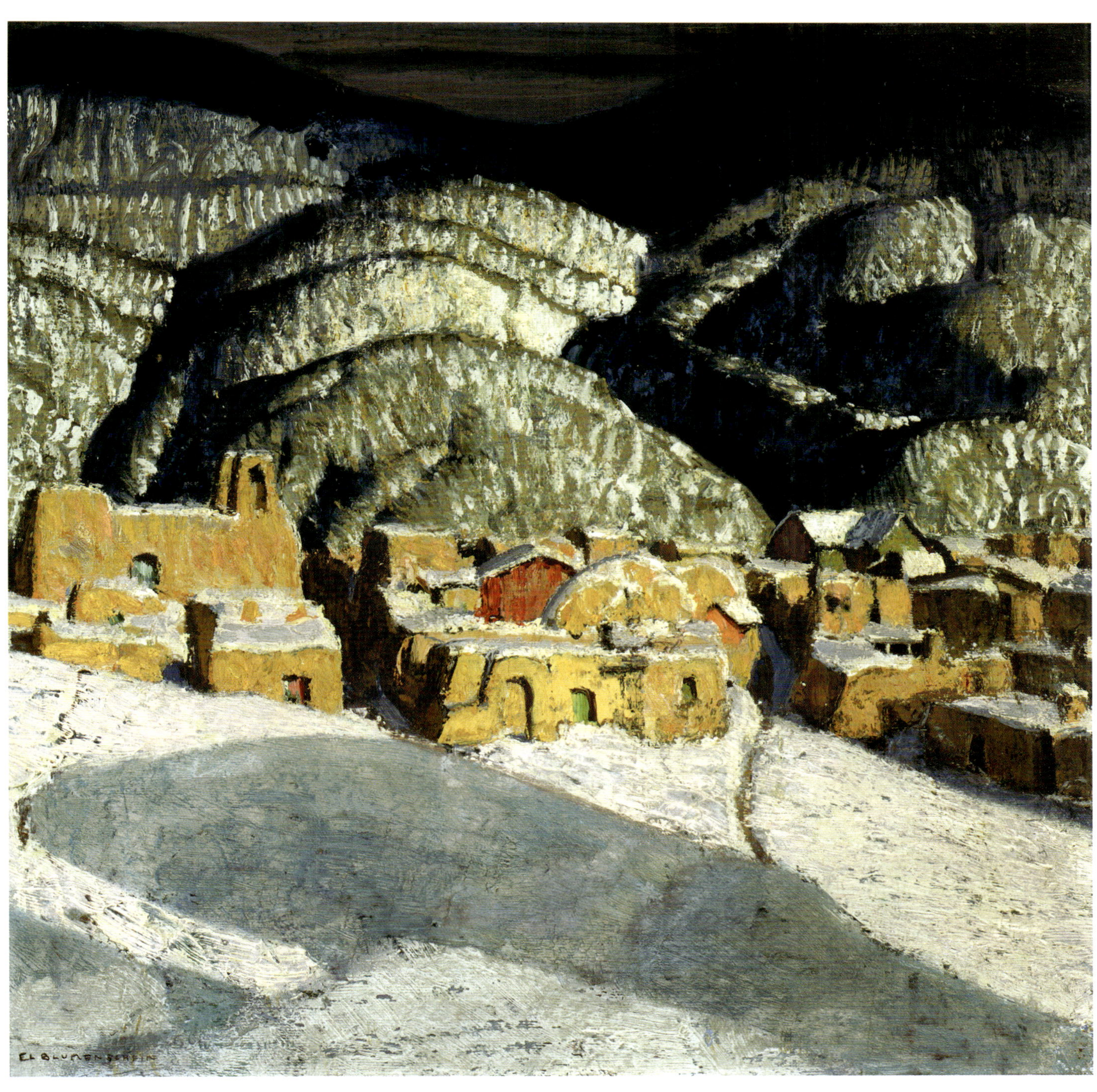

Village in Winter (study for *Sangre de Cristo Mountains*), 1925
Oil on panel, 13½ × 13½ inches
Private collection

masses of the town's adobe buildings closely fit Mowat's observation. When the *New York Times* reviewed the painting, it confirmed Blumenschein's prime aspiration. "Here we get design cast for the leading part," it concluded.[88]

In the mid-1920s Blumenschein began a series featuring a single Pueblo Indian model. The beauty of Taos women had been proclaimed from the days of the French fur trappers in the 1700s. The model for *Girl in Rose,* whose name has not yet been discovered, appears in two other paintings, *Woman in Blue* and *Indian Girl Seated by Oven.* Audiences across the country were exposed to the beauty that Blumenschein captured when these three portraits traveled throughout the United States from 1927 to 1931 as part of the Grand Central Art Galleries' exhibition of his work. Here, as in *Woman in Blue*, the artist paints a half-length frontal portrait against a tepee liner with glyphic designs, putting the woman in a context much like the art nouveau portraits of another painter, Winold Reiss, a contemporary chronicler of Montana's Blackfeet people.

After Blumenschein had executed the three paintings of a Pueblo woman, he may have thought to offset the feminine with his *Portrait of a Taos Indian.* The setting—architectonic rectangles of adobe walls—places the model outdoors but still confined to a more intimate space, enclosed within the pueblo village, with spruce forests rising beyond. The repetition of rounded forms in the head and encircling blanket play against the blocks of adobe, with the verticality of bluffs and trees leading the eye to the top of the picture plane. This shows Blumenschein's use of repetitive patterns, a modernist device he adopted.

Once Blumenschein had separated himself from the Taos Society of Artists, he was increasingly more open for experimentation. He, along with Higgins, explored new and innovative approaches to landscape painting. Blumenschein's oil study *Green Aspens* dates from around 1925. Its naturalism is sufficiently selective and reductive in view to make it a logical precursor for a boldly abstract larger allegorical painting that took shape that year, *Decorative Landscape with Figures—Adam and Eve.* As a mythic construct, this oil resembled a number of biblical theme paintings that Higgins produced around that time such as *Adam and Eve.*[89] Reminiscent of Arthur Davies's fantasies that were seen at the Armory

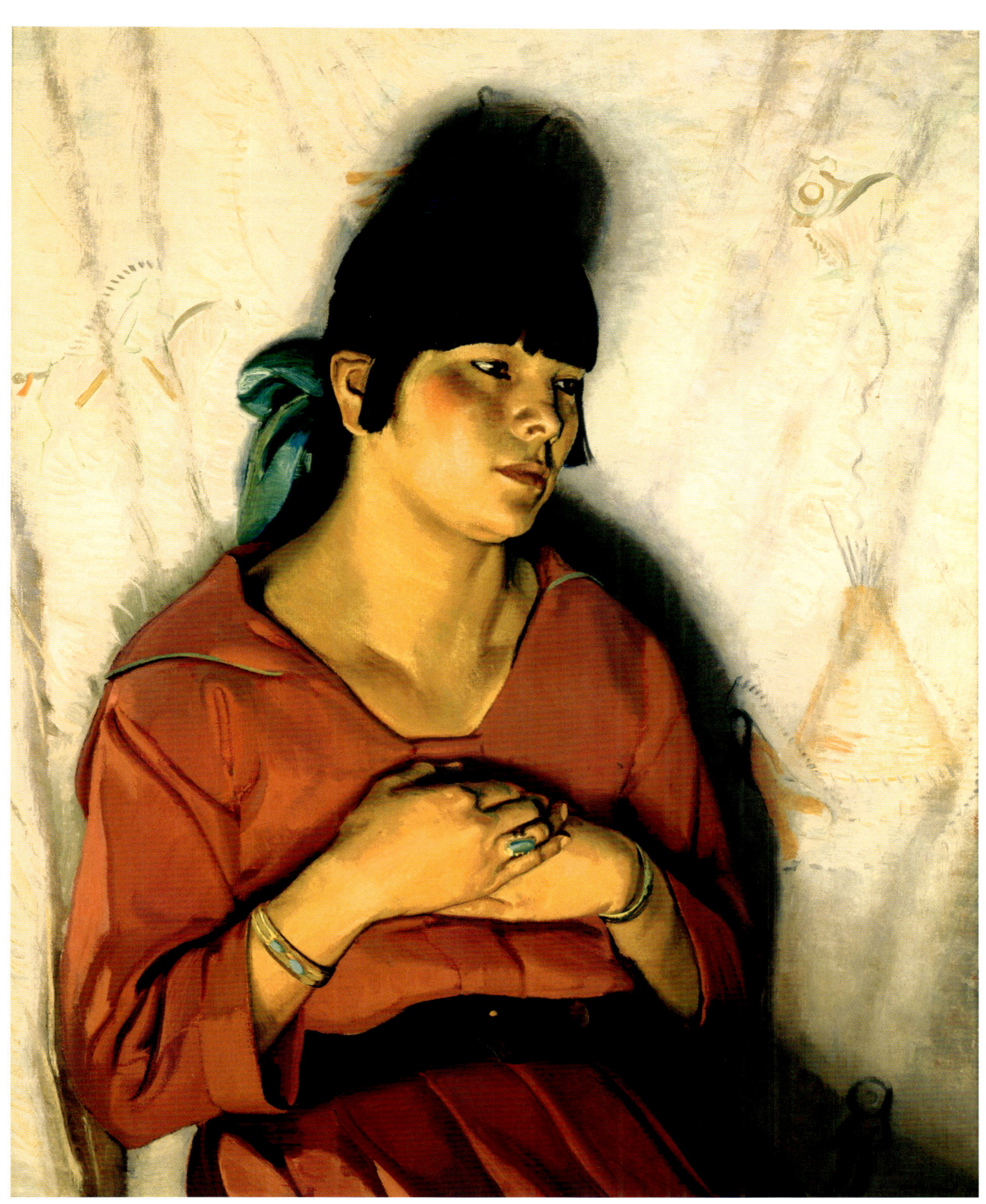

Girl in Rose, 1926
Oil on canvas, 30 × 25 inches
Courtesy of the Lunder Collection,
Colby College Museum of Art, Waterville, Maine

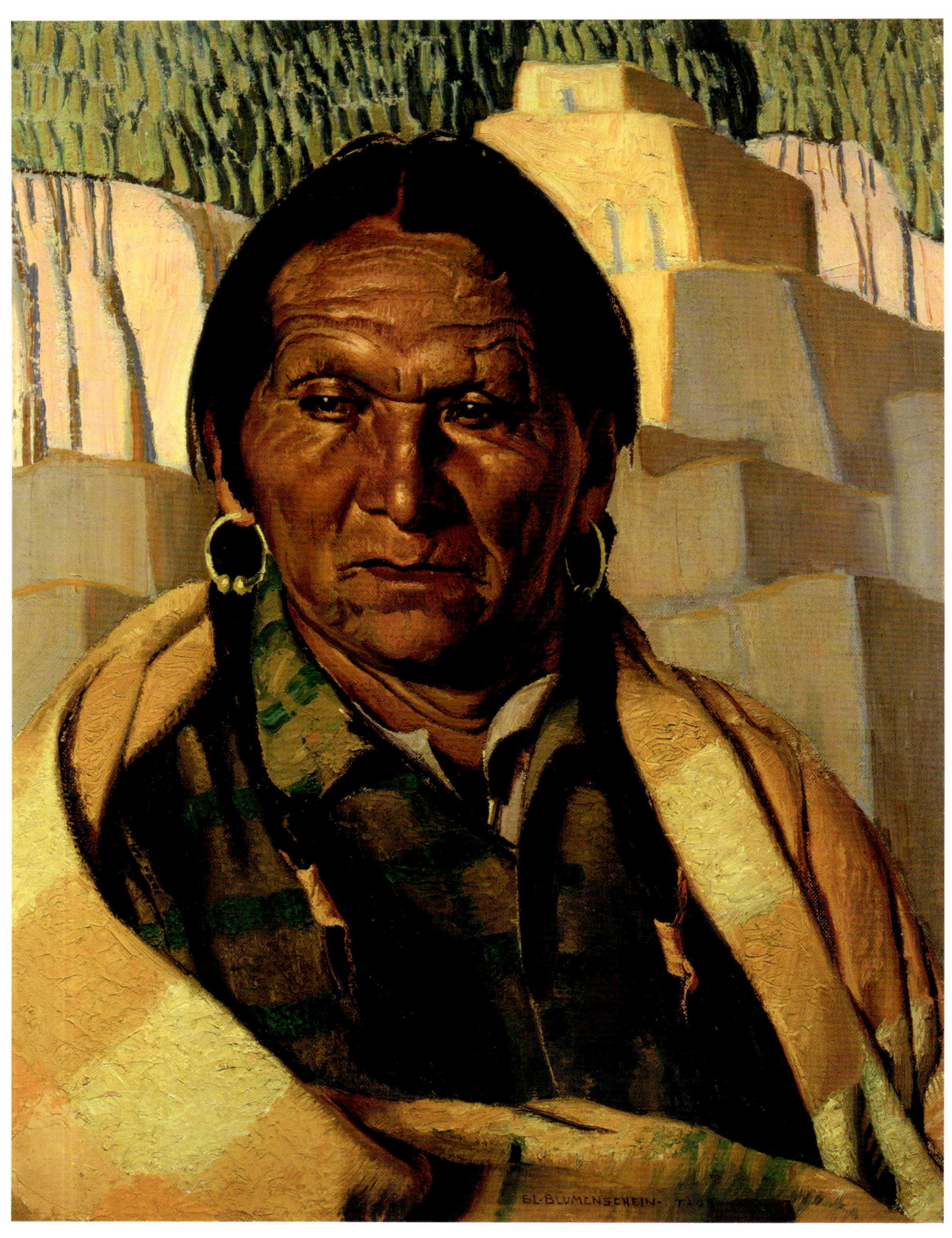

Portrait of a Taos Indian, ca. 1929
Oil on canvas, 20¼ × 15¼ inches
Courtesy of the Gerald Peters Gallery, Santa Fe, New Mexico

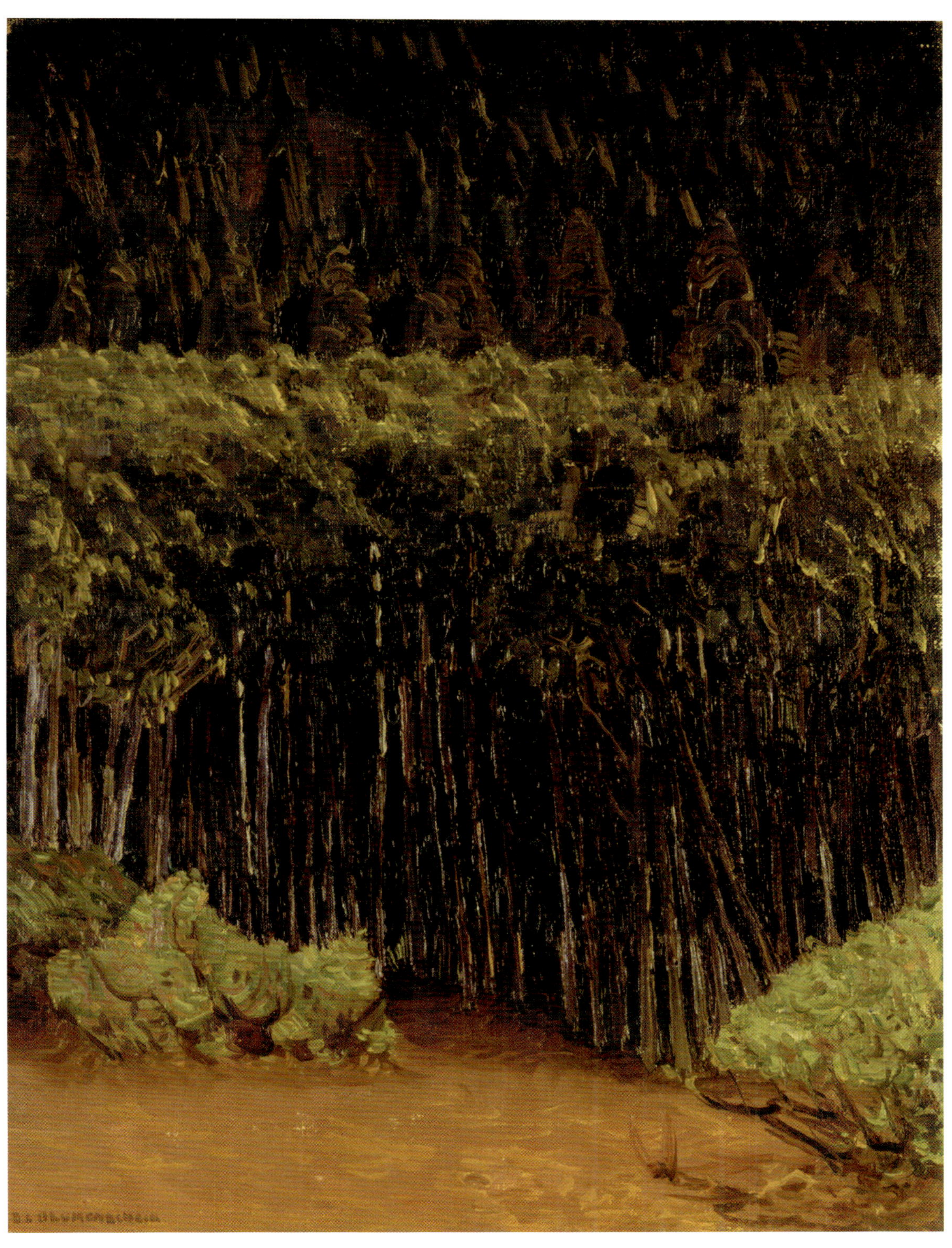

Green Aspen, 1935
Oil on canvas mounted on board, 15⅞ × 12 inches
Courtesy of the Stark Museum of Art, Orange, Texas (31.30/1)

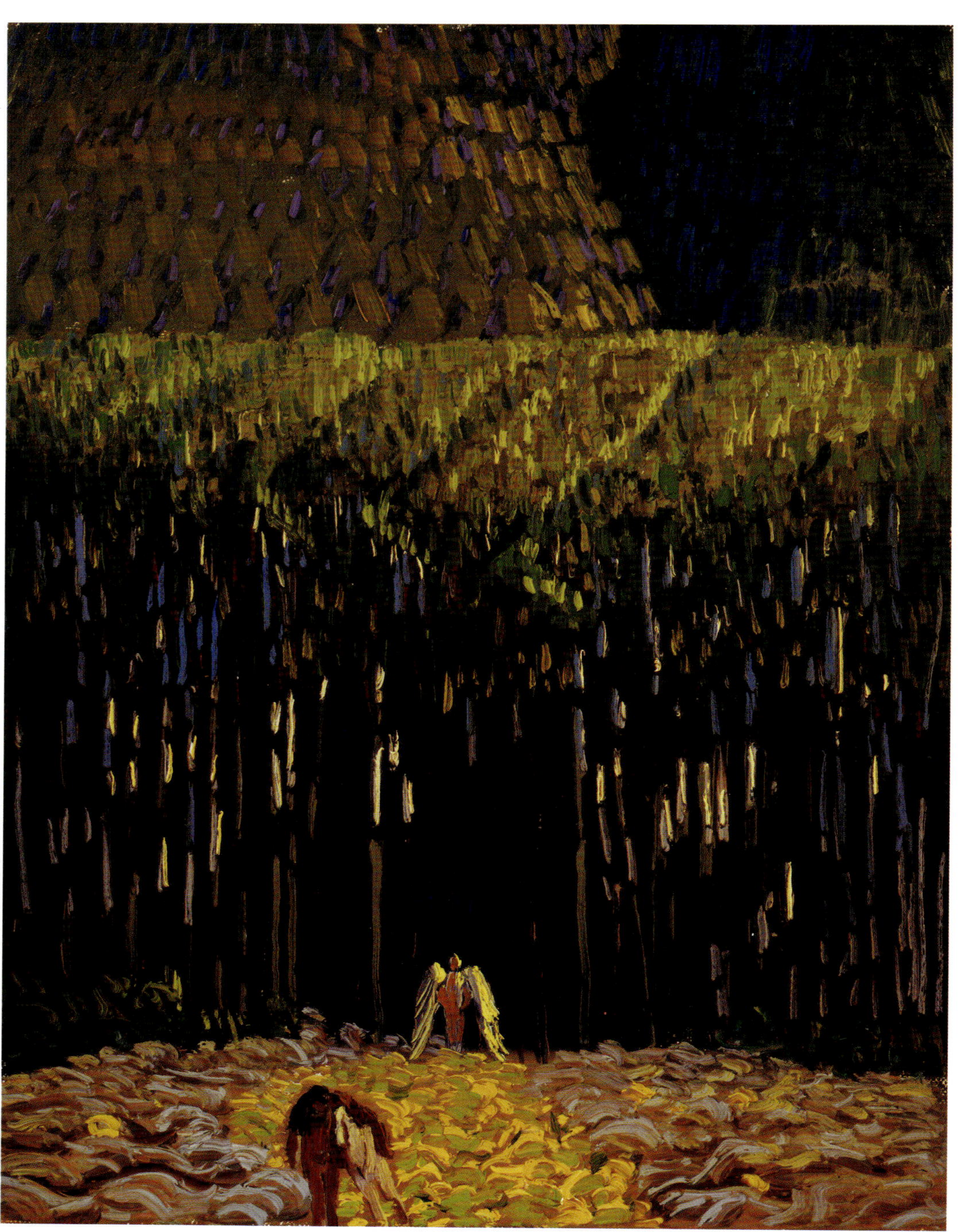

Untitled (study for ***Decorative Landscape with Indians***), 1935, oil on panel, 16 × 12 inches. Collection of the New Mexico Museum of Art, Santa Fe. Gift of Helen Greene Blumenschein, 1964.

Show a decade earlier, Higgins's mythological paintings were whimsical and dainty. Blumenschein's, to the contrary, were bold and pointedly focused. The powerful linear interplay of the aspen trunks surrounding the Avenging Angel (taken from Milton's *Paradise Lost*) and the cantilevering foliage are abstract and planar, though rooted in the naturalism of sketches like *Green Aspens* or another untitled similar study taken from nature.

Over the next several years *Decorative Landscape* continually positioned Blumenschein as a modernist. For example, when exhibited at the Noonan and

Kocian Gallery in St. Louis in 1928, it was touted in a headline of the local *Post-Dispatch* as modernistic art with a rare element of meaning. "St. Louisans," wrote the reviewer, will have to "revise their opinions" of the "modernistic in art" after seeing some of Blumenschein's recent canvases on display: "With a handling of colors that in some of the canvases brings [the British muralist Frank] Brangwyn to mind, a high skill in draftsmanship, and a remarkable genius for novel composition, Blumenschein rescues the modern tendency in painting from the often justified charges of sloppiness, flatness and even childishness."[90] In 1929 the artist repainted the foreground, replacing Adam and Eve with another depiction of the Deer Dance and titled it *Enchanted Forest*. The avenging angel was also eliminated, with the result, according to his daughter, Helen, of a "much more appropriate" theme.[91]

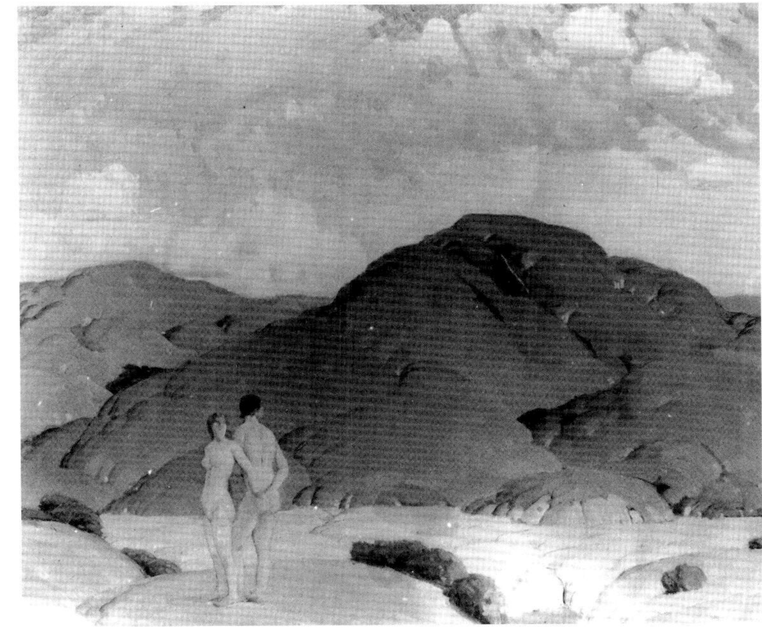

Victor Higgins, ***Adam and Eve***, ca. 1922–23, oil on canvas, 24 × 27 inches. Present location unknown. Photograph courtesy of the New Mexico Museum of Art. Gift of the Joan Higgins Reed Estate, 1984.

While most people thought that academic and modernist art were readily distinguishable and distinctly separate modes of expression, Blumenschein comfortably embraced both. In his own work he employed solid naturalistic, academic drawing, yet his designs were based on imagination and his color and use of light were boldly creative. He had left the conservative Taos Society of Artists for the more innovative New Mexico Painters, yet he had retained an allegiance, at least as an expedient, to the former that could not be broken. And this sense of accommodation went well beyond New Mexico. When he went east in December to be with Mary during a serious operation, he found an opportunity to help unite the ever-increasingly divided camps of artists in New York. His target in that case was the National Academy of Design, where he had been an associate member for several years. In an opinion piece published in the *New York Times* in February 1926, Blumenschein called for equal recognition for the academics and what he referred to as the "moderns." He pleaded that the National Academy adopt an open door policy, not unlike that employed by the Museum of New Mexico

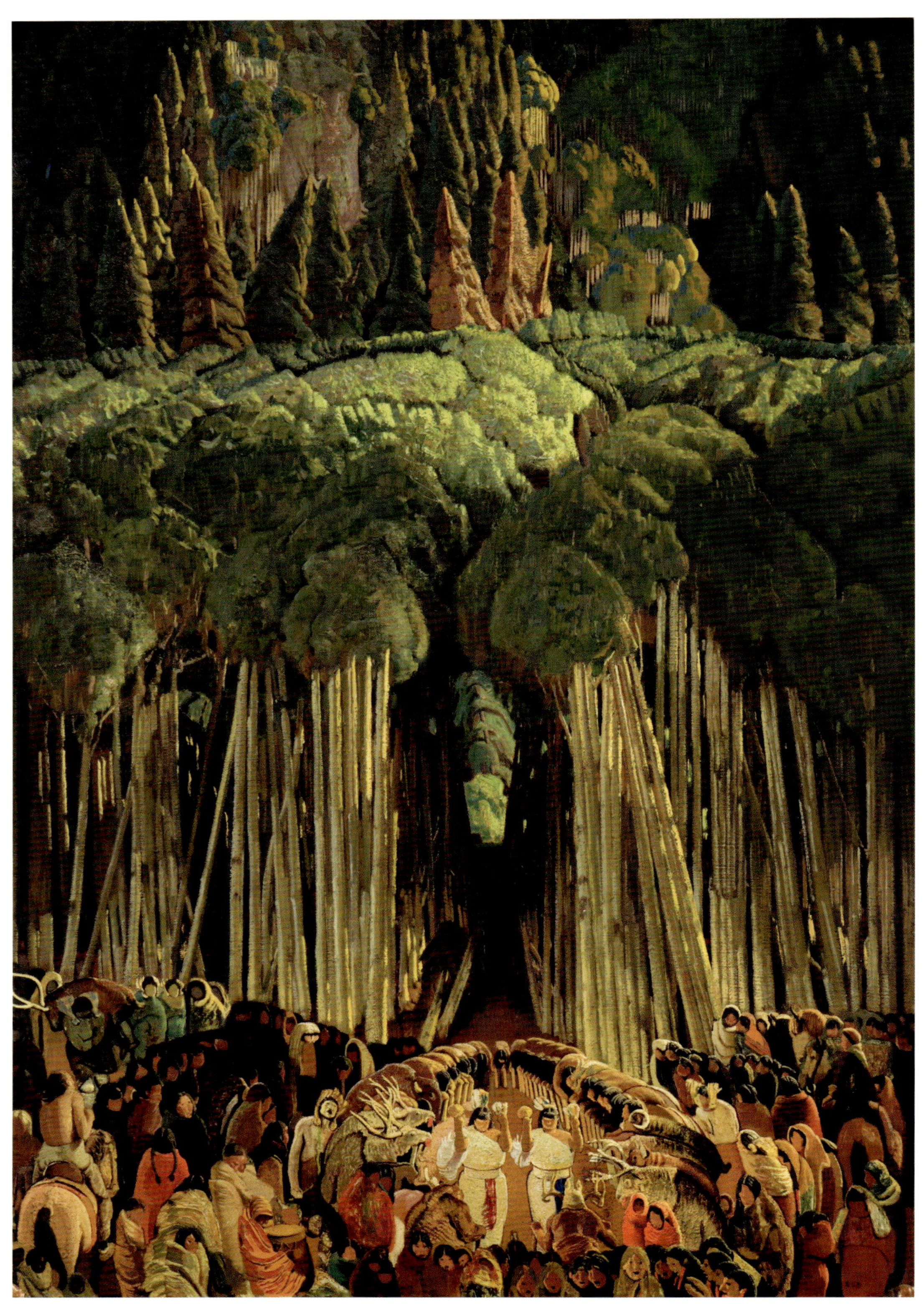

Enchanted Forest (originally *Decorative Landscape with Figures,* 1925; later *Aspen Grove,* 1929), finished 1946
Oil on canvas, 51 × 35¼ inches
Courtesy of the Gilcrease Museum, Tulsa, Oklahoma

over the previous decade through the inspiration of Robert Henri, John Sloan, and others, that would accommodate both camps. He pointed out that with few exceptions, like the Carnegie in Pittsburgh and the Brooklyn Museum, most art museums also suffered from closed minds and galleries when it came to admitting moderns. It would be good for the institutions and the public, he argued and would enliven the national creative culture, just as it had invigorated him as an artist.

"I can speak personally of my increased enthusiasm for work, an added courage to express myself, a quadrupled interest in art of all kinds and a broader appreciation, since the radical ideas led me away for the strict religion of the Academic," he wrote.[92] Even when he returned to New Mexico in March, he carried the message west, lavishing his ideas on the ladies of the State Teachers Convention in Santa Fe.[93] At the same time, Blumenschein was preparing a fondly sentimental remembrance on the beginnings of the Taos art colony that would be published in multiple venues later that spring.[94] By inference he acknowledged the New Mexican moderns when he concluded that there was an "equally famous" art colony in Santa Fe, but primarily he wanted to champion the Taos traditionalists as being genuinely "serious and honorable factors" in the cultural and economic development of New Mexico.[95]

Even within his own work, Blumenschein served dual masters. Later in May, the *Taos Valley News* reported on three of his landscapes exhibited at the Museum of New Mexico that spring. Two of them appeared to have been of the same scene, one naturalistic and the other with a modernist bent. "The first," the newspaper wrote, "was a mountain scene at dusk after a snowfall [that] has [as] a counterpart the same scene in decorative pattern, a veritable magic carpet, warm in color and harmonious in design."[96] Exactly which paintings were referenced here is uncertain, but probably the naturalistic one was *Untitled (Mountain Wood Gatherers)* and the more modernistic counterpart, an early version of *Mountain near Taos*. A small oil study for the latter, owned by the Stark Museum of Art, may suggest in its faceted planar construction what *Mountain near Taos* originally looked like. This work was retained by Blumenschein, who altered it over the years, not being satisfied with it until the mid-1950s.[97]

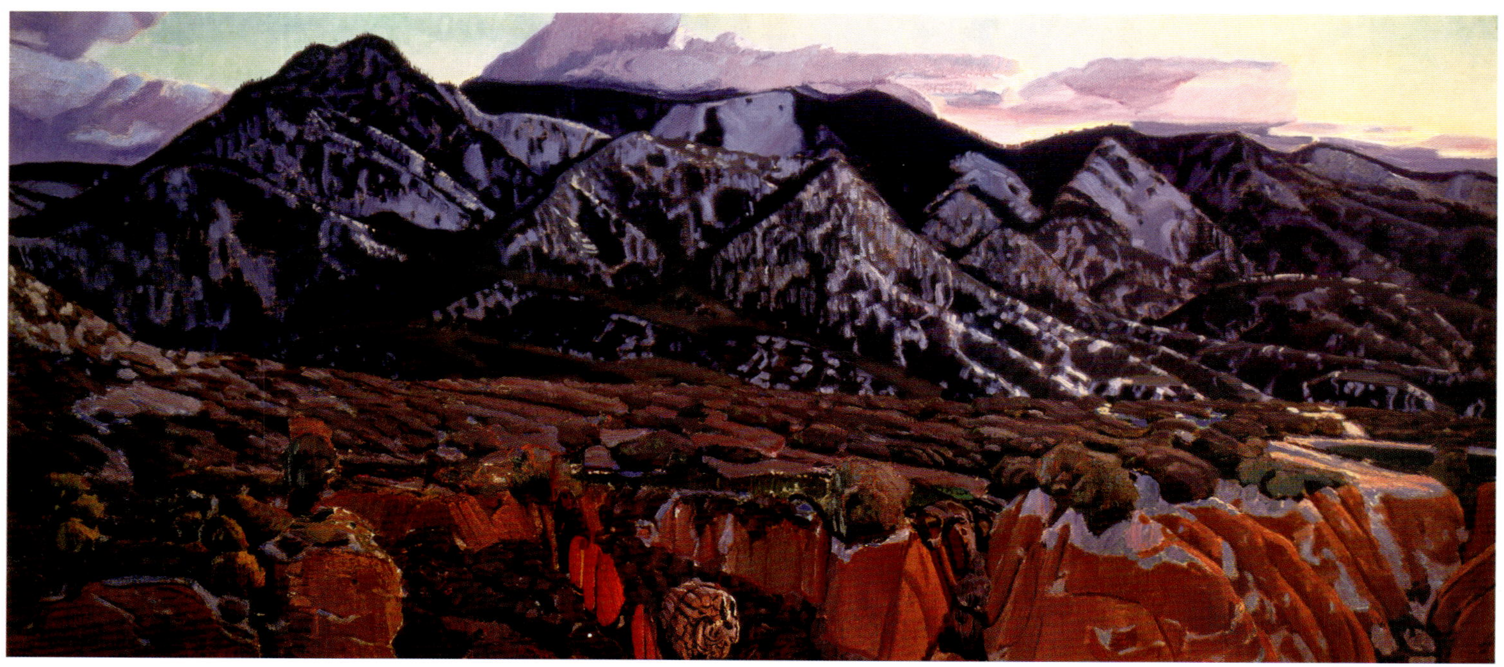

Untitled (Mountain Wood Gatherers), ca. 1926, oil on canvas, 23 × 50 inches. Courtesy of the Gerald Peters Gallery, Santa Fe, New Mexico.

Mabel Dodge Luhan once wrote that Leo Stein, who had visited her in Taos in 1917, commented that New Mexico "is the most aesthetically-satisfying landscape I know." To Luhan, it was more than that. She asserted, "It had a splendid, silent terror, and a vast far-and-wide magnificence which made it way beyond mere aesthetic appreciation."[98] For Blumenschein, the mountains represented the quintessence of all that was Taos. "One can't tell about Taos," he had written in 1917, "without dwelling on the mountains that box in the valley on three sides."[99] All this may explain why he devoted so much attention to those granite monoliths. His decorative celebration of them, with the "glowing colors and distinctive form," as the *Taos Valley News* described *Mountain near Taos* later that fall, provided the essence of all Blumenschein gloried in by being a resident artist in their shadow.[100] "Even in direct landscape he feels at liberty to adjust and modify the natural scene in the interest of decoration," remarked a reviewer in the *New York Herald Tribune* the next year when he exhibited the painting at the Grand Central Galleries there.[101] For Blumenschein and much of his audience, pure decoration—the patterned, rhythmic staccato and the elegant, linear definition of his forms—equated with modern.

He summed up his feelings on the matter for DeWitt Lockwood in describing his reaction to a John Singer Sargent exhibition at Grand Central Galleries in 1926.[102] "After a careful study during four visits to this show," he told Lockwood,

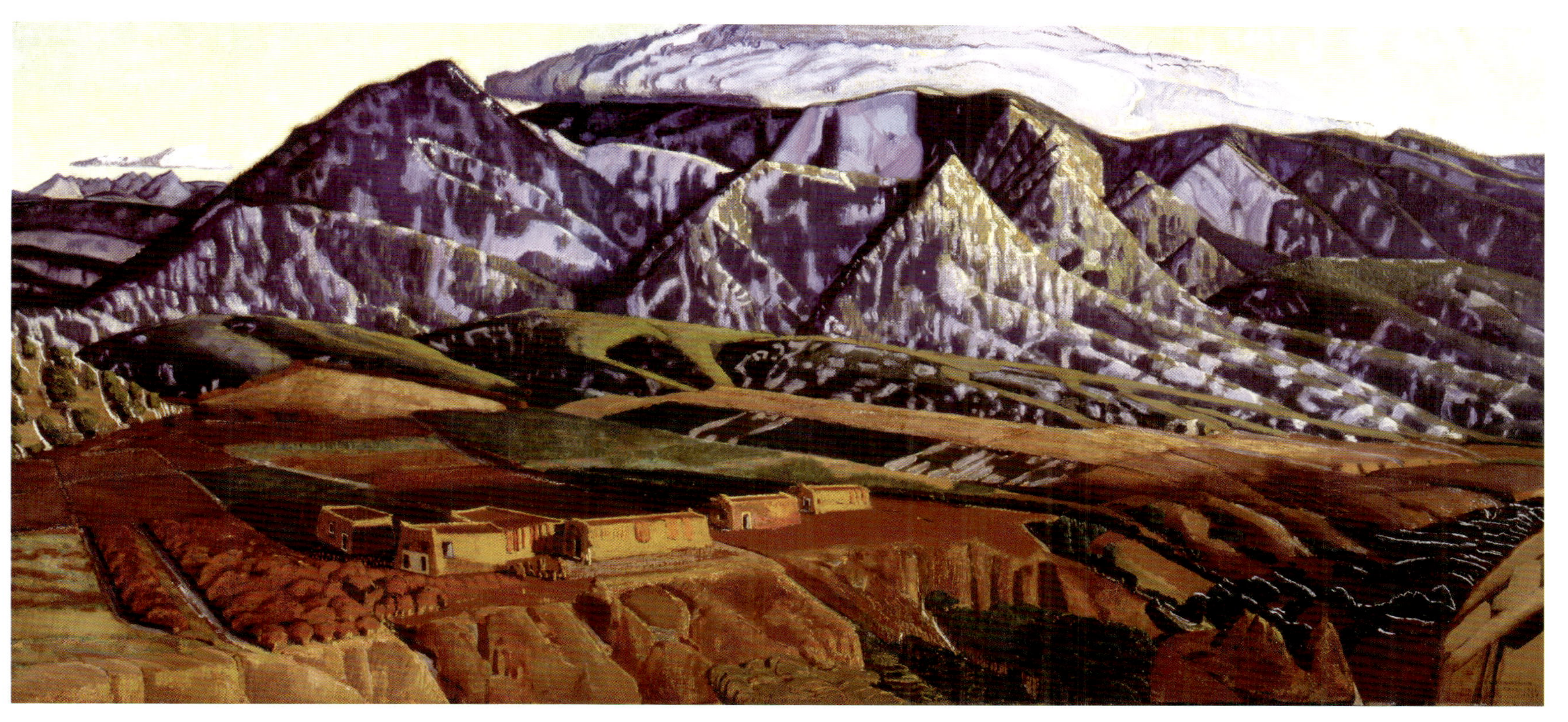

Mountains near Taos, 1926, reworked 1954
Oil on canvas, 22½ × 49½ inches
Courtesy of the Dallas Museum of Art, Dallas, Texas
Gift of Helen Greene Blumenschein

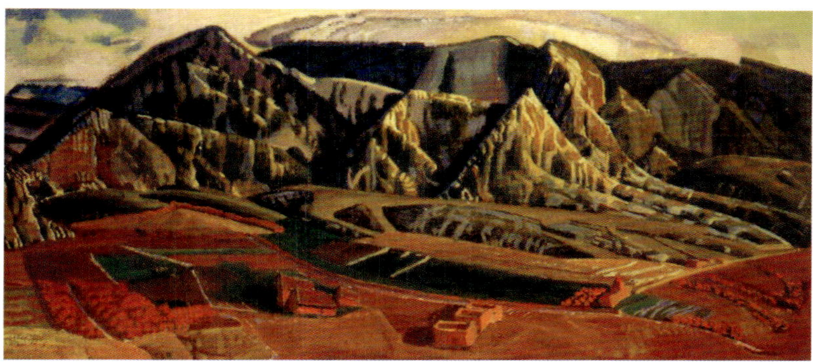

Mountains near Taos, ca. 1926, oil on board, 12 × 27 inches. Courtesy of the Stark Museum of Art, Orange, Texas

"I concluded that Sargent created no beautiful shapes—had no sense of design, a poor timbre of color and never considered rhythm of line. I am positive that design is the greatest element of the imagination—the creative quality. Design is architecture from the human literal element. The so-called modern movement is accentuated design."[103]

At exactly the same time that the New York press was applauding *Mountain Near Taos*, in 1927, Blumenschein was gratified to see that the National Academy of Design had heeded his pleas and invited selected modernists to show in the spring exhibition. He had brought some of the two camps together in an uneasy but worthy alliance.

In the winter exhibition of the academy, Blumenschein entered one of the most vigorous, dynamic, and highly decorative paintings of his mid-career. He called it "my best painting," and he put an asking price on it of five thousand dollars, twice what he normally charged for canvases of this size.[104] It bore the title *The Extraordinary Affray* and was actually a reworking of a painting known as *Indian Battle* that dated from around 1920.[105] The *Taos Valley News* announced that the new version was just completed in late July 1926. They termed it "truly wonderful," a pictorial rendition of "furious combat" that presented the "full . . . spirit of the battle and with perfect artistic curve."[106] It placed Blumenschein, already known as an arbiter between the representational conservatives and the more abstract modernists, somewhere outside, if not above, the art fray in America. In discussing this work when it was exhibited early the next year in New York, the *Brooklyn Daily Eagle* observed that "Mr. Blumenschein has remained apart from either group. If his first pictures were chiefly concerned with realistic, but always decorative studies of Indian types, his recent tendency is all toward the dramatic and imaginative. He invests a realistic setting with a strong, suggestive symbolism."[107] And while not all critics agreed—Henry McBride, who was typically unsympathetic to Blumenschein, felt he was squarely back among the academics, "plodding rather than inspired" with "paint that is heavily applied and

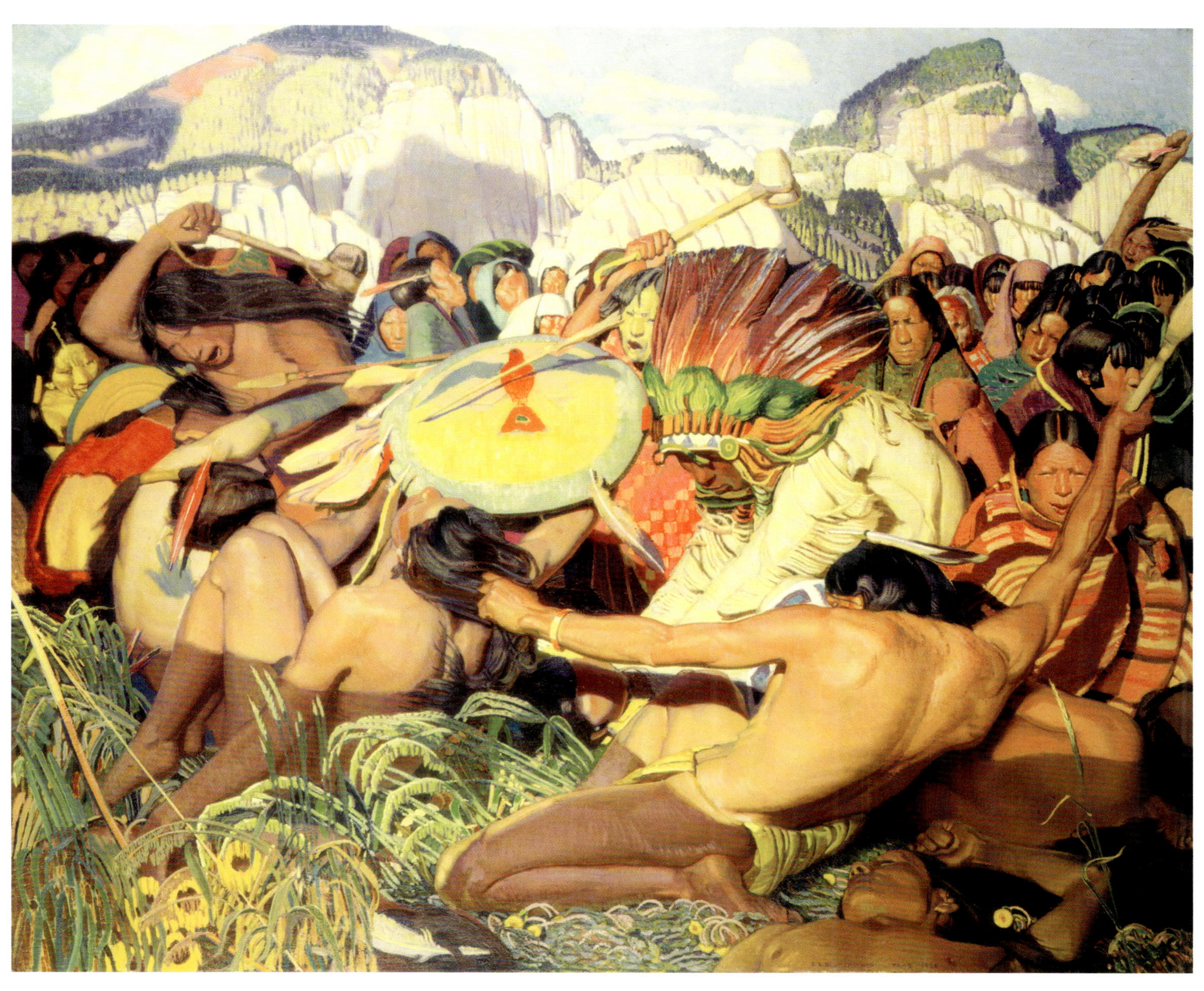

The Extraordinary Affray (originally ***Indian Battle,*** 1920), reworked 1927
Oil on canvas, 50 × 60 inches
Courtesy of the Stark Museum of Art, Orange, Texas (31.30/13)

lethargic"—most viewed his latest work as remarkable and fresh.[108] Paintings like *The Extraordinary Affray* are "only second in vigor and individuality to that of George Bellows," remarked a more affirming reviewer.[109]

If *The Extraordinary Affray* is fundamentally an expression of symbolism, no one at the time, including the artist, expressed how. Perhaps, it might be suggested, the combating Indians represented the lingering tensions imposed on the Native communities by Burke's efforts, through the BIA, to introduce a bill in Congress in 1926 outlawing dances and many religious practices. It continued to divide the Pueblos between those who, once exposed to other cultures and the outside world, desired change and those who sought to preserve traditional ways. Both the painting and the contemporary political scene were truly pictures of cultural death struggle.[110]

Beyond seeking to retain Native traditions among the Pueblos, Blumenschein continued to work to preserve the Hispanic, Pueblo Revival, and Territorial architectural integrity of Taos. He had earlier that year argued at length before members of the local Chamber of Commerce about the virtues of keeping Taos an adobe village.[111] The artists had pressing financial concerns of their own. The historic charm of the old town helped, as did the vast number of tourists it brought in.

The artists' studios, like the town and the pueblo, became popular attractions for visitors from out of town. To some, as Blumenschein put it, they were "a great nuisance."[112] Ada Rainey, an art writer for the *Washington Post*, for example, found a sign on Ufer's studio door: "Dangerous, Keep Out. High Explosives Within."[113] On the other hand, Blumenschein observed, tourists were an important "source of income to certain of the artists who have now reached a point where they can practically support themselves by sales of their work in Taos."[114]

The Santa Fe modernist artist Frank Applegate viewed this trend as serving to diminish the standards of high art. Most opulent tourists, he claimed, tended to buy "a colored illustration in oil by some one of the more gifted illustrators." Applegate equated illustrators with the plethora of "reproducers of romantic subjects," like Couse or Sharp, who "make very skillful illustrations and reproductions of these subjects and win great local acclaim thereby."[115] He felt arrogantly that while they might bond with the tourists, they knew nothing of real appreciation for art. But Blumenschein was convinced, to the contrary, that there was room for both traditions. He was probably less gratified to read Applegate's comments than to see an especially appealing puff piece by Fred Hamilton Rindge promoting the Taos artists and their colony, including plaudits for Phillips, Sharp, and Couse, as well as Higgins, Ufer, and himself.[116] Blumenschein was proud of his association with all the Taos artists, proud of his role in promoting New Mexico through art to tourists who, in his words, were "frequently" genuinely "interested in art" and felt especially rewarded with the opportunity to "buy directly from the artist."[117]

At the same time, Blumenschein embarked on a program to market his art outside Taos. Back in 1924, when he was secretary of the New Mexico Painters, he had written to the Albright Art Gallery arranging for an exhibition of the group's work. In his letter, Blumenschein lamented that Higgins had withdrawn his paintings from the traveling show "in order to use them in a one man show" of his own. "I can't get a word from him," Blumenschein concluded, as "he's so busy secretarying for himself."[118] By 1927 Ufer had decided to go the solo route as well, and now it was time for Blumenschein to follow suit.[119] The Taos Society of Artists ceased to function after March 1927 (in the past few years they had "failed to get satisfactory recognition from critics or purchasers"[120]), and the New Mexico Painters would stop their traveling shows in 1927 as well. So it was apt that Blumenschein would step out on his own.

His first solo show in New York, titled "30 Paintings by Ernest L. Blumenschein," opened on February 7, 1927, to rave notices at the Grand Central Art Galleries, a New York venue that had been founded four years earlier to promote American artists. It was a retrospective sampling, giving credence to the *New York Times*' assessment of the show as a "harvest of many years of study and work." Over three hundred people attended the opening, and the artist termed it "quite a success."[121] The prominent *Times* critic Elizabeth Cary, particularly drawn to the artist's more recent things, asserted that "the new paintings wear an aspect of great authority."[122] The *New York Herald Tribune* applauded his "potent imagination" and the power he brought to "glorifying the rather severe beauty of the land of mesas and adobe villages."[123] The show boasted an "all American" flavor, assuring Blumenschein's recognition as a national art figure, not simply a regional talent. And it attracted a national, indeed international, audience as it graced the galleries of more than twenty major museums and galleries over the next three years. In his hometown, Dayton, where the exhibit had expanded to forty-two works by April 1927, the newspaper referred to the artistic homecoming as a "most astounding and overpowering collection of paintings," and in Toronto later that fall, one critic noted it as "one of the most unforgettable one-man shows ever seen in Toronto."[124] Blumenschein had truly found his artistic voice and he, like many of his fellow painters in Taos, felt convinced that the future of American art lay solidly in the Southwest.[125]

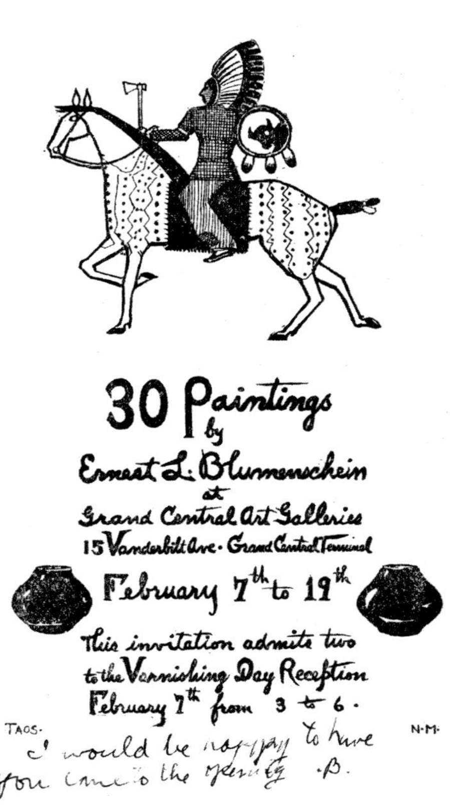

Invitation to the exhibition 30 Paintings by Ernest L. Blumenschein, 1927. Courtesy of the DeWitt Lockman Papers, Nita Stewart Haley Memorial Library, Midland, Texas.

Shortly after his show closed in New York and started on its lengthy tour, Blumenschein was made a full National Academician. Ufer had been accorded the same honor. The two men, who observers felt represented "the more liberal modes of expression in . . . Taos art," had achieved a rewarding pattern in their careers.[126] Yet Ufer, who questioned his own artistic purpose as well as his basic virility, tried to make Blumenschein share in a cloud of self-doubt. He wrote to Blumenschein in 1927:

> If I had money—much of it, I mean—I believe that I would be doing something more manly than paint pictures. One has to associate with too many women in the game. . . . My regret is that I cannot compete with strong men—real towering men. Such a regret is natural too—I would like to be strong like a locomotive or something like it. But I did not know this when I was young and in the making. I was simply a damned fool—but I believe you were one too. You started with the violin—then switched over to the paint box—and

Blumey, such things are nothing to compete with in this Industrial and "Modern" Age.[127]

But Blumenschein would not be swayed by such cynicism. Although now in his mid-fifties, and unable any longer to play baseball, he competed heartily on the tennis courts, winning a three-state veterans tennis championship in 1927. When he revisited his hometown, Dayton, local papers recognized his past athletic prowess on an equal par with his current artistic renown. In April 1927 the *Dayton Herald*, for example, promoted his paintings, "which have made him famous throughout the country" and were available for viewing at the Dayton Art Institute, while announcing Blumenschein's return as a "homecoming reunion" for one of their favorite "former football stars."[128] His ego and his manhood were firmly intact. Ever searching for competitive venues, in fact, he now took up the game of bridge. One of his most dramatic landscapes, *Haystack, Taos Valley,* was reputedly a gift to Mrs. K. F. Moore, who taught him how to play.[129] (Blumenschein's ledgers, however, show he sold the painting to Mrs. C. H. Burkarrt.)

If the notion that art is nature filtered through an artist's temperament holds credence, then *Haystack, Taos Valley,* is fine proof. The vigor of the brushwork and vibrancy of the palette speak to Blumenschein's vitality of spirit and physical energy as a man. Compared with the quiet, lyrical quality of landscape depiction practiced by other Taos artists, especially E. Martin Hennings, Blumenschein wanted to be seen as physically active and personally a bit on the cantankerous side, always ready for a match or a spat.

As in the previous several years, Blumenschein painted many of his landscapes in series. Such is the case with *Rock of Fire—Morning*, part of a set of three works that traveled with his one-man show. The artist and Denver Art Museum's director, Arnold Rönnebeck, referred to the three works (the other two are *Rock of Fire—Afternoon* and *Apache Country*) as painted in the manner of the French Impressionists, at various times of day and under various weather conditions. They illustrate, Rönnebeck concluded, "what a penetrating and passionate way this artist seeks to find out about the light of New Mexico and the atmospheric

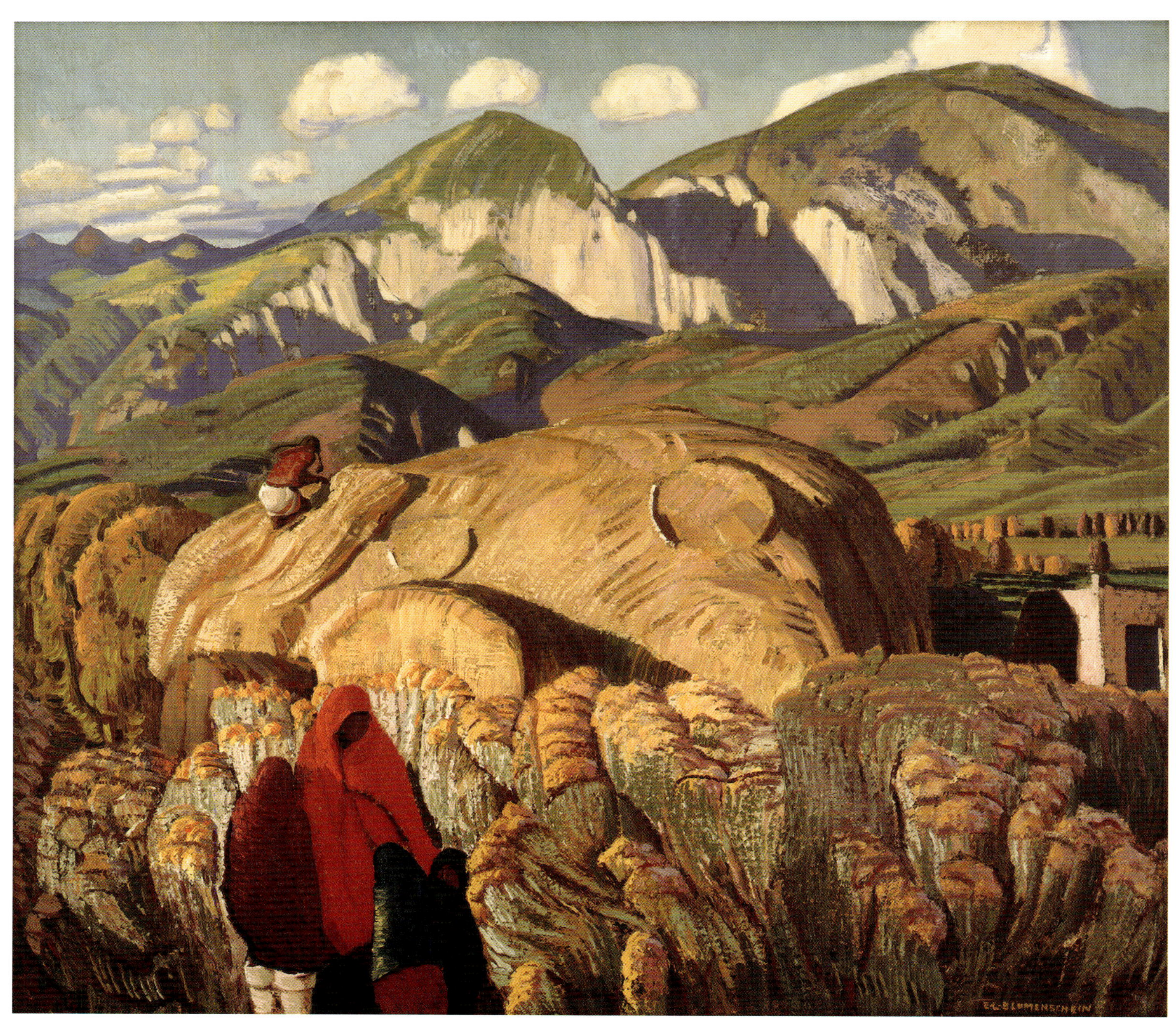

Haystack, Taos Valley, prior to 1927, reworked 1940
Oil on canvas, 24 × 27 inches
Courtesy of the Fred Jones Jr. Museum of Art, the University of Oklahoma, Norman
Given in memory of Roxanne P. Thams by William H. Thams, 2003

peculiar to this very country."[130] The vitality of Blumenschein as a man translated into the freshness and potency of his art.

Cortissoz wrote in 1927 that the Taos painters "tended to a certain hardness and they have maintained, too, in spite of obvious relations with nature, a . . . studio atmosphere."[131] Yet Marguerite Williams of the *Chicago Daily News*, when standing before landscapes like *Rock of Fire—Afternoon* at the Art Institute in January 1928, disagreed. She argued that while some of his heavily symbolic paintings of Indian life had a "certain dangerous literary element (which might be taken as a studio weakness)," the landscapes were different. In them she found "a strong keynote of emotionalism and a tendency to abstraction." She acknowledged a personal artistic response to nature, one not constrained by representational obligations or studio formulas.[132] As another Chicago critic proclaimed, "The mountains are massive. The far-reaching foothills and valleys between them are of the earth itself."[133] His was certainly no patterned repetition.

That said, Blumenschein *did* have a set of what he called "fundamental principles" that he applied to all his work. The color needed to "sing," as he put it, and needed to be used instead of perspective to establish planes. The design should be vigorous, not soft or pretty. Lines should be "rhythmical" and "masses large" and in "good proportion." Depending on the sentiment of a picture, line should also convey a sense of "nobility," "chastity," or "dynamics." The most important element, though, and one that for Blumenschein "comes from within oneself," was ingenuity of design. It was like "the architecture of a picture" and included "rhythm of line," "rhythm of movement," "proportion of space," and the essential building block, color. The last great quality for a painting, according to Blumenschein, was depth. For him, it naturally expressed itself in relation to music. It was, he said,

> Depth of the nature that creates a work of art—expressed by design and color. Depth in design as shown by ingenuity and balance and vigor. Depth in color as shown by the quality—by the timbre—as they judge the quality of the voice or a musical instrument. A full rich tone in music

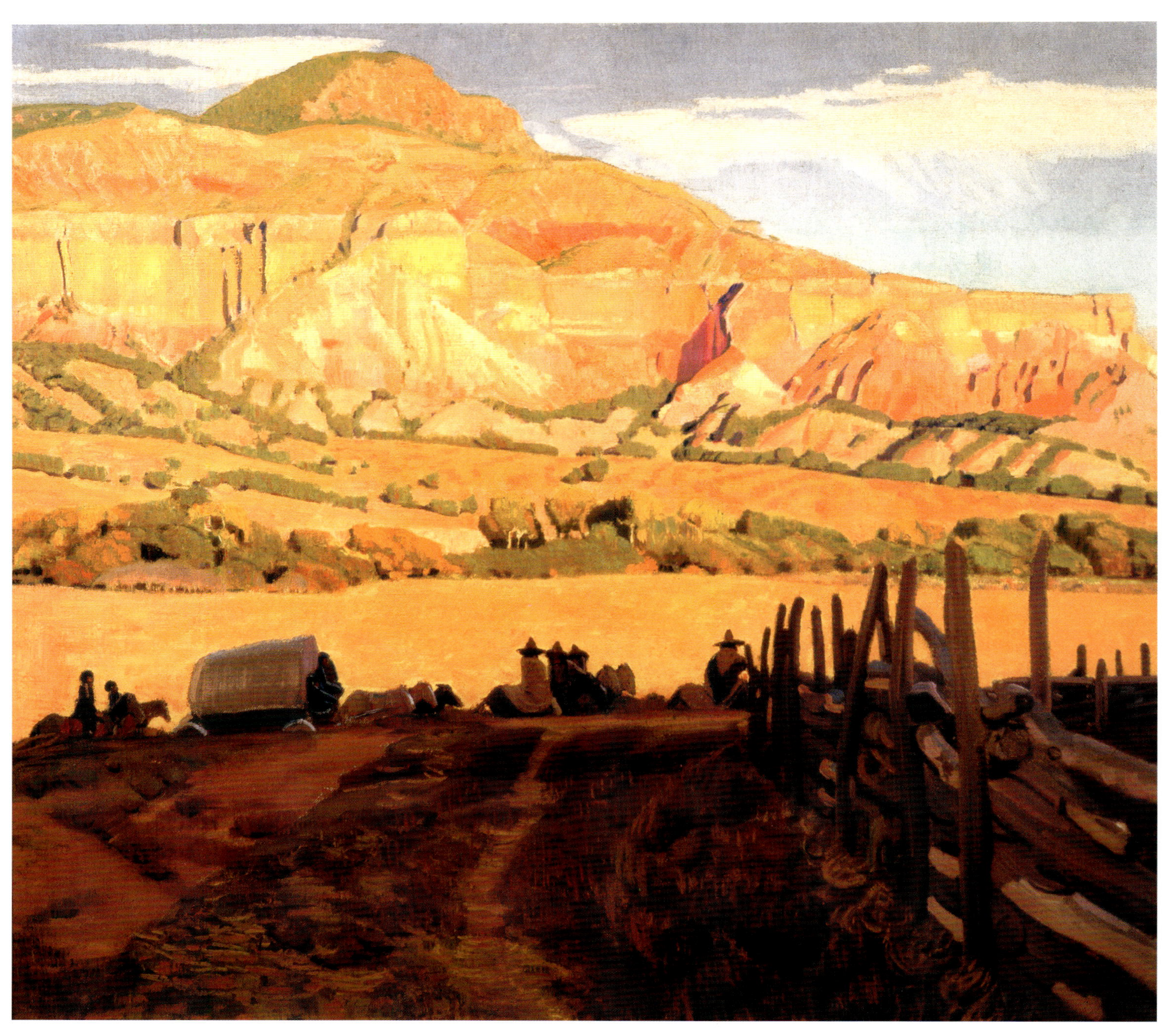

Rock of Fire—Afternoon, prior to 1927
Oil on canvas, 24 × 27 inches
Private collection, Washington, D.C.

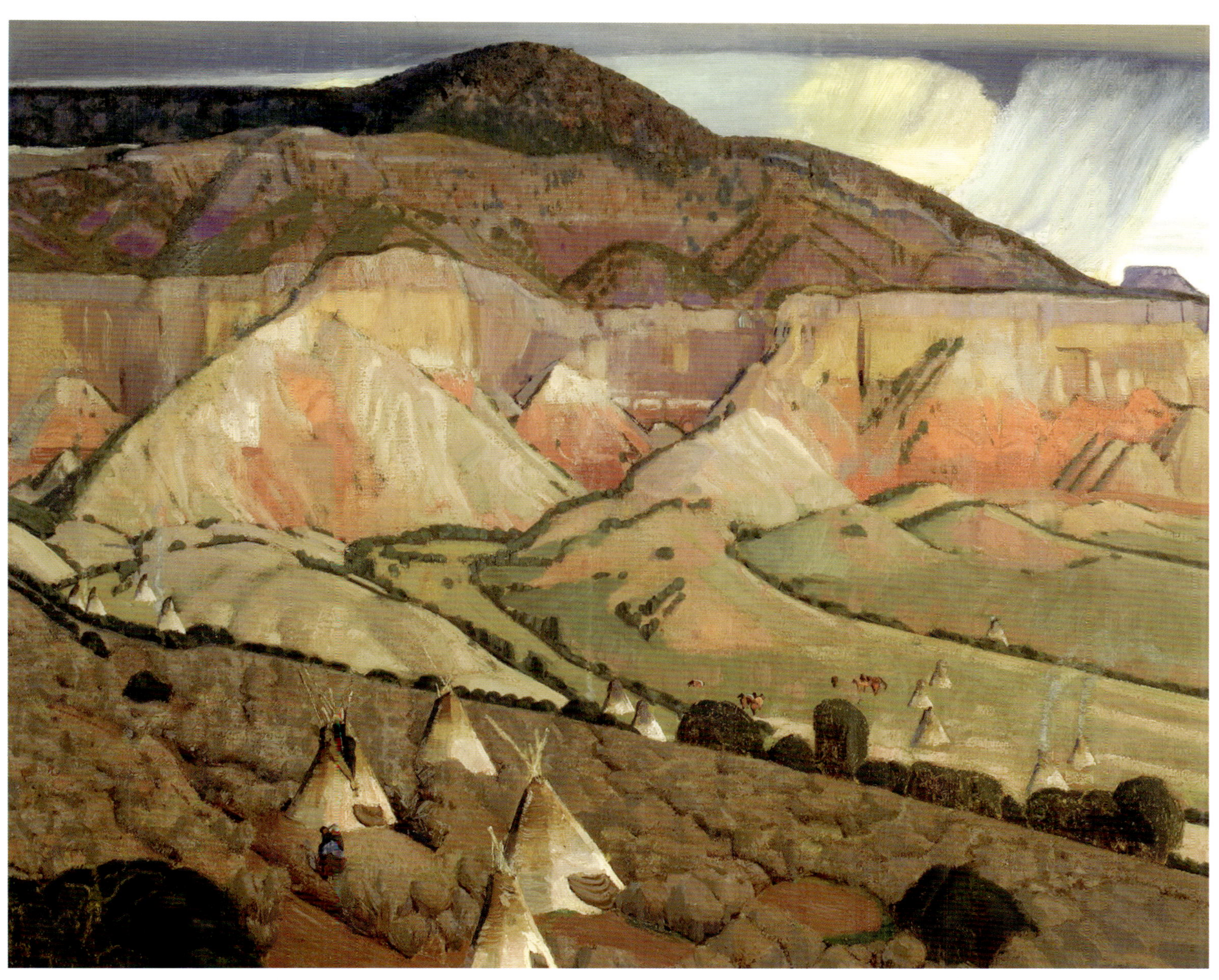

Apache Country, prior to 1927
Oil on canvas, 25 × 30½ inches
Private collection

> is comparable with a full rich note in color, and a thin squeaky tone to a color that does not sing. The greatest use of color is to establish your planes. Here is probably the biggest point in the painter's technique. The establishment of plane by means of color.

That was his technical credo. That was what he called "my religion."[134] These were qualities that now, in his mature work, became broadly recognized. When, for example, his one-man show stopped at the museum in Santa Fe in August 1928, the staff wrote that "his talent for design, decoration, his genius for color and atmosphere, place Blumenschein in the foremost rank of contemporary artists and assure that his work will live."[135]

Blumenschein was left in Taos alone over the winter of 1928–29. Mary and Helen had sailed for Europe in December 1928 so that Helen could study art under similar circumstances afforded her parents years earlier. Blumenschein, as the *Taos Valley News* reported, would stay home: "Taos will hold him with his work ahead."[136]

One of the works that he set out to create suggested how much he missed his family. It represented something of a biographical essay in paint, a portrait of a burro in the Taos landscape. Burros had long been Helen's pets, so Blumenschein's portrayal of a chubby, wind-blown foundling in *The Burro* was as much a remembrance of his daughter as a chilling testament to his own loneliness and to New Mexico's harsh winter clime.

One of the paintings Blumenschein is thought to have completed that winter is a stunning smaller version of *Adobe Village—Winter* that has been titled *Village, Northern New Mexico*. Another of the works inspired by Blumenschein's winter solitude, *Adobe Village—Winter*, was no less the result of a highly personalized vision. *Adobe Village—Winter*, like *The Burro,* was autobiographical as well as a southwestern reverie. When he eventually sold it to the major California collector Paul Grafe in the 1940s, Blumenschein described the pictured village as Taos, saying that "somewhere up that street is where I live." He remembered the scene as a "magnificent, exciting, lonely winter."[137]

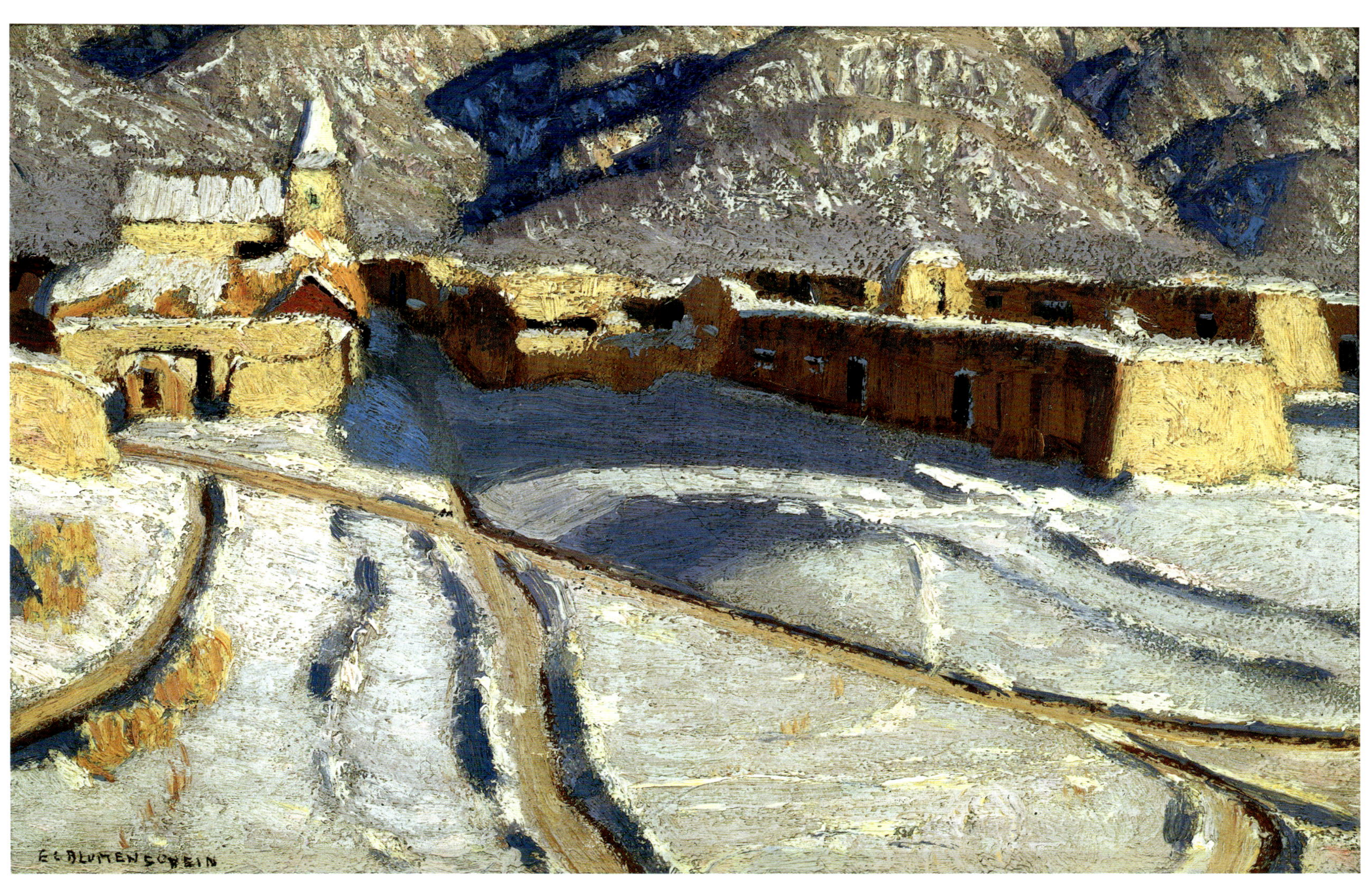

Adobe Village — Winter (sketch for ***Adobe Village — Winter***), 1929
Oil on board, $6\frac{1}{8} \times 8\frac{7}{8}$ inches
Courtesy of the Gerald Peters Gallery, Santa Fe, New Mexico

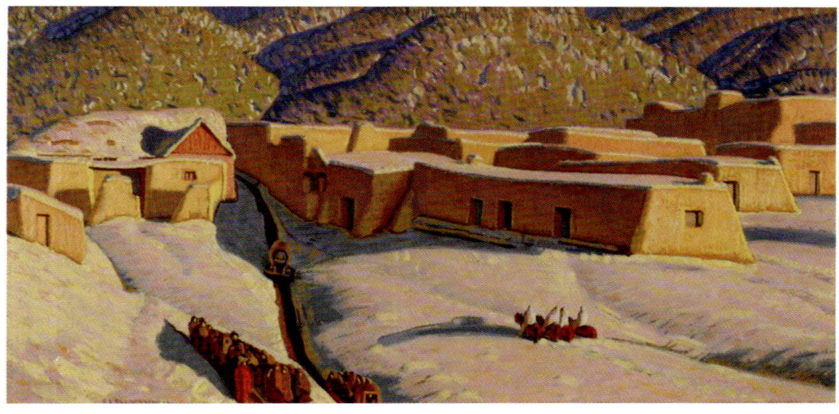

Village, Northern New Mexico (study for *Adobe Village—Winter*), ca. 1929, oil on panel, 9 × 17¾ inches. Courtesy of The Eugene B. Adkins Collection at the Fred Jones Jr. Museum of Art, University of Oklahoma, Norman, and the Philbrook Museum of Art, Tulsa, Oklahoma.

In establishing a motive for the painting, he had once again complained, this time in February 1929 to the local Lion's Club, that the town was deteriorating—adobe building styles were not being perpetuated. Taos, he remonstrated, had looked far better when he and Phillips arrived, the buildings then being far "more attractive in the older type."[138] So like *Sangre de Cristo Mountains*, this new canvas, finished one day before his presentation to the Lion's Club, was inspired by the artist's dream of architectural legacies. In spirit, his efforts were not much different than Grant Wood's at the time; Wood, in paintings like *Arbor Day* of 1932, endeavored to celebrate and preserve relics of midwestern life against an increasingly indifferent modern insurgency.

Blumenschein's comments to Grafe, a description of his aesthetic response, visual memory, and enthusiasm for plein air painting and the creative process speak clearly of his frame of mind and working method:

> I saw the scene in 1929—not exactly as I have painted it, for I had to rebuild considerably. I was strongly moved by the effect of the brilliant low light on the adobe walls, the elegant tones of the mountains, and the superb modeling of the deep snow. I cannot describe my powerful impressions of the beauty of the color, the exotic charm of the place, the simple long lines in the buildings, and rhythmic construction at the mountains. Perhaps my painting can convey what I felt. The finer emotions I try to express are impossible for me to explain in words. Let me instead write only of the painting method I use: When I get a "jolt" from Nature, I know from many experiences that I must study the reasons, in order to pass it along in a picture. It is not a matter of putting up your easel and copying the scene. It is far deeper. Perhaps I don't exactly see the scene, but am affected more by the light, or the drama, or whatever you want to call it. Anyway, I have to get right down to

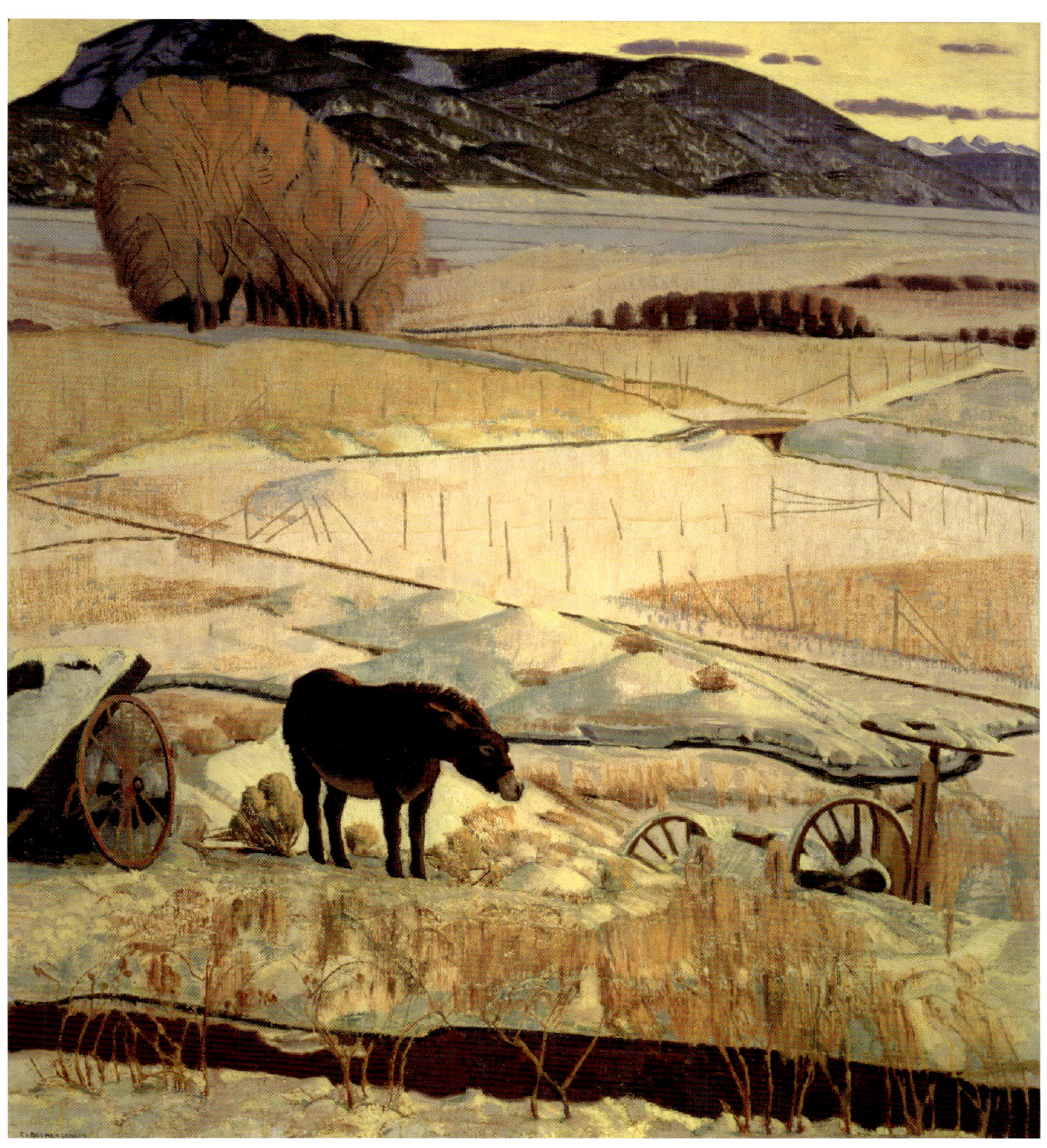

The Burro, 1929
Oil on canvas, 34¼ × 30¼ inches
Courtesy of the Smithsonian American Art Museum, Washington, D.C. (1975.85)
Bequest of Henry Ward Ranger through the National Academy of Design, New York, New York

earth and analyze, to find out what makes the music. And this is how I do it. While the impression is vivid I immediately make a pencil sketch of the whole.

In the case of "Adobe Village—Winter" I also painted a thumb box note of the color effects. By the time that was completed, I had to jump up and down to keep from becoming part of the landscape. I hurried home, and, after my evening meal, started my small composition in pencil and ink. This is the most important detail of all, as this composition must not only give my emotional reaction, but also be well built structurally. That is, the combination of lines and masses must not only make acceptable "architecture," well balanced construction and good anatomy, but must convey by the "movement" the dramatic sense of a cold winter in a rather theatrical town below the rolling mountains. The general idea of the picture grew from that live little composition. I returned to Nature each day as long as the snow lasted, and made more studies. My chief recollection of these cold excursions is of my two suits of heavy woolen underclothes, my heavy socks, shoes and galoshes, and my cold hands. But, when the heat of ambition is on, a fellow can take a lot of punishment that usually nets results. I jotted down in paint, pencil, and mentally, the main facts of the relations of color in the foreground snow with that in the mountains, the difference in blue between the color of the deep shadows cast by the buildings and those in the rolling hills; the rapport between the golden light on the buildings and the violet quality of the light on the background. I had to paint the foreground snow with the glowing light so that it still remained a solid mass in the background; and that, I believe, was my most difficult problem.

"Adobe Village—Winter" moved smoothly after being transferred to the large canvas which was painted in the studio, taking altogether about two months to execute. Then it was framed and sent on its journey. And did it travel![139]

Blumenschein entered both *The Burro* and *Adobe Village—Winter* in the spring 1929 exhibition of the National Academy of Design. *The Burro* won the Henry Ward Ranger Purchase Fund Prize of $1,600 (the last award he would receive from the academy, although he kept showing there through 1950) and was placed on loan at the Brooklyn Museum. His *Adobe Village—Winter* was later shown at the Grand Central Galleries, where it received the Frank C. Logan Prize for the best landscape painting. It brought a cash award of $1,000. Blumenschein must have felt gratefully flush as the nation began to strain under the early pressures of the Depression.

Some intriguing narrative elements weave through the scene in *Adobe Village—Winter* and in a smaller version, illustrated here, but the artist never described them on the record. A road meanders forward in the center of the composition, and two trucks, one perhaps full of workers, steers its course. To the left a procession, maybe a funeral, presses forward as well. But most of the space is devoted to a sunlit, snowy bench and three riders headed for town, reminiscent, if not symbolic, of the three Blumenscheins who had arrived in Taos a decade earlier. But fundamentally this painting was not about stories. It was an exercise of those rhythmical masses, the music of color and how color establishes opposing planes and achieves depth and mood. It relays a sense of chastity in its whiteness and mobility in its figures. It represented Blumenschein's aesthetic credo writ large and supremely accomplished. Even Cortissoz, who finally relented, would conclude that "his color is strong but in light . . . the result is a series of impressions having a quietly rich harmony. Best of all . . . his canvases have always a pictorial interest, balanced, unified, and finally, individualized. A particularly attractive quality in his works is a sense of still vastness which it conveys."[140]

The Museum of New Mexico, upon learning of Blumenschein's winning the Logan Prize, proclaimed him without doubt to be the foremost among all the southwestern artists of the day.[141] That local praise combined with his ascendant national reputation must have been welcome affirmation of his vision and effort. He left Taos that fall, heady with pride and anxious for a reunion with his family.

He would rendezvous with Helen and Mary that winter in Europe for a prolonged tour of France and Italy.

The rainbow he had been chasing, the one that had connected New York and Taos for the Blumenschein family in 1919, had revealed a veritable pot of gold for the artist at its western end. It had proven to be an inspired and fortuitous decision to move to New Mexico, and the 1920s surely resulted in the most ambitious and productive creative decade of his long career. Pursuing that rainbow had been well worth the journey.

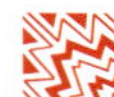

The Extraordinary Affray Indians and Identity

Sarah E. Boehme

A four-column, seven-inch reproduction of Ernest L. Blumenschein's painting *The Extraordinary Affray* illustrated a *New York Times* review of the artist's 1927 exhibition at the Grand Central Art Galleries.[1] The illustration, even in black and white on newsprint, conveyed the bold brush and vision of Blumenschein at this crucial period in his career. The accompanying review praised the artist's pictorial accomplishments in the exhibition and used *The Extraordinary Affray* as a prime example. In the art-critical language of the twenties, the reviewer lauded Blumenschein's design within a naturalistic approach but eschewed any analysis of narrative content. Blumenschein himself reportedly dismissed the relevance of the subject, referring to the painting only in pictorial terms. Yet the complex subject asserts itself in any analysis of the painting. In *The Extraordinary Affray,* Blumenschein painted a work with a dense and complex composition. He portrayed a battle scene of Indian warriors surrounded by other Indians against a mountain backdrop. The warring figures, most of them only partially visible, seem to be nude, one with a breechcloth, whereas one prominent figure wears a fringed buckskin warshirt and warbonnet. These figures are enveloped by blanket-wearing Indians. Space in the painting is compressed so that warriors, bystanders, and mountains are pushed to the picture plane. Both the subject and the pictorial design combine to create one of Blumenschein's most compelling works of art.[2]

Blumenschein's daughter, Helen, colorfully and yet uncomfortably relayed confusion about the subject, and she also reported a reaction from

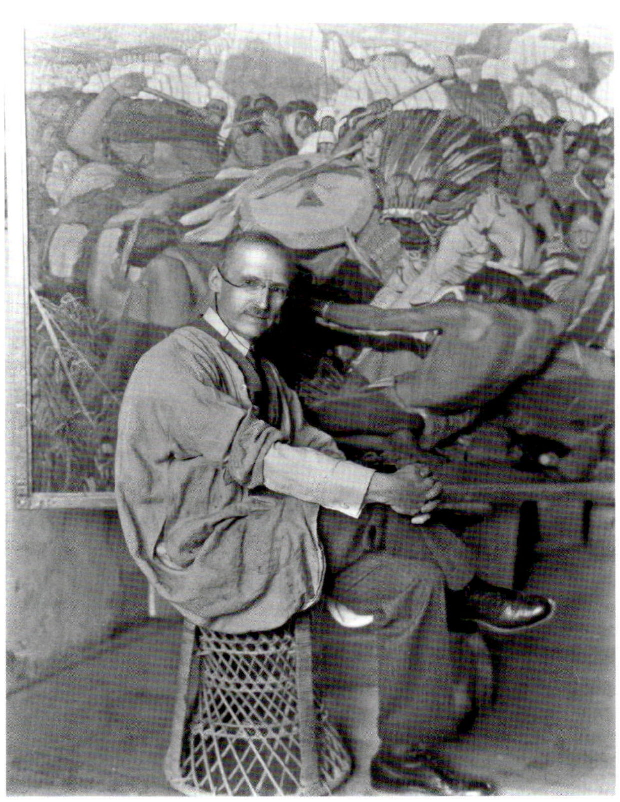

Studio portrait of Ernest L. Blumenschein seated in front of ***The Extraordinary Affray.*** Courtesy of the Peter A. Juley and Son Collection, Photograph Archives, Smithsonian Institution, Washington, D.C.

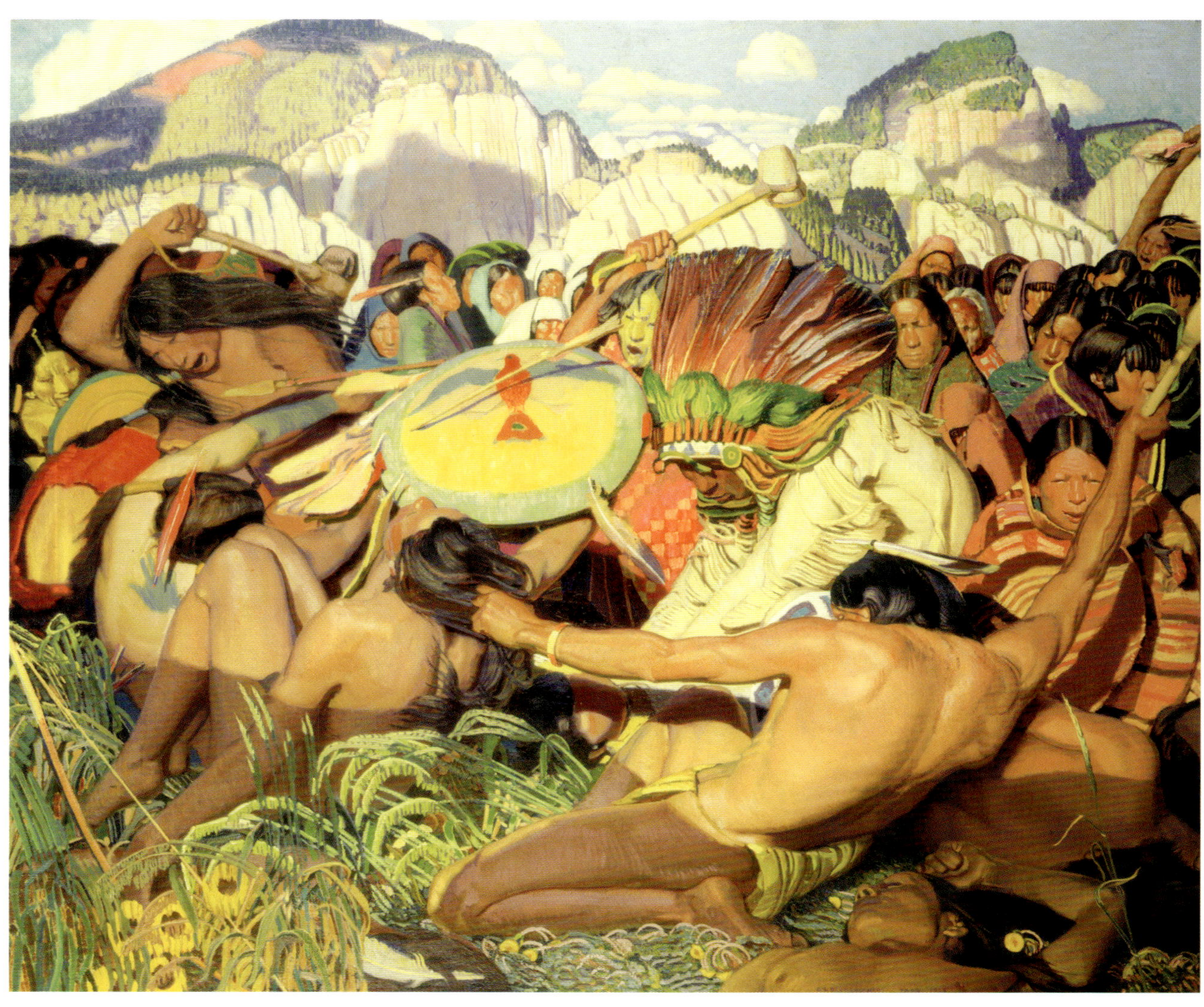

The Extraordinary Affray (originally *Indian Battle,* 1920), reworked 1927, oil on canvas, 50 × 60 inches. Courtesy of the Stark Museum of Art, Orange, Texas (31.30/13).

her father when she described the painting in her unpublished biography: "Another large, spectacular Indian picture done in the 1920's was called *Extraordinary Affray*, a battle scene with two Indian nude figures with a G-string striking at each other. They were surrounded by many onlookers—Indians who were just watching the scene. This brought some criticism from several people who asked why these men would be watching this contest, and they were told [by Blumenschein] because it was more artistic and the lines went the way he wanted them to go."[3]

Thus Blumenschein himself avoided commenting on the subject and projected the painting's meaning as residing in the pictorial elements. The modeling of the warriors' bodies strikes a balance between realism, in the artist's evocation of anatomy, and abstraction, in the elegant linear design. The power of those lines, notwithstanding, the intriguing subject asserts itself.

The *New York Times* reviewer betrayed a modernist focus on pictorial elements alone yet recognized that effective use of line, space, and color could be done within a visual vocabulary of mimetic reality. In fact, the article asserted that the marriage of design and representation was Blumenschein's strength, saying about the exhibition as a whole that "the best examples have the double quality of faithfulness to nature and imaginative design." The reviewer then singled out *The Extraordinary Affray* as "one in which the painter lets himself work directly through nature, without, that is, imposing symbolism or literature upon the material he has chosen. His material is a mass of fighting savages, bare limbs and backs, slithering into battle. . . . No accusation possible of excessive cerebration, of a technique overmastering the lively human interest of a good fight." In confronting the insistent subject matter of Blumenschein's work, the 1927 reviewer denied narrative or symbolism and reduced the subject to a good fight, perhaps linking Blumenschein with his Ashcan school contemporaries in portraying pugilistic bouts.

The pictorial means used by Blumenschein to construct his imaginative design nevertheless lead back to questions about the subject matter. There are two distinct groupings of Indian peoples in the painting—the warriors with weapons and painted shields (one featuring a thunderbird design) and the bystanders wrapped in woven blankets. The cultural artifacts identify the first group as Plains Indians, the second as Southwestern, and within the particular landscape setting, Pueblo Indians. Blumenschein's compression of space, which pictorially creates an all-over patterning and a rhythm of shapes, brings the Pueblo onlookers almost into the melee. They are a part of it, yet separate. Blumenschein's composition is reminiscent of European history paintings, his Indian warriors paralleling in the "piled on" compositions of battle scenes of an artist such as Nicolas Poussin. His modeling of figures evokes the emphasis on human anatomy in traditional academic painting, yet Blumenschein's work breaks from the traditions of the past. The painting conveys representations of reality in the human figures and identifiable objects, yet the scene itself is unreal. The artificiality is theatrical, and Blumenschein's *The Extraordinary Affray* must have drawn its inspiration from the enactments of ritual drama and dance.

In the early twenties, Blumenschein had the opportunity to witness dances and performances that related to the complex history of the New Mexico region, its Native inhabitants, and the incursions of outsiders. Among these was the folk drama *Los Comanches*, which dramatized the defeat of Comanche warriors who had raided New Mexico by the Spanish.[4] *Los Comanches* was performed as a large outdoor enactment and is known to have been enacted in the plains between Taos and Ranchos de Taos and to have featured Pueblo Indians who dressed in buckskins and beads to take the roles of Comanches.[5] *The Extraordinary Affray* is not a literal transcript of that drama; *Los Comanches* pitted the Comanches against Spanish soldiers on horseback, not the Indian conflict on the ground of Blumenschein's painting. Yet the folk drama's significance points to the intertwined history of the Comanches with the peoples of the New Mexican region. Other dances and songs performed in New Mexico draw upon Comanche elements, such as

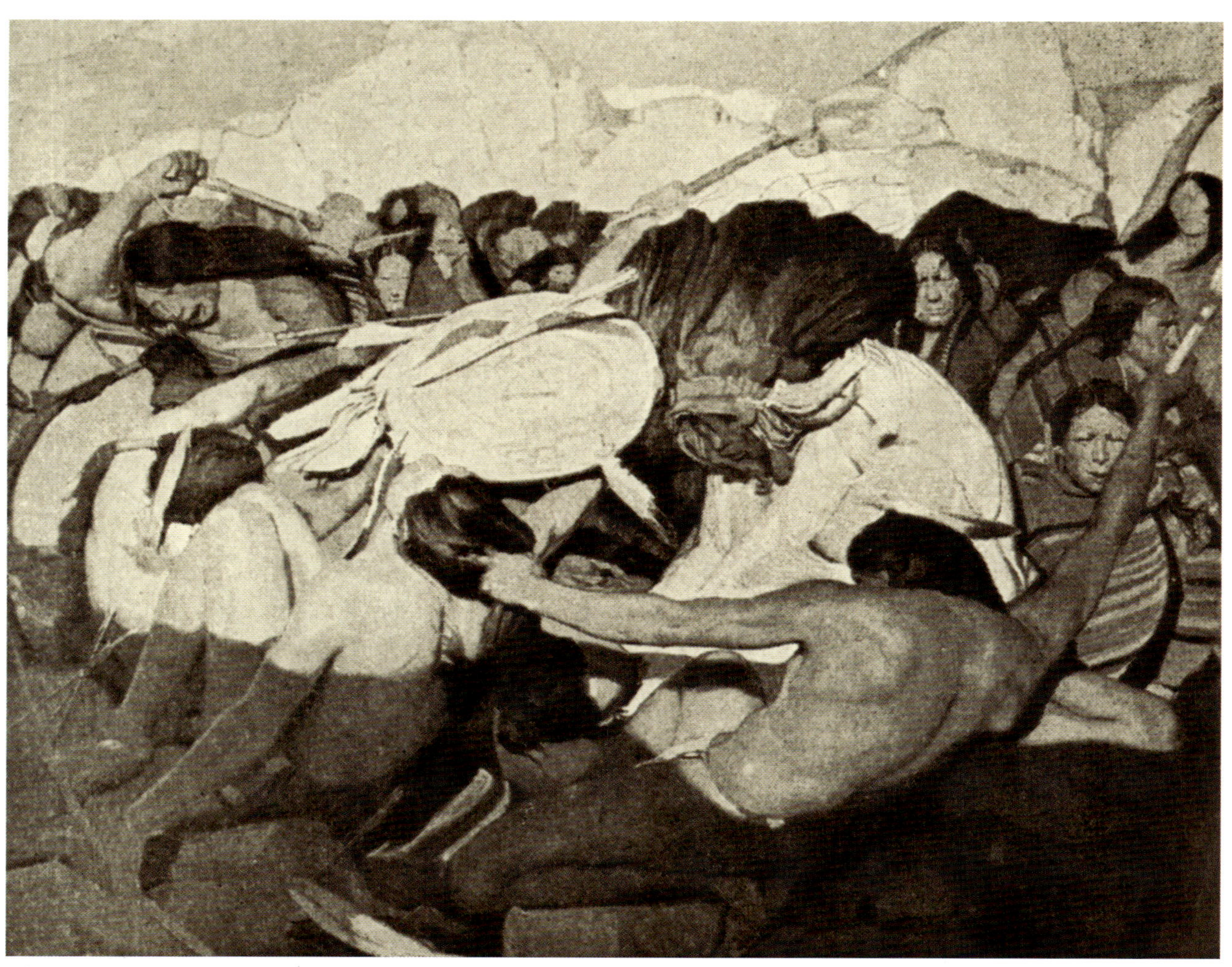

Indian Battle from Fifteenth Annual Exhibition of Paintings by American Artists, City Art Museum, St. Louis, Missouri, September 15–October 31, 1920. Courtesy of the St. Louis Art Museum, St. Louis, Missouri.

the song sung in Ranchos de Taos that "features a combat scene between the Numunuh (Comanche) and Apaches in which each has equal footing and prowess."[6] Blumenschein may have changed and combined elements so that he would not portray any specific ritual.

The title of the painting points to the work's significance. *The Extraordinary Affray* was a consciously chosen title by the artist.[7] Early in its history, the painting was simply titled *Indian Battle* and was exhibited as early as 1920. In 1926 Blumenschein submitted it to the National Academy of Design with a message he wanted conveyed to the jury: "It is called 'Extraordinary Affray.' In its 1st state it was called 'Indian Battle' and exhibited about 5 years ago. On receiving it back I decided to repaint it and have spent 3 months doing so. Every inch has been repainted; the background completely changed, also the foreground. The general lines of the grouping I have kept, although the detail was done over."[8] Blumenschein was clearly eager to have the painting regarded as a new work.[9] The new title gives it not only a new identity but a different emphasis. The words "extraordinary affray"

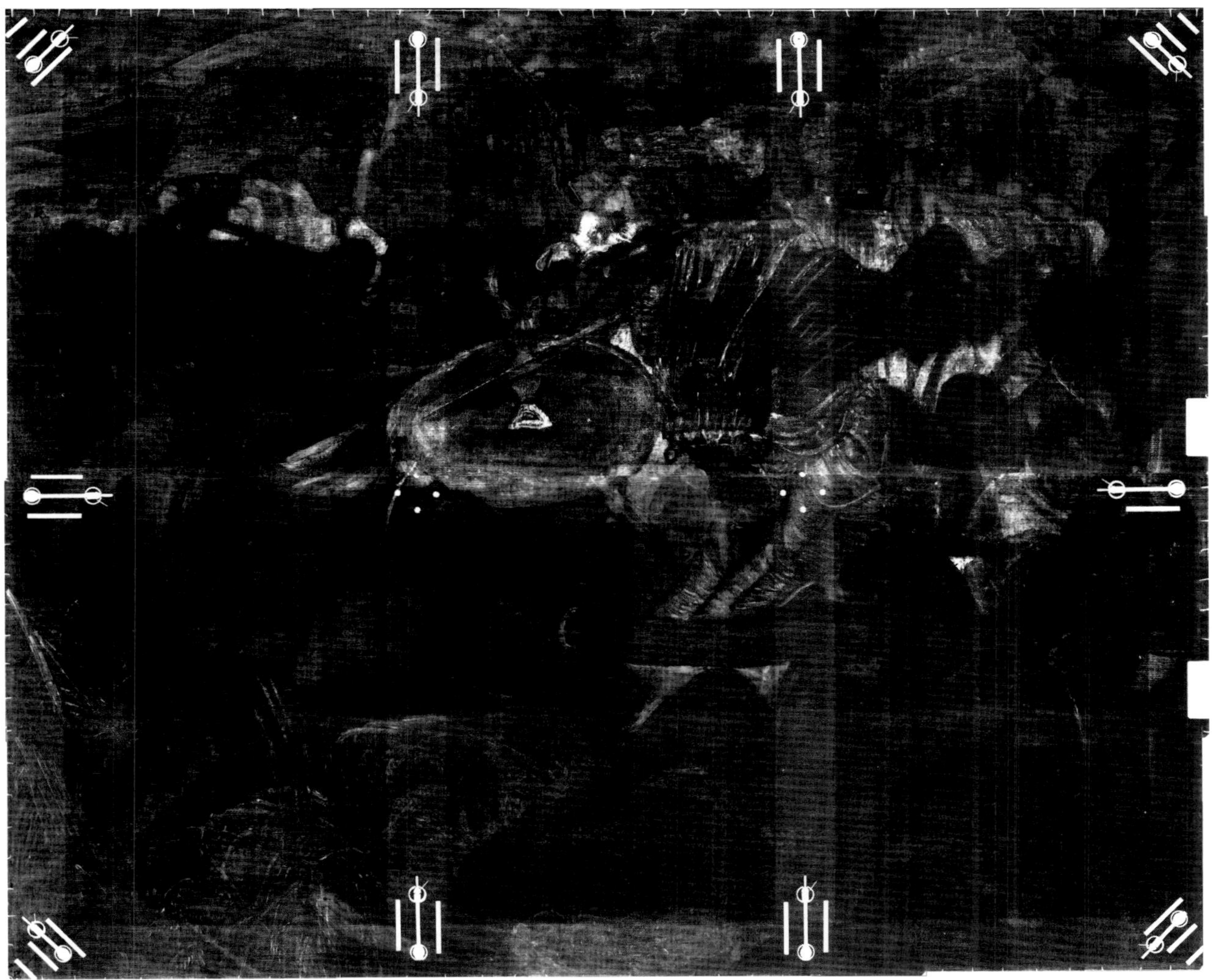

The Extraordinary Affray. X-Ray photography by Bert E. Samples. Courtesy of the Museum of Fine Arts, Houston, Texas, 2007.

formed a combination that Blumenschein might have encountered in literature or contemporary journalistic accounts. In a legal meaning, an affray consists of "the public fighting of two or more persons to the terror of the people."[10] A ritual drama certainly corresponds with the concept of a fight, outside the ordinary realm, in a public space that gives rise to an emotional response. In *The Extraordinary Affray,* Blumenschein powerfully evoked the dramas and songs of the Pueblo people that provide meaning through community and tradition.

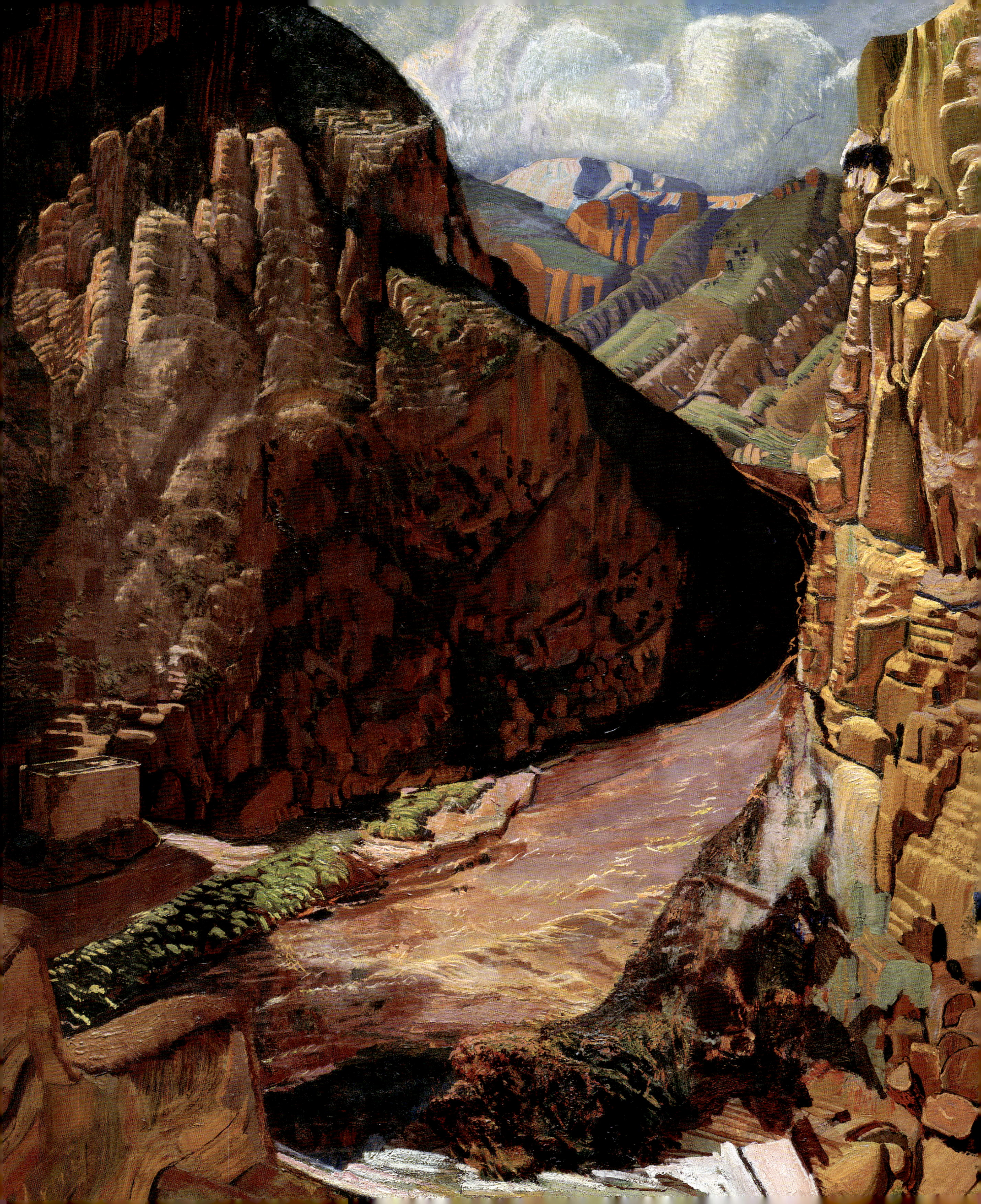

Chapter 4
Blumenschein, Modernism, and National Art in the 1930s

Elizabeth J. Cunningham

Called upon in August 1930 to reflect on his past decade of work, Blumenschein drafted a list of the paintings he considered his ten best. Of those the artist named, five—*Sangre de Cristo Mountains*, *The Burro*, *The Gift*, *Superstition*, and *Adobe Village*—had won major prizes in the 1920s. Yet even as he recalled these accomplishments, Blumenschein looked not to the past but to the future. In that light, he would write Mr. Derby, who had requested the list, "Mind you, these are the best 10 to date, but am expecting to far surpass them very soon."[1]

As the first year of the new decade opened, Blumenschein's vision expanded. He saw modernism, Europe, and his own painting with fresh eyes. In early January he said he had "new art" on his mind. The establishment of the Museum of Modern Art in 1929 impelled him to keep up with the times. In the spirit of the moment, Blumenschein decided to lobby once more, as he had in the mid-1920s, for more modernist representation in the exhibition program of the National Academy of Design. His efforts, however, went largely unrewarded. New York architect Cass Gilbert (then president of the academy), while lauding Blumenschein's role in the academy as a worthy exhibitor and critic, concluded in response that the academy was not ready to formally commit to future trends in art. "Sometimes," he wrote Blumenschein, "it is not progress to throw away all the accumulated wisdom and traditions of the past for untried experiments of the moment."[2]

Determined to respond to the emerging art trends, Blumenschein moved his own art forward alone. Fresh, modernist tenets could be clearly recognized in

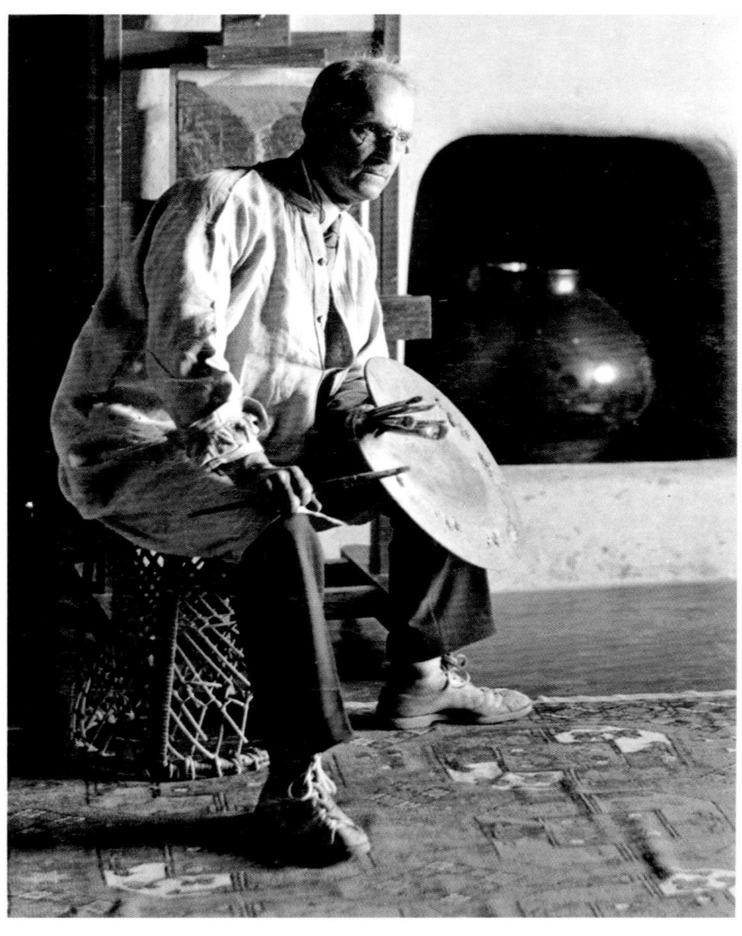

Blumenschein in studio, 1932. Courtesy of the Palace of the Governors, Museum of New Mexico, New Mexico Department of Cultural Affairs, Santa Fe (neg. 59758).

works that he included in a one-man show circulated by Grand Central Art Galleries through 1930. Critics acknowledged his evolving aesthetic. Observing, for example, an edginess to his recent oeuvre, a review in the *Shreveport Louisiana Times* noted "a boldness, a dynamic something about his paintings that defies definition. Done in the modernistic spirit they are tempered by a certain trend toward classicism."[3] This was exactly the artistic direction in which Blumenschein thought his colleagues and large art organizations like the National Academy of Design should go. He stood ready to lead them, though it was a difficult path for most others of his traditionalist ranks.

Gilbert had addressed his January 1930 reply to Blumenschein at the National Arts Club, where the artist had stopped en route to Paris. Missing his family, Blumenschein was scheduled to board the *Aquatania*, sailing to France. In 1928 he and Mary had agreed to sponsor Helen for two years of art education in Paris. The couple's years spent studying abroad had benefited their careers, and Helen would be the third generation of Blumenscheins to enjoy artistic training abroad. Mary planned to accompany Helen as chaperone, the same arrangement of propriety that had governed Mary's student days in Paris. Mother and daughter would build a life similar to the one Mary had experienced with her mother decades earlier. Each would be free to concentrate on her artistic endeavors away from the distraction and demands of caring for husband and father.

Mary and Helen had sailed for France in December 1928. The year of separation had been a long one for Blumenschein. A few months after their reunion, his comments on Paris appeared in the *Taos Valley News*. He found the city to be much cleaner and the architecture as magnificent as ever, but the people were dressed so much like Americans that he could not tell the French from his countrymen.[4] The newspaper reported the family's intended itinerary to Italy and Germany.

The Blumenscheins spent a week in Rome, then, in search of family roots, they took the train to the agricultural village of Brensbach, Germany. They wandered the cobblestone streets and met several relatives—farmers who still resided there. At Reichelsheim Odenwald near Darmstadt, their genealogical quest blossomed when Pastor Schaffnit showed them the names of Blumenscheins that went back to 1640. In Germany, Blumenschein also reconnected with his musical heritage when the family attended the "finest opera . . . a modern version of Tannhäuser."[5] In May, satisfied with his European sojourn, Blumenschein boarded the *Il-de-France* bound for New York and then continued on to New Mexico.

When the University of New Mexico opened its Field School of Art in Taos that summer, Blumenschein was asked to give critiques. As part of the August session, students spent Monday through Thursday mornings painting outdoors in the Twining area or other locations typifying the "motifs of Taos"; in the afternoons they worked from life, often with Pueblo Indian models. The field school bulletin boasted that students would "receive stimulating and profitable instruction from the leading artists of Taos, a group of mature painters, outstanding in the field of contemporary American Art."[6] Critiques with Taos artists were held Friday mornings during the four- to eight-week summer sessions.[7]

Blumenschein hosted his assigned art students in his studio. They placed their paintings on the studio floor, and he critiqued each one's work in turn; sometimes a student would come to him on a private basis.[8] They found him an exacting teacher, one who adhered to high aesthetic and technical standards. Blumenschein taught for the UNM field schools until the mid-1950s. When asked about his advice to young artists, he passed on the standard that had served him so well: "Learn to draw and to draw well. That's the foundation, just like the scales are in music."[9] As years progressed and abstraction gained a foothold in American art, such counsel must have sounded somewhat tedious and old-fashioned; he nonetheless adhered to the artistic principles that guided him. In the late thirties, advising his daughter in similar matters, he pressed for accuracy of construction, precision of drawing, and "elegant contour" of line.[10] His critiques could be stinging, and he justified them to Helen as well as his field school students by stating that "the approach I had was from high standards, and you must be able to take it—and improve."[11]

For Blumenschein the painter, recognition and honors abounded in 1931. During Helen and Mary's absence, he had more time to devote to conceptualizing and experimenting with new compositions. His efforts were rewarded that year when his *Indian Girl Seated by Oven* won the National Academy's First Logan Prize and the Salmagundi Club's Shaw Purchase Prize of one thousand dollars. The latter commendation was especially revered by Blumenschein, as it placed him in the vortex of national art life. Art patron Samuel T. Shaw supported living American artists through art purchases and annual cash prizes. Paintings from his American collection graced the walls of his Grant Union Hotel, located at Forty-second Street and Park Avenue. His association with the National Academy of Design, the Society of American Artists, and the Salmagundi Club brought him into contact with member artists like Blumenschein.

Each year Shaw hosted a dinner party for the winner of his prize. He and the winner sat at the center surrounded by tables of painters in formal attire. Blumenschein related that the "honor guest at this dinner is not allowed to make a speech—which is a relief—but he is obliged to wear a laurel wreath on his brow during the entire evening."[12] Blumenschein valued the experience. He had won not only approval from Shaw but also acknowledgement from his artist peers. The highlight of the evening came when artists in attendance signed a limited edition print of *Indian Girl Seated by Oven.*[13]

In 1931 the Carnegie Institute paid tribute to Blumenschein's stature in the American art community, selecting him as one of the jurors for its Thirtieth Annual International Exhibition. This prestigious honor was bestowed only on the most highly respected, established American artists. Over the past dozen years Blumenschein had served as juror at the National Academy of Design, the Corcoran Gallery of Art, and the Art Institute of Chicago, but the Carnegie was particularly alluring. In contrast to annual shows of American artists at those other institutions, the Carnegie included both Americans and Europeans in its yearly survey. When Andrew Carnegie founded the institute in 1895, his plan included

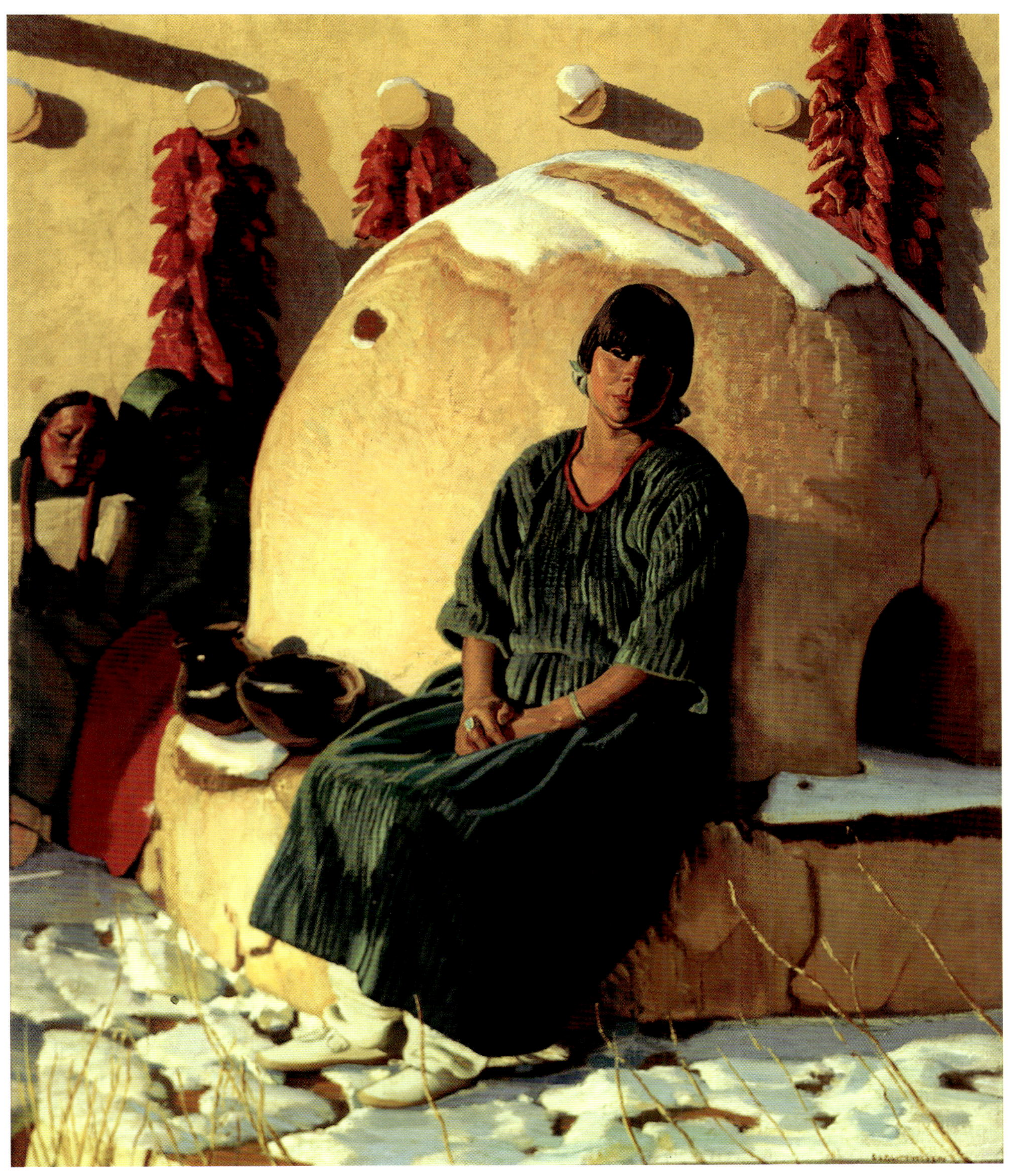

Indian Girl Seated by Oven (originally *Girl Seated by Oven,* 1926), reworked 1931
Oil on canvas, 30 × 25 inches
Private collection

a museum of modern art to celebrate the latest trends, or what he called the "old masters of tomorrow."

The exhibition opened on October 14, and the *Christian Science Monitor* applauded the jurors' efforts, calling it a "notable gathering on the walls of the Carnegie Institute." Of special note, according to the reviewer, was the representation of "those apostles of the Southwest, Walter Ufer and Ernest L. Blumenschein."[14] Blumenschein's two works, *New Mexico Interior* and *Moon, Morning Star, Evening Star*, garnered positive acclaim. *New York Times* critic Edward Alden Jewell called Blumenschein's New Mexico canvases "imaginatively, often glowingly, ingenious."[15] Jewell thought his works showed distinctly modern tendencies, despite Blumenschein's self-characterization as a "somewhat radical conservative" painter at the time.[16] But the 1931 International reflected Carnegie's desire to showcase even more aggressive forms of modern art, and the three-thousand-dollar prize went to Taos Protocubist painter Andrew Dasburg.

Throughout the 1930s, Blumenschein often had to juggle paintings between the numerous exhibitions he entered. For a painter who was not prolific, this often proved challenging. In 1931 when the schedules for four autumn annuals overlapped, Blumenschein had to strategize—of the museum-class paintings in his studio, which would best represent him at each venue? He had only one new painting, *New Mexico Interior,* at hand. He chose to send it and *Moon, Morning Star, Evening Star* to the more prestigious Carnegie International.

The remaining paintings, less venturesome canvases from the twenties, found their way into other venues; *Adobe Village—Winter* went to the St. Louis City Art Museum, *Adobe Church* to the Art Institute of Chicago, and *Mountains near Taos* to the National Academy of Design. Just as some of Blumenschein's paintings received recognition for their modernist proclivities, other more traditional works that were making the national circuit countered the formative contributions he was making. This confused some writers. In *The History and Ideals of American Art*, for example, Stanford University art historian Eugene Neuhaus included him in a chapter titled "The Painters of Indian and Frontier Life" and reproduced Blumenschein's painting *The Peacemaker*, from 1913, as representative of his western painting.[17] The Whitney Museum of American Art's Virgil Barker listed Blumenschein, along with Higgins, Ufer, and Frederic Remington, under the heading of "Painters of Western Life," while modernists like Marsden Hartley, Georgia O'Keeffe, and John Marin, as well as regionalist painter Thomas Hart Benton, were regarded as "Contemporary."[18] In 1931, as Blumenschein's paintings were receiving recognition for their modernist tendencies, this restrictive categorization cut off his work with his academic paintings of the 1910s. This occurred when he had nearly three decades of painting left in him, when in fact he would develop two more modernist series: monumental southwestern landscapes and Albuquerque cityscapes.

To escape the world of art critiques and competitive institutional exhibitions, Blumenschein retreated to his beloved Southwest, where he occasionally worked side-by-side with his favorite student, Helen Blumenschein. He found that travel outside New Mexico, sometimes in conjunction with tennis tournaments, offered fresh subject matter and painting opportunities. A new approach to the landscape began with a two-week sketching trip in October 1932, where Helen accompanied him. (Mary stayed home: her first camping trip in pouring rain just after the family moved to Taos was also her last.) Following a weekend of tennis in Phoenix, they spent two weeks near the Superstition Mountains. Their destination was Roosevelt Dam, an "amazing structure built between the rock masses of the cañons sides." The trip to the isolated area was slowed by narrow winding roads and, as he reported to Mary, "the most difficult driving along precipices" that he had ever experienced.[19] But once situated, father and daughter settled into sketching the "barren and magnificent" scenery and the "rocky savage landscape" of the Salt River Canyon.[20]

Blumenschein brought several sketches, no larger than a postcard, and three watercolors back from this excursion. These carefully rendered studies were subsequently developed into large pictures, often 3-by-4 feet, for exhibition purposes.[21] The abstract power of nature and the essential geometry of the canyon cliffs and boulders were combined with what one observer noted as a "strong sense of drama in his lighting effects" and his preoccupation with the play of light on natural forms.[22]

A change of scene provided Blumenschein with novel subject matter—"I usually brought back an art inspiration from these trips in the Southwest"—and launched new approaches to painting.[23] In his records, Blumenschein referred to *Arizona Cañon* as one of his "best [and last] academic works."[24] When a transition occurred in his painting, he returned to the classic academic model to work out formal problems. In *Sangre de Cristo Mountains* and *Adobe Village—Winter* of the late twenties, the mountains in the background had loomed large over the human drama in the foreground. At Roosevelt Dam the mass of concrete and steel set against the massive reach of canyon walls fueled his paintbrush. The mammoth proportions of the canyon walls pushed Blumenschein to paint "pure landscape."

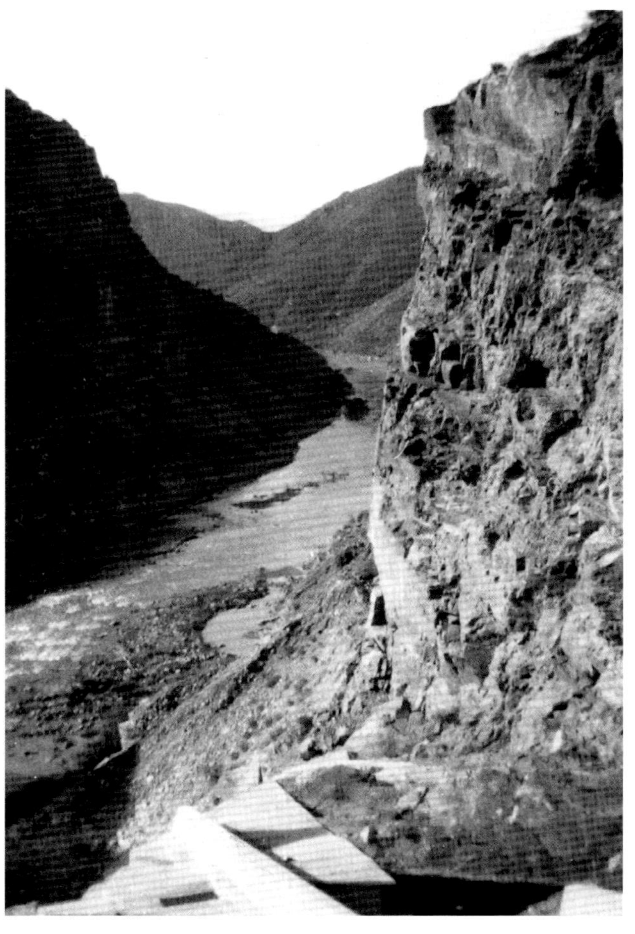

Roosevelt Dam, Arizona. Courtesy of the Palace of the Governors, Museum of New Mexico, New Mexico Department of Cultural Affairs, Santa Fe (neg. HP.05.25-R).

Starting with *Arizona*, Blumenschein began a series of landscapes that occupied him throughout much of the 1930s.[25] His work took on another dimension as he left the lessons of Post-Impressionism behind. His style changed. Nature still influenced him, but the scenes he portrayed displayed more emotion. The use of bold patterning and pure, bright colors in his paintings increased. He applied color more broadly, and his forms became increasingly more abstracted. This brought a different expression and balance to his work, as he explained at the time: "Regarding my technique: I believe it is as unconscious (that is the manipulation of brush and paint) as any man's language. But the composition, the choice of lines, the harmony and quality of color, the balance of masses are all guided by the sentiment or motif of the painting. How much these elements are emotion, how much intellectual, is beyond me to state. I know they are both emotional and intellectual and draw on every resource in your mind and body."[26]

In 1933 Blumenschein completed a second exhibition-size landscape based on California's Mojave Desert region, the result of another tennis trip, this time to Pasadena.[27] He had visited the nearby Mojave Indian Reservation in late November 1898 on assignment from *McClure's*. Apparently that basin-and-range landscape with its jagged, angular rock formations made a lasting impression: "I saw the desert from a hill in the afterglow and was very impressed and affected. I memorized the color and light from the brief moment it lasted, then went sixty miles where we could sleep and made memory sketches in pencil and paint. I spent the next two days going back to the spot, getting the structure of hills and material for the painting. There was never a tennis trip that did not yield a picture."[28] It was as if the physical exertions and competitive tensions of the tennis tour combined with the physical dynamics and geomorphic tensions of the desert drove him to the heights of creativity, which as it surged forth, engaged him fully.

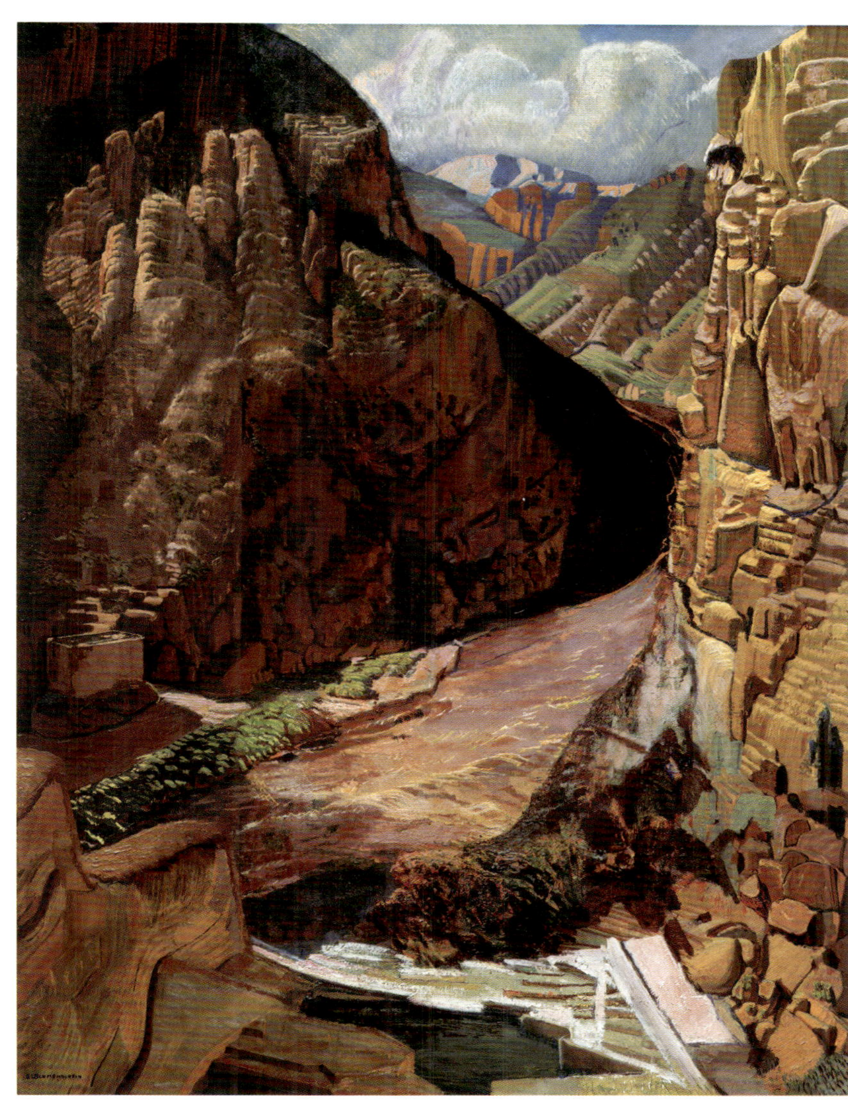

Arizona Canyon (originally ***Arizona,*** 1931; later ***Red Symphony,*** 1939), finished 1957, oil on canvas, 51 × 39 inches. Courtesy of the Nedra Matteucci Galleries.

The structure of the hills Blumenschein confronted there were ridges interspersed with *bajadas*, or broad alluvial aprons. These poured forth millions of years ago, when volcanic activity created the Mojave, the most arid desert in North America. The sun setting between these areas made them appear orange-hot, as if fiery molten lava still flowed. The artist was looking due north at sunset, the time when the raking light made dust-filled valleys beyond appear to glow from within. This effect is made more dramatic by the contrasting deep red-purple monolithic mountain, possibly a cinder cone, in the foreground. *Mojave Desert* exemplified Blumenschein's stylistic progression and the artistic depth and maturity he had achieved. His friend Taos modernist artist Howard Cook would later comment on his compatriot's triumphal coup:

> *Mojave Desert* [is] a majestic picture large and mural in feeling. It is an epic experience, a thoroughly realized creative expression of the inner spiritual beauty of the desert, finally summing up all experience and thought of the country that Blumenschein loves. Intellectually conceived and designed with sensitive architectural form appropriate to the character of mountain-desert, here is a tremendously moving symbol of the forces of nature as they thrust out rock shapes to meet the line of receding hills. The canvas is illuminated with a deep reverence for these forces of the infinite. It is a religious tribute to the mysteries and the glorious wonder of the world about us.[29]

Blumenschein later rated *Mojave Desert* as one of his "top notchers"—it earned a star in his ledger book. Fellow Taos Society artist Kenneth Adams agreed: "That canvas is an experience I shall ever remember. Think it rates among your best works."[30] Adams, whose paintings and prints were more abstract, appreciated the painting's modern quality.

The two tennis trips from the early thirties brought Blumenschein face to face with stunning new geographies. Once he finished what he referred to as the "foreign" challenge that painting the Arizona and California desert backcountry had presented, he developed a deeper, renewed vision for his own backyard. Taos Mountain, sacred to Taos Pueblo people, had formed the decorative backdrop for *Sangre de Cristo Mountains* and *Adobe Village—Winter* in the twenties. Blumenschein had written in 1927 about the valley "surrounded on three sides by mountains and [on] the west by the great desert" replete with "almost continual sunshine."[31] Now, in February 1934, just in time for his second solo show in New York, he completed *Taos Valley*, which more than either of his earlier landscape masterpieces fit that description.

Knolls painted in warm browns and reds, held to neutral tones, form a montane foreground looking down onto the broad sweep of land below. A rutted dirt road, giving the illusion of depth, leads into one end of the valley. Foreshortened by the view from above, the tawny valley unfurls, dotted with

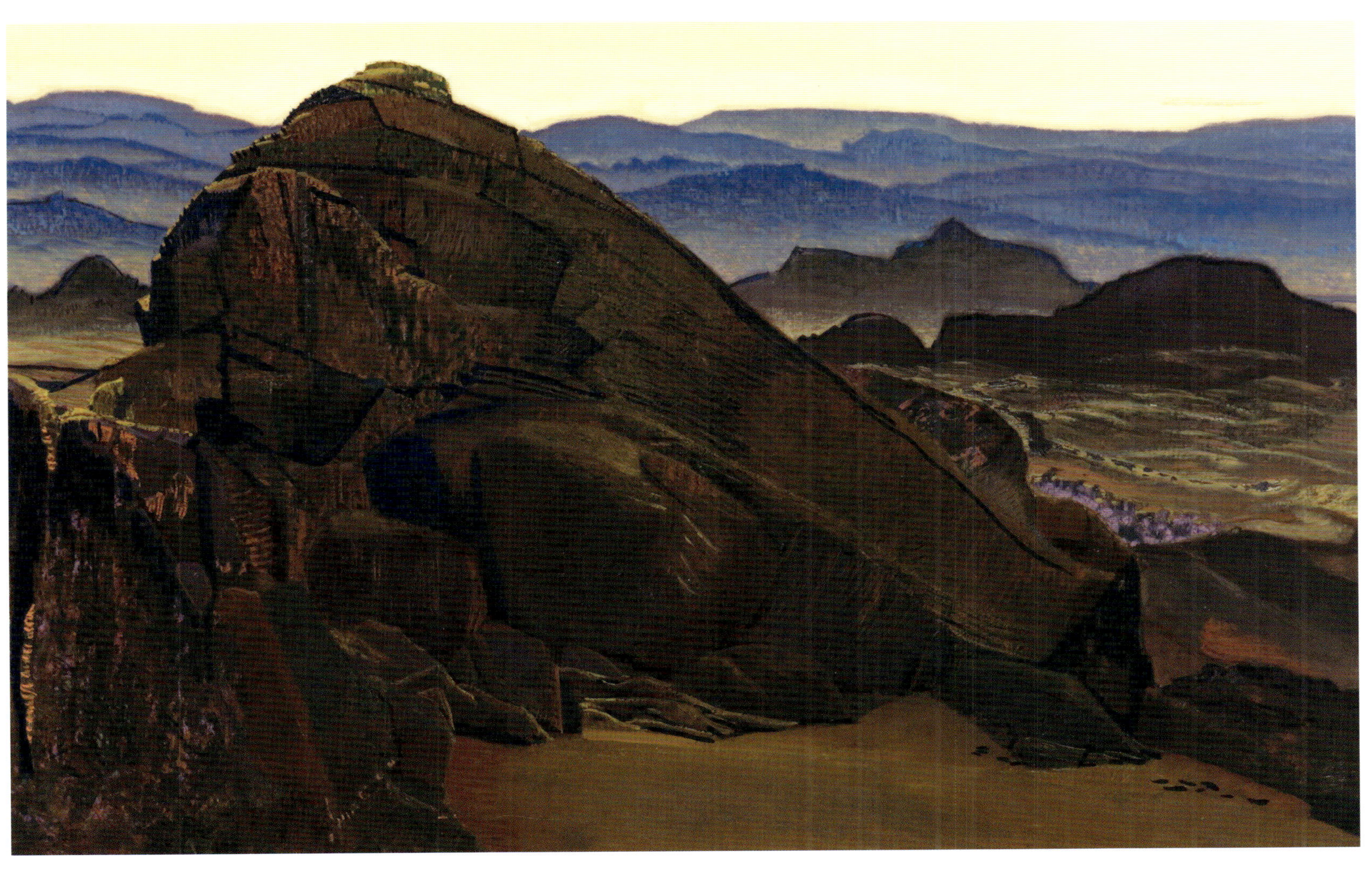

Mojave Desert, 1933, reworked ca. 1949
Oil on canvas, 32½ × 50¾ inches
Courtesy of the Gilcrease Museum, Tulsa, Oklahoma

minute adobe structures and filled with straw-colored sunlight. A rose-gold evening light climbs up the red "Blood of Christ" (Sangre de Cristo) Mountains in the background. So far the viewer finds tranquility in this seeming pastoral setting—that is, until the eye focuses on storm clouds, painted sheer as a watercolor and heavy with rain, that threaten overhead. This creates a tension in the painting, the kind of drama quickly changing weather conditions in northern New Mexico present, the very scene Blumenschein liked to portray. But these qualities of light, drama, and tension were little different from his earlier two landscapes. What makes this new is its fundamentally architectonic power, its lack of elegant design, and its subordination of human presence. Entering what some would call his period of "monumental landscape painting," he observed, shaped, and transformed nature to convey a fresh vision. In turn, the landscape shaped him, as Howard Cook observed:

> Stern canyons, great mountain ranges, desert space have moulded the character of this artist who is so sensitively tuned to nature's moods, and have ultimately shaped the symbols and the manner of expressing them on canvas. He went to nature directly, spending years camping, fishing, and hunting, loving the harsh, exciting color and elemental structure of the quiet, monumental country. These experienced associations have been absorbed into his spirit, and he has painted with a touch of their precious, mystical guiding.[32]

In *Taos Valley,* as in many of his later landscapes, Blumenschein employed a new painting device: he placed warm colors in the foreground and cool colors in the background to give his paintings both depth and weight.[33] During this period he also commented on how much beauty and drama moved him; getting those elements on canvas was his "happy job."[34]

Modernity of a practical as well as aesthetic nature made inroads in remote Taos. In the 1930s a motor-driven power generator supplied the town with its first electricity, and phone service provided the isolated residents with immediate

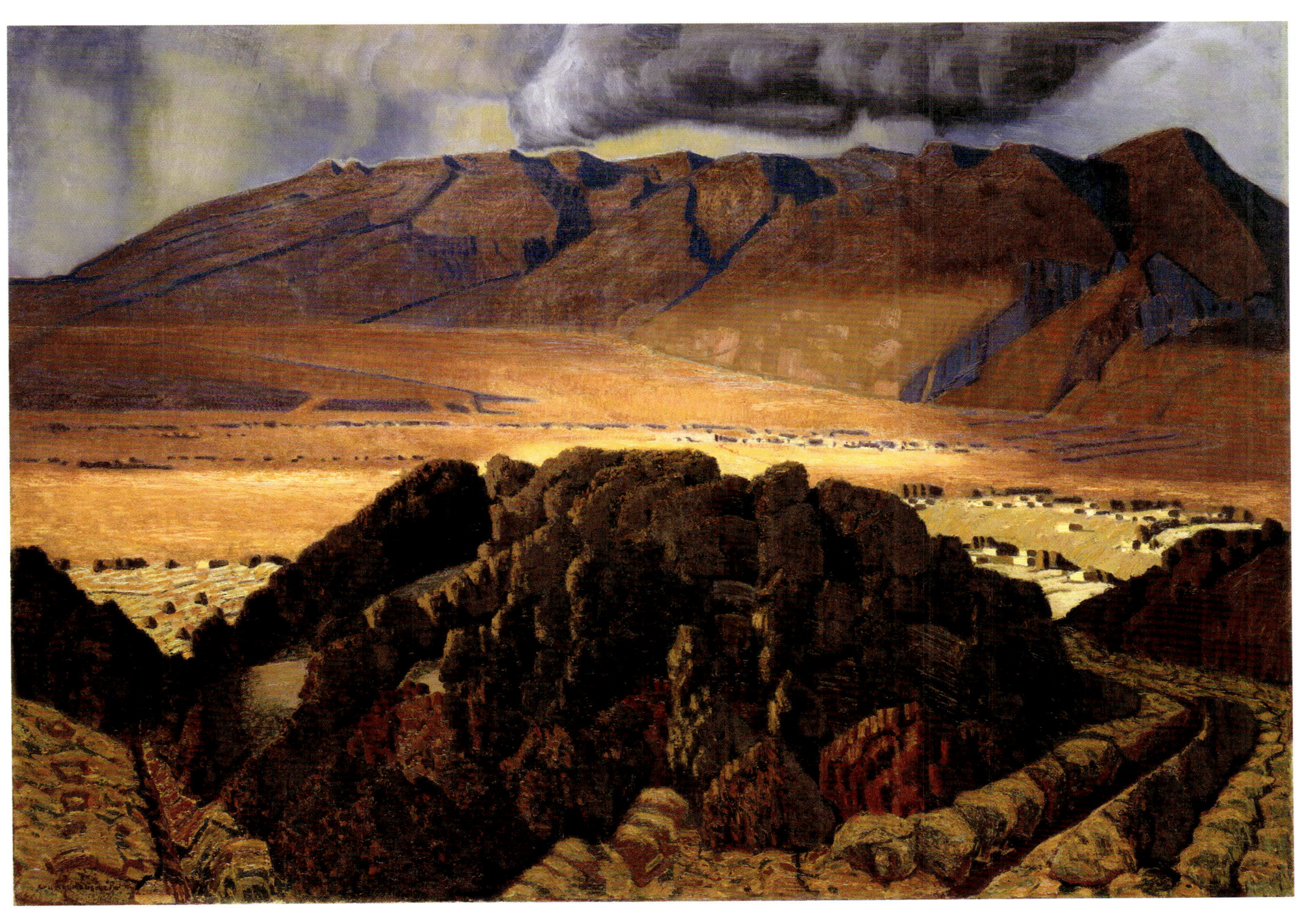

Taos Valley, 1933
Oil on canvas, 25 × 35 inches
Courtesy of The Metropolitan Museum of Art, George A. Hearn Fund, 1934 (34.61)

communication to the outside world.[35] When the state paved the road between Taos and Santa Fe in 1934, motorists had quicker, easier access. As hotels and private residences obtained electricity, phone service, and running water, it became easier to entertain. Gerson Gusdorf, whose converted mercantile business became the Don Fernando Hotel in 1926, held a yearly formal dinner for the artists, replete with amusing postprandial speeches. He also offered the hotel walls for displays of their work.[36] The *Taos Valley News* reviewed a Blumenschein exhibition there in May 1929.

In 1932, after study in Mexico with Diego Rivera on a Guggenheim Fellowship, Emil Bisttram settled in Taos. He and Blumenschein became acquainted and discovered that they had each abandoned commercial work to pursue painting in Taos and that both advocated modernism. They also liked to fish. In May Blumenschein wrote that he had invited Bisttram to the opening of fishing season at Eagle Nest Lake: "I feel indebted to him. So it will not be a cheap outing."[37] One reason for his gratitude became clear the following year.

With Blumenschein and four other painters, Bisttram organized the first gallery in Taos dedicated solely to work by artists with modernist leanings. The Heptagon Gallery opened at the Don Fernando in May 1933. The artists' styles differed widely, but a common purpose bound them. In December the hotel burned to the ground in a fire that destroyed most of the plaza's southwest corner. The Taos volunteer fire department members, many of them artists, managed to save the paintings.[38] The following June the gallery reopened in a new space at the La Fonda Hotel.

Bisttram moved to Taos during the Depression, when the bottom had dropped out of the art market. Like many others, he needed a job to sustain him through these hard times. He decided to apply the spiritual-in-art and Dynamic Symmetry theories learned from his New York mentors Nicholas Roehrich and Jay Hambidge to a classroom setting in Taos. Blumenschein brought in art students to help him launch his Taos School of Art just months later. In his teachings, Bisttram stated his belief that abstract work could convey more meaning through symbolism than paintings that depicted physical objects. Around this time, Bisttram invited the old-timers to attend a lecture on Dynamic Symmetry. Perhaps there he let it be known that he created "pot boiler" representational art to earn his living but that abstractions were the only true art.[39] This undoubtedly vexed the older artists like Blumenschein; indeed, this may have prompted his departure from the Heptagon Gallery. The two men differed in philosophy: Bisttram excluded other art styles, where Blumenschein, based on his training at the Art Students League, was more inclusive.

In 1938 Bisttram and Albuquerque modernist Raymond Jonson formed the Transcendental Painting Group. Alfred Morang explained the group's purpose: "to carry painting beyond the appearance of the physical world, through new concepts of space, color, light, and design, to imaginative realms that are idealistic and spiritual."[40] The group included some well-known abstract painters and three of Bisttram's students. In 1939 the Transcendental Painting Group exhibited at the Golden Gate Exposition, and the following year they showed in New York at the Guggenheim Museum and the Museum of Modern Art.[41] Their activities aroused such unease among representational artists that by 1939, the year surrealist painter Tom Benrimo arrived in Taos, a "committee of three, led by Blumenschein," called on him to ferret out his artistic "intentions."[42] The same thing happened in 1944 to Louis Ribak, who showed at New York's Whitney Studio Club alongside the well-known abstractionist Stuart Davis when he came on the Taos scene in 1941.[43]

Bisttram, on the leading edge of a modernist wave of artists who would soon make their own history in northern New Mexico, continued teaching at his Taos School of Art through the 1940s. However popular with his students, he fell out of favor with some of the older artists. Within five years of their meeting, Blumenschein's opinion of the younger man had flipped. By 1937 he considered Bisttram "a four-flushing, self-pushing, narrow-minded individual."[44] Nonetheless, Blumenschein benefited from Bisttram's and other modernists' presence in Taos. Years later he admitted that "modern art [had] helped his painting." His style changed, "making him more free as a painter and helping him break with academicism."[45]

In 1933, at the height of the Depression, the Century of Progress Exposition opened in Chicago. The fair celebrated the city's centennial and advances in science and industry over the last century. New technology gave people hope of an easier life and a rising standard of living. Architects carried the idea of progress in this modern age into their designs of the pavilions. They eschewed the classical architecture of Chicago's 1893 Columbian Exposition, preferring more modern, functional buildings based on European modernist models like the Bauhaus. Judging from the attendance, the fair spoke to the heart of the American people. From its opening in May 1933 until its close in October 1934, thirty-nine million people visited.

Tourism numbers swelled throughout the city, setting records at places like the Art Institute of Chicago. In preparation for the Century of Progress, the museum had cancelled its annuals in order to host special exhibitions. The 1933 special show echoed the World's Fair centennial theme—it stressed, in its selection of painting and sculpture, "a hundred years of progress in American picture collecting." Blumenschein and five other artists represented New Mexico in the 1933 exhibition—Randall Davey, John Sloan, Nicolai Fechin, Victor Higgins, and Walter Ufer.

The 1934 Century of Progress exhibition had two objectives: to showcase the museum's permanent collection and to highlight the "characteristics and development of American painting" from the eighteenth century to the 1930s. It featured loans from museums, including the newly opened Whitney Museum of American Art, and from galleries, private collectors, and younger artists representing themselves. A room devoted solely to George Bellows, William Glackens, and George Luks paintings flowed into the Contemporary American Painting section. In this section, works by painters born in the 1890s and early 1900s hung next to the older generation. The works of these established younger artists, like Arnold and Lucile Blanch, John Steuart Curry, and Grant Wood, who had studied at the time of the Armory Show, were decidedly modernist in nature. So was Blumenschein's entry, *Canyon Red and Black*.

Blumenschein loved to fish in the canyon of the Rio Grande and did many sketches there. He chronicled painting in the canyon at Christmastime. The temperature was near freezing, the sun warm, the air still. The landscape, beautifully lit by "the low sun of winter," produced yellow, brown, tan, and gray, a palette of hues that he regarded as particularly "fine in quality." Back in the studio, as was often his custom, he executed a medium-size study to put down the composition, color, and design he had in mind. The study suited him, but when he began the final, exhibition-sized canvas, things did not go well. His canvas, a month's work, proved disappointing.

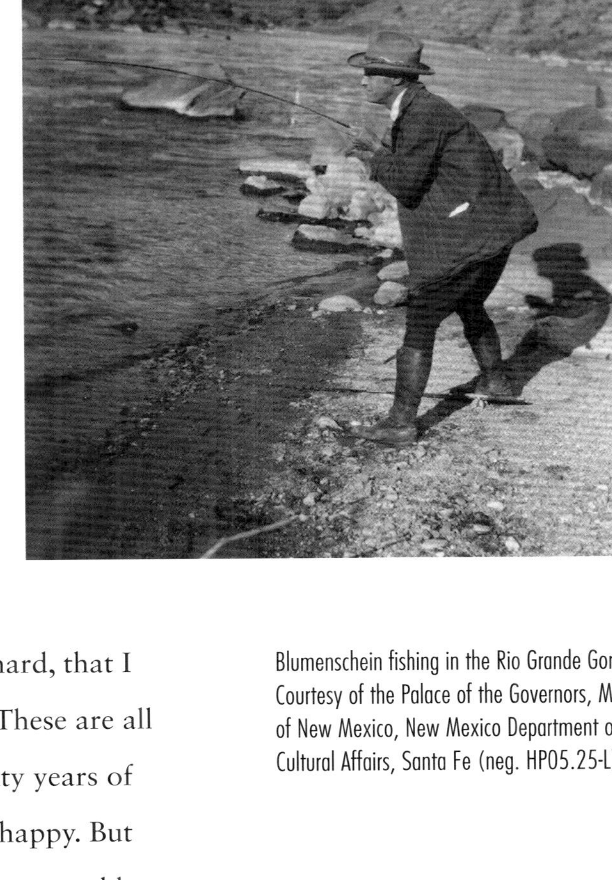

Blumenschein fishing in the Rio Grande Gorge. Courtesy of the Palace of the Governors, Museum of New Mexico, New Mexico Department of Cultural Affairs, Santa Fe (neg. HP05.25-L).

> I have struggled with every angle of the composition and while I have some beautiful passages, the painting as a whole does not possess a moving quality. Some days of the last month I worked on after dark, in the studio, with electric light always on this same picture of the Rio Grande Cañon then I would eat my supper at 10:30 at night. And one day I was so interested, or struggling so hard, that I did not eat any lunch, but continued to paint until dark.—These are all intimate details of how foolish a painter can be, even at sixty years of age. If I get a good picture as the result of my efforts, I am happy. But sometimes even after several months' work I have to give it up, and burn the canvass or destroy it.[46]

In the end, Blumenschein triumphed. He achieved the perfection he was seeking in *Canyon Red and Black*. Enveloped in sunset light and shadow, Blumenschein's canvas captured the drama of dusk and the structural play between color and form. By dividing the picture plane diagonally, so that monolithic basalt boulders in the foreground darkness contrast with the vivid colors in the sunlit cliffs behind, Blumenschein provided an all-encompassing statement of nature's universal breadth and power. Painted in the low light of winter sky, the ambient and predominate reds and yellows reflect off the black basalt canyon walls. Blumenschein heightened and intensified the colors and the geology to deliver the full emotional effect this landscape had on him.

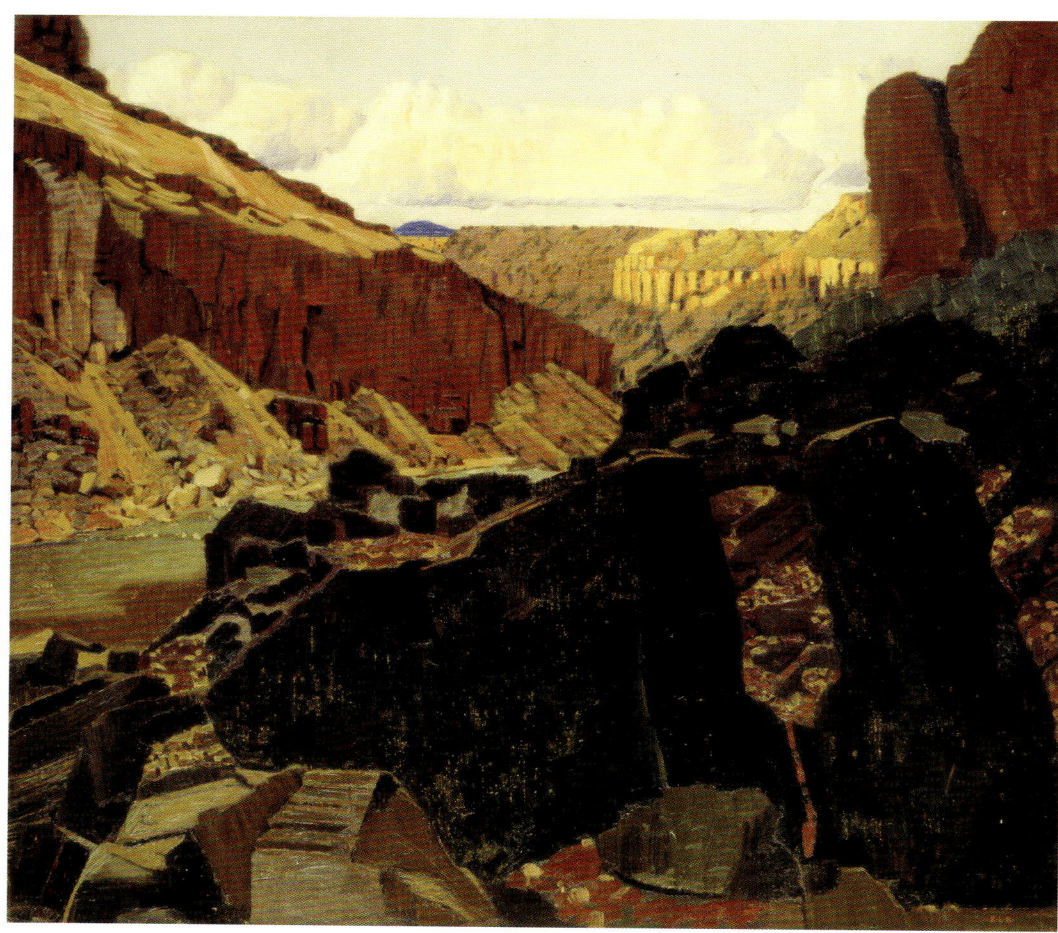

Canyon Red and Black (study), 1933, oil on canvas, 24⅛ × 27 inches. Courtesy of Stark Museum of Art, Orange, Texas (31.30/10).

None of Blumenschein's paintings were faithful replications of a scene. In the landscapes, he literally moved mountains or canyon walls to create in his compositions the sensation it evoked in him. Nonetheless, his daughter, Helen, remarked on her father's success in depicting the canyon as no other painter had done. He could simplify it and still convey the rocks' depth and weight and the light of the receding color.[47] As in *Arizona,* flat masses of color defined his composition. The architectonic painting implies the space, volume, and depth that exists within the flattened picture plane. As Blumenschein worked to uphold his credo—keeping masses large and forms plastic, moving, and alive—in *Canyon Red and Black*, it is as if he were retelling a symphonic narrative with an orchestra conductor's back hovered over the players while the audience views the scene from the front few rows below.[48] When *Canyon Red and Black* was given to the Dayton Art Institute in 1935, the local papers noted its rich color and "huge blocks of river-carved rock and cliffs barren of trees." It had taken

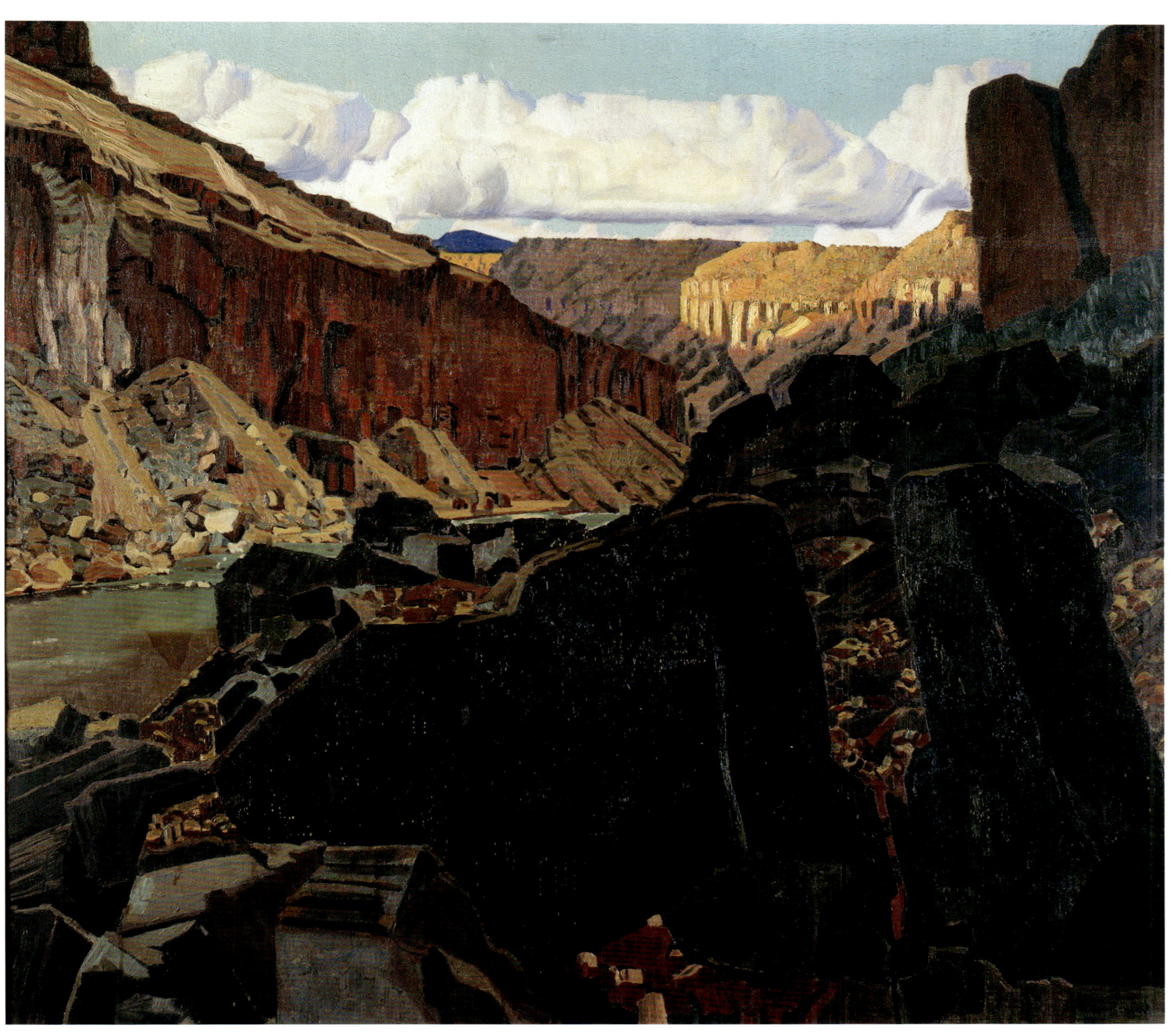

Canyon Red and Black, 1934
Oil on canvas, 39½ × 44½ inches
Courtesy of The Dayton Art Institute, Dayton, Ohio (1935.14)
Gift of Mr. John G. Lowe

the competence and potent best efforts of "one of America's finest painters" to capture the scene.[49]

From the canyons, Blumenschein looked again to the mountains. He composed a series of paintings devoted to the Picurís Mountains south of Taos. Previously they had appeared in truncated form in the background of his painting *The Burro*. Blumenschein also painted an early version of them in 1926, *Mountains near Taos*. It was reworked in 1954 with enriched color and several modifications in detail, but in its initial form it was the "mother study of others." Blumenschein subsequently painted five more canvases featuring "the same beautiful background."[50] When snow covered the gaps of bare, rocky ground between patches of forested land, the resultant design reminded him of Indian blanket patterns. He repeated the elements—stylized clouds and snow-covered mountains reaching pyramidal peaks—for the background. In *Indians in the Mountains*, he mirrored the patterning of "highly colored" Navajo and Rio Grande blankets as decorative motifs weaving his Pueblo subjects into the conifer and snow-striped mountains.[51] The horses—buckskin, dun, sorrel, dark bay—and their riders add natural movement and rhythm to the undulating plains in the middle and right foreground. They seem to grow out of the boulders at the left, imparting the landscape with an organic unity.

In spite of the Depression, 1934 provided another successful benchmark for Blumenschein. Besides the inclusion of *Canyon Red and Black* in Chicago's Century of Progress exhibition, the Carnegie International featured his landscape *Arizona* in its dual showing in Pittsburg and San Francisco. *Arizona* won Blumenschein his second National Arts Club medal in January.[52] In March Grand Central Art Galleries issued a press release for Landscapes of New Mexico and Arizona, Blumenschein's second solo exhibition. The release boasted of him as "one of the most distinguished American artists and winner of nearly all important prizes." New Yorkers would come to see the decidedly new trend of his painting.

The exhibition drew notice in two of *Art Digest*'s March editions. For one reviewer, Blumenschein's latest canvases offered the opportunity for the public to "evaluate anew this artist's undoubted ability to express his love for nature in its most beautiful and powerful aspects."[53] Nearly all the paintings evoked a spiritual eminence, "an apocalyptic quality," as if the artist had so immersed himself in his subject that they meant "something more to him than mere landscapes." Returning to the musical analogy, the magazine singled out *Allegro Maestoso* for "the curved segments of the hill . . . akin to the symphonic vibrations of its title." No "glib description of travelogue" these, but "a reflection of a long, intimate acquaintance [that captures] the salient character of each one," concluded a reviewer in the *New York Evening Post*. Viewers were to "marvel at the temerity of the painters who attempt to put any part of its colossal panorama on record."[54]

Modernist critic Henry McBride, acerbic, patronizing, and condescending in most of his Blumenschein reviews, viewed Blumenschein's new landscapes no differently than usual. There was in his mind no elemental abstract formalism here but rather the typically faithful, literal replications of nature's countenance. McBride described *Canyon Red and Black* as "too literally and rigidly painted to suit my private taste." He went on to suggest that Blumenschein, was pandering to the masses. With the world so constituted of people who preferred such "a literal landscape" to a "highly emotional poem" like El Greco's *View of Toledo*, he wrote, "well, the artist was not to be pitied," for he had "the majority [of the public] with him."[55]

Ironically in light of McBride's criticism, the major sale of the year came not from the Grand Central Gallery exhibition but from other quarters. In April the Metropolitan Museum of Art purchased Blumenschein's entry, *Taos Valley*, from the National Academy's spring annual.[56] Blumenschein considered this a major coup. Counting the Metropolitan's acquisition, Blumenschein paintings in museum collections now numbered fourteen.

Blumenschein always strove for excellence, and such recognition from the Metropolitan Museum of Art was confirmation of his expectations for himself. Yet, during the Depression, when there was a severely diminished demand for easel paintings, he had to find other venues to exercise such ambitions and to keep his skill and eye fresh.[57] Among the programs initiated by the Roosevelt administration

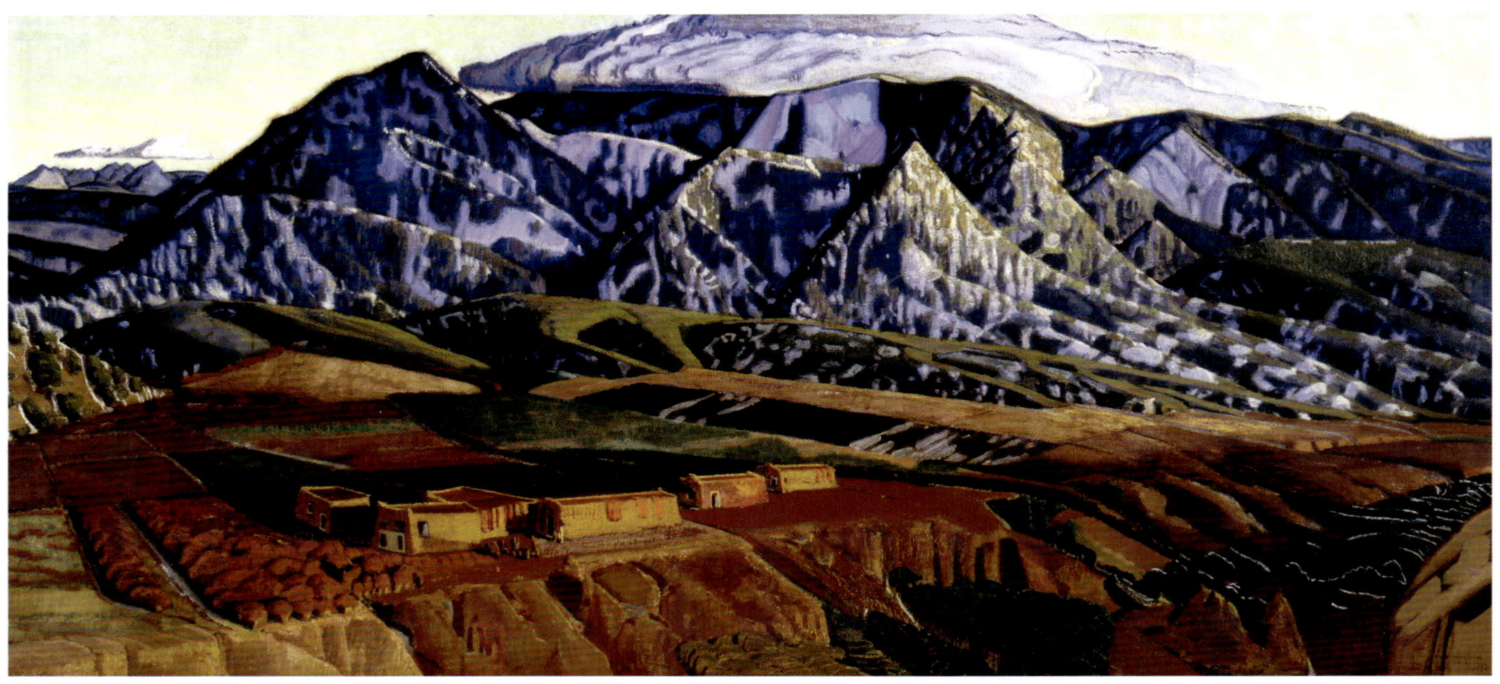

Mountains near Taos, 1926, reworked 1954, oil on canvas, 22½ × 49½ inches. Courtesy of the Dallas Museum of Art, Dallas, Texas. Gift of Helen Greene Blumenschein

to help artists like Blumenschein through these hard times was a federal program that succeeded the Public Works Art Project (PWAP) in 1934, known as Section of Painting and Sculpture.[58] This was not a relief program like the PWAP. The Section, charged with commissioning paintings and sculpture of "the highest quality" to decorate new federal buildings, established democratic procedures that required artists to submit sketches anonymously to a jury of selection.[59] The jury awarded commissions to the best designs. Between 1934 and 1943, the Section created "the world's largest art gallery" in federal buildings and 1,100 post offices.[60] This was governmental art patronage for the discriminating artist, and while it and other programs kept artists from starving and provided the American people with cultural amenities, it also engendered their best efforts.

New Mexico had the highest percentage per capita of artists working on such projects. Four Taos artists received the state's earliest and largest commission in 1934—a ten-panel mural for their town's new county courthouse.[61] Others followed in 1935 when the Section announced that year's competition winners. Of the forty-four painters named, four were from New Mexico, and Blumenschein was one of them.[62]

Ed Rowan, who headed the Section of Painting and Sculpture, informed Blumenschein of his commission before December 1935 newspaper reports reached him. Rowan wrote that, "on the basis of his competent design," the artist

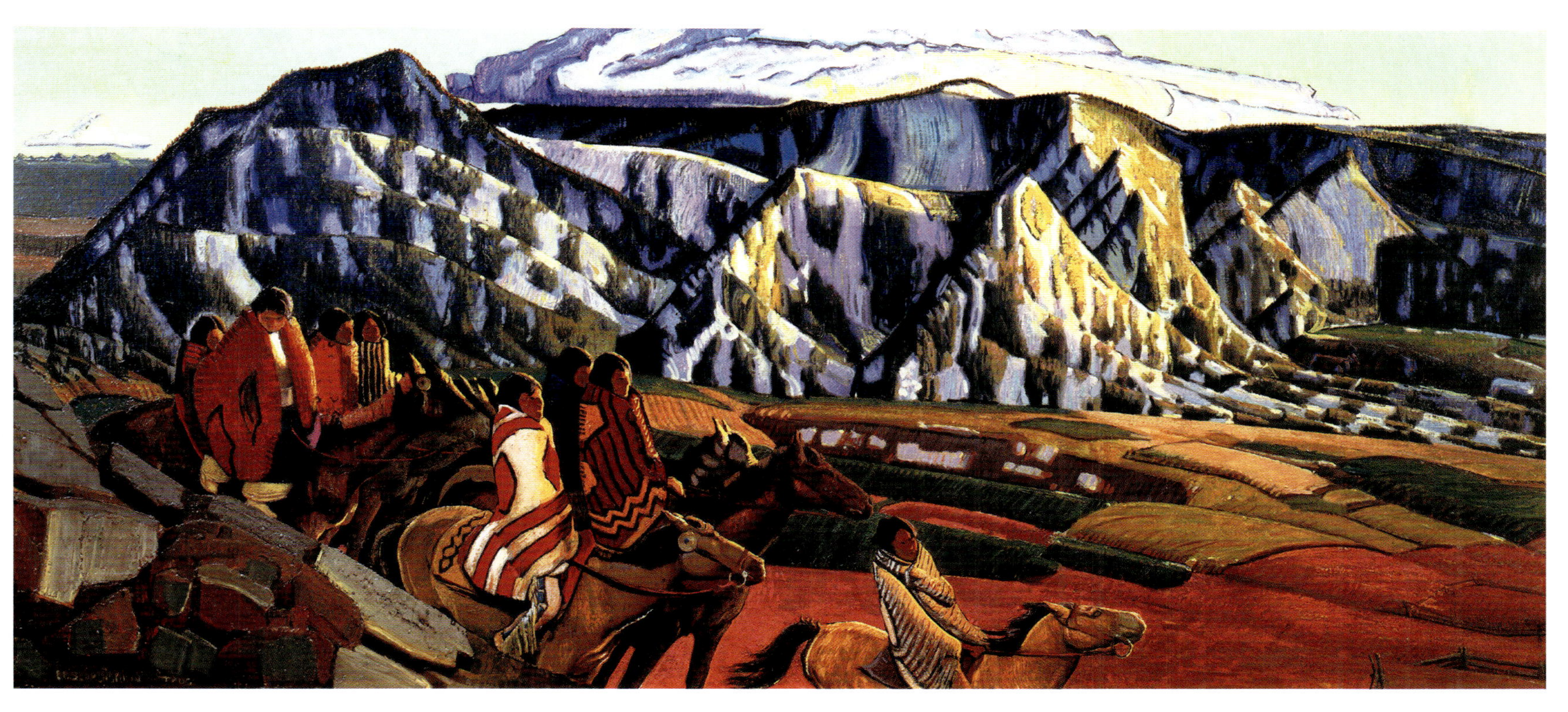

Indians in the Mountains (originally *Landscape with Indians,* 1936), reworked 1938
Oil on panel, 20 × 44½ inches
Courtesy of the J. N. Bartfield Galleries, New York, New York

had been appointed to execute a mural for the new post office in Walsenburg, Colorado. He would receive $580 for a mural designed to fit a space measuring 11 feet 9½ inches by 4 feet 1¾ inches. Blumenschein needed to complete the work in twelve to eighteen months and should choose subject matter appropriate to the locale.[63]

Blumenschein had long admired and wanted to paint the Spanish Peaks near Walsenburg, so he chose them as his subject. With this in mind, he let Rowan know that he "could get something that would please [himself] as well as the citizens of that community." Due to zero-degree winter weather, though, Blumenschein had to delay a sketching trip until spring. In the meantime, he began to question his allotted funding. He had learned that Kenneth Adams's commission for a comparable mural would pay nine hundred dollars. And while he was glad for Adams, who needed the job and should be well compensated, he wondered if a mistake had been made.[64] Rowan responded that compensation varied according to the cost of the building, which caused a variation in the amount each artist received.[65]

In February 1936 Rowan notified the Walsenburg postmaster of Blumenschein's appointment. The artist hoped to get to the area by March or April to make sketches. A commission for an overmantel in Pittsburg, however, delayed him until October.[66] In December Rowan informed Blumenschein that his sketches had been approved. The work, which Rowan described as a "dignified type of landscape mural" suitable to the purpose, had been "enthusiastically received" for "its fine monumentality" in design. Rowan encouraged him to maintain the palette suggested in his sketch. Blumenschein received his contract and a voucher for two hundred dollars in January 1937. Before executing the mural, he planned to make a large study.[67]

An inspiration for a "portrait group" of what he called a "notorious Taos freaks" struck Blumenschein in the summer of 1937. This so distracted him that it promised to delay work on the mural. He confessed his whim to Rowan in mid-September, when only a month and a half of his contract remained, and asked for a two- to three-month extension. Rowan was not sympathetic. He told Blumenschein

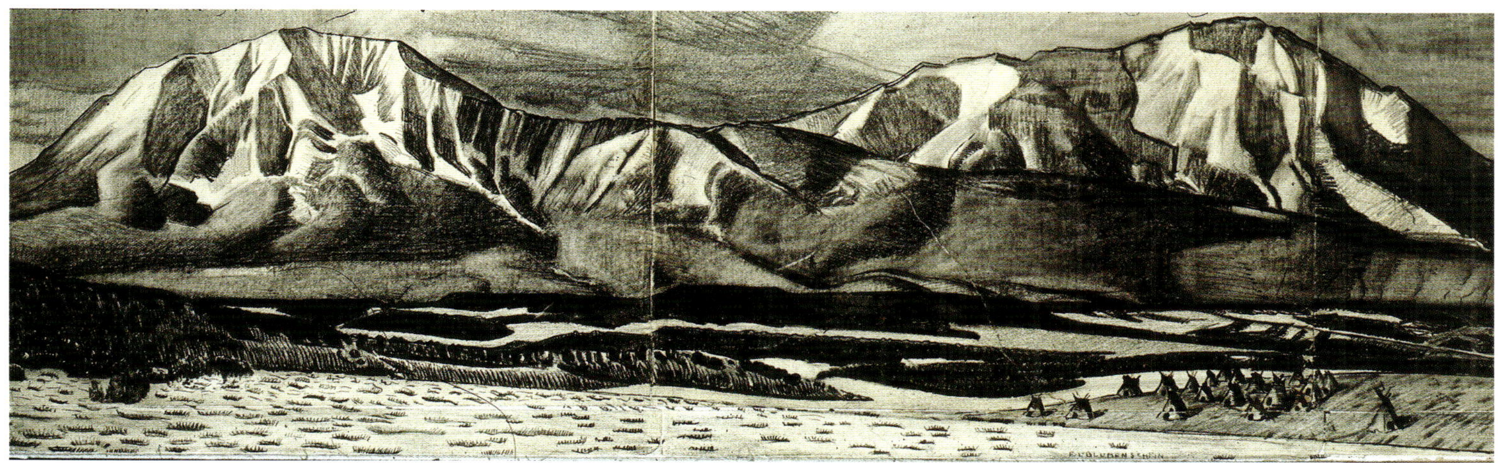

Spanish Peaks, mural study, ca. 1937, pencil and ink on paper, 19 × 7 inches. Courtesy of the Taos Historic Museums, Taos, New Mexico. Photograph by Anthony Richardson.

that he "very much regretted" hearing this report and flatly instructed him to proceed at once on the mural.[68] By late October the mural was finished. It only had to dry, and then it could be transported and installed to meet the November 2 deadline.

For weeks Blumenschein had worked from daylight to dark, allowing time only to eat and sleep. After the painting was finished, the artist made his feelings known: "You took all the joy out of life and turned me into a driving mechanical machine." For its installation, Blumenschein asked Rowan to "*telegraph at once* to that curious specimen of a Postmaster," who regarded the artist variously as someone who would mess up his lobby or "just some boob from a small town in New Mexico."[69] In December Rowan acknowledged the mural was in place and declared it a "most competent and handsome piece of work."[70]

Although the Roosevelt initiatives had spared many of Blumenschein's associates from undue hardships, the thirties were tough on his Taos bunch. Three of the old guard were missing by the time Blumenschein completed the Colorado mural. W. Herbert Dunton, Eanger Irving Couse, and Walter Ufer of the "old Taos society" all died in 1936. Blumenschein, who was particularly close to Ufer, conducted the memorial service in his good friend's honor. The local paper recounted friends and admirers gathered amid paintings on easels and flowers surrounding Ufer's portrait. Blumenschein introduced the speakers. Taos artists—Kenneth Adams, E. Martin Hennings, and Eleonore Kissell—spoke of Ufer's encouragement and support, especially of young artists. After the service, former models Bob Abbott and Jim Mirabal released Ufer's ashes to the land at sundown, fulfilling their friend's final request.[71]

With Dunton's death, Blumenschein lost both friend and fishing companion. One place they liked to fish was thirty miles northeast of Taos. Completion of a dam had created the 2,400-acre Eagle Nest Lake in 1918. The lake rapidly became a favorite among fishermen—and inspired a series of Blumenschein's finest late landscapes. One he had painted in 1933 featured his friend Dunton carrying a large lake trout and wearing his signature white cowboy hat. The painting, executed without a preliminary composition, was atypical of Blumenschein, who usually worked from studies. This time the finished piece came directly "from Nature," with Blumenschein consciously choosing to reproduce the "lyrical charm of a pleasant scene on a happy vacation day" rather than convey "any deep emotion."[72]

Blumenschein painted the lake "at least five times in different moods."[73] When he created a series, he often used similar compositional elements that, although inspired by the same subject, differed in viewpoint. Automobiles and grouped fishermen appeared in two of these paintings. In *Eagle Nest Lake, No. 4*, the row of fishermen dominate the center foreground, while the automobile, possibly Blumenschein's 1924 Ford, hunched black among red boulders, waits patiently to the left of the fishermen, anchoring the left foreground. The view is from above the shoreline looking west with Mount Wheeler looming under gauzy, sun-splashed rain clouds in the distance. Waves crash and splash in crescent patterns that are repeated in the wrinkles of the peak above.

Mountain Lake (Eagle Nest) differs in viewpoint—an aerial perspective looking from the slope above down onto the lakeshore, east across the lake, and up the slope across the foothills into the mountains. The patterns and forms of the sage and rabbit brush in the foreground, illumined by the New Mexican sun, recur in forested foothills in the background. The V-shaped wedges of flying ducks break up the flat rippled surface of the lake.

The artist employs a similar palette in *The Lake,* with the blue water and blue of the mountains in the background. The crest of the waves creates movement that is repeated by flattened versions of the snow-capped peaks in the far distance. The conifers along the canyon walls in the middle ground emerge right out of the water. Although Blumenschein took artistic liberties here, this painting's viewpoint is from the dam at the head of Cimarron Canyon looking down onto the lagoon from just behind the boat in the foreground. In this painting, he exaggerates the canyon walls' height and slope and makes the distant peaks look jagged rather than rounded (from that vantage point, they more closely resemble peaks like Wheeler in *Eagle Nest Lake, No. 4*).

A dramatic slanting light on the peak after a rain shower prompted Blumenschein to abandon fishing one evening in order to start on a fourth Eagle Nest Lake painting, one that would be known as *Lone Fisherman*: "Toward evening the sun's rays broke through in spectacular fashion that brought out my thumb-box sketching outfit," he later wrote. In less than an hour, he had captured the feeling of that stirring moment. Later, back in his studio, Blumenschein struggled with the painting. At one time, he had placed a ten-pound trout jumping out of the water in the middle of the canvas. Deeming the fish too small in proportion to the lake's expanse, he painted it out, replacing it with the figure of Don Mondragon from Taos Pueblo, Blumenschein's companion and camp tender on these fishing trips.[74]

Perhaps Blumenschein's love of the wilds was in part an excuse for escaping the routine of studio life and certain frustrations involving his social and professional associations. One story that developed at this time was exemplary. Some of Blumenschein's paintings from his 1934 show at Grand Central Galleries were on exhibition in Dayton. On this occasion, two hometown clubs asked him to speak. The *Dayton Journal* reported on his address before the Lawyer's Club. Hamming it up in the course of delivering his talk, Blumenschein made some imprudent remarks about his Taos neighbors: he described Mabel Dodge Luhan as a big, spoiled baby whose "business was building houses and upsetting plans" and said that his fellow painter Irving Couse painted one squatting Indian for a calendar company and spent the next thirty years depicting the same subject. He closed his address with the remark that people in Taos would be the happiest ones on earth

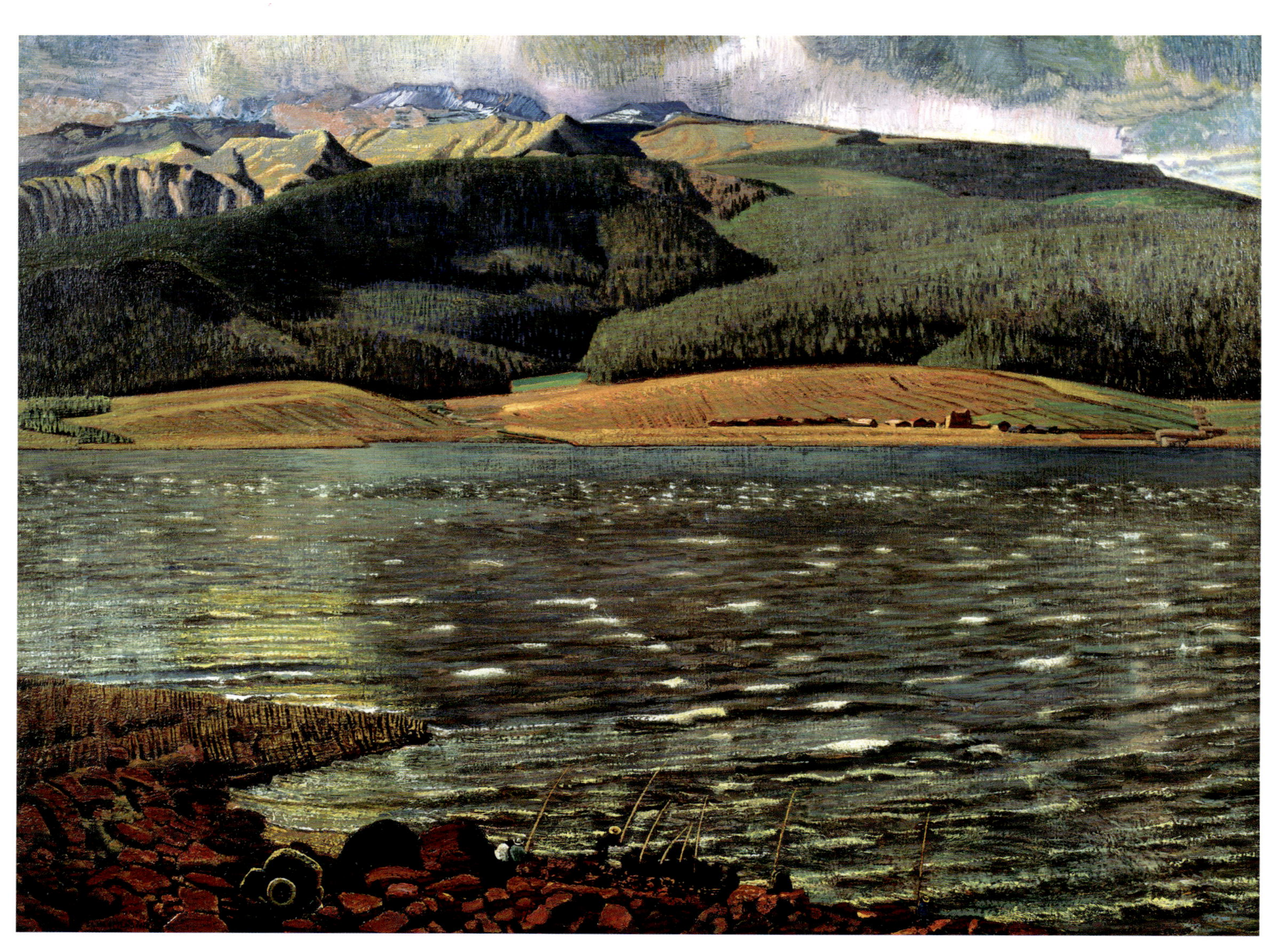

Eagle Nest Lake, No. 4, 1933
Oil on canvas, 30 × 40 inches
Courtesy of Michael and Andrea Frost

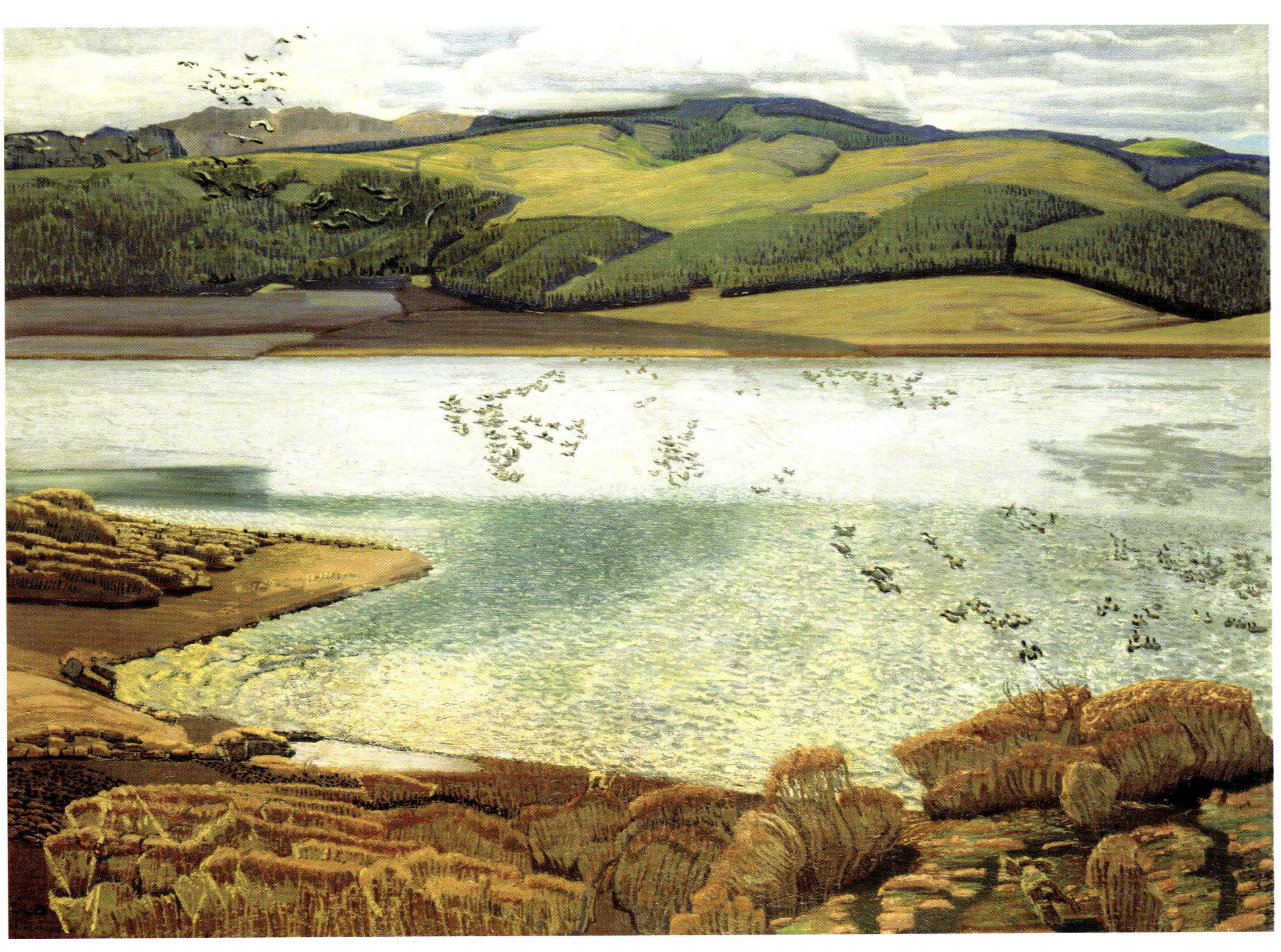

Mountain Lake (Eagle Nest), 1935
Oil on canvas, 29 × 39½ inches
Courtesy of the Denver Art Museum,
William Sr. and Dorothy Harmsen Collection, Denver, Colorado (2001.458)

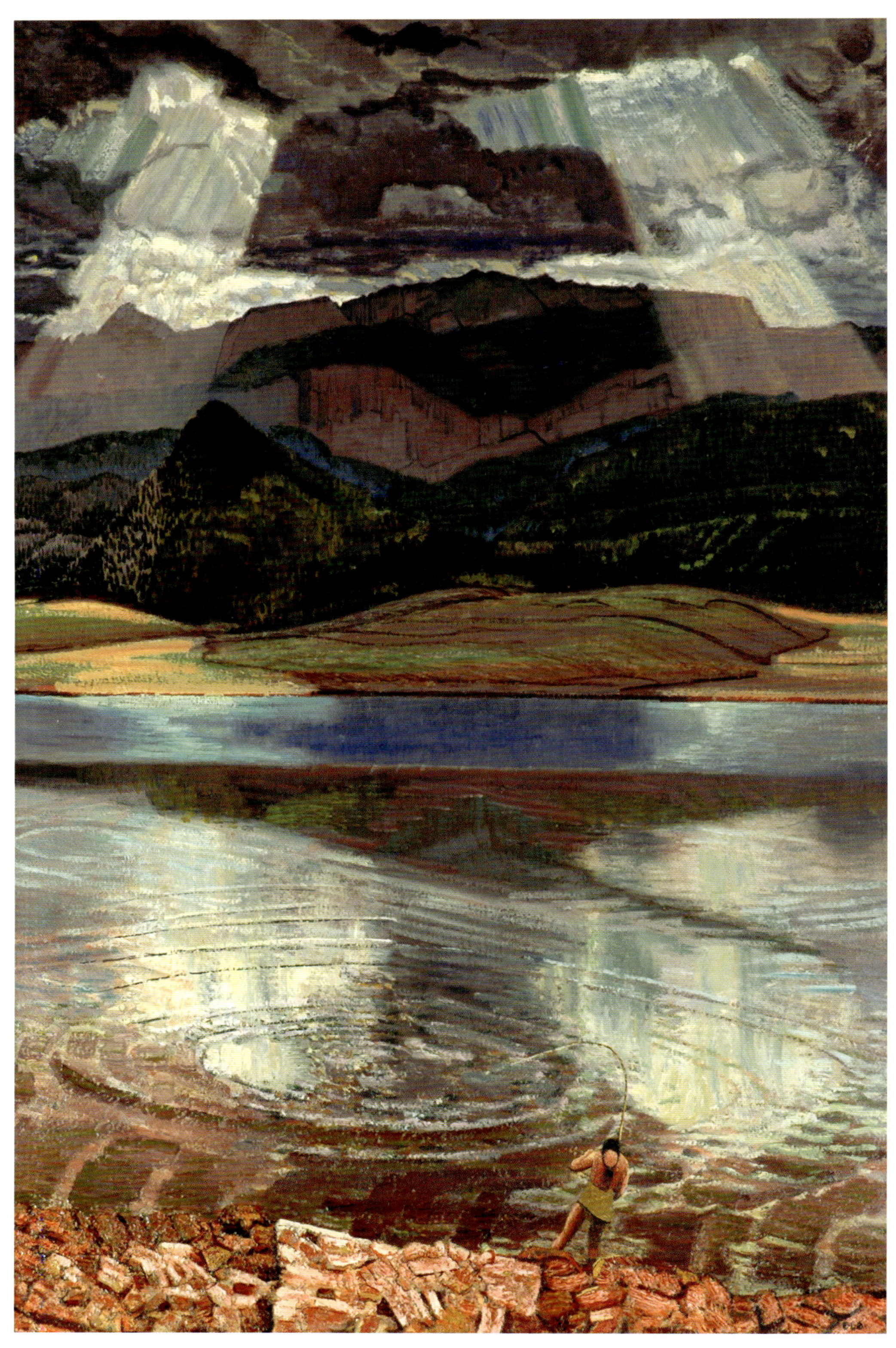

The Lone Fisherman, 1933
Oil on canvas, 40 × 27 inches
Private collection

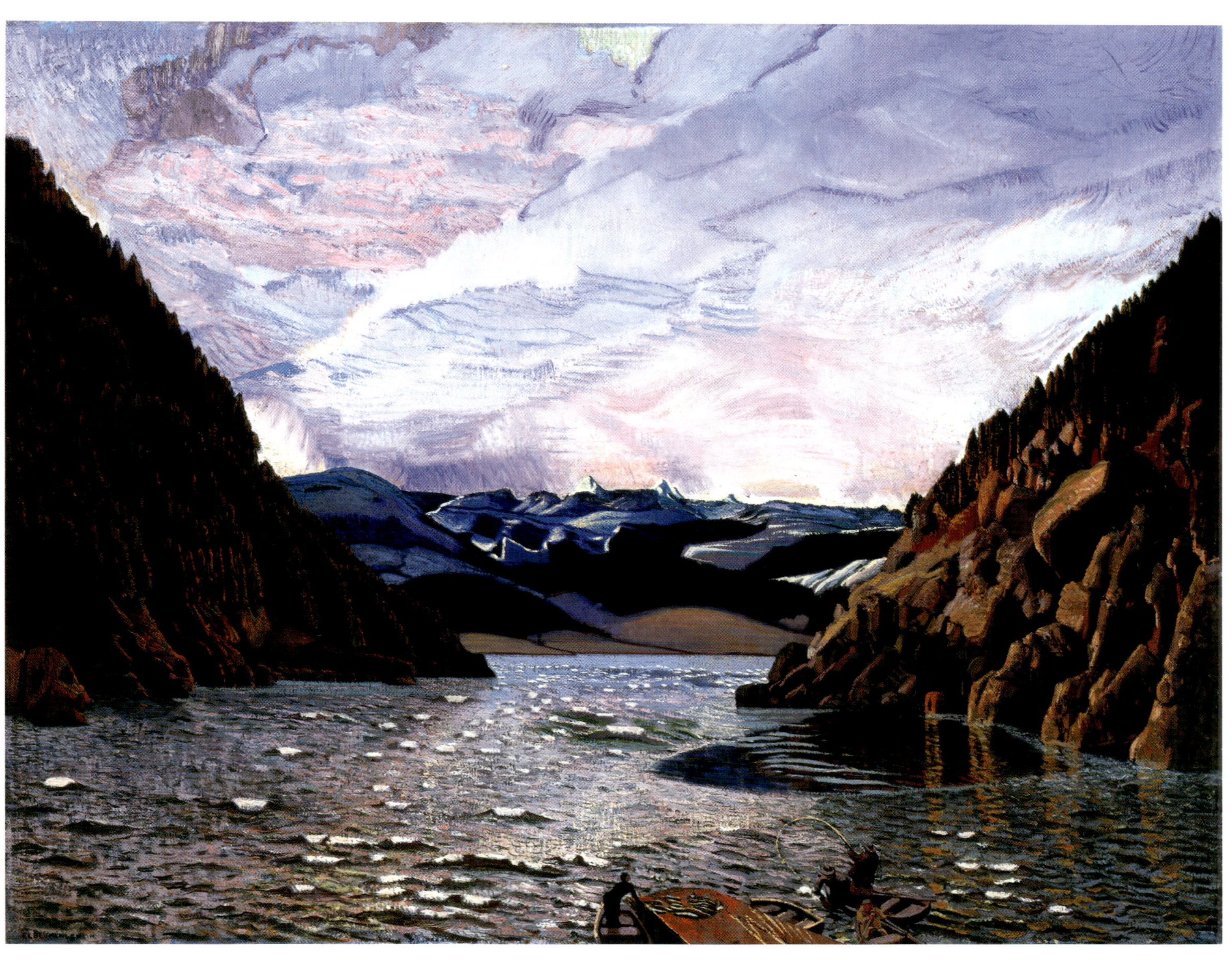

The Lake (Fishing on Eagle Nest Lake), 1931
Oil on canvas, 30 × 38 inches
Collection of Phoenix Art Museum, Phoenix, Arizona
Museum Purchase with Funds Provided by the Men's Arts Council Western American Endowment Fund

if it were not for the abrasive professional jealousies among its residents.[75] A month later, the Taos paper caught wind of the story. Headlined "Blumenschein Indiscreet in Home Town," it made the front page.[76] Luckily for him, the offender was miles away in Chicago working on a portrait for the Butler family when the story broke.

Elsie Butler Waller, daughter of the Ellis Butlers, wanted a family portrait like that of her parents, something to match Blumenschein's *Portrait of Ellis Parker Butler and Family* in size and in subject matter—husband, wife, and child. Elsie's husband, Harold, had wanted to have Elsie painted with their daughter, Nancy, at age six, the same age his wife had been when Blumenschein painted the first Butler family portrait in 1908.[77] Part of that plan went awry when business matters conflicted with Harold's time to sit for the portrait. His solution was to have the artist memorialize his wife, daughter, and their two-year-old son, Harold. As in the Butler portrait, Blumenschein arranged the figures in the Waller portrait so that the three heads formed a triangle that immediately draws the eye to them. He utilized similar curvilinear shapes to define the Waller grouping. There the similarities end, however. Blumenschein used color instead of a monotone background to accentuate the figures, and the portrait is decidedly modern, more abstract and loosely painted. The background includes furniture and decorations in the Waller home, lending a feeling of domesticity as well as specificity. The painting reflects the artist's stylistic transformation.

Elsie's diary and the artist's letters home to Mary and Helen divulged the trials incurred on both sides of the creative process. Like her mother before her, Elsie had to figure out ways to keep the children occupied during the tedious posing process. Reading stories to them held their attention the longest. Blumenschein, for his part, once he laid out the composition, worked first to capture Elsie's charm. He had no trouble painting baby Harold, "an Italian Renaissance cupid." Painting wriggly-worm Nancy, however, was another story: "When she tires, she calls me a 'dumb-bell' and calls the portrait a 'dumb-bell' then goes into the kitchen and calls the maid a 'dumb-bell'!"[78] Blumenschein recovered in afternoons spent cheering on the Chicago Cubs.

The Waller family commission reintroduced multiple-figure pictures into Blumenschein's oeuvre just at a time when he was contentedly concentrating on landscape. The change may have sparked ideas for his next two major paintings, both figure work: *Jury for the Trial of a Sheepherder for Murder* (1936) and *Ourselves and Taos Neighbors* (1937). Like the Waller family portrait, each is quietly static in mood and structure. The setting for both was the east studio of his Taos residence, where Blumenschein had worked on his recent mural commissions. In 1931 that studio, emptied of all paintings, was the subject of *New Mexico Interior*. Most likely it served as a 41-by-50-inch "study" for *Jury*. In the summer of 1937 Blumenschein was struck with the notion of peopling its empty interior. And so it became a work in progress.

The augmented composition, retitled *Ourselves and Taos Neighbors*, was exhibited at the 1938 Carnegie and National Academy shows. It initially included Ernest, Mary, and Helen Blumenschein along with a handful of Taos associates. By 1948 the number of friends totaled sixteen, and ultimately the ranks swelled to twenty-four of what he now affectionately referred to as "notorious Taos characters," including Mabel Dodge Luhan. The resulting painting stirred Howard Cook to reminisce:

> Coming upon that remarkable group painting of his friends, artists, and neighbors gathered around his family seated in his studio in Taos—"Ourselves and Taos Neighbors"—we find a record of the epic days when Taos was in the full bloom of its pioneer members. With the exception of D. H. Lawrence and Walter Ufer, who had already died, the work was completed from the friends themselves as they strolled into the studio and were fitted into a place in the arrangement. . . . The spatial setting and exaggeration of depth helps to surround the people with the dignity with which the artist wished to invest his friends.[79]

The second figurative work set in the studio space, completed in 1936, resulted from a darker moment—a brutal murder that took place near Taos.

In August 1927 the lives of newlywed Russell Dewese and his bride had been shattered when he was shot and killed by a young sheepherder in the mountains near Taos. A jury of twelve men from the Hispanic community later found the sheepherder, Jose Cruz Maestas, guilty of second-degree murder.

Eight years later, in 1935, Blumenschein exorcized the incident, which had haunted him, transforming it into *Jury for the Trial of a Sheepherder for Murder*. To lend authenticity to the picture, Blumenschein had sketched "mountain types" on the Taos plaza and from the nearby Peñasco area. He used a single model to strike various poses for each man sitting in the jury box. Their clothing is typical of the place and time—sturdy boots, sheepskin and wool coats, sweaters, and jackets. *Con respecto*, they hold felt hats in their hands. Blumenschein has narrowed the studio space so it contains the men sitting in the jury box, with just enough room for the court clerk in the foreground and an onlooker just behind. The men in the front row are lit as if on a stage; the back row recedes in shadow. The artist builds an atmosphere of tension through his choice of a pronounced vertical format, dim light, and shadowy tints—the room is darkened by the low *viga* ceiling—contrasted with the spotlighted and highly defined individual jurymen, giving weight to what the law asks of them, to judge one of their own under an unfamiliar American legal system.

The National Arts Club awarded *Jury for the Trial of a Sheepherder for Murder* a medal in 1937. The same year, it was displayed in the Second National Exhibition of American Art, which featured paintings from all states of the Union, as well as from the Virgin Islands and American Samoa. The exhibition celebrated art from the Depression-era programs and was one of the first comprehensive assemblages of American art to take place outside museum and world's fair venues. Each state's governor appointed an art committee to select art works that represented them.[80] The resulting exhibition, according to a critic in the *New York Times*, afforded the public "the opportunity of seeing both the critical and creative temper of the entire country."[81] *Time* magazine's Emily Genauer summed up the exhibition, saying it made clear that "art in America is now a sturdy growth, like an elm tree which spreads its roots slowly but far, and eventually reaches great lasting solidity and height."[82]

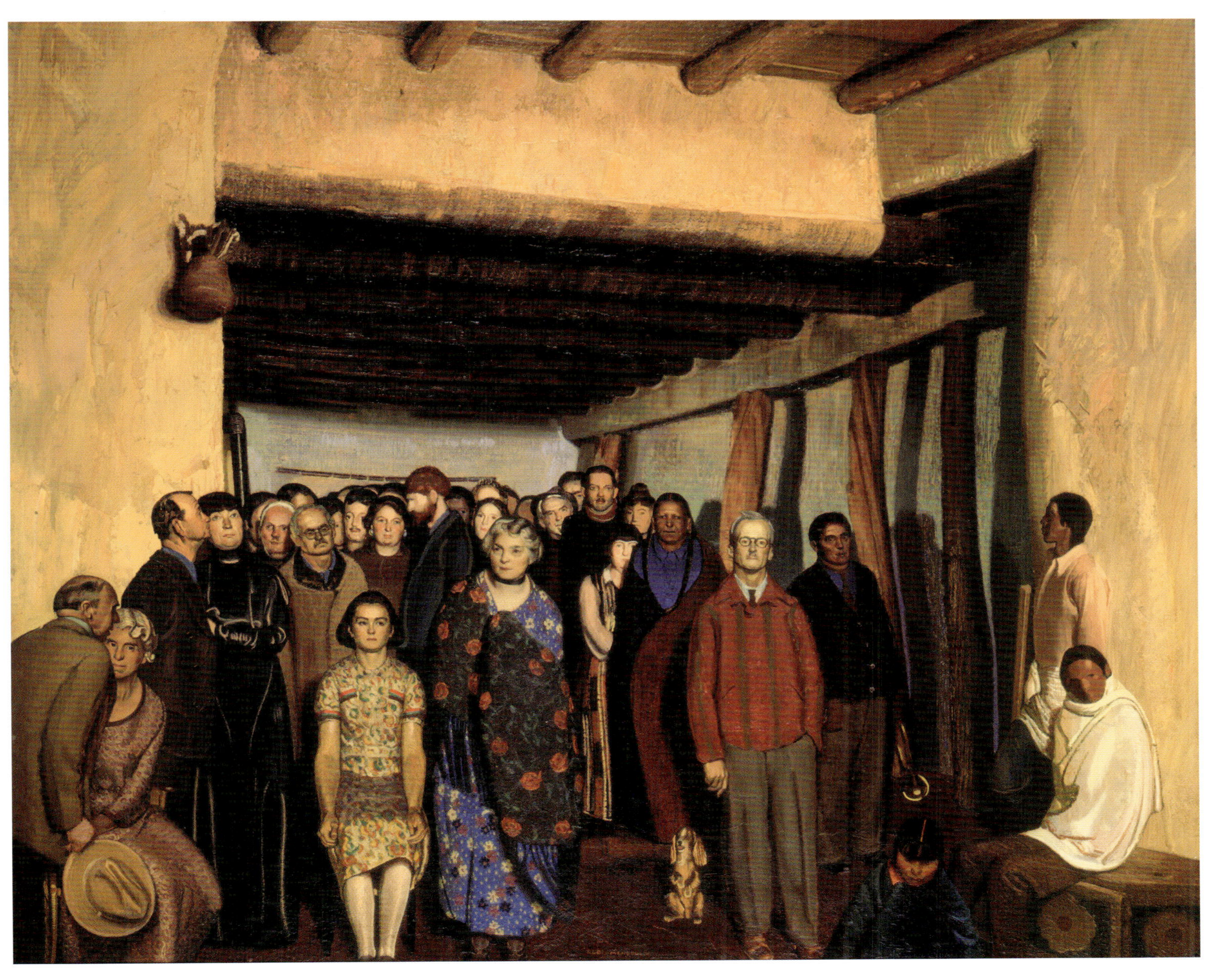

Ourselves and Taos Neighbors (originally ***New Mexico Interior*** or ***New Mexican Interior,*** 1931), reworked 1937 and 1938, finished ca. 1948
Oil on canvas, 41 × 50 inches
Courtesy of the Stark Museum of Art, Orange, Texas (31.30/12A)

When the national exhibition opened in New York, the *New York Herald Tribune* mentioned Blumenschein's *Jury for the Trial of a Sheepherder for Murder* in its Sunday edition and reproduced it the following Sunday.[83] *Time* magazine singled out *Jury for the Trial of a Sheepherder for Murder* as "among the ablest pictures technically" and, from over five hundred artworks, chose it as one of three works reproduced for the article.[84] The painting was then invited to the annual exhibition at the Art Institute of Chicago. The president of the Museum of Modern Art, A. Conger Goodyear, saw it there and suggested it for inclusion in his museum's forthcoming exhibition in Paris.

Two exhibitions took American art to Europe in 1938. Grand Central Art Galleries organized a selection of masterworks by past and present American painters and printmakers to represent the United States at the Twenty-first Venice Biennale. *Art Digest* called it "one of the largest international exhibitions in the world," and it was broadly touted as the consummate venue for contemporary art.[85] Gallery director Erwin Barrie chose three of Blumenschein's paintings: *Moon, Morning Star, Evening Star, The Peon: Portrait of Pedro* (location unknown), and *Deserted Mining Camp* (Harwood Museum of Art, Taos). Blumenschein was one of thirty-four American painters in that exhibition.

The second exhibition, Trois Siècles D'Art Aux État-Unis (Three Centuries of American Art), hung in Paris's Jeu de Paume Museum over the early summer of 1938. It illustrated the development of American art from 1609 to 1938 in one of the "most comprehensive showings . . . ever sent to Europe."[86] Museum of Modern Art director Alfred H. Barr, Jr., along with his boss, A. Cougar Goodyear, and curator Dorothy C. Miller, made the selection of contemporary painting and sculpture for the Twentieth-Century American Painting section.[87] He included Blumenschein's canvases with what he called the "American Scene paintings." To illustrate his essay, Barr elected to reproduce *Jury for the Trial of a Sheepherder for Murder* next to Grant Wood's nationally iconic *Daughters of the Revolution*.

Back home, when *New York Times* art critic Edward Alden Jewell reviewed the Paris exhibition, he reproduced *Jury for the Trial of a Sheepherder for Murder*

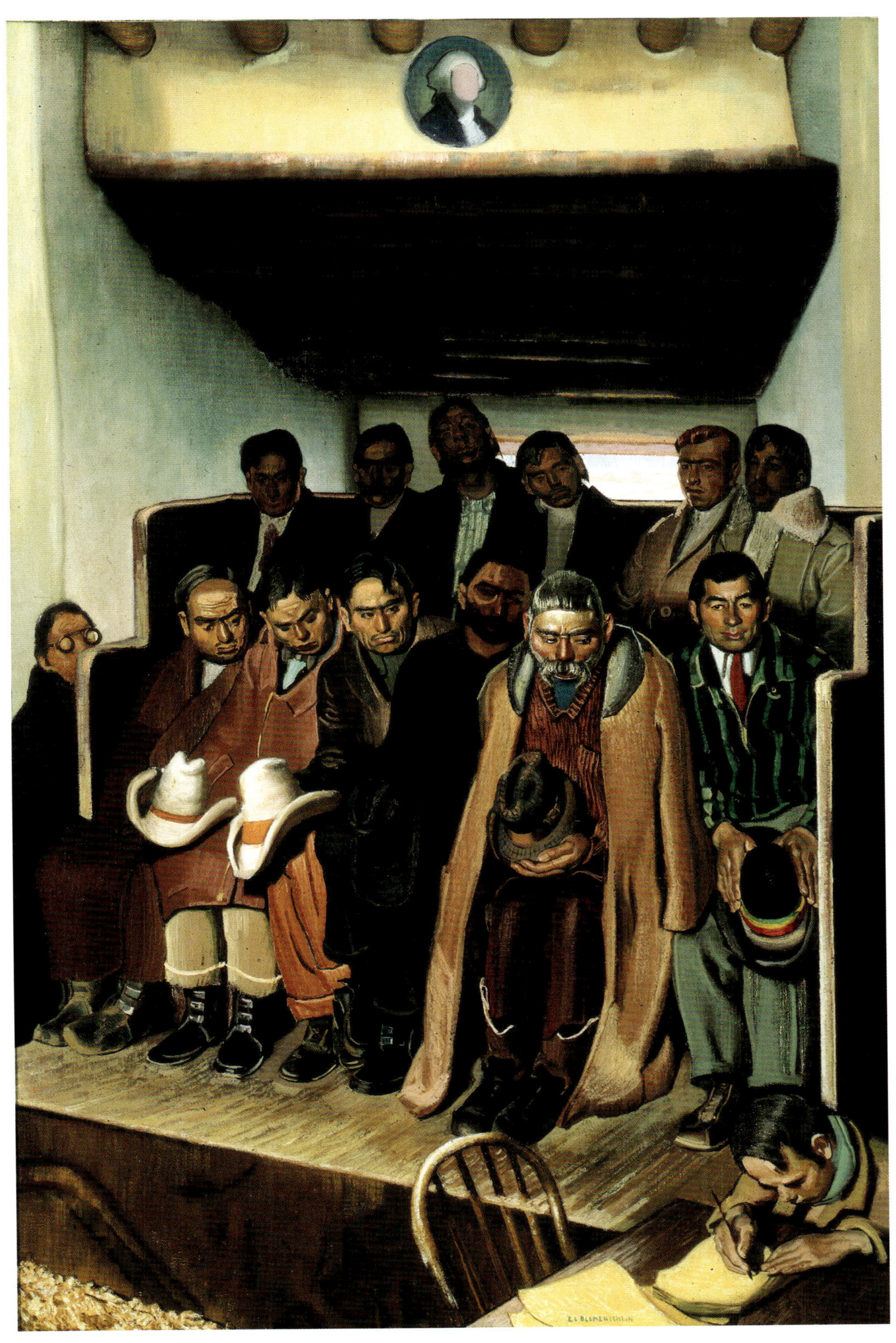

Jury for Trial of a Sheepherder for Murder, 1936
Oil on canvas, 46 × 30 inches
Courtesy of the Rockwell Museum, Corning, New York
Clara S. Peck Fund purchase (97.13)

alongside works by John Sloan, George Bellows, and Charles Burchfield as quintessentially American examples.[88] Later, after its acquisition by the Museum of Modern Art, Barr chose to include the painting in a catalog published in tribute to the museum's tenth anniversary and the first exhibition in its new building. Pleased and honored at his inclusion, Blumenschein commented that he felt "encouraged to continue putting on the gloves with the many schools of modern artists." It signified to him a broadening, more accommodating, view in art since he still insisted that the artist needed a sound foundation, especially in drawing and composition, to produce a "really good painting."[89]

Blumenschein, by no means an animalier painter, was nonetheless intrigued by animal subjects for his art, especially when they were native to his beloved New Mexico. He incorporated burros, goats, and sheep into many of his canvases of the period in order "give a little animal life to the great big landscape."[90] Halfway down the Rio Grande Gorge, a trail enclosed by dark basalt boulders and red-gold canyon walls attracted his attention during one of his outings. In the resulting painting, *The Pass,* the setting sun casts diagonal shadows where the light hits unseen rocks from above, almost obscuring a lone black goat topping one of the boulders. Where the sun still breaks through, it illuminates the sheep in the right-hand corner and middle ground. The same amber light catches puffy, wool-skein clouds that mirror the bunched sheep below.

In *Afternoon of a Sheepherder*, a larger picture from 1939, a herder looks down on his flock, keeping all in sight, except for the ever-present goat behind him.[91] Blumenschein depicts the characteristic canyon and its broad expanse plunging down into the winding fault line of the Rio Grande Rift eight hundred shadowy feet below and then up the tawny slopes past vertical basalt walls to flat-topped mesas beyond. In the background rise the Sangre de Cristo Mountains. The famed blue sky of New Mexico tops elongated cloud streams, and a rising full moon crowns the vista. Blumenschein plays the linear verticality of canyon walls against the long horizontal sweep of the canvas and accents the view with the texture and undulating patterning of the sheep. And all is captured in a moment of light so typical, so elusive.

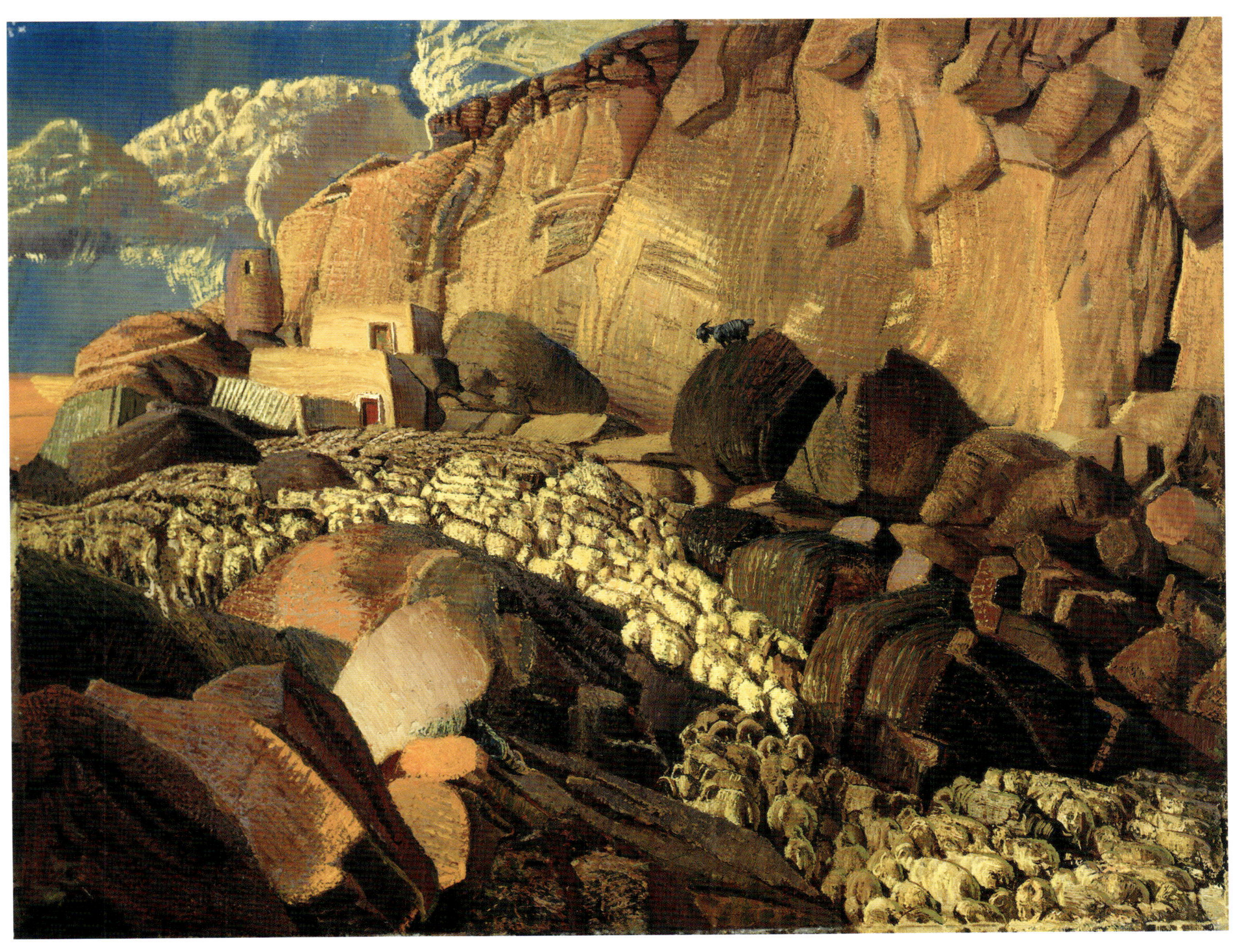

The Pass, 1929, reworked 1939
Oil on canvas, 22 × 28 inches
Collection of the Arizona State University Art Museum, Tempe
Gift of Oliver B. James

The decade of the great national exhibitions closed with a virtual explosion of contemporaneous art. A huge, comprehensive exhibition and catalog, *American Art Today*, materialized in tandem with the 1939 New York World's Fair. Its mission was to showcase the nationwide range of artistic ability that included the work of "the advanced, the moderate, and the conservative schools."[92] For this exhibition—"the most extensive competition between 20th century American artists" to date, selection committees from six regions labored to choose 1,200 works from over 25,000 submitted entries. World's Fair President Grover A. Whalen described the resulting exhibition as the "best expression of all phases and schools in painting, sculpture, and graphic arts."[93]

The New Mexico committee, charged with choosing works characteristic of the New Mexico art spectrum, selected paintings by both Blumenscheins. For the exhibition, Blumenschein repainted *Arizona*, and retitled it *Red Symphony*. Mary's entry, *Acoma Legend*, had previously won Honorable Mention at the Denver Art Museum in 1934. Blumenschein was included in other important shows organized around the World's Fair extravaganza.[94]

American Art Today consciously procured paintings representative of other regions for a first-time showing in New York. Besides introducing new artists to World's Fair audiences in New York City, it also showed the growth of regionalist art in the United States. In 1937 artist and Dallas museum director Jerry Bywaters observed both the rise in regional exhibitions and new opportunities for art students that the growth of American art had fostered. Aspiring students no longer had to travel abroad or to large urban areas for art education. Now they could get adequate training in Cleveland, Kansas City, Los Angeles, Denver, and "other provincial cities." Many practicing artists who had trained in New York and elsewhere in the early 1900s—like Thomas Hart Benton, Grant Wood, and John Steuart Curry—had returned to their native states to teach. Art instruction had shifted to the provinces. Bywaters observed that American art had gradually become decentralized.[95] As art schools and museums in those cosmopolitan areas grew in stature, they promoted regional exhibitions. This would prove true in New Mexico, as an ambitious, statewide exhition in 1940 would demonstrate.

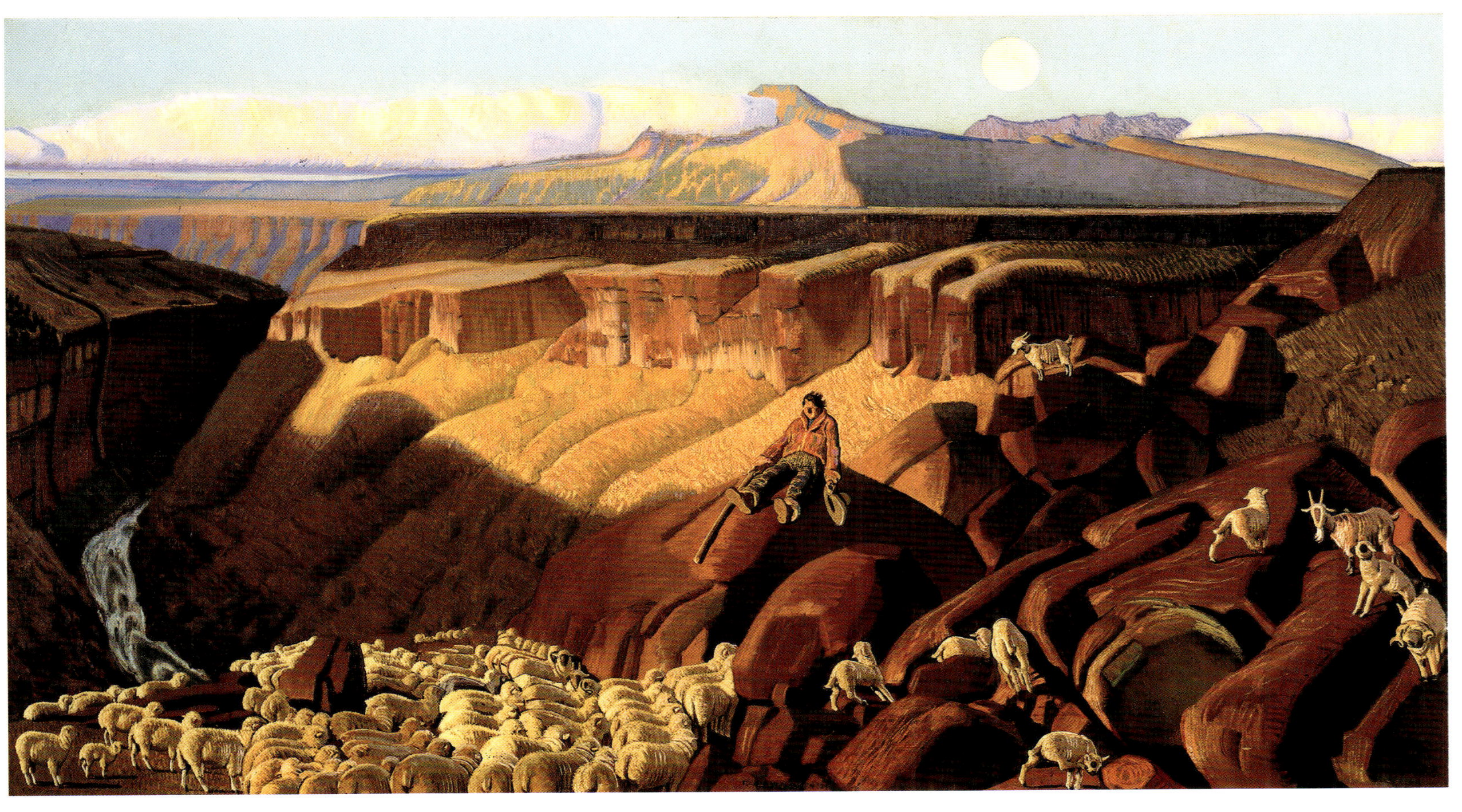

Afternoon of a Sheepherder, 1939
Oil on canvas, 28 × 50 inches
Courtesy of the National Cowboy and Western Heritage Museum,
Oklahoma City, Oklahoma (1976.32)

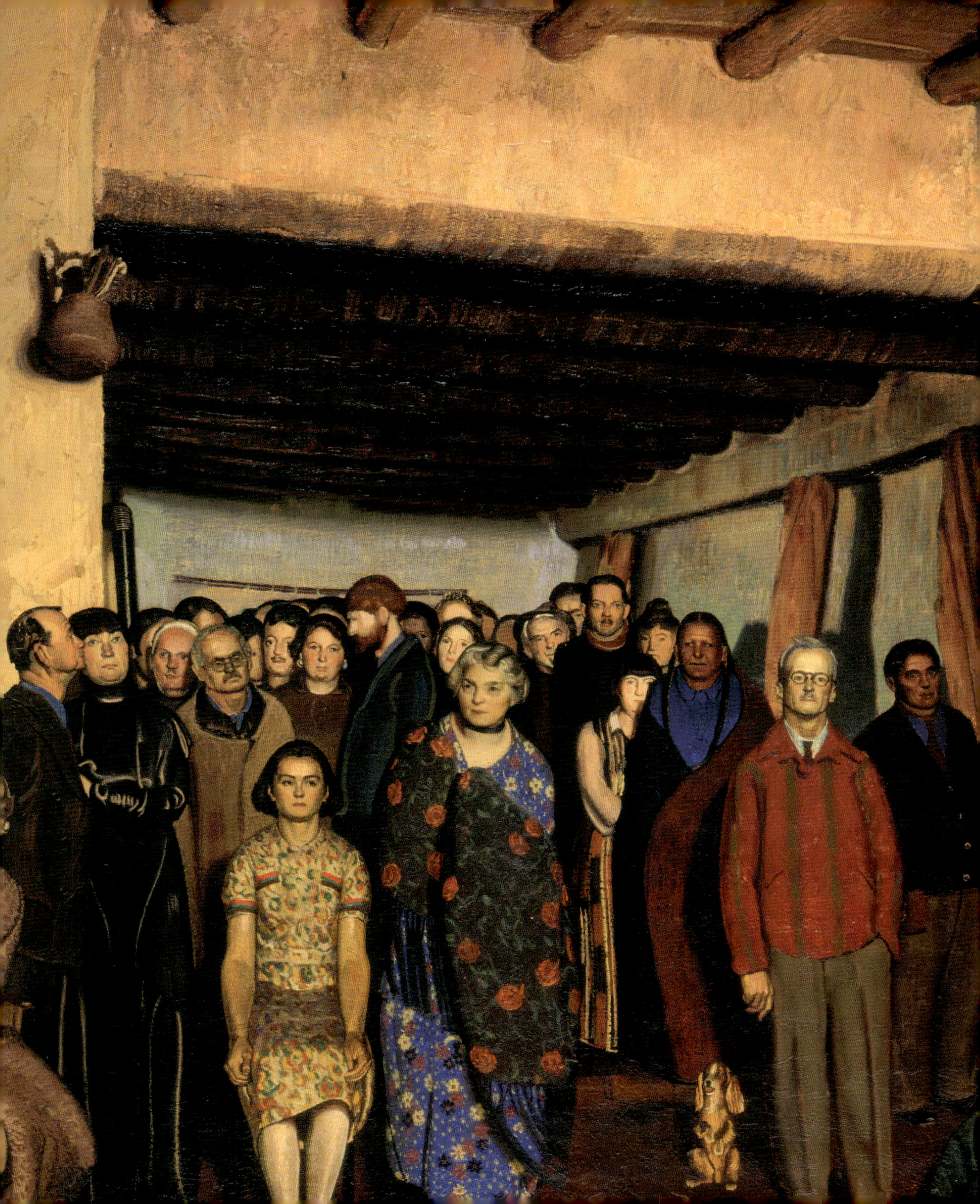

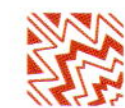

Ourselves and Taos Neighbors

Portrait Group of "Notorious Taos Freaks"

Skip Keith Miller

In 1931 Blumenschein completed a canvas titled *New Mexico Interior* (in some reviews and Blumenschein's own ledger it was also called *New Mexican Interior*), which was exhibited the same year at the Museum of New Mexico in Santa Fe and at the Thirtieth International Exhibition of Paintings at the Carnegie Institute in Pittsburgh. In 1934 it was exhibited in Blumenschein's one-man show, Landscapes of New Mexico and Arizona, at Grand Central Art Galleries in New York. One critic noted this nonlandscape painting: "Among the best canvases in this exhibit was 'The New Mexican Interior,' distinguished by simplicity of design from the others, which are in general, detailed."[1] A year later, the picture was also included in the 130th Annual of the Pennsylvania Academy of the Fine Arts.

This rather odd (even by Blumenschein standards) yet remarkable competition-size painting (40 × 50 inches), being neither landscape nor truly figurative, reads very much like an almost empty stage set, ready to be filled by actors with a story to tell. At this point the only "actors" in the painting are a single person (a Pueblo Indian model) bent over working on a rug (or something on the floor) in the lower center of the painting and a cat, tail held straight in the air, boldly walking toward the Indian and away from the viewer.[2] The painting was an exceedingly accurate depiction of the east studio sometime after the Blumenscheins had acquired this and two other rooms from Epimenio Tenorio, or his estate, around 1924.[3] Tenorio had been the family's neighbor and handyman and the model for *The Plasterer*, *New Mexico Peon,* and a destroyed canvas titled *The Half Breed and His Family (The Genízaro)*. When they bought the Tenorio rooms, the Blumenscheins extended the easternmost room and raised the ceiling on the north end several feet in order to accommodate the installation of a large, multipane, north-facing window. This studio was where Blumenschein completed the Missouri State Capitol murals and later the Walsenburg, Colorado, post office mural.[4] Prior to completion of the east studio, he had painted in the former W. Herbert "Buck" Dunton studio with the massive adobe fireplace, which was the backdrop for several paintings including *The Plasterer* and *Portrait of Jim Romero,* both completed in 1921. After construction of the new studio was completed, the old studio became the family's living room.[5]

Exactly when Blumenschein began the process of repainting *New Mexico Interior* is not precisely known. However, the last documented exhibition

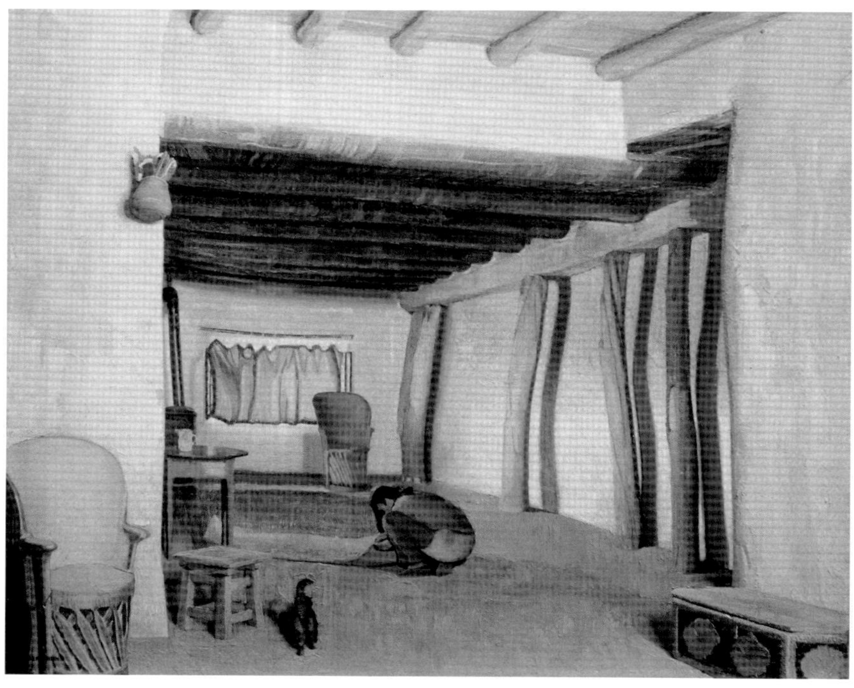

New Mexican Interior. Photograph courtesy of the Ernest L. Blumenschein Papers, 1889–1960, Archives of American Art, Smithsonian Institution, Washington, D.C.

of *Interior* was at the Pennsylvania Academy of the Fine Arts, which closed on March 3, 1935. Sometime after the painting arrived back in Taos and Blumenschein returned home in late May of 1935 from painting the *Waller Family Portrait* in Winnetka, Illinois, he must have been stimulated to take up figurative work once again. Beginning in the mid-1920s, he had focused increasingly on the landscape, and by the 1930s he began producing works that concentrated solely on the monumentality of the Southwest. Blumenschein's art evolved from the emphasis on figure to the expression of forms in the landscape to almost pure landscape images—all a natural and deliberate progression for him. In discussing Blumenschein's long career, Howard Cook captured this sense of continuous transformation:

> For a moment travel back along the road of Blumenschein's subject matter. Think of his early Indian paintings, then of the period of richly tapestried, decorative, highly colored and stylized allegorical subjects, the beginning of his decorative approach to landscape, a beginning which grew to his present powerful interpretations, in contemporary rhythm, of the Southwest. Then come the Indian religious rituals, followed by a change of scene producing the railroad paintings, fanciful episodes in public parks, and urban aspect in California. In between, portraits and a few mural designs—not a static moment during his long, hard-working life. Never a repetition for the sake of capitalizing on popular acclaim.[6]

In 1908 Blumenschein painted a family portrait of one of his dearest friends and early patrons. The *Portrait of Ellis Parker Butler and Family* also won him his first major prize for work in oil. In 1935 Butler's daughter, Elsie Butler Waller, sat for a portrait of herself and her children at the same age that her mother and she had been in the original Butler picture. Ellis Parker Butler was ill at the time Blumenschein was completing the *Waller Family Portrait*. He died the next year. These related circumstances may have prompted a desire in Blumenschein to again take up figurative work as well as planted the seed to document his own "family" as the intimate connections to his past were shifting with the rapidly accelerating flight of time.[7]

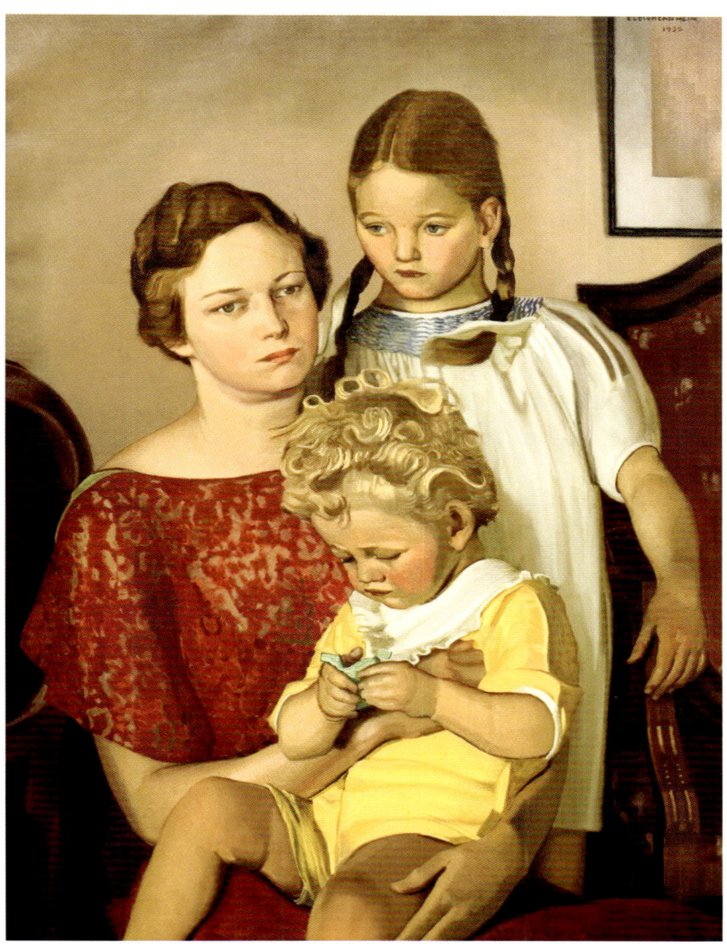

Waller Family Portrait, 1935, oil on canvas, 39½ × 29½ inches. Private collection.

Parker Butler and fellow artists and friends W. Herbert "Buck" Dunton, E. I. Couse, and Walter Ufer in 1936, as Blumenschein was completing *Jury*. These significant personal losses must have impelled him to capture for posterity his family and those intimate friends within the community that he held dear. Perhaps as a consequence of the death of these friends he completed a finely detailed compositional study for *Ourselves and Taos Neighbors* that contained twenty-seven figures.[8] Not unexpectedly, Blumenschein must have considered both *Jury* and *Ourselves* as related stylistically and compositionally: each uses the same interior space (albeit the former vertically and the latter horizontally), each contains superbly executed portraits, and each is quietly static in mood and structure. Although figures in the landscape appear in Blumenschein's later work, *Jury* and *Ourselves*, respectively, proved to be the last great purely figurative works that he produced in his long career.

Shortly after Blumenschein returned from completing the Waller portrait in the spring of 1935, and while he worked on the Walsenburg mural commission, the empty stage of *New Mexico Interior* stared him in the face. The homecoming of *Interior* may have been the impetus to begin work on the *Jury for the Trial of a Sheepherder for Murder*, which, based on Blumenschein's ledgers, was completed in 1936. The idea for *Ourselves* must have percolated for months.

The ultimate motivation for the large group portrait *Ourselves and Taos Neighbors* probably stemmed from the deaths of his close friend Ellis

During the summer of 1937, when Blumenschein was supposed to be finishing the mural for the Walsenburg, Colorado, post office, he was industriously at work on *Ourselves*. In a September 15, 1937, letter to Mr. Ed Rowan, of the Treasury Department's Section of Painting and Sculpture, he wrote: "Suppose you are wondering what has happened to the Walsenburg, Colo. P.O. I had an inspiration—a real one—to paint a portrait group of notorious Taos freaks and could not resist.

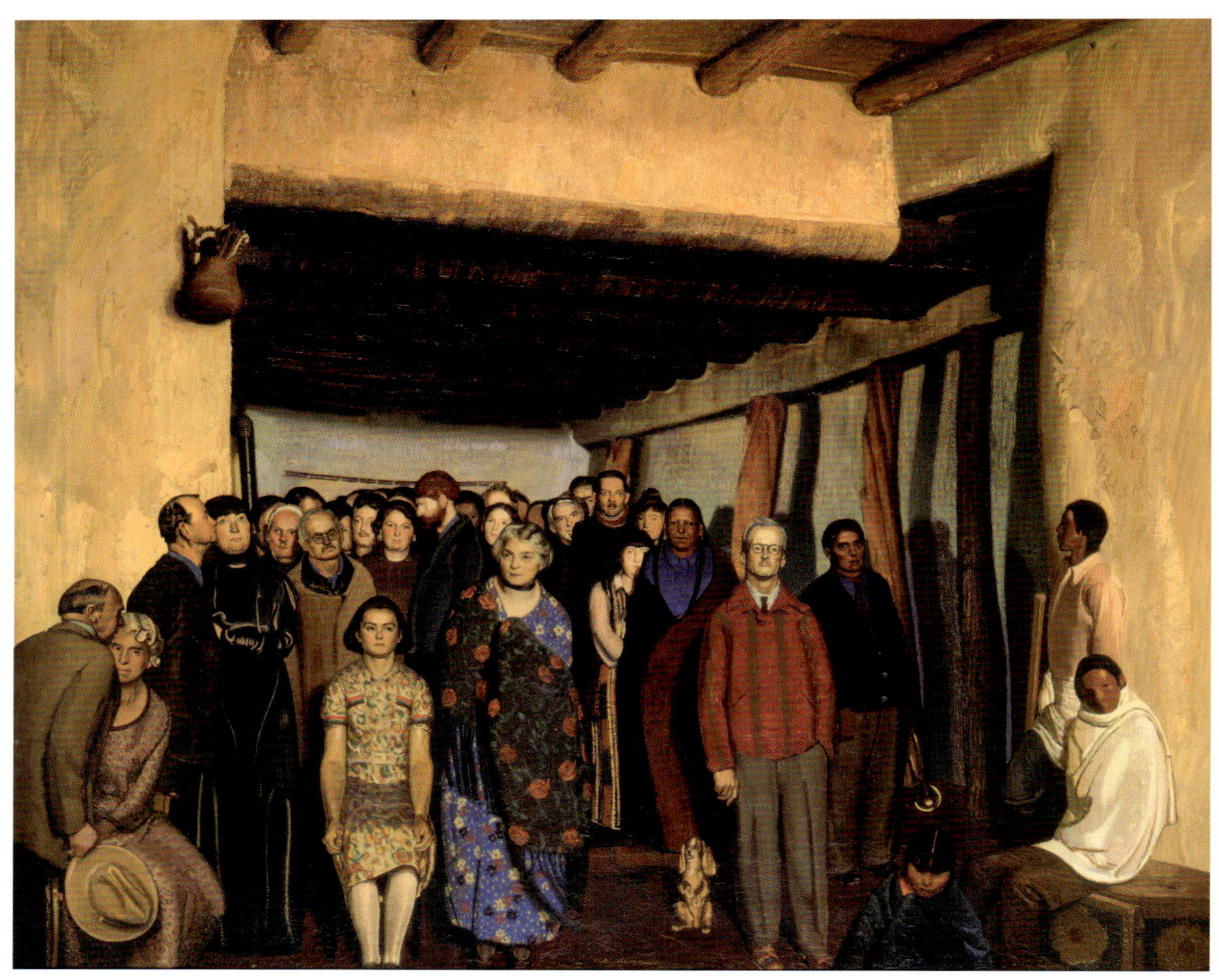

Ourselves and Taos Neighbors (originally ***New Mexico Interior*** or ***New Mexican Interior,*** 1931), reworked 1937 and 1938, finished ca. 1948, oil on canvas, 41 × 50 inches. Courtesy of the Stark Museum of Art, Orange, Texas (31.30/12A).

Put in the hardest working summer of many years and believe I accomplished a good picture. Now the deck is completely cleared for work on the mural."[9] He goes on to ask if the mural contract can be extended two or three months as only six weeks were remaining within which to complete the mural. In his painting ledger notes regarding *Ourselves*, Blumenschein wrote, "formerly 'New Mexican Interior' (1931) figures now fill bottom of canvas (as originally intended) Finished (almost) Aug 25–27 . . . to be worked on again in Oct." as he did not get the requested extension on the mural.[10] Not surprisingly for Blumenschein, at the time he wrote the letter to Mr. Rowan *Ourselves* was already on exhibit at the Twentieth Anniversary Exhibition, 1917–1937, at the Museum of New Mexico.[11]

Exactly how many figures were in the painting in 1937 is not clear. In a 1948 *El Palacio* article discussing the Blumenschein retrospective, Dr. Reginald Fisher wrote:

> *Ourselves and Taos Neighbors* requires separate mention as a documentary painting of the Blumenschein family. This rich-colored 40" × 50" oil was begun in 1938 [*sic*] as group portrait of his family and Taos associates. Since then, several portraits have been added until it now includes some sixteen figures.[12] There is room for about three more, Mr. Blumenschein says.[13] In the foreground of a viga-ceilinged room stand the artist, Mrs. Blumenschein, and their daughter, Helen. Grouped behind them are their "Taos Neighbors"—Bert Phillips, Oscar Berninghaus, Walter Ufer, Leon Gaspard, Victor Higgins, D. H. Lawrence, J. H. Sharp, Kenneth Adams, Mabel Luhan, and others. This picture is one of Mr. Blumenschein's cherished possessions. He says he plans to finish it soon. It has been exhibited widely in its various stages of completion—first at the MNM in 1938 [*sic*], then at the NAD the same year, then in the Corcoran Gallery in Washington, D.C., the Grand Central Galleries in NY, and elsewhere.[14]

There are a number of problems with Dr. Fisher's chronology, but the idea that Blumenschein continued to add characters to the group portrait over time is quite evident. Further, the painting is, as Fisher notes, a "documentary painting of the Blumenschein family." Blumenschein frequently referred to Mary and Helen as "his girls." Nearly from the time they moved to Taos, both Mary and Helen spent a good portion of each year in New York. There Helen attended school, first public and later art school, and Mary studied and maintained her connection with friends and family. Where Helen and Mary are depicted in close proximity is an accurate presentation of their relationship (in fact, Helen often felt that she and her mother were early feminists); the considerable space between them and Blumenschein is also telling of the often strained nature of the emotional and intellectual connections among this family of independent artists and strong personalities. Helen is painted in a rigid pose with her arms held tight to her sides, looking away from the viewer (and indeed, the artist, as he paints the image). Likewise, Mary is wrapped up in her shawl and quite self-contained in demeanor. She is also looking away. Blumenschein, on the other hand, is staring mildly out of the canvas directly at the viewer. Interestingly, Floppy, one of a succession of cocker spaniels the family owned, is presented closer to Blumenschein than "his girls" but definitely looking at Mary and Helen, in effect reconnecting the family and representing their strong ties.

In a sketched, india ink key to the painting dated March 21, 1957, produced for Mr. and Mrs. H. J. Lutcher Stark, purchasers of the piece, Blumenschein identified all of the "Taos Neighbors" and wrote a brief description of the portrait group:

> Bert Phillips was companion of E.L.B and arrived in Taos with him, Sept. 1898. Together they are known as the Founders of the Taos Art Colony. When they came to this now famous town not an artist lived

> in New Mexico. Today many painters (and also writers) are doing important work, much of which will live.
>
> Reading from left to right, are
>
> Bert Phillips—Mrs. Eliz. Harwood who with her husband built the huge Harwood building, which was left to the town as a community center and now owned by the University of New Mexico. Next in order is Oscar Berninghaus, a delightful entertainer at our gatherings, and a very faithful recorder (on his canvases). Then comes Dr. Light—next, three of the top artist[s], Gaspard, Ufer, Higgins.[15] Following is Mrs. Lucille Couse—and then the famous English author, D. H. Lawrence. Mrs. Ward Lockwood, J. H. Sharp, Kenneth Adams, Mabel Luhan (partially hidden by her husband (who refused to pose). Mary Austin, an excellent writer is shown between Mabel and Tony.[16] The three figures in front center, are "Ourselves," all artists, Helen G. B., Mary Greene, and Ernst L.—(and Floppy). At extreme right are a Spanish Trumpeter and three Pueblo Indian Friends.[17]—Most of the "neighbors" posed for me. Ufer and Lawrence I painted from memories of these most talented men.[18]

Blumenschein's daughter, Helen, would later note, "The ones he did from life in this painting are Dr. Gertrude Light, Mr. O. E. Berninghaus, and

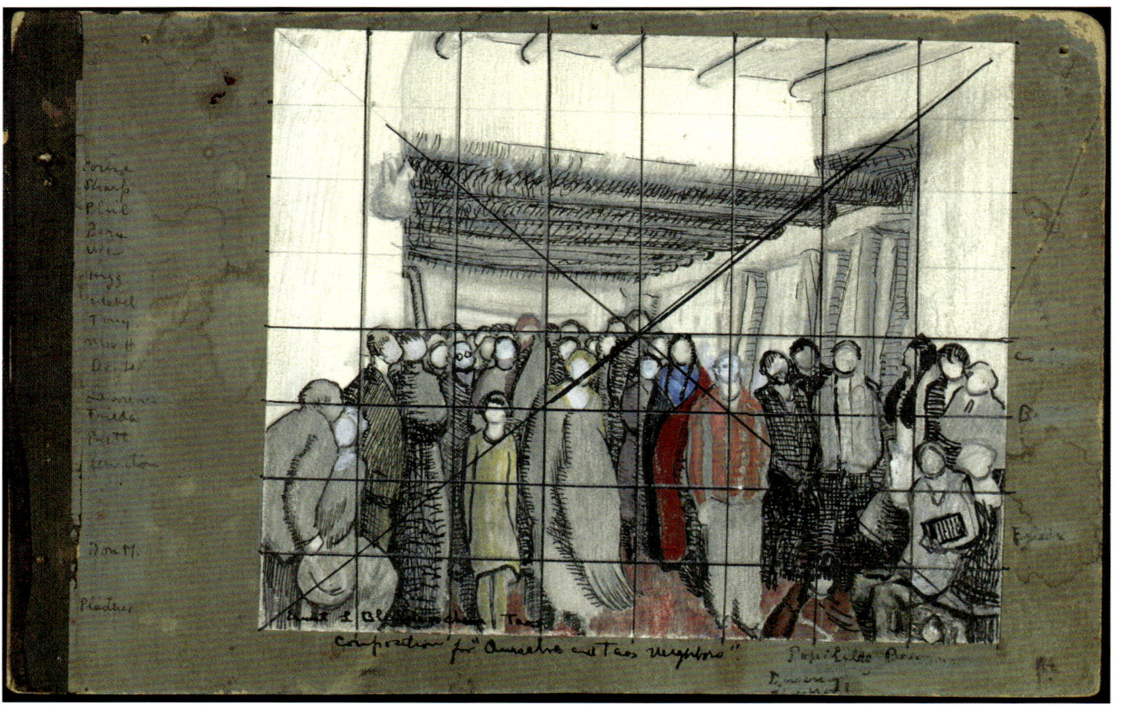

Gridded preliminary sketch for ***Ourselves and Taos Neighbors***, n.d., pencil, pen and gouache on paper, 5 × 6 inches. Private collection.

Mrs. Elizabeth Harwood, Kenneth Adams, and Mrs. Ward Lockwood. He put in Mary Austin, D. H. Lawrence and several others including all three members of our family, in a very stylized and rather stilted way. But again, when criticized for this, he said it went with the composition."[19]

When trying to make sense of the sequence and timing for when the various characters were added, or even what decisions were made by the artist on whom to include in the painting, it is of note that Ufer, who died in August of 1936, is included. But neither Dunton nor Couse, both friends and colleagues of Blumenschein, are present, though they both died in 1936 as well. However, Lucille Couse, wife of E. I. Couse, is there.[20] Why would Blumenschein include a portrait of the wife but not her husband and his fellow artist when he states that he painted Ufer from memory?[21] The painting, especially when compared to the original sketch of twenty-seven figures, leaves a multitude of unanswered questions about the choices Blumenschein made through time of whom to include and whom not to depict as he brought the painting to completion—at least in his mind.

Ourselves and Taos Neighbors remains one of the great story pieces of Taos art, as each of the characters have a remarkable tale to tell in their own right in addition to their connections with the Blumenschein family and history of the artist community. Howard Cook noted in his 1952 essay on the painting, "A gentle honesty characterizes the friendly group which is, naturally, of real interest and value to the region since this period is soon to be gone forever."[22] This painting remained one of Blumenschein's most cherished possessions until he sold it to Mr. and Mrs. Stark for inclusion in their extensive collection of Taos art. In the letter accompanying the key and guide to the painting written to the Starks on October 21, 1957, he says of the picture: "I believe it is a first class work. I really like it; and strange to say am satisfied as it is."[23] That Blumenschein received in 1957 the highest price he ever got for any work within his lifetime from the Starks for *Ourselves and Taos Neighbors* is also testament to the painting's continued significance to the artist.

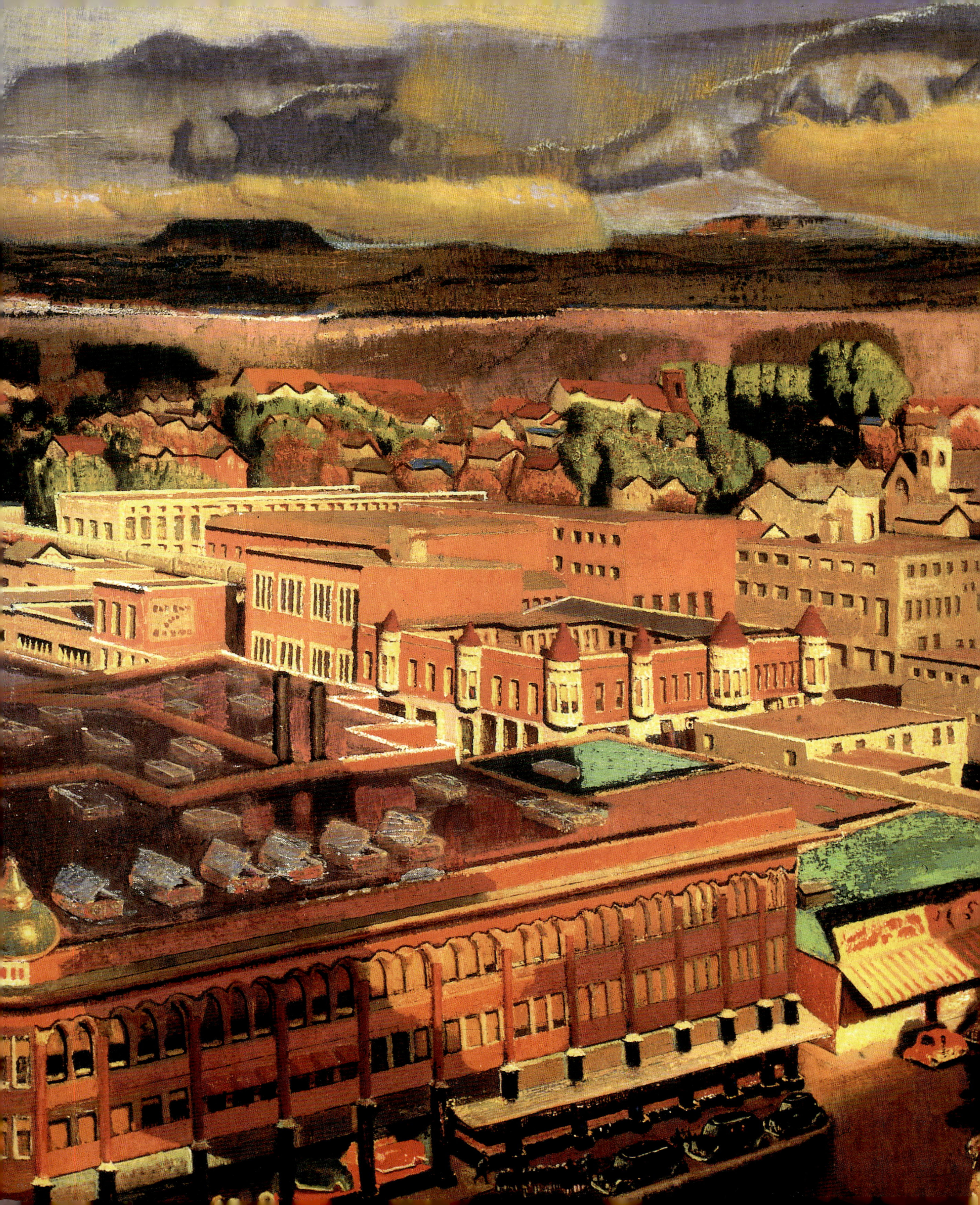

Chapter 5

In Contemporary Rhythm

The Search for Final Perfection

Elizabeth J. Cunningham

New Mexico celebrated four centuries of making art in 1940. The state had created the Cuarto Centennial Commission in 1938 to plan the commemoration of Francisco Vásquez de Coronado's 1540 explorations of New Mexico. Eighteen pageants, different but unified in theme, would highlight other historical and anthropological events and exhibits, some reaching the neighboring states of Colorado and Arizona. For its part, the Museum of New Mexico organized an exhibition that would "give a thrilling panorama view of the state's three distinctive art cultures."[1]

The exhibition, retrospective in scope, included paintings by all three members of the Blumenschein family, and so did a special edition of the *Santa Fe New Mexican,* which featured a forty-four-page Artists and Writers section in June 1940. It boasted that "in no other state of this union is the trend of life so clearly shaped by art as in New Mexico." Although by percentage the population of artists and writers was small, their influence in the state was noticeable everywhere.[2] To honor its artistic luminaries, the newspaper supplied their biographies and examples of their paintings and sculpture, prose pieces, and poems. Blumenschein, who spent the preceding decade striving to cement his place in the national and international art scene, was now invited to reflect on the local art scene and his place within it. He wrote about the founding of the Taos art colony and opened the Fine Arts portion of the Coronado Congress with a speech on the colony's genesis and growth and on Indian art in the Taos region.[3]

The Coronado exhibition's success inspired the Museum of New Mexico to send works by Santa Fe and Taos artists outside the region. From its Twenty-eighth Annual Exhibition of Painters and Sculptors of the Southwest, the museum assembled one painting from each of thirty-five New Mexico artists. It traveled to "leading galleries" in Minneapolis, Kansas City, Tulsa, Philadelphia, Rochester (New York), and Boston. In its November 1941 issue, *El Palacio* reported that such exhibitions served as "a reminder that this state is the seat of two of the best known art groups in the United States."[4] The *Kansas City Star* agreed when it ventured, "The exhibition of paintings by New Mexican artists now at the Nelson Gallery contains . . . a higher percentage of widely-known names than any regional show that's come this way in a long time." The reviewer singled out "a couple of first-class landscapes by Blumenschein and [Cady] Wells."[5]

Not content with past achievements and accolades, Blumenschein looked for fresh scenes in New Mexico to inspire him. Beginning in the late 1930s, he sought relief from northern New Mexico's harsh, cold winters, and as he moved south to a lower elevation, away from the craggy canyon and mountain country of Taos, he found new subject matter in Albuquerque. He embarked on a new set of images that reflected his fascination for modern life in a western setting. Blumenschein often stayed at the Fred Harvey Company's Alvarado Hotel overlooking the railroad yards. The tracks and telephone wires strung along poles set against the rectangular forms of locomotives, freight cars, and station buildings caught his eye and stirred his imagination. Touted for its "subtle but powerful appeal through its splendid color harmonies," Blumenschein's *Box Cars and Railroad Tracks* introduced a new series of paintings streamlined to fit the spare modernist lines those forms and patterns evoked.[6]

On December 7, 1942, the anniversary of the bombing of Pearl Harbor, a "mammoth nation-wide" exhibition, Artists for Victory, opened at New York's Metropolitan Museum of Art. The stated purpose was to show the best works by U.S. artists "one year after the war came." The exhibition was the largest assemblage of contemporary art the Metropolitan Museum had ever shown. The museum offered fifty-two thousand dollars in purchase prize money and opened twenty-eight rooms to house over 1,400 objects.[7]

After the exhibition opened, *New York Times* art critic Edward Alden Jewell noted that the Whitney Museum's concurrent annual show had attracted "nothing short of the best" and regarded many works by well-known artists in the Metropolitan as tired old veterans because they had already been shown in other exhibition venues. Of Blumenschein's entry, *New Mexico Peon*, that was true, but only partly so. He had repainted a work called *Taos Plasterer* that had been painted for exhibition at the Corcoran seven years earlier. In preparation for Artists for Victory, he completely reworked the background and retitled the painting *New Mexican Peon*.

Helen once criticized her father for taking "an old egg" and repainting it.[8] Howard Cook saw the matter in a different light: "[Blumenschein's] method of painting reveals an extraordinary determination, a tremendous effort of will to achieve final perfection."[9] If a painting had not sold, as *The Plasterer* had not by 1942, that opened the way to artistic reconsideration when it returned to his studio. In these years the artist reasserted himself time and again in similar ways, always questing after final perfection.

In the original painting, *Taos Plasterer*, Blumenschein depicted Epimenio Tenorio, the same model used in *The Plasterer* (1921), taking a break, arm raised and leaning against a wooden support rail. Mud cakes his trousers and the trowel in his hand. Thickly applied paint, brushed on as if with a trowel, imitates the texture of adobe, creating a near-sculptural effect. In front of Tenorio, buckets for adding water to dirt and straw on one side balance the mud boat for mixing adobe on the other. He stands on a platform, surrealistically suspended over an apparently deep chasm beyond and against the abstracted triangular and pyramidal forms of mountains and clouds. The painting's background appears entirely abstract, similar in feeling to contemporary modern paintings by Victor Higgins or the backdrop for Blumenschein's own *Superstition*.

The alterations to the painting, retitled *New Mexico Peon* in 1942, created a painting dramatically different in style, color, and setting. Blumenschein lowered Tenorio's hand so that the float, or plastering tool, rested on an adobe wall. He enlarged and broadened the coat and hat, widened the shirt collar, added a belt

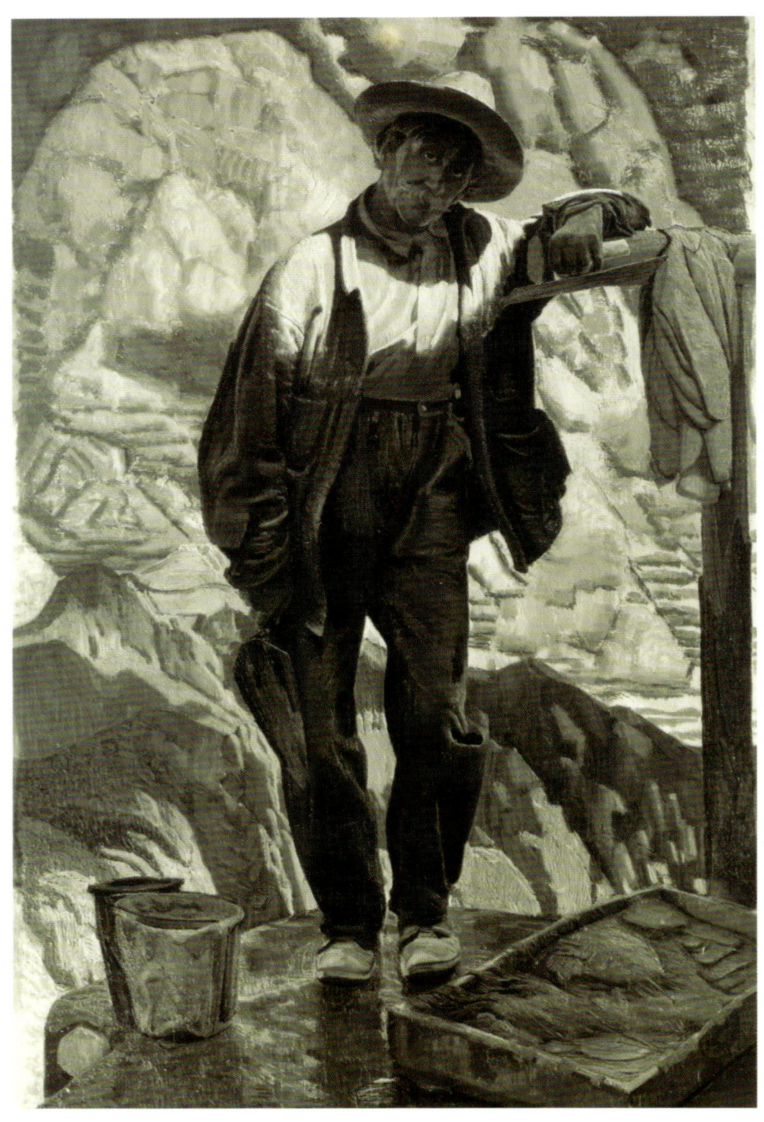

Taos Plasterer, original state. Photograph courtesy of the Ernest L. Blumenschein Papers, 1889–1960, Archives of American Art, Smithsonian Institution, Washington, D.C.

with a gleaming buckle, and darkened the shoes. To create interest and extend the painting's verticality, the artist added a shovel and other adobe-working implements to the mud boat. The platform became the earth that Tenorio stands on, and two cabbage-leafed plants replaced the buckets. The dark blue-green of denim clothing makes the figure stand out against the golden wheat, where the receding stalks created additional vertical movement. The texture of the tawny wheat field obscures the former background; the yellow straw color flows into buff-hued peaks on one side and contrasts with dark blue mountains on the other. At the top of the picture, a cerulean blue sky broken by billowy white cumulus clouds creates horizontal tension. In this painting, Blumenschein allowed the canvas to show through around the shoes, an effect that adds to their worn appearance. His efforts made an impression. After the Artists for Victory show, the Art Institute of Chicago selected *New Mexican Peon* for its Annual Exhibition of American Paintings and Sculpture in 1943.

By spring of 1943 the war occupied the minds of the Blumenschein family: their focus became especially acute because Helen had enlisted in the Women's Army Auxiliary Corps. After basic training, she began officer candidate school. She reached lieutenant grade in July, then attended specialist school in December. In May 1944 Helen sailed from San Francisco for an unnamed assignment in the Pacific. By way of V-mail, her concerned parents sent her tidings from Taos. Almost daily they also shared news of the nation and the war in Europe. Mary kept Helen abreast of family members, mutual friends, and New York's cultural life.

In his letters, Blumenschein apprised his daughter of artists' activities, like Howard Cook's assignment as war correspondent to the Salomon Islands. He also

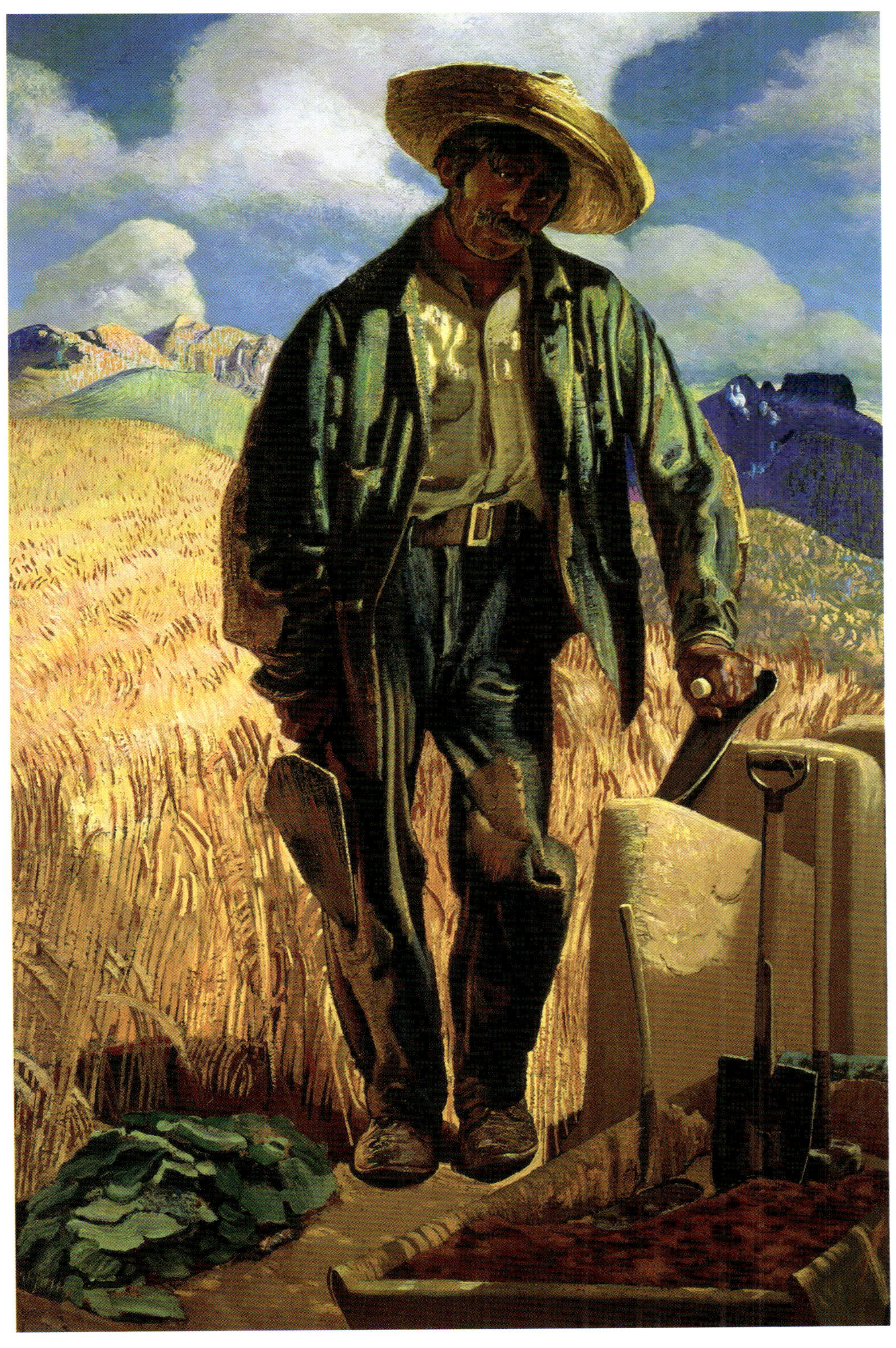

New Mexico Peon (originally ***Taos Plasterer,*** 1930), reworked 1934, finished 1942
Oil on canvas, 40 × 25 inches
Courtesy of the Gerald Peters Gallery, Santa Fe, New Mexico

complained about the lack of sales. In 1943 and 1944, during Helen's first two years in the army, the royalties from *Indian Boyhood* provided Blumenschein's only income. In 1945 he sold *Star Road and White Sun* to Albuquerque High School for a sacrificial price of $250 (about one-tenth its value at the time). He expressed his disappointment to Helen: "No one seems to want to buy my paintings except at most ridiculous low prices. Could have sold everything in my studio to Albuquerque people, if I would charge twenty-five to fifty dollars a picture. But I would rather leave the batch to my heir and hope that some of them will fetch a decent price. There is no promise of even that, for the vogues in art change so rapidly."[10] The dilemma, then, was multifaceted; in those war years sales were understandably soft, tastes were changing, and the acceptance of Blumenschein's style proved uncertain. Underlying his words to Helen lay a deeper concern. How would his work hold up for posterity when the new trends in art threatened to tear away the very foundations upon which it was built?

In the winter of 1944, Helen asked Blumenschein why he had turned to doing just pure landscapes.[11] The answer lay in the solace and inspiration he found in the hills and mountains around Albuquerque. These fresh images inspired new paintings. From the city he looked out on the Sandia Mountains to the east, and he often took drives up into their rugged embrace. Those trips invariably yielded new paintings. The artist liked the geology but found the ground cover of sagebrush and chamisa even more intriguing. In *Sandia Mountains*, painted in 1942, these ubiquitous plants fill two-thirds of the canvas. Their rounded forms, resembling the bunched sheep in *The Pass*, flatten as they recede toward the foothills, as the rose-gold evening light splashes its glow across the bold escarpments. In Spanish *sandia* means "watermelon," an apt name that describes how, in certain light, the mountains appear pink. Blumenschein could not resist the combined splendor of this sight.

To add to Blumenschein's worries, Mary's heart problems became a growing concern. Lengthy travel and the winter climate of Manhattan had taken their toll on her, so her customary annual trips to New York ended. She settled in at the Alvarado with her husband. There she began a series of colored pencil drawings

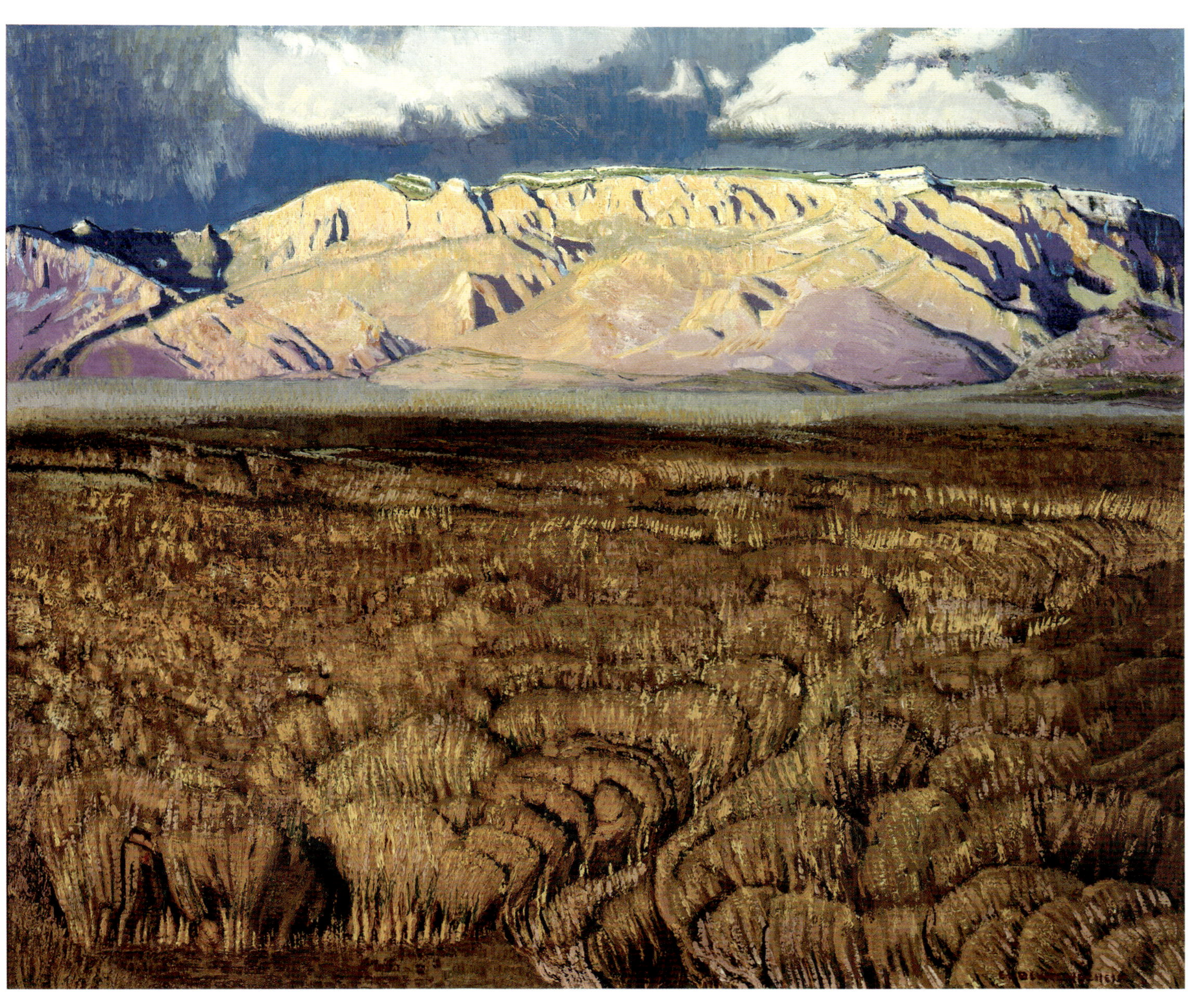

Sandia Mountains, 1942
Oil on canvas, 21 × 25 inches
Private collection

of stories from *The Arabian Nights*. She and Blumenschein attended meetings of the New Mexico Art League and enjoyed visits with Taos friends who stopped in Albuquerque. They kept up a lively exchange about their artwork during this time, a practice that seemed to distract them from anxieties of war (Mary reported that Blumenschein was "overwhelmed," e.g., by the POW atrocities in Germany) and their concerns about each other and especially for Helen's safety in the Pacific theater.

To their relief, the war came to a close in August 1945. Helen was on her way home by October. With her safe return, the family's spirits revived, and they resumed their lives in Taos. Now, once again, they could devote time to one another and to their art. (Although, as Helen once remarked, having three adult artists under one roof could be trying at times. It was good that each had a separate workroom.[12]) Blumenschein promptly stepped back into the national exhibition scene. He sent a group of new paintings out on the road in 1945: *The Strength of the Earth* to the National Academy of Design, *The Oven* to the Corcoran's Nineteenth Biennial, and *Railroad Yard* to the Carnegie's Painting in the United States. That same year the Museum of New Mexico began to organize traveling exhibitions within the state, including a solo show of twelve Blumenschein paintings sent to Las Cruces and Las Vegas, New Mexico. That summer the Metropolitan Museum included *Taos Valley* in its traveling exhibition, America Paints Outdoors.

In 1946 the Carnegie Institute announced the resumption of its internationals, and Blumenschein embarked on another major figure painting. Remembering the critical success of his *Moon, Morning Star, and Evening Star,* he decided to rework a dramatic canvas from the mid-1920s, *Decorative Landscape with Figures Adam and Eve*, into a more powerful figurative statement. The painting, "a careful study of an aspen forest with overhead evergreens on side of a cañon," depicted the figures of Adam and Eve in a larger-than-life primeval landscape, which made them diminutive in scale.[13] As he set about reworking the painting, Blumenschein chose to eliminate these biblical icons to reexplore the wonders of Pueblo ceremonials. Helen had recalled the happenstances of the original 1925 inspiration:

> Papa came back from his work . . . [one] afternoon laughing. He had been doing a large painting, some four feet by two feet, vertical, of the aspen forest at that time (1920s). In the foreground he had Adam and Eve coming out from a pristine forest. He had left his canvas for a short time and came back to find, as though the hand of the Lord had aided him, a flame coming up behind these two figures! It turned out that a cow had come by at this point and slapped its tail plunk against the canvas. This he accentuated with his brush and then called it "Adam and Eve Leaving the Garden of Eden."[14]

After its inclusion in his 1927 solo show at Grand Central Art Galleries in New York, the painting traveled with Blumenschein's three-year circuit show as *Decorative Landscape with Figures*. In a review, the *St. Louis Post-Dispatch* called it the "most striking of all" and regarded the "small and chaste figures" emerging from the grand, sublime forest canopy as homage to Milton's *Paradise Lost*.[15]

Once back in the studio, Blumenschein determined that the painting needed a more "moving group of people who belonged in the forest." He would replace Adam and Eve with a group from the Deer Dance and compose the scene so that instead of recounting banishment, the figures would fit "beautifully with the well painted background." The group of dancers took the artist "over two months to execute, and required great 'restraint,'" he said, "as I had hundreds of studies and drawing from life to use for reference."[16] When the Oklahoma oilman and collector Thomas Gilcrease bought the painting, retitled *Enchanted Forest*, he asked Blumenschein to write about it. But the artist had little to say: "as I believe it is all very evident that I combined the Deer Dance (this time including the Deer Mothers, as their perpendicular lines harmonize with the Aspens), and above, Spruce and Pine, because it was a great setting for a primitive festival." Blumenschein also believed that the color was finer now than in the companion work, *Moon, Morning Star, and Evening Star,* an assessment confirmed when he recounted that many of the Taos artists considered *Enchanted Forest* his best painting.[17] He had succeeded in making this complex conjunction of abstraction and figuration, sculptural and flat forms, moving and still elements, and light and dark passages into a brilliantly cohesive unit.

Blumenschein effectively combined old and new in his quest for a synthesis of human and natural forms and that final perfection that had pushed him earlier to alter *Taos Plasterer* so dramatically. He said that *Enchanted Forest* was "invited without being first seen (which is unusual) by Carnegie, Pittsburgh. I endeavored to do my utmost on this painting, as I was fascinated by the conception of primitive people in the right setting and by the intricacies of the composition."[18] Homer St. Gaudens, then at the Carnegie's helm, appreciated having it for exhibition in his Painting in the United States, 1946. He complimented Blumenschein: "Your *Enchanted Forest* is a good, colorful job, and makes a handsome center to one of our gallery panels."[19]

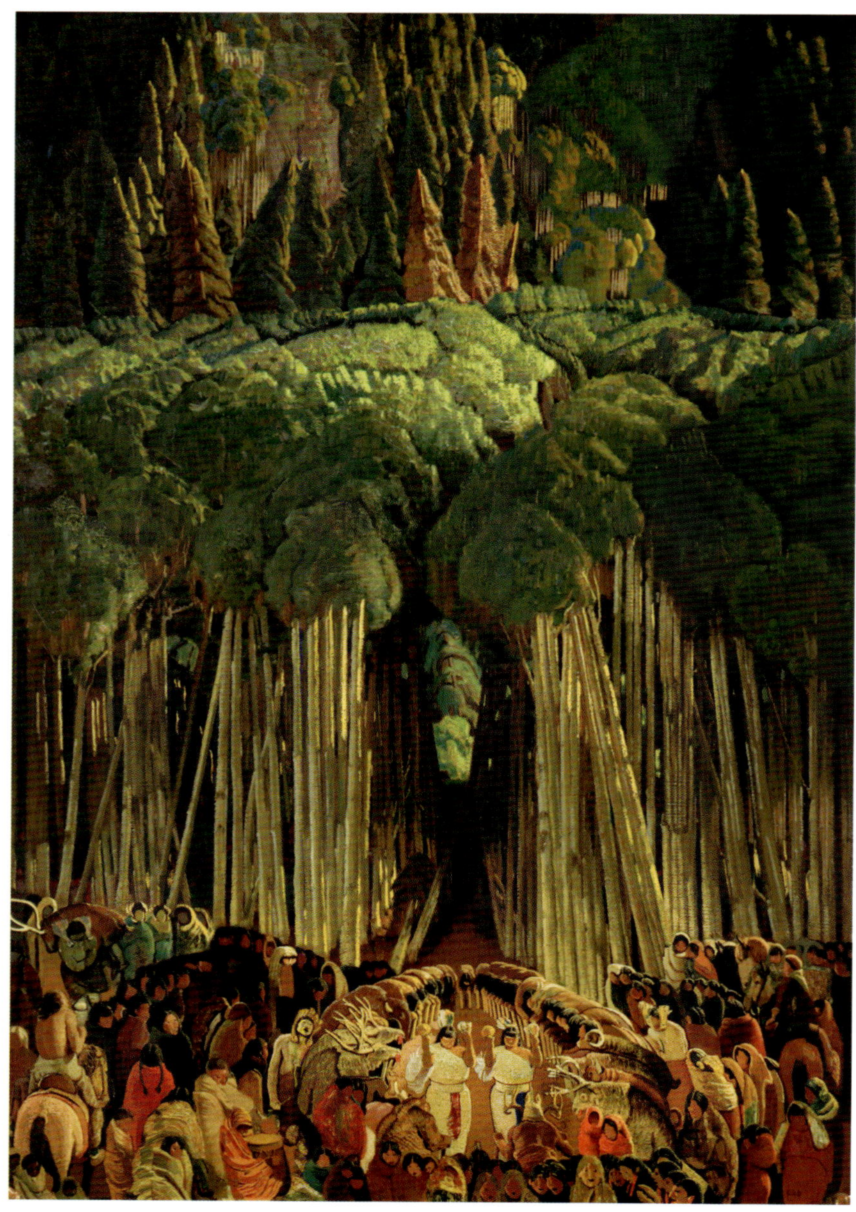

Enchanted Forest (originally ***Decorative Landscape with Figures,*** 1925; later ***Aspen Grove,*** 1929), finished 1946, oil on canvas, 51 × 35¼ inches. Courtesy of the Gilcrease Museum, Tulsa, Oklahoma.

Sales and recognition resumed fairly rapidly after the war. In 1945 Thomas Gilcrease, who was building an Indian-related art collection for his museum in San Antonio (later to be moved to Tulsa), visited Taos in order to purchase paintings. He bought Blumenschein's *Ranchos Church with Indians* from the Blue Door Gallery. He met Blumenschein on that visit as well, a memorable rendezvous for the artist, although the two did not immediately see eye to eye on aesthetic matters: "Mr. Gilcrease didn't believe I was right to take any liberties with the ethnological truths, in order to make a picture that conveyed a bigger truth, as well as moved the onlooker in an emotional way."[20]

A year later, however, when Blumenschein offered to sell Gilcrease his more historically accurate painting *Taos Entertains the Cheyenne*, the collector declined. The disappointment was short-lived, though: in November 1946 Paul Grafe, a Los Angeles businessman, purchased four important oils, *Adobe Village—Winter; Woman in Blue; The Lone Fisherman;* and *Eagle Nest Lake*.

Elation at his good fortune was tempered that fall when Blumenschein became seriously ill. A medical examination revealed a prostate condition that required specialized surgery. Blumenschein was admitted to the Good Samaritan Hospital in Los Angeles, and though the operation was deemed a success, it took him months to recuperate. Then, in early 1947, follow-up surgery became necessary. Blumenschein spent another three months recuperating in Los Angeles. His prognosis was disheartening. He could not expect a return to his previous vigor, and he began to realize, as he told Helen, that at age seventy-two he was "beginning to be an old man."[21]

Blumenschein grew despondent, a state as much explained by his physical health as by current art trends. He was aging, and so was his artistic vision. The preceding fall he had written to Helen: "Can't see my way for first time in my life. . . . And am as upset over the complete swing in Art to abstract and non-objective! Feel out of competition entirely, while doing my best."[22] He noted that Pepsi Cola had awarded a big prize to "exceedingly wildly modern art," and the Carnegie had awarded its First Prize to "an entirely abstract picture." There was no use denying that objective painters, even those who championed abstract design elements in their figural constructions, would be relegated to the background for some time.[23] For Blumenschein, that meant directing energy and time to painting potboilers, "yellow trees for tourists," as he called them, to help pay expenses after his hospitalization in Los Angeles.[24]

Several events conjoined to help revive Blumenschein's spirits once he returned to Taos. In May 1947 a letter from University of New Mexico president J. P. Wernette announced that Blumenschein had been awarded an honorary master of fine arts degree.[25] Two other distinguished New Mexicans, architect John Gaw Meem and historian Fray Angélico Chávez, joined him when the sheepskins were handed out.

The 1947 publication of Mabel Dodge Luhan's book *Taos and Its Artists* also gave him a boost. His old sparring partner brought renewed national attention to the art colony and affectionately acknowledged Blumenschein and Phillips for their pioneering efforts in Taos. To Blumenschein, she mixed the old and the new in a balanced, nonprejudicial way. Cubists like John Marin and Expressionists like Marsden Hartley had "commemorated the countryside" with the same vigor as the earlier founders.[26] Critics deemed the book a piece of fluff that avoided the true analytical view of art colonies and their inherent shortcomings. One reviewer in the *Christian Science Monitor* spoke of artists so gathered in lonely, faraway places as being potentially out of touch. Besides becoming self-satisfied and losing contact with the mainstream art, such artists ran the danger of becoming old-fashioned, especially as represented in the works of their "maturer, more venerated members."[27] Blumenschein no doubt found such assessments rather pointed. Still Luhan had been objective and openly celebrated the art colony, concluding that it was as much about the "manner of living cultivated by painters of Taos [that was] exemplary and enviable" as it was about the resulting art.[28]

At the Museum of Fine Arts in Santa Fe's Museum of New Mexico, Luhan's warm estimation of the colony's importance struck a resonant chord. According to the museum's curator, Reginald Fisher, the artists of Taos were worthy of great tribute. In order to pay them proper homage, especially the mature ones, he set out to develop a new exhibition series. He later explained that his museum believed "New Mexico's deserving artists should be recognized and honored during their life time, while they are still here to meet their friends and together look back upon their life's work and evaluate its accomplishments."[29] These annual shows would honor eminent artists "on the basis of nation-wide distinction and the increase of recognition brought to New Mexico art."[30] Fisher chose Blumenschein to inaugurate the program.

Fisher's invitation set off a flurry of preparations and press coverage. Blumenschein spent over fourteen months organizing the show. For this exhibition, essentially a retrospective, he selected representative works that revealed his artistic development, repainted some old canvases to his current satisfaction, and procured loans from various owners.[31] The *Santa Fe New Mexican* heralded the opening in 1948 with a reproduction of *Jury for the Trial of a Sheepherder for Murder*, which they termed the "artist's most outstanding work." The reviewer did not distinguish in importance, though, between such old and renowned Blumenschein paintings as *The Chief Speaks*, lent by the Cincinnati Art Museum, or *The German Tragedian*, from the Herron Institute of Art in Indianapolis, and more recent prizewinners like *Superstition* and *Taos Entertains the Cheyenne*.[32]

The "first show of its kind" opened on May 30, 1948, four days after Blumenschein's seventy-fourth birthday.[33] The afternoon festivities began with the School of American Research bestowing on him the first Honorary Fellow award ever granted to an artist. Fellow painters Bert Phillips, Kenneth Adams, and Theodore Van Soelen spoke on aspects of his art career and work.[34] In "A Critique of the Exhibition," the last speaker, Howard Cook, articulated Blumenschein's true place in the scheme of regional and national art:

> The concrete means of expression which distinguishes the painting of Ernest Blumenschein stems directly from his knowledge of and love for the Southwest. And, because of his awareness of the necessity of strong underlying design structure which suggests a contributing abstract quality, his work forms a connecting link between today and the traditional art of the past. From the static envelope of the past he has succeeded in his purposeful search for the richer values of creative form, into the fascinating realms animated by imaginative, complicated rhythms with design asymmetrical or subtly balanced, and color as rich as the earth of old Spanish and Indian civilizations.[35]

Cook described the scope of Blumenschein's oeuvre: portraiture; figure, history, and urban scene paintings; landscapes; even a few mural designs. He discussed individual paintings in the exhibition—from early works like *Moon, Morning Star, and Evening Star* to those from the 1940s like *Box Cars and Railroad Tracks*—and Blumenschein's range of subject matter from the early Indian pictures through landscapes, which began as decorative and evolved into "his present powerful interpretations, in contemporary rhythm, of the Southwest."[36]

The exhibition received accolades and applause. Newspapers in Santa Fe and Albuquerque reported capacity crowds at the opening. The Transcendentalist painter Alfred Morang penned approvingly in the *Santa Fe New Mexican,* "Here is painting that is utterly honest. These paintings show deep thought and long hours of the most serious work . . . each canvas is a lesson in the application of abstract principles." Morang called Blumenschein one of America's greatest living American artists and urged art students to make repeated visits to study his paintings.[37] So popular was the exhibition that the La Fonda Hotel listed it as Santa Fe's number one attraction for the month of June.

In tandem with attention from the press and other quarters, Blumenschein received kudos from friends far and near. "My congratulations!" wrote Lionel Barrymore from California.[38] Unable to attend the opening, Taos modernist Ward Lockwood expressed delight in the "privilege of seeing the show, and re-seeing a number we had seen in the process of development in your studio."[39] Mabel Dodge Luhan congratulated Blumenschein on his distinguished lifework.[40]

At the time of the exhibition's close, the Museum of New Mexico organized two pared-down versions of the retrospective for travel. The return of museum loans narrowed the selection, as did Thomas Gilcrease's return to Taos in September. With elation tempered by concern, the artist wrote to Reginald Fisher:

> Had a great break last week!! The Gilcrease Foundation of Tulsa purchased four of my big ones! . . . My only regret, if I have one, is that the loss of four of my very best will make a big difference in my traveling show, opening at Kansas City. The ones sold and already sent to Tulsa, are: *Enchanted Forest*, *Moon, Morning Star and Evening Star*, *Superstition*, and *Mojave Desert*. Mr. Gilcrease insisted on the *best works*, as he wants a permanent representation of what I can do, and one that will last a long time in his museum which is for the recording of the American Indian. His inclusion of *Mojave Desert* was a big surprise as that is pure landscape.[41]

Even the absence of seven major paintings did not diminish the viewer's experience of the smaller Blumenschein exhibitions. In October 1948 the larger of the two shows, numbering twenty-seven paintings, opened at the Nelson Gallery of Art in Kansas City, then traveled for a year to four other regional museums.[42] A smaller assemblage of fourteen drawings and paintings traveled simultaneously to venues within New Mexico.[43]

Just as Blumenschein's world seemed to gather some equilibrium, however, he suffered another physical setback in December 1948, when his appendix ruptured. It took until spring the next year to recover. When he did, he returned to his studio, where a five-year-old canvas, a large landscape titled *Strength of the Earth* from 1944, challenged him to pick up his brushes again and move forward. The painting, now reworked to Blumenschein's satisfaction and retitled *Rio Grande Gorge Near Taos*, was originally somewhat more expansive, showing the canyon appearing to recede from view as it wound into a bluff with mountains in the background. In the repainted version, Blumenschein changed the bluff to extend the river in a lightning design reminiscent of petroglyphs pecked into the canyon walls that suggests the Rio Grande Rift was about to continue expansion. Dark browns divide the picture near the center and up the canyon until it intersects with a diagonal downslope topped by juniper and piñon. The dark blue of cliffs and highlighted mountains contrast with pink clouds against a robin's egg blue sky. All the geomorphic forms, though recognizable, are reduced to essentials of design and structure.

Perhaps his painting retrospective, combined with health issues and advancing age, drove Blumenschein to review his own life's career as he stepped into the new decade of the 1950s. Although dedicated solely to painting by the 1920s, his illustrations were still in demand. When his Albuquerque friend Will Keleher had completed manuscripts, he asked Blumenschein to provide illustrations for his two books, *Turmoil in New Mexico* (1952) and *Violence in Lincoln County* (1957). The artist consented to Keleher's request as well as to Grace Glueck's for use of his illustration *The Merry-Go-Round Comes to Taos* (1899) for the *New York Times Book Review* in 1957.[44] Earlier, in 1951, Helen Card, "an enthusiast of American Illustration of my period," corresponded with Blumenschein. She had assembled

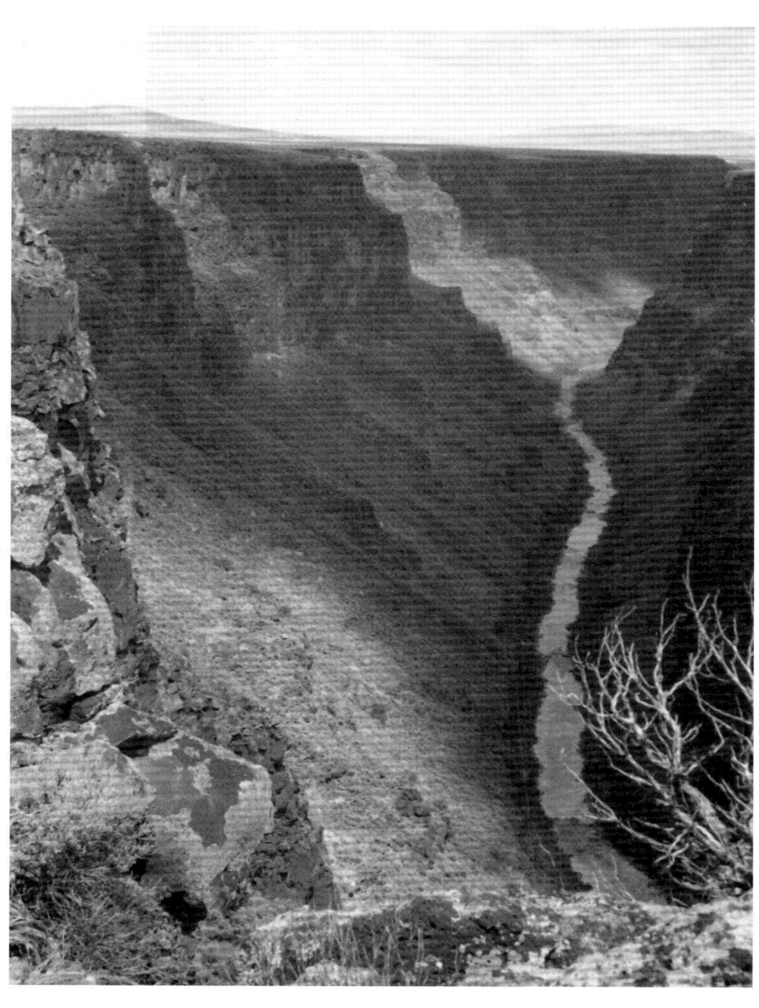

Rio Grande Gorge. Courtesy of the Palace of the Governors, Museum of New Mexico, New Mexico Department of Cultural Affairs, Santa Fe (neg. ACP.008-A).

clippings of Frederic Remington illustrations, enough to fill five scrapbooks that she donated to the Metropolitan Museum of Art in the 1940s. Card now wished to make a similar permanent record of Blumenschein's work. She had assembled some of his drawings and magazine illustrations, and sent him a letter with the list of the works she collected. In closing, she added: "Do you know, some of the earliest work of 'top men' was more attractive in spirit than their later work." She applied this to some of Norman Rockwell's work and the rudimentary work Remington did in his twenties. Blumenschein's drawings were not only good "but full of the love of it." Card liked that.[45]

Demands for his paintings also came from disparate quarters, sometimes asking him for historic work and sometimes for current efforts. When—as in the case of the Colorado Springs Fine Arts Center and their 1952 exhibition, Taos Painting, Yesterday and Today—he was asked to submit *Ranchos Church*, a painting from the twenties, he felt out of sync with the times. Representational works of nine early Taos artists, including Blumenschein, Sharp, and Couse, hung side by side with twenty-one "painters of today" like Howard Cook, Emil Bisttram, and Andrew Dasburg. The latter were touted as coming forward with "all varieties of current expression." And the old-timers got credit for having provided "powerful and influential expression" for younger artists, but that was faint praise for someone of Blumenschein's ambition and self-estimation.

Another painting exhibited that August placed him among the contemporary modernist painters. The Museum of New Mexico chose to feature his painting *Downtown Albuquerque*, completed in 1952, on the cover of that year's Thirty-ninth Annual Exhibition catalog. Blumenschein's painting was even among fifteen

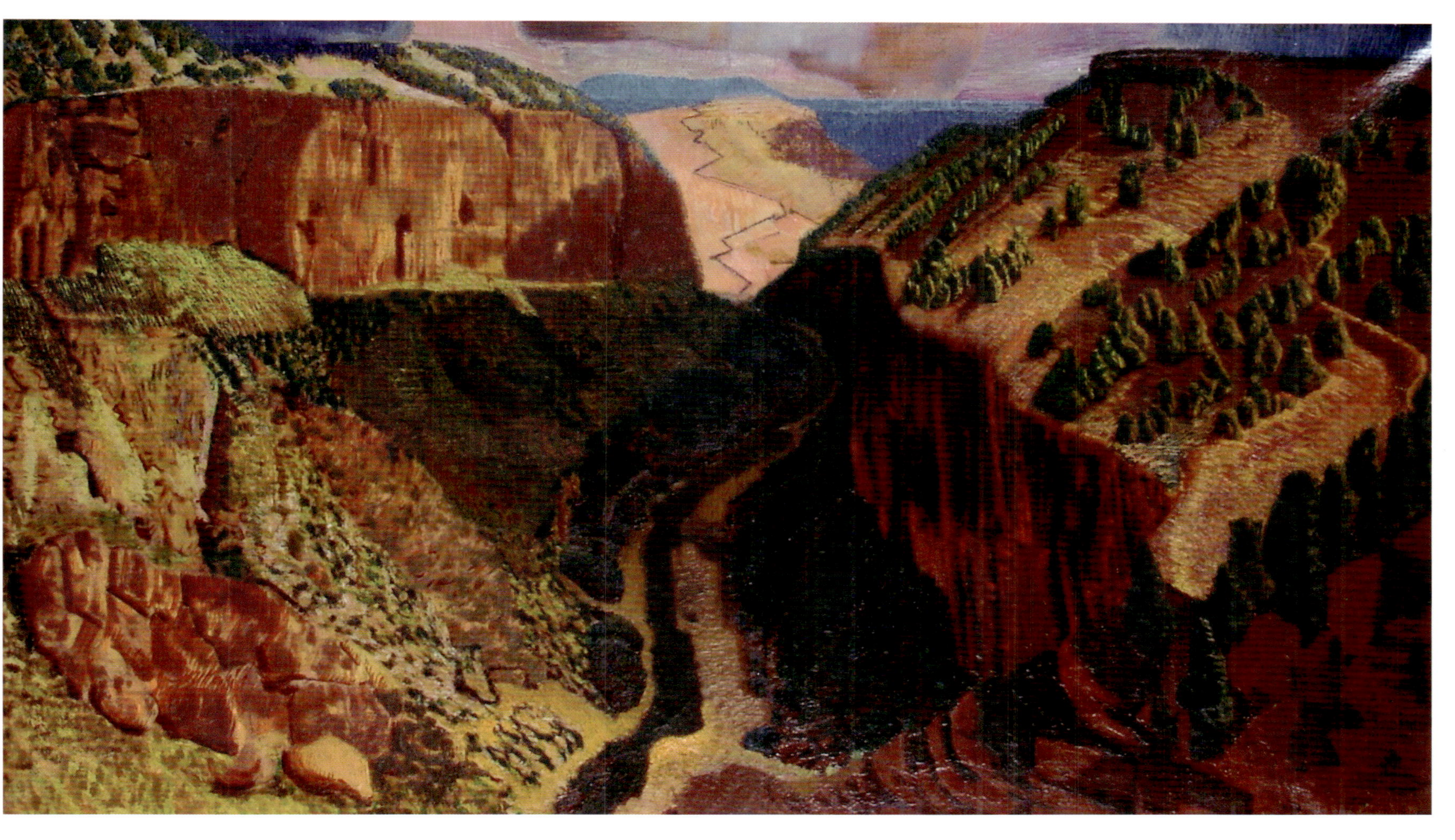

The Canyon (originally ***Strength of the Earth,*** 1944; cross-referenced as ***Rio Grande Cañon at Taos***), reworked 1949
Oil on canvas, 27 × 47 inches
The Eugene B. Adkins Collection at the Fred Jones Jr. Museum of Art,
University of Oklahoma, Norman, and the Philbrook Museum of Art, Tulsa, Oklahoma

selected for museum purchase consideration. Unfortunately, his was not purchased. However, *Downtown Albuquerque* was one of thirty-five works picked for the ensuing national traveling exhibition.

In his later years, Blumenschein painted more in the red range. Accordingly to Helen, his paintings "became very rich with a beautiful Indian red," a color prevalent in *Downtown Albuquerque*.[46] His later city and train yard paintings also reveal a powerful sense of abstract design. *Downtown Albuquerque* is set on a diagonal, with the city's buildings reduced to simplified, yet ornamented linear rectangles and squares, divided by the repeated geometry of the windows. Rounded turrets, light poles, smokestacks, and church steeples provide vertical accents to mitigate the open, horizontal plateaus of the rooftops. Reds in various shades predominate and link the buildings together as a unified entity. The foreground is peopled with rooftop observers who watch a marching band led by two tubas on the street below. *Downtown Albuquerque*, a masterful study of abstract geometries enlivened with shadow and light, caused reviewer Dorothy Morang to call it "splendidly integrated in color and composition."[47]

In the 1952 shows in Colorado Springs and Santa Fe, more purely abstract works dominated the galleries. As a stylistic change it seemed sufficiently extreme to engender public outrage, uproar, and incomprehension. On a national scale, this situation had compelled New York's Museum of Modern Art and the Whitney Museum of American Art to issue a joint statement in 1950 with Boston's Institute of Contemporary Art to "clarify the current controversial issues of modern art." They, however, deplored what they viewed as the public's pervasive "tendency to identify American art exclusively with popular realism, regional subject and nationalistic sentiment." The museums' function was not to wrest control of "the course of art" or to tell an artist what to do or to "impose tastes dogmatically on the public" but simply to recognize diversity of expression. In a manifesto titled "A Statement on Modern Art," the museums laid down perhaps the most comprehensible proclamation of their time about their mission regarding modern art: "The field of contemporary art is immensely wide and varied, with many diverse viewpoints and styles. We believe that this diversity is a sign of vitality and

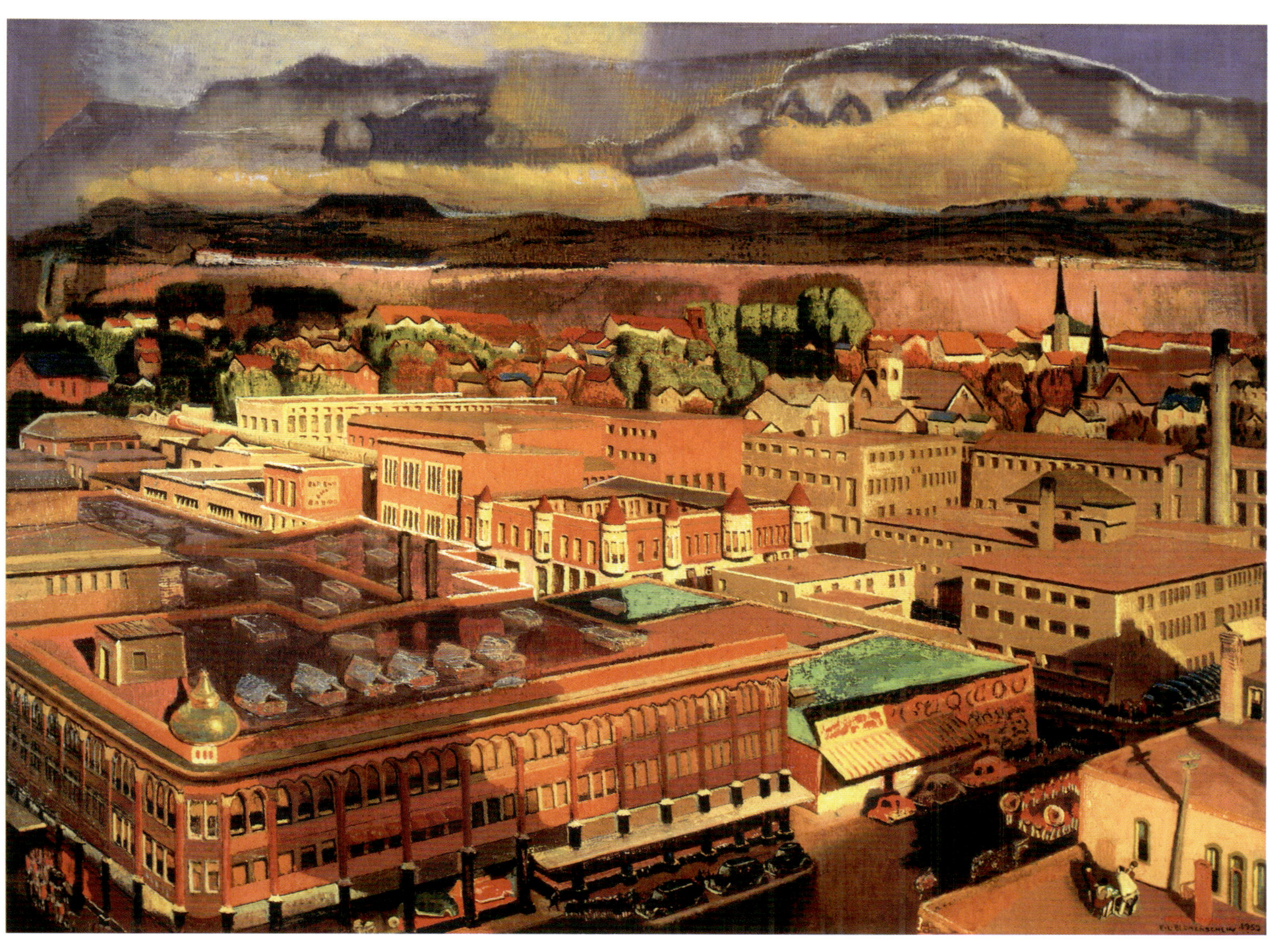

Downtown Albuquerque, 1952
Oil on canvas, 29 × 39 inches
Courtesy of the University of New Mexico Art Museum, Albuquerque (63.13)
Gift of Helen Blumenschein

of freedom of expression inherent in a democratic society. We oppose any attempt to make art or opinion about art conform to a single point of view."[48]

This sounded reasonable and open-minded enough; though when the modern in art moved toward the extreme of pure abstraction, Blumenschein was vexed. After visiting San Francisco and looking at modern art, including a Kandinsky exhibition that he confessed to appreciating, Blumenschein began to turn a critical eye on the whole current art scene. In a 1952 interview, quoted later in the New Mexico press, he expressed his opinion by recalling his Paris years and by retreating even from the acquiescent stand he had taken in 1914 after viewing the Armory Show. Just as Impressionism, with its theories of broken light, reached its peak, the "octopus we call Modernism was born." That's when Matisse, with whom Blumenschein had reconciled in his younger mind, upset the proportions of the human body; Gertrude Stein published "her gibberish"; and music composers "decided to throw harmony and counterpoint downstairs and put dissonance and syncopation on the pedestal. . . . Then Publicity, the huge giant, reached out and embraced all modernism, separated the parts, dropping some in our Universities and scattering the rest to the hungry world that wanted new thrills."[49]

Blumenschein had retrenched, casting his spirit of accommodation aside. He now figured that "after all we cannot burst the links of the traditional ideals of man, and with a flood of propaganda endeavor to create new ideals that lack the depth of centuries." He admitted to appreciating "skillful ingenuity" and to occasionally finding works of "extraordinary color or design" that pleased him among those who sanctioned or created abstract works, but he would resolutely "never again compare these works that build no form, with the grandeur of thought and feeling which have been expressed in our masterpieces of architecture, music and painting."[50]

Increasingly Blumenschein would be called upon for his reminiscences on the Taos art colony. By the 1950s he functioned as its senior spokesman and would thoughtfully address its history when called upon by circumstances to do so. Following the deaths of fellow Taos Society artists Oscar Berninghaus (1952) and Joseph Henry Sharp (1953), Blumenschein was asked to deliver a memorial speech on Sharp in September 1953. Evidently the information he requested on his fellow artist from the Museum of New Mexico arrived too late. When it did come, Blumenschein objected to its content. The record, he complained to Fisher, gave Sharp far too much credit for starting the Taos colony: "But for 'Gawd's Sake' do get Sharp's place correct. What he told me in Paris had little influence except to induce Phil and me to want to see the Taos Pueblo if we ever passed that way. . . . Sharp visited Taos in 1893 for two weeks—not the first artist by any means. . . . Most credit as an anchor-pioneer must go to Bert Phillips, for he never left the village of Taos. . . . Kindly get the facts understood by newspapers and public—and those whose interests include Taos in the art world."[51]

To keep his increasingly precious values and high standards before art students, Blumenschein continued to give critiques for the University of New Mexico's field school in Taos. In the early 1950s, the university also recruited Howard Cook, Andrew Dasburg, Emil Bisttram, and Ward Lockwood for their modernist perspectives. The field school bulletin in 1953 illustrated paintings by that year's instructors and showed the diversity of style and aesthetic penchant among the faculty. Blumenschein's *Railroad Yard* matched Kenneth Adams's modernist portrait of a woman—both were objective representations of recognizable figures. Pictures by Dasburg and Cook, while still recognizable, were more reductive and abstracted. Those by Bisttram and Lockwood had by then evolved into pure abstractions. In accompanying biographical statements, the bulletin lauded Blumenschein, "considered by many [as] the 'Dean' of New Mexico artists." Students could count on his "quick and keen understanding and tolerance of their artistic efforts."[52] Howard Cook commented on Blumenschein's encouragement of New Mexico's younger artists: "An indication of Blumenschein's contemporary feeling is his interest in fostering younger talent. Many are the younger painters who have received encouragement from him to persevere in their individual idiom. After wielding a verbal whiplash, he urges in his junior companions integrity and the love for secure values. It is fine to feel his appreciative and keen attempts at analysis of another's work, his reaching out for a common understanding of the fundamentals of artistic expression."[53]

Blumenschein's interest in younger artists extended beyond the classroom and could be as derisive as it was decisive. He evidently critiqued Freddie O'Hara's work following the younger artist's solo show of abstracts at Galerie Escondida. O'Hara replied that he appreciated the criticism and encouragement from one "whose artistic integrity I admire."[54] When modernist painter and printmaker Doel Reed lived in one of the Harwood studios, Blumenschein often dropped by to see his works in progress and talk art one on one. Reed also once received an all-too-public critique from his older compatriot. Taos modernist Wolcott Ely recalled Blumenschein arriving at one of Reed's openings. Standing next to Ely, he said, "These all look like they came out of the same pot." Startled, Ely tried to quiet him, fearing Reed, at the center of the room, had overheard. Unabashed, the outspoken Blumenschein repeated, loud enough for the whole room to hear, "Reed, these all look like they came out of the same pot."[55]

Blumenschein regarded most abstract artists as lacking or indifferent to traditional training, and when he saw this failing as blatant, he rebelled. In 1952 Emil Bisttram revived the Taos Artists Association and with its members developed a new community art gallery called the Stables. Simultaneously, conservative artists met with "their natural enemies, the moderns, to clear the smoke from the air." The two factions drafted a code of conduct designed to end "open hostilities" between the groups. When in September 1954 the *Chicago Tribune* reported the two factions had reached a peace accord, the paper also noted that there were still some holdouts, expressly, a band of 17 artists, out of the 490 members, known as the La Fonda Group. The leader of those traditionalist renegades, Ernest Blumenschein, gave the reason: "Half of those people"—referring to the association—"have no talent and no gift."[56]

Brazenly, Blumenschein even carried his crusade nationally. He soon took on his old friend Daniel Caton Rich, director of the Art Institute of Chicago. Blumenschein accused Rich of undergoing "some sea change or transformation" in supporting abstract art, and his parry put the director on the defensive. The museum, Rich responded, was simply endeavoring to expose what was "*happening* without too much *final judgment.*" While he recognized the presence of some shallow work in the contemporary art scene, he also found a genuine "striving towards a new conception . . . which science (especially physics and chemistry)" had opened to the art world. Thus he believed that true artists would find new forms, techniques, and tools (different from but no less important than Blumenschein's tradition of academic training) and, like their predecessors, would continue to "express the old tension of hate and love and faith and dismay."[57] Blumenschein's point was made but not won.

Winning for Blumenschein, he knew in his heart, would not come from resistance to new art trends or from political maneuvering. Winning would come from work, long and hard hours with brush in hand, and a determination to find that exhilarating sense of achieving "final perfection." In the 1950s Blumenschein reworked nearly all the canvases still in his possession. Howard Cook considered the self-investigation and self-criticism this took admirable: "Such soul searching reassures us that each picture that goes out to the public will be as close to perfection as possible. It is responsible for the smaller number of pictures painted but guarantees more lasting qualities for the benefit of the future."[58]

Sometimes when Blumenschein felt he had reached completion on a reworked canvas, though, the results were not always clear to his audience. This occurred over his *Railroad Yard, No. 5*. An attentive viewer, seeing the painting in the Museum of Fine Art's 1953 Fiesta Show, seemed to find no difference between it and one titled *Railroad Yard* illustrated by the museum in 1951. He could not understand how an artist could try to fool the public by exhibiting old work as new. This incident and similar remarks on the reworked painting forced Blumenschein to respond. The *Santa Fe New Mexican* published photos of both paintings, captioned "Look Closely—There IS a Difference," and the artist published a rebuttal. Inspiration had struck him, he recalled, when he crossed the overpass on Coal Avenue above Albuquerque's freight yard. He saw in the scene below him "a dramatic movement of the masses and lines with certain qualities of light and color" and worked diligently to capture on canvas the mood with the character, strength, and virility this first impression evoked. Blumenschein sent a photo of the finished work, *Railroad Yard,* to the Carnegie, and they had invited the painting to be included in their exhibition Painting in the United States, 1945. Once back in his studio, the picture had a hardness and dryness the artist did not like: "I felt deeply that the composition of that long diagonal line, the circular group of figures, the color, the smoke, had produced a mood that deserved improvement—and I would stay with it until fairly satisfied with the result."[59] He remodeled it twice in 1950 and again in 1951.

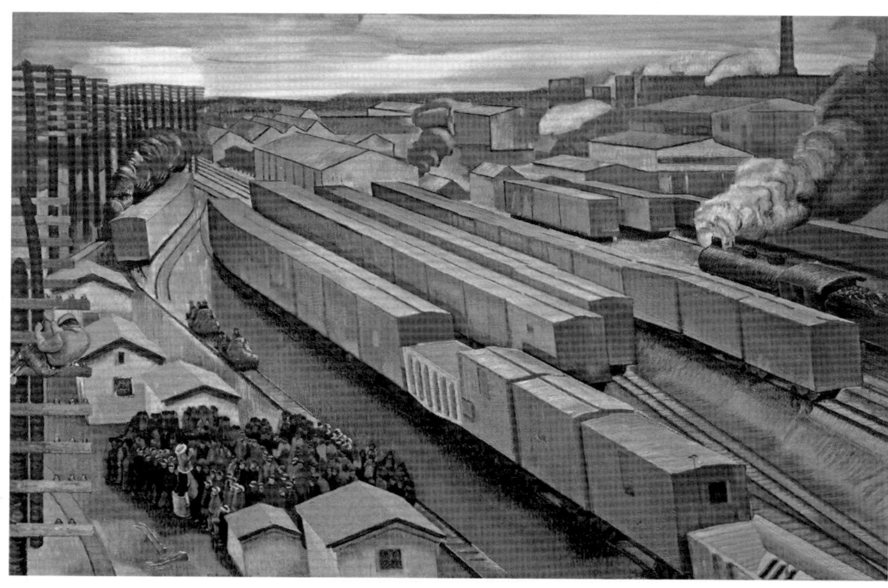

Railroad Yard, original state, oil on canvas, 31 × 48 inches. Courtesy of the Palace of the Governors, Museum of New Mexico, New Mexico Department of Cultural Affairs, Santa Fe (neg. HP05.25-G).

Still not entirely satisfied, he started on version number five in 1953. It took six months' work until he could lay down his brushes, wipe his palette clean, and enter it in his record book as finished. The resulting *Railroad Yard, No. 5*, concluded Blumenschein, moved, lived, and captured the mood that had first motivated him to consider the scene. He entered the "new" painting in the fall 1953 Fiesta Show.[60]

Blumenschein's patience and persistent reworking of his canvases ultimately paid off for him. During one of Blumenschein's absences from Taos in the fall of 1954, Texas millionaire H. J. Lutcher Stark had stopped by the studio and purchased four of the artist's finest paintings.[61] All of the paintings—*Box Cars and Railroad Tracks, Extraordinary Affray, Taos Entertains the Cheyennes*, and *Rio Grande, No. 2*—had been in major exhibitions; all were striking examples of his best mature work. When the magazine *El Crespusculo* interviewed Blumenschein for his reaction, the artist responded with self-assured satisfaction: "One makes sales of this kind because he has established a reputation." He advised younger artists to keep their good pictures, whether or not they had received recognition. Eventually they would achieve the success due them.[62]

Blumenschein enjoyed further confirmation of his own success when he received an invitation to the Museum of Modern Art's twenty-fifth anniversary show in New York. He accepted and attended the opening reception of Paintings

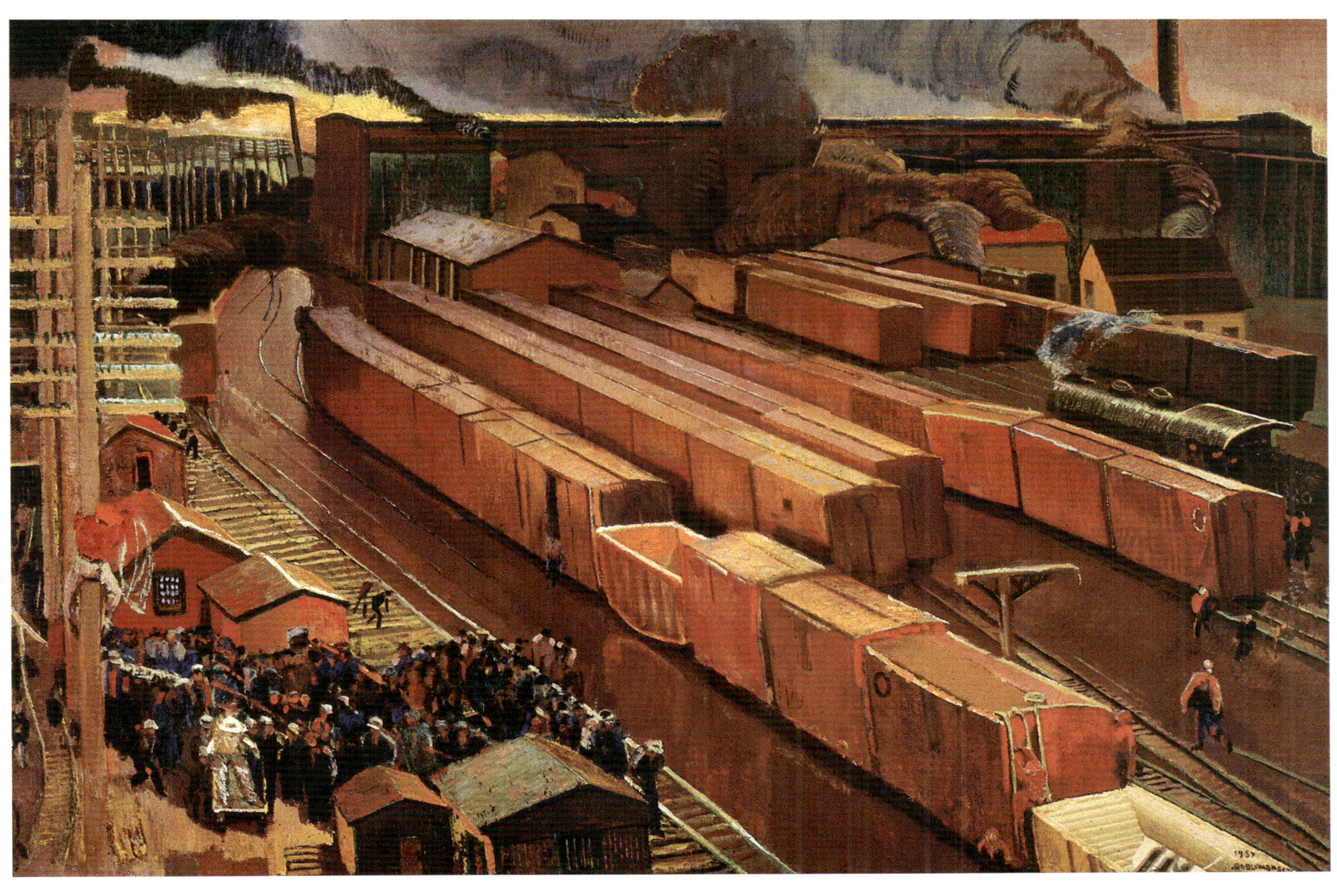

Railroad Yard—Meeting Called (originally ***Railroad Yard,*** 1945; later ***Railroad Yard, No. 3***, 1951; then ***Railroad Yard, No. 5***, 1953), finished 1958
Oil on canvas, 31 × 48 inches
Courtesy of the Taos Historic Museums, Taos, New Mexico
Photograph by Anthony Richardson

from the Museum Collection. At the height of abstract expressionism's ascendancy in New York, he saw his prize painting *Jury for the Trial of a Sheepherder* hung alongside others by the country's leading modern artists. He said the biggest compliments in his art life were the purchases of two paintings placed in "the two leading Art Museums of our country," the Museum of Modern Art and the Metropolitan Museum of Art.

Although Blumenschein was a proud man with a substantial ego, he was ever willing to share credit where it was due. So when a local nurse named Laura Bickerstaff embarked on research for the first volume ever dedicated exclusively to the Taos Society of Artists, he made sure that the limelight was broadly shared. She had chosen to highlight the six charter members, Blumenschein, Phillips, Couse, Berninghaus, Sharp, and Dunton, and using their letters and other written work, she sketched the artists' lives and listed their honors. When she asked Blumenschein to write an introduction to the book, he found some important figures missing, Ufer and Higgins, so he included personal recollections on the lives and careers of both compatriots in his essay. After its publication in early 1955, the Taos Bookshop hosted a coming out party for the book. The shop's owners assembled members of the artists' families to pour tea and invited the whole town to attend.[63] Bickerstaff and the two surviving founding members, Phillips and Blumenschein, autographed books.

Blumenschein wintered in Albuquerque that year. In February the National Arts Club announced him as recipient of their 1956 medal. *El Crespusculo* reported that he had received the honor for the fourth time, after winning it three times in the 1930s. The artist had begun work on this 1956 award winner, *Indian Sheep Herder*, ten years previously. According to *El Crespusculo*, the painting depicted an "old streambed with the shepherd and some of his flock in the center. Mr. Blumenschein repainted the center portion several times. When he finished the sheep herder, he thought he had a good picture at last. The national award judges agreed."[64] Later that year Stark bought the painting for his collection, now retitled *Rocky Trail*. Blumenschein wrote him about the painting and the award it had garnered. Of the latter he said, "Am of course proud of it—and to think I received it in my late years. So I am encouraged to believe I am not aging artistically as I am physically."[65]

In 1924 Blumenschein painted a portrait of himself, Higgins, and Ufer. A phantasmagoric painting, it depicts a whimsical donkey with angel's wings flying above three vultures perched side-by-side on stylized clouds; the birds peer down at three men balanced on popsicle-rounded peaks. Almost cartoonish, the painting drew ridicule from modernist critic Henry McBride, then art editor for the *New York Herald*: "Mr. Blumenschein's 'Idealist, Dreamer, Realist' is, like the title to the picture, turgid and overcharged with fomentation."[66] An argument with McBride ensued, and a few years later the artist's ledgers showed the painting's destiny: "Destroyed."[67]

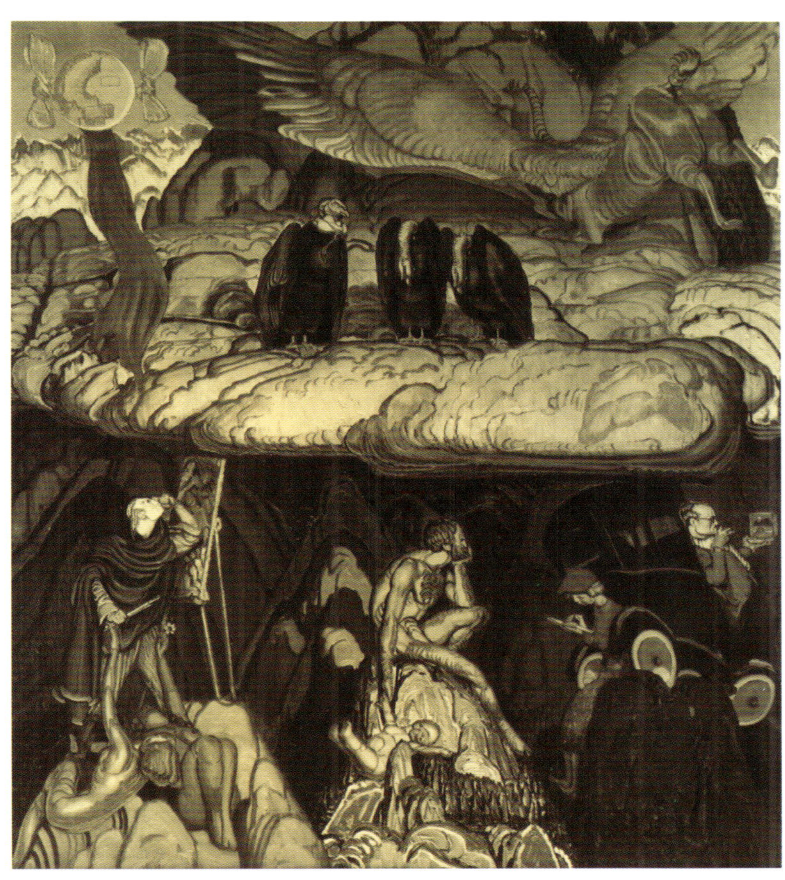

Idealist, Dreamer, Realist, 1924. Photograph courtesy of the Ernest L. Blumenschein Papers, 1889–1960, Archives of American Art, Smithsonian Institution, Washington, D.C.

In *Rocky Trail* he played with scale and reality. No matter where placed on the canvas, the sheep are the same size, nearly as large as the trees. For their size, the sheepherder could be driving cows. Lopsided boulders reminiscent of whales and walruses are strewn among blocks and rounds of rocks and stepped stairs of stone. With its masklike face and striped belly, the enigmatic goat, its horns, the shepherd's stick, and bare tree branches contrast perpendicular to the canyon's breadth and the horizontal and diagonal rows of sheep. Light shines as if emanating from the painter, in a cruciform glow of heightened reds and lighter reddish-brown. The crowning joke in this delightful late work is the blanketed Pueblo herder. In Taos only Hispanic people tended sheep.

When Stark visited Blumenschein's studio to purchase *Rocky Trail*, he saw another painting in progress. Even in its unfinished state, Stark recognized its quality—and a new note in the artist's work. The moment he saw it, Stark asked to buy it and Blumenschein agreed to sell it, a "painting of the R.R. Yard (under Diesel power)," on one condition: he could send it to two exhibitions in the East.

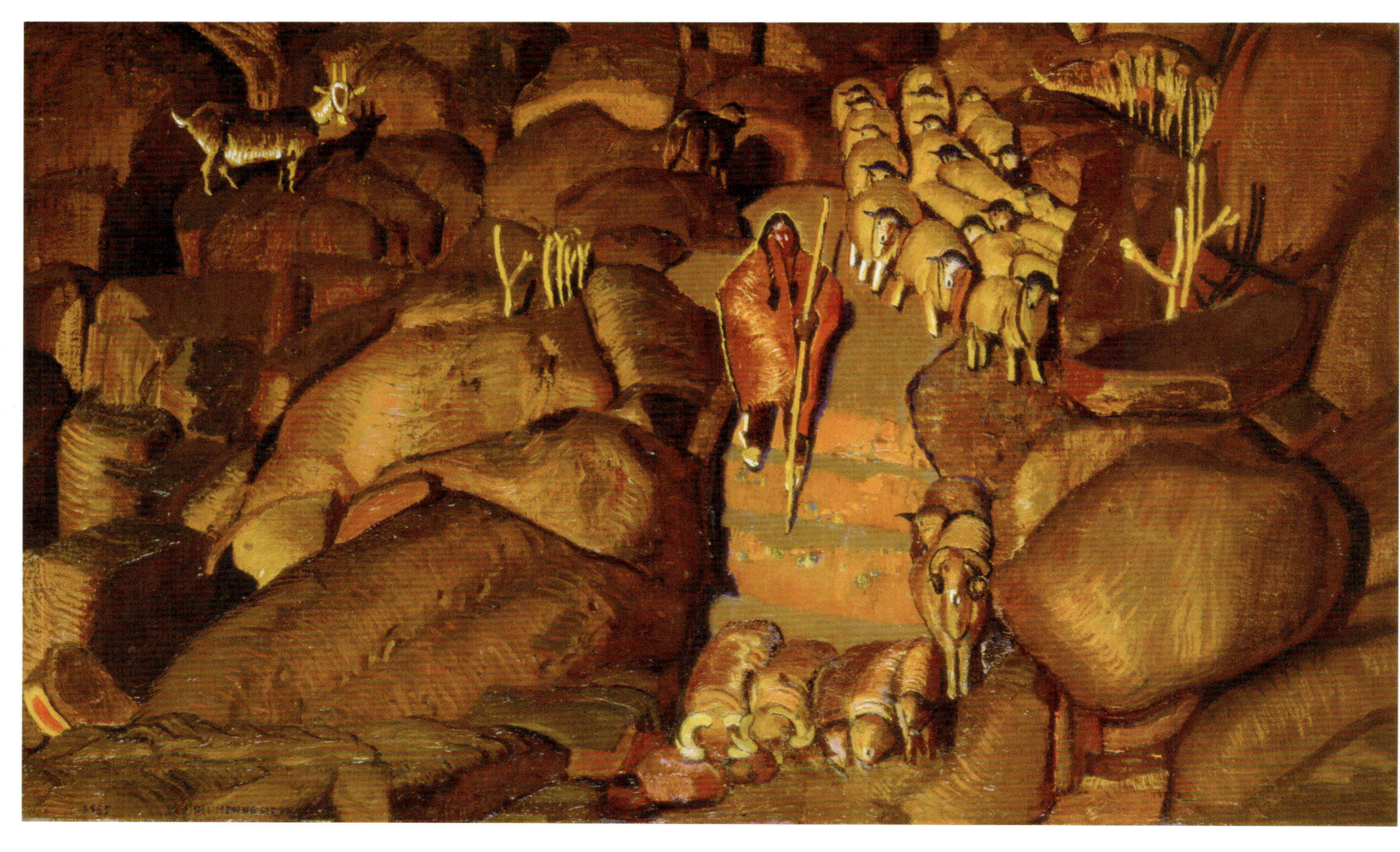

Rocky Trail (originally ***Sheepherder among the Rocks*** or ***Indian Sheep Herder,*** ca. 1944), reworked 1955
Oil on canvas mounted on Masonite, 16⅜ × 27⅛ inches
Courtesy of the Stark Museum of Art, Orange, Texas (31.30/5)

Stark consented. To seal their deal, Blumenschein placed Mr. and Mrs. Stark's names under the painting's stretcher—he would set a price later.[68]

As was his practice, Blumenschein had continued to observe the railroad yards from his rooms at the Alvarado Hotel during his winter stays in Albuquerque. For more than fifteen years he had watched as the Santa Fe Railway modernized its locomotives and passenger cars. Competition with other railroads and the transition from steam to diesel power made the Santa Fe look at redesigning and modernizing its passenger trains to suggest power and speed and to advance a new, progressive image. In 1956 the company debuted the new Super Chief, an "over-the-road consist"—railroad terminology for the train's composition of sleek-sided F7 locomotives, lounge and chair cars, diners, and baggage and baggage-dormitory cars. Blumenschein stayed current with the evolving aerodynamic design of the railcars. He modeled his most linear, streamlined painting, *The Chief Goes Through*, on the railroad's latest prototype of the future. Both the railroad and Blumenschein had progressed with the times.

In October 1956, after six months of "work at a fascinating motif," Blumenschein declared the painting finished. He reported its studio debut: Lawrence Sithman, the Nelson Art Gallery's director, "had a fine appreciation"; painter Dorothy Brett, Mabel Dodge Luhan's friend, declared it beautiful. Cook weighed in, pronouncing it "as fine as any picture you ever painted. One of your top works." Blumenschein too was convinced *The Chief Goes Through* was one of his lifetime bests.[69]

As he prepared to send *The Chief Goes Through* to the National Academy and the National Arts Club, he was confident, as he told fellow painter Leon Kroll, that now "*all* the boys" could see his "top-notch picture"; both his colleagues and the public too would know he was on his "art toes!"[70]

When it returned from New York in late spring 1957, Blumenschein entered *The Chief Goes Through* in a local venue, Santa Fe's Southwestern Artists Annual. Since, in his mind, "modern artists . . . completely monopolized the Art World" by then, he took quite a gamble by submitting this modern, albeit representational picture. Yet even though what he termed a "strict jury of

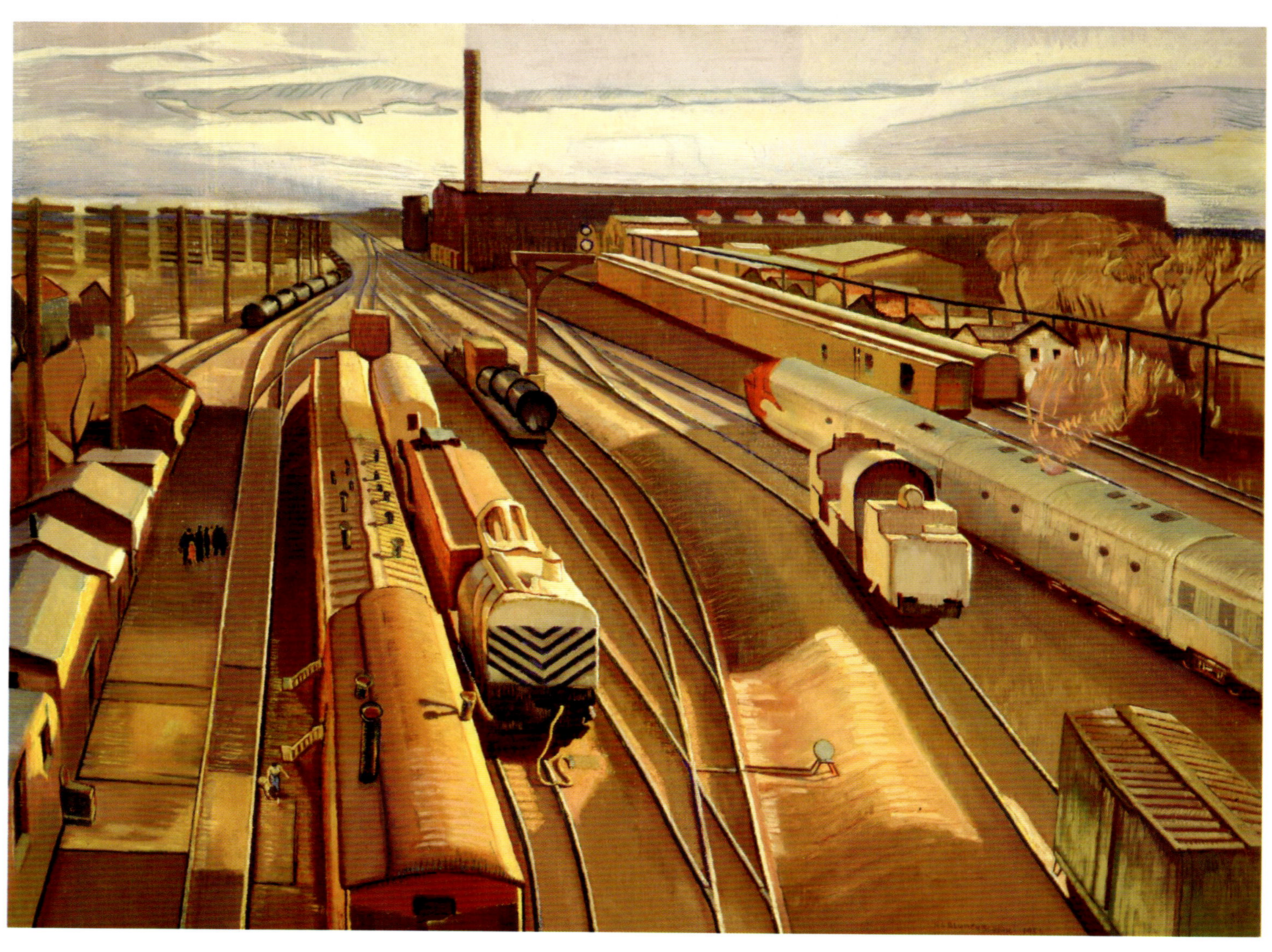

The Chief Goes Through, 1956
Oil on canvas, 30 × 40 inches
Courtesy of the Stark Museum of Art, Orange, Texas (31.30/9)

moderns" rejected two-thirds of the two hundred works submitted, they selected *The Chief Goes Through*. This, of course, pleased Blumenschein greatly, especially because in his experience "this type of jury," unlike those in charge of the National Academy or the National Arts Club, usually accepted only "the latest fad."[71]

But in fact, he was not giving himself much credit for his ability, at age eighty-three, to compete shoulder to shoulder with all manner of artists at home and beyond. Earlier that year, in the Museum of New Mexico's Tenth Annual Graphics Exhibition, a study for *The Chief Goes Through* had won a purchase award. That study was reviewed in the *New Mexico Magazine* by Ina Sizer Cassidy, who recognized something extraordinary in the drawing, something that spoke to a personal autobiographical connection as well as a vision for the whole region and the nation:

> The straight steel tracks [fan] out in purely engineered elongated curves from the embarking and discharging center to the final exit onto the main line leading to adventure. . . . This is more than merely a presentation of a railway yard. It could as well symbolize the life of an individual; or the history of this industrial city . . . [beginning] with but one line of track . . . a picture of progress, of a people combining their efforts to build a city, or a nation. . . . It proves also the thorough study of a chosen subject which this artist gives to all of his work. . . . But to the realist, this print is but another presentation of a railroad, well organized and [intelligently] presented, to be easily understood. There will be many who view it, enjoy it and count each gleaming track. But this artist is never satisfied with this outward appearance, he delves deeper into the very heart of his subject, taking time and pains to feel it all.[72]

After the southwestern show closed, Blumenschein notified Stark to expect receipt of *The Chief Goes Through*. He reported that the painting had been well received on the East Coast and that his many friends had admired his latest creative triumph. In recounting the jury story from the Southwestern Artists Annual,

Blumenschein spoke disparagingly of abstract painting and how unjust he felt he was being treated by the younger generation of artists. To Stark Blumenschein ventured to predict that it might take as much as fifty years before "painting, architecture, music, and literature [would] return to the noble proportions of form understandable." Neither he nor Stark would see that day, but he wanted it understood that he, Ernest Blumenschein, would uphold high aesthetic standards to the very end.[73]

In July Stark wrote, "The Chief Came Through" and went on to say that if Blumenschein ever painted another one "along this line," he wanted to see it before someone else purchased it.[74] Blumenschein just happened to have something in mind, one he proffered as "a very good painting artistically as well as a most valuable historical picture." Although not exactly along the same line, the painting, he assured his patron, would "stand up in any museum of art."[75] In a 1952 article for *El Crepusculo*, Regina Cooke had mentioned a canvas titled *My Neighbors,* which depicted the three Blumenscheins and twenty-one of their Taoseño friends and colleagues. The extraordinary canvas had been "long coveted by the State Museum, Santa Fe," which valued the painting for its portrayal of early celebrities, many of whom were now gone.[76]

The painting spoke to Stark's connoisseur heart. Just months after acquiring *Rocky Trail* and receiving *The Chief Goes Through*, he stepped forward to purchase *Ourselves and Taos Neighbors*. Blumenschein wrote Stark: "Am sure it is at last in good hands for safekeeping, as everyone believes it to be a most important cog in the history of art in New Mexico and the Southwest particularly."[77] He added that he could not believe that most of his models were deceased, "excepting 'ourselves'!"[78] Mary, now eighty-eight, had grown feeble, and he was all too aware of old age creeping up on him. Yet he told Stark that he sensed his work was better than ever—at least he felt more satisfied with it. His active mind desired the challenge of work at the easel, but with his physical complaints he doubted he could keep painting much longer.[79]

Blumenschein would soon set health concerns aside. Sometime in mid-1957, Reginald Fisher decided to host a second Blumenschein retrospective. It was to open the next fall and travel in the area for many months. Exactly when Fisher announced his intention is not clear, but the artist spent the fall and winter months before the show reworking several large paintings. Sensing that this might be his "very last," Blumenschein had "really put on the screws" in preparation.[80]

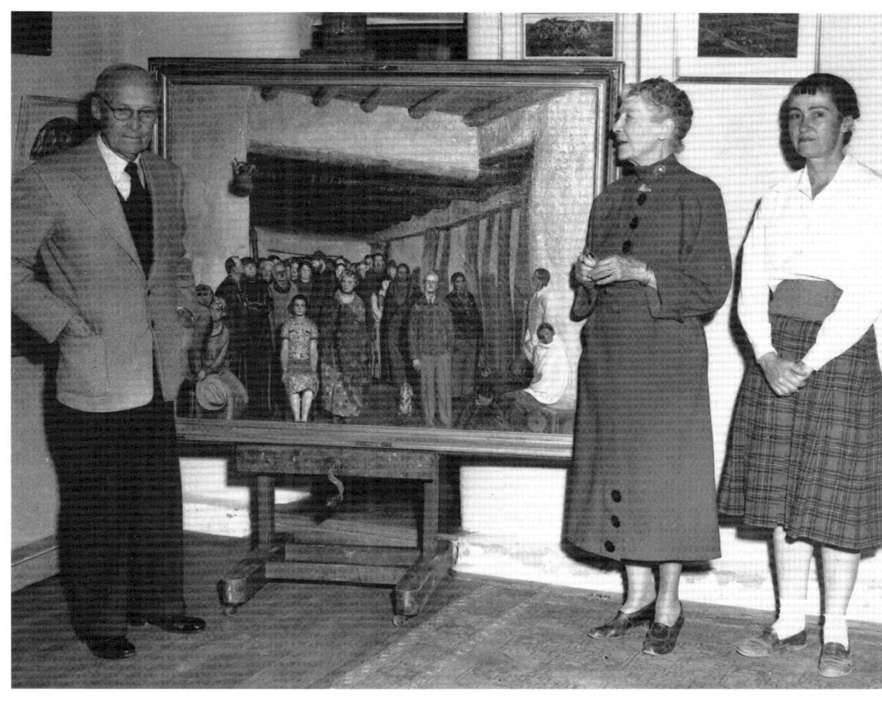

Ernest, Mary, and Helen Blumenschein in studio with ***Ourselves and Taos Neighbors*** on easel. Courtesy of the Palace of the Governors, Museum of New Mexico, New Mexico Department of Cultural Affairs, Santa Fe (neg. 40381).

Blumenschein was not prepared for "the very last" of a different and tragic sort that befell him the day before his eighty-fourth birthday. On May 24, 1958, after a lengthy illness, Mary succumbed to the effects of degenerative heart disease at St. Vincent Hospital in Santa Fe. With her passing, Blumenschein lost his companion of fifty years, the woman who had stood by him, as difficult as he could be, and supported his career from the time she took her marriage vows. In her memory, Ernest and Helen arranged for the posthumous exhibition of Mary's *Girl with Fan* at the National Academy of Design in 1959, the same year they gave her painting *Husking Corn* to the Harwood Museum in Taos.

By summer Blumenschein's forthcoming retrospective had him working again. He finished repainting *The City* in August and, with Helen's assistance, asked collector friends to lend pictures to the exhibition.[81] Blumenschein called the resulting assemblage of thirty-three paintings My Life's Story. They ranged from the Love of Life illustrations from 1904 to the latest variation on *Railroad Yard, Meeting Called* (the repainted *Railroad Yard, No. 5*), finished in 1958. The Museum of Modern Art, the National Academy of Design, and the Museum of New Mexico each loaned a painting; half of the remaining loans came from private collectors.

Helen reported on the inaugural showing held at the Harwood Museum in September and told family members that she would accompany her father to the other openings—in Albuquerque in early November, Santa Fe later that month, and Las Cruces over the holidays.[82] The *Santa Fe New Mexican* described Blumenschein as "probably the most vital figure" of all the pioneer artists of Taos.[83] Erwin Barrie, director of Grand Central Art Galleries, wrote his congratulations from New York: "I am so glad you had a successful show and there is no question in my mind regarding the originality and individuality of your work. It certainly deserves a place for all time in American Art."[84] Of all the accolades, Blumenschein found Barrie's remarks to be the most profoundly meaningful. He *did* deserve a place in American art for all time.

Quite by coincidence, Enrique Lafuente, the director of the Museum of Modern Art in Madrid, Spain, was on hand in Albuquerque the day of Blumenschein's opening. Lafuente had seen some representative reproductions of the Taos school of painting and had traveled to New Mexico to witness the scene firsthand. Lafuente met Fisher just as the curator was putting the finishing touches on the Blumenschein installation. After Lafuente toured the exhibition, Fisher introduced him to Blumenschein. Lafuente spent two hours interviewing the artist at the Alvarado Hotel. In January 1959, the Madrid director sent an article he had written for the *Albuquerque Journal.* In it he named Blumenschein as the "representative head of the Artistic School, a true patriarch of painting." He had possessed "an artistic rectitude [that enabled him to maintain] his proper conceptions across a most agitated epoch . . . of art history." Earlier, in his home country, Lafuente had made an extensive study on the life work of Ignacio Zuloaga, a contemporary of Blumenschein's. Lafuente saw parallels between the two artists' work. They were "painters of character [who] aspired to monumental painting [and] grand composition." Both represented the generation that "resisted heroically [what] the great Spanish writer, Ortega y Gasset called 'The Dehumanization of Art.'"[85]

In May, on the anniversary of Mary's death, the *Albuquerque Journal* reported Blumenschein and Helen's first joint exhibition. Just after his eighty-fifth birthday, the *Santa Fe New Mexican* told of what he termed his "last show," adding, "We listen to these words with due respect but hasten to remind 'Blumey' that H. Hoover says the same thing at every election-time."[86] The two-person show at the Stables Gallery featured twelve of Blumenschein's works, most of them recent. The critic singled out three of his paintings and found them "suffused with the magical warmth, the vibrant, liquid vitality" typical of the Taos founder. Helen's sketches and watercolors of local subject matter showed a more "carefree approach [with] a verve of their own." The reviewer asked Helen's forgiveness, though, for devoting the lion's share of the article to her father, adding, "but Blumey is a lion; besides, anyone sharing gallery space with him [already suffers] a handicap."[87]

The reviewer mentioned *The Funeral*, a repainted version of *Alas Proud Mansion*, a painting begun in 1947 while Blumenschein was convalescing in Los Angeles. A cormorant in the picture's foreground adds a somber tone to the subject—a California mission-style building in a state of decay. Ina Sizer Cassidy had referred to the ornate mansion with its leaning pillars and crumbling walls and a "huge bird of prey [waiting] its time to pick the bones." She stated that Blumenschein often expressed himself through such symbolism.[88] In the literature of Milton or Shakespeare the cormorant represented death. Blumenschein had used that symbol too as he confronted his own mortality after major surgery in California. Now, after Mary's death and in the face of his own infirmities, he worked out more feelings around death—with his signature touch of visual humor. In repainting the picture, he added a man and a woman looking off into the far distance, away from the coffin with angel, depicted as a curious, derby-hatted butler, hovering over it. The latter addition confirmed that the laughter and wit his dear friend Ellis Parker Butler had brought to the Blumenscheins' lives triumphed in the end, providing the transcendant humor that helped Blumenschein reconcile the loss of Mary. Although the artist's ledgers show that he reworked the canvas in December 1957, he evidently touched up the painting one more time, for the stretcher bears its final title, *The Cormorant Attends Funeral of His Friend the Butler, June 6, 1959*.

This was the last painting Blumenschein worked on. He grew so progressively weak that it became impossible for even Helen to care for him, and she was forced to place him in the Sandia Ranch Sanatorium near Albuquerque in October

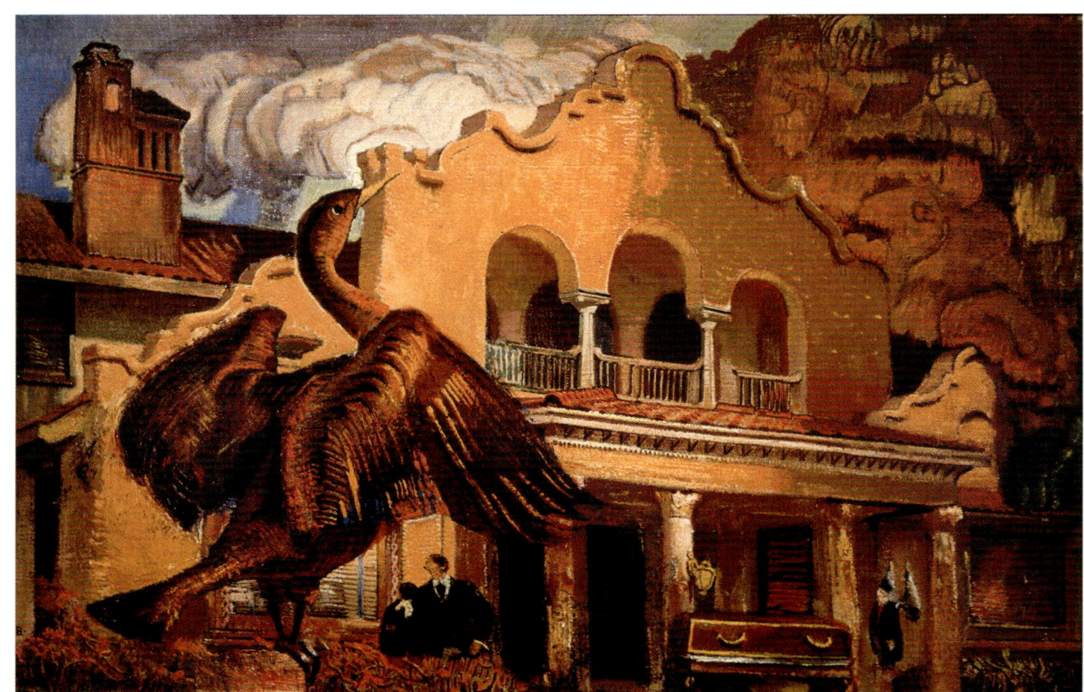

The Cormorant Attends Funeral of His Friend the Butler, June 6 1959, (originally *Alas Proud Mansion,* 1947; later *The Funeral,* 1957), finished 1959, oil on canvas. Courtesy of the Taos Historic Museums, Taos, New Mexico.

1959. She also withdrew all paintings from sale at this point, wishing to keep the few that remained.[89] Regular letters from Blumenschein's physician kept Helen apprised of her father's occasional visitors, his activities, and his continued deterioration. He died of bronchial pneumonia in Albuquerque on June 6, 1960—a year to the day after he signed his last reworked painting. As her father had requested, Helen scattered his ashes on Taos Pueblo Indian ground in the heart of a landscape that had inspired him for over sixty years and amid a people he had admired, defended, and loved.

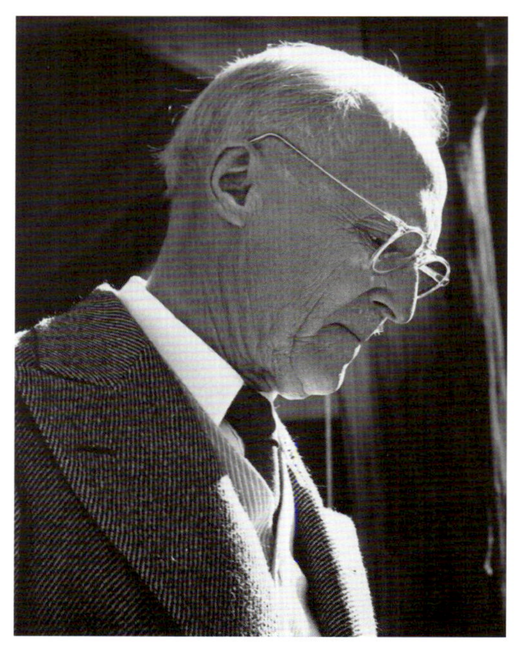

Ernest Blumenschein, 1950s. Courtesy of the Palace of the Governors, Museum of New Mexico, New Mexico Department of Cultural Affairs, Santa Fe (neg. 40410).

A myriad of obituaries rolled out with countless accolades in the pages of *Time* magazine, the *New York Times,* and elsewhere. They spoke of his role as a founder of the Taos art colony, his formidable successes as an American painter in an age of change, and his lifelong adventure in New Mexico.[90] But they did not find the real man nor reveal the all-embracing spirit or uncommon genius of the artist. They did not tell of his inspired ways with light and line and design, his disquieting disdain for mediocrity, or his dedication to new visions and perfection. He was gone and no longer able to defend the bulwarks of his righteous self-determination and perfectionism as a creative force. All that was left were his voice from the past and his paintings.

The latter have proven themselves as remarkable exercises of unbridled genius. The former reveals how he shaped that genius to serve American art. The pages of this book preserve the wonders of his art and the voice of the man. They stand in testament to his friend Reginald Fisher's final comment about Ernest Blumenschein, that he was not just a true artist but "one of the great among Twentieth Century Americans."[91]

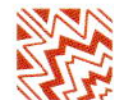

Twelve Men, Listening
Blumenschein's Struggle with Murder, Justice, and the Inarticulate Soul of America

James Moore

The painting is large. At almost four feet tall, it is too large to fit comfortably in a room of an average house. Ernest L. Blumenschein would have considered this to be an exhibition picture meant to travel the museum circuit, a painting he hoped would boost his standing in major art circles in the East, although his reputation was already substantial by 1936. It is a painting about life in his community, the small village of Taos, New Mexico, but it is a painting made for a sophisticated, urban audience. It is a public painting but not one done in the manner of most public art of the period. The painting is ambitious, illustrating a scene with fourteen persons, but Blumenschein does not approach the subject with the illustrator's normal repertoire of dramatic action and rhetorical gesture. These figures are still. The painting appears to be a view into a narrow room of an adobe house, its low ceiling of dark *vigas* bearing down on the people inside. But this is not meant to be someone's house. Twelve men, diverse in age, dress, and demeanor sit on benches in two rows, one above the other. An oval portrait of George Washington hangs above the center of the scene; its placement declares the space to be a public one, within the jurisdiction of the United States of America. It becomes clear that this is a courtroom and that the men are a jury. A young court reporter, seated at a table in front of the group, writes, and his hand, moving across the paper, is the only hint of action in the scene. At the opposite wall a mysterious figure in a black coat and glasses peers into the room over the edge of the jury box. He seems strangely out of place, an enigma. Large size is not the only factor that suggests a public purpose for this painting; its puzzling nature and ponderous feeling makes it seem inappropriate as a decoration for someone's home. This is a painting about a serious subject. A window on the far wall reveals a distant winter landscape. Some of the men have their heavy coats on. In this cold room they are trying to understand what happened on a beautiful summer's day less than three months earlier.

In late August in New Mexico, the days start out bright and warm, but as midday approaches, the clouds build up in the mountains and the rains come. In particularly wet years the land fairly bursts open with pent-up energy as wildflowers emerge in abundance as if in celebration of release from long drought. The upper meadows of the high mountains near Taos are breathtakingly beautiful in their

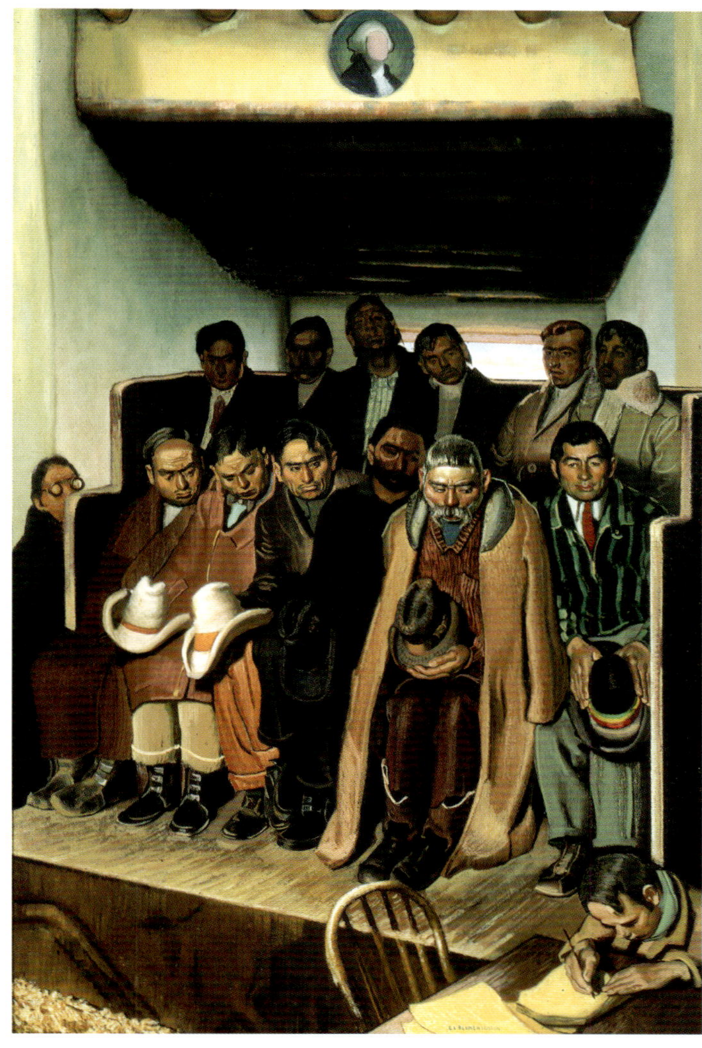

Jury for the Trial of a Sheepherder for Murder, 1936, oil on canvas, 46 × 30 inches. Courtesy of the Rockwell Museum, Corning, New York.

dazzling color: giant red paintbrush, purple western monkshood, blue gentian, the bright yellow of heartleaf arnica, and the subtle whites of lousewort. In these wet years the high country holds unique rewards for those who venture up, but the hiker must be well prepared and, like a good sailor, keep a weather eye out for trouble, for storms can come up quickly and move in on the unwary with great violence.

Sunday, August 28, 1927.[1] Russell DeWese and his young bride of two months met their new friend Henry Moburg for a hike up to the fire lookout station on Gold Hill.[2] A thirty-year-old professor of modern languages, DeWese and his wife, Evelyn, had just moved from Indiana to Dallas, Texas, where he had taken a faculty position at the Terrell School for Boys, a prestigious, Yale-connected prep school. Life was unfolding new for them, and they were spending their summer vacation and honeymoon in the mountain town of Red River, New Mexico. Moburg, the son of a local miner, grew up in Red River and knew the mining camps and the mountain trails like they were part of his own backyard.[3]

At midday, and about halfway up the trail, they spotted a shepherd's camp at the edge of a large meadow. He had a fire going, so Mrs. DeWese persuaded her husband and Moburg to stop for lunch and warm themselves.[4] There, they met José Cruz Maestas, who was tending livestock for Don Antonio Vargas of Arroyo Hondo, a village some twelve miles north of Taos.[5] They asked permission to stop and get warm, and Maestas agreed, so they invited him to share their lunch. The group stayed together eating for more than an hour, enjoying the expansive view.[6] As they talked, they spoke of the beautiful panorama of nature, the abundance of wood, and the richness of mineral deposits. About two in the afternoon they packed up to leave. They thanked Maestas and gave him fruit to eat later.

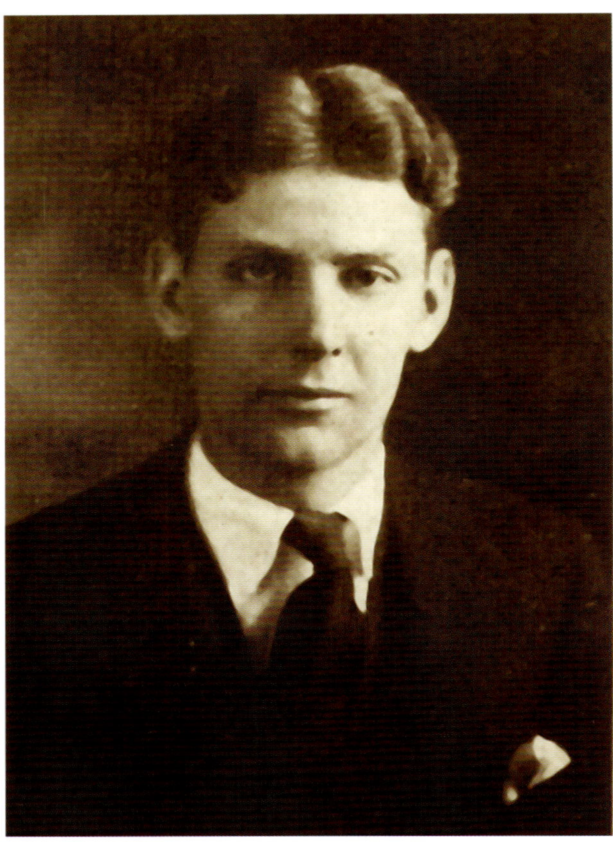

Russell P. DeWese photograph, 1927, *The Terrellian* yearbook. Courtesy of Special Collections, the University of Texas at Arlington Library.

They happily continued up the trail, Moburg in front, followed by Mrs. DeWese, with DeWese bringing up the rear. Suddenly they heard a shot behind them and turned in horror to see DeWese covered in blood. As he fell he shouted, "Oh my God!" Initially Mrs. DeWese and Moburg thought there had been an accident, but then they saw that Maestas was now pointing his rifle at Moburg. Moburg, seeing that Mrs. DeWese was between the two of them, begged Maestas not to kill her as he grabbed her and placed her behind him. Maestas fired again, hitting Moburg in the right shoulder. Throwing away his rifle, which was now empty, Maestas grappled with Moburg and threw him down an embankment. Mrs. DeWese ran to her husband, saw that he was indeed dead and, after kissing him, fled into the dense forest in order to escape detection. She walked for some time before coming to a mining camp, where she asked for help. The miners took her down to Red River, and a posse was assembled to search for the killer and retrieve the bodies.[7]

In the meantime, Maestas returned to Arroyo Hondo and told his employer he had shot "an Americano who wanted to steal their sheep," and on Monday morning Don Antonio Vargas went back up to the camp with several other shepherds. The constable, meanwhile, had called Sheriff Antonio Gonzales, who, with his deputy Malaquias Martinez, joined up to follow the trail up to the camp. Gonzales returned to Arroyo Hondo that, evening and Martinez quickly arrested Maestas, who gave up without resistance. He wept as the handcuffs were placed on him.

Maestas was placed in the Taos county jail late in the evening of the twenty-ninth. Interviewed Tuesday morning in jail by the editor of *La Revista Popular*, Maestas gave his mother's name as Lázara Gurulé and said that he had two sisters in Arroyo Hondo but that he had been raised by Don Nicolas Duran and his wife in the village of Arroyo Seco.[8] When questioned about his motive for such a crime he stated in all seriousness that he intended to kill both men and attack the woman. When asked what he thought he would do with her afterward, he simply stated, "Kill her also."[9] The frail-looking boy stated that, ever since he was young, he had been wicked and addicted to quarrelling. Maestas was arraigned for preliminary hearing on August 30

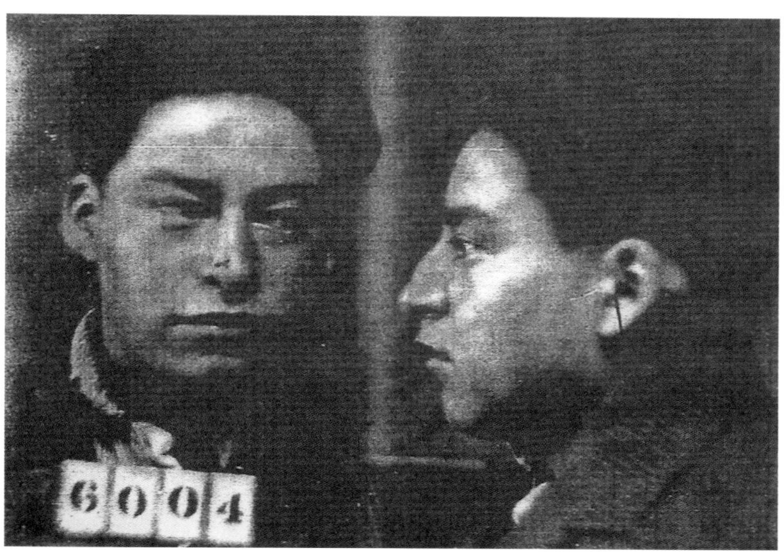

José Cruz Maestas, November 1927, intake record. Courtesy of the New Mexico State Penitentiary, State of New Mexico, State Records Center and Archives, Santa Fe.

by Justice of the Peace Miguel A. Perrinia. District Attorney T. H. Whalen stated that the boy had made a full confession, and Maestas was bound over to district court on a first degree murder charge.[10] When angry residents of the county assembled at the jail, it was feared that there would be an attempt to lynch Maestas, so officials placed additional guards at the jail.[11] In an attempt to defuse the situation, Taos County Judge Henry J. Kiker quickly ordered that Maestas be moved to the state penitentiary in Santa Fe.[12] The sheriff carried out the order that night.

November 17, 1927.[13] In Taos County, the twelve jurors held their hats on their laps but kept their heavy coats on. As they were sworn in by Judge Kiker, they huddled closely together as if they were one body, gaining warmth from one another against the cold in the courtroom.[14] Attorneys for the prosecution from the office of District Attorney T. H. Whalen were prepared to make short work of the case. William J. Barker and his partner Beutler, who had come up from Santa Fe to defend Maestas, must have been anxious to see how the prosecution would argue the case.[15] Maestas was a small, skinny boy who hardly appeared to have been one to commit such a vicious crime, but the odds certainly seemed against him.[16] Defending a client who had confessed so explicitly would be difficult, but Barker thought there were a couple of avenues of argument available to them.

Seeking to thwart an insanity defense, the state brought forward two alienists, Dr. A. J. Massie of Santa Fe and Dr. H. M. Smith of the New Mexico State Hospital in Las Vegas.[17] Both testified that they had evaluated Maestas and that he was sane. Although the insanity defense was not particularly common at the time, there were a couple of possible reasons for this legal maneuver. One was the case of George Remus, a Cincinnati lawyer and notorious bootlegger who murdered his wife on October 6, 1927. Remus's trial and successful insanity defense were front-page news nationwide for about a month.[18] Added to this, in the local context of northern New Mexico, there was the notion that sheepherders could go insane from the long periods of isolation entailed by their difficult work in remote locations.[19] It is difficult to document this as fact and even harder to demonstrate it as commonplace, but it was, nevertheless, shared folklore, including a story about a sheepherder who won his case in court.[20] Although such stories were normally classed with other humorous folklore about sheepherders, the defense did attempt the argument for insanity.[21] While the actions of the prosecuting attorneys indicate that they took this defense seriously, their tactics to forestall the argument were more likely due to the notoriety and widespread publicity of the Remus case. The state felt that they had proved Maestas's guilt beyond any doubt and demanded that the jury return a decision of first degree murder, which would mean he would go to the gallows.

The state's witnesses certainly weakened any insanity defense; however, Barker brought to the stand Sheriff Antonio Gonzales and Senator José Montaner, who claimed that Maestas was intoxicated when he attacked the men. Although New Mexico had voted to become dry in 1918 and federal prohibition laws had been in force for seven years, liquor was not difficult to obtain.[22] Although many people who drank had some vicarious sense of lawlessness, only those who manufactured and distributed liquor broke the law, not those who consumed it. In New Mexico, "it was commonplace for people to own a hip flask and offer someone a drink."[23] Barker must have argued that the DeWese couple and Moburg had provided the liquor, or at least had instigated the drinking; even if Maestas had liquor, it certainly would seem unlikely that he would have been the one to offer up toasts to the beauty and rich resources of the mountains.[24] When Barker put Maestas on the stand, the boy testified that liquor and "the devil in me" made him do it.[25] It was a defense that had been seldom used in Taos, and with it Barker hoped to gain a decision of second degree murder by persuading the jury that Maestas's intoxication cast doubt on the issue of premeditation. He hoped that this would counter the weight of the confession and the arguments of the prosecution, resulting in a decision of second degree murder. This became the dilemma that the jury faced.

The jury deliberated for less than an hour before coming back with a verdict of guilty of second degree murder.[26] Although they might have based their decision on the defense argument, they also might have been influenced by Maestas's youth, his lack of education, and his appearance on the stand, for, even as he testified, he did not seem to be aware of what was happening. Many people felt that the jury's decision was wise and humanitarian, but it angered Judge Kiker.[27] He dismissed the jury without thanking them and sentenced Maestas to ninety to ninety-nine years in the penitentiary, stating his opinion that the murder was deliberate and that Maestas should hang for it. Looking at the defendant he declared, "No governor should pardon you, and your only trip from the prison should be your funeral."[28]

Everyone in Taos and the small communities around it, as well as many in the major cities in New Mexico, knew of the murder by mid-September. Although it could have been coincidence, Blumenschein was inspired that autumn to take up a new subject. In early November, his wife, Mary, wrote to their daughter, Helen, "Yesterday E.L.B. and I went to Rio Grande & Hondo for him to paint on his sheep picture which is much improved thereby."[29] In spite of his interest in this subject of sheepherding and sketching in the area near Arroyo Hondo, where Maestas's employer lived, Blumenschein produced no major painting related to the dramatic events of the late summer.[30] The painting that resulted from this excursion, *Sheep Herd in Hondo Canyon,* was of a herd of sheep in a dramatic landscape. Its abstracted forms drew notice in a review: "Among the recent canvases by this artist is a very striking painting, 'Sheep Herd in Hondo Canyon.' The colors are featured in grey tint from the crowding herd which fills the canyon to the cliffs rising at the side, and the sky effect beyond. There are no bright colors depicted, but the result is most fascinating and the impression left is very pleasing as the lines throughout the picture are drawn with most artistic finish and rhythm that gives it a peculiar charm."[31]

The events of 1927, however, must have remained in Blumenschein's mind for several years. He seems to imply this when, in 1932, he wrote Mary and Helen about "another" murder in a village southeast of Taos: "Another murder has recurred in Peñasco. It took place in the court room during a session."[32]

In 1935, eight years after the DeWese murder and the hostility of the community over Maestas's arrest and court proceedings, Blumenschein began to think of painting the jury for the trial of José Maestas.[33] Blumenschein had not witnessed the trial itself, so he composed an imaginative version of the scene. Titled *Jury for the Trial of a Sheepherder for Murder*, it would become one of his most successful efforts, and the painting he considered late in life to be his best. The painting was finished in early 1936 and sent to New York to the 111th annual exhibition of the National Academy of Design; in a review of the exhibition, *New York Times* critic Edward Alden Jewell called *Jury for the Trial of a Sheepherder for Murder* "vivid."[34] It was shown again in New York in January 1937 in the National Arts Club members' exhibition, where it received one of the five prizes given that year.[35] The paintings in that exhibition were nominated by the governors of all forty-eight states, as well as the territories and possessions, and were to be representative of each region.[36] This probably made the honor even more moving to Blumenschein, to see the painting considered symbolic of New Mexican culture, and to have it chosen by Governor Clyde Tingley, who had by then become a close friend of President Roosevelt. In addition, the painting was one of the few in this large exhibition to be singled out for favorable critical mention in the national press.[37] In November of that year the painting was shown again, this time in the Forty-eighth Annual Exhibition of American Paintings and Sculpture at the Art Institute of Chicago. In 1938 it was selected to be in the exhibition Trois Siècles D'Art Aux État-Unis, organized by the Museum of Modern Art in New York and shown at the Musée du Jeu de Paume in Paris; Blumenschein commented that it was "the highest honor I have ever received."[38] Later that year it was acquired by the Museum of Modern Art with funding from the Abby Aldrich Rockefeller Fund.[39] When the Museum of Modern Art loaned the painting to the Museum of Fine Arts in Santa Fe for Blumenschein's retrospective in 1948, its return to New Mexico was greeted with enthusiasm and great pride, a symbol not only of Blumenschein's success but also of the importance of New Mexico's role in the mainstream of American art.[40] The painting was a centerpiece in one of the crowning events of Blumenschein's career.

The painting is still, quiet, actionless. In a small, cramped room, twelve men sit tightly packed together in two rows in the jury box, so close that they are all touching, twelve distinctive individuals locked together as one. Some of them have their attention focused into the room and slightly to their left. Two men in the back row look straight ahead. One man in the front row, appearing older than the others, seems to be the strong focal point of the scene. He directs his gaze downward, as if deep in thought. The younger man to his right leans toward him and also looks down; the two men at the far end of the row do the same. The man to his left looks directly out into the courtroom. Most hold their hats on their lap, and their coats have been left on to ward off the November chill of the courtroom. In the foreground a court reporter sits at a table and writes, an empty chair to his right. From the other side of the room an anonymous man in a black coat and glasses casts a vacant-eyed look over the edge of the jury box. The winter landscape is visible through a small window at the back of the room. On the wall above the jury hangs a reproduction of the well-known Gilbert Stuart portrait of George Washington, sketched in with the features left blank. Familiar to any American of almost any age from its presence on the dollar bill to countless reproductions hanging in schoolrooms across the country, it is a unifying national symbol. In the courtroom context, Blumenschein's summary treatment of it seems to stand for the concept of the belief in blind justice.

The interior of the courtroom was based on Blumenschein's studio at the east end of his house on Ledoux Street. Although the jury members appear as unique, identifiable individuals, they are not portraits of the actual jury members. To create these likenesses, Blumenschein sat out on the Taos plaza and memorized faces, which were drawn later in the studio in what he called "memory portraits."[41] At the time of the exhibition in Paris, Blumenschein spoke openly with his friend Spud Johnson about his inspiration and the process of making the painting:

> "The picture was suggested by a real trial of a Taos sheepherder for murder," says Blumenschein in explanation of his creation. "I felt I could carry out the dramatic suggestion by the characters in the jury box alone; I studied for that purpose the rougher element of the mountain Spanish people in the vicinity.
>
> "I made no actual portraits—yet my characters so closely resemble those of Peñasco, Arroyo Seco, and other out-of-the-way places, that they are, I believe, convincing as far as realism goes.
>
> "In spite of this," he added, "I trust that the human element is not more marked than the art element to be found in the composition. This latter, I hope is not commonplace."[42]

The impression of portraiture in the painting was certainly convincing to viewers. In 1947, when the painting was included in a traveling exhibition from the collection of the Museum of Modern Art, a reviewer noted:

> Blumenschein so precisely illustrates his story that the account seems journalistic. Yet the painting is not a literal reconstruction of the way a group of people looked. Blumenschein attended a trial, a year before he began work on the composition; he changed the background from the courthouse to his own studio and used one model, a Spanish laborer, for all the figures. Although the heads were executed from memory of mountain types of northern New Mexico, the individual characterization is so literal that the spectator is tempted to construct a case history for each member of the jury.[43]

Blumenschein knew that it was important to underscore the realism of the painting, and thereby the event, through the means of portraiture. However, what he called the "art element" in his conversation with Johnson was of paramount importance to him in his major paintings, and these formal aspects of composition and color were his means of adding greater significance to the painting.

That "art element" was the focus of fellow artist Howard Cook's remarks on the painting in an insightful essay on Blumenschein's work:

> Probably Blumenschein's greatest figure painting is the large "Jury for the Trial of a Sheepherder for Murder," owned by the Museum of Modern Art of New York. A classic grace distinguished the group of forceful characters, while the construction of the painting is founded on a solid background of precise abstract planning. The rich, deep color in the garments, giving somber emotional quality, unites harmoniously into a flowing background for the brighter notes of the faces. One is reminded of the early Italians' use of large color volumes and their feeling for spatial design to stimulate emotive characterization. This is indeed the artist's peak as a masterful designer and a painter of sympathetic human attributes. It is a picture rewarding careful study and calls for much returning to.[44]

Harmonies of rhythmic pattern abound in the painting, from the back of the bentwood chair to the stripes of the green coat on one of the jurors to the *vigas* in the ceiling to the jurors themselves. There is unity and regularity of rhythm here in the architectural forms, yet they are broken slightly by the subtle differences in position of the jurors themselves. The human element is the area in which there is a hint of unpredictability. The regularity of the nearly squared-off, centralized view of the room itself is played against an illogically diagonal placement of the table, chair, and the jury box, creating an unresolved sense of tension. This uneasiness is heightened by the fact that none of the figures in the composition look out at the viewer. Similarly, in his treatment of the palette of the painting, Blumenschein sets the green-striped jacket and red tie of one juror in a bold and striking contrast to the limited range of earth tones in the rest of the composition. Will he be the one to disagree with the others?

Blumenschein clearly had a public purpose in mind when he conceived this painting, and the public exposure of the painting brought him great accolades, but just as there are unresolved tensions in the composition and color of the painting, unanswered questions remain about what Blumenschein's more personal intentions might have been. Why did this subject suggest itself eight years after the event and not in 1927, when he was working on his "sheep picture"?[45] And why did he not choose to depict some dramatic moment connected to the murder and arrest of Maestas, settling instead on the jury that decided his fate?

During the late twenties and early thirties, Blumenschein had turned his attention primarily to landscape painting; and as the Depression deepened in the early thirties, sales of art lagged. Some of these landscapes, however, were major pictures, and in 1934 Blumenschein was delighted when *Taos Valley* was acquired by the Metropolitan Museum in New York. In early 1935 Blumenschein received a major portrait commission to paint the family of Elsie Butler Waller. This not only helped his finances but also rekindled an interest in figure painting.

The primary motivation, however, for Blumenschein's painting came from the newly created federal art programs. These programs offered relief, and they were also vigorously discussed and critiqued by artists across the country; Taos was no exception.[46] The mixing of art and politics did not set well with all artists, and moreover, the new programs definitely favored realist painting at a time when there was much discussion in the art world over the relative virtues of realism versus abstraction. Blumenschein was not involved in the short-lived Public Works of Art Project (PWAP) in the winter of 1933–34, but in 1935 he was invited to apply in a limited competition for a mural commission for the Department of Justice under the Treasury Department's Section of Painting and Sculpture.[47] Blumenschein was one of six Taos artists to apply for the prestigious commissions to paint murals in the new post office and in the Department of Justice building in Washington, D.C.[48] The drawings he submitted were ones that ultimately became the *Jury for the Trial of a Sheepherder for Murder*.[49] The two commissions were treated separately; for the Department of Justice commission, fifty-five artists submitted a total of ninety sketches.[50] According to the call for entries, the proposals for the Department of Justice murals were to deal with the subject of the "administration of Justice in contemporary American life," specifically, "Justice Toward Labor," "Emancipation of Women," and "Protection of the Child."[51] Certainly *Jury for the Trial of a Sheepherder for Murder* would have fit that theme; and, as Maestas was a minor, Blumenschein may well have considered his proposal to fit the criteria of "Protection of the Child." For some reason, though, Blumenschein's title for the painting did not explicitly convey this notion, and that might have had some bearing on the reason that the concept for his proposal did not pass the selection committee.[52]

In fact, all entries for the Department of Justice were rejected, and the committee decided to follow up with a limited competition in which nine artists would be invited to participate.[53] Addressing the decision, a letter from Forbes Watson stated that "the more difficult and abstract subject of Justice was not interpreted, or visualized, with as clear a grasp as was the simpler subject matter suggested by the history of the Post."[54] This problem of giving modern visual form to traditional abstract concepts was noted by others as well, and this was particularly germane to the Department of Justice competition. The blindfolded lady holding a scale was certainly considered a hackneyed concept, one to be avoided at all costs. In an essay on the contemporary problems of mural painting, Arthur Millier stated this in no uncertain terms when he wrote that the "day of meaningless ladies styled Truth, Justice, Virtue, and so forth, is over," but he acknowledged that because of this the artist faced a more difficult problem. "His task," Millier wrote, "is to search the inarticulate soul of a people for those universal characteristics which make and sustain its greatness."[55] Writing several months later about the two competitions for the post office and the Department of Justice, Inslee Hopper summarized the differences between the two projects: "In general, the painters show a lack of creative power when faced with the demand for an ideology, but their adaptability to historical or factual subject matter is in many cases surprising."[56] The selection committee probably would not have suspected that Blumenschein's solution to the problem was to attempt to address the former by means of the latter, to represent ideology by means of an actual story about twelve real men pondering the facts of a case involving an unfortunate young teacher and an uneducated sheepherder the age of his students. In a contentious exchange with Olin Dow of the section, William C. Palmer, secretary of the Mural Painters' Society in New York, called Department of Justice the competition a "colossal and expensive failure." [57] As a senior member of the Taos art colony Blumenschein must have been a bit disappointed in October when two of his colleagues, Ward Lockwood and Kenneth Adams, succeeded in the Washington, D.C., competition.[58]

In the latter part of 1935 it also seemed that Blumenschein was fading a bit from the local art scene. A list of New Mexico artists compiled by Lester Raines of New Mexico Normal School (now Highlands University) in Las Vegas, New Mexico, counted 152 in the state, with 37 in Taos. Both Mary and Helen Blumenschein were listed, but as the local paper pointed out, there was "no mention whatever of Papa Ernest L."[59] That fall *El Palacio*, the magazine of the Museum of New Mexico, covered the exhibition at the Museum of Fine Arts; Blumenschein was included in the exhibition but the only reproductions were of paintings by Bert Phillips, Buck Dunton, and Oscar Berninghaus.[60] When a reporter in December interviewed Bert Phillips, calling him "the Inventor of Taos" and saying that, under the PWAP program a few years earlier, a panel in the Taos courthouse had been "handed over" to him to paint, Blumenschein may well have wondered if his career was on the wane.[61] Nevertheless, the time was ripe that autumn for

Blumenschein to finish a major painting, and by December he was working on one that he seems not to have mentioned to people.[62] Since he had submitted the concept to competition, it is unlikely that he would have started a major easel painting of the subject before the end of October, when the results of the competition were announced. The rejection by the selection committee probably strengthened his resolve to continue with this subject, which he felt was too important to leave. He saw *Jury for the Trial of a Sheepherder for Murder* as complex figure painting that was both modernist and political, one that would rival his earlier successful ventures in that area.[63]

Courtroom drama and notions of justice were not unique subjects for artists in the first half of the twentieth century. Both Guy Pène du Bois and John Sloan had addressed the theme.[64] Perhaps the best-known example in American art is Ben Shahn's interest in the early 1930s in the notorious case of Sacco and Vanzetti.[65] In 1934 Everett Shinn covered the Millen brothers' trial in Massachusetts for the *Boston Traveller*.[66] Early in 1936, Louise Rönnebeck produced her most important work of that decade, a large painting titled *The People vs. Mary Elizabeth Smith*.[67] Blumenschein's painting is significantly different from Shinn's and Rönnebeck's treatments, both in composition and concept. One of Shinn's drawings shows the chief of police and district attorney holding the slain patrolman's coat; in familiar visual rhetoric, the left arm of the coat hangs limply, as does the arm in images of the dead Christ.[68] Rönnebeck's is more in the style and feeling of a New Deal mural, with attention centered on the defendant; the prosecutor, in a dramatic gesture, waves the rifle for the entire courtroom to see. Blumenschein's jury, in contrast, is motionless; no rhetorical action is evident in either their bodies or their faces. Although the product of memory and imagination, the jury, in its stillness, is similar in feeling to the look of journalistic reportage evident in Shahn's double portrait *Bartolomeo Vanzetti and Nicolo Sacco*.[69]

This was not the first time Blumenschein had taken up legal issues in his paintings, although *Jury for the Trial of a Sheepherder for Murder* is

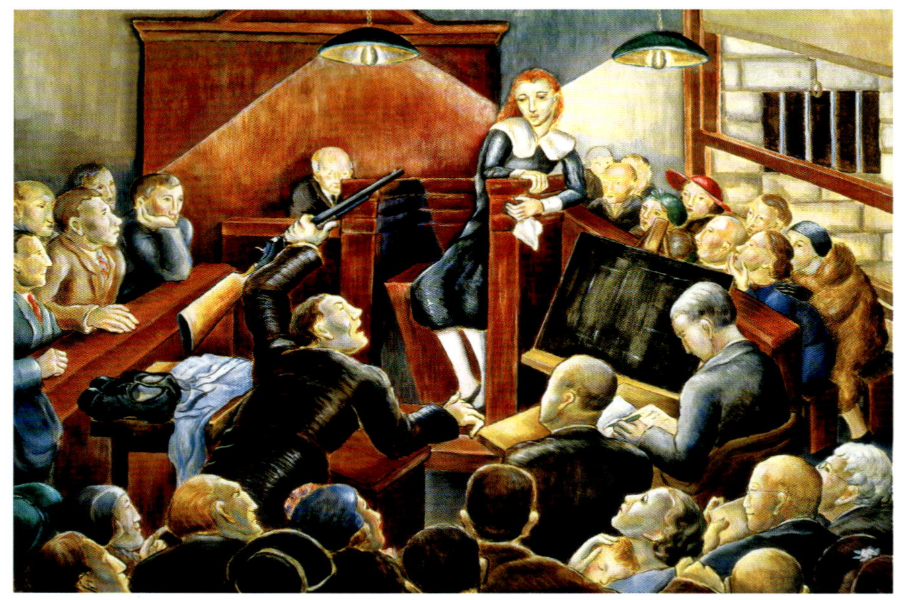

Louise Emerson Rönnebeck, ***The People vs. Mary Elizabeth Smith***, 1936, oil on canvas, 34 × 50 inches. Collection of Bruce and Jaren Ducker. Used by permission of the Estate of Arnold and Louise Rönnebeck.

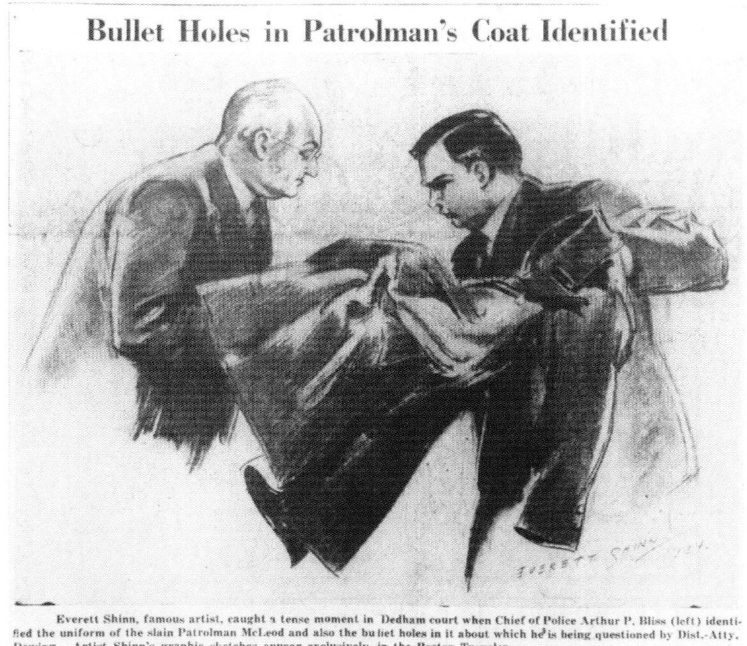

Bullet Holes in Patrolman's Coat Identified

Everett Shinn, famous artist, caught a tense moment in Dedham court when Chief of Police Arthur P. Bliss (left) identified the uniform of the slain Patrolman McLeod and also the bullet holes in it about which he is being questioned by Dist.-Atty. Dewing. Artist Shinn's graphic sketches appear exclusively in the Boston Traveler.

Everett Shinn, ***Bullet Holes in Patrolman's Coat Identified,*** *The Boston Traveler,* 1934. Courtesy of the Everett Shinn Papers, Delaware Art Museum, Wilmington.

the most explicit and is unique in its focus on the jury.[70] Blumenschein's talent as an illustrator would have lent itself to an image of high action, either in the courtroom or a depiction of the murder itself, and this is just the kind of subject that provided his support for his family for many years. However, when Blumenschein made the move to Taos in 1919, he was determined to leave behind the work of the illustrator in favor of a higher form of art, one that sought nobler purposes and greater artistic effect. He wanted to address issues in his major paintings that engaged matters of the intellect and the heart, and this, in part, is probably what led him to this subject. Moreover, since *Jury for the Trial of a Sheepherder for Murder* was intended for the Department of Justice mural competition, an illustration of the action of the murder itself would not have been appropriate. In making the jury the center of attention, Blumenschein focused the subject of the painting on the abstraction of the idea of justice, and he inevitably led the viewer to wonder about the thoughts of the jury as they pondered the arguments of the prosecution and the defense and about the notion that they represented the stability and purpose of a living community.

It has been suggested that under the old system of jurisprudence, Maestas would likely have been pardoned of his crimes.[71] However, this is not at all certain. Although English common law was not immediately instituted in New Mexico at the beginning of the territorial period, it had long been the practice by the time of Maestas's trial.[72] In 1837 the Mexican system placed adjudicatory powers with a justice of the peace, who would gather verbal and written testimony on a case and render a decision. Although a case might have a prosecutor and an advocate for the defense, there was not a jury trial. It was not always easy to find individuals who would undertake this role, because this sort of decision making in small communities was often very sensitive and these judges were led in their decisions by their sense of the greatest good for the whole community. This, in turn, was an extension of legal concepts in Spanish colonial law in which the notions of local custom and *equalidad* were primary guidelines in the justice system.[73] Although

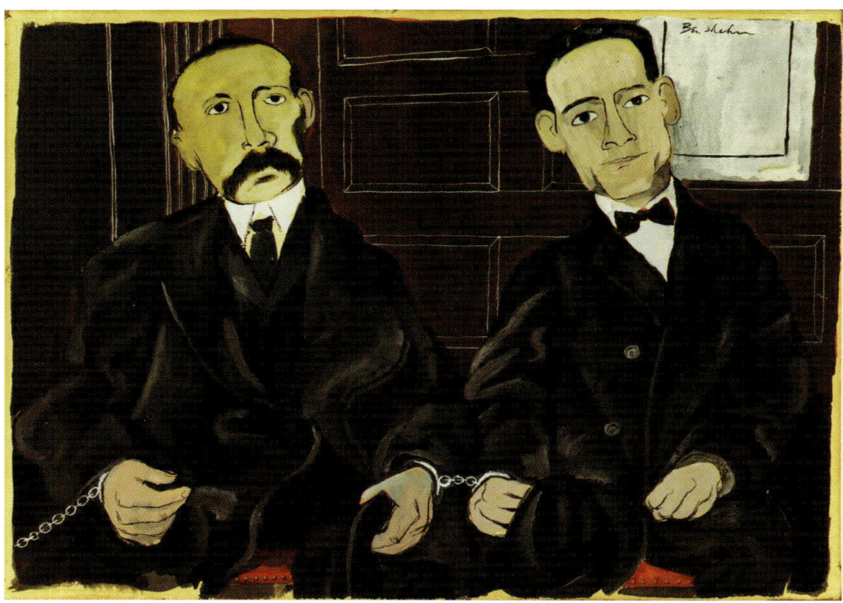

Ben Shahn, *Bartolomeo Vanzetti and Nicola Sacco*, 1931–32, gouache on paper mounted on board, 10⅞ × 14⅝ inches. The Museum of Modern Art, New York, New York (144.1935). Gift of Abby Aldrich Rockefeller. Digital Image © The Museum of Modern Art/Licensed by SCALA/Art Resource, New York. Art © Estate of Ben Shahn/Licensed by VAGA, New York, New York.

Anglo-American newcomers to the West complained about the system, it was not the case that outsiders were treated less fairly than resident citizens, and cases in which foreigners were killed brought the death penalty if circumstances warranted it.[74] Given the nature of Maestas's admission of a history of violent behavior in his confession, it is at least conceivable that the Mexican system could have held that his continued presence in the community threatened others and that he might have received a harsher penalty than the one returned by the jury. In the end, common law, with its system of rulings based on legal precedents, may have allowed the jury a legal technicality on which to base a lenient decision in the fate of this young, frightened man. These things,are of course unknowable, since we cannot actually penetrate the minds of the jury. And although Blumenschein knew what the verdict had been, as did everyone in Taos, he sensed the real drama to be in the life of the mind of the jury before the verdict was rendered.

Nevertheless, there was a larger story here, and Blumenschein, ever the illustrator, left clues to its telling. The title is deceptively straightforward, a simple description, yet it introduces an element of exoticism and mystery in revealing the defendant as a sheepherder. This fact gives some context for the scene, for, unlike the notorious trials that gained the attention of Shahn or Shinn, the event in Taos would not have been known to an audience in the East. It is the longest title Blumenschein ever gave a painting; in fact, it reads much like a caption for a book illustration. It establishes that there is a narrative here and in encapsulating a part of it, encourages the viewer to imagine the rest of the story.

Blumenschein does not show Judge Kiker or José Maestas in the picture, for in our tight view of the room we cannot see the judge's bench or the witness stand, as the jury can. Yet the empty chair, which faces the judge, by implication directs attention to that part of the room. The chair can only be that of the defendant. That the court reporter is writing indicates that someone is speaking. This must be the moment of Maestas's testimony, and we are allowed to see what he saw from the witness stand: the jury, his own empty chair, and a strange figure peering over the jury box. This man's face is generic, partially covered, and lifeless compared to the individuality of the jurors. The glasses turn his eyes into a blank stare and contribute to his mysterious presence. They seem to identify him as an outsider, but they perhaps also signify a stereotype, that of an academic. The strange man is like a specter of the young Professor DeWese, who has come to hear the proceedings and confront his murderer.[75] In spite of his odd placement in the room (no spectator in the audience for the trial would have been allowed to stand there) and his proximity to the jury box, the man in glasses draws no attention from any of the jurors. We can see him, and so can Maestas. The room is filled with dread, and it is cold.

In the end, Blumenschein passed no judgment on whether the jury made the right decision in Maestas's case. This was not his issue. He sought simply to show the faces of Hispanic Taos as a unified group acting together for the good of the community, and he sought to make this humble group of men in a remote New Mexican village stand for the highest values of rendering honest justice in American society. Like the inarticulate soul of a country undergoing difficult times and painful decisions, they were simply trying to find a way to do the right thing, in this case, to do the right thing for a young man who had gone so wrong. Blumenschein came close to placing the real story of José Maestas and the jury of his peers in the halls of justice in the nation's capitol, but perhaps, in the eyes of the selection committee, he was both too explicit and too subtle. Who are these men of the jury who look so real, and why are they just sitting there? We see no bold, noble actions. We hear no passionate arguments. There is no crying or pleading that justice be done for the disenfranchised, just the stillness and tension of twelve men, listening.

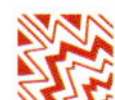

Modernism and the Art of Ernest L. Blumenschein

Jerry N. Smith

Ernest L. Blumenschein lived during a remarkably complex period in the history of art. Born ten days after the close of the first Impressionist exhibition in Paris in 1874, he studied art in a traditional academic setting at a time when the academies were beginning to be overshadowed creatively by modern artists working in individual means of expression. During his lifetime, the art world witnessed an array of radically changing artistic movements, from Impressionism and Post-Impressionism to the earliest achievements in Minimalism, through Cubism to Surrealism, and Dada to Neo-Dada. Blumenschein stayed aware of modern art trends and regularly expressed an appreciation for the production of younger, innovative artists. Despite the rapid changes taking place, he remained true to his own artistic vision, working in a figurative manner even when such work was no longer valued by a majority of American art critics and contemporary museum curators. Yet because of his interests in modern art, his creations never grew stale or formulaic—a statement that cannot be made for many who painted in strict accord with various isms. "I've lived through four vogues, and learned from each one," Blumenschein claimed.[1] Indeed, few artists of his era were equally capable of wedding academic conventions and modernist ideas with the same aplomb. Reexamination of his paintings and particularly his writings and lectures on modernism and art history reveals an artist who carefully balanced his love of artistic traditions with a genuine interest in exploring new ideas in his own work and encouraging it in others.

Blumenschein's paintings do not, or more appropriately should not, easily fit into an art-historical category. He spent the majority of his career working in Taos, New Mexico, and routinely made paintings of the region's landscape and the Hispanic, Pueblo Indian, and Anglo cultures there. As such, Blumenschein's name is today associated almost exclusively with western American artists, a defining label that carries with it a large degree of conservative, or nonmodern, baggage. Of the Taos Society of Artists, of which Blumenschein was a founding member, in 2002 art historian Erica Doss stated that the group displayed "nostalgic and anti-modernist longings for a pre-industrial past."[2] In similar fashion, for the text accompanying his 1999 PBS special *American Visions*, critic Robert Hughes summarily dismissed Blumenschein as one of the "minor academic artists" who founded the Taos artists' colony "years before any modernists got there."[3] Despite such categorization, Blumenschein was not a minor figure; nor did he ignore modernism in his painting. In his time he was highly regarded in art circles from New Mexico to New York, and his paintings were frequently honored and rewarded. Described in the 1910s as "one of the foremost of the American artists" and "a recognized authority on modern art and on the trend of Post-Impressionism," Blumenschein was an early defender of modern artists, writing on their behalf in the press and campaigning to his more conservative peers at the National Academy of Design for their inclusion at the academy's annual exhibitions.[4] Neither a strict academician nor a full-blown modern, Blumenschein felt that he belonged somewhere in between. He wrote, "It is some solace to be an artist in the transitional stage—between movements" and to "naturally form the bridge between the conservatives and the moderns."[5] More succinctly, he once stated, "I'm somewhat radical conservative in painting."[6]

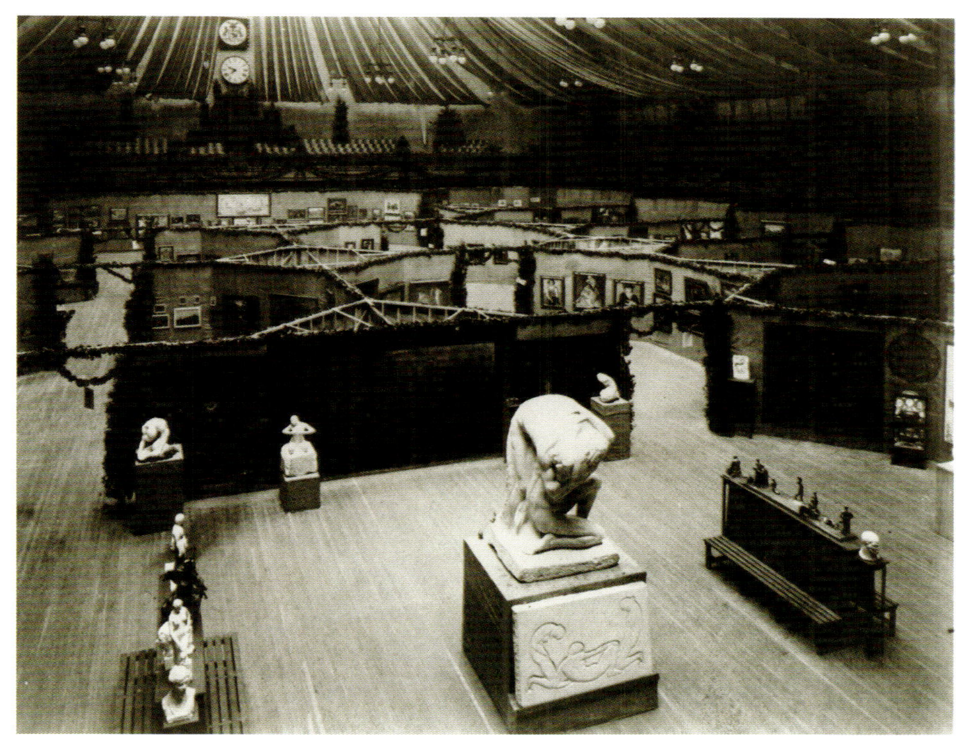

Sixty-ninth Regiment Armory, during the Armory Show, 1913. Photograph courtesy of the Walt Kuhn Family Papers and Armory Show Records, 1859–1978 (bulk 1900–1949), Archives of American Art, Smithsonian Institution, Washington, D.C.

Blumenschein held strong opinions about art, made clear in his writings, but he rarely addressed his own work in detail. "I do not like to talk about my pictures—I wish the pictures to do the talking," he informed reporters.[7] He was more forthcoming, however, in sharing his views in the press and in lectures on the history of art and the work of others. His insights into modernism are detailed in his longest published essay, a reflection on the 1913 International Exhibition of Modern Art, better known as the Armory Show. The exhibition was filled with more than 1,300 works of art in various media, and in the month it was on view in New York there were more than one hundred thousand paid admissions. For the first time, a large number of Americans became aware of trends in European modernism. While not the first exhibition of modern art held in the United States—the French Impressionists were originally shown at Paul Durand-Ruel's gallery in Boston as early as 1883 and other examples of modernism were shown in several smaller exhibitions after—yet the Armory Show had a remarkable effect among the general public and in the national press.

A plethora of negative criticism was levied against the large exhibition, particularly in opposition to European modernists, including Henri

Matisse, Constantin Brancusi, and Marcel Duchamp. Editorials appeared around the country, and criticism came from more than just the customary art critics. It seemed that everyone wanted to speak out against the exhibition, including former president Theodore Roosevelt. He weighed in on the art of the "lunatic fringe" in an article for *Outlook*, unfavorably comparing Duchamp's cubist *Nude Descending a Staircase*, #2 (1912; Philadelphia Museum of Art) with Navajo rug designs.[8] Even John Sloan, one of the infamous Eight who rankled critics with his paintings of the unglamorous side of everyday life, used the opportunity to poke fun at the cubists with an illustrated poem for *The Masses*.[9]

Waiting one year for the excitement and heated opinions to settle, *Century* magazine published its "Modern Art Number" in April 1914. The magazine intended to "consider dispassionately all of these phases, from the conservative to the radical," in the art presented at the Armory.[10] *Century* presented five articles and included black-and-white illustrations of varying styles and degrees of modernism by American artists.[11] It featured impressionist works by Frederic Frieseke and Robert Reid, tonalist imagery by Dwight Tryon and Charles Dewey, and realist designs by George Bellows and George Luks. It also pictured the Europeans who garnered the bulk of the negative reaction for their "primitive," abstract, and cubist compositions, despite representing only one-third of the total works on display. Among the authors was John White Alexander, an artist known for his eloquent and fashionable female portraits. Alexander wrote of "this ultra-modern experiment that is really a menace even to the strong."[12] In similar fashion, academically conservative artist Edwin Blashfield detailed the "fatuous contempt for the lesson of the past" presented by the moderns.[13] Included was Blumenschein's essay "The Painting of To-morrow," an impassioned and insightful article on behalf of the seriousness of modern art.[14] Aimed at a general audience, it demonstrates an ability to explain difficult artistic ideas in a thoughtful and intelligent manner. Unlike the many reactionary responses, Blumenschein enthusiastically described the exhibition as "a very healthy affair, the influence of which will work for good in the art of to-morrow." Writing in a personal manner, he even explained the conflicts he personally faced in applying modern concepts into his own painting practices.

Appreciative of the fact that, by and large, the American public had only recently come to accept Impressionism, Blumenschein laid out a history of modern art that led to the current styles. This outline traced the Impressionism of Claude Monet to the Post-Impressionism of Paul Cézanne, Paul Gauguin, and Vincent Van Gogh. Blumenschein felt that the art of the Post-Impressionists led, "strangely enough, to the primitive in art." Recognizing that "archaic is one of the passwords" of the moderns, he understood this to be a starting point for future advancement. "After some reflection, I came to the conclusion that these men were going far back in order to go ahead," he stated, adding the honest biographical note, "It was too far back for me." Admiring the moderns' willingness to seek the new, Blumenschein commented, "it takes a tremendous amount of courage to be different from our fellow-sheep, and to be frank where it implies facing derision, contempt, and a diminished income."[15]

Blumenschein described his initial encounter with modern art, which occurred in Paris in 1907 or 1908 through a chance encounter on a Parisian street with the collector Leo Stein. He is unnamed in the article, but identified as the "American apostle and 'angel' of Post-Impressionism."[16] Stein invited Blumenschein to come to the apartment he shared with his sister, avant-garde author Gertrude, at the now infamous 27 Rue de Fleures. The apartment "rapidly was becoming a rendezvous for the restless in art," observed Blumenschein. It was there that he first saw paintings by Matisse, "about twenty or more," including today's well-known icons of modernism *Portrait of Mme Matisse / The Green Line* (1905; Statens Museum for Kunst, Copenhagen), *The Woman with the Hat* (1905), and a study for *The Joy of Life* (1905–1906; both at San Francisco Museum of Modern Art). The Stein collection also included Pablo Picasso's protocubist *Portrait of Gertrude Stein* (1906; Metropolitan Museum of Art), as well as canvases by Cézanne, Edouard Manet, Pierre-August Renoir, Henri de Toulouse-Lautrec, Pierre Bonnard, and several others. "It was my first sight of this new art," Blumenschein explained, "and as my mind was not thoroughly liberated from the prevailing idea of what constituted good pictures and bronzes, I was shocked."[17]

Although "shocked" by the encounter, he apparently was not captivated enough to revisit the Steins or to seek out further examples of modernism while in Paris or after his return to America in 1908. The interest in staying in touch with modern

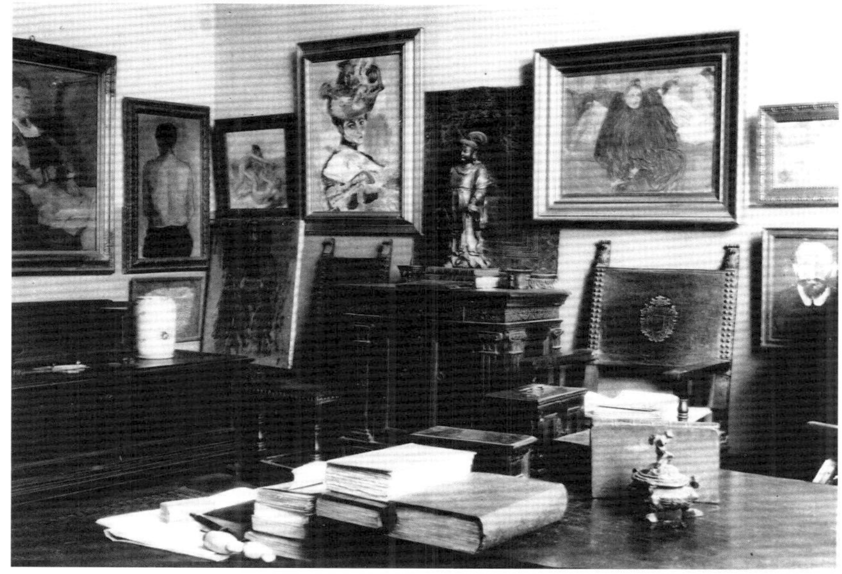

Leo and Gertrude Stein apartment, 27 rue de Fleurs, Paris, 1906. Courtesy of the Dr. Claribel Cone and Miss Etta Cone Papers, Baltimore Museum of Art, Baltimore, Maryland.

trends had yet to develop in the artist. By his own account, five years would pass after his visit to the Stein apartment until Blumenschein next saw modernist paintings at the Armory Show, although the opportunities were present. Alfred Stieglitz's Little Galleries of the Photo-Secession in New York, better known as the 291 Gallery for its Fifth Avenue address, had been exhibiting modern art as early as 1907. Prior to the landmark Armory Show, Steiglitz had already exhibited Cézanne and Matisse and had given Picasso his first solo exhibition. Arthur Dove, Marsden Hartley, and Max Weber were among the Americans exhibiting at 291 who demonstrated in their work the influence of the European moderns. Despite Blumenschein's lack of a prolonged exposure to modern art, to his own stated surprise, "I no longer doubted the new creeds." He wrote that there was life in modernism, "and if it had life, it had beauty; for they are inseparable." With great foresight, he realized that this new art would have a lasting effect, emphasizing "that a new truth has been added to our knowledge, and *one which will be welded into all future art.*"[18]

Blumenschein was in the minority when it came to his appreciation and support of modern art. "Clearly, there were few critics who sought to understand this new artistic language and make it intelligible to viewers," wrote art historian Sylvia Yount in 1996.[19] Yet this is precisely what Blumenschein accomplished, despite being an academically trained and established artist about to turn forty years old. It was not a one-time event, as he continued throughout his life to write and speak on various aspects of modernism. In 1919 the *Albuquerque Evening Herald* described Blumenschein as "a recognizable authority on modern art and on the trend of post-impressionism."[20] His interest in modern art led him to be a leading force and founding member of the progressive group from Santa Fe known as the New Mexico Painters, a move that resulted in his ultimate resignation from the more conservative Taos Society of Artists.

The tone of appreciation and acceptance for modern artists found in Blumenschein's *Century* magazine article became a cause for the artist in the following decade that blossomed into a public debate regarding the conservative exhibitions of the National Academy of Design. Blumenschein wrote a call for acceptance of modern artists by the academy that appeared in the *New York Times* as a lengthy letter to the editor on February 7, 1926. In the letter, titled "Modern Art and the Academy," Blumenschein opined that the "so-called moderns do not submit their works to the large national exhibitions of the country because the juries and directors will not allow them to be admitted."[21] Taking an unflattering tone against institutional collections, he noted, "Unfortunately the trustees and directors of Museums, very often the officers of large art societies, have not the time to continue their education in art . . . hence they do little to encourage new art, new thoughts, youthful vigor and hopes." He envisioned the National Academy as the ideal place to correct this national trend. "If the Academy takes the initiative, and it is just that it should, the entire country will soon follow." To accomplish this goal, he suggested "that the National Academy of Design at its forth-coming show offer one of its few rooms for exhibition of carefully chosen modern painting." With all expenses paid. When presenting this same paper later that month at the New Mexico State Teachers Convention, he added, "This paper is a frank effort to bring together in pleasant relations the two schools of painting and sculpture that we now find in the United States."[22]

Given the conservative nature of the National Academy of Design and its supporters, it is not surprising to find that the immediate response was less than favorable. "Treason in the Academy," was the title of an article the following week in the *New York Telegram*, which mockingly likened Blumenschein's proposal as "giving aid and comfort to the enemy."[23] Suggesting that Blumenschein had disingenuously written on behalf of fellow academicians, the writer questioned why the infusion of modern art would need to be installed in a separate room. He asked, "Do Mr. Blumenschein and the rest fear that if the vigorous work of the wild men were shown beside the mild productions of the Academy the latter would die a violent death?" The writer added, "And why 'carefully chosen modern paintings' if the selection is to be made by the bearded ancients who make up the juries of West Fifty-seventh street?" Even if the moderns were included, the writer expressed doubt that the academy would be forthcoming in the sharing of prizes, concluding, "In vain is the net spread in the sight of any bird."

Blumenschein did not allow his proposal to end there. He countered with a second letter, this time to the *New York Telegram*. Picking up on the editorialist's equating artists with birds, Blumenschein recounted a trip taken into the mountains where he saw beautiful birds of varying species, all "fighting among themselves . . . and I wonder why they must fight for the worm, why 'love your neighbor' has not had a greater effect, and why education results in so many people remaining ignorant. And this ignorance that exists among artists (I am told I should say lack of appreciation, but ignorance is the word) is what causes most of the disagreement."[24] Blumenschein also felt it necessary to counter the suggestion that he had written on behalf of others. "And do get this right—I am not an Academician, as you stated. I am an A.N.A. [Associate National Academician]. That, as you know, is an almost Academician."

This acknowledgment of his place at the academy hints at the fact that there was a certain level of professional risk Blumenschein was taking for the benefit of others. As an elected associate member since 1910, he had experienced success and won awards at the academy's exhibitions. He was twice presented with the Benjamin Altman Prize for American-born artists, arguably the most prestigious and coveted prize given by the academy, with *Superstition* (1921; this volume, p. 143) being recognized with the first Altman Prize in 1921 and *Sangre de Cristo Mountains* (1925; p. 167) awarded the second Altman four years later. With such a high level of success earned, he was clearly an associate candidate on the verge of acceptance as a full academician. He would earn this honor the following year, although there was no way he could have known this with certainty in advance. Thus the energy spent on the behalf of others is rather remarkable. "At the age of fifty-four, when most artists are beginning a decline, Ernest Blumenschein, N.A. is still a young man," observed fellow artist Alexandre Hogue in 1928.[25]

Remarkably, the call by Blumenschein to bring modernists into the academic fold proved a success. At the academy's spring exhibition of 1927, "the new art rubbed shoulders with the old in democratic fashion," as a room was indeed set aside where invited modernists were displayed.[26] On view were works by artists who were largely unknown to the public at the time but would become major figures in the development of American modernism, including Charles Sheeler, Joseph Stella, Reginald Marsh, and Blumenschein's fellow New Mexico painter Andrew Dasburg.

After this initial gesture by the academy, Blumenschein continued to campaign for even greater acceptance on the behalf of modern artists, although he had serious doubts about the chances for greater success. In private he expressed deep frustration with the continued conservative nature prevalent among those running the organization. A few months after his election as full academician, he attended an academy board meeting on March 14, 1928, which left him disillusioned about the organization's board members. Blumenschein wrote a scathing personal observation following the meeting. In a handwritten note, he observed, "More than ever convinced of ever closing circle of men who for self-preservation attend the control meetings. This circle composed of poorest artists, with very few exceptions."[27] He described the academy's president, architect Cass Gilbert, as "very able, but standing too much on dignity to get below the surface," while the first vice president, artist Harry Watrous, was "absolutely ignorant of Amer[ican] art outside the Academy walls." His strongest criticism was leveled at the secretary, artist Charles Curran, described as "the shallowest of all." This private note points to the continued importance of adding quality modern artists to the academy body, realizing that the only way to do so "is to organize voters and use political methods," though he expressed doubt of the "continued success." Despite his strong interest in the matter and previous willingness to take up the cause, he conceded, "I do not feel that I can be of service." He named three reasons as drawbacks to his ability to help. One was being in New York only a few months of the year, "second, because I do not like [to] fight except to defend myself, and third, because I really doubt the possibility of obtaining permanent results."

Regardless of the tone of resignation at the conclusion of his personal message, Blumenschein did continue to campaign on behalf of others. Two years following his personal condemnation of the academy's officers he wrote a direct letter to Gilbert, making a final appeal for modern artists. This letter has not been identified, but the meaning is suggested through Gilbert's typed, five-page response. Although respectful in tone, Gilbert maintained the academy's conservative stance against innovative, individual styles. "I would not discourage experimentation," Gilbert claimed, "but I would not accept its vagaries as standards, as for me, I prefer beauty and clarity to crudity and confusion."[28] He called upon Blumenschein to refrain from making public criticism, perhaps recalling the media attention given his letters to the *New York Times* and *New York Telegram* four years earlier. "We do not want a 'defeatist party' in the Academy and, frankly, I think it is up to you and thoughtful men like you to discourage every word you hear which is damaging to the Academy." Despite his personal feelings, Blumenschein apparently took the note to heart and discontinued his public call for greater inclusion of the moderns at the academy. The role he played in having modern artists accepted appears to have been largely selfless, as he had little or nothing to gain professionally from his efforts. Artistic gains, however, could be a different matter. Blumenschein apparently felt that exhibiting alongside modern artists would allow his own interests in progressive means of visual expression to grow. Presenting his art alongside those of younger moderns was a point of pride, indicating that his work had not become dated with age.

In 1936 Blumenschein created *Jury for the Trial of a Sheepherder for Murder* (this volume, p. 239), a painting that would garner considerable attention in both academic and modern art circles. Artist Howard Cook described the image as "a solid construction of basic abstract design."[29] The painting of uneasy jurors sitting tightly together is a disquieting look at American justice. Based on an actual case, the jurors were selected from the Hispanic community of Taos. Through their discomfort, they appear to be the ones on trial. The focus on the jurors rather than the accused was a modern concept in painting, and it proved to be a major success for Blumenschein. *Jury* was included in the 1938 Paris exhibition Three Centuries of Art of the United States. Showing his work as an example of contemporary painting alongside younger, modern artists, including Alexander Calder, Stuart Davis, Arshile Gorky, and Georgia O'Keeffe, was a great thrill for the sixty-three-year-old. He expressed his pleasure to a reporter, who wrote that Blumenschein "feels encouraged to continue putting on the gloves with many schools of modern artists."[30] He also used the opportunity to stress the importance of "sound fundamentals." The Museum of Modern Art purchased *Jury* following its Paris exhibition.

When *Jury* traveled to Europe, Blumenschein returned to the issue of modern art in a lecture likely delivered to art students. Revisiting the ideas he originally detailed in his 1915 article "The Painting of To-morrow," Blumenschein detailed a history of modernism, from Cézanne's "reaction to the cold photographic point of view of Ingres," through Cubism and Surrealism, which "climaxed the era of French influence on Modern Art in the U.S.A."[31] He wrote, "Art has returned to a normal expression and illustration of our daily life" and that "cubism and the abstract painting of twenty years ago reflected with great intensity the agonies and confusion of mind the world underwent as result of the World War." He added, "Economic factors are as vital in fashioning art as the inspiration of the individual. In fact the individual is only a 'tool' for the expression of his period." The notion that an artist is merely a "tool" of his time is an insightful passage that prefigures by thirty years the writings on discourse and original thought by theoreticians such as Michel Foucault and Roland Barthes.[32]

Jury for the Trial of a Sheepherder for Murder sums up what Blumenschein had been doing for several years. It demonstrates an exploration into modernist concepts of design while working in a figurative and narrative style. Ten years after its completion, William S. Lieberman in *Art News* compared it to a cubist design "that approaches complete abstraction" by the French artist Ferdnand Léger. Of *Jury*, Lieberman writes, "today, with the revaluation of the possibilities of realism and the storytelling picture, Léger's *Breakfast*, painted in 1920 at the very vanguard of its time, seems no more modern."[33]

Throughout his career, Blumenschein routinely took part in regional, national, and international exhibitions. His paintings received awards and were purchased by private collectors and acquired by institutions that included the conservative Metropolitan Museum of Art as well as the progressive Museum of Modern Art. "The modernist as well as the academician will recognize the constant research and problematic thoughtfulness in the work of Blumenschein's very interesting personality," wrote the director of the Denver Art Museum, artist Arnold Rönnebeck.[34] Noting his strengths in compositional design and bold coloration, one critic described Blumenschein's canvases as displaying a "savage love of color" and a "manner of formalizing everything into a pattern which takes on everywhere a mystic meaning."[35] He combined the classic and the modern, prompting one critic to write that "he aims to grasp at Michaelangelean feelings" while at the same time "is to the Southwest what Gauguin was to the South Seas."[36]

The "Michaelangelean feelings" come through in Blumenschein's intense attention to compositional design. "Art to be art must emphasize design," he claimed.[37] Fellow artists, Blumenschein's contemporaries, greatly admired the design element of Blumenschein's work. Howard Cook noted that Blumenschein's paintings exhibited a "love of architectural formal order" and "an unmistakable feeling for strong architectural design."[38] Theodore Van Soelen observed that "every picture he has painted is carefully designed."[39] And Alexandre Hogue wrote that the painting *Sangre de Cristo Mountains* displayed "superb composition and highly sophisticated technique."[40]

The importance of strong composition was a major aspect of Blumenschein's conception of fine art. As early as 1915, he had expressed that the key to understanding good design and quality art was "to get a solid foundation under the guidance of a first class artist in the study of form, anatomy, color and composition" at a major art academy, such as the National Academy of Design in New York, the Art Institute of Chicago, or the Pennsylvania Academy of the Fine Arts.[41] The earlier a student began instruction the better. However, he felt the ability to appreciate and understand the underlying force of quality design was largely inherent, not something learned in a classroom. Schooling would only reinforce what was already inside the student. In an interview in 1927, Blumenschein elaborated on the qualities of design: "rhythm of line—rhythm of movement—and proportion of spaces. In fact, it could be termed the architecture of a picture and just as it is with architecture, this power of design comes from within oneself. It indicates conception or vision which quality is about fifty percent of the virtue in any art work. It also indicates your sense of proportion, your elegance, or lack of elegance, your emotional vigor or your sentimentality, your knowledge derived from observation or your ignorance. In fact, design in your work of art tells what you are."[42]

One design element frequently employed by Blumenschein was the use of repeating elements within a single composition. In *Moon, Morning Star, and Evening Star,* (1931; this volume, p. 151) for example, figures are not shown as unique individuals, but rather become part of a unified mass in a series of generalized, echoing forms. Hogue noted that Blumenschein was generally faithful to his models, "but when he is interested in the great gatherings at Indian ceremonials he turns to the abstract. It is then that the seething mass of human beings, robed in brilliant colors and going through fantastic movements, becomes a great design which fulfills two distinct purposes—to present on close inspection a maze of authentic detail in an epic subject, and at a distance to have this all appear as a colorful Indian design, causing a sensation somewhat akin to that produced by the marvelous beauty of an Indian blanket. To enjoy this last quality of a Blumenschein we must forget subject matter and revel in fantastic shapes and harmonious color."[43] Speaking in 1948 of the painting *Moon, Morning Star, and Evening Star,* Blumenschein said, "I could have sold this painting had I included one of the main figures in the dance in it. But it would have spoiled the design. I am not an anthropologist, I am a painter, but the buyer wanted an anthropologist picture, so I still have it." He continued, "The great emphasis today is on *creative* art. Imitating nature is not art. Art is beyond nature."[44] Frequently, hills or trees are aligned within a composition to provide a desired visual rhythm rather than strictly adhering to observations in nature. Speaking on the qualities of a late landscape painting, possibly *Enchanted Forest* (1946; this volume, p. 176), Blumenschein wrote, "I had to arrange and rearrange, many times shuffling my trees like a deck of cards."[45]

For Blumenschein, good design was equally important as color, what he referred to as "the Man Friday of Design."[46] He explained, "Color is the instrument of the design idea and is usually born with the design. It cannot be separated from form because it is the clay that form is made of. Color too expresses your nature." The expressive use of color became important early on. He kept in his studio a well-worn card from his days as a student that read, "Search Beautiful Color," a reminder of something that would remain important for the artist throughout his career.[47] In 1937 he wrote, "Today, we all recognize and use color for emotional effect."[48] Fifteen years later, he repeated the sentiment, claiming "I depict the emotional side entirely by color."[49] This personal combination of design and color, of carefully considered, classically influenced composition used together with emotive application of color, is found in Blumenschein's art and affirmed in his statement that "The two most important influences on my painting career were from the Louvre in Paris—and later from the Impressionist school in Paris."[50]

From the Impressionists, Blumenschein learned to appreciate the potential in returning to a location to paint at different times of the year under various effects of atmosphere and light. One of his favorite fishing haunts and painting sites to which he frequently returned was Eagle Nest Lake, a lake created in 1918 and located about twenty-five miles from Taos. "I have painted it at least five times in different moods."[51] In bright daylight of summer or under cloud cover in winter, each painting presents a dramatically different impression. For his painting *The Lake* (*Fishing on Eagle Nest Lake*) (1931; this volume, p. 233), the sharp angles of the Sangre de Cristo Mountains frame the scene. Textured clouds in shades of purple and pink fill the sky and match the contours of the tree-covered cliffs and the choppy water below.

These carefully crafted images use color for emotional effect, which is further enhanced by the artist's painting technique of applying layer upon layer of thick paint on a canvas. Brushwork is always evident in Blumenschein's paintings, as the layers of paint provide a visceral effect separate from the actual image. In this regard, the surfaces of his paintings are perhaps best compared to the heavily worked canvases of the American Impressionist Ernest Lawson, one of the innovative Eight working out of New York. Blumenschein's technique led critics to frequently comment on the "very plastic landscape of plane after plane of weather carved mountains," of designs made up of "quilted hills," and of work that "gives the effect of an Oriental rug."[52]

Critics were not alone in recognizing the textural quality of Blumenschein's paintings, and fellow artists also admired his technique. Arnold Rönnebeck wrote, "The given space of each canvas is always animated to the last square inch. Nothing is incidental."[53] In *The Plasterer* (1921; this volume, p. 146), a painting praised by Howard Cook for its "surprisingly modern basic design," dense patches of paint, applied as if with a trowel, are used to describe areas of the plaster depicted, providing a physical presence to the surface of the work. In a review of Blumenschein's 1948 retrospective, Theodore Van Soelen wrote, "[*The Plasterer*] is well worth studying. It shows plainly how Blumenschein works—how he scrapes and repaints, sometimes with heavily loaded brushes such as the full strokes of solid blue, and at other times with great restraint and delicacy as in the painting of the fireplace."[54] Van Soelon notes that as Blumenschein progressed through his career, he "discarded undiluted realism and was giving his imagination rein."

One imaginative aspect of Blumenschein's oeuvre was his frequent descriptive and conceptual linking of visual imagery with musical qualities. "The standards that touch me deepest and that I have constantly held before me are those of Beethoven, Michelangelo, and Shakespeare," he claimed.[55] As an accomplished violinist reared in a musical household who had to make a difficult decision as a young adult between music and painting, it is not surprising to find that Blumenschein frequently used musical terminology to discuss his images. "I have to get right down to earth and analyze, to find out what makes the music," was a typical statement from Blumenschein.[56] In a letter from 1901, just three years after his first visit to Taos, he praised the beauty of the Southwest, and then went into great detail about the musical impulses he received from nature:

> Music is all I miss. Be we have that in the storms that tune all the instruments of nature to noble harmonies, and in the quiet nights that fill a man's soul with a calm rhythm in accord with all that is serene and beautiful. The cottonwoods and the pines are the violins, the sweeping grass of the prairies play the cello, a plunging brook is a silver flute, the quivering aspen leaves a tremulous oboe, and the Master Musician blows through the cañons from afar across the desert, and the music wavers in the gulches and ravines and modulates in rarest harmonies. There are no singing bards, save the quail that plays his

two tones, and the dove. But many a harp is strung in the cedars.[57]

The concept of one sensory perception stimulating a response of another sense is known as synaesthesia, and in the late nineteenth century music was frequently linked to visual sensations. Art historian Charles Eldredge observed, "Although interest in such translated sensory responses extended well back into history, the synaesthetic state was first examined 'scientifically' by Francis Galton in his *Inquiries into Human Faculty*, published in 1883. . . . Painters, like writers and composers, were fond of the cultivation of synaesthetic response which advanced the analogical relationship between disparate things toward complete unity."[58] The artists of the Romantic and Symbolist movements at the turn of the century considered such associations as vital to their imagery and this progressed into modern art. "In effect, the idea of synaesthesia served to mediate between music and visual art in the early twentieth century and proved essential to the development of abstraction," wrote Jeremy Strick for the 2005 study and exhibition *Visual Music*.[59] Artists noted for the musicality of their imagery include Russian Vasily Kandinksy and Americans James Abbott MacNeil Whistler, Morgan Russell, Arthur Dove, and Blumenschein's friend and fellow New Mexico artist Emil Bisttram. Like Blumenschein, these artists also provided musical titles for paintings at various stages in their careers.

One of Blumenschein's most significant examples of providing a visual image of music came about when he was commissioned by the Steinway Piano Company in 1918 to make a painting for advertisement purposes. While other images in the Steinway collection feature likenesses of famous composers, Blumenschein instead created a painting inspired by Edward Alexander MacDowell's *Indian Suite* (this volume, p.96), a composition for orchestra written in 1896. In the similarly titled painting, a central figure holding a drum towers above a field of combatants, arrows filling the distance between the two warring factions like so many musical notes. The painting is a visualization of the music and illustrates that Blumenschein did not embrace in his own art the complete abstract qualities found in works by artists such as Kandinsky or Dove. He explained in an interview, "I once studied the violin and I crave emotion when I go to a recital. But emotion should be restrained. I might here mention that Rembrandt shows restrained powerful emotions. Certainly, the great artist must control his emotions."[60]

The attention of the art world, however, would rapidly change in the late 1940s, and critics began to recognize the achievements of artists who exhibited an apparent lack of control in their art. The emphasis on figurative painting popularized in American scene and regionalist art was quickly replaced by purely nonrepresentational art of Abstract Expressionism, and for the first time in his life Blumenschein felt unsure of his future. In 1946, three years before *Life* magazine asked if Jackson Pollock was the country's greatest living artist, Blumenschein had expressed his displeasure at the altering artistic landscape. In a letter to his daughter,

Helen, he wrote of his unhappiness with prizes going to "wildly modern art" and observed there was "no use denying that objective painters are put in the background for quite a while."[61] He added, "Can't see my way for the first time in my life. And am so upset over the complete serving in Art to abstract and non-objective! Feel out of competition entirely, while doing my best work."

While in Albuquerque, New Mexico, in 1952, Blumenschein spoke on the city's lagging intellectual development in a tone that addressed a national concern, claiming that its "fine art standards are being weakened by the low form of art of the movies and television."[62] Later that year, he spoke in Taos on his opinion of the modern art he had seen during a recent visit to San Francisco. Apparently for the first time, he was critical of modernism and the teaching of modern art to students. Upon seeing an exhibition of paintings by Kandinsky, he praised the artist's "ability to make a composition that had an emotional kick and beautiful technique," yet he found it "hard to believe that he was a large influence in setting off the modern movement."[63] The work was personal, yet apparently "easy for imitators to follow." Likening modernism to "the primitive sex appeal" of jazz music, Blumenschein claimed "it was an easy escape for many; there were no scales to practice, no hours of tedious training. . . . I am sorry for the generation that is now being educated on these modern ideals. They will be a pretty lop-sided lot."

The great art he encountered in San Francisco was not inside the galleries and museums but outside in the city's architecture, "which is as magnificent and overwhelming as the flow of a symphony orchestra." The trip to San Francisco strengthened Blumenschein's growing unease with modernism. "Before this experience," he claimed, "I was not sure of my opinions; I liked all art that men created but had no scale of values I could trust." He closed on a conservative note: "To the blessed few whose works will live because their gifts were rich, their souls great, and their intellects profound, Modernism was a spur. Yet it did not make them lose sight of the fundamentals of order, form, proportion, and color that sings."[64]

The final major exhibition of Blumenschein's work during his lifetime was his 1958 retrospective held at the Museum of New Mexico, Santa Fe. The catalog states, "In the final analysis Blumenschein is progressive. Born in an earlier generation he stands abreast of the 'modern.'"[65] Blumenschein used the opportunity of the retrospective to reach out to the curator of American art at the Metropolitan Museum of Art, Robert Beverly Hale, to whom he sent a copy of the exhibition catalog. On its cover, Blumenschein included a personal note. It is written in a slightly unsteady hand, but it stresses a sharp intellect. He begins and ends in a sarcastic tone: "Ever since I cancelled my subscription to the art mags of N.Y. my name is rarely mentioned. Therefore I humbly request you to give this brochure a quiet glance-over." Pleased with his latest paintings, yet understanding that he was at the end of his long career, he added, "I completed most of the important paintings (for the last time) last summer, the happiest working year of my life." Likely intended as a humorous comment on his own longevity, he dated this note "Jan. 10, 1859."

At the time of his death in 1960, a friend wrote, "Though a conventional, old-school, realistic painter, he was invariably intrigued by what younger artists were doing, and was endlessly active himself in exploring new approaches to color and composition."[66] Ernest L. Blumenschein was a gifted artist, trained in the academic traditions, who appreciated and incorporated modernist ideas, in doses, into his own distinctive style. As such, his art does not fit easily into generalized categories. He was a modern among his fellow western American artists and a conservative among the moderns. Yet, instead of trying to fit the mold of either camp, Blumenschein remained true to his own artistic desires, which were developed out of the conventions of the nineteenth century and nurtured in the turbulent twentieth century.

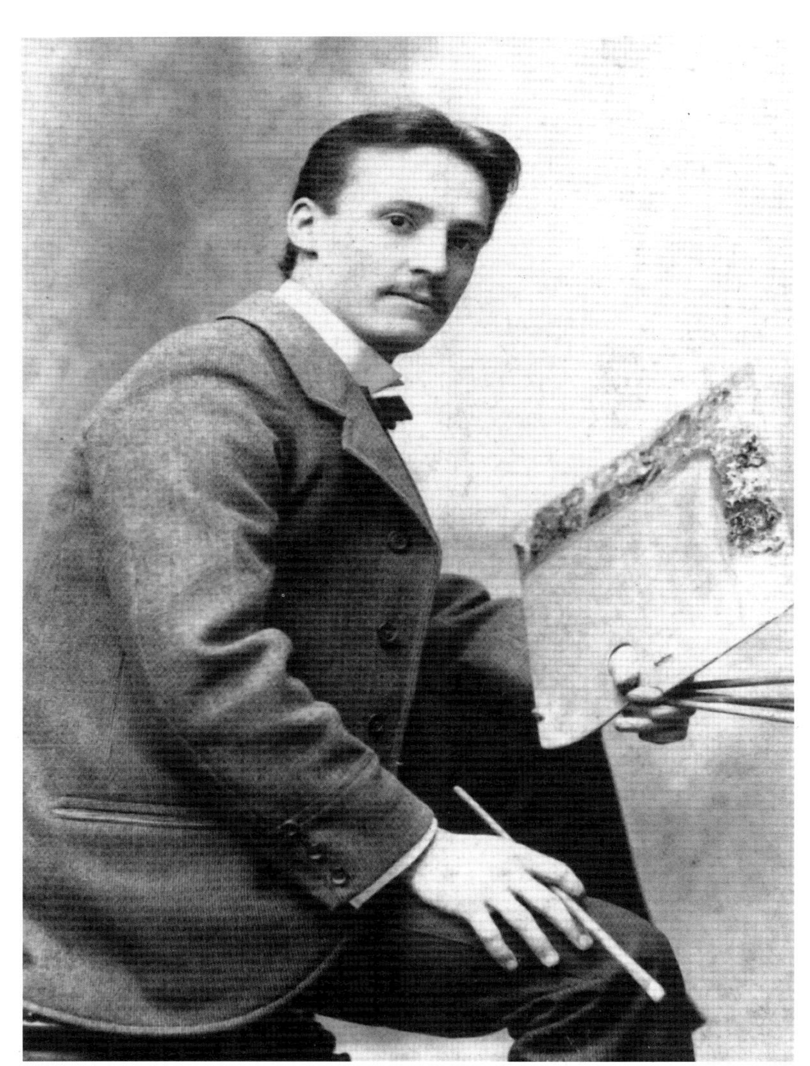

Chronology

Compiled by Elizabeth J. Cunningham

1874 May 25: Born in Pittsburgh, Pennsylvania, to William Leonard and Leonore Chapin Blumenschein.

1878 Family moved to Dayton, Ohio; father employed as director of the Dayton Philharmonic Society.

1881 February 15: Mother, Leonore Chapin Blumenschein, died; began violin study at age seven.

1887 Attended Central High School, where he was classmates with the poet Paul Laurence Dunbar and the Wright brothers; did sketches of family and Dayton environs.

1889 Created and illustrated *Tomfoolery*, based on *Puck* and *Life* magazines; included classmate Paul Dunbar in illustration for high school Philomathean Society (literary organization); played football and tennis.

1891 Illustrated *High School Times* for the school's Philomathean Society; final year of *Tomfoolery* editions; June: graduated from Central High School; father wrote to *McClure's Young People* magazine inquiring about his son's illustrating talent and the field of illustration; played violin in the Ayght Orchestra; received violin scholarship at the Music Academy of Cincinnati.

1892 After one year study at the music academy, persuaded father to transfer to the Art Academy of Cincinnati, where he was classmates with Charles Ebert; won prize for illustration in Fernand Lungren's class.

1893 Fall: Moved to New York to attend classes at Art Students League; roomed with Ebert; studied with John Twachtman, J. Carroll Beckwith, and Kenyon Cox; fellow students included Ebert and Lionel Barrymore; enrolled in Jeanette Thurber's National Conservatory of Music, where he played first violin under the conservatory's second director, Antonin Dvořák.

1894 Finished study at Art Students League; placed illustrations with *McClure's* magazine; September: departed New York accompanied by Ebert and others for study in Paris; studied two years at the Académie Julian under Jean-Paul Laurens and Jean-Joseph Benjamin-Constant; awarded three prizes for drawings; spent summers in Crecy-en-Brie.

1896 Finished study at Académie Julian; Spring: exhibited *Le Flutiste* (*The Flute Player*) and *Le Lac* (*The Lake*) at the Paris Salon; participated in the American Art Club Minstrels show; September: returned to New York; received commission from *Scribner's* to illustrate "The Business of a Factory."

1897 January: Arrived at Ft. Wingate, New Mexico, on commission to cover Navajos; illustrated for *McClure's*, including Rudyard Kipling's story "The Tomb of His Ancestors"; met Ellis Parker Butler when both roomed at New York boarding house; exhibited watercolors at the Art Institute of Chicago (AIC).

1898 Lived at 120 West Fiftieth Street in New York; shared studio with Bert Geer Phillips; April–May: received commission for illustrations and traveled to Kansas to meet with author William Allen White; Summer: traveled with Phillips to Denver, Colorado, for sketching trip, intending to go south into Mexico; September: landed in Taos, New Mexico, due to broken wagon wheel, sketched Taos Pueblo Indians, and attended and recorded the San Geronimo Feast Day at Taos Pueblo; November: went on commission to Mojave Indian Reservation; December: returned to New York; among *McClure's* stories illustrated were Stephen Crane's "The Bride Comes to Yellow Sky" and Hamlin Garland's "General Custer's Last Fight as Seen by Two Moon"; *Harper's Weekly* illustrations included *The New Orleans Carnival* and *A Strange Mixture of Barbarism and Christianity—The Celebration of San Geronimo's Day among the Pueblo Indians*; showed watercolors in American Watercolor Society (AWS), National Academy of Design (NAD), and Pennsylvania Academy of the Fine Arts (PAFA) exhibitions.

1899 Met Booth Tarkington; elected member of the Salmagundi Club, and member of Society of Illustrators; May: exhibition at Dayton Club included Indian ghost dance illustrations and *Trail to the Golden North* for Hamlin Garland articles in *McClure's*; September: returned to Paris for advanced study at Académie Julian; began correspondence Ellis Parker Butler and with Butler and Phillips developed scheme to establish artist and writer colony in Taos; illustrations included James

Mooney's story "Quivera and the Wichitas" for *Harper's Monthly* and *Wards of the Nation—Their First Vacation from School* for *Harper's Weekly*.

1900 Painted color sketches of Isadora Duncan; March: received commission from *Harper's Weekly* to illustrate the Paris Exposition; Spring: saw Paris Exposition's contemporary exhibitions of European and American art; June: played baseball with American art students; August: returned to New York; met Richard Watson Gilder, editor, and began illustrating for *Century* magazine; sent by *Century* to Minnesota and Pennsylvania for series on iron; illustrations included Lincoln Steffens's story "The Old Jim Horse" in *McClure's* and six issues on the Paris Exposition for *Harper's Weekly*.

1901 Exhibited western pictures in Carnegie building studio in New York; Summer: sent by *Century* to Sioux country in Dakota territory to illustrate Dr. Charles Eastman's book *Indian Boyhood*; played baseball with the Sioux; September: spent two months in Taos; December: received *Century* commission to illustrate articles on the Northwest; received illustration commissions for two books: Robert Amis Bennett's *Thyra* and Samuel Merwin's *The Road to Frontenac*; magazine illustrations included Jack London's story "The God of His Fathers" in *McClure's* and the iron series in *Century*.

1902 April: Played in Salmagundi Club vaudeville; May–ca. October: traveled with author Ray Stannard Baker to Montana, Oregon, Washington, Wyoming, and Utah to get material to for *Century*'s Great Northwest article series; returned to Taos; November: exhibited at the Salmagundi Club.

1903 August: Returned to Paris; September–October: traveled to Italy, where he was influenced by Italian primitives; in Paris took criticisms from Lucien Simon and Rene Menard.

1904 April: Met Mary Shepard Greene; July: began portrait of Booth Tarkington; finished illustrations for London's story "The Love of Life" for *McClure's*.

1905 March: Portrait of Tarkington appeared in *The Bookman*; June 29: married Mary Shepard Greene; December: Dayton press covered illustrations of London's story "The Love of Life" in *McClure's*.

1906 Illustrated London's story "The Unexpected" in *McClure's*; July: traveled to New York to reconnect with editors; August: worked on commission for Willa Cather's story "The Namesake" in Frederick MacMonnies's studio in Giverny; December 26: son, Ethan Allen Blumenschein, born, and died two days later.

1907 Second summer in Giverny, hosted by the Frederick Friesekes; published illustrations for O. Henry story in *American Magazine* and for Joseph Conrad and Willa Cather stories in *McClure's*; exhibited *Portrait de Mme Tarkington* at the Paris Salon and *Portrait of a Man* at the Carnegie Institute, Pittsburgh, Pennsylvania; Ellis Parker Butler family visited Paris, commissioned family portrait.

1908 Worked on illustrations for centenary edition of Edgar Allan Poe's *Tales*; exhibited *Portrait d'un artiste dramatique* at the Paris Salon; completed *Portrait of Ellis Parker Butler and Family.*

1909 March: Began Lionel Barrymore family portrait; May: Blumenscheins departed Paris for New York; November 21: daughter, Helen Greene Blumenschein, born; December: *Century* reproduced *Portrait of Ellis Parker Butler and Family* as part of their American Artists series; Poe's *Tales* was published; exhibited Butler portrait at NAD.

1910 Tarkington purchased *The German Tragedian*; Joseph S. Isidor bought small painting from Salmagundi Club exhibition; April: elected Associate Academician (ANA) at NAD; August–November: painted in Taos; "Love of Life" illustrations won Beck Prize at PAFA; *Portrait of Ellis Parker Butler and Family* won Salmagundi Club's Isidor Prize for best portrait; exhibited *The German Tragedian* at NAD; illustrated Edith Wharton story for *Century*.

1911 April: submitted required painting, *Self-Portrait*, and received ANA certificate and status at NAD; August–September: painted in Taos; September: began teaching at the Art Students League; suggested formation of Southwest painter organization to W. H. Simpson, advertising agent for the Atchison, Topeka and Santa Fe Railway (Santa Fe Railway); *Lady in Black* (Mrs. Greene) won Salmagundi Club's Isidor Prize for best portrait; exhibited *Allegory in Honor of a Barrymore Child* at PAFA and AIC.

1912 June–August: Painted in Taos; August–September: joined Mary in Ogunquit, Maine, art colony; *Wise Man, Warrior, and Youth* received Isidor Medal for best figure composition at NAD.

1913 Elected member of AWS (member until 1944); sold *Evening at Taos Pueblo* to Santa Fe Railway; June: Mary and Helen joined Blumenschein in Taos and returned to New York one week later; October: first solo show at the Palace of Governors, Santa Fe; November: returned to New York; exhibited *Semi-Decorative Composition: The Peacemaker* at NAD.

1914 March: Exhibited *The Peacemaker* at PAFA; April: published modernist article "Painting of To-morrow" in *Century*; May: concluded teaching at the Art Students League; June–September: painted in Taos.

1915 *The Peacemaker* and *Wise Man, Warrior, and Youth* awarded silver medal at the Panama-Pacific Exposition (one of twelve artists to receive this award); exhibited *Family Group* [*Portrait of Artist and Family*] in Cincinnati; July–September: painted in Taos; became founding member of the Taos Society of Artists (TSA); exhibited for the first time with painter group the Society of Men Who Paint the Far West.

1916 March 27: Father, W. L. Blumenschein, died in Dayton; elected member National Arts Club; selected juror AWS, chairman of the art committee, Salmagundi Club; July–ca. September: painted in Taos; September: wrote "The Taos Society of Artists," published in *American Magazine of Art*; Santa Fe Railway purchased *Church at Ranchos de Taos*.

1917 Exhibited *The Chief's Two Sons* with the Society of Independent Artists; selected juror for NAD; ca. August–October: painted in Taos; November: won Potter Palmer Gold Medal and $1,000 for *The Chief Speaks* at AIC; *The Oracle* (another title for *The Peacemaker*) was one of three paintings exhibited in Dedication Exhibit of Southwestern Art (for the opening of the new art museum at Santa Fe); exhibited *Juanita of Taos* in Summer Exhibition of Paintings by Contemporary American Artists (loaned by Mr. and Mrs. William Preston Harrison in Los Angeles); exhibited *The Chief Speaks* at PAFA, St. Louis City Art Museum, and Detroit Institute of Art annuals.

1918 Cincinnati Art Museum purchased *The Chief Speaks*; exhibited with Taos Society of Artists at Hotel Majestic Literary and Art Salon in New York; April–October: painted in Taos; participated in Taos artists raffle–Red Cross fund-raiser; solicited range finder paintings for Salmagundi Club's War Service Committee; participated in Liberty Loan program; exhibited *Albedia of Taos* in Fourth Annual Exhibit of

Taos Society of Artists; juror at NAD and for Society of Illustrators' Fourth Special Exhibition at NAC; commissioned by Steinway and Sons for *Indian Suite*, one of series by American painters honoring the great composers.

1919 January–April: Painted at southern Pueblos in Albuquerque; April–June: took painting trip with Phillips to Laguna, Zuni, Painted Desert, and Phoenix; May: exhibited with Victor Higgins, Walter Ufer, and Alexander Phimister Proctor in Paintings and Sculpture by Four Artists of Taos at AIC; July: toured Colorado with Mary and Helen before arrival in Taos; painted portrait of Santa Fe artist Sheldon Parsons; November: bought W. Herbert Dunton's home and returned to New York; *Indian Suite* reproduced in James G. Huneker's *The Steinway Collection of Paintings by American Artists*, together with prose portraits of the great composers.

1920 Moved from New York to New Mexico; January: solo exhibition at Fakir's Club, ASL, New York; three-person exhibition with Ufer and Higgins at Carson Pirie Scott & Co. in Chicago, Milch Galleries in New York, and Buffalo Fine Arts Academy in New York; exhibited *The War Captain in Times of Peace* (original version of *The Gift*) at Corcoran.

1921 *Superstition* won First Altman Prize at NAD.

1922 Won medal for best figure painting for Steinway advertisement (*Indian Suite*) at Art Directors Club's Second Annual Exhibition.

1923 June 6: Founded New Mexico Painters; *The Gift* received prize at NAC.

1924 Chosen to work on Missouri State Capitol murals and executed three murals; exhibited *Superstition* at Fourteenth Venice Biennial.

1925 *The Gift* won Ranger Fund Purchase Prize, NAD; *Sangre de Cristo Mountains* won Second Altman Prize for landscape, NAD; served as juror for NAD.

1926 *Sangre de Cristo Mountains* received one of twelve U.S. silver medals at the Sesquicentennial International Exposition in Philadelphia; opinion piece "Modern Art and the Academy" published February 7, 1926, in the *New York Times*; May: "Origin of the Taos Art Colony," appeared in *Albuquerque Herald*, *Taos Valley News,* and *El Palacio*; served as juror for NAD.

1927 Elected Academician at NAD and gave *The Lake* to NAD as diploma presentation; first solo show, Thirty Paintings by Ernest L. Blumenschein, at Grand Central Art Galleries, New York (show travels through 1931; Art Gallery of Toronto purchased *Sangre de Cristo Mountains*.

1928 October: received Missouri state mural commission to paint portraits of artist George Caleb Bingham and General John A. "Blackjack" Pershing; served as juror for Corcoran Gallery of Art, Washington, D.C.; exhibited *Night Street Scene* in Fourteenth Annual Exhibition of American Art at the Detroit Institute of Arts; exhibited twenty paintings as part of the Southwest exhibition at San Francisco's Palace of the Legion of Honor; exhibited *Star Road and White Sun* at Corcoran Biennial.

1929 *The Burro* awarded Ranger Fund Purchase Prize, NAD; *Adobe Village—Winter* received GCAG's Frank G. Logan Prize ($1,000) for best landscape; participated in NAD exhibition of Ranger Fund paintings at the National Gallery of Art, Washington, D.C.

1930 January–May: Joined Mary and Helen in Paris, and family traveled to Italy and Germany; April: sold small portrait of White Sun to Charles G. Dawes, vice president of the United States (1925–29); began giving art critiques for University of New Mexico's Taos Field School; featured in Virgil Barker's *A Critical Introduction to American Painting* and Eugene Neuhaus's *History and Ideals of American Art*; *Adobe Church* (1929) traveled to Stockholm, Budapest, and Venice.

1931 Provided illustration for Erna Fergusson's, *Dancing Gods: Indian Ceremonials of New Mexico and Arizona*; *Indian Girl Seated by Oven* won Shaw Purchase Prize at the Salmagundi Club and First Logan Prize at NAD; served as juror for Thirtieth Annual Exhibition at Carnegie Institute; October: took two-week painting trip with Helen to Roosevelt Dam, Arizona; completed *Arizona* (later *Arizona Dam*) in studio.

1932 March: Honored with Salmagundi Club dinner hosted by Samuel T. Shaw for *Indian Girl Seated by Oven*; served as juror for NAD and Kansas City Art Institute; exhibited *Adobe Village—Winter* in American Pavilion at Eighteenth Venice Biennial; exhibited *Arizona* at the Thirteenth Exhibition of Contemporary American Oil Paintings at the Corcoran.

1933 Completed *Mojave Desert*; May: became founding member of Heptagon Gallery, first Taos gallery dedicated to modernist art; October: exhibited *Mojave Desert* at Carnegie's Thirty-first Annual; exhibited *Adobe Village—Winter* at 1933 Century of Progress show, AIC.

1934 Exhibited *Canyon Red and Black* in 1934 Century of Progress at AIC; *Eagle Nest Lake* selected for Exhibition of Contemporary Paintings by Artists of the United States at the National Gallery of Canada, Ottawa, Ontario (opened in Ottawa, then traveled); broke with Heptagon Gallery; March: solo exhibition, Landscapes of New Mexico and Arizona, at GCAG; April: Metropolitan Museum of Art purchased *Taos Valley*; received NAC medal for *Arizona*; *Canyon Red and Black* given to Dayton Art Institute.

1935 Submitted sketch of *Jury for the Trial of a Sheepherder for Murder* for Department of Justice mural commission (not accepted); April–May: worked on and completed *Waller Family Portrait* commission in Chicago; December: submitted sketch and won government commission for mural at Walsenburg, Colorado.

1936 Completed *Jury for the Trial of a Sheepherder for Murder*; government approved sketches for Walsenburg Post Office mural.

1937 *Jury for the Trial of a Sheepherder for Murder* awarded medal at NAC, exhibited in Second National Exhibition of American Art, under the auspices of the Municipal Art Committee, New York; October: completed Walsenburg mural; November: installed Walsenburg mural; Ellis Parker Butler died.

1938 May: exhibited *Jury for the Trial of a Sheepherder for Murder* in Museum of Modern Art's Trois Siècles D'Art Aux État-Unis (Three Centuries of American Art); exhibited *Moon, Morning Star, Evening Star*, *Portrait of Pedro*, and *Deserted Mining Camp* at the Twenty-first Venice Biennale; October: Museum of Modern Art purchased *Jury for the Trial of a Sheepherder for Murder*; exhibited *Landscape with Indian Camp* in Golden Jubilee Exhibition, Texas State Fair, Dallas; exhibited *Taos Entertains the Cheyenne* in Paintings and Lithographs by Members of the Original Taos Society of Artists, Tulsa Art Association.

1939 Exhibited *Sheep in Rio Grande Canyon* in Special Exhibition National Academy at NAD; exhibited *Red Symphony* (the retitled *Arizona* painting) at 1939 World's

Fair American Art Today exhibition, New York; MOMA showed *Jury for the Trial of a Sheepherder for Murder* in their Tenth Anniversary Exhibition; exhibited *The Plasterer* in 1939 Golden Gate Exposition, San Francisco; exhibited *The Chief Speaks* in AIC's Half a Century of American Art.

1940 Exhibited *Moon, Morning, and Evening Star* at 1940 Golden Gate International Exposition, Palace of Fine Arts, San Francisco; exhibited *Pedro* in Coronado Exhibition: Contemporary and Retrospective Show, Art Museum, Santa Fe; exhibited *Mountains near Taos* in IBM's Contemporary Art of the United States at Golden Gate International Exposition.

1941 Tarkington gave *The German Tragedian* to the Herron Art Institute, Indianapolis; exhibited *Jury for the Trial of a Sheepherder for Murder* in Sixty Paintings That Won Sixty Prizes, GCAG.

1942 Exhibited *New Mexico Peon* in Artists for Victory show at the Metropolitan Museum of Art (commemorating first anniversary of bombing of Pearl Harbor).

1943 Exhibited *Eagle Nest Lodge* in Fifty Years on 57th Street show at ASL, New York (benefit for the American Red Cross); exhibited *Box Cars and Railroad Tracks* in Painting in the United States at Carnegie; April: Helen enlisted in WAAC.

1944 May: Helen sailed from San Francisco on unnamed WAAC assignment.

1945 Sold *Adobe Village—Winter*, *Woman in Blue*, *The Lone Fisherman*, and *Eagle Nest Lake* to Paul Grafe, Los Angeles; sold *Star Road and White Sun* to the Albuquerque High School; Thomas Gilcrease bought *Ranchos Church with Indians*; exhibited *Railroad Yard* at Carnegie's Painting in the United States; October: Helen discharged from WAAC, returned to Taos.

1946 Exhibited *Enchanted Forest* in Painting in the United States at Carnegie; May: Booth Tarkington died; royalty income from Eastman's *Indian Boyhood* ceased when publisher Little, Brown, and Company decided to forego reprint; October: diagnosed with prostate condition, had surgery in Los Angeles.

1947 January: second surgery in Los Angeles; April: returned to Taos; awarded honorary master of fine arts at the University of New Mexico (UNM); featured with Phillips for pioneering effort in Mabel Dodge Luhan's *Taos and Its Artists*.

1948 Honored with first New Mexico artist retrospective show at Art Museum, Museum of New Mexico (Santa Fe); at opening received honorary fellowship from the School of American Research, Santa Fe (part of retrospective traveled to Kansas City Art Institute); September: Gilcrease purchased *Enchanted Forest*, *Moon, Morning Star, and Evening Star*, *Superstition*, and *Mojave Desert*; December: surgery for ruptured appendix.

1949 Repainted *Rio Grande Gorge Near Taos* (formerly titled *Strength of the Earth*).

1950 Exhibited *Taos Valley* in Metropolitan Museum of Art's Twentieth Century Painters.

1951 Mary suffered heart attack; corresponded with Helen Card regarding illustration career; sent *Self-Portrait* (1948) to Gilcrease; gave critiques at UNM Field School, Taos.

1952 Provided illustration for William A. Keleher's *Turmoil in New Mexico*; exhibited *Adobe Church* (formerly titled *Church at Ranchos* 1929) in Taos Painting Yesterday and Today; exhibited *Downtown Albuquerque* in Museum of New Mexico's Thirty-ninth Annual Exhibition.

1953 Controversy over repainted *Railroad Yard, No. 5*; delivered memorial lecture for Joseph Henry Sharp; gave critiques at UNM Field School, Taos.

1954 H. J. Lutcher Stark purchased *Box Cars and Railroad Tracks*, *Extraordinary Affray*, *Taos Entertains the Cheyennes*, and *Rio Grande, No. 2*; controversy over lack of training in paintings exhibited at revived Taos Artists' Association exhibition at the Stables Gallery in Taos; invited artist to the Museum of Modern Art's Twenty-fifth Anniversary Exhibition, where *Jury for the Trial of a Sheepherder for Murder* was shown; gave critiques at UNM Field School, Taos; wrote introduction for Laura Bickerstaff's *Pioneer Artists of Taos*.

1955 May: Attended debut of Bickerstaff's *Pioneer Artists of Taos* at Taos Bookshop with Phillips.

1956 Elected honorary member of New Mexico Art League; *Indian Sheep Herder* (later titled *Rocky Trail*) received medal of honor from NAC; October: finished new painting, *The Chief Goes Through*.

1957 Exhibited study for *The Chief Goes Through* at the Museum of New Mexico's Tenth Annual Graphics show and won a purchase award; sent painting of *The Chief Goes Through* to NAD and NAC; *The Chief Goes Through* juried into the Museum of New Mexico's Southwestern Artists Annual in Santa Fe; exhibited and spoke at opening of Fifty Years of Art in Taos in Albuquerque; Stark purchased *Ourselves and Taos Neighbors*; provided illustration for William A. Keleher's *Violence in Lincoln County.*

1958 Museum of New Mexico sponsored second Blumenschein retrospective in Taos, Santa Fe, Albuquerque, and Las Cruces; *The Burro* featured in Henry Ward Ranger Centennial Exhibition, sponsored jointly by the Smithsonian Institution and NAD.

1959 Recognized by Madrid's Museum of Modern Art director Enrique Lafuente as "representative head of the Artistic School, a true patriarch of painting," and compared to Spanish artist Ignacio Zuloaga; final exhibition (two-person with daughter, Helen, at Taos Artists' Association's Stables Gallery), Taos.

1960 June 6: Died in Albuquerque.

Exhibition Checklist

Ernest Blumenschein had a penchant for repainting, retitling, and altering his paintings. This idiosyncrasy of his is reflected in the list: the title by which each work is now known is the last title that Blumenschein gave it; earlier titles given to paintings are shown in parentheses. Dates listed indicate when the artist first completed the canvas through the last known repainting.

Ghost Dancer, 1898
Illustration for "Rising Wolf, Ghost Dancer," by Hamlin Garland, *McClure's*, 1899
Gouache and ink on paper
32 × 20 inches
Collection of the Cheekwood Museum of Art, Nashville, Tennessee

Isadora Duncan—Paris Opera, 1900
Gouache on paper
9 × 5 inches
Collection of the New Mexico Museum of Art, Santa Fe
Gift of Helen Greene Blumenschein, 1964

Untitled (Isadora Duncan), 1900
Gouache on paper
9 × 11½ inches
Collection of the New Mexico Museum of Art, Santa Fe
Gift of Helen Greene Blumenschein, 1964

Sitting for a Photograph on Pulpit Terrace, 1903
Illustration for "A Place of Marvels: Yellowstone Park as It Is Now," by Ray Stannard Baker, *Century*, 1903
Gouache on paper
17½ × 12⅞ inches
Courtesy of the Print and Picture Collection, Free Library of Philadelphia, Pennsylvania

Yet the Life That Was within Him, 1904
Illustration for "The Love of Life," by Jack London, *McClure's*, 1905
Oil on canvas
30 × 19 inches
Used with permission of the Kelly Collection of American Illustration

Notre Dame, Paris, 1906
Oil on canvas
10½ × 14¼ inches
Courtesy of the University of New Mexico Art Museum, Albuquerque (74.204)
Gift of Mrs. Julius L. Rolshoven

Our Paris Apartment, ca. 1906
Oil on board
13 × 9¼ inches
Courtesy of Carlsbad Museum and Art Center, Carlsbad, New Mexico (CMAC 1047)
Gift of William and Christine McAdoo

Paris Apartment, ca. 1906
Oil on panel
10 × 8 inches
Courtesy of the Fred Jones Jr. Museum of Art, the University of Oklahoma, Norman
Purchase, Richard H. and Adeline J. Fleischaker Collection, 1996

Portrait of a German Tragedian, 1907
Oil on canvas
57½ × 33 inches
Courtesy of Indianapolis Museum of Art, Indianapolis, Indiana (41.32)
Gift of Booth Tarkington

Untitled (Nude with Drapery), 1907
Oil on canvas
15 × 12 inches
Courtesy of The Albuquerque Museum, Albuquerque, New Mexico
Museum purchase, 1993 General Obligation Bonds (1994.15.1)

Self-portrait, 1911
Oil on canvas
30 × 20 inches
Courtesy of National Academy Museum, New York (111-P)

Evening at Pueblo of Taos, 1913
Oil on canvas
30 × 40 inches
Courtesy of the BNSF Railway

The Peacemaker (also exhibited as *The Orator*), 1913
Oil on canvas
44¼ × 45 inches
Courtesy of The Anschutz Collection

Portrait of the Artist and Family, 1913
Oil on canvas
46 × 45 inches
Collection of the New Mexico Museum of Art, Santa Fe
Gift of Helen Greene Blumenschein, 1982

Church at Ranchos de Taos, 1916
Oil on canvas
45½ x 47½ inches
Courtesy of The Anschutz Collection (exhibited at Denver Art Museum)

The Chief Speaks, 1917
Oil on canvas
47 × 44½ inches
Private Collection

Old Man in White, 1917
Oil on canvas
25½ × 25½ inches
Courtesy of the Museum of the American West and the Institute for the Study of the American West, Autry National Center, Los Angeles, California (98.108.1)

Fifty-seventh Street, New York, 1917
Oil on canvas
14 × 14 inches
Courtesy of the North Carolina Museum of Art, Raleigh
Gift of the North Carolina Art Society (Robert F. Phifer Bequest)

Indian Suite, 1918
Oil on canvas
55½ × 37½ inches
Courtesy of the Steinway Collection, New York

Portrait of Albedia, ca. 1918
Oil on canvas
20 × 16 inches
Courtesy of the Gerald Peters Gallery, Santa Fe, New Mexico

The Gift (*The War Captain in Times of Peace*, 1919), reworked 1922
Oil on canvas
40½ × 40¼ inches
Courtesy of the Smithsonian American Art Museum, Washington, D.C. (1975.86)
Bequest of Henry Ward Ranger through the National Academy of Design, New York

Eagle Fan (left half of *The Chief's Two Sons*, 1915), reworked 1920s
Oil on canvas
34 × 40 inches
Courtesy of the Denver Art Museum, William Sr. and Dorothy Harmsen Collection, Denver, Colorado (2001.446)

Eagle Feather, Prayer Chant (right half of *The Chief's Two Sons*, 1915), reworked 1920s
Oil on canvas
34 × 30 inches
Courtesy of the Lunder Collection, Colby College Museum of Art, Waterville, Maine

The Extraordinary Affray (*Indian Battle*, 1920), reworked 1927
Oil on canvas
50 × 60 inches
Courtesy of the Stark Museum of Art, Orange, Texas (31.30/13)

Star Road and White Sun, 1920
Oil on canvas
42 × 51 inches
Courtesy of The Albuquerque Museum, Albuquerque, New Mexico
Museum purchase, 1985 General Obligation Bonds, Albuquerque High School Collection (1986.50.3)
Gift of the classes of 1943, 1944, and 1945

The Plasterer, 1921
Oil on canvas
48⅛ × 30⅛ inches
Courtesy of the Eiteljorg Museum of American Indians and Western Art, Indianapolis, Indiana

Superstition, 1921
Oil on canvas
41¼ × 45 inches
Courtesy of the Gilcrease Museum, Tulsa, Oklahoma

White Robe and Blue Spruce, 1922
Oil on linen mounted on paperboard
34 1/8 × 28 1/8 inches
The Wichita Center for the Arts Collection, Wichita, Kansas (1928.1)
Purchased with funds provided by the Wichita Art Association Patron Group Subscription

Moon, Morning Star, and Evening Star (*Legend*, 1923), reworked 1931
Oil on canvas
50 × 40 inches
Courtesy of the Gilcrease Museum, Tulsa, Oklahoma

First Snow, ca. 1924
Oil on canvas
17 1/8 × 21 inches
Courtesy of Robert Stamm

Enchanted Forest (*Decorative Landscape with Figures*, 1925; *Aspen Grove*, 1929), finished 1946
Oil on canvas
51 × 35¼ inches
Courtesy of the Gilcrease Museum, Tulsa, Oklahoma

*Penitente Procession (*study for *Sangre de Cristo Mountains)*, ca. 1925
Ink, watercolor, Chinese white on paper mounted on paper
12 × 8 7/8 inches
Collection of the New Mexico Museum of Art, Santa Fe
Gift of Helen Greene Blumenschein, 1985

Sangre de Cristo Mountains, 1925
Oil on canvas
50¼ x 60 inches
Courtesy of The Anschutz Collection; (exhibited at Denver Art Museum)

Two Burros, ca. 1925
Oil on canvas
30 × 25 inches
Private Collection

Village in Winter (study for *Sangre de Cristo Mountains*), 1925
Oil on panel
13½ x 13½ inches
Private Collection; (exhibited at The Albuquerque Museum and Denver Art Museum)

Girl in Rose, 1926
Oil on canvas
30 × 25 inches
Courtesy of The Lunder Collection, Colby College Museum of Art, Waterville, Maine

Indian Girl Seated by Oven (originally *Girl Seated by Oven*, 1926), reworked 1931
Oil on canvas
30 × 25 inches
Private Collection

Mountains near Taos, 1926, reworked 1954
Oil on canvas
22½ × 49½ inches
Courtesy of the Dallas Museum of Art, Dallas, Texas
Gift of Helen Greene Blumenschein

Apache Country, prior to 1927
Oil on canvas
25 × 30½ inches
Private Collection

Haystack, Taos Valley, prior to 1927, reworked 1940
Oil on canvas
24 × 27 inches
Courtesy of the Fred Jones Jr. Museum of Art, University of Oklahoma, Norman
Given in memory of Roxanne P. Thams by William H. Thams, 2003

The Lake, ca. 1927
Oil on canvas
24 1/8 × 27 inches
Courtesy of National Academy Museum, New York (112-P)

Rock of Fire—Afternoon, prior to 1927
Oil on canvas
24 × 27 inches
Private Collection, Washington, D.C.

Adobe Village, Winter (sketch for *Adobe Village, Winter*), 1929
Oil on board
6 1/8 × 8 7/8 inches
Courtesy of the Gerald Peters Gallery, Santa Fe, New Mexico

The Pass, 1929, reworked 1939
Oil on canvas
22 × 28 inches
Collection of the Arizona State University Art Museum, Tempe
Gift of Oliver B. James

Portrait of a Taos Indian, ca. 1929
Oil on canvas
20¼ × 15¼ inches
Courtesy of the Gerald Peters Gallery, Santa Fe, New Mexico

New Mexico Peon (*Taos Plasterer*, 1930), reworked 1934, finished 1942
Oil on canvas
40 × 25 inches
Courtesy of the Gerald Peters Gallery, Santa Fe, New Mexico

The Lake (Fishing on Eagle Nest Lake), 1931
Oil on canvas
30 × 38 inches
Collection of Phoenix Art Museum, Phoenix, Arizona
Museum purchase with funds provided by the Men's Arts Council Western American Endowment Fund

Ourselves and Taos Neighbors (*New Mexico Interior* or *New Mexican Interior,* 1931), reworked 1937 and 1938, finished ca. 1948
Oil on canvas
41 × 50 inches
Courtesy of the Stark Museum of Art, Orange, Texas (31.30/12A)

Canyon Red and Black (study), 1933
Oil on canvas
24⅛ × 27 inches
Courtesy of the Stark Museum of Art, Orange, Texas (31.30/10)

Eagle Nest Lake, No. 4, 1933
Oil on canvas
30 × 40 inches
Courtesy of Michael and Andrea Frost

The Lone Fisherman, 1933
Oil on canvas
40 × 27 inches
Private Collection

Mojave Desert, 1933, reworked ca. 1949
Oil on canvas
32½ × 50¾ inches
Courtesy of the Gilcrease Museum, Tulsa, Oklahoma

Taos Valley, 1933
Oil on canvas
25 × 35 inches
Courtesy of the Metropolitan Museum of Art, George A. Hearn Fund, 1934 (34.61)

Canyon Red and Black, 1934
Oil on canvas
39½ × 44½ inches
Courtesy of The Dayton Art Institute, Dayton, Ohio (1935.14)
Gift of Mr. John G. Lowe

Green Aspen, 1935
Oil on canvas mounted on board
15⅞ × 12 inches
Courtesy of Stark Museum of Art, Orange, Texas (31.30/1)

Mountain Lake (Eagle Nest), 1935
Oil on canvas
29 × 39½ inches
Courtesy of the Denver Art Museum, William Sr. and Dorothy Harmsen Collection, Denver, Colorado (2001.458)

Untitled (study for *Decorative Landscape with Indians*), 1935
Oil on panel
16 × 12 inches
Collection of the New Mexico Museum of Art, Santa Fe
Gift of Helen Greene Blumenschein, 1964

Indians in the Mountains (*Landscape with Indians,* 1936), reworked 1938
Oil on panel
20 × 44½ inches
Courtesy of the J. N. Bartfield Galleries, New York, New York

Jury for the Trial of a Sheepherder for Murder, 1936
Oil on canvas
46 × 30 inches
Courtesy of the Rockwell Museum, Corning, New York
Clara S. Peck Fund purchase (97.13)

Afternoon of a Sheepherder, 1939
Oil on canvas
28 × 50 inches
Courtesy of the National Cowboy and Western Heritage Museum, Oklahoma City, Oklahoma (1976.32)

Sandia Mountains, 1942
Oil on canvas
21 × 25 inches
Private Collection

The Canyon (originally *Strength of the Earth*, 1944, cross-referenced as *Rio Grande Cañon at Taos*), reworked 1949
Oil on canvas
27 x 47 inches
The Eugene B. Adkins Collection at The Fred Jones Jr. Museum of Art, University of Oklahoma, Norman, and the Philbrook Museum of Art, Tulsa, Oklahoma

Rocky Trail (*Sheepherder among the Rocks* or *Indian Sheep Herder*, ca. 1944), reworked 1955
Oil on canvas mounted on Masonite
16 3/8 × 27⅛ inches
Courtesy of the Stark Museum of Art, Orange, Texas (31.30/5)

Railroad Yard—Meeting Called (originally *Railroad Yard*, 1945; later *Railroad Yard, No. 3*, 1951; then *Railroad Yard, No. 5*, 1953), finished 1958
Oil on canvas
31 x 48 inches
Courtesy of the Taos Historic Museums, Taos, New Mexico

Downtown Albuquerque, 1952
Oil on canvas
29 × 39 inches
Courtesy of the University of New Mexico Art Museum, Albuquerque (63.13)
Gift of Helen Greene Blumenschein

The Chief Goes Through, 1956
Oil on canvas
30 × 40 inches
Courtesy of Stark Museum of Art, Orange, Texas (31.30/9)

Notes

1. BUILDING COLOR MUSCLE: THE PATH TO PAINTING, 1874–1909

1. Ernest L. Blumenschein (ELB) to Anne [surname unknown] (sweetheart and fellow art student), June 4, 1904, Ernest L. Blumenschein Papers, Archives of American Art, Smithsonian Institution, Washington, D.C. (hereafter cited as ELB Papers, AAA).
2. Ernest L. Blumenschein, interview by DeWitt M. Lockman, January 18, 1927, Ernest L. Blumenschein File, Dewitt M. Lockman Collection, Nita Stewart Haley Memorial Library, Midland, Tex. (hereafter cited as ELB, Lockman interview 1).
3. Ibid.
4. Ibid.
5. A family photo taken in the mid-1880s when Ernest was about twelve, depicts two more Blumenschein children, Jennette and Carl. The photo and death certificates are the only documentation located to date on Jennette and Carl Blumenschein. Ted Schwarz Papers, Southwest Artists Collection, Special Collections, Archives and Special Collections, Arizona State University, Tempe (hereafter cited as Southwest Collection, Schwarz Papers). Several undated clippings from Dayton newspapers suggest family visits between the Kumler and Blumenschein families. Ernest L. Blumenschein Collection (AC 354), Fray Angélico Chávez History Library, New Mexico History Museum, Santa Fe (hereafter cited as ELB Collection, FACHL). A few drawings showing a Kumler family picnic in the collection of the New Mexico Museum of Art date to the late 1880s. Ernest L. Blumenschein Collection, New Mexico Museum of Art, Santa Fe.
6. ELB, Lockman interview 1; photo of Dayton's 1891 championship football team, *Dayton Daily News*, March 14, 1954, ELB Collection, FACHL.
7. ELB, Lockman interview 1; Helen Greene Blumenschein (HGB), unpublished manuscript, Helen Blumenschein Collection (AC 376), Fray Angélico Chávez History Library, New Mexico History Museum, Santa Fe (hereafter cited as HGB Collection, FACHL). Orville Wright and the Patterson brothers, who founded the National Cash Register Company, would later help establish the Dayton Art Museum.
8. The poem was "Our Martyred Soldiers," published on June 8, 1888. Virginia Cunningham, *Paul Laurence Dunbar and His Song* (New York: Biblio and Tannen, 1969 [c1947]), 28. Courtesy of Nancy Horlacher, local history specialist, Dayton Metro Library, Dayton, Ohio.
9. Dunbar was also class president. He graduated with honors from Central High and wrote the class song, which was printed on the back of the commencement program and was sung at commencement on June 16, 1891. ELB Collection, FACHL; Dayton Metro Library, "Paul Laurence Dunbar Collection: Images," http://home.dayton.lib.oh.us/Archives/Dunbar/ExhPaulDunbar.html.

10. ELB, Lockman interview 1. The drawing can be seen at http://home.dayton.lib.oh.us/Archives/Dunbar/art/DPhilom1-ex.JPG.

11. ELB, Lockman interview 1. Eugene "Zim" Zimmerman (1862–1935), one of the late nineteenth century's most respected cartoonists, worked first for *Puck*, then for *Judge* magazine. A true original, he was known as the developer of the grotesque school of caricature. He founded the American Association of Cartoonists and Caricaturists, and was its first president.

12. Puzzle Editor, *Harper's Young People,* to ELB, June 4, 1891, ELB Collection, FACHL.

13. "At the Art School," *Cincinnati Tribune*, June 1, 1893, Art Academy of Cincinnati Archives, Mary R. Schiff Library, Cincinnati Art Museum, Cincinnati, Ohio.

14. ELB, Lockman interview 1.

15. Ibid.

16. After the trial period, this class was officially added to the curriculum. The class description appeared in the *Art Academy of Cincinnati Catalogue*, *1893–1894*, copy in the Art Academy of Cincinnati Archives.

17. ELB, Lockman interview 1.

18. Ibid. See Emanuel Rubin, "Jeanette Meyers Thurber and the National Conservatory of Music," *American Music* (Autumn 1990): 294–325.

19. For an overview of the school's history, see "A Brief History of the League's Early Years," www.theartstudentsleague.org.

20. There were over a dozen art schools and clubs that offered studio instruction in New York by 1893. The Art Students League was both the finest and the most accommodating. See Raymond J. Steiner, *The Art Students League of New York: A History* (Saugerties, N.Y.: CSS Publications, 1999), 59–67.

21. Ibid., 67.

22. "Exhibitions Nearing a Close: Narrow Policies of the Academy as Regards New Members," *New York Times*, May 12, 1893.

23. "The Splendid School Exhibit: New York Takes the Lead, Particularly in the Work of Its Art Classes," *New York Times*, May 27, 1893.

24. ELB, Lockman interview 1.

25. Tucker began studying with Twachtman in 1890. He later became an instructor at the Art Students League. Allen Tucker, "The Art Students League: An Experiment in Democracy," 13, Art Students League Records, 1875–1955, reel NY59-207: 23, Art Students League of New York Archives (hereafter cited as Art Students League Records).

26. For a discussion of Twachtman's critical stature and emotional status in the early 1890s, see Lisa Peters, *John Twachtman (1853–1902): A "Painter's Painter,"* (New York: Spanierman Gallery, 2006), 19–29, 62–66.

27. Lionel Barrymore, *We Barrymores* (New York: Grosset and Dunlap, 1951), 44.

28. Beckwith taught at the Art Students League between 1878 and 1897. He was noted for his love of "everything to do with the League." After he retired, he often visited his old classroom, where he would talk to the students, look at their work, and make drawings for them. Christian Buchheit, "Recollections of Christian Buchheit, ASL Instructor from 1893–1900," Art Students League Records, reel NY59-207: 82.

29. See Alexander Phimister Proctor, *Sculptor in Buckskin* (Norman: University of Oklahoma Press, 1971), 86–87.

30. Buchheit, "Recollections," 81.

31. H. Wayne Morgan, *Kenyon Cox, 1856–1919: A Life in American Art* (Kent: Kent State University Press, 1994), 86.

32. See Steiner, *Art Students League*, 84, 89, 91–92.

33. ELB, Lockman interview 1.

34. Alphaeus Cole, "An Adolescent in Paris: The Adventure of Being an Art Student Abroad in the Late 19th Century," *American Art Journal* 8, no. 2 (1976): 114.

35. This is recounted in a handwritten biographical outline, "Ernest L. Blumenschein," thought to have been compiled by Reginald Fisher, curator of art at the Museum of Mexico in 1948. ELB Papers, AAA.

36. Edwin H. Blashfield, "Jean-Paul Laurens," in *Modern French Masters*, ed. John C. Van Dyke (New York: Century, 1896), 90.

37. Barrymore, *We Barrymores*, 118.

38. Cole, "An Adolescent in Paris," 112.

39. Ibid., 112, 114.

40. Ernest L. Blumenschein, handwritten script, Southwest Collection, Schwarz Papers; see also Laura M. Bickerstaff, *Pioneer Artists of Taos* (1955; reprint, Denver: Old West Publishing, 1983), 33–34.

41. ELB, Lockman interview 1; scrapbook, ELB Collection, FACHL.

42. Unidentified Dayton newspaper clipping [May 1896]: L. B. Gunkel, letter to the editor, "Two Dayton Boys: Something of What They Have Accomplished in the Old Country: George Compton and Ernest Blumenschein, Who Are Now Studying in Paris, France," May 14, 1896. ELB Papers, AAA.

43. The painting is listed as *Devant Saint-Antoine* in the *Catalogue Illustre de Peinture et Sculpture: Salon de 1896* (Paris: Librairie D'Art, 1896).

44. Unidentified Cincinnati newspaper clipping [probably the *Cincinnati Enquirer*]: "Honored: Cincinnati Painters: Who Have Won Recognition in Paris Salons: Pictures by Sharp, Winters, and Blumenschein Find Place," [May 1896], ELB Papers, AAA.

45. ELB Papers, AAA; ELB, Lockman interview 1.

46. Quote from Albert Keiser, author of *The Indian in American Literature* (New York, 1933), cited in Owen J. Reamer, "Hamlin Garland and the Indians," in *Critical Essays on Hamlin Garland*, comp. James Nagel (Boston: G. K. Hall, 1982), 301n1.

47. Hamlin Garland, "General Custer's Last Fight as Seen by Two Moon," *McClure's* 11, no. 5 (1898): 443–48.

48. Garland continued to write in this vein and to attract Blumenschein in similar fashion. See Garland's "Sitting Bull's Defiance," *McClure's* 19, no. 1 (1902): 35–40. For a thoughtful discussion of the two perspectives, see Brian W. Dippie, "Brush, Palette and the Custer Battle," *Montana Magazine* 24, no. 1 (1974): 55–63.

49. Blumenschein's illustration *Wards of the Nation—Their First Vacation from School* appeared on the cover of the June 17, 1899, *Harper's Weekly*. It accompanied a report titled "Wards of the State—Their First Vacation from School."

50. Garland finally found a publisher for his Indian tales in the early 1920s. When Harper and Brothers published his collection as *The Book of the American Indian* in 1923, the company chose Frederic Remington's works to illustrate the volume. Garland disapproved of Remington's depictions of Indian people: "I

don't like him or his illustrations. His red men and trappers are all drawn from one model. . . . [H]is red men are savages without being graceful. He does not see the Western men and Indians as I see them." Reamer, "Hamlin Garland," 289. On the federal assimilation policy, see Skip Keith Miller, "*Superstition* and the Artist's Defense of Native Rights," this volume.

51. Gerhard Keller, rev. of *The Indian Man: A Biography of James Mooney,* by L. G. Moses (University of Illinois Press, 1984), *American Anthropologist* 88 (March 1986): 239. Among other books, anthropologist James Mooney authored *The Ghost Dance and the Sioux Outbreak of 1890* (Smithsonian Institution, 1896), *Calendar History of Kiowa Indians* (Smithsonian Institution, 1898), and *Myths of the Cherokee* (Smithsonian Institution, 1900). His work must have inspired Garland's western journeys to the same locales to gather information for his Indian stories. Garland knew Dr. Charles A. Eastman; in the early 1900s he recommended that Roosevelt appoint Eastman to carry out social reform field work under the Bureau of Indian Affairs. See Reamer, "Hamlin Garland"; and Lonnie E. Underhill and Daniel F. Littlefield, Jr., *Hamlin Garland's Observations on the American Indian* (Tempe: University of Arizona Press, 1976), 46–47. Blumenschein illustrated James Mooney's "Quivera and the Wichitas," which appeared in *Harper's Monthly*, June 1899.
52. ELB Papers, AAA.
53. Benjamin Eisenstat qtd. in Walt and Roger Reed, *The Illustrator in America, 1890–1900: A Century of Illustration* (New York: Published for the Society of Illustrators by Madison Square Press, 1984), 28. See also Arpi Ermoyan, *Famous American Illustrators* (New York: Watson-Guptill, 1997), 6–7.
54. ELB, Lockman interview 1.
55. Bert Phillips, "The Broken Wheel, or How Art Came to New Mexico," typescript, 1948, Southwest Collection, Schwarz Papers.
56. Their inexperience led to the death of the third horse. They had improperly tethered the animal, and it strangled while trying to get to water. Helen Greene Blumenschein, "Introduction to the Taos Artists Era," unpublished manuscript, HGB Collection, FACHL; Ernest L. Blumenschein, "Origins of the Taos Art Colony," *Albuquerque Herald*, May 10, 1926.
57. ELB, Lockman interview 1.
58. Ibid.
59. Blumenschein wrote on the back of a photograph of the broken wheel, "and a history making episode began." Blumenschein Papers, Gilcrease Museum Archives, Tulsa, Okla. (hereafter cited as ELB Papers, Gilcrease).
60. Ernest L. Blumenschein, interview by DeWitt M. Lockman, January 22, 1927, Ernest L. Blumenschein file, Dewitt M. Lockman Collection, Nita Stewart Haley Memorial Library, Midland, Tex. (hereafter cited as ELB, Lockman interview 2); quote in Mason Sutherland, "Adobe New Mexico," *National Geographic* (December 1949): 785. Courtesy of Nancy Butler Waller Nadler.
61. ELB, Lockman interview 1; ELB, Lockman interview 2.
62. *The Taos Cresset*, November 24, 1898.
63. Blumenschein's article, "San Geronimo: The Pueblo Indian's Holiday," took up most of page

1207; his illustrations appeared on pages 1204 and 1205. *Harper's Weekly*, December 10, 1898.

64. Ernest L. Blumenschein, handwritten biographical account, reel 270, frame 167, ELB Papers, AAA.

65. Typescript, ELB Papers, AAA; *Dayton Daily News*, May 12, 1899, ELB Collection, FACHL.

66. Ibid.; unidentified newspaper clipping: "Interesting Exhibit—Blumenschein's Pictures at Dayton Club," n.d., ELB Collection, FACHL.

67. Unidentified Albuquerque newspaper clipping, scrapbook, ELB Collection, FACHL.

68. Butler's articles appeared under this byline in *Redbook*. Katherine Harper, "The Man from Muscatine: A Bio-Bibliography of Ellis Parker Butler," (PhD diss., Bowling Green State University, August 2000), 11.

69. Ibid., 14.

70. "Ernest Blumenschein," *Dayton Daily Journal*, January 9, 1899.

71. Blumenschein and Phillips included Butler in their plans for establishing an art colony. Phillips also wrote about Butler in this regard. See Phillips to ELB, January 15, March 30, September 25, and November 26, 1899, in Julie Schimmel and Robert R. White, *Bert Geer Phillips and the Taos Art Colony* (Albuquerque: University of New Mexico Press, 1994), appendix B.

72. ELB to Butler, January 16, 1900, ELB Collection, FACHL.

73. Cole, "An Adolescent in Paris," 114.

74. ELB notes, courtesy of Shirley Greene Davis.

75. ELB to Butler, September 20, 1899; October 1899; November 26, 1899; January 16, 1900; March 5, 1900, ELB Collection, FACHL.

76. *Harper's Weekly* 44, no. 2263 (1900): 214–15.

77. ELB, handwritten biographical account; ELB, Lockman interview 1.

78. ELB to Butler, September 30 and October 8, 1900, ELB Collection, FACHL.

79. Rosamond Gilder, ed., *Letters of Richard Watson Gilder* (Boston: Houghton Mifflin Company, 1916), 102.

80. ELB, Lockman interview 1.

81. Ibid.

82. Eastman and his wife, Elaine Goodale Eastman, later collaborated on *Wigwam Evenings: Sioux Folk Tales Retold*. (Boston: Little, Brown, 1909). The book was illustrated by Edwin Willard Deming.

83. ELB to Butler, September 4, 1901, ELB Collection, FACHL.

84. Ernest L. Blumenschein, handwritten dedication for Charles Eastman's *Indian Boyhood*, Center for Southwest Research, University of New Mexico, Albuquerque.

85. Ibid.

86. Rev. of *Indian Boyhood*, by Charles Eastman, *New York Times*, September 27, 1902.

87. ELB to Drake, September 1, 1901, ELB Papers, AAA.

88. Ibid.

89. Ibid.

90. ELB, handwritten biographical account.

91. Ibid.

92. Ibid.

93. ELB to Butler, October 31, 1903, ELB Collection, FACHL.

94. Ibid.

95. ELB, Lockman interview 1.

96. The author is indebted to painter and sculptor George Carlson for his illuminating remarks on the technical aspects of painting and the painter's perspective. Carlson and the author

have had a running conversation about the painter's perspective that has informed painting discussion here and in other of the author's painting descriptions.

97. ELB to Butler, October 31 and December 5, 1903, and February 7, 1904, ELB Collection, FACHL.

98. Helen Greene Blumenschein, interview with the author, fall 1986.

99. ELB to Butler, May 3, 1904, ELB Collection, FACHL.

100. Raymond Bouyer, "L'Indépendance au Salon official de la Société des Artistes français," *Revue Bleu*, May 10, 1902, Mary Greene Blumenschein Collection (AC 410), Fray Angélico Chávez History Library, New Mexico History Museum, Santa Fe (hereafter cited as MGB Collection, FACHL).

101. Nourse to Mary Greene Blumenschein (MGB), June 2, 1901, MGB Collection, FACHL.

102. See discussion in "Tradition and Professionalism: North America" in Delia Gaze, ed., *Dictionary of Women Artists*, vol. 1 (Chicago: Fitzroy Dearborn, 1997).

103. "Medals and Diplomas for American Artists in Europe Awaiting Distribution," August 1, [1904], Elizabeth Nourse Papers, Archives of American Art, Smithsonian Institution, Washington, D.C. (hereafter cited as Nourse Papers).

104. Unidentified newspaper clipping: "Art Awards at St. Louis Fair," [1904], MGB Collection, FACHL.

105. William Leonard Blumenschein to ELB, January 12, 1905, Ernest L. Blumenschein Collection, Taos Historic Museums, Taos, N.M. (hereafter cited as ELB Collection, THM).

106. ELB to Butler, April 30, 1905, ELB Collection, FACHL.

107. *New York Herald*, June 30, 1905, Nourse Papers; *Brooklyn Daily Eagle*, May 28, 1905, MGB Collection, FACHL.

108. ELB to Butler, September 3, 1905, ELB Collection, FACHL.

109. Ibid.

110. Boyden to ELB, November 29, 1905, ELB Collection, THM.

111. London to ELB, November 23, 1905, ELB Collection, THM.

112. Unidentified Dayton newspaper clippings: "Success" and "E. L. Blumenschein," [1905], ELB Collection, THM.

113. Pound to ELB, December 13 [1905], ELB Collection, THM.

114. ELB to Butler, April 27, 1906, ELB Collection, FACHL.

115. ELB to Butler, December 13, 1906, ELB Collection, FACHL.

116. ELB to Butler, January 15, 1905, ELB Collection, FACHL.

117. Jack London, "The Unexpected," *McClure's*, August 1906; O. Henry, "The World and the Door," *American Magazine*, August 1907; Joseph Conrad, "The Brute," *McClure's*, November 1907; Willa Sibert Cather, "The Namesake," *McClure's*, March 1907.

118. Other books included *The Praying Skipper and Other Stories,* by Ralph D. Paine (1906), and *Come and Find Me,* by Elizabeth Robins (1908).

119. MGB to the Butlers, ca. June 8, 1908, ELB Collection, FACHL.

120. A full-length, full-page portrait of Mary, under the caption "She Read from the New Testament," appears in *McClure's* August 1906 issue. Sometime, probably before their move to Taos in 1919, Blumenschein so altered the painting that only Mary's face from that

portrait survived. It is now in the collection of the New Mexico Art Museum in Santa Fe.

121. Mary also painted a portrait of Louisa. It won acclaim later in New York and is now in the collection of the Indianapolis Art Museum.

122. Nicholas Kilmer (grandson of the Friesekes), correspondence with the author, October 19, 2006.

123. Nicholas Kilmer et al., *Frederick Carl Frieseke: The Evolution of an American Impressionist* (Savannah, Ga. : Telfair Museum of Art, 2001), 32.

124. ELB to Butler, May 1906, ELB Collection, FACHL.

125. The story "The Namesake," appeared in *McClure's* in March 1909.

126. See Polly Duryea, "Paintings and Drawings in Willa Cather's Prose: A Catalogue Raisonné" (PhD diss., University of Nebraska, Lincoln, 1993).

127. ELB to Butler, September 10, 1907, ELB Collection, FACHL.

128. MGB to the Butlers, ca. June 8, 1908, ELB Collection, FACHL.

129. Qtd. in Van Deren Coke, *Taos and Santa Fe: The Artist's Environment, 1882–1942* (Albuquerque: University of New Mexico Press, 1963), 22.

130. Peter H. Hassrick was the first to recognize the unnamed collector as Leo Stein.

131. Ernest L. Blumenschein, "The Painting of To-morrow," *Century* 87, no. 6 (1914): 847–48. See Jerry N. Smith, "Modernism and the Art of Ernest L. Blumenschein," this volume.

132. ELB to Butler, December 13, 1908, and January 18, 1909, ELB Collection, FACHL.

133. ELB, Lockman interview 1.

134. ELB to Butler, [March] 22, 1909, ELB Collection, FACHL.

135. Ibid.

136. ELB to "Folks," May 10, 1909, ELB Collection, THM.

137. ELB to Butler, June 27, 1909, ELB Collection, FACHL.

138. ELB to Butler, July 20 and August 6, 1909, ELB Collection, FACHL; Methodist church concert program, Ogunquit, Maine, August 9, 1909, ELB Collection, FACHL.

139. Birth announcement on Salmagundi Club letterhead, 1909, ELB Collection, FACHL.

140. "A Few Excellent Figure Subjects in the Academy Exposition" *New York Times*, December 19, 1909, ELB Papers, AAA.

141. This article on celebrated Daytonians included biographies of Blumenschein's father and his former schoolmates the Wright brothers and Paul Laurence Dunbar. "Father and Son: Composer and Artist," *Dayton Daily News*, June 16, 1909, ELB Collection, THM.

2. IN SEARCH OF THE REAL THING: BLUMENSCHEIN IN THE 1910S

1. ELB, Lockman interview 2, p. 3.

2. See Peter Hastings Falk, ed., *The Annual Exhibition Record of the National Academy of Design, 1901–1950* (Madison, Conn.: Sound View Press, 1990), 85–86; and M. F. Robinson, "The Fall Academy in Detail," *Craftsman* 23, no. 5 (1913): 564–65. The duo also exhibited in Philadelphia in 1909 and 1910. See Falk, *Annual Exhibition Record*, 95.

3. Unidentified newspaper clipping, 1909: "A Few Excellent Figure Subjects in the Academy Exposition—J. W. Alexander's Fine 'Sunlight,'" ELB Papers, AAA. See also Robinson, "Fall Academy," 565, for a comparison of Blumenschein's submission with that of his wife, Mary, and two paintings by his cohort E. Irving Couse.
4. Blumenschein had earlier expressed a similar, unrealistic desire. In a letter to Butler he indicated that his studies at the Louvre might hopefully result in his being able to abandon illustration for a career in painting. No such ambition occurred until the late 1910s. See ELB to Butler, January 16, 1900, Southwest Collection, Schwarz Papers.
5. Arthur Hoeber, "National Academy of Design, Winter Exhibition," *Art and Progress* 1 (February 1910): 92.
6. Julie Schimmel, *The Art and Life of W. Herbert Dunton* (Austin: University of Texas Press, 1984), 35–36.
7. ELB, Lockman interview 2, p. 3.
8. Edgar Allan Poe, *Tales* (New York: Duffield, 1909).
9. Gilder, *Letters of Richard Watson Gilder,* 402.
10. ELB, Lockman interview 2, pp. 3–4.
11. "Prize Pictures at Academy," *New York Times*, March 13, 1910.
12. Unidentified New York newspaper clipping: "The Spring Academy," March 16, 1910, ELB Papers, AAA.
13. See Betty Blythe, "Genius of Tarkington Revealed Again in Home Decorations," *Indianapolis Star*, January 19, 1913, Women Section, p. 1; "The Artist Colony Corner," *Taos Valley News*, November 12, 1910.
14. I am grateful for these insights to Barrymore biographer Margot Peters.
15. Gest to ELB, April 6, 1910, Southwest Collection, Schwarz Papers.
16. Blanche C. Grant, *When Old Trails Were New* (Chicago: Rio Grande Press, 1963), 259.
17. ELB, Lockman interview 2, p. 3.
18. Ibid.
19. Ernest L. Blumenschein, interview by Reginald Fisher, 1948, p. 7 (hereafter cited as ELB, Fisher interview), ELB Papers, AAA.
20. "The Artists' Colony Corner," *Taos Valley News,* August 20, 1910.
21. ELB to Butler, October 1899, Southwest Collection, Schwarz Papers.
22. See Chas. F. Lummis, "The Artists' Paradise," part 2, *Out West* 22, no. 3 (1908): 191; Nina Spalding Stevens, "Pilgrimage to the Artist's Paradise," *Fine Arts Journal* (February 1911): 113.
23. ELB to Simpson, October 26, 1910, Burlington Northern Santa Fe Railroad Archives, Fort Worth, Tex.
24. "The Artist's Colony Corner," *Taos Valley News,* November 12, 1910.
25. I am grateful to David A. Kiehn for providing information about the original format and use of this image.
26. These qualities were discussed in "The Artist's Colony Corner," *Taos Valley News,* December 9, 1911.
27. See James Moore, foreword to *Eanger Irving Couse: Image Maker for America,* by Virginia Couse Leavitt (Albuquerque: Albuquerque Museum, 1991), ix.
28. For a discussion of the complex nature of this painting, see Schimmel and White, *Bert Geer Phillips*, 147.

29. ELB to Simpson, June 11, 1911, Southwest Collection, Schwarz Papers.

30. Everett Carroll Maxwell, "Genre and Figure Painters of the Southwest," *Fine Arts Journal* (April 1911): 249.

31. I am grateful to Annie McDonald of the Taos Historic Museums for information about the Scheurich House.

32. Bert Phillips, "The Taos Art Colony," published in Schimmel and White, *Bert Geer Phillips*, 321–22.

33. For Blumenschein's accounting of the event, see Ernest L. Blumenschein, interview by DeWitt M. Lockman, January 24, 1927, Ernest L. Blumenschein file, Dewitt M. Lockman Collection, Nita Stewart Haley Memorial Library, Midland, Tex. (hereafter cited as ELB, Lockman interview 3).

34. J. M. Bernal, "Blumenschein in the Early Days," *The Horse Fly, Smallest and Most Inadequate Paper Ever Published*, June 23, 1960, Southwest Collection, Schwarz Papers.

35. For more information on this relationship, see Schimmel, *Art and Life of W. Herbert Dunton*, 35–36.

36. Royal Cortissoz, *Annual of the Society of Illustrators* (New York: Charles Scribner's Sons, 1911), x, xii.

37. Ibid., xiv.

38. Helen Greene Blumenschein, "Recuerdos: Early Days of the Blumenschein Family," unpublished typescript, 1979, 8, College of Santa Fe Library, Santa Fe, N.M.

39. One such reference is quoted in Laura M. Bickerstaff, *Pioneer Artists of Taos* (Denver: Old West Publishing, 1983), 38.

40. See Nancy Mowll Mathews, *Mary Cassatt* (New York: Harry N. Abrams, 1987), 113.

41. E. Blumenschein, "Painting of To-morrow," 846.

42. See William T. Henning, Jr., *Ernest L. Blumenschein Retrospective* (Colorado Springs: Colorado Springs Fine Art Center, 1978), 18.

43. I am grateful to Jim Moore for providing some of these insights into the interpretation of this painting.

44. Ibid.

45. *Taos Valley News*, August 17, 1912.

46. If Denver provided an impetus, two other organizations supplied the structural armature on which to build the concept of an artists' society. Blumenschein and other Taos artists were familiar with the Society of Western Artists in Chicago and the Society of Men Who Paint the Far West in New York. Blumenschein belonged to the latter. See Dean Porter, Teresa Hayes Ebie, Suzan Campbell, et al., *Taos Artists and Their Patrons, 1898–1950* (Notre Dame, Ind.: Snite Museum of Art, 1999), 30–39.

47. One critic compared the Blumenschein to Couse paintings of the period as follows: *Wise Man, Warrior, and Youth* was regarded as "excellent in composition, excellent in color, excellent in characterization. The portraiture of race has been properly subordinated to the pictorial quality and the relations of the dark masses to the light have been so well considered that the arrangement has a monumental character and the dignity in which the Indian picture by E. Irving Couse . . . is deficient. The drawing of the individual figures, the youth, in particular, is spirited, however, and suggests the ideal of the type without disregarding realism. Mr. Couse's picture, 'Making Pottery,' is illustrative in tendency,

and somewhat overmodeled, but it has popular interest and tells its story entertainingly." See unidentified newspaper clipping: "Art Jury to Judge Paintings Tomorrow," [ca. 1913], ELB Papers, AAA.

48. ELB to Simpson, March 26, 1913, Southwest Collection, Schwarz Papers.
49. The final sales agreement was completed on October 28, 1913. Southwest Collection, Schwarz Papers.
50. "Two Other Celebrated Artists Arrive in Taos to Join the Artists' Colony," *Taos Valley News*, June 7, 1913.
51. H. Blumenschein, "Recuerdos," 18.
52. "A Successful Art Colony on the Edge of the Desert That Had Its Beginning as an Adventure on an Overland Trip," *New York Evening Post*, January 30, 1920.
53. "Blumenschein's Fine Exhibition," *Santa Fe New Mexican*, October 24, 1913. See also "Fine Art Exhibit in the Museum," *El Palacio* 1, no. 1 (1913): 4, which predicted that one of the paintings, *The Peacemaker,* would create a critical stir in the East.
54. Ibid. The *Taos News,* March 24, 1914, also refers to this work for its "decorative note."
55. Ernest Peixotto, "The Field of Art," *Scribner's* 54, no. 2 (1913): 258–59.
56. E. Blumenschein, "Painting of Tomorrow," 846.
57. See Patricia Trenton, *Picturesque Images of Taos and Santa Fe* (Denver: Denver Art Museum, 1974), 30.
58. Charles C. Eldredge, "Ernest Blumenschein's *The Peacemaker:* Native Americans, Greeks, and Jurisprudence circa 1913," *American Art* 15, no. 1 (2001): 37.
59. E. Blumenschein, "Painting of To-morrow," 845. Couse, who had executed a similarly ambitious painting, *Return of War Party* (ca. 1910), expressed a preference for golden hues, thus suggesting a passing era, reverie and remembrance rather than the promise of a fresh future.
60. Qtd. in Bickerstaff, *Pioneer Artists of Taos*, 46.
61. Walter Pach, "The Point of View of the 'Moderns,'" *Century* 89, no. 6 (1914): 851–64. Kuhn is quoted in Barbara Rose, *American Art Since 1900: A Critical History* (New York: Frederick A. Praeger, 1967), 70.
62. John W. Alexander, "Is Our Art Distinctively American?" *Century* 89, no. 6 (1914): 827.
63. Kenyon Cox, "Artist and Public," *Scribner's* 55 (April 1914): 512–20. For a full discussion of the traditionalist viewpoint, see Morgan, *Kenyon Cox,* 220–23.
64. Richard Gilder, "This Transitional Age in Art," *Century* 89, no. 6 (1914): 825.
65. E. Blumenschein, "Painting of To-morrow," 845–50.
66. See Max Weber, "The Fourth Dimension from a Plastic Point of View," *Camera Work* (July 31, 1910): 25.
67. Morton Schamberg, "Post-Impressionism Exhibit Awaited," *Philadelphia Inquirer*, January 19, 1913.
68. "Blumenschein Interviewed," *El Palacio* 6, no. 6 (1919): 84.
69. See *Taos Valley News*, June 1, 1915, July 6, 1915.
70. ELB to Simpson, July 11, 1915, Southwest Collection, Schwarz Papers.
71. Arrell Morgan Gibson, *The Santa Fe and Taos Colonies: Age of the Muses, 1900–1942* (Norman: University of Oklahoma Press, 1983), 29.
72. The Taos Society of Artists' constitution and by-laws are quoted in full in Robert W. White,

The Taos Society of Artists (Albuquerque: University of New Mexico Press, 1998), 17–19.

73. Kenneth M. Adams, "Los Ocho Pintores," *Mexico Quarterly* 21, no. 2 (1952): 148.

74. ELB to Simpson, July 11, 1915, Southwest Collection, Schwarz Papers.

75. "Exhibit of Taos Artists Will Be Notable," *Taos Valley News*, September 7, 1915.

76. "Artists' Rule for Success—Begin Young, Work Hard, and Keep at It," *Dayton Journal*, October 3, 1915.

77. Ibid.

78. See, e.g., the National Arts Club's shows 3rd Special Exhibition, Society of Illustrators (New York, October–November 1912), 4th Special Exhibition, Society of Illustrators (New York October–November 1913), and Retrospective Exhibition of Life Members (New York, January 1919) in which Blumenschein participated.

79. Henry Z. Steinway, correspondence with Elizabeth J. Cunningham, December 18, 2002. *Indian Suite* appeared in *The Steinway Collection of Paintings by American Artists*, by James Huneker, in 1919. Steinway used Blumenschein's painting *An Interpretation of MacDowell's* Indian Suite to illustrate a full-page ad placed in the March 1922 issue of *Literary Digest*.

80. Paul A. F. Walter, "The Santa Fe–Taos Art Movement," *Art and Archaeology* 4 (December 1916): 330.

81. Ibid. Similar sentiments were finding voice in other venues such as Frederic J. Haskin's article "New Mexican Village Becomes Art Colony," *The Railroad Red Book* 34, no. 4 (1917): 11 (Western History Collection, Denver Public Library), in which the author presents Taos as "a center of American art" whose artists represent "a new and native school of painting" and are realizing a truly "American art form."

82. See Virginia Couse Leavitt, "Taos and the American Art Colony Movement: The Search for an American School of Art," *Ayer y Hoy en Taos* (Winter 1987): 3–8.

83. Birger Sandzen, "The Southwest as a Sketching Ground," *Fine Arts Journal* 33, no. 2 (1915): 333.

84. Phillips, "Taos Art Colony," 1.

85. See Walter Ufer, "Taos, New Mexico—It's Artist Colony," *The Railroad Red Book* 39, no. 1 (1922): 323. Others wrote along similar lines; see, e.g., J. Keely, "Real American Art—At Last!" *Chicago Sunday Herald*, April 25, 1917.

86. Sandzen, "Southwest as a Sketching Ground."

87. See Reginald Fisher, "Museum's First Retrospective Exhibition," *El Palacio* 55, no. 6 (1948): 163–68; and Howard Cook, "Ernest L. Blumenschein: The Artist in His Environment," *New Mexico Quarterly* (Spring 1949): 21.

88. Edward Watts-Russell, "Chicago Institute Exhibition," *American Art News* 16, no. 7 (1917): 1.

89. Lena M. McCauley, "30th Annual Exhibibion: An Index of Change," *Chicago Evening Post*, November 13, 1917.

90. Ernest L. Blumenschein, *Blumenschein: A Self-Portrait* (San Francisco: Richard Finnie, 1946), [16].

91. "Art Circles," *Cincinnati Enquirer*, October 27, 1918.

92. John Sloan, *Gist of Art* (New York: American Artists Group, 1939), 13.

93. Ernest L. Blumenschein, "The Taos Society of Artists," *American Magazine of Art* 8, no. 11 (1917): 448–49.
94. Ibid.
95. Couse to Blackton, May 5, 1916, Couse Family Archives, Taos, N.M. For a full discussion of this painting, see Leavitt, *Eanger Irving Couse*, 176–79.
96. Henry McBride, "Taos Society Exhibition," *New York Herald*, November 1920.
97. See E. Blumenschein, *Blumenschein*, [2]; and ELB to Thomas Gilcrease, August 7, 1951, ELB Papers, Gilcrease. Eldredge, "Ernest Blumenschein's *The Peacemaker*," 37–38, provides an interesting discussion on how Blumenschein's feelings about acculturation changed from the late nineteenth century to the mid-1910s.
98. See Simpson to ELB, January 4, 1917, and ELB to Simpson, March 27, 1917, Burlington Northern Santa Fe Railroad Archives, Fort Worth, Tex.
99. For architectural historian George Kubler, artists who recorded its contours did so in order to "capture something essential about the nature of New Mexico." See Kubler's foreword to *Spirit and Vision: Images of Rancho de Taos Church,* by Sandra D'Emilio and Suzan Campbell (Santa Fe: Museum of New Mexico Press, 1988).
100. E. Blumenschein, "Taos Society of Artists," 445.
101. Frederic J. Haskin, e.g., refers to "the town of Taos" as a true "old time city of adobe built in the purest American style." Haskin, "New Mexican Village," 11.
102. "Taos Art Colony," *Taos Valley News*, March 24, 1913.
103. Qtd. in J. Keeley, "Real American Art—At Last," *Chicago Sunday Herald*, April 15, 1917.
104. Carlos Vierra, "New Mexico Architecture," *Art and Archaeology* 7 (January/February 1918): 42. See also D'Emilio and Campbell, *Spirit and Vision*, 7.
105. See Trenton, *Picturesque Images*, 30; and D'Emilio and Campbell, *Spirit and Vision*, 5.
106. ELB, Lockman interview 3, p. 3.
107. E. Blumenschein, *Blumenschein,* [2]
108. Royal Cortissoz, *The History of American Painting* (New York: Macmillan, 1927), 575.
109. See Marianne Doezema, "The 'Real' New York," in *The Paintings of George Bellows,* by Michael Quick et al., 99–135 (New York: Harry N. Abrams, 1992), 129.
110. ELB, Lockman interview 3, p. 1. Blumenschein illustrations, despite this comment, continued to appear for the next two years, into 1919.
111. E. Blumenschein, "Taos Society of Artists," 451.
112. See Patricia Trenton and Patrick Houlihan, *Native Faces: Indian Cultures in American Art* (Los Angeles: Los Angeles Athletic Club, 1984), 44–49.
113. bid., 45.
114. Qtd. in White, *Taos Society of Artists,* 25–26.
115. "A Taos Artist 1st Honored," *Taos Valley News*, November 13, 1917.
116. Qtd. in White, *Taos Society of Artists,* 26.
117. Walter, "Santa Fe–Taos Art Movement," 333.
118. "Artists Portraying Taos Indians Form New School," *Kansas City Times*, February 18, 1918; and "Indian Pictures in Majority in Library Exhibit," *Denver Times*, May 1, 1918.
119. Qtd. in "Art News from Summer Colonies," *American Art News*, September 14, 1918.

120. ELB to Walter, October 4, 1918, Southwest Collection, Schwarz Papers.

121. Qtd. in Stephen L. Good, "Walter Ufer: Munich to Taos, 1913–1918," in Bickerstaff, *Pioneer Artists of Taos*, 158.

122. Ibid., 160.

123. ELB to Henry J. Koch, October 3, 1918, Southwest Collection, Schwarz Papers. The painting was deaccessioned from the museum in the 1990s.

124. Paul A. F. Walter, "New Mexico in the Great War," *New Mexico Historical Quarterly* 1 (October 1926): 417. See also Paul A. F. Walter, "Art in War Service," *Art and Archaeology* 7, no. 9 (1918): 395–403.

125. Ibid., 395.

126. Blumenschein in "Art News from Summer Colonies."

127. For a complete account of the controversy, see Robert R. White, "Ernest Blumenschein and the Great War," *Ayer y Hoy en Taos* (Winter 1986): 3–6.

128. "Art Proceeds for Red Cross," *El Palacio* 5, no. 13 (1918): 217–18.

129. Qtd. in "Fourth Annual Exhibit of Taos Society of Artists," *El Palacio* 5, no. 6 (1918): 83.

130. When Albedia Marcus married Manuel Reyna, the *Taos Valley News*, February 11, 1919, claimed that "the bride was one of the most beautiful models, painted by many of the Taos artists and, by her Americanized manner and proficient use of English, is a general favorite among the inhabitants of Taos."

131. "Exhibit by Taos Artists," *Santa Fe New Mexican*, August 3, 1918.

132. "Fourth Annual Exhibit of Taos Society of Artists," 88–89.

133. See Valerie Ann Leeds, *My People: The Portraits of Robert Henri* (Orlando: Orlando Museum of Art, 1994), 33–36.

134. "A Taos Art Society Exhibit," *El Palacio* 7, nos. 5–6 (1919).

135. "Art Circles," *Cincinnati Inquirer*, October 27, 1918.

136. "News about Artists," *Taos Valley News*, October 22, 1918.

137. See Blumenschein's introduction to Bickerstaff, *Pioneer Artist of Taos*, 25.

SUPERSTITION AND THE ARTIST'S DEFENSE OF NATIVE RIGHTS

1. *Portrait of Jim Romero* may have been a full-size study on the confrontational aspect that would be wholly realized in *Superstition*. Although depicted wearing a hat and placed in front of the same fireplace Blumenschein used for his other 1921 portrait, *The Plasterer*, Romero is shown conspicuously staring out of the canvas directly at the viewer.

2. See, e.g., Hamlin Garland "Rising Wolf—Ghost Dancer." *McClure's* 12, no. 3 (1899): 241–48; and "Wards of the Nation—Their First Vacation from School," *Harper's Weekly* 43, no. 2217 (1899): 587, 609.

3. Eastman was a member of the Wahpeton Dakota Tribe, educated at Dartmouth College, and he graduated with honors from Boston University Medical School. www.kstrom.net/isk/stories/authors/eastman.html.

4. See also James C. Moore's excellent discussion of *Star Road and White Sun* in

"Ernest Blumenschein's Long Journey with Star Road," *American Art* 9, no. 3 (1995): 6–27.

5. The blackware wedding vase form is not a Taos pottery style but was developed and produced among some of the Tewa Pueblos to the south: San Juan, Santa Clara, and San Ildefonso.
6. The surface of this painting, like so many of Blumenschein's signature works, is luxuriantly textured with juicy applications of thick, beautifully modulated bits of color in every brushstroke of paint. He further pushed the extraordinary textural quality of this picture when he used a prominent dark green line of color extruded directly from the paint tube as a visual accent in the arrangement of marigolds in the Tewa vase to the lower left of Romero.
7. Blumenschein once noted in an unidentified manuscript, ca. 1928, "Mr. Blumenschein is vehement in his declaration that he does not like titles for his pictures, he believes titles come under the head of literature and would prefer to leave something for the imagination of the person looking at the picture. 'I should rather number pictures,' he said, 'than give them titles because everyone would be left to his own interpretation.'" Paul Albright Collection, Taos Historic Museums Archives, Taos, N.M. However, it appears throughout his career that Blumenschein labored over his painting titles, frequently changing them after they had been exhibited, to provide the necessary narrative clues by which viewers might begin to make sense of the works.
8. By 1800 one-third of the population of New Mexico were *genízaro,* that is, people of Indian descent (the children and grandchildren of Native American slaves) who had been essentially detribalized as they spoke only Spanish, practiced Spanish customs, and were Catholic. Most of the remaining population was considered *mestízo*, literally "mixed-blood."
9. It is my belief that the rise and development of the Penitente Brotherhood provided a social mechanism by which these basically classless people, the *genízaro,* could gain acceptance and become integrated into the Hispanic culture of New Mexico starting at the end of the eighteenth century (c.f. James F. Brooks, *Captives and Cousins: Slavery, Kinship, and Community in the Southwest Borderlands* [Chapel Hill: University of North Carolina Press, 2002]).
10. The arguments of continued use for agriculture and pasturage were the crux of the Pueblo's position in the New Mexico Supreme Court in the struggle to gain title to the Tenorio Tract in 1917. See *Pueblo de Taos v. A.R. Manby et al.,* New Mexico Supreme Court, 1917, Francis Cushman Wilson Paper on Legal Issues, 1913–1956, MSS 305 BC, Folder 2, Zimmerman Library Center for Southwest Research, University of New Mexico, Albuquerque. I wish to thank Jim Moore for identifying this citation and making the connection to my discussion of the wedding vase imagery.
11. "Academy Prize Winners: Altman Award of $1,000 to E. Blumenschein for His 'Superstition,'" *New York Times,* November 19, 1921.
12. *New York Herald,* November 18 (14, 16, 19?), 1921, ELB Collection, THM. Although the work is anything but a "tawdry Indian painting," the reviewer ironically captured the

very essences of Blumenschein's intent while totally missing the point.

13. *Dayton Journal*, May 14, 1927. Courtesy of Marianne Richter.

14. See Tisa Wenger, "Land, Culture, and Sovereignty in the Pueblo Dance Controversy;" *Journal of the Southwest* (June 2004): 381–412, esp. footnote 33. Charles Burke, "Circular No. 1665: Indian Dancing," April 26, 1921, Reel 40, Indian Rights Association Papers, 1868–1968, Glen Rock, N.J. The primary policy regulating Indian dances was the 1883 Religious Crimes Code, a portion of the Department of the Interior's Rules Governing the Court of Indian Offenses (Washington, D.C.: Government Printing Office, 1883).

15. John Collier, "Pueblos and Religious Persecution," letter to the editor, *New York Times*, November 14, 1924.

16. I wish to express my thanks to Peter Hassrick for suggesting a look at these two images and comparing them with *Superstition* and to Dr. Dean Porter for his generous sharing of his Ufer research and material.

17. See Good, "Walter Ufer," 156.

18. Ibid.

19. Ibid.

20. Dean A. Porter, manuscript in progress on Walter Ufer, 2007.

21. Ruben Salazar Márquez, *New Mexico: A Brief History* (Albuquerque: Cosmic House, 1999), 441.

22. In three of Ufer's large self-portraits, *Fantasy*, *Paint and Indians*, and *Artist and Model*, he is again making social comments regarding the eventual disappearance of the Indian and the conflict and tension between the artist and models and the appropriation of images.

23. ELB to Mr. Teenor, December 18, 1951, ELB Papers, Gilcrease.

24. On February 14, 1923, a supplement to Circular 1665 was issued. Some of the main features of the amendment were that "Indian dances be limited to one day in the midweek and at one center of each district; the months of March, April, June, July and August being exempted (no dances in these months). That none take part in the dances or be present who are under 50 years of age. That a careful propaganda be undertaken to educate public opinion against the (Indian religious) dance." www.cr.nps.gov/history/online_books/5views/5views1e.htm.

25. Jaime de Angulo's first wife, Carey Fink, worked for a period of time starting in 1921 for Jung in Zurich, Germany. Jaime would bring Jung to Taos in 1925 and introduce him to Antonio Mirabal (Mountain Lake), who had provided Jaime with material on the grammar of the Taos language. Gui de Angulo, *Jaime in Taos: The Taos Papers of Jaime de Angulo* (San Francisco: City Lights Books: 1985), 7–8, 85–87. I wish to thank Allen Ferguson and Lucy Whyte-Ferguson for introducing me to this book.

26. Ibid., 57–58.

27. The Bursum Bill had its inception in May 31, 1921, when former senator of New Mexico Albert Fall, then secretary of the interior, convinced Senator Holm Bursum of New Mexico to draft legislation that would remove lands from the Pueblos that were being squatted on by non-Indian people that had been held for more than ten years prior to New Mexican statehood, thus giving quiet title to the squatters (the bill came out of committee

in 1922 and was then brought before the Senate, although none of this information seemed to reach the newspapers of New Mexico). Additionally, the bill directed that any future Pueblo water or land rights issues would "fall under the jurisdiction of the unfriendly state courts." Marc Simmons, *New Mexico: An Interpretive History* (Albuquerque: University of New Mexico Press, 1988), 171–72. See also Vine Deloria, Jr., and Clifford Lytle, *The Nations Within: The Past and Future of American Indian Sovereignty* (New York: Pantheon Books, 1984), 39–40.

3. CHASING RAINBOWS: TAOS IN THE 1920S

1. Qtd. in Frederick Lewis Allen, *Only Yesterday: An Informal History of the Nineteen-Twenties* (New York: Harper and Brothers, 1981), 11.
2. ELB, Fisher interview, p. 7.
3. Allen, *Only Yesterday,* 247.
4. See "Art News," *Taos Valley News*, March 11, 1919, 1, April 15, 1919, 1.
5. ELB to MGB, March 6, 1919, ELB Papers, AAA.
6. "Art News," *Taos Valley News*, July 8, 1919, 1.
7. ELB, Lockman interview 3, p. 2. Mary had visited New Mexico before 1919. She and Helen had spent a brief part of the summer of 1913 in Taos. See *Taos Valley News*, June 7, 1913, announcing their arrival.
8. "Blumenschein Interviewed," *Albuquerque Evening Herald,* article reprinted in *El Palacio* 6, no. 6 (1919): 85.
9. Ibid., 86.
10. "An Appreciation of Indian Art," *Albuquerque Evening Herald,* article reprinted in *El Palacio* 6, no. 12 (1919): 178.
11. Ibid., 178–79.
12. Newspaper clipping: J. Keeley, "Real American Art—At Last," *Chicago Sunday Herald*, 1917, Joan Higgins Reed Archives, Museum of Fine Arts, Museum of New Mexico, Santa Fe.
13. Goerge Vaux, Jr., "Pueblos Object to Disturbing Bones of Ancestors," *Santa Fe New Mexican*, December 28, 1919.
14. "Locals," *Taos Valley News*, October 14, 1919.
15. "Blumenschein Interviewed," 85.
16. Qtd. in White, *Taos Society of Artists,* 56–57, 62.
17. The film may be viewed at the New Mexico State Records Center and Archives, Santa Fe. See ibid., 112–13.
18. "A Unique Art Colony," *Christian Science Monitor*, February 10, 1919.
19. ELB, Lockman interview 3, p. 2.
20. ELB to J. H. Gest, March 12, 1919, Ernest L. Blumenschein File, Mary R. Schiff Library, Cincinnati Art Museum, Cincinnati, Ohio. Gest was director of the Cincinnati Art Museum, and Blumenschein was writing to borrow *The Chief Speaks,* which he felt would be "the 'clou' [main attraction] of my section." Gest consented and asked to have the show.
21. H. Blumenschein, "Recuerdos," 9.

22. "E. L. Blumenschein's Paintings," *New York Times*, January 4, 1920.

23. Henry McBride, "Recent in the World of Art," *New York Sun*, January 11, 1920.

24. See W. F. Morris to ELB, January 16, 1920, Southwest Collection, Schwarz Papers.

25. See notice in "Western Painters at the Milch Galleries," *Taos Valley News*, May 18, 1920, quoting an article from *American Art News*, April 10, 1920.

26. Taos Society of Artists minutes for July 12, 1920, qtd. in White, *Taos Society of Artists*, 64. See also "Artist Couse Resigns," *Taos Valley News*, July 20, 1920.

27. I am grateful to Virginia Couse Leavitt for this information on the Blumenscheins' itinerary.

28. "Blumenscheins Entertain," *Taos Valley News*, July 27, 1920. Jean Allard Jeançon worked in Colorado, Arizona, and New Mexico, including the Rio Grande region (in 1919) and the Taos Valley area (1920). His books include *Excavations in the Chama Valley, New Mexico* and *Archeological Investigations in the Taos Valley, New Mexico, during 1920*.

29. H. Blumenschein, "Recuerdos."

30. See "Distribution of Paintings, 1920," [6], ELB Papers, AAA. The painting continued to travel widely through the 1930s.

31. See Dean Porter, "Picturing Taos Indians: Artists and Their Models," in *Enchanted Visions: The Taos Society of Artists and Ancient Cultures* (Spokane: Northwest Museum of Arts and Culture, 2005), 17.

32. For a full discussion of Star Road's peyote use and a definitive discussion of the painting's history, see James Moore, "Ernest Blumenschein's Long Journey with Star Road," *American Art* (Fall 1995): 7–27.

33. Mary Carroll Nelson, *The Legendary Artists of Taos* (New York: Watson-Guptill, 1980), 31.

34. H. Blumenschein, "Recuerdos," 19.

35. Incomplete newspaper clipping: "The Week in Art Circles," *Cincinnati Enquirer*, 1925, ELB Papers, AAA.

36. See "Distribution of Paintings, 1920," [6].

37. Sharp to Kanst, August 25, 1920, Sharp Papers, McCracken Research Library, Buffalo Bill Historical Center, Cody, Wyo., gift of Forrest Fenn.

38. From Blumenschein's introduction to Bickerstaff, *Pioneer Artists of Taos*, 27.

39. ELB to Mr. Schenber at the National Academy of Design, November 5, 1925, ELB Papers, AAA.

40. ELB to a Miss Howe, October 1, 1920, Library of the Albright-Knox Art Gallery, Rochester, N.Y.

41. Qtd. from Walter Ufer's "Report of the Secretary" in the society's minutes, qtd. in White, *Taos Society of Artists*, 71.

42. Henry McBride, "The Society Exhibition," *New York Herald*, November 15, 1920.

43. ELB to Mr. Teenor, December 18, 1951, ELB Papers, Gilcrease.

44. Patricia Janis Broder, *Great Paintings of the American West* (New York: Abbeville Press, 1979), 128.

45. From a review of the National Academy of Design winter exhibition, 1921, in an unidentified newspaper clipping, ELB Papers, AAA.

46. Theodore Van Soelen, "Blumenschein Exhibition Sets Important Precedent," *Santa Fe New Mexican*, June 4, 1948.

47. Helen Greene Blumenschein, in "Recuerdos," 19, explains that the family purchased Tenorio's room after his death. Blumenschein used it as a mural studio, and from 1931 until 1960 it served as a studio for Helen.
48. ELB to Mabel Dodge Luhan, December 9, 1947, Southwest Collection, Schwarz Papers.
49. See Wanda Corn, "Grant Wood's American Gothic," in *Reading American Art*, ed. Marianne Doezema and Elizabeth Milroy (New Haven: Yale University Press, 1998), 401.
50. Howard Cook, "Ernest L. Blumenschein: The Artist in His Environment," *New Mexico Quarterly Review* 19, no. 1 (1949): 21.
51. ELB, Fisher interview, p. 8.
52. "Blumenschein," *Santa Fe New Mexican*, June 7, 1959.
53. "Art News," *Taos Valley News*, March 28, 1922.
54. ELB to Gilcrease, January 6, 1948, ELB Papers, Gilcrease.
55. Ibid.
56. Incomplete newspaper clipping: *Christian Science Monitor*, August 9, 1920, ELB Papers, AAA. The article suggests that the oil was first painted in 1920 and two years later reworked.
57. Alexandre Hogue, "Ernest L. Blumenschein," *Southwest Review* 13, no. 4 (1928): 472.
58. Qtd. in *El Palacio* 12, no. 12 (1922): 14.
59. See White, *Taos Society of Artists*, 66–67.
60. W. Herbert Dunton, "The Painters of Taos," *American Magazine of Art* 13, no. 8 (1922): 249–52. These sentiments differ little from those expressed by the director of the Museum of New Mexico, Edgar L. Hewett, in "Recnt Southwest Art," *Art and Archaeology* 9, no. 1 (1920): 31–33. For a formal statement of mission for the Taos Society of Artists, see their by-laws published in White, *Taos Society of Artists*, 19–20.
61. E. Blumenschein, "Taos Society of Artists," 451.
62. See White, *Taos Society of Artists*, 80–81; and Schimmel, *Art and Life of W. Herbert Dunton*, 38.
63. Qtd. in "Art News," *Taos Valley News*, May 9, 1922.
64. See Robert R. White, *The New Mexico Painters* (Santa Fe: Gerald Peters Gallery, 1999), 9–10, for a detailed account of these events. Regarding Blumenschein's dismissal from the society, see White, *Taos Society of Artists*, 88–89, which quotes the July 31, 1923 minutes.
65. Amy Scott, "Ernest L. Blumenschein," in White, *New Mexico Painters*, 35.
66. ELB to Mrs. Quinton, January 23, 1924, Albright-Knox Gallery Library, Buffalo, N.Y.
67. "The New Mexico Painters," *Taos Valley News*, June 16, 1923.
68. ELB to Cortissoz, February 25, 1923, and February 27, 1923, Yale University Library, New Haven, Conn.
69. John H. McGinnis, "Taos," *Southwest Review* 13 (October 1927): 41.
70. "The Artist Colony Corner," *Taos Valley News*, June 16, 1923.
71. For particularly succinct explanations of these government efforts, see Mark Thompson, *American Character: The Curious Life of Charles Fletcher Lummis* (New York: Arcade Publishing, 2001), 311–12; and Lois Palken Rudnick, *Mabel Dodge Luhan: New Woman, New Worlds* (Albuquerque: University of New Mexico Press, 1984), 175–82, 186–87.

72. Qtd. in Dean A. Porter et al., *Taos Artists and Their Patrons, 1898–1950* (Notre Dame, Ind.: Snite Museum of Art, 1999), 213.

73. "Taos Artists Honored," *Taos Valley News*, February 9, 1924. Regarding confirmation of the national significance of these commissions for the Taos group, see also Fred Hamilton Rindge, "Taos—A Unique Colony of Artists," *American Magazine of Art* 17, no. 9 (1926): 452.

74. "The Artist Colony Corner," *Taos Valley News*, October 11, 1924.

75. John Pickard, *Report of the Capitol Decoration Commission, 1917–1928* (Jefferson City: State of Missouri, 1928), 113.

76. "The Artist Colony Corner," *Taos Valley News*, March 3, 1924, March 8, 1924, 1.

77. See "The Artist Colony Corner," *Taos Valley News*, March 8, 1924, May 17, 1924, June 14, 1924, 4.

78. J. Pennington, "Taos: An Art Center on the Edge of the Desert," *The Mentor* 12, no. 6 (1924): 24.

79. Ibid., 27. For a fuller, contemporary description of the artists' adobe houses, see Rose Henderson, "The Artist Colony Corner," *Taos Valley News*, November 8, 1924.

80. H. Blumenschein, "Recuerdos," 9–10.

81. Ibid., 30.

82. Qtd. from "Art News" in "The Artist Colony Corner," *Taos Valley News*, March 15, 1924. See Dean Porter, "Picturing Taos Indians: Artists and Their Models," in *Enchanted Visions*, 25, for an informed discussion on Indian subjects in art of this time.

83. "The Artist Corner," *Taos Valley News*, March 8, 1924.

84. Martha K. Schaver, "Art and Artists," *Dayton Journal*, May 5, 1927.

85. Hogue, "Ernest L. Blumenschein," 470–71.

86. Ibid., 471.

87. Jean Mowat, "The Artist in the Southwest," reprinted from the *Chicago Evening Post* in *El Palacio* 20, no. 10 (1926): 194.

88. Partial newspaper clipping: *New York Times*, April 5, 1925, ELB Papers, AAA.

89. Higgins also produced an Adam and Eve painting at this time. It is now lost. See Dean A. Porter, *Victor Higgins: An American Master* (Salt Lake City: Peregrine Smith Books, 1991), 99.

90. Partial newspaper clipping: "Exhibit of Paintings by E. L. Blumenschein," *St. Louis Post-Dispatch*, 1925, ELB Papers, AAA. See also Helen Appleton Read, "Brooklyn Museum Inaugurates New Wing with American Exhibition," *Brooklyn Daily Eagle*, November 22, 1926, for a similar assessment.

91. H. Blumenschein, "Recuerdos," 23.

92. Ernest L. Blumenschein, "Modern Art and the Academy," *New York Times*, February 7, 1926.

93. "Modern Art and the Art Academy: Address by Ernest L. Blumenschein at Luncheon by Art Section of State Teacher's Convention," *Santa Fe New Mexican*, March 8, 1926.

94. See Ernest L. Blumenschein, "Origin of the Taos Art Colony," *Taos Valley News*, May 15, 1926, and "Origin of the Taos Art Colony," *El Palacio* 20, no. 10 (1926): 190–93.

95. Ibid., 193.

96. "The Artists Colony Corner," *Taos Valley News*, May 29, 1926.

97. A label on the back of the painting at the Dallas Museum of Art states, in Blumenschein's hand, that it was "Finished 1954."

98. Mabel Dodge Luhan, "Taos—A Eulogy," *Creative Art* 9, no. 4 (1931): 295.

99. E. Blumenschein, "Taos Society of Artists," 445.

100. "The Artist Colony Corner," *Taos Valley News*, October 2, 1926.

101. Untitled newspaper clipping: *New York Herald Tribune*, February 13, 1927, ELB Papers, AAA.

102. See "Conservative Arts Citadel Yields to Modernists," *New York Herald Tribune*, February 13, 1927.

103. ELB, Lockman, interview 2, 5.

104. "Distribution of Paintings, 1920," [16].

105. The painting *Indian Battle* was exhibited in the Carnegie Museum's spring 1920 exhibition. See ELB to Miss Beatrice Howe, April 23, 1920, Southwest Collection, Schwarz Papers. In an October 24, 1926, letter from Blumenschein to the painter Charles Curran, then NAD secretary, he mentions spending three months repainting *Indian Battle*. Artist file, National Academy of Design, New York.

106. See "A Striking Canvas," *Taos Valley News*, July 24, 1926. They used the title *The Extraordinary Battle*. For description of *The Indian Battle*, see "Santa Fe–Taos Artists in Chicago Exhibition," *Taos Valley News*, January 25, 1921.

107. "New Mexican Paintings by Ernest Blumenschein," *Brooklyn Daily Eagle*, February 13, 1927.

108. Henry McBride, "Blumenschein's Paintings of American Indians," *New York Sun*, February 12, 1927.

109. "Ernest L. Blumenschein, Famous Desert Painter, Addresses Art Institute Here," *Dayton Journal*, April 27, 1927.

110. It has been suggested that this may be based on the reenactment in Taos in the 1920s of a famous battle between the Taos Indians and the Comanches that took place in 1779. See Marta Weigle and Peter White, *The Lore of New Mexico* (Albuquerque: University of New Mexico Press, 1988).

111. "Commercial Club Dinner," *Taos Valley News*, May 1, 1926.

112. ELB, Lockman, interview 3, p. 3.

113. Ada Rainey qtd. in "The Artists Colony Corner," *Taos Valley News*, November 27, 1926.

114. ELB, Lockman interview 3, p. 3.

115. Frank G. Applegate, "Tourists and Art," *Southwest Review* 12, no. 1 (1926), 23–24.

116. Fred Hamilton Rindge, "Taos—A Unique Colony of Artists, *American Magazine of Art* 17, no. 9 (1926): 447–53.

117. ELB, Lockman interview 3, p. 3.

118. ELB to Mrs. Quinton, January 12, 1924, Library of the Albright-Knox Art Gallery, Buffalo, N.Y.

119. On Ufer's decision, see White, *Taos Society of Artists*, xxv, 12–13.

120. McGinnis, "Taos," 40.

121. ELB notes for February 7, 1927, ELB Papers, AAA.

122. Elizabeth L. Cary, *New York Times,* qtd. in "Exhibitions," *National Art Club Bulletin* 11, no. 1 (1927): n.p.

123. *New York Herald Tribune,* qtd. in ibid.

124. "Ernest L. Blumenschein; Famous Desert Painter" and Fred Jacob, "One-Man Show by Blumenschein Should Not Be Overlooked," *Toronto Mail and Empire*, November 12, 1927.

125. E.g., see Ufer's comment that "the future of American art will be spelt and finished, not along the Atlantic or Pacific coast but in the Southwest," in Marion Murray, "Art in

the Southwest," *Southwest Review* 2, no. 4 (1926): 281.

126. McGinnis, "Taos," 40.

127. Qtd. in Van Deren Coke, *Taos and Santa Fe: The Artists' Environment, 1882–1942* (Albuquerque: University of New Mexico Press, 1963), 28.

128. "Artist, Ex-Daytonian, Returning," *Dayton Herald*, April 23, 1927.

129. Eric McCanley Lee and Rima Canaan, *The Fred Jones Jr. Museum of Art: Selected Works* (Norman: University of Oklahoma Press, 2002), 117.

130. Arnold Rönnebeck, "Blumenschein Exhibits 43 Fine Paintings," *Rocky Mountain News*, June 10, 1928.

131. Royal Cortissoz, "Picture Making Old and New," in *The History of American Painting*, by Samuel Isham and Royal Cortissoz (New York: Macmillan, 1927), 575.

132. Undated newspaper clipping: Marguerite B. Williams, "Here and There in the Art World," *Chicago Daily News*, [January 1928], ELB Papers, AAA.

133. Lena M. McCauley, "Surveys Hawthorne, Blumenschein Shows," *Chicago Evening Post*, January 3, 1928.

134. ELB, Lockman interview 2, pp. 4–5, 8.

135. "The Blumenschein Exhibit," *El Palacio* 25, nos. 6–7 (1928): 95. For another confirmation of Blumenschein's technical success and sophistication, see Hogue, "Ernest L. Blumenschein," 470–72.

136. "The Artist Colony Corner," *Taos Valley News*, December 1, 1928.

137. E. Blumenschein, *Blumenschein*, [7]. Grafe was an important collector of works by Higgins and Maynard Dixon as well as Blumenschein.

138. "Pleasure and Profit," *Taos Valley News*, February 16, 1929.

139. E. Blumenschein, *Blumenschein*, [7–9].

140. Royal Cortissoz qtd. in "Blumenschein, Out of the West," an unidentified newspaper clipping illustrating *Adobe Village—Winter*, Artist file, Saint Louis Art Museums Library, St. Louis, Mo.

141. "Another Prize for Blumenschein," *El Palacio* 27, nos. 21–22 (1929): 252.

THE EXTRAORDINARY AFFRAY: INDIANS AND IDENTITY

1. "In New Mexico: Some Paintings of Taos by Ernest Blumenschein Exhibited," *New York Times*, February 6, 1927.

2. Elizabeth Cunningham, Skip Keith Miller, and James Collins Moore have all contributed ideas, resources and references that were crucial in the formation of this essay. My thanks go to them.

3. Helen Greene Blumenschein, "ELB," unpublished manuscript, HGB Collection, FACHL.

4. See Enrique R. Lamadrid, *Hermanitos Comanchitos: Indo-Hispano Rituals of Captivity and Redemption* (Albuquerque: University of New Mexico Press, 2003).

5. See Arthur Campa as quoted in Weigle and White, *Lore of New Mexico*, 359–60.

6. Lamadrid, *Hermanitos Comanchitos*, 147.

7. Handlettered on cardboard on verso: THE EXTRAORDINARY AFFRAY ERNEST L. BLUMENSCHEIN TAOS NEW MEXICO.

8. ELB to Charles Curran, October 24, 1926, Artist file, National Academy of Design, New York.
9. A current x-ray of the painting does not reveal the extent of repainting that x-rays of his *Ourselves and Taos Neighbors* show.
10. Thomas Weldburn Hughes, *A Treatise on Criminal Law and Procedure* (Indianapolis: Bobbs Merrill, 1919), 435.

4. BLUMENSCHEIN, MODERNISM, AND NATIONAL ART IN THE 1930S

1. ELB to George Derby, August 12, 1930, ELB Collection, THM.
2. Gilbert to ELB, January 23, 1930, ELB Papers, AAA.
3. "Fine Paintings on Exhibition: Blumenschein's Work on Display at Woman's Department Club," *Shreveport Louisiana Times*, March 16, 1930, ELB Papers, AAA.
4. *Taos Valley News*, April 10, 1930.
5. Helen Greene Blumenschein, "E. L. Blumenschein: The Taos Story, 1898–1960," unpublished manuscript, 1982, HGB Collection, FACHL; HGB notation on MGB to ELB, May 23, 1930, ELB address book notes, ELB Collection, FACHL.
6. *University of New Mexico Field School Bulletin,* 1939, University Archives, University of New Mexico, Albuquerque.
7. Other artists offering critiques were Joseph Henry Sharp, Walter Ufer, Herbert Dunton, Oscar Berninghaus, and Kenneth Adams. *Taos Valley News*, June 12, 1930.
8. According to his daughter, Helen, Blumenschein charged one dollar for private critiques. H. Blumenschein, "E. L. Blumenschein."
9. Ernest L. Blumenschein, interview by Mary McDonald, KOB Radio, Albuquerque, November 1958, ELB Papers, Gilcrease.
10. ELB to HGB, February 2 and March 24, 1939, ELB Collection, FACHL.
11. ELB to HGB, February 21, 1945, ELB Collection, FACHL.
12. ELB to Roy Allen Stamm, March 22, 1932, Southwest Collection, Schwarz Papers.
13. For these occasions, Shaw printed one hundred copies of the prize-winning painting, which were distributed to his dinner guests.
14. "The Carnegie International," special to the *Christian Science Monitor*, n.d.
15. Edward Alden Jewell, "American Art Climbs the Bright Hill of Renaissance . . . The American Section at Pittsburg," *New York Times*, October 25, 1931.
16. *Taos Valley News*, October 26, 1931.
17. Neuhaus also included and reproduced the following works by other painters: *The Wise Men,* by Maynard Dixon; *Sacred Birds,* by E. Irving Couse; and *Fiesta Day,* by Victor Higgins.
18. Among the artists listed under the "Contemporary Period," modernists Edward Hopper, Maurice Sterne, Stuart Davis, and Andrew Dasburg had connections to New Mexico during that time period. New York painters Yasuo Kuniyoshi, Arnold Blanch, and Ernest Fiene later taught at the Broadmoor Art Academy (now the Colorado Springs Fine Art Center) in Colorado.

19. ELB to MGB, October 28, 1931, ELB Collection, FACHL.
20. ELB to MGB, November 6, 1931, ELB Collection, FACHL.
21. H. Blumenschein, "E. L. Blumenschein."
22. Ibid., 57.
23. Bickerstaff, *Pioneer Artists of Taos,* 40.
24. ELB Ledgers, ELB Collection, FACHL.
25. Blumenschein exhibited this work first as *Arizona*; later for the 1939 World's Fair exhibition he repainted it and retitled the painting *Red Symphony*. The painting is now titled *Arizona Dam*.
26. ELB to George Derby, August 12, 1930, ELB Collection, THM.
27. Blumenschein created his best works for exhibition purposes. These paintings, sized larger to command space and notice, typically ranged from 3 x 4 feet to 4 x 5 feet.
28. Bickerstaff, *Pioneer Artists of Taos*, 40.
29. Howard Cook, "Ernest L. Blumenschein: The Artist and His Environment," in *New Mexico Artists*, series no. 3 (Albuquerque: University of New Mexico Press, 1952), 23.
30. Adams to ELB, June 19, 1948, ELB Papers, AAA.
31. ELB, Lockman interview 2.
32. Cook, "Ernest L. Blumenschein," 17–18.
33. Helen Greene Blumenschein, hand-corrected manuscript, 15, HGB Collection, FACHL.
34. ELB to Mr. Stark, July 30, 1957, Blumenschein File, Stark Museum of Art Archives, Orange, Tex.
35. H. Blumenschein, "E. L. Blumenschein."
36. Ibid.
37. ELB to MGB and HGB, May 18, 1932, ELB Collection, FACHL.
38. "Don Fernando Hotel in Ruins," *Taos Valley News*, December 21, 1933.
39. David Witt, *Modernists in Taos: From Dasburg to Martin* (Santa Fe: Red Crane Books, 2002), 67–68.
40. Alfred Morang, "Transcendental Painting Group," *New Mexican*, January 17, 1939, reprinted in ibid., 255n.
41. Witt, *Modernists in Taos,* 66.
42. Earl Stroh account in ibid., 74.
43. Ibid., 107–108.
44. ELB to Edward Rowan, November 5, 1937, Records of the Public Building Service, Records of Federal Art Activities, Textual Records of the Section of Fine Arts, Public Building Administration and Its Predecessors, Case Files Concerning Embellishments of Federal Buildings, 1934–1943, CO [Colorado], RG 121, Box 11, Entry 133, National Archives, Washington, D.C. (hereafter cited as Records of the Public Building Service).
45. Ann Conger, "City Needs Great Leaders Who Have Big Dreams—Blumenschein" *Albuquerque Tribune*, February 25, 1950, ELB Collection, FACHL.
46. Ernest L. Blumenschein, handwritten manuscript, 1934, Southwest Collection, Schwarz Papers.
47. See H. Blumenschein, "E. L. Blumenschein."
48. *Taos Painting—Yesterday and Today* (Colorado Springs: Colorado Springs Fine Arts Center, March 1952).
49. "Blumenschein Painting of Stupendous Canyon Scene Is Given to Art Institute," *Dayton Journal*, June 28, 1935, courtesy of Mary Ann Richter.
50. ELB Ledgers, ELB Collection, FACHL.
51. ELB, Lockman interview 2.
52. "Wider Cooperation among Artists Found," *New York Times,* January 18, 1934.

53. "Blumenschein Brings Southwest to New York," *Art Digest*, March 15, 1934, 19, ELB Papers, AAA.

54. *New York Evening Post*, March 27, 1934. While no painting list has been found for this exhibition, various sources indicate paintings in this exhibition, besides those listed in the reviews, included *The Lone Fisherman*, *Adobe Village—Winter*, *The Lake*, *Landscape with Indian Camp*.

55. *New York Sun*, March 24, 1934.

56. Mary's entry in the 1934 National Academy show, *Acoma Legend*, won an Honorable Mention at the Denver Art Museum's Fortieth Annual Exhibition later that year. The other prizewinner was Denver painter and muralist Louise Emerson Rönnebeck. *Fortieth Annual Exhibition Catalogue* (Denver: The Denver Art Museum, 1934), Western History Department, Denver Public Library, Denver, Colo.

57. Ernest L. Blumenschein, handwritten manuscript, 1934, Southwest Collection, Schwarz Papers.

58. This was later renamed the Section of Fine Arts.

59. Virginia M. Mecklenburg, *Roosevelt's America: New Deal Paintings form the National Museum of American Art* (Washington, D.C.: Smithsonian Institution Press, c1982), Fine Arts Library, University of New Mexico, Albuquerque.

60. Peyton Boswell qtd. in *Democratic Vistas: Post Offices and Public Art in the New Deal*, by Marlene Parks and Gerald E. Markowitz (Philadelphia: Temple University Press, 1984), xviii.

61. The artists were Emil Bisttram, Victor Higgins, Bert Geer Phillips, and Ward Lockwood. See Peter Bermingham, *The New Deal in the Southwest* (Tucson: University of Arizona Museum of Art, 1980).

62. The others that year were Kenneth Adams, Victor Higgins, and Randall Davey. The paper also named artists chosen for future appointments, including New Mexico painter W. Herbert Dunton and sculptor Eugenie Shonnard. Others listed from the region were Arnold Rönnebeck from Colorado and Paul Sample from California. Among the jurors for the painting awards were Edward Bruce, Olin Dows, Leon Kroll, Jonas Lie, Ernest Peixotto, and Eugene Speicher. "63 Artists Named for Federal Work," *New York Times*, December 14, 1934.

63. Rowan to ELB, December 2, 1935, and December 6, 1935, Records of the Public Building Service.

64. ELB to Rowan, December 18, 1935, Records of the Public Building Service.

65. Rowan to ELB, December 22, 1935, Records of the Public Building Service.

66. ELB to Mr. Hoppe, October 17, 1936, Records of the Public Building Service.

67. ELB to Rowan, January 14, 1937, Records of the Public Building Service.

68. ELB to Rowan, September 15, 1937; Rowan to ELB, September 22, 1937, Records of the Public Building Service.

69. ELB to Rowan, October 24, 1937, Records of the Public Building Service.

70. Rowan to ELB, December 1, 1937, Records of the Public Building Service.

71. "Friends Pay Tribute to Walter Ufer," *Taos Review and the Taos Valley News*, August 13, 1936, 1, Records of the Public Building Service.

72. E. Blumenschein, *Blumenschein.*

73. Ibid.

74. Ibid.

75. "Widely-Known Artist Is Speaker," *Dayton Journal*, April 12, 1935, ELB Collection, THM.

76. "Blumenschein Indiscreet in Home Town," *Taos Review* and *Taos Valley News*, May 2, 1935, courtesy of David L. Witt.

77. See Skip Keith Miller, "A Matter of Time and Friendship: The Ernest L. Blumenschein and Ellis Parker Butler Letters," *Taos Lightnin'* (Summer 1996): 2–5; and Skip Keith Miller, "Elsie's Story," *Taos Lightnin'* (Winter 1998): 1, 4–5.

78. ELB to MGB and HGB, April 28, 1935, ELB Collection, FACHL.

79. Cook, "Ernest L. Blumenschein," 22.

80. The regulations designated that the number of works be chosen by percentage according to each state's population. Thus, New Mexico, with its many fine artists and thriving art communities, could only send five paintings and one sculpture.

81. Howard DeVree, "American Cross Section," *New York Times*, June 20, 1937.

82. Emily Genauer, "National Show," *Time*, June 28, 1937.

83. *New York Herald Tribune*, June 13, 1937, Southwest Collection, Schwarz Papers.

84. Genauer, "National Show."

85. "Venice Biennial" *Art Digest*, May 1, 1938, 13.

86. Besides paintings, sculpture, and graphics, the thousand-item selection included architectural and photographic displays and motion pictures, plus folk art from Mrs. John D. Rockefeller, Jr.'s, collection and graphic art assembled from works of Currier and Ives, Audubon, James Whistler, George Bellows, and Mary Cassatt. "Americans in Paris," *Art Digest*, May 1, 1938, 1.

87. Ibid.

88. Edward Alden Jewell, "Truly Ours: Roots of Painting in Nation's Culture," *New York Times*, August 14, 1938.

89. Unidentified newspaper clipping: "Blumenschein to Be Included in Paris Exhibition" 1938, ELB Papers, AAA.

90. ELB to Harold Waller, January 20, 1948, ELB Collection, FACHL.

91. A goat appears in every sheep painting of his later years.

92. A. Conger Goodyear, preface to *American Art from the New York World's Fair* (1939; reprint, 1987), 13–16.

93. Ibid.

94. The paintings and exhibitions included *The Chief Speaks* in Half a Century of American Art at the Art Institute of Chicago; *Moon, Morning Star, Evening Star* at the Golden Gate International Exposition, Palace of Fine Arts, San Francisco; and *Sheep in Rio Grande Canyon* at the National Academy of Design.

95. Jerry Bywaters, "Art Comes Back Home," *Southwest Review* (October 1937): 80–82.

OURSELVES AND TAOS NEIGHBORS: PORTRAIT GROUP OF "NOTORIOUS TAOS FREAKS"

1. "Ernest Blumenschein—Grand Central Galleries Fifth Avenue Branch," *Art Digest*, March 24, 1934.
2. In a March 14, 1936, letter to Mary, Blumenschein commented on their cat: "The cat is the same disagreeable personality, beautiful to watch."
3. This room was my office for over six years while I was a codirector and curator for the Taos Historic Museums, which accounts in part for my great fondness for the painting.
4. After completion of the Missouri murals, Blumenschein had to cut a large, narrow slice out of the adobe wall next to the north window in order to remove the murals.
5. Some years later Blumenschein could no longer tolerate the cool bluish-green light from the north window of the east studio and reclaimed the living room as his studio because it had south-facing windows that retained the warm colors he preferred, especially in later life.
6. Cook, "Ernest L. Blumenschein," 18–19.
7. In Elsie Butler Waller's manuscript on the time Blumenschein spent painting her family's portrait she remembered, "Blumenschein said he would never paint children again and certainly never again paint anyone except in his own studio—after our portrait." March 17, 1974, ELB Collection, THM.
8. This study is privately owned. Unfortunately, there is no date on the gridded sketch, but as Blumenschein frequently completed detailed studies prior to initiating his larger canvases I feel the sketch predates his work on the painting.
9. Blumenschein to Rowan, September 15, 1937, Records of the Public Building Service.
10. Unnumbered pages in ELB Ledgers, ELB Collection, FACHL.
11. School of American Research, Museum of New Mexico, Santa Fe, September 1937.
12. This seems an unlikely number as there should have been more like twenty-two figures in 1948, as Blumenschein considered the painting finished then.
13. This statement is also curious, as the original study for the picture depicts twenty-seven figures.
14. In 1948 Dr. Reginald Fisher was head associate in charge, Department of Fine Arts and Extension, Museum of New Mexico, Santa Fe; later he became director. As of June 2007 the Museum of Fine Arts, Museum of New Mexico, has changed its name to the New Mexico Museum of Art.
15. Dr. Gertrude Light is superbly portrayed in an essay titled "A Misadventure," by Frank Waters in his book *Pure Waters: Frank Waters and the Quest for the Cosmic*, ed. Barbara Waters (Athens: Swallow Press/Ohio University Press, 2002): "an unmarried, childless, and careworn woman of sixty or more. Not too much was known about her, remarkable and loved as she was. Apparently she received early medical schooling in Europe, worked in Russia, and was the first woman doctor to graduate from John Hopkins. When she began her practice, she found doors closed to her; for in those days women practitioners were regarded with disfavor. Perhaps that is

why she eventually landed in the backward village of Taos, only to encounter the same prejudices. The town's two doctors were young and inexperienced, without her sound medical and surgical qualifications. But they controlled the small hospital and refused to admit her patients. Nevertheless, Dr. Light built up a practice among the Spanish-American villagers too poor to afford large doctor's fees and hospital costs. None minded her occasional vagueness and brief lapses from work. Gradually she became more widely known for her devoted care and profound knowledge of the illness and rare diseases of children" (112).

16. Tony Luhan, a Taos Pueblo Indian, was Mabel Dodge Luhan's fourth and final husband.

17. The question is often asked why the two male Indians on the far right, one standing and one seated on a carved chest, are totally lacking in individualized detail. An examination of the original study for this painting shows several more characters (seven) on the right side of the painting, both standing and seated, that Blumenschein never got around to completing. He probably painted the anonymous Indians at first as visual placeholders for the intended figures. The finely depicted kneeling Pueblo woman in the extreme foreground is the Blumenscheins' longtime housekeeper and family friend Popthlee Romero; she is identified on the bottom margin in the original study for the painting. The study also listed Taos Pueblo model and handyman Don Mondragon (written as "Don M," and possibly indicated on the sketch as the figure in side view [like D. H. Lawrence] with very long dark hair). Also the word "Plasterer" is in the left margin, suggesting that Blumenschein perhaps had intended to include Epimenio Tenorio or another of his Hispanic helpers. And there is no mention in the study of the Taos Trumpeter, but the figure that becomes the Trumpeter in the final painting is indicated with a distinct moustache (but no trumpet) in the study—just like Epimenio Tenorio, ironically the original inhabitant of the room.

18. Letter and guides in the Stark Museum of Art Archives.

19. H. Blumenschein, "E. L. Blumenschein," 7.

20. Based on the study for the painting, it appears that Blumenschein had intended to include Dunton (who is more than likely the figure wearing a long scarf in the study and identified in writing) among the characters on the right side of the painting, which he never completed. The study indicates the inclusion of "Frieda" (Lawrence), (D. H.) "Lawrence," and (Dorothy) "Brett" as figures; they have no distinguishing visual characteristics, but their names, in barely legible script, appear on the sides of the study. The study also appears as if some of the names may have been erased and written over, suggesting Blumenschein was having a hard time deciding whom to include in the painting.

21. The study also lists simply "Couse" along the left border of the study, and since the same list includes "Mrs. H." (Mrs. Harwood), it appears that Blumenschein had every intention of including E. I. Couse but ended up substituting Mrs. C. (Mrs. Couse) instead. Also puzzling is that on the left right side margin of the study there is an erased area that only shows clearly "Co," perhaps where he had originally intended to place Couse, or Mrs.

Couse, as several of the nonincluded figures from the study appear to be women. "Frieda" has also been partially erased from the right margin as well.

22. Cook, "Ernest L. Blumenschein," 22.

23. Letter in the Stark Museum of Art Archives.

5. IN CONTEMPORARY RHYTHM: THE SEARCH FOR FINAL PERFECTION

1. The exhibition would feature paintings by Pueblo Indians from Dr. Edgar Hewett's collection, Spanish colonial ecclesiastic art (based on writer Mary Austin's collection), and a fifty-year retrospective of painting in New Mexico.
2. "Artists and Writers," *Santa Fe New Mexican*, June 26, 1940.
3. Unidentified newspaper clipping: "Conference Hears Taos Painter," ELB Papers, AAA.
4. "New Mexico Artists' Show on Tour," *El Palacio,* November 1941, 246.
5. Review qtd. in *El Palacio,* January 1942, 13.
6. "New Mexico Artists' Show on Tour," 246.
7. The exhibition included 557 paintings, 581 prints, and 309 sculptural works. Edward Alden Jewell, "Artists for Victory," *New York Times*, December 6, 1942.
8. HGB to ELB, July 17, 1930, ELB Papers, AAA.
9. Cook, "Ernest L. Blumenschein," 21.
10. ELB to HGB, May 2, 1944, ELB Collection, FACHL.
11. HGB to ELB, December 18 and 19, 1944, ELB Collection, FACHL.
12. HGB, interview with the author, Taos, N.M., 1986.
13. ELB Ledgers, ELB Collection, FACHL.
14. H. Blumenschein, "E. L. Blumenschein"; see also Helen Blumenschein qtd. in Kit Egri, "Ernest L. Blumenschein: Intellect and Growth," *American Artist* (January 1978).
15. Partial newspaper clipping: "Exhibit of Paintings by E. L. Blumenschein," *St. Louis Post-Dispatch*, 1925, ELB Papers, AAA.
16. ELB Ledgers, ELB Collection, FACHL.
17. ELB to Gilcrease, January 6, 1948, ELB Papers, Gilcrease.
18. ELB Ledgers, ELB Collection, FACHL.
19. Homer St. Gaudens to ELB, November 29, 1946; Blumenschein wrote a letter to Mary and Helen on this letter, dated December 7, 1946, ELB Collection, FACHL.
20. ELB to Mrs. H. J. Lutcher Stark, October 17, 1954, Blumenschein File, Stark Museum of Art Archives, Orange, Tex.
21. ELB to HGB, December 6, 1946, ELB Collection, FACHL.
22. ELB to HGB, October 24, 1946, ELB Collection, FACHL.
23. Ibid.
24. ELB to HGB, November 10, 1946, ELB Collection, FACHL.
25. Wernette to ELB, May 28, 1947, ELB Papers, AAA.
26. Gerald Sykes, "Gem-Like Flame, New Mexican Décor," *New York Times*, February 15, 1948.
27. Dorothy Adlow, "Mabel Dodge Luhan Writes of Taos," *Christian Science Monitor,* February 14, 1948, WM12.

28. Ibid.
29. Ina Sizer Cassidy, "Blumenschein in Retrospect," *New Mexico Magazine* 26 (July 1948): 28, 57.
30. Fisher, "Museum's First Retrospective Exhibition," 163.
31. Cassidy, "Blumenschein in Retrospect," 28, 57.
32. The Herron Art Institute is the former name of the Indianapolis Art Museum. "Blumenschein Painting Arrives from New York," *Santa Fe New Mexican,* May 26, 1948, ELB Collection, THM.
33. "Blumenschein Exhibition Sets Important Precedent," *Santa Fe New Mexican*, June 4, 1948, ELB Collection, FACHL.
34. Fisher, "Museum's First Retrospective Exhibition," 163.
35. The *New Mexico Quarterly Review* published Howard Cook's paper in its spring 1949 issue. This citation is taken from its later inclusion in *New Mexico Artists*, series no. 3. (Albuquerque: University of New Mexico Press, 1952), 17.
36. Ibid., 19, 21–22.
37. Alfred Morang, "Art in the News," *Santa Fe New Mexican* [ca. June 1948], ELB Collection, THM.
38. Barrymore to ELB, May 30, 1948, ELB Papers, AAA.
39. Lockwood to ELB, June 3, 1948, ELB Papers, AAA.
40. Lujan, River House, Embudo, to ELB [1948], ELB Papers, AAA.
41. ELB to Fisher, August 24, 1948, Museum of Fine Arts Library, New Mexico Museum of Art, Santa Fe.
42. The other venues were Wichita Art Association, Wichita, Kansas, December 15, 1948–January 15, 1949; Museum of Fine Arts, Dallas, Texas, January 30–February 20, 1949; Oklahoma Art Center, Oklahoma City, Oklahoma, February 27–March 27, 1949; and Joslyn Memorial Art Museum, Omaha, Nebraska, April 6–27, 1949. Museum of Fine Arts Library, New Mexico Museum of Art, Santa Fe.
43. *Santa Fe New Mexican*, May 15, 1949, Museum of Fine Arts Library, New Mexico Museum of Art, Santa Fe.
44. Grace H. Glueck to ELB, May 13, 1957, ELB Papers, AAA. Reproduced in the *New York Times Book Review*, May 19, 1957.
45. Helen Card to ELB, June 9, 1951, ELB Collection, FACHL.
46. H. Blumenschein, "E. L. Blumenschein."
47. Dorothy Morang, "39th Annual Exhibition for New Mexico Artists-A Review and Historical Comparison," *El Palacio,* September 1952, 271.
48. "A Statement on Modern Art," March 1950, Museum of Modern Art Library, 1.07 B67, Museum of Modern Art, New York.
49. Copy of Blumenschein's written work "Modernism," October 1952, for Associated Press interview, ELB Papers, AAA.
50. Ibid. See also "Blumenschein Regrets Generation Is Educated on Modern Art Ideas," *Albuquerque Journal*, November 16, 1952; and "Blumenschein Expresses Views on Modernism," *El Crepusculo*, November 27, 1952.
51. ELB to Reginald Fisher, September 6, 1953, ELB Collection, FACHL.
52. The University of New Mexico Taos Field School of Art, June 22–August 14, 1953, Center for Southwest Research, University of New Mexico, Albuquerque.

53. Cook, "Ernest L. Blumenschein," 19.

54. O'Hara to ELB, July 26 [no year given], ELB Collection, FACHL.

55. Wolcott Ely, interview with the author, summer 1993.

56. I am indebted to Amy Scott for this information. "Peace Reigns between Taos' Art Factions: Conservatives, Moderns Reach Accord," *Chicago Tribune*, September 13, 1954, courtesy of Amy Scott.

57. Rich to ELB, November 29, 1954, ELB Collection, FACHL.

58. Cook, "Ernest L. Blumenschein," 19.

59. "Blumenschein Explains: What Makes a Painting New?" *Santa Fe New Mexican*, September 13, 1953, courtesy of Mary Leonard, librarian, Dallas Museum of Fine Art, Dallas, Tex.

60. Ibid.

61. Mary wrote her husband that he could thank Mr. Hennings for urging Mr. Stark to stop by the studio. MGB to ELB, September 26, 1954, ELB Collection, FACHL.

62. "Blumenschein Comments on Important Sales," *El Crepusculo*, October 21, 1954, 2.

63. Family members present were Phillips's daughter, Mrs. Floyd Beutler; Mrs. Berninghaus and daughter, Mrs. Jack Brandenburg; Dunton's daughter, Vivian; and Mary and Helen Blumenschein. *El Crepusculo*, May 19, 1955.

64. *El Crepusculo*, February 2, 1956, Stark Museum of Art; "National Arts Group Honors Blumenschein," *Albuquerque Tribune*, January 26, 1956.

65. ELB to Mr. Stark, October 18, 1956, Stark Museum of Art.

66. Henry McBride, "New Mexico Painters Prove Disturbing," *New York Herald*, October 25, 1924.

67. In his ledgers Blumenschein wrote, "Sorry," under "Destroyed"; Helen later added "me, too." ELB ledgers, ELB Collection, FACHL.

68. Blumenschein had not yet titled the painting. ELB Collection, FACHL.

69. ELB to Mr. and Mrs. Stark, September 21 and October 31, 1956, Stark Museum of Art.

70. Ibid.; ELB to Leon Kroll, February 19, 1953, Leon Kroll Papers, reel D326, Archives of American Art, Smithsonian Institution, Washington, D.C.

71. ELB to Mr. Stark, June 30, 1957, courtesy of the Stark Museum of Art, Orange, Tex.

72. Ina Sizer Cassidy, "Tenth Annual Print Show," *New Mexico Magazine* (April 1957): 33.

73. ELB to Mr. Stark, June 30, 1957, Stark Museum of Art.

74. Stark to ELB, July 23, 1957, Stark Museum of Art.

75. ELB to Stark, October 12, 1957, Stark Museum of Art.

76. Regina Cooke, "The Blumenscheins: A First Family," *El Crepusculo*, September 25, 1952, ELB Collection, FACHL.

77. ELB to Stark, October 12, 1957, Stark Museum of Art.

78. ELB to Stark, January 13, 1958, Stark Museum of Art.

79. Ibid.

80. ELB to Stark, November 20 [1958], Stark Museum of Art.

81. Ibid.; ELB Ledgers, ELB Collection, FACHL.

82. HGB to Florence Rowe, October 23, 1958, courtesy of Gail Curry Fish.

83. "Scores of Long-Time Friends of Ernest Blumenschein Greet Taos Artist at Opening of Retrospective Show," *Santa Fe New Mexican*, November 24, 1958, ELB Collection, FACHL.

84. Barrie to ELB, November 26, 1958, ELB Papers, AAA.

85. Handwritten translation from Spanish by Helen G. Blumenschein, ELB Collection, FACHL; "Blumenschein Paintings Acclaimed," *Albuquerque Journal*, May 17, 1959. This was not the first time Blumenschein's work had been compared with that of Zulaoga. In its coverage of the 1937 National Exhibition of American Art in New York, *Time* magazine remarked on the similarity of the two painters. "National Show," *Time*, June 28, 1937.

86. "Blumenschein, Daughter Arrange Joint Exhibition," *Albuquerque Journal*, May 24, 1959; Martin Elkort, "Blumenschein," *Santa Fe New Mexican*, June 7, 1958, ELB Collection, FACHL.

87. Ibid.

88. Cassidy, "Blumenschein in Retrospect."

89. HGB to Gilcrease, December 10 [1959], ELB Papers, Gilcrease Museum Archives.

90. See, e.g., "Ernest L. Blumenschein Dead: A Founder of Taos Art Colony," *New York Times*, June 8, 1960.

91. Reginald Fisher, "Commentary," in *Blumenschein: A Retrospective Exhibition, 1902–1958*, exhibition catalog, ELB Collection, THM.

TWELVE MEN, LISTENING: BLUMENSCHEIN'S STRUGGLE WITH MURDER, JUSTICE, AND THE INARTICULATE SOUL OF AMERICA

1. Between 1912, the year of New Mexico's statehood, and 1930, the highest August precipitation at Red River occurred in the years 1916, 1929, and 1927, respectively. U.S. Historical Climatology Network Monthly Temperature and Precipitation Data, http://cdiac.esd.ornl.gov/ndps/ushcn/ushcn.html#TOP.

2. Newspaper accounts in New Mexico give his name as DeWeiss; in *The Terrellian*, the annual for the Terrell School for Boys, his name is spelled "DeWese." At 12,711 feet above sea level, Gold Hill is the second highest mountain in New Mexico; Wheeler Peak, to the south of Gold Hill, stands at 13,020 feet.

3. For the most complete account of the day's events, see "Brutal Asesinato en Red River," *La Revista Popular de Nuevo Mexico,* September 3, 1927, 1. The first coverage appeared two days after the incident: "Professor DeWeiss Killed, Friend Shot Down in Taos County," *Santa Fe New Mexican*, August 30, 1927, 1. On the following day, the story was front-page news in Albuquerque: "Taos Herder Confesses to Murder," *Albuquerque Journal*, August 31, 1927, 1, 3. Another account of this event was given by a young man who was interviewed at the Museum of Modern Art in 1939. The man was a friend of the DeWese couple and had intended to go on the hike that day, but family obligations kept him at home. He claimed that he was a member of the posse that went up to recover DeWese's body and that they captured the sheepherder. He noted that Moburg was Swedish. "Memo to Mr. Barr RE: Blumenschein: Jury for the Trial of a Sheepherder for Murder. From Miss Knowles (Dorothy)," 1939, Blumenschein Permanent

Collection File, Museum of Modern Art, New York.

4. Although she is mentioned often in the media accounts of the murder and trial, Mrs. DeWese's first name is never given in the Taos or Santa Fe coverage; the *Albuquerque Journal*, quoting a Dallas AP report, gives her maiden name as Evelyn Convere.
5. José Cruz Maestas is the young man's full name, although some reports in the *Santa Fe New Mexican* refer to him as José Cruz. Newspaper accounts give Maestas's age variously from seventeen to nineteen years; his penitentiary record states it as sixteen years. New Mexico Department of Corrections Records, New Mexico State Records Center and Archive, 2.1.3, Inmate Intake Records, 7203, Inmate # 6004 (hereafter cited as Department of Corrections Records).
6. There are three trails up Gold Hill from the Red River side: west of the town, Columbine Creek to Placer Fork; from the east, up Placer Creek to Goose Lake, south of the peak; and from the town itself, up Pioneer Creek, along which there are a number of mining claims. The latter route is the most direct, and probably the one Moburg, who grew up around the mining camps, chose for the hike. About a mile after the trail leaves the Pioneer Creek watershed, it skirts the eastern edge of a large open meadow in the forest below timberline; such high meadows were ideal grazing land, and this is the likely site of the shepherd's camp.
7. What happened exactly between Moburg and Maestas is not clear; Moburg survived the attack and apparently either made it back to Red River or met the group coming up. He was taken to the hospital. According to Mrs. DeWese, Moburg had been thrown down the embankment after grappling with Maestas, who had used his only two cartridges in the attack. See "Professor DeWeiss Killed, Friend Shot Down in Taos County"; "Woman Tells of Murder of Her Husband by Man near Red River," *Albuquerque Journal*, November 17, 1927, 1; and "Getting Jury for Maestas Trial at Taos," *Santa Fe New Mexican*, November 16, 1927, 1. "Brutal Asesinato en Red River" gives a somewhat different account, stating that Moburg jumped down the embankment in desperation and evaded Maestas in the rocky terrain.
8. The editor was José Montaner; he was also a state senator from Taos. In the record for the New Mexico State Penitentiary, Maestas gave his mother's name as Josefita Duran of San José; another reference Maestas gave was Antonio Baros of Arroyo Hondo. (While Josefita was probably Nicolas's wife, it is not clear which San José in New Mexico this refers to, or whether the information is accurate.) Department of Corrections Records, Inmate Intake Records, Inmate # 6004.
9. "Professor DeWeiss Killed, Friend Shot Down in Red River," states that Maestas intended to "kidnap" Mrs. DeWese. In the account in "Brutal Asesinato en Red River," Maestas uses the term "atacar" rather than "violar," but the context seems to indicate that his intention was to rape her.
10. Maestas's confession was taken by State Senator José Montaner and Sheriff Antonio Gonzales. See "Sheepherder was Drinking," *Santa Fe New Mexican*, November 17, 1927, 2.
11. "Heavy Guard over Taos County Jail," *Santa Fe New Mexican*, August 31, 1927, 1.

12. "Getting Jury for Maestas Trial at Taos."
13. Scholars assumed for years that the trial took place in 1935, although no evidence of this was published. The first instance of the incorrect dating of the trial comes from William S. Lieberman, "The Painter Looks at People," *Art News*, September 1947, 29. Bickerstaff, *Pioneer Artists of Taos*, 43, repeats this information. I would like to thank Elizabeth Cunningham, who, in 2002, located the article "Sheepherder Was Drinking," which clearly established the date of the trial and led to the discovery of the other documents related to this event. Transcripts of testimony in the trial, if they existed, were probably destroyed; the Taos County Courthouse burned in the spring of 1932. See Schimmel and White, *Bert Geer Phillips*, 102.
14. The jurors were Salvador Santistevan, Samuel M. y Lavadie, Alfredo Romero, Valentin Gonzales, Ruben Cortés, Carlos Romero, Manuel Fresquez, Federico Cárdenas, J. E. Ortega, Romulo Vigil, Melquiades Madrid, and Daniel Esquivel. "Corte de Distrito: José Cruz Maestas Culpable en 2do Grado," *La Revista Popular de Nuevo Mexico*, November 19, 1927, 2.
15. Beutler's first name is not given in the media reports.
16. "Brutal Asesinato en Red River." This is Senator Montaner's impression of Maestas when he interviewed him in the jail in Taos. The record for the New Mexico State Penitentiary describes Maestas as five feet tall and 123 pounds. Department of Corrections Records, Inmate Intake Records, Inmate # 6004.
17. An alienist is a medical doctor serving as an expert witness in an insanity argument.
18. The Remus trial received front-page coverage in the *Santa Fe New Mexican* starting on October 7 and running through the end of the trial in December. See esp. "Remus Insanity Hearing Waived," *Santa Fe New Mexican*, November 4, 1927, 1; "Remus Smiles upon Arriving in Courtroom," *Santa Fe New Mexican*, November 14, 1927, 1; and "Remus Granted Right to Quiz Jury," *Santa Fe New Mexican*, November 15, 1927, 1.
19. William T. Henning, Jr., *Ernest L. Blumenschein Retrospective* (Colorado Springs: Colorado Springs Fine Arts Center, 1978), 21; and Sherry Clayton Taggett and Ted Schwarz, *Paintbrushes and Pistols: How the Taos Artists Sold the West* (Santa Fe: John Muir Publications, 1990), 231. Both treat this as fact. The young man interviewed at the Museum of Modern Art in 1939 also mentions this. After characterizing Maestas as "rather degenerate," the memo notes that "apparently it is a common occurrence for herders thus isolated to go mad." "Memo to Mr. Barr." They all suggest that Penitente membership also played a role in favoritism in the jury's decision, but there is no evidence that this was the case.
20. Julian Josue Vigil, *Vamos a la Borrega: La Vereda—The Sheeptrail* (Las Vegas: Institute of Research, New Mexico Highlands University, 1980), unpaginated. Vigil comments: "Se dice que el pobre borreguero hasta pierde su sentido en el campo, como en el cuento del que fue abogado en corte y ganó el caso porque lo que respondía juez era 'BAA!'" (It is said that the poor sheepherder even loses his mind out there, as in the tale about the sheepherder that went to court and won his case, since all the judge could get out of him was "BAA!")

21. Vigil, in this context, cites two other humorous anecdotes about sheepherders. Archer B. Gilfillan, *Sheep* (Boston: Boston, Little, Brown, 1929), 151–52, states that "the most common slander on the herding profession [is] that no one can herd for any length of time without losing his mental equilibrium," but he goes on to point out that "I never knew one of them to avail himself of this privilege and I never heard of an authentic case of its being done." He refers to "other slanders," and recounts other humorous anecdotes, including a courtroom story similar to the one noted by Vigil. This folklore is so ubiquitous that Gilfillan begins his book *Sheep* with this tongue-in-cheek commentary: "it should be stated at the outset that there are two general theories about herding. Some hold that no man can herd for six months straight without going crazy, while others maintain that a man must have been mentally unbalanced for at least six months before he is in fit condition to entertain the thought of herding" (3). On the more serious side, Gilfillan notes that a sheepherder is, "like other solitary workers, apt to be introspective, sensitive to outside contacts when they come, and he broods over trifles that a man in a normal life would quickly forget" (151). On the defense insanity argument, see "Maestas Is Sent Up for 90 Years: He Should Hang, Judge Declares," *Santa Fe New Mexican*, November 18, 1927, 6.

22. "Los Prohibicionistas en Taos," *La Revista Popular de Nuevo Mexico*, November 26, 1927, 1, gives an account of the arrest of four Anglo-American bootleggers in Questa, just downriver from Red River.

23. David J. McCullough, "Bone Dry? Prohibition New Mexico Style, 1918–1933," *New Mexico Historical Review* 63, no. 1 (1988): 41.

24. The record for the New Mexico State Penitentiary indicates that Maestas smoked but did not drink. Department of Corrections Records, Inmate Intake Records, Inmate # 6004.

25. "Maestes Is Sent Up," 6.

26. "Corte de Distrito."

27. Ibid.

28. "Life in Prison for Slayer of School Man on Red River, N.M.," *Albuquerque Journal*, November 18, 1927, 1.

29. MGB to HGB, November 6, 1927, MGB Collection, FACHL. "Hondo" here refers to the area around the village of Arroyo Hondo, north of Taos. The ELB Collection, FACHL, contains miscellaneous magazine clippings, photographs, and art reproductions of sheep and sheepherding.

30. Blumenschein's large painting *Afternoon of a Sheepherder*, now at the National Cowboy and Western Heritage Museum, was done in 1939, three years after *Jury for the Trial of a Sheepherder for Murder* was first exhibited. Two other drawings in the collection of the Museum of Fine Arts, Santa Fe, are close in conception to the 1939 painting, but none in that collection are related to *Jury for the Trial of a Sheepherder for Murder*.

31. "The Artists Colony Corner," *Taos Valley News*, January 7, 1928, 1. *Sheep Herd in Hondo Canyon* (present whereabouts unknown) may have been a work that was repainted and retitled *The Pass*, now at the Arizona State University Art Museum. In 1930, Blumenschein listed *The Pass Landscape with Sheep* as one of his "top ten." ELB to George

Derby, August, 12, 1930, ELB Collection, THM.

32. ELB to MGB and HGB, April 11, 1932, folder 2, ELB Collection, FACHL.

33. One of the sketches for the painting, dated 1935, was shown in Blumenschein's 1948 retrospective exhibition at the Museum of Fine Arts in Santa Fe. *Retrospective Exhibition of the Lifework of Ernest L. Blumenschein, May 30–June 30, 1948, Art Gallery, Museum of New Mexico, Santa Fe*, ELB Collection, FACHL, scrapbook.

34. Edward Alden Jewell, "The Old Familiar Faces," *New York Times*, March 22, 1936, X8.

35. "Arts Club Makes Awards," *New York Times*, January 27, 1937, 24.

36. "National Show," *Time*, June 28, 1937, 44–45. *Jury for the Trial of a Sheepherder for Murder* was one of five paintings that represented New Mexico in the exhibition. See Spud Johnson, "Parisians to Get Glimpse of Northern New Mexicans on Blumenschein Canvas at Summer Show," *New Mexico Sentinel*, June 5, 1938, 3.

37. "Among the ablest pictures technically is *Jury for the Trial of a Sheepherder for Murder* by Ernest Blumenschein of New Mexico." In "National Show," 45.

38. Johnson, "Parisians to Get Glimpse," 3.

39. "Modern Art Works Added by Gallery," *New York Times*, October 25, 1938, 24. Deaccessioned by the museum in April 1981, it was purchased By William Foxley of Denver, and in 1997 it was purchased by the Rockwell Museum of Western Art, Corning, New York, with funding from the Clara S. Peck Fund.

40. See "Blumenschein Painting Arrives From New York," *Santa Fe New Mexican*, May 26, 1948, 6; "Exhibition Sets Important Precedent," *Santa Fe New Mexican*, June 4, 1948, 7.

41. In all likelihood Blumenschein did not know the individuals whose faces he studied on the plaza; if he did, their identities were not documented, as they would have been irrelevant to the subject of the actual jury. An "original memory sketch" for the jury was exhibited in Blumenschein's 1948 retrospective exhibition. See *Retrospective Exhibition of the Lifework of Ernest L. Blumenschein, May 30 - June 30, 1948, Art Gallery, Museum of New Mexico, Santa Fe*, ELB Collection, FACHL. The ides of depicting "types" of faces has its precedent in Blumenschein's career as an illustrator.

42. Johnson, "Parisians to Get Glimpse."

43. William S. Lieberman, "The Painter Looks at People," *Art News*, September 1947, 29.

44. Cook, "Ernest L. Blumenschein" (1952), 21–22.

45. "Memo to Mr. Barr" states that Maestas "served seven or eight years and was paroled." While this could suggest that Maestas's parole could have prompted Blumenschein to take up an interest in this subject, this is not the case. Maestas's penitentiary record indicates that on March 5, 1946, his sentence was commuted to "50 to 99 years," and on December 23 of that same year it was again commuted to "27 years, 6 months, and 28 days." Department of Corrections Records, Governor's Inmate Notebooks, 17164–17165. If Maestas served out his term, he would have been released in mid-June of 1955.

46. Although Blumenschein participated in the federal programs, he was also one to question decisions made by arts administrators.

He complained about the removal of Emil Bisttram, Loren Mozley, Joseph Fleck, and Barbara Latham from mural commissions, stating he was "having a mad time over artists on relief." ELB to MLB and HGB, March 28, 1936, folder 2, ELB Collection, FACHL.

47. The competition was announced in April. Eleven artists had been preselected by a special advisory committee to participate in the Department of Justice project; the artists selected were Thomas Hart Benton, George Biddle, John Stuart Curry, Rockwell Kent, Leon Kroll, Reginald Marsh, Henry Varnum Poor, Boardman Robinson, Eugene Savage, Maurice Sterne, and Grant Wood. The remaining spaces were to go to artists who were to be selected from a "limited competition." "U.S. Projects," *Art Digest* 9, no. 13 (1935): 7. Blumenschein was among those invited. "Competition letters sent out to the Following artists on Justice and P.O. buildings—March 30, 1935," NA RG 121, Records Concerning Federal Art Activities, Entry 133, Case Files Concerning Embellishments of federal buildings, Box 121, Folder: Justice Dept. Building—Advisory Committee Recommendations.

48. The others were Kenneth Adams, Emil Bisttram, Buck Dunton, Victor Higgins, and Ward Lockwood. "Gossip from the Artist Colony: Competition," *Taos Valley News* 24, no. 34 (1935): 1. The *Taos Valley News* refers to the Department of Justice building as the "Federal Building."

49. Applicants were requested to submit two drawings, one in color, and were encouraged to send as many as four. The whereabouts of the compositional drawings for *Jury for the Trial of a Sheepherder for Murder* is unknown, but the concept for this painting was definitely triggered by the federal competition; the proportions of *Jury for the Trial of a Sheepherder for Murder* are consistent with those given for the panel dimensions in the Department of Justice building. "National Competition for Mural Decoration in the Department of Justice Building, Washington, D.C.," NA RG 121, Records of the Public Buildings Service, Entry 133, Records of the section of Fine Arts, Case Files Concerning Embellishments in Federal buildings, Box 121, Folder Justice Dept. Building—Competition #2, p. 3. (This is a copy of the prospectus sent out on January 26, 1936, for the second round; the National Archives does not have the 1935 prospectus, although the criteria were undoubtedly the same.) Blumenschein would have received the first prospectus in April; the Waller portrait was finished in May. The "memory sketches" done on the Taos plaza would have been done in the summer months, so the concept of the *Jury for the Trial of a Sheepherder for Murder* would have been well along for the August submission to the competition. In December of 1935 Blumenschein did receive a commission to paint a mural (a view of the Spanish Peaks) in the post office in Walsenburg, Colorado; he was sketching in the area in October of that year, before the Washington D.C. competition results would have been announced. The Walsenburg commission was finished in 1937.

50. There were eight murals proposed for the post office and three for the Department of Justice. Edward Alden Jewell, "Under Federal Guidance: Sculpture and Murals Produced in

the Treasury Department's Competitions," *New York Times*, October 27, 1935, X9.

51. "National Competition for Mural Decoration," 3–4.

52. All rejected entries were photographed; however, a search in the National Archives has not turned up any visual documentation of Blumenschein's entry. Forbes Watson proposed that the Corcoran mount an exhibition of all the studies submitted. Forbes Watson to Edward Bruce, August 28, 1935, NA RG 121, Series 122, Box 36. An exhibition of "Sketches for Mural Designs for the Post Office Department and Department of Justice Buildings, and Sketch Models of Figures to be Used in the Postmaster General's Reception Room" was shown from October 29 to November 21, 1935, but it is not clear whether these works were only related to the final selections or whether it included all submissions, as Forbes suggested. www.corcoran.org/exhibitions/archive_results.asp?Year=1935. A 1938 exchange of letters between Blumenschein and Edward Rowan, superintendent of the Section of Painting and Sculpture, refers to a photo of *Jury for the Trial of a Sheepherder for Murder.* Blumenschein inquired whether the section had a photo of the painting, and, if not, he offered to send one. Rowan replied that the section did have a photo; however, it is not clear whether he was referring to a photo of the finished painting or the photo of the sketch. ELB to Edward Rowan, April 1938; Edward Rowan to ELB, May 3, 1938, NA RG 121, Box 11, Entry 133.

53. This prospectus was sent out on January 28, 1936. "National Competition for Mural Decoration in the Department of Justice Building, Washington, D.C.," NA RG 121, Records of the Public Buildings Service, Entry 133, Records of the Section of Fine Arts, Case Files Concerning Embellishments in Federal Buildings, Box 121, Folder Justice Dept. Building—Competition 2. Emil Bisttram, Blumenschein's colleague in Taos, was one of the artists selected. His mural is titled *Contemporary Justice and Woman.* Other artists, including Blumenschein, were listed for consideration for other projects. "Complete List of Painters and sculptors Receiving Appointments as a result of the Competition for the Post Office and Justice Department Buildings," NA RG 121, Box 18, Folder T.R.A.P. Projects. From Bulletin, Treasury Department Art Projects, No. 7, December 1935.

54. Jewell, "Under Federal Guidance." Art critic and administrator Forbes Watson was a close advisor to Edward Bruce, the head of the Section of Fine Arts in the Works Progress Administration. It was decided that the Department of Justice commission proceed with a limited competition in which nine painters would be invited; apparently Blumenschein was not among those. See Edward Alden Jewell, "Many Countries Send Murals Here," *New York Times*, November 26, 1935, 23.

55. Arthur Millier, "Murals and Men," *Art Digest* 9 (September 1935):6.

56. Inslee Hopper, "America in Washington; Designs to Be Executed under the Supervision of the Section of Painting and Sculpture," *American Magazine of Art* 28 (December 1935): 721.

57. "Olin Dow Replies to Questions Raised by Mural Painters Group," Bulletin, Treasury

Department Art Projects, No. 7, December 1935, NA RG 121, Box 18,Folder T.R.A.P. Projects.

58. "Gossip from the Artist Colony: Ward Wins," *Taos Valley News* 24, no. 44 (1935): 1. Lockwood won one of the mural commissions for the post office; Adams was recommended for a future project.
59. "Gossip from the Artist Colony: 37 Varieties," *Taos Valley News* 24, no. 35 (1935): 1.
60. "Gossip from the Artist Colony: Santa Fe Show," *Taos Valley News* 24, no. 41 (1935): 1.
61. "Gossip from the Artist Colony: B.C.P. Says PWA is N.G.," *Taos Valley News* 24, no. 49 (1935): 1. For Phillips's involvement in the Taos County Courthouse murals, see Schimmel and White, *Bert Geer Phillips*, 102–104, 113.
62. There is no indication in correspondence or in local art news that Blumenschein was working on a major painting at that time, but the painting must have been well under way in the latter months of 1935. Since the concept for *Jury for the Trial of a Sheepherder for Murder* was submitted and rejected in the Department of Justice commission, it seems likely that the large painting would have become his major activity in November and December of 1935.
63. Major examples of earlier paintings that dealt with political issues include *The Peacemaker* (1913), *Star Road and White Sun* (1920), and *Superstition* (1921).
64. See Betsy Fahlman, "Louise Emerson Rönnebeck: A New Deal Artist of the American West," *Woman's Art Journal* 22, no. 2 (2002): 18.
65. Shahn's depictions postdate the 1920 events of the trial by more than a decade.
66. This was also a trial with a controversial decision. In 1934, two cab drivers in Boston were accused of killing a bill poster at a theatre. Three weeks into the trial, Irving and Murton Millen and an accomplice, Abraham Faber, confessed to the crime. The cab drivers were acquitted, and the Millens and Faber were executed. Although Blumenschein's letters make no mention of this case, it was well known outside of legal circles. Judge John Crawford Crosby's lengthy opinion in *Commonwealth v. Millen* was widely read and discussed by laypersons and lawyers alike. www.massreports.com/memorials/318ma800.htm. The trial was also the basis for a story by Joseph F. Dinneen, "Murder in Massachusetts," *Harpers* 172 (March 1936): 401–15; in 1939 Dinneen's story was adapted as the screenplay for the movie *Let Us Live*, starring Henry Fonda and Maureen O'Sullivan.
67. The Denver trial in January of 1936 involved domestic abuse and murder, and Mary Elizabeth Smith was acquitted on an insanity defense. Fahlman, "Louise Emerson Rönnebeck." Rönnebeck's painting is not a direct source for Blumenschein, since his idea for *Jury* dates from 1935; however, the Rönnebecks and Blumenscheins were acquainted because the Rönnebecks often summered in Taos, and it seems likely they would have been interested in one another's work.
68. Twelve of Shinn drawings appeared in *The Boston Traveller.* Most of them are quite melodramatic, although there is one, of four of the jurymen being taken to breakfast by two officers, that is low-key and nonrhetorical in comparison to the others.

69. Shahn's painting is based on a photograph. It is not known whether Blumenschein knew Shahn's painting before he conceived of *Jury for the Trial of a Sheepherder for Murder*, although it was in the collection of the Museum of Modern Art, a gift of Abby Aldrich Rockefeller. It may be that Rockefeller's earlier gift of the Shahn painting might have influenced the museum to use her fund to acquire the Blumenschein painting.

70. There are other examples in which Blumenschein addressed the legal system in major paintings, but the connections with legal issues, however deeply felt by the artist, are less obvious and more embedded within symbolic structures. See esp. Charles C. Eldredge, "Ernest Blumenschein's *The Peacemaker*: Native Americans, Greeks, and Jurisprudence circa 1913," *American Art* 15, no. 1 (2001), 34–51; and Skip Keith Miller, "*Superstition* and the Artist's Defense of Native Rights," this volume.

71. Henning, *Blumenschein Retrospective.* My own previously published remarks on the painting followed Henning's conclusions. James Moore, "Ernest Blumenschein's Long Journey with Star Road," *American Art* 9, no. 3 (1995): 12.

72. See Gordon M. Bakken, "The English Common Law in the Rocky Mountain West," *Arizona and the West* 11 (1969): 109–28.

73. The concept of *derecho indiano* evolved in New Spain as a means of dealing with the complexities of interaction with diverse indigenous populations. It was a flexible system of justice rather than a strict system of ruling by precedents in written law. The system is discussed in detail in Charles R. Cutter, "Community and the Law in Northern New Spain," *The Americas* 50, no. 4 (1940): 467–80. Cutter notes, "Finally, judicial decisions were to be equitable solutions that not only satisfied the aggrieved party, but that also considered the well-being and harmony of the community" (469).

74. David J. Langum, *Law and Community on the Mexican California Frontier: Anglo-American Expatriates and the Clash of Legal Traditions, 1821–1846.* (Norman: University of Oklahoma Press, 1987). See esp. the discussion of cases in chapter 3, "Criminal Litigation." See also Jill Mocho, *Murder and Justice in Frontier New Mexico, 1821–1846* (Albuquerque: University of New Mexico Press, 1997), "Part Three: Extranjeros," 124–78, for similar examples.

75. Blumenschein would not have known what DeWese looked like or whether he wore glasses (he did not). Although Blumenschein often depicted real people, places, and events in his paintings, throughout his career there are major paintings that are enigmatic or contain symbolic details that are set against the realism of the picture. See, e.g., *The Peacemaker* (1913), *Superstition* (1921), New Mexico (1921), *The Extraordinary Affray* (1925), and *The Funeral (Alas Proud Mansion)* (1944–59).

I would like to extend my gratitude to Elizabeth Cunningham for her kindness, expertise, and collegial attitude in sharing her years of research with me as I prepared this essay. Thanks also go to Peter Hassrick and Skip Miller for their thoughts and observations on Blumenschein's paintings, to Forrest Fenn for thoughtfully sharing his bibliographic material on Blumenschein, and to my wife, Vickie Hamilton-Smith, for her keen editorial suggestions.

1. Unidentified newspaper clipping: Ina Sizer Cassidy, "Art and Artists of New Mexico," July 1948, Southwest Collection, Schwarz Papers.
2. Erica Doss, *Twentieth-Century American Art* (Oxford: Oxford University Press, 2002) 89.
3. Robert Hughes, *American Visions: The Epic History of Art in America* (New York: Alfred A. Knopf, 1999), 388.
4. "Artists' Rule for Success"; "Blumenschein Is Interviewed," *El Palacio* 6, no. 6 (1919): 84.
5. "Modern Art and the Art Academy," *Santa Fe New Mexican*, February 1926.
6. "Blumenschein's Job Was Not Easy, He Says" [*Taos Valley News*, October 26, 1931], ELB Papers, AAA.
7. [Brian Boru Dunne,] "Blumenschein Blooms Again" [*Santa Fe New Mexican*, November 29, 1939], ELB Papers, AAA.
8. Roosevelt wrote, "Take the picture which for some reason is called 'A naked man going down stairs.' There is in my bath-room a really good Navajo rug which, on any proper interpretation of the Cubist theory, is a far more satisfactory and decorative picture." See Theodore Roosevelt, "A Layman's View of an Art Exhibition," *Outlook* 53 (March 29, 1913): 718–20.
9. John Sloan's poem *A Slight Attack of Third Dimentia [sic] Brought on by Excessive Study of the Much Talked of Cubist Pictures in the International Exhibition at New York*, originally published in *The Masses*, April 1913, reads, "There was a cubic man / And he walked a cubic mile / And he found a cubic sixpence upon a cubic style / He had a cubic cat, which caught a cubic mouse / And they all lived together in a little cubic house." Reproduced in *Echoes of Revolt: The Masses 1911–1917*, ed. William L. O'Neill (Chicago: Quadrangle Books, 1966), 115.
10. Robert Underwood Johnson, "This Transitional Age in Art," *Century* 87, no. 6 (1914): 825.
11. The other essayists were artists and writers John W. Alexander, Edwin H. Blashfield, Walter Pach, and Jay Hambridge writing with Gove Hambridge.
12. Alexander, "Is Our Art Distinctively American?" 827.
13. Edwin H. Blashfield, "The Painting of To-day," *Century* 87, no. 6 (1914): 837.
14. Blumenschein, "Painting of To-morrow," 845–50.
15. Ibid, 847–48.
16. My appreciation goes to Peter Hassrick for sharing his insight in identifying Leo Stein as the unnamed art collector described by Blumenschein.
17. Blumenschein, "Painting of To-morrow," 847.
18. Ibid., 849–50, italics in the original.
19. Sylvia Yount, "Rocking the Cradle of Liberty: Philadelphia's Adventures in Modernism," in *To Be Modern: American Encounters with Cézanne and Company*

(Philadelphia: University of Pennsylvania Press, 1996), 11.

20. "Blumenschein Is Interviewed," *El Palacio* 6, no. 6 (1919): 84.
21. Ernest L. Blumenschein, "Modern Art and the Academy," *New York Times,* February 7, 1926, XX14.
22. Ernest L. Blumenschein, "Modern Art and the Academy," *Santa Fe New Mexican,* February 1926.
23. "Treason in the Academy," *New York Telegram,* February 10, 1926.
24. Ernest L. Blumenschein, "Quarrelling Artists and Fighting Birds," *New York Telegram,* February 19, 1926.
25. Hogue, "Ernest L. Blumenschein," 474.
26. "New Art Greets Olds at Academy Show," *New York Times,* March 23, 1927, 24.
27. ELB to self, "Conclusions after attending my 1st Meeting of N.A.D.," March 14, 1928, ELB Papers, AAA.
28. Cass Gilbert to ELB, January 23, 1930, ELB Papers, AAA.
29. Cook, "The Art of Ernest L. Blumenschein."
30. Unidentified newspaper clipping, 1937: "Blumenschein to Be Included in Paris Exhibition," ELB Papers, AAA.
31. Ernest L. Blumenschein, "Modern Art," 1937 lecture, ELB Papers, AAA.
32. Blumenschein's description of artists being nothing more than a "tool" of their environment touches on what Michel Foucault's calls the "author-function," detailed in his seminal essay of 1969, "What Is an Author?" Roland Barthes depicts authors as being of a time and place, for "it is the language which speaks, not the author." Michel Foucault, "What Is an Author?" *Bulletin de la Societé Française de Philosophie* 63, no. 3 (1969), reprinted in *The Art of Art History: A Critical Anthology*, ed. Donald Preziosi, 299–314 (Oxford: Oxford University Press, 1998); Roland Barthes, "The Death of the Author," *Image, Music, Text* (New York: Hill and Wang, 1977), 142–48.
33. William S. Lieberman, "The Painter Looks at People," *Art News* 46, no. 7 (1947): 28–29.
34. Arnold Rönnebeck, "Blumenschein Exhibits 43 Fine," *Rocky Mountain News* (Denver), June 10, 1928.
35. Newspaper clipping: *Cincinnati Enquirer*, 1928, ELB Papers, AAA.
36. Unidentified clipping: Nick John Matsoukas, 1936, ibid.
37. Cassidy, "Art and Artists of New Mexico," 28.
38. Howard Cook, "The Art of Ernest L. Blumenschein," lecture, presented at Museum of New Mexico, Santa Fe, on occasion of Blumenschein retrospective, May 30, 1948.
39. Theodore Van Soelen, "Blumenschein Exhibition Sets Important Precedent," *Santa Fe New Mexican,* June 4, 1948.
40. Hogue, "Ernest L. Blumenschein," 471.
41. In the original text, the Pennsylvania Academy of the Fine Arts is listed as the "Philadelphia Academy of Fine Arts." See "Artists' Rule for Success."
42. ELB, Lockman interview 3.
43. Hogue, "Ernest L. Blumenschein," 472.
44. Cassidy, "Art and Artists of New Mexico," 28, 57 (italics in original).
45. ELB, unidentified letter possibly for retrospective, ELB Papers, AAA.
46. ELB, Lockman interview 3.

47. Hogue, "Ernest L. Blumenschein," 470.

48. Cassidy, "Art and Artists of New Mexico" 28.

49. Katy Marvin, "City's Intellectual Growth Lags, Says Blumenschein," *Albuquerque Tribune*, February 27, 1952.

50. ELB to Dr. Reginald Fisher, March 19, 1948, Ernest L. Blumenschein Files, Museum of Fine Arts Library, New Mexico Museum of Art, Museum of New Mexico, Santa Fe.

51. ELB, unidentified notes on art, ELB Papers, AAA.

52. Unidentified newspaper clipping: Marjorie C. Bush-Brown, "Paintings by Blumenschein Inspired by Mexican Life," ELB Papers, AAA; Elisabeth Luther Cary, "A Tasty Meal Offered," *New York Times*, March 24, 1929, 142; Unidentified newspaper clipping, "In the World of Art," October 15, 1927, 13, ELB Papers, AAA.

53. Rönnebeck, "Blumenschein Exhibits."

54. Theodore Van Soelen, "Blumenschein Exhibition Sets Important Precedent," *Santa Fe New Mexican*, June 4, 1948.

55. "Blumenschein Brings Southwest to New York," *Art Digest*, March 15, 1934, 19.

56. Ernest L. Blumenschein, personal manuscript, c. 1950, ELB Papers, AAA.

57. ELB, Taos, N.M., to Mr. Drake, art editor of *Century* magazine, New York, N.Y., September 15, 1901, ELB Papers, AAA.

58. Charles C. Eldredge, *American Imagination and Symbolist Painting* (New York: Grey Art Gallery and Study Center, 1979), 84.

59. Jeremy Strick, *Visual Music: Synaesthesia in Art and Music Since 1900* (Washington, D.C.: Thames and Hudson, 2005), 16.

60. [Dunne,] "Bloomenschein Blooms Again."

61. ELB to HGB, October 24, 1946, ELB Papers, AAA.

62. Katy Marvin, "City's Intellectual Growth Lags, Says Blumenschein," *Albuquerque Tribune*, February 27, 1952, Southwest Collection, Schwarz Papers.

63. Ernest L. Blumenschein, "On Modernism," lecture, October 1952, Southwest Collection, Schwarz Papers.

64. bid.

65. *A Retrospective Exhibition* (Museum of New Mexico, Santa Fe, 1958), with personal note from ELB to Robert Beverly Hale, January 10, 1959, ELB Papers, AAA.

66. Unidentified newspaper clipping: Victor White, "The Man I Knew: A Tribute to E. L. Blumenschein," ELB Papers, AAA.

Selected Bibliography

ARCHIVAL SOURCES

Art Academy of Cincinnati Archives. Mary R. Schiff Library, Cincinnati Art Museum, Cincinnati, Ohio.

Art Students League Records, 1875–1955. Art Students League of New York Archives, New York.

Blumenschein, Ernest L., Collection (AC 354). Fray Angélico Chávez History Library, New Mexico History Museum, Santa Fe.

Blumenschein, Ernest L., Collection. Taos Historic Museums, Taos, N.M.

Blumenschein, Ernest L., File. Dewitt M. Lockman Collection. Nita Stewart Haley Memorial Library, Midland, Tex.

Blumenschein, Ernest L., File. Museum of Modern Art, New York.

Blumenschein, Ernest L., File. National Academy of Design, New York.

Blumenschein, Ernest L., Files. Elizabeth Cunningham and Skip Miller, Joseph, Ore.

Blumenschein, Ernest L., Files. Forrest Fenn Files, Santa Fe, N.M.

Blumenschein, Ernest L., Files. Gerald Peters Gallery, Santa Fe, N.M.

Blumenschein, Ernest L., Files. Museum of Fine Arts Library, New Mexico Museum of Art, Museum of New Mexico, Santa Fe.

Blumenschein, Ernest L., Papers. Archives of American Art, Smithsonian Institution, Washington, D.C.

Blumenschein, Helen, Collection (AC 376). Fray Angélico Chávez History Library, New Mexico History Museum, Santa Fe.

Blumenschein, Mary Greene, Collection (AC 410). Fray Angélico Chávez History Library, New Mexico History Museum, Santa Fe.

Blumenschein File. Mary R. Schiff Library, Cincinnati Art Museum, Cincinnati, Ohio.

Blumenschein File. Stark Museum of Art Archives, Orange, Tex.

Blumenschein Papers. Gilcrease Museum Archives, Tulsa, Okla.

Burlington Northern Santa Fe Railroad Archives, Fort Worth, Tex.

Center for Southwest Research. University of New Mexico, Albuquerque.

National Archives. RG 121, Records of the Public Building Service, Records of Federal Art Activities, Textual Records of the Section of Fine Arts, Public Building Administration and Its Predecessors, Case Files Concerning Embellishments of

Federal Buildings 1934–43, CO [Colorado], Box 11. Washington, D.C.

New Mexico State Records Center and Archives, Santa Fe. Exhibition catalogs of the Art Museum of New Mexico shows, various locations.

Schwarz, Ted, Papers. Southwest Artists Collection. Special Collections. Archives and Special Collections. Arizona State University, Tempe.

BOOKS AND ARTICLES

"Another Prize for Blumenschein." *El Palacio* 27, nos. 21–22 (1929): 252.

Applegate, Frank G. "Tourists and Art." *Southwest Review* 12, no. 1 (1926): 23–27.

"Artist, Ex-Daytonian, Returning." *Dayton Herald,* April 23, 1927.

"Artists' Rule for Success—Begin Young, Work Hard, and Keep at It." *Dayton Journal,* October 3, 1915.

"Artists and Writers." *Santa Fe New Mexican,* June 26, 1940.

Bickerstaff, Laura M. *Pioneer Artists of Taos.* 1955. Reprint, Denver: Old West Publishing, 1983.

"Blumenschein." *Santa Fe New Mexican,* June 7, 1959.

Blumenschein, Ernest L. *Ernest L. Blumenschein: A Self-Portrait, with Notes on Four Paintings in the Paul Grafe Collection.* San Francisco: Richard Finnie, 1946.

———. "Modern Art and the Academy." *New York Times,* February 7, 1926.

———. "Origins of the Taos Art Colony." *Albuquerque Herald,* May 10, 1926.

———. "The Painting of Tomorrow." *Century Magazine* 87, no. 6 (1914): 845–50.

———. "Quarrelling Artists and Fighting Birds." *New York Telegram,* February 19, 1926.

———. "San Geronimo: The Pueblo Indian's Holiday." *Harper's Weekly,* December 10, 1898, 1207.

———. "The Taos Society of Artists." *American Magazine of Art* 8, no. 11 (1917): 445–51.

Blumenschein, Ernest L., and Bert Geer Phillips. "An Appreciation of Indian Art." *El Palacio* 6, no. 12 (1919): 178–29.

Blumenschein, Helen G. *Recuerdos: Early Days of the Blumenschein Family.* Silver City, N.M.: Tecolote Press, 1979.

"The Blumenschein Exhibit." *El Palacio* 25, nos. 6–7 (1928): 95–96.

"Blumenschein Exhibition Sets Important Precedent." *Santa Fe New Mexican,* June 4, 1948.

"Blumenschein Explains: What Makes a Painting New?" *Santa Fe New Mexican,* September 13, 1953.

"Blumenschein Expresses Views on Modernism." *El Crepusculo,* November 27, 1952.

"Blumenschein Is Interviewed." *El Palacio* 6, no. 6 (1919): 84–86.

"Blumenschein Paintings Acclaimed." *Albuquerque Journal,* May 17, 1959.

"Blumenschein Regrets Generation Is Educated on Modern Art Ideas." *Albuquerque Journal*, November 16, 1952.

"Blumenschein's Fine Exhibition." *Santa Fe New Mexican,* October 24, 1913.

Bywaters, Jerry. "Art Comes Back Home." *Southwest Review* (October 1937): 80–82.

Cassidy, Ina Sizer. "Blumenschein in Retrospect." *New Mexico Magazine* 26 (July 1948): 28, 57.

Coke, Van Deren. *Taos and Santa Fe: The Artists' Environment, 1882–1942.* Albuquerque: University of New Mexico Press, 1963.

Cook, Howard. "Ernest L. Blumenschein: The Artist in His Environment." *New Mexico Quarterly Review* 19, no. 1 (1949): 18–25.

Dunne, Brian Boru. "Blumenscgein Blooms Again." *Santa Fe New Mexican,* November 29, 1939.

Dunton, W. Herbert. "The Painters of Taos." *American Magazine of Art* 13, no. 8 (1922): 249–52.

Egri, Kit. "Ernest L. Blumenschein: Intellect and Growth." *American Artist* (January 1978).

"E. L. Blumenschein's Paintings." *New York Times,* January 4, 1920.

Eldredge, Charles C. "Ernest Blumenschein's *The Peacemaker*: Native Americans, Greeks, and Jurisprudence Circa 1913." *American Art* 15, no. 1 (2001): 34–51.

"Ernest Blumenschein." *Dayton Daily Journal,* January 9, 1899.

"Ernest L. Blumenschein Dead; A Founder of Taos Art Colony." *New York Times,* June 8, 1960.

"Ernest L. Blumenschein, Famous Desert Painter, Addresses Art Institute Here." *Dayton Journal,* April 27, 1927.

"Fine Art Exhibit in the Museum." *El Palacio* 1, no. 1 (1913): 4.

Fisher, Reginald. "Museum's First Retrospective Exhibition." *El Palacio* 55, no. 6 (1948): 163–68.

Gibson, Arrell Morgan. *The Santa Fe and Taos Colonies: Age of the Muses, 1900–1942.* Norman: University of Oklahoma Press, 1983.

Grant, Blanche C. *When Old Trails Were New.* 1934. Reprint, Chicago: Rio Grande Press, 1963.

Haskin, Frederic J. "New Mexican Village Becomes Art Colony." *The Railroad Red Book* 34, no. 4 (1917): 11–12.

Henning, William T., Jr. *Ernest L. Blumenschein Retrospective.* Colorado Springs: Colorado Springs Fine Arts Center, 1978.

Hewett, Edgar L. "Recent Southwest Art." *Art and Archeology* 9, no. 1 (1920): 31–33.

Hogue, Alexandre. "Ernest L. Blumenschein." *Southwest Review* 13, no. 4 (1928): 469–74.

Jewell, Edward Alden. "Artists for Victory." *New York Times*, December 6, 1942.

——— "Truly Ours: Roots of Painting in Nation's Culture." *New York Times*, August 14, 1938.

Leavitt, Virginia Couse. *Eanger Irving Couse: Image Maker for America*. Albuquerque: Albuquerque Museum, 1991.

———. "Taos and the American Art Colony Movement: The Search for an American School of Art." *Ayer y Hoy en Taos* (Winter 1987): 3–8.

Luhan, Mabel Dodge. "Taos—A Eulogy." *Creative Art* 9, no. 4 (1931): 288–95.

McBride, Henry. "Blumenschein's Paintings of American Indians." *New York Sun*, February 12, 1927.

McGinnis, John H. "Taos." *Southwest Review* 13 (October 1927): 36–47.

Miller, Skip Keith. "Elsie's Story." *Taos Lightnin'* (Winter 1998): 1, 4–5.

———. "A Matter of Time and Friendship: The Ernest L. Blumenschein and Ellis Parker Butler Letters." *Taos Lightnin'* (Summer 1996): 2–5.

"Modern Art and the Art Colony: Address by Ernest L. Blumenschein at Luncheon by Art Section of State Teacher's Convention." *Santa Fe New Mexican*, March 8, 1926.

Moore, James. "Ernest Blumenschein's Long Journey with Star Road." *American Art* 9, no. 3 (1995): 6–27.

Morang, Alfred. "Art in the News." *Santa Fe New Mexican*, June 11, 1948.

Mowat, Jean. "The Artist in the Southwest." *El Palacio* 20, no. 10 (1926): 194–96.

Nelson, Mary Carroll. *The Legendary Artists of Taos*. New York: Watson-Guptill, 1980.

"New Mexican Paintings by Ernest Blumenschein." *Brooklyn Daily Eagle*, February 13, 1927.

"The New Mexico Painters." *Taos Valley News*, June 16, 1923.

Pennington, J. "Taos: An Art Center on the Edge of the Desert." *The Mentor* 12, no 6 (1924): 23–28.

Peixotto, Ernest. "The Field of Art." *Scribner's* 54, no. 2 (1916): 257–60.

Pickard, John. *Report of the Capitol Decoration Commission, 1917–1928*. Jefferson City: State of Missouri, 1928.

Porter, Dean A. *Enchanted Visions: The Taos Society of Artists and Ancient Cultures*. Spokane: Northwest Museum of Arts and Culture, 2005.

Porter, Dean A., Teresa Hayes Ebie, Suzan Campbell, et al. *Taos Artists and Their Patrons, 1858–1950*. Notre Dame, Ind.: Snite Museum of Art, 1999.

Rindge, Fred Hamilton. "Taos—A Unique Colony of Artists." *American Magazine of Art* 17, no. 9 (1926): 447–53.

Rönnebeck, Arnold. "Blumenschein Exhibits 43 Fine Paintings." *Rocky Mountain News,* June 10, 1928.

Sandzen, Birger. "The Southwest as a Sketching Ground." *Fine Arts Journal* 33, no. 2 (1915): 333.

Schaver, Martha K. "Art and Artists." *Dayton Journal,* May 5, 1927.

Schimmel, Julie. *The Art and Life of W. Herbert Dunton.* Austin: University of Texas Press, 1984.

Schimmel, Julie, and Robert White. *Bert Geer Phillips and the Taos Art Colony.* Albuquerque: University of New Mexico Press, 1994.

Steiner, Raymond J. *The Art Students League of New York: A History.* Saugerties, N.Y.: CSS Publications, 1999.

"A Taos Art Society Exhibit." *El Palacio* 7, nos. 5–6 (1919).

Taggett, Sherry Clayton, and Ted Schwarz. *Paintbrushes and Pistols: How the Taos Artists Sold the West.* Santa Fe: J. Muir Publications, 1990.

Trenton, Patricia. *Picturesque Images of Taos and Santa Fe.* Denver: Denver Art Museum, 1974.

Ufer, Walter. "Taos, New Mexico." *The Railroad Red Book* 39, no. 1 (1922): 322–27.

Walter, Paul A. F. "The Santa Fe–Taos Art Movement." *Art and Archeology* 4 (December 1916): 330–38.

White, Robert R. "Ernest Blumenschein and the Great War," *Ayer y Hoy en Taos* (Winter 1986): 3–6.

———. *The New Mexico Painters.* Santa Fe: Gerald Peters Gallery, 1999.

———. *The Taos Society of Artists.* Albuquerque: University of New Mexico Press, 1998.

Witt, David. *Modernists in Taos: From Dasburg to Marin.* Santa Fe: Red Crane Books, 2002.

Index

In Contemporary Rhythm: The Art of Ernest L. Blumenschein

Frontmatter illustrations: p. i: *Indian Girl Seated by Oven* (originally *Girl Seated by Oven*), 1926, reworked 1931, oil on canvas, 30 × 25 inches, private collection; p. ii: *Indians in the Mountains* (originally *Landscape with Indians,* 1936), reworked 1938, oil on panel, 20 × 44½ inches, courtesy of the J. N. Bartfield Galleries, New York, New York ; p. iv: *Two Burros*, ca. 1925, oil on canvas, 30 × 25 inches, private collection; p. xiv: Ernest L. Blumenschein seated in front of *The Extraordinary Affray*, courtesy of Peter A. Juley & Son Collection, Photograph Archives, Smithsonian Institution.

Copyedited by Renae Morehead
Text design and composition by David Alcorn,
Alcorn Publication Design
Set in Sabon, with display heads set in Syntax
Jacket design by Tony Roberts
Color separations by University of Oklahoma Printing Services
Printed by Everbest Printing, China, through Four Colour
Imports, Louisville, Kentucky
Printed on 128 gsm Gold East Matte